ON TRIAL

waldenu.edu/grad.

800.457-7811

ON TRIAL

Master's &
Ph.d's online

PREVIOUSLY TITLED *MAN ON TRIAL*

GERALD DICKLER

A LOU REDA BOOK

GRAMERCY BOOKS
NEW YORK • AVENEL

Originally published under the title *Man on Trial*
Copyright © 1962 by Gerald Dickler
All rights reserved

This 1993 edition published by Gramercy Books
distributed by Outlet Book Company, Inc., a Random House Company,
40 Engelhard Avenue, Avenel, New Jersey 07001

Random House
New York • Toronto • London • Sydney • Auckland

Printed and bound in the United States of America

Library of Congress Cataloging-in-Publication Data
Dickler, Gerald.
[Man on trial]
On trial / by Gerald Dickler.
p. cm.
Originally published: Man on trial. 1st ed. Garden City, N.Y.
Doubleday, 1962.
Includes bibliographical references and index.
ISBN 0-517-09317-0
1. Trials. I. Title.
K540.D5 1993
345'.07—dc20
[342.57] 93-19324
CIP

8 7 6 5 4 3 2 1

PREFACE

"The law sharpens the mind," Justice Oliver Wendell Holmes once said, "by narrowing it."

If there is any truth in that rather crusty observation, this is not a book for lawyers. They will find little to help them win their next case, or explain why they lost their last. The niceties of legal maneuvers and the intricacies of judicial systems are dealt with only to the extent necessary to advance the narrative and enhance the dramatic impact of each trial.

Nor is this volume likely to transport the devotees of true crime chronicles. No "foul and midnight murder" is celebrated here; when bodies are found, they must be counted in the thousands.

The trials recorded in these pages have been selected for the imprint they left upon Western history, and the illumination they cast upon their own troubled times. Each represents a phenomenon seldom seen and generally unrecognized, which makes its appearance when society is at war with itself, when fresh ideas and new values are being born on the tangled bed of social upheaval.

In such periods of tension, the forces dominating the community display a remarkable propensity for resorting to the judicial process to relieve themselves of their ideological bellyaches. Assassination or lynching or some less drastic but equally expeditious disposition of the problem might well have served, without fear of retribution; yet in each instance judicial machinery is rolled ponderously into place (or invented if it does not exist), the ceremonials observed with due solemnity, often at unnecessary length, and if nothing goes amiss, the prevalent political or religious principle is suitably embalmed as truth.

In these cases, the trial may be seen as an aspect of mankind's dependence on ritual. Specifically, the ritual employed is that of expurgation—to rid the body politic of an irritant, an alien substance, or a poison. Without inviting odious comparison, it may be said that Stalin and Cromwell, for example, shared an instinctive need for judicial endorsement of their bloodlettings, although each held absolute sway in his realm. Ironically, in the eye of history these trials failed to cure the maladies for which they were prescribed.

Whatever the fate of the defendants, in the larger view it was less consequential than the judgments rendered on the societies which tried them—judgments implicit in the trials themselves. Although they were nominally the losers, Socrates and Galileo had the last cosmic word. And those who prevailed but were nevertheless consumed by the ordeal, like Dreyfus and Andrew Johnson, had the satisfaction in the winter of their lives of witnessing the condemnation of the forces which had led them to the sacrificial altar.

All ritual is theater; and the drama inherent in these trials could scarcely be conveyed without quoting at length from the proceedings. But so that the narrative might not be retarded, quotations in the text have been held to a minimum; and there has been appended to each chapter the best available verbatim account of the highlights of each case.

It would be presumptuous to suggest that this collection is comprehensive; limitations of space have dictated that it be, at best, representative. If the omission of a number of cases of equal or even greater interest distresses the reader, it may comfort him to know that the feeling is shared.

A final note: the term "trial" is used here in its dictionary meaning—the formal examination of an issue of fact with a view to its determination. That the judgment may be a foregone conclusion is a factor which will interest historians, but not lexicographers—and least of all lawyers, who cannot permit themselves to ponder such morbid distinctions as they mount the steps to the courthouse.

New York City
March 30, 1962

CONTENTS

PREFACE   5

SOCRATES (399 B.C.)   15

JESUS (30 A.D.)   33

JOAN OF ARC (1431)   43

GALILEO GALILEI (1633)   61

CHARLES I (1649)   75

SALEM WITCHCRAFT TRIALS (1692)   91

ANDREW JOHNSON (1868)   111

THE DREYFUS CASE (1894)   137

THE SCOPES TRIAL (1925)   173

THE REICHSTAG FIRE TRIAL (1933)   201

THE MOSCOW TRIALS (1936–1938)   233

THE NUREMBERG TRIAL (1945–1946)   323

THE OPPENHEIMER HEARING (1954)   375

BIBLIOGRAPHY   427

INDEX   439

ACKNOWLEDGMENTS

For service above and beyond the call of conjugal duty, in translating voluminous material from German sources and in typing and criticizing my manuscript, I owe more than mere gratitude to my wife, Ruth.

Irving R. Levine and John H. Rich, Jr., both of the National Broadcasting Company, gave unstinting assistance in locating useful research material abroad. The excellent translation of the Galileo proceedings is the work of Professor Irma Brandeis of Bard College. Leonard Raulston generously checked doubtful points concerning the Scopes trial, over which his grandfather presided. From Louis Lochner came a keen first-hand appraisal of Marinus van der Lubbe, whose arrest and trial he covered. Helpful insights into the Nuremberg case were furnished by Benevenuto von Halle.

Space does not permit me to name the many others to whom I am indebted for their interest and encouragement, but I cannot fail to single out my old friend, H. V. Kaltenborn, who applied a constant and benign spur to speed the completion of this book.

G.D.

Mostly for Ruth, but also for three young women of a generation whose trial has just begun.

SOCRATES
(399 B.C.)

To a society in which the word "soul" is rarely heard except on Sundays and "truth" is no longer printed with a capital "T," Socrates is an alien and puzzling figure. Saintliness makes us uneasy. Accustomed as we are to daily appeasements to avoid unpleasantness, we are baffled by anyone who refused to compromise with his own conscience, even in the face of death.

Joan of Arc bowed to expediency and temporarily denied her voices. Even Jesus on the Cross had his moment of doubt: "My God, My God! Why hast Thou forsaken me?" But Socrates moved in a straight line to the cup of hemlock; the manner of his dying was simply an affirmation of his way of life.

That life had been devoted to a one-man war against hypocrisy and loose thinking in fifth-century (B.C.) Athens. His battle cry was the inscription on the temple wall at Delphi, "Know thyself." In the gymnasium, in the market place, or in the fields, he would proceed to demolish his fellow Athenians' pet notions about nature or virtue, pricking the balloons of their prejudices and convictions with the rapier of his logic. Using a question mark as a scythe, he cut a wide swath through the undergrowth of hypocrisy and loose thinking in other people's gardens. Man's intellect was his vineyard, and he labored there joyfully, with no hope or expectation of material reward.

Although he frequently spoke of an "inner voice" that guided his course, Socrates was not a religious man in the modern sense. The virtue he looked for in his fellow Athenians was not otherworldly; his objective was positive good this side of the River Styx, achieved through reason and discourse.

Earnest though he was about his mission, he pursued it with wit and skepticism, and a decidedly unsaintly love of fun and of the pleasures of the flesh.

He was no mean contestant at the banquet table. Far into his sixties,

he could still outdrink a company of men many years his junior, and outtalk those who stayed sober. His eye for an attractive dancing girl was not dulled by age, although he always had to reckon with his wife, the fabled shrew, Xanthippe. "I chose Xanthippe," he once said, "because I knew if I could get on with her, I could with anyone."

Fame came to Socrates before he was forty, and it was not diminished in later years by the prodigious endurance and courage he displayed as a middle-aged infantryman in the Peloponnesian War. Tourists to whom he was pointed out on the streets of Athens could not easily forget the broad satyrlike face—pugnosed, thick-lipped, and bearded—the potbelly bulging under his shabby robe, the bare feet which belied his fairly comfortable circumstances.

Over the years, two generations of leaders of thought and action had flocked to his circle: intellectuals like Plato; the tragic poets, Euripides and Agathon; the wealthy Crito, who helped Socrates eke out his earnings as a stonecutter by investing his small inheritance for him—and a few politicans whose passage through his orbit would figure significantly in his trial.

Alcibiades, for example. This handsome and ill-starred military genius was scarcely twenty when Socrates saved his life on the field of battle. The youthful warrior's gratitude and admiration took the form of frank homosexual overtures to the older man; and although Athens did not condemn such relationships, Socrates staved off his advances by gently diverting him into abstract discussions.

Alcibiades' career is a study in paradox. In his twenty-five years as an adult, he lived intensely enough for two men, and indeed he seemed like two men. He was twice the darling of Athens, a hero who could do no wrong in the eyes of its citizens, and twice a refugee fleeing death at their hands for sacrilege and treason. After leading his native city to brilliant victories on land and sea against Sparta, he turned coat and showed Sparta how to conquer Athens. He could spend an evening discussing love and virtue in melting and ingratiating discourse with Socrates, and devote the following day to ramming through the Assembly a resolution to slaughter the entire male population of a conquered enemy city. In Athens he lived a life of sybaritic luxury; after going over to the Spartans, he denied himself all worldly comforts—except the love of their queen, who bore him a son.

Alcibiades met a violent death in a foreign land; Sparta, not Athens, saw to that. And although he and Socrates had long since parted company, their names were inextricably linked in the minds of the judges at the philosopher's trial.

Then there was the power-hungry Critias, who threw in his lot with

Sparta during the Peloponnesian War and headed the puppet government of Athens after her crushing defeat in 404 B.C. During the eight months that he and his so-called Council of Thirty held sway, they conducted a reign of terror in which thousands were killed and exiled, the temples plundered, and civil rights suppressed. Socrates himself almost fell victim to the tyranny. A government spy overheard him remarking that a herdsman should not pride himself on the decrease in the number of his cattle, and Critias and his bloody-handed colleagues got the point. Summoned before the Thirty, Socrates was threatened with a ban on further conversations with younger men—in his case, a virtual death sentence. But with his usual argumentative acuity, he demonstrated how absurdly such an order might work out in practice, and was let off with a warning. The ruling clique then tried to involve him with their own criminality—a familiar totalitarian tactic today—by ordering him and four others to seize a wealthy man named Leon of Salamis, who was slated for death. The others obeyed, but Socrates refused to take part in the deed. He would have answered for his defiance with his own life, but for a timely democratic counterrevolution which overthrew the terror and brought death to Critias.

But the memory of his sanguinary rule lingered on; and Socrates' repeated collisions with his former pupil were not enough to erase the public bitterness and suspicion engendered by the old association between them. Although both Alcibiades and Critias had passed from the scene when Socrates was brought to trial, their names remained a stench in the nostrils of his judges.

It was a former disciple of a different sort who stood on the accusers' platform in the year 399 B.C.: Anytus, a prominent and apparently sincere moderate politician who had spent most of his fortune in the struggle against the Thirty and had served with distinction in the city's liberation from their rule. Once democracy was restored, he had sponsored the enactment of a merciful general-amnesty statute, which barred any accusation against his old teacher for consorting with traitors. A most unlikely candidate for the role of Socrates' nemesis; and some historians have been puzzled enough to look for an element of personal vengefulness in his action. Anytus' son has been suggested as the key to the enigma. Socrates had once told Anytus that the boy was fit for better things than the family tanning business—a compliment to the son, no doubt, but an affront to the father. Staying behind in Athens with Socrates when his father fled the city during the reign of terror, the lad apparently took to drink in the company of dissolute young aristocrats, and Socrates may have been held responsible.

What little is known of Anytus, however, supports the view that he acted against Socrates not as an irate father, but as a misguided patriot. For Socrates was outspoken in his criticism of the new democracy and its leaders, most of whom he considered crude politicians lacking in wisdom and ill-equipped for high office. He believed in government by the well-educated and well-informed, and made no secret of his disdain for Athens' system of election to public office by lot—a mechanism which, he felt, entrusted the city's fate to a grab bag.

Anytus' sensitivity to these opinions can only be understood in the light of conditions in Athens during the closing years of the fifth century. Although the nightmare of the bloody days of the Thirty had begun to recede, the city's leadership felt far from secure. Twenty-seven years of almost continuous hostilities against her sister city-states had brought plague, famine, and class warfare in their wake. Her once-mighty fleet lay at the bottom of the sea or rotting in the harbor, and her commerce was barely worthy of the name. Prices were high, necessities scarce. The Athenian government subsisted on the sufferance of Sparta, which had reluctantly given the nod to an orderly democratic regime to supplant the anarchy of the Thirty. Threats of war from outside kept the city on edge; and within, it was uncertain that the reactionaries would not make another bid for power.

As so often happens in times of postwar stress, the anxiety of the city was reflected in excessive religious and political orthodoxy. Those who pursued the cult of the individual and who substituted doubt for certainty were bound to be suspect; and the name of Socrates led the list.

Anytus was neither a fanatic nor a fool. His own government had restored to its citizens freedom of speech in the political arena. That same government had adopted his proposal of a general amnesty, prohibiting any charges against Socrates based on his former associations with traitors and oligarchs. He was determined to drive Socrates from Athens, and he needed to concoct a case of sufficient gravity to warrant exile for the aged savant.

A law prohibiting impiety—long in disuse and never taken seriously —furnished the hook to hang a case on. Although Athens had never punished as heretics those who repudiated the traditional myths of Homer and Hesiod, and had on the whole looked tolerantly on deviations from dogma, Socrates, with his constant references to the inspiration of a "divine voice" and his calculated sowing of doubt in the minds of his listeners, might be accused of violating the ancient statute—and he would probably flee into exile rather than face trial, just as Alcibiades had done. Or so Anytus assumed.

He must have weighed carefully, however, the chances that there would be a trial and that it might result in an acquittal. Under Athenian

18

law he would be penalized heavily as the accuser if one fifth or more of the jury did not vote for conviction. (This mechanism was designed to prevent frivolous prosecutions; the state left the bringing of criminal charges to individuals, except in matters like draft-dodging or tax-evasion, which directly affected Athens' interests.) And there was also the question of political prestige.

To insulate himself against an untoward result, Anytus enlisted two other Socrates-haters as fellow prosecutors—Meletus, a cadaverous poet who qualified as a religious zealot, and Lycon, a professional orator. Meletus could be relied upon to supply gusto to the attack, and Lycon finesse, for there were no lawyers in Athens: parties had to plead their own cases.

Still, the evidence was not too strong, and Anytus might have thought better of the entire venture but for the nature of the jury system under which Socrates would be tried.

Juries were chosen by lot from a panel of citizens over thirty who had volunteered to serve. Out of 30,000 citizens, about 6000 volunteered each year; and considering that the pay was less than a day laborer's, the chances for a moderately intelligent jury were not too good. At least 201 jurors sat in each trial; in very serious cases the number sometimes exceeded 1000. Mob rule reigned supreme in the courts of Athens.

Thus popular prejudices and misconceptions played a prodigious part in the votes that juries cast (without retiring to deliberate) by dropping shells into "guilty" and "not guilty" ballot boxes. The more so, because the magistrates who presided over the proceedings had no function except to maintain order and see to it that the parties stayed within their allotted time—all cases had to be completed within the span of a single day. Even if the magistrates had been something more than monitors, it would have availed little, because there was no written text of legal rules or precedents, and the presiding magistrate was not required to possess any particular qualifications as a jurist.

Under these circumstances, the maverick Socrates would be tried by the herd. To an alert politician like Anytus, the outcome was not too difficult to predict: in a very real sense Socrates had been on trial before the Athenian public for a generation, and had been all but condemned.

Back in 423 B.C., long before the city's fortunes began to decline, the comic poet-playwright Aristophanes had fixed in the minds of the populace a stereotype of Socrates which was destined to plague him to the end of his days. Before an audience of about 15,000 people in the Theater of Dionysius, Socrates had been cruelly and falsely caricatured in the young dramatist's *The Clouds*; and it was more than happenstance that the charges brought against the philosopher twenty-four years later

19

coincided squarely with Aristophanes' satiric attack on him. In the play Socrates was portrayed as denying the existence of the gods and worshiping the clouds instead:

> To them we owe all thoughts, speeches, trickery, roguery, boasting, lies, sagacity.

The echo of this speech (and many of the same tenor) would be heard by Socrates in the accusation before the Court:

> Socrates is guilty of crime, first, for not worshiping the gods the city worships, and for introducing new divinities of his own . . .

The second count of the indictment read:

> . . . and next, for corrupting the youth.

Aristophanes' vicious lampoon covered this ground, too:

> SOCRATES. *Well, then, do you take away your son or do you wish me to teach him how to speak?*

> STREPSIADES (A RICH MAN). *Teach him, chastise him, and do not fail to sharpen his tongue well, on one side for petty lawsuits and on the other for important cases.*

> SOCRATES. *Make yourself easy. I shall return to you an accomplished Sophist.*

Although the practice of ridiculing public figures was widespread in Aristophanes' day, *The Clouds* can hardly be excused as having been written in the spirit of good clean fun. A revised version presented and published a few years later heaped the coals of abuse still higher; and in *The Birds* (414 B.C.) and *The Frogs* (405 B.C.) the playwright renewed the assault on "the odious Socrates," warning the audience to "beware of jabbering" with him.

Aristophanes' gravest offense against Socrates lay in identifying him with the Sophists—the much-despised verbal fencers and teachers of logic who sold their talents at exorbitant prices, writing speeches for use in lawsuits. They had brought to Athens from other parts of Greece a critical attitude toward the conventional morality and religious convictions of the people. Socrates had nothing in common with the Sophists except a gift for manipulating ideas; he disavowed them and their practices. But the jurors who sat in judgment on his case were incapable of nice distinctions; and many of them had undoubtedly been bested in court proceedings by litigants who had bought clever briefs from those "blackguards" (as Aristophanes called them) who could "make the poorer cause seem the better."

20

Such was the climate of opinion Anytus could count on, when he took his place among the accusers on a balmy spring day in 399 B.C. for the trial of his old friend. Into the jury enclosure trooped 501 good men and true, who seated themselves under the open sky on ranks of wooden benches, separated by a railing from the spectators. Following the customary offering of incense and the invocation to the gods, the presiding magistrate put the jury to an elaborate collective oath. The water clock was started, timing each speaker, to make certain that the trial would be concluded by nightfall.

All of the evidence had previously been prepared in the form of affidavits in a preliminary hearing before the magistrate, held after Socrates had been summoned by his accusers. The witnesses appeared at the trial, but only to authenticate their oaths on these papers; they could not be cross-examined. Socrates disdained to produce any witnesses in his behalf, although in the course of his defense speech he occasionally turned to his friends in the audience to attest the truth of his statements.

All three prosecutors, mounting in turn the raised platform reserved for them, addressed the jury court. Their speeches have not been preserved, but they are partly mirrored in Socrates' reply, as reported by Plato and Xenophon. Meletus probably led off, pointing to Socrates' acknowledged belief in his "divine voice" and vaguely referring to his early and long-abandoned speculations in physical science as proof of the introduction of "novel religious practices." The elderly Anytus stressed the corruption of youth and led the jurors into a rusty trap, saying that if Socrates were not guilty, he would not have been prosecuted in the first place. He warned the jurors that if the old man were released, he would go right back to corrupting their sons by his example. There is no indication of the content of Lycon's speech, for Socrates' defense ignores him. He was, after all, only a professional orator.

Socrates was at a distinct disadvantage, aside from the size and poor quality of the jury and the muddled prejudices of the populace against him. The crime of impiety does not appear to have been defined, although it had long been recognized as an offense which could be punished by death. The standards for judgment were therefore hazy and intangible; and he was compelled to contend with the pious instincts of his jurors, rather than with commonly accepted criteria. This was not his dish of intellectual tea.

Socrates' defense speech was eloquent enough, but it was unnecessarily abrasive. So much so, in fact, that the theory has been advanced in some quarters that he was deliberately committing judicial suicide. To this approach Xenophon lends some support in his account of a dis-

21

cussion between Socrates and one of his friends shortly before the trial. The seventy-year-old philosopher is explaining why he cannot exert himself to prepare a defense:

Do you think it surprising that even God holds it better for me to die now? Do you not know that I would refuse to concede that any man has led a better life than I have up to now? . . . But now, if my years are prolonged, I know that the frailties of old age will inevitably be realized— that my vision will be less perfect and my hearing less keen, that I shall be slower to learn and more forgetful of what I have learned. If I perceive my decay, and take to complaining, how could I longer take pleasure in life?

Much as modern historians distrust Xenophon's account (he was away from Athens during the trial and wrote his narrative long after the event), its spirit is consistent with Socrates' state of mind at the time as revealed by the more reliable Plato: a determined stand for a just verdict, underlaid by philosophic acceptance of whatever fate might hold in store for him.

His interest in setting the record straight before his countrymen is plain enough as he prods them in the direction of truth with irony and wit, and with that peculiar mixture of conceit and self-depreciation which he employed in discoursing with his students. But he appears throughout as the lecturer rather than the advocate, more interested in abstract justice than in his own skin.

His cross-examination of Meletus—for accusers could be questioned by both the prisoner and the jurors—illustrates the point sharply. Through sheer cleverness he forces Meletus to overstate his accusation until it borders on the absurd; he leaves Meletus shorn of dignity and probity; but he ignores the fact that the crimes of which he is accused are the by-product of that very cleverness.

All things considered, the vote against him was fairly close—281 to 220. Thirty-one ballots in his favor would have swung an acquittal.

Socrates was then asked, as Athenian procedure required, to propose a penalty as an alternative to the death sentence demanded by his accusers. The jurors had no power to compromise. They had to choose between the two, by marking with their fingernails on a wax tablet either a long line (for the punishment suggested by his prosecutors) or a short line (for the defendant's proposal).

It is probable that if Socrates had suggested banishment, the jury would have concurred, and Anytus at least would have breathed a sigh of relief. Respect for the gods of the state was not so deeply ingrained in the Athenian of 399 B.C. that a technical breach of the law against impiety would have normally called for the extreme penalty. But Socrates cleaved to his own impeccable (and irritating) logic. Again he spoke as a teacher; his position as a convicted criminal was merely a springboard for further mental acrobatics. He had served the state so well, he said quite seriously, that he deserved the recognition given to Olympic victors, eminent warriors, and such: free board for life in the town hall.

Sensing that he was making no headway with this audacious gambit, he finally relented:

Well, perhaps I could afford a *mina*, and therefore I propose that penalty; Plato, Crito, Critobulus, and Appollodorus, my friends here, bid me say thirty *minae*, and they will be the sureties. Let thirty *minae* be the penalty . . .

Thirty *minae* was no trifling sum; equivalent to about $600 in today's currency, it was considered a handsome dowry for a middle-class girl in fifth-century Greece. But by the time he closed his speech with this elaborately casual offer, Socrates had already lost whatever sympathy his years and his eminence might have earned him, with words like these:

I will not say to myself that I deserve any evil, or propose any penalty. Why should I? Because I am afraid of the penalty of death which Meletus proposes? When I do not know whether death is a good or an evil why should I propose a penalty which would certainly be an evil? Shall I say imprisonment? And why should I live in prison, and be the slave of the magistrate of the year—of the Eleven? Or shall the penalty be a fine, and imprisonment until the fine is paid? There is the same objection. I should have to lie in prison, for money I have none, and cannot pay. And if I say exile (and this may possibly be the penalty which you might choose), I must indeed be blinded by the love of life, if I am so irrational as to expect that when you, my fellow citizens, cannot endure my discourses and words and have found them so grievous that you will have no more of them, others are like to endure me.

No compromise. The jury voted the death penalty by eight more votes than had been cast for the verdict of guilty.

Now Socrates could see the horizon close at hand; it had stopped receding. In his farewell to the jurymen, he rose to heights of tragic and heroic eloquence seldom equaled in history:

Often in battle there can be no doubt that if a man will throw away his arms, and fall on his knees before his pursuers, he may escape death; and in other dangers there are other ways of escaping death, if a man is willing to say and do anything. The difficulty, my friends, is not to avoid death, but to avoid unrighteousness; for that runs faster than death. I am old and move slowly, and the slow runner has overtaken me, and my accusers are keen and quick, and the faster runner, who is unrighteousness, has over-taken them.

The unfriendly jurors, their eyes cast down, were leaving the court as he spoke; and typically, he turned to a message of consolation for those who voted in his favor:

Now if you suppose that there is no consciousness, but a sleep like the sleep of him who is undisturbed even by dreams, death will be an un-speakable gain . . . for eternity is then but a single night. But if death is the journey to another place, and there, as men say, all the dead abide, what good, O my friends and judges, can be better than this? If indeed, when the pilgrim arrives in the world below, he is delivered from the pro-fessors of justice in this world, and finds the true judges who are said to sit in judgment there . . . that pilgrimage will be worth making. . . . Nay, if this be true, let me die again and again . . .

The hour of departure has arrived, and we go our ways—I to die, and you to live. Which is better God only knows.

His closing words signified the arrival of officers of the Eleven, who supervised the small body of jailers, executioners, and torturers main-tained by the state. Generally, executions were carried out without de-lay, but Socrates' case was an exception. A "sacred boat" had been sent to the shrine of Apollo in Delos, as part of an annual religious celebra-tion, and the rules of ceremonial purity barred executions until the ves-sel returned. Adverse winds delayed the return of the boat, and Socrates remained chained in a prison cell for thirty days.

His friends meanwhile laid plans for his escape. Bribing his guards was a simple matter, and funds had been raised from as far away as Thebes to silence possible informers. When the subject was broached to Socrates, he balked: yes, the verdict was unjust and founded on perjury; but it was the judgment of a legally constituted court and the state would be wronged if it were not enforced. Not Athens, but Anytus and Meletus had wronged him; and if he should flee, he would be un-faithful to his obligations as a citizen and truly guilty of a crime against the state.

He had been spending his time composing verses and engaging in spirited colloquies with his friends, no different from those which had occupied his days as a free man. His final day on earth he faced with equanimity. Many of his friends thronged into his cell, where they found him with Xanthippe and their son, both of whom had apparently spent the night in the prison. He sent them home at once and settled down to a final discourse designed to comfort his disconsolate followers. Pain and pleasure, knowledge and poetry, truth and beauty, they discussed—and death. Plato has preserved this session in his *Phaedo*, and we see a Socrates alternately impish and grave, turning his hearers' arguments back upon themselves, confounding all (even his jailer, who was in tears) with his wisdom and good nature.

The conversation ended, Socrates calmly turned to the business of the day. First a bath, to save the women the trouble after he was dead. Then the final fond farewells. And suddenly there was no more time. Crito, to whom he had given instructions for his burial: "In any way that you like; but you must get hold of me and take care that I do not run away from you!"—returned with the jailer, who brought in the cup of hemlock. Asking the gods "to prosper my journey from this to the other world," Socrates drained the cup without emotion. His friends were in tears, and he quieted them with a few well-chosen words. After walking about the room a while, he felt his legs begin to fail and lay down, and covered his face. Death came to him shortly.

Virtuous men have been many, both before and after Socrates. But few have, by their deaths and the manner of their dying, provided so vivid a vision of sacrifice in the cause of truth and freedom. His legacy to the world was not merely in the body of ideas which sprang from his mind and those of the schools of philosophy which he spawned, but in the image of heroism in the service of a just cause which he stamped on the soul of posterity.

Had he behaved more like a man and less like a god after the verdict was handed down; had he asked for exile instead of contemptuously offering the jury thirty pieces of silver; had he listened to the invitation to flee—his defense speech to the jury court would have sounded preposterous and pretentious, the vain strutting of a self-indulgent intellectual. Seen through the glass of subsequent events, the following excerpts from Socrates' speech shine with a purity of soul that was not to be equaled on earth for 400 years:

How you, O Athenians, have been affected by my accusers, I cannot tell; but I know that they almost made me forget who I was—so persuasively did they speak; and yet they have hardly uttered a word of truth. . . .

And first, I have to reply to the older charges and to my first accusers . . . who began when you were children, and took possession of your minds with their falsehoods. . . .

And hardest of all, I do not know and cannot tell the names of my accusers; unless in the chance case of a comic poet. All who from envy and malice have persuaded you—some of them having first convinced themselves —all this class of men are most difficult to deal with; for I cannot have them up here, and cross-examine them, and therefore I must simply fight with

25

shadows in my own defense, and argue when there is no one who answers. . . .

I will begin at the beginning, and ask what is the accusation which has given rise to the slander of me . . . and I will sum up their words in an affidavit: "Socrates is an evildoer, and a curious person, who searches into things under the earth and in heaven, and he makes the worse appear the better cause; and he teaches the aforesaid doctrines to others."

Such is the nature of the accusation: it is just what you have yourselves seen in the comedy of Aristophanes, who has introduced a man whom he calls Socrates, going about and saying that he walks in air, and talking a deal of nonsense concerning matters of which I do not pretend to know either much or little—not that I mean to speak disparagingly of anyone who is a student of natural philosophy. . . . But the simple truth is, O Athenians, that I have nothing to do with physical speculations. Very many of those here present are witnesses to the truth of this, and to them I appeal. . . .

As little foundation is there for the report that I am a teacher, and take money; this accusation has no more truth in it than the other. Although, if a man were really able to instruct mankind, to receive money for giving instruction would, in my opinion, be an honor to him. . . .

I dare say, Athenians, that someone among you will reply, "Yes, Socrates, but what is the origin of these accusations which are brought against you: there must have been something strange which you have been doing? All these rumors and this talk about you would never have arisen if you had been like other men: tell us, then, what is the cause of them, for we should be sorry to judge hastily of you." . . .

And here, O men of Athens, I must beg you not to interrupt me, even if I seem to say something extravagant. . . . I will refer you to a witness who is worthy of credit; that witness shall be the God of Delphi—he will tell you about my wisdom, if I have any, and of what sort it is. You must have known Chaerephon; he was early a friend of mine, and also a friend of yours, for he shared in the recent exile of the people, and returned with you. Well, Chaerephon, as you know, was very impetuous in all his doings, and he went to Delphi and boldly asked the oracle to tell him whether . . . anyone was wiser than I was, and the Pythian prophetess answered, that there was no man wiser. Chaerephon is dead himself; but his brother, who is in court, will confirm the truth of what I am saying.

Why do I mention this? Because I am going to explain to you why I have such an evil name. When I heard the answer, I said to myself, What can the God mean? and what is the interpretation of his riddle? . . . For I know that I have no wisdom, small or great. What then can he mean when he says that I am the wisest of men? And yet he is a god, and cannot lie; that would be against his nature. After long consideration, I thought of a method of trying the question. I reflected that if I could only find a man wiser than myself, then I might go to the god with a refutation in my hand.

I should say to him, "Here is a man who is wiser than I am; but you said that I was the wisest."

Accordingly I went to one who had the reputation of wisdom, and observed him—his name I need not mention; he was a politician whom I selected for examination—and the result was as follows: When I began to talk with him, I could not help thinking that he was not really wise, although he was thought wise by many, and still wiser by himself; and thereupon I tried to explain to him that he thought himself wise, but was not really wise; and the consequence was that he hated me, and his enmity was shared by several who were present and heard me. . . .

Then I went to another who had still higher pretensions to wisdom, and my conclusion was exactly the same. Whereupon I made another enemy of him, and of many others besides him.

Then I went to one man after another, being not unconscious of the enmity which I provoked, and I lamented and feared this: but necessity was laid upon me—the word of God, I thought, ought to be considered first. And I said to myself, Go I must to all who appear to know, and find out the meaning of the oracle. And I swear to you, Athenians, by the dog I swear!—for I must tell you the truth—the result of my mission was just this: I found that the men most in repute were all but the most foolish; and that others less esteemed were really wiser and better. . . .

After the politicians, I went to the poets; tragic, dithyrambic, and all sorts. . . . I took them some of the most elaborate passages in their own writings, and asked what was the meaning of them—thinking that they would teach me something. Will you believe me? I am almost ashamed to confess the truth, but I must say that there is hardly a person present who would not have talked better about their poetry than they did themselves. . . . So I departed, conceiving myself to be superior to them for the same reason that I was superior to the politicians.

At last I went to the artisans. I was conscious that I knew nothing at all, as I may say, and I was sure that they knew many fine things; and here I was not mistaken, for they did know many things of which I was ignorant, and in this they certainly were wiser than I was. But I observed that even the good artisans fell into the same error as the poets—because they were good workmen they thought that they also knew all sorts of high matters, and this defect in them overshadowed their wisdom; and therefore I asked myself on behalf of the oracle whether I would like to be as I was, neither having their knowledge nor their ignorance, or like them in both; and I made answer to myself and to the oracle that I was better off as I was.

This inquisition has led to my having many enemies of the worst and most dangerous kind, and has given occasion also to many calumnies. And I am called wise, for my hearers always imagine that I myself possess the wisdom which I find wanting in others; but the truth is, O men of Athens, that God only is wise; and by his answer he intends to show that the wisdom of men is worth little or nothing; he is not speaking of Socrates, he is only using my name by way of illustration, as if he said, He, O men, is the wisest, who, like Socrates, knows that his wisdom is in truth worth nothing. And so I go about the world obedient to the god, and search and make enquiry into the wisdom of anyone . . . who appears to be wise . . . and my occupation quite absorbs me, and I have not time to give either to any public matter of interest or to any concern of my own, but I am in utter poverty by reason of my devotion to the god.

There is another thing—young men of the richer classes, who have not much to do, come about me of their own accord; they like to hear the pretenders examined, and they often imitate me, and proceed to examine others; there are plenty of persons, as they quickly discover, who think that they know something, but really know little or nothing; and then those who are examined by them instead of being angry with themselves are angry with me: This confounded Socrates, they say; this villainous misleader of youth!—and then if somebody asks them, Why, what evil does he practice or teach? they do not know, and cannot tell; but in order that they may not appear to be at a loss, they repeat the ready-made charges which are used against all philosophers about teaching things up in the clouds and under the earth, and having no gods, and making the worse appear the better cause; for they do not like to confess that their pretense of knowledge has been detected—which is the truth; and as they are numerous and ambitious and energetic, and are drawn up in battle array and have persuasive tongues, they have filled your ears with their loud and inveterate calumnies. And this is the reason why my three accusers, Meletus and Anytus and Lycon, have set upon me; Meletus, who has a quarrel with me on behalf of the poets; Anytus, on behalf of the craftsmen and politicians; Lycon, on behalf of the rhetoricians: and, as I said at the beginning, I cannot expect to get rid of such a mass of calumny all in a moment. . . .

I have said enough in my defense against the first class of my accusers; I turn to the second class. They are headed by Meletus, that good man and true lover of his country, as he calls himself. Against these, too, I must try to make a defense:

Let their affidavit be read: . . . It says that Socrates is a doer of evil, who corrupts the youth; and who does not believe in the gods of the state, but has other new divinities of his own. Such is the charge; and now let us examine the particular counts. He says that I am a doer of evil, and corrupt the youth; but I say, O men of Athens, that Meletus is a doer of evil, in that he pretends to be in earnest when he is only in jest, and is so eager to bring men to trial from a pretended zeal and interest about matters in which he really never had the smallest interest. And the truth of this I will endeavor to prove to you.

Come hither, Meletus, and let me ask a question of you.

Q. You think a great deal about the improvement of youth?

A. Yes, I do.

Q. . . . Speak, then, and tell the judges who their improver is.

A. The laws.

Q. But that, my good sir, is not my meaning. I want to know who the person is, who, in the first place, knows the laws.

A. The judges, Socrates, who are present in court.

Q. What, do you mean to say, Meletus, that they are able to instruct and improve youth?

A. Certainly they are.

Q. What, all of them, or some only and not others?

A. All of them.

Q. By the goddess Hera, that is good news! There are plenty of improvers, then. And what do you say of the audience—do they improve them?

A. Yes, they do.

Q. And the senators?

A. Yes, the senators improve them.

Q. But perhaps the members of the Assembly corrupt them?—or do they improve them?

A. They improve them.

Q. Then every Athenian improves and elevates them; all with the exception of myself; and I alone am their corrupter? Is that what you affirm?

A. That is what I stoutly affirm. . . .

Q. But still I should like to know, Meletus, in what I am affirmed to corrupt the young. I suppose you mean, as I infer from your indictment, that I teach them not to acknowledge the gods which the state acknowledges, but some other new divinities or spiritual agencies in their stead. . . .

A. Yes, that I say emphatically.

Q. Then, by the gods, Meletus, of whom we are speaking, tell me and the Court, in somewhat plainer terms, what you mean! For I do not as yet understand whether you affirm that I teach other men to acknowledge some gods, and therefore that I do believe in gods, and am not an entire atheist —this you do not lay to my charge—but only you say that they are not the same gods which the city recognizes—the charge is that they are different gods. Or, do you mean that I am an atheist simply, and a teacher of atheism?

A. I mean the latter—that you are a complete atheist. . . .

Q. Can a man believe in spiritual and divine agencies, and not in spirits or demigods?

A. He cannot.

SOCRATES: How lucky I am to have extracted that answer, by the assistance of the Court! But then you swear in the indictment that I teach and believe in divine or spiritual agencies (new or old, no matter for that); at any rate, I believe in spiritual agencies—so you say and swear in the affidavit; and yet if I believe in divine beings, how can I help believing in spirits or demigods—must I not? To be sure I must; and therefore I may assume that your silence gives consent.

29

ǫ. Now what are spirits or demigods? Are they not either gods or the sons of gods?

A. Certainly they are.

SOCRATES: But this is what I call the facetious riddle invented by you: the demigods or spirits are gods, and you say first that I do not believe in gods, and then again that I do believe in gods; that is, if I believe in demigods. . . . You have put this into the indictment because you had nothing real of which to accuse me. But no one who has a particle of understanding will ever be convinced by you that the same men can believe in divine and superhuman things, and yet not believe that there are gods and demigods and heroes.

I have said enough in answer to the charge of Meletus: any elaborate defense is unnecessary; but I know only too well how many are the enmities which I have incurred, and this is what will be my destruction if I am destroyed—not Meletus, nor yet Anytus, but the envy and detraction of the world, which has been the death of many good men, and will probably be the death of many more; there is no danger of my being the last of them.

Someone will say: And are you not ashamed, Socrates, of a course of life which is likely to bring you to an untimely end? To him I may fairly answer: There you are mistaken: a man who is good for anything ought not to calculate the chance of living or dying; he ought only to consider whether in doing anything he is doing right or wrong—acting the part of a good man or of a bad. . . .

For the fear of death is indeed the pretense of wisdom, and not real wisdom, being a pretense of knowing the unknown; and no one knows whether death, which men in their fear apprehend to be the greatest evil, may not be the greatest good. . . . And in this respect only I believe myself to differ from men in general, and may perhaps claim to be wiser than they are: that whereas I know but little of the world below, I do not suppose that I know: but I do know that injustice and disobedience to a better, whether God or man, is evil and dishonorable, and I will never fear or avoid a possible good rather than a certain evil. And therefore . . . if you say to me, Socrates, this time we will not mind Anytus, and you shall be let off, but upon one condition, that you are not to enquire and speculate in this way any more, and that if you are caught doing so again you shall die—if this was the condition on which you let me go—I should reply:

Men of Athens, I honor and love you; but I shall obey God rather than you, and while I have life and strength I shall never cease from the practice and teaching of philosophy, exhorting anyone whom I meet and saying to him after my manner: You, my friend—a citizen of the great and mighty and wise city of Athens—are you not ashamed of heaping up the greatest amount of money and honor and reputation, and caring so little about wisdom and truth and the greatest improvement of the soul, which you never regard or heed at all? And if the person with whom I am arguing says: Yes, but I do care; then I do not leave him or let him go at once; but I proceed

to interrogate and examine and cross-examine him, and if I think that he has
no virtue in him, but only says that he has, I reproach him with under-
valuing the greater, and overvaluing the less. And I shall repeat the same
words to everyone whom I meet, young and old, citizen and alien, but especially to the citizens, inasmuch as they are my brethren. For know that
this is the command of God; and I believe that no greater good has ever
happened in the state than my service to the God. For I do nothing but go
about persuading you all, old and young alike, not to take thought for your
persons or your properties, but first and chiefly to care about the greatest
improvement of the soul. I tell you that virtue is not given by money, but
that from virtue comes money and every other good of man, public as well
as private. This is my teaching, and if this is the doctrine which corrupts
the youth, I am a mischievous person. But if anyone says that this is not my
teaching, he is speaking an untruth. Wherefore, O men of Athens, I say to
you, do as Anytus bids or not as Anytus bids, and either acquit me or not;
but whichever you do, understand that I shall never alter my ways, not even
if I have to die many times. . . .

And now, Athenians, I am not going to argue for my own sake, as you
may think, but for yours, that you may not sin against the God by condemning me, who am his gift to you. For if you kill me you will not easily
find a successor to me, who, if I may use such a ludicrous figure of speech,
am a sort of gadfly, given to the state by God; and the state is a great and
noble steed who is tardy in his motions owing to his very size, and requires
to be stirred into life. I am that gadfly which God has attached to the state,
and all day long and in all places am always fastening upon you, arousing
and persuading and reproaching you.

You will not easily find another like me, and therefore I would advise
you to spare me. . . .

When I say that I am given to you by God, the proof of my mission is
this: if I had been like other men, I should not have neglected all my own
concerns or patiently seen the neglect of them during all these years . . .
but now, as you will perceive, not even the impudence of my accusers dares
to say that I have ever exacted or sought pay of anyone; of that they have
no witness. And I have a sufficient witness to the truth of what I say—my
poverty.

Someone may wonder why I go about in private giving advice and busy-
ing myself with the concerns of others, but do not venture to come forward in public and advise the state. I will tell you why. You have heard
me speak at sundry times and in divers places of an oracle or sign which
comes to me, and is the divinity which Meletus ridicules in the indictment.
This sign, which is a kind of voice, first began to come to me when I was a
child; it always forbids but never commands me to do anything which I am
going to do. This is what deters me from being a politician. And rightly, as
I think. For I am certain, O men of Athens, that if I had engaged in
politics, I should have perished long ago, and done no good either to you or

to myself. And do not be offended at my telling you the truth: for the truth is, that no man who goes to war with you or any other multitude, honestly striving against the many lawless and unrighteous deeds which are done in a state, will save his life; he who will fight for the right, if he would live even for a brief space, must have a private station and not a public one. . . .

Well, Athenians, this and the like of this is all the defense which I have to offer. Yet a word more. Perhaps there may be someone who is offended at me, when he calls to mind how he himself on a similar, or even a less serious occasion, prayed and entreated the judges with many tears, and how he produced his children in court, which was a moving spectacle, together with a host of relations and friends; whereas I, who am probably in danger of my life, will do none of these things. The contrast may occur to his mind, and he may be set against me, and vote in anger because he is displeased at me on this account. Now, if there be such a person among you—mind, I do not say that there is—to him I may fairly reply: My friend, I am a man, and like other men, a creature of flesh and blood, and not "of wood or stone," as Homer says; and I have a family, yes, and sons, O Athenians, three in number, one almost a man, and two others who are still young; and yet I will not bring any of them hither in order to petition you for an acquittal. And why not? Not from any self-assertion or want of respect for you. Whether I am or am not afraid of death is another question, of which I will not now speak. But, having regard to public opinions, I feel that such conduct would be discreditable to myself, and to you, and to the whole state. One who has reached my years, and who has a name for wisdom, ought not to demean himself. Whether this opinion of me be deserved or not, at any rate the world has decided that Socrates is in some way superior to other men. And if those among you who are said to be superior in wisdom and courage, and any other virtue, demean themselves in this way, how shameful is their conduct!

I have seen men of reputation, when they have been condemned, behaving in the strangest manner: they seemed to fancy that they were going to suffer something dreadful if they died, and that they could be immortal if you only allowed them to live; and I think that such are a dishonor to the state. . . .

Do not then require me to do what I consider dishonorable and impious and wrong, especially now, when I am being tried for impiety on the indictment of Meletus. For if, O men of Athens, by force of persuasion and entreaty I could overpower your oaths, then I should be teaching you to believe that there are no gods, and in defending should simply convict myself of the charge of not believing in them. But that is not so—far otherwise. For I do believe that there are gods, and in a sense higher than that in which any of my accusers believe in them. And to you and to God I commit my cause, to be determined by you as is best for you and me.

JESUS

(30 A.D.)

Arnold Toynbee was not the first to point out the remarkable parallels in the biographies of Socrates and Jesus of Nazareth. A number of learned historians have found the similarities sufficiently impressive to suggest that their life stories draw on a common stream of heroic tradition. But their trials deviate from the pattern: they more closely approximate mirror images of each other. Socrates was called to account on religious grounds for political reasons, while Jesus was condemned on political grounds out of religious motives.

If Jesus' death on the Cross was preordained, he could hardly have been born at a more appropriate time and place: Galilee, in about 6 B.C.[1] Galilee was an outlying district of Palestine, then a remote but strategically important outpost of Rome's sprawling Mediterranean empire. To Rome and its puppet rulers, the Herods, it had long been a trouble spot. The imperial spy system had for decades kept a wary eye on this center of seething Jewish nationalism, from which Zealot hotheads had drawn much of their support in their spasmodic efforts to throw off the yoke of their conquerors. When Jesus was a boy, these extremists had led a countrywide uprising that ended with 2000 Jews on the cross and 20,000 sold into slavery. Jesus' association with the area would count heavily against him at his trial; when his accusers identified him as a Galilean to the Roman Procurator, Pontius Pilate, they were making a political point.

Pilate never quite fathomed what made these stubborn Jews tick. And although he had managed, after a few false starts, to work out an accommodation with their religious and temporal leaders, he kept half a Roman legion of infantry and a cohort of cavalry permanently stationed in Jerusalem as a precautionary measure.

[1] The Christian Era got off to a late start, thanks to the loose arithmetic of a sixth-century monk.

33

Most of the Jews within his realm managed to slake their thirst for release from bondage by drinking deeply of the Scriptures. Like the Egyptians before them, the Romans would pass; if Israel could only resist assimilation and remain worthy in the sight of God, the Book told them that the world would sooner or later be purged of evil. Enoch and Amos had predicted the coming of a Messiah who would restore the Jews to their rightful place among the nations. These prophecies were replenished and nurtured through daily observances of the distinctive rituals of the Faith, reinforced by the majestic symbol of the Temple that dominated Jerusalem's landscape.

But even among the quietists, there was anything but complete accord. At the opposite pole from the fiery Zealots stood the reactionaries of the ancient Jewish world—the wealthy and aristocratic Sadducees, who had traded collaboration with Rome for a substantial measure of religious and civil authority over their coreligionists. Appointed from among their number by the Procurator, the chief priests used the Law—which they considered confined to the five books of Moses—as a whip to keep the faithful in line. Ritual purity was held all-important; and with every aspect of Jewish life equating in one way or another with ritual, the chief priests and elders wielded enormous power among the Chosen People. And since the Messiah was not even mentioned in the first five books of Moses, the Sadducees could conscientiously lend a hand to the Procurator in thwarting the ambitions of the next self-styled liberator to come along.

The moderate middle-class group known as the Pharisees, to which Jesus' family vaguely adhered, held a generally more liberal religious outlook. Like the Sadducees, they adopted a passive attitude in politics, although they could be militant enough when their religious autonomy was threatened. They shared the Zealots' belief in the Messiah who would restore Israel to her rightful place in the family of nations, but they rejected violence as a means to that end.

All of these righteous Judeans looked with considerable scorn on Galilee, a land with a motley population including many Gentiles, where the nearly untouchable *amhaaretz*, the unlearned peasants and workers, predominated among the Jews, and ritual practices gave way to the necessities of wringing a daily subsistence from the land and sea. Even the few monastic Essenes there were regarded with distaste: they made no blood sacrifices, and they washed too much.

Rejecting the legalism of the Sadducees and Pharisees, the radicalism of the Zealots, and the unworldliness of the Essenes, Jesus preached in a welcome tongue to those who found no spiritual home under the roof of any of these sects. For reformation of Israel through ritual, he

34

substituted transformation through love; for outward observance, inward faith.

Although he saw eye to eye with much of theoretical Pharisaism, he found that it had degenerated into an inflexible and puritanical obsession with the Word, as interpreted by the scholarly scribes and elders, with little regard for the spirit. He sought to break down the barriers built up through centuries of orthodoxy between the people and their religion, between the chosen and the dispossessed. To the lowly *amhaaretz*, to outcast courtesans and hated tax collectors, and to the equally despised Gentiles, he opened doors which had hitherto been closed against them. He came to the people as a rabbi who kept no fasts, violated the Sabbath, ignored ritual washing, and disregarded the dietary laws—yet left no doubt of his essential piety and righteousness.

Had he confined himself to castigating the sterile and exacting legalism of the priestly groups, exhorting his followers to prepare for the kingdom of God, and healing the sick, he might have passed into history merely as a singularly poetic and inspired minor Jewish prophet. In about two years of active ministry, he had enlisted few followers and had attracted only a handful of enemies. Even in his native territory of Galilee he had won little acclaim and no disciples. Although he had not escaped the attention of the religious and civil authorities, he was not considered a threat to the established order; else he would never have spent a day in Jerusalem as a free man.

But his ceremonial entry into that city in the year 30 A.D. served notice that he was committed to a course of action which could readily spell trouble. Until then he had confided to no one but his intimates—and then only under a pledge of secrecy—his conviction that he was the Messiah. Now he was bent on fulfilling his mission, if at all possible, in the proper setting and on the proper occasion: Jerusalem at Passover.

Precisely what he meant when he spoke of himself as the Messiah defies analysis; and, ironically, Jesus' fate may have turned on the ambiguity in the meaning of that word. To most Jews, including his ambitious disciples, it meant the earthly king of the house of David who would restore Israel's independence. Jesus himself probably had somewhat less militant intentions and thought of himself simply as the herald of God who would warn Israel that it must return to the path of righteousness before it could be redeemed. Whatever his purpose, he never openly proclaimed his messianic role until his last day on earth, when the High Priest put the question to him squarely; and even then he refused to define its precise nature. Instead he spoke in the parables and metaphors characteristic of his time and calling, leaving it to his hearers to interpret them as they chose.

35

His conduct in Jerusalem did nothing to resolve the issue. Five days before the Passover festival, Jesus had found the city thronged with a polyglot assortment of pilgrims from the outlying districts of Palestine and from the Jewish communities of other lands. Within the city walls, and in tent camps on the surrounding hills, the pious were eagerly preparing for the holiday. Pilate had arrived from Caesarea to spend the festival season as usual in Jerusalem and had reinforced the Roman garrison at Fort Antonia, just in case. Herod Antipas had likewise moved his household into the city from Tiberias, capital of his tiny domain of Galilee.

As Jewish law prescribed, Jesus went immediately to the Temple. In the outer court surrounding the Temple area, sheep stood tethered and doves were displayed for sale in wicker baskets. Money-changers announced in many tongues the rates at which foreign currencies could be exchanged for the officially approved Tyrian coinage.

Jesus' violent reaction to this sight was understandable, but not altogether justified. The portion of the Temple grounds devoted to these commercial activities, known as the Forecourt of the Heathen, was especially set aside for those who, for various reasons, could not gain admission to the sacred precincts of the inner Temple. Although orthodox doctrine forbade trading on the grounds, the high priests allowed sacrificial fowl and cattle to be kept in the Forecourt compound and sold there as a matter of public convenience; but since all such Temple offerings required the approval of an official censor, the arrangement may very well have been extortionate, as the high prices prevalent at the time would seem to indicate.

By the same token, money-changers probably qualified as a necessary evil. The Romans permitted only small copper coins to be minted in Palestine. The more precious currency that came from Rome was stamped with the Emperor's image, and hence barred as "unclean" for Temple use. Foreign pilgrims brought in money of every description, varying so greatly in value that the Jerusalem authorities had proscribed its use to pay or purchase seals for the various Temple offerings. The exchange of this heterogeneous coinage for uniform Palestinian money made sense; the utilization of the Temple Forecourt for the purpose was expedient, but might well be interpreted as proof of the hypocrisy of the high priests and elders who regulated the affairs of the Temple.

To Jesus, it was just that; but he did nothing that day. A night's repose failed to blunt the edge of his indignation. When he returned to the scene the following morning, he was no longer the "gentle Jesus, meek and mild," of the hymnbooks. With the aid of some of his followers, he overturned the tables of the money-changers and the seats of the pigeon merchants and started to expel the traders. Paradoxically, and just this once, he emerged as a militant Jew enforcing the letter of the Law, at which the usually puritanical Sadducees had chosen to wink. His forceful action won him new supporters and lent some credence to the notion that this newcomer might be the aggressive Messiah of the prophecies.

The next day, when he arrived at the Temple, the scribes and elders, backed up by the priests on duty, were ready for him. By what authority had he acted the day before? Responding with a parable, Jesus intimated that he had come as the Messiah, and that it was forbidden to kill him. Cautiously feeling their way, they took another tack and tried to entrap him into a seditious statement: Is it lawful to give tribute unto Caesar? Pointing to Caesar's likeness on a Roman coin, Jesus sidestepped the snare and deftly implied the antithesis between the Emperor and God: "Give unto Caesar the things which are Caesar's, and to God the things which are God's." This soft reply may well have puzzled some of his new-found adherents who had looked to him as the potential leader of an insurrection. But except for the hardened Zealots, those who stayed on to hear more were not disappointed. The Nazarene launched into a bitter diatribe against the Pharisees and Sadducees, seemingly reckless of the consequences that must inevitably follow upon his defiance of the hierarchy. Then, to cap the climax, he turned to one of his disciples, who was awed by the splendor of the Temple, and exclaimed prophetically: "Seest thou these great buildings? There shall not be left one stone upon another that shall not be thrown down!"

Jesus might have been arrested on the spot, but the chief priests and scribes preferred to avoid any public uproar. The job had to be done in secret. That night Judas betrayed his hiding place at Gethsemane, and the soldiery moved in. He was taken promptly to the nearby detention chambers of Caiaphas, the High Priest.

Under Jewish law, capital cases were not supposed to be tried at night, and it is particularly unlikely that this rule would have been waived on the eve of a feast day. Jesus was, therefore, probably held in close custody until daybreak, while the Sanhedrin was being assembled on short notice—no easy task, for it had seventy-one members, and it took twenty-three to fill a quorum.

The Sanhedrin was comprised of priests, elders, and scribes, with a sprinkling of the heads of important families, all appointed by the High Priest. Its jurisdiction was limited to religious crimes. The hearing, therefore, must have been designed to establish proof of blasphemy, heresy, or sorcery. The trial of cases punishable by death was scrupulously hedged about by formalities, and any death sentence required the approval of the Procurator.

At first the hearing went well for Jesus. Two witnesses were required to prove the commission of a crime, and no two could be found who would agree. Although there had been witnesses galore to the cleansing of the Temple, it did not qualify as an offense: the structure itself had not been harmed, and the incident had not occurred within its sacred area. Jesus himself stood silent, possibly knowing of the practice of concealing eavesdroppers who could then corroborate each other's testimony concerning admissions made by the prisoner.

But, at length, two witnesses testified that Jesus had stated that he would destroy the Temple and rebuild it "without hands" in three days. This perversion of his words was all that could be brought to bear against him, and while it had the ring of blasphemy, it was still pretty thin to warrant a death sentence.

Caiaphas then turned to Jesus and put the direct question: "Art thou the Messiah?"

The moment of decision had arrived; if Jesus answered in the negative, his mission would dissolve in a thundering echo of derision. The query was a challenge to fulfill his destiny. He answered: "I am He."

Direct and unequivocal; and he added: "And ye shall see the Son of Man sitting at the right hand of Power and coming with the clouds of Heaven."

This was Caiaphas' cue. Dramatically rending his garments, he cried that they had heard enough of such blasphemy and called for a consensus from his colleagues. Had they followed his lead and torn their tunics "the length of the palm of the hand," in accordance with prescribed practice in the presence of a blasphemer, it would have signified that they concurred. But the members of the Sanhedrin could not bring themselves to find Jesus guilty of blasphemy.

The reasons were, like the offense itself, peculiarly technical. The crime of blasphemy consisted of an insult to the majesty of God. Messianic claims did not fall into that category; and so Caiaphas obviously rested his case as prosecutor (and chief judge) on the reference to the Deity in Jesus' reply. But under the Law, it was not considered blasphemous or even disrespectful to speak of God unless the accused used the sacred name that God had revealed to Moses—"Yahweh." As a well-indoctrinated rabbi, Jesus had circumvented that pitfall by employing one of the many synonyms current at the time, "Power"—just as others referred to God as "the Almighty" or "the Blessed One." And so Caiaphas' ruse failed—although it was unanimously agreed that Jesus was, nevertheless, "worthy of death."

This was not a verdict in any judicial sense. Had Jesus been found guilty of blasphemy, it would only have been necessary to inform Pilate, who would have complaisantly rubber-stamped the decision. The life of one Jew, more or less, meant nothing to this notoriously ruthless administrator; he would have been happy to oblige his friends, the Sadducees, who dominated the Sanhedrin. The Nazarene would then have died by one of the permissible Jewish modes of punishment: stoning, strangling, decapitation, or the stake.

Unable to find in the sacred law grounds for convicting Jesus of blasphemy, the Sanhedrin nevertheless realized that his fate as a political offender was a foregone conclusion. The Procurator was bound to regard a potential Messiah as a threat to the peace of his domain—enough, under the Roman statutes, to justify his condemnation for treason.

At about eight o'clock on the morning of April 3, therefore, Jesus was brought to the gaudy marble palace of Herod the Great, where Pilate had been conducting official business since daybreak. At the foot of the agate and azurite steps, the bound Nazarene was turned over to Roman guards. The Jewish dignitaries remained outside; they could not enter a Roman house before Passover without becoming unclean.

Roman law at that time provided elaborate guarantees of a fair trial, but Pilate apparently felt that the customary procedure need not hold good for a Jew. His reputation for cruelty, which later contributed to his removal from office, was matched only by his contempt for those curious religionists whom he had been dispatched to govern; and it is difficult to understand why he exhibited as much patience with Jesus as the Gospels attribute to him. The charge of blasphemy was not once mentioned before Pilate. He would certainly have taken it amiss if he had known that the prisoner had escaped conviction by the Sanhedrin that very morning. Instead, resting on Jesus' admission of a messianic mission, the chief priests told the Procurator that the Galilean was claiming to be King of the Jews.

Confronted with the charge, Jesus replied cryptically: "Thou sayest." From then on, he refused to answer the Procurator's questions. Pilate must have been puzzled, both by the attitude of the accused and by the persistent demands for his crucifixion from the small group at the foot of the palace steps. The enthusiasm of a Jewish crowd for the death of a would-be liberator might well have led him to conclude that he had been cast as a cat's-paw.

This supposition, if correct, lends some substance to the story of Barabbas. According to the Gospels, this Zealot insurrectionist and murderer had been condemned to death that morning, and, in accordance with a supposed custom at Passover time, Pilate offered to release to the assembled Jews any prisoner they desired. The crowd, it is said, spurred by the chief priests, called for Barabbas, and he was freed. In this fashion Pilate might have confirmed his suspicions about the role he was playing in the Sanhedrin's plans.

But no historical foundation exists for the Barabbas story. The Passover custom of releasing a felon is not mentioned outside of the Gospels; and under Roman law the privilege of pardon was reserved to the Emperor and not exercisable by his underlings. Pilate might have dropped a case before sentence, but his hands were tied once judgment was pronounced. And it is hardly credible that he would have released to the Jews a hard-bitten revolutionary caught in the act.[2]

In any case, he turned Jesus over to his soldiers for scourging and crucifixion, the typically Roman penalty for political crimes. It is most unlikely that he was merely bowing to a Sanhedrin threat to appeal over his head to Caesar; Pilate could not be intimidated by his Jewish vassals. His sole concern was to maintain order. Jesus stood before him accused of messianic pretensions—a charge which he did not deny. Policy dictated that if there were the least prospect that he was guilty, he should be liquidated.

So passed half an hour of an impatient Roman governor's time.

The ordeal that followed is now graven in the minds of one third of humanity—the scourging, the ridicule, the painful passage to the skull-shaped hill of Golgotha amid the gathering crowds, the six hours on the Cross, parched, half-conscious and, toward the last, despairing. By mid-afternoon it was over.

The death of Jesus paved the way for the genius of Paul. In time, the Jesus of history would be transformed into the Christ of faith, and his sufferings on the cross would become to countless millions a symbol of man's hope of salvation.

The earliest of the Gospels, *Mark*, contains an account of the trial which is distinguished in the King James version by the economy and grace of its prose:

[2] The Gospels are at odds concerning two other episodes in the progress of the trial, both generally discounted by lay scholars. Only two of the Gospel accounts refer to Pilate's symbolic washing of his hands to signify his innocence of the blood of Jesus. The story is probably apocryphal. The handwashing ritual was a peculiarly Jewish practice connected with the sacrifice of cattle and seems out of character for a Roman Procurator. And *Matthew's* account has Pilate speaking words strongly reminiscent of the Book of Samuel, an anachronism that strains credulity to the breaking point. Similarly, *Luke's* story that Pilate sent Jesus to Herod has no support from the other Gospels and probably reflects another attempt to emphasize Pilate's belief in the Nazarene's innocence.

And they led Jesus away to the High Priest: and with him were assembled all the chief priests and the elders and the scribes. . . .

And the chief priests and all the council sought for witness against Jesus to put him to death; and found none.

For many bare false witness against him, but their witness agreed not together.

And there arose certain, and bare false witness against him, saying,

"We heard him say, 'I will destroy this temple that is made with hands, and within three days I will build another made without hands.'"

But neither so did their witnesses agree together.

And the High Priest stood up in the midst, and asked Jesus, saying, "Answerest thou nothing? which is it which these witness against thee?"

But he held his peace, and answered nothing. Again the High Priest asked him, and said unto him, "Art thou the Christ, the Son of the Blessed?"

And Jesus said, "I am: and ye shall see the Son of Man sitting on the right hand of Power, and coming in the clouds of Heaven."

Then the High Priest rent his clothes, and saith, "What need we any further witnesses?"

"Ye have heard the blasphemy: what think ye?" And they all condemned him to be guilty of death.[3]

And some began to spit on him, and to cover his face, and to buffet him, and to say unto him, "Prophesy": and the servants did strike him with the palms of their hands. . . .

And straightway in the morning the chief priests held a consultation with the elders and scribes and the whole Council, and bound Jesus, and carried him away, and delivered him to Pilate.

And Pilate asked him, "Art thou the King of the Jews?" And he answering said unto him, "Thou sayest it."

And the chief priests accused him of many things: but he answered nothing.

And Pilate asked him again, saying, "Answerest thou nothing? behold how many things they witness against thee."

But Jesus yet answered nothing; so that Pilate marveled.

Now at that feast he released unto them one prisoner, whomsoever they desired.

And there was one named Barabbas, which lay bound with them that had made insurrection with him, who had committed murder in the insurrection.

And the multitude crying aloud began to desire him to do as he had ever done unto them.

But Pilate answered them, saying, "Will ye that I release unto you the King of the Jews?"

For he knew that the chief priests had delivered him for envy.

[3] None of the other Gospels speaks of the death sentence. And *John* (18:31) has the Jews reminding Pilate: "It is not lawful for us to put anyone to death."

But the chief priests moved the people, that he should rather release Barabbas unto them.

And Pilate answered and said again unto them, "What will ye then that I shall do unto him whom ye call the King of the Jews?"

And they cried out again, "Crucify him."

Then Pilate said unto them, "Why, what evil hath he done?" And they cried out the more exceedingly, "Crucify him."

And so Pilate, willing to content the people, released Barabbas unto them, and delivered Jesus, when he had scourged him, to be crucified.

JOAN OF ARC
(1431)

Five centuries after Joan of Arc was burned at the stake as a heretic and sorceress, she was proclaimed a saint by the Roman Catholic Church. Both actions were opposite sides of the same coin. Much of the evidence which brought about her condemnation was used to support her canonization. The premise in each instance was identical: that Joan possessed supernatural powers. The difference in result stemmed from the attribution of those powers by the Holy Inquisition to Satan, and by the contemporary Church to God.

Seen in this light, Joan's trial is not too difficult to comprehend. An illiterate farm girl, proclaiming that she is sent by God, suddenly bounds onto the stage of history and promptly reverses the course of the Hundred Years' War. She is captured by the enemy and turned over to a quisling ecclesiastical court. The outcome is a foregone conclusion: a "show trial" for propaganda purposes, dictated by military necessity. For the crown of France hung in the balance; her captors had to demonstrate, with an elaborate show of legality, that God was on the side of the English invader and that the coronation of Joan's beloved Dauphin was the work of the Devil.

But for these considerations, the English would undoubtedly have disposed of their curious captive by tying her in a sack and tossing her into the nearest river. With the sure instinct they have always displayed in such matters, they realized that they were dealing with no ordinary prisoner but with a living legend. Her trial was designed to break the grip of that legend on the medieval mind on both sides of the Channel.

Only a few misguided souls considered it possible that Joan's claims of divine guidance might be explained away as hysterical delusions or the symptoms of organic illness. Scientific skepticism had not penetrated the fifteenth-century mind; and even if it had, a satisfactory diagnosis would probably not have been forthcoming. Even in her own lifetime the figure of Joan was larger than life. Ever since, her story has defied every attempt to reduce her to human dimensions.

The difficulty springs from the fact that it is one of the best-documented legends of all time. Apart from contemporary chronicles, there is the awe-inspiring record of her trial, containing thousands of words from her own mouth; and her so-called "rehabilitation trial" twenty-five years later recorded the recollections of hundreds with whom she had personally associated. Neither the idolators nor the iconoclasts—and least of all the scientists—have managed to alter her stature. She remains a three-dimensional figure—heroic, pathetic, and, in many aspects, intensely human.

She was born in 1412 at Domremy, on the extreme eastern boundary of France. This sleepy hamlet in the Meuse Valley typified the condition of the entire country during her childhood: divided in allegiance between the House of Valois and the pro-English Burgundians. Northern and eastern France were occupied by the British invaders and their French allies, with the balance of the country, for the most part, loyal to the debauched and imbecilic King of France, Charles VI.

Shakespeare immortalized in *Henry V* that bold young monarch's revival of the Hundred Years' War "in order to busy giddy minds with foreign quarrels." By his crowning coup, the Treaty of Troyes, Henry was designated heir to the throne of France by the enfeebled Charles. The French Queen, Isabelle de Beauvière, admitted that her son, the Dauphin, was illegitimate and was awarded an annuity of 24,000 francs for her candor.

Henry V died before he could enjoy the fruits of this bargain, and Charles soon followed him to the grave. On the latter's death, Henry VI of England was installed on the throne of France, but he was still too young to sit up. His uncle, the Duke of Bedford, carried on as Regent the war which the Dauphin and his followers refused to discontinue.

Joan's family was pro-French, and had been forced to flee Domremy when the victorious Anglo-Burgundian forces swept through the Meuse Valley. As a pious child, she naturally looked to God to redress the balance of power. She had not long to wait for an answer.

"I was thirteen," she later testified, "when I heard a Voice from God for my help and guidance. The first time I heard the Voice, I was very much frightened; it was midday, in the summer, in my father's garden. I had fasted the day before. I heard the Voice to my right, towards the Church; rarely do I hear it without its being accompanied by a light. This light comes from the same side as the Voice."

Thereafter her visions appeared with increasing frequency. She recognized her first visitor as Saint Michael—his figure stood in the village church. Saint Margaret, who was an old friend for the same reason, and Saint Catherine, whose image graced the church at Maxey across the river, soon joined him.

She could touch them, embrace them; they spoke French (of course) and smelled good. Their messages were direct and persistent: God had chosen her to go to the aid of the Dauphin—"and thou shalt restore his kingdom." She must lead him to Rheims to be anointed, so that all of France would recognize him as its rightful ruler. Soon after the siege of Orléans began, she was instructed to relieve this last great stronghold of the Dauphin's domain.

Many attempts have been made during the last century to find a scientific basis for Joan's apparitions. Some have pointed to her pubescence, and to the one physical abnormality she is known to have had: she never menstruated. Others have concentrated on psychiatric causes. A recent medical view speculates that she may have been suffering from a brain abscess due to bovine tuberculosis, a very common malady in the Middle Ages. This disease sometimes causes an organic abnormality on the left side of the brain which is characteristically attended by mixed sensations of visions and voices on the right side.

Provocative though it may be, this area of inquiry goes no further than to question the miraculous character of Joan's visitations. It does not touch upon the extraordinary career that followed upon Joan's obedience to her saints' commands. It suffices for our purposes that Joan believed in her visions. Of that there can be no doubt.

Yet for four years she listened to them without making a move or even speaking of them to anyone. She may have been overwhelmed by a sense of inadequacy: as she told them, she "knew nothing of riding or making war." And she later said that she kept silent about her visitations for fear of her father, who would not have understood, and of the Burgundians in the vicinity, who might have.

But at length she took up the challenge. She was probably encouraged by a popular legend that the wizard Merlin had prophesied that France would be desolated by a woman (the Dauphin's mother) and saved by a *pucelle*—a virgin—from Lorraine. Conscious of this, she took a vow of chastity and from that time forth referred to herself as *La Pucelle*, a term which has since been used synonymously with Joan in the French language.

In the solemn recital of miracles credited to the Maid, her most remarkable accomplishment goes unnoticed: the comparative ease with which she convinced seasoned soldiers, the jaded and dissolute Dauphin, and his skeptical entourage that she could lead France to victory. The fact that she succeeded is a fair measure of the desperate plight of the

French court at the time. The Dauphin, a listless, pasty-faced youth with heavy-lidded eyes, pendulous nose, and deformed legs, had holed up in his castle at Chinon. His treasury was bankrupt, his supporters' ranks thinned out by disaffection. The bar of illegitimacy clouded over his claim to the throne. He was ripe for a miracle, and a miracle is what Joan offered him.

Dressed in male garb, her hair cut like a boy's, she had traveled 350 miles in eleven days on horseback to see him, journeying through flooded lands largely held by the enemy. Not once had her party been molested along the way. The hardened warriors who accompanied her bore witness to her piety and virtue. Her persistent demands to hear Mass had twice forced them to risk capture by the English. And although she and her companions had slept side by side every night, "I felt so much respect for her," one of them later testified, "that I would not have dared to make her an unseemly proposal, and I declare under oath that I never felt an evil desire towards her, nor was aware of any sensual thought." The Maid seems to have had this emasculating effect on all Frenchmen, but not, as later events proved, on the usually more cold-blooded English.

The Dauphin, however, could not accept supernatural assistance without first ascertaining from which direction it came. Joan was promptly sent to Poitiers to be questioned by learned theologians who were evidently baffled by this saucy but dedicated teenager, but took a practical approach: "We decided that in view of the necessity and the danger of Orléans, the King might allow the girl to help, and might send her to Orléans." Next, her virginity had to be established, for it was generally believed that the Devil could have no dealings with a virgin. Some ladies of the court took care of this problem. Present-day physicians would like to know how they went about it, since modern medical methods are still inadequate to this particular task.

Once over these hurdles, Joan was ready for her rendezvous with the British. She was fitted out with a complete suit of white armor, banners, and a horse. For her sword she insisted on sending to Fierbois, where her voices told her a weapon once belonging to Charles Martel was buried, behind the altar of the Church of St. Catherine. No one, so the story goes, had ever heard of the whereabouts of this sword; but it was found at the spot she specified, and as soon as it was rubbed, a twenty-year incrustation of rust fell away, revealing five crosses (a common decorative motif). The circulation of this account boosted Joan's stock at court sharply. Had she not testified to this incident at her trial, it might be dismissed as the counterpart of the legendary tales of Excalibur, Nothung, and Durandel. But barring the possibility that she had heard of the practice of leaving weapons as votive offerings in churches on her trip through Fierbois en route to Chinon, the incident stands as a singular example of clairvoyance.

Her military career had begun. In the company of over 3000 men she departed for Orléans, leaving the Dauphin behind to pray and philander as the mood seized him. Her male garb was suited to the occasion and in keeping with her vow of chastity; and skeptics who are inclined to look for Freudian explanations in the drive to lead a masculine existence are confronted with repeated instances of childish femininity in her behavior, even at the moments of her greatest triumphs.

Strange as it seems, no clear picture of her appearance has survived to the present day. Contemporary descriptions by her French companions dwell on her godliness, her skill in the art of war, and on what must have been her outstanding physical attribute, her shapely bosom. It can only be assumed that hers was a plain countenance, undistinguished by any single feature comely enough to fix itself in one's memory.

When Joan arrived at Orléans on April 29, 1429, the city had been under siege for six months. The military situation stood at stalemate. Greatly as they outnumbered their attackers, the French forces were too demoralized to fight a pitched battle to break the deadlock. The English had widely dispersed their troops at fortified points commanding only three sides of the city and had failed to cut off its supplies effectively enough to force surrender. The Duke of Bedford, in command of the siege, was disheartened by the desultory support he was receiving from the home country.

Joan had little difficulty in entering the city. Although not technically in command, she behaved as though she were. After vainly bombarding the English troops with threatening messages, reinforcing her reputation for piety by repeatedly attending Mass, prohibiting foul language among the troops, and driving the prostitutes out of the vicinity, the Maid went into action.

Within four days—on one of which she decreed no hostilities, it being Ascension Day—the British were in full retreat. The French victory stemmed largely from the improved morale of the troops, thanks to Joan's mere presence on the field. But it was at least partly attributable to her personal fearlessness and indomitability in the face of danger. What man dared not follow where a woman led?

The British, too, had fallen under the spell. As their commander wrote three months later, they suffered "a lack of sad belief and unlawful doubt that they had of a disciple and limb of the Fiend, called *La Pucelle*, that used false enchantments and sorcery." His agitation is betrayed in his syntax.

47

Joan was wounded on the last day of the battle of Orléans, and thereby hangs a curious tale. She prophesied, according to a letter written *before* the battle, that she would be wounded there and would survive. Toward midday she was struck by an arrow which penetrated six inches above the left breast, and returned to the fray that afternoon, little the worse for wear.

Orléans was saved. The French had destroyed a large part of the British force with an idea—the idea that a seventeen-year-old girl possessed supernatural powers. She had fulfilled the first promise she had made to her "gentle lord."

Military genius had little to do with the case. About a month later, Joan led an inspired French force to slashing victories at Jargeau and Patay, taking thousands of prisoners, including two of the outstanding British leaders. Had the demoralized remnants of the defeated army been pursued, she stood a good chance of marching straight into Paris. But she missed this opportunity, as she missed others yet to come; Joan's voices were calling the turn, and the next item on their agenda was the coronation of the Dauphin.

With some difficulty she tore him loose from the sanctuary of his court, and he trailed her in a triumphant procession toward Rheims, with town after town swearing allegiance to the Valois colors along the way. On July 17, less than five months after she had left Domremy, she proudly stood beside her monarch while the Archbishop of Rheims anointed him King of France.

Another prophecy fulfilled; now she must press on to Paris. To start with, all went as before: Beauvais, Compiègne, and St. Denis toppled before her banners. At the walls of Paris, however, her fortunes changed. First she was wounded in the thigh by an arrow; and when she wanted to resume the assault she found herself balked by orders from her King to rejoin him at St. Denis.

In the next two months she saw action sporadically, with mixed results, exhibiting reckless courage in the face of the enemy; but winter set in and Joan returned to court to wait out the weather. Returning to the fray in the spring at Melun, she heard her voices foretell her capture before the feast of Saint John (June 24).

At Compiègne, on May 23, 1430, the prophecy was fulfilled. Fighting against an advance guard of the Anglo-Burgundian besiegers outside the city walls, Joan was surprised by enemy reinforcements who chanced on the scene. Her force was hopelessly outnumbered, and its retreat to the safety of the city would have been cut off if she had not fought a desperate rearguard action, almost alone, against the enemy. When she was but a few yards from the city gate, the drawbridge was raised from within, choking off all possibility of escape for the Maid. One of John of Luxembourg's archers pulled her from her horse, and the curtain rose on the last act of the tragedy of Joan.

John of Luxembourg was a vassal of the Duke of Burgundy in the employ of the British Crown. The value of his prize was easy to estimate, although he must have been surprised (as have all chroniclers of Joan since) that Charles VII thought so little of her that he made no attempt to ransom or exchange her, as was customary in cases of important prisoners. Charles may have yielded to the persuasion of the Archbishop of Rheims, his chancellor, who let the people of his see know that Joan was captured because of her willfulness and "on account of her great pride and the rich clothes she wore." Besides, another divinely inspired young warrior had appeared on the scene—a shepherd boy whose body bore the stigmata of Christ! This lad left no lasting mark on history; not long afterwards he fell into English hands and ended up in a sack in the Seine.

But active bidders for the precious *Pucelle* could be found closer at hand. All the majesty of the Church resided in the faculty of the University of Paris, which had assumed supreme power over French Christendom while the strength of the Papacy was sapped by factional disputes. Its leading theologians had been outraged by Joan's conduct, and frightened, too; for the University had thrown in its lot with the English, and could expect no mercy from Charles if he emerged victorious. Joan's surrender to the Inquisition was demanded by it within a few days after her capture.

But John had to deal with his English master, the Duke of Bedford, as well. The Duke was not altogether comfortable about leaving Joan to the mercies of the Inquisition, despite the fact that the University had labeled her "an enemy of the realm." Lodged in a Church prison for women, she might escape; tried as a heretic, she might recant and be let off lightly. Yet Bedford realized that if the brand of Satan could be attached to the Maid, it would deprive Charles' crown of much of the luster of divine right she had brought to it.

A bargain was struck. The Maid would be bought from John with English funds (raised by levying a tax on the Duchy of Normandy). She would be held in an English prison. If not convicted by the Inquisition she would be turned over to the English military.

The negotiations were handled by an ambitious prelate on the invader's payroll, Pierre Cauchon, Bishop of Beauvais, who had a special interest in the matter, for Joan's recent sweep through France had deprived him of the revenues of his diocese. After six months of trading

49

with John, he gained possession of the prize in exchange for 10,000 gold livres.

Meanwhile Joan had twice tried to escape. The second of these efforts came close to putting her out of her misery. At Beaurevoir, to which John had removed her for greater security after her first bid for liberty, she was allowed to walk the castle tower for exercise, unattended by guards because of the height of the structure. Disregarding the advice of her voices, she jumped from the tower, a distance of sixty or seventy feet. Apparently she suffered no injuries except a slight concussion, which caused her a few days' loss of appetite.

This incident has often been cited in support of the case for Joan's miraculous powers. But medical authorities say that a fall of this kind can be sustained without serious consequences, depending on what the body lands on and in what position. Still, in company with the other chapters of Joan's life, it tends to sustain the proponents of sainthood—despite the lingering suspicion that she was attempting suicide, and thereby committing sacrilege.

Her intransigence as a prisoner may have given Cauchon the excuse he needed to commit the first of many breaches of canon law in Joan's case, once he got possession of her. She was entitled to be held in an ecclesiastical place of detention, such as he maintained at Rouen, with a room where women were placed under the care of female warders. But the Bishop had sealed his compact with the English. The Maid was thrown in irons into a damp, fetid cell, guarded day and night by five English soldiers. Had Cauchon not yielded to the Duke of Bedford on this score, Joan might have discarded her male clothing, and her trial might have taken on a somewhat different cast. She was in fact frequently molested by visiting curiosity-seekers from the English garrison, as well as by her warders. Her complaints to the Bishop went unheeded; but on one occasion, the Earl of Warwick heard her cries during an attempted rape, and replaced the two chief offenders.

Common rumor was enough to justify the holding of a prisoner by the Inquisition, pending a preliminary inquiry. Cauchon gathered evidence from all over France, tracing Joan's career from childhood to the day of her capture. His investigation was primarily directed toward proving Joan a witch by the conventional tests with which the Inquisition was so familiar, and between the falsehoods and half-truths garnered in six weeks of nosing about, he accumulated evidence at least as strong as that upon which many an innocent had gone to the stake in that superstitious age: a tree of fairies and a magic spring at Domremy, which Joan sometimes visited in the summertime; a mandrake root reputed to have grown in the vicinity; predictions made by her and fulfilled, and lost articles found by supernatural aid; the finding of the sword at Fierbois (by consulting demons); the use of her ring and standard to cast spells; the revival of a presumably dead baby by invocation of the Devil—all grist for the mill which ground out thousands of executions in the fear-ridden fifteenth century.

None of the witnesses interrogated in this process was brought to Rouen to confront Joan. No formal accusation was drafted until later. Inquisition procedure called for a preparatory trial, a series of sessions in which the prisoner alone was questioned by the full Court, with a view to formulating the so-called Articles of Accusation. In actuality, by the time this process was completed, the fate of the accused was sealed, even though the semblance of a trial followed.

The Court which tried Joan consisted of two judges—Cauchon and a deputy for the Grand Inquisitor of France—and seventy-one assessors, as against the normal complement of six to eight, indicating the importance attached to the case by the Bishop. The assessors were clerics, lawyers, and doctors handpicked by Cauchon, many of them in the pay of the English. But the safety usually to be found in numbers did not hold true in Joan's case; not all of the assessors were content to serve as rubber stamps. A few protested the irregularity of the proceedings and tried to revise the composition of the Court to counterbalance the obvious bias against the Maid. Threats of reprisal took care of some of these troublesome customers, while others were simply denied further attendance at the trial. After the first six sessions, Cauchon solved his problem by removing the scene of the inquiry from the Chapel Royal of the Castle of Rouen to Joan's cell, where only a few selected assessors could crowd in, along with the prosecutor, the judges, the clerks, and the prisoner. Here he committed another breach of canon law, since the accused was entitled to be heard by the full Court.

Cauchon soon discovered that he had little need to prove the usual pattern of witchcraft to secure a conviction. Joan had not been afforded counsel, although Inquisition law required that it be offered whenever the prisoner's ability to conduct her defense personally was open to question. Had she been properly advised (and been willing to listen) she might have made Cauchon's task a little more difficult. She might not have appeared in court on the morning of February 21, 1431, for the first session, clad as a male and with her hair cropped short, in violation of the strict prohibition of the Book of Deuteronomy. She might not have insisted on the reality of her visions and the divine source of their revelations. She might have been better attuned to the difference between the Church Triumphant and the Church Militant and agreed to bow to the authority of the latter. She might not have refused to repeat the Pater Noster and Ave Maria in open court, insisting that she first be heard in confession. Before the second sitting was over, Joan had qualified herself for burning by her own words.

But Cauchon was not content with a brief trial, impatient as his English masters were to have the case over. He had his eye on the central purpose of the case: to discredit Joan—and through her Charles VII—beyond redemption. And so, the preparatory hearings stretched into sixteen sessions, until on March 17th they came to a halt.

Apart from her naive insistence on self-destruction, Joan gave a good account of herself. Steadfastly she refused to incriminate her beloved Dauphin, or to attribute to her voices her own mistakes and failures. Repeatedly she asked that the record of the Poitiers proceedings be produced, undoubtedly recognizing among the assessors some of the clerics who had questioned her there. But if any record was ever kept, it had disappeared. She offered to submit her case to the Pope; but when asked whether she would submit to the Church Militant, which he headed, she replied:

I came to the King of France from God, from the Blessed Virgin Mary, from all the Saints of Paradise, and the Church Victorious above, and by their command. To this Church I submit all my good deeds, all that I have done or will do.

Sometimes she hurled a shrewd barb in the direction of her English captors, as when she replied to the charge of mortal sin in wearing male garb:

I did better to obey and serve my sovereign Lord, who is God.

And when asked whether Saint Michael appeared before her naked (with plain implications of witchcraft), she retorted sharply:

Do you think God has not wherewithal to clothe him?

Thrust and parry, parry and thrust; and throughout, the simple piety of an ignorant girl against the calculated and sophisticated entrapment of her accusers. Her transparent honesty was no shield against their sanctimonious legalisms. Private revelation could not be accepted as superior to the judgment of God's representatives on earth—this was the "first principle of schism," and Joan was obdurate on that point. Standing by itself—ignoring the male clothing and the petty charges of magic and spells—this was enough to doom her, English or no English.

The reading of the seventy articles of the Act of Accusation, which was then drawn up, was a perfunctory procedure. Technically, this constituted the trial proper; but Joan simply repeated in abbreviated form what had been gone over before, or referred the Court to her previous testimony. It is noteworthy, however, that this was the first occasion on which she was offered counsel; and she rejected it, saying simply, "I have no intention of desisting from the counsel of Our Lord."

Cauchon then boiled down the seventy articles of accusation and Joan's replies to them into a handy condensation for consideration by the assessors. Consisting of twelve articles in all, it did not accurately reflect Joan's answers, and, in fact, attributed to her confessions which she had never made. Granted that this was a grave act of injustice, it can hardly be supposed that it had any effect upon the outcome. The twenty-two assessors Cauchon consulted considered her guilty. A few outside lawyers and theologians suggested appeal to higher authority, and the shortened version was sent off to the faculty of theology of the University of Paris for its opinion.

In the meantime, every possible device to make the Maid recant was employed. Joan only once showed signs of wavering, when she was threatened with denial of confession and the sacraments, and burial in unhallowed ground. But neither these dire prospects nor the imminence of torture could make her break faith with her voices:

Truly, if you were to tear me limb from limb and separate soul and body, I would tell you nothing more; and if I were to say anything else, I should always afterwards declare that you had made me say it by force.

The verdict from Paris finally arrived and surprised no one: Joan must retract or be treated as a sorceress, heretic, apostate, and schismatic. Upon hearing this dire pronouncement, she stood firm.

If I were condemned, and if I saw the fire lighted, and the faggots prepared and the executioner ready to kindle the fire, I would not say otherwise, and would maintain to the death all I have said.

The trial was over. The following day was fixed for sentence. It was exactly one year since Joan had been taken prisoner at Compiègne.

The fate which was in store for Joan was brought home to her vividly the next morning, when she was taken, still in chains, to the cemetery of the abbey of St. Ouen. On a large platform erected for the occasion stood Henry Beaufort, Cardinal of England, surrounded by French Church dignitaries. Lord Warwick and other Englishmen were also in attendance. Joan, in her ragged boy's clothes, mounted a smaller stand, where Guillaume Erard, Canon of Rouen, awaited her. But her eyes must have been riveted on a high plaster pedestal, heaped high with branches crosswise in tiers, in front of an iron stake, which stood between the two wooden structures.

As was customary with condemned heretics, Joan was to be favored with a sermon before sentence was pronounced. Erard's words on this occasion are lost to us, but it is known that he excoriated Charles VII for having listened to her, and that she interrupted him, crying heatedly, "I swear that my King is the noblest of all Christians! I charge no one, neither my King nor any other; if there is any fault, it is mine alone!" Not even the imminence of death would blemish the hallowed image of her faithless Monarch.

Once more she appealed to have her words and deeds referred to the Pope for judgment. But this plea was brushed aside: the Holy Father was too far away, and her judges were well qualified to pass on her case.

Finally, the Bishop of Beauvais rose and began delivering sentence. As he neared the end, saying, "For these causes, as obstinate in thy crimes, excesses, and errors, we declare thee of right excommunicated and heretic . . . ," the Maid's courage failed. The strain had lasted too long and been too severe. She would submit herself to the Church, she cried, and would no longer support her apparitions or believe what they told her.

An Act of Abjuration had been prepared for just such a contingency— a document of six or seven lines confessing "that I have grievously sinned, in falsely pretending that I have had revelations from God and his angels, Saint Catherine and Saint Margaret, etc.," and revoking all her words and deeds "which are contrary to the Church." She signed it with a cross, although she could write her name.

The wily Cauchon, not content with this brief admission of error, later substituted in the official record of the trial a full-dress Act of Abjuration some 500 words long. All witnesses agree that it was spurious; but Cauchon wanted a self-indictment on record which would blacken Joan's name beyond redemption.

The Bishop was not completely taken aback by this sudden turn of events, but it posed a dilemma. The English had paid well for this prisoner, and had already told him that their monetary and political investment would be cashed in, no matter what the Court decided. Yet she had recanted; mercy was indicated as a matter of course. Cauchon turned to the English cardinal for advice and was told he must receive Joan as a penitent. This cleared the way to impose sentence on the Maid from a previously prepared document: perpetual imprisonment.

The English military gentlemen were furious. "The King is ill-served," was Warwick's angry comment. "Joan has escaped us."

The Maid was returned to her cell. The English guards remained— three in her cell, two outside. The fetters stayed on. That afternoon her head was shaved and she put on a long gray robe, discarding her tunic and hose. Curiously, these sinful garments were kept in her cell in a sack, raising a plain implication that the ensuing events were manipulated by the English.

She was not permitted to go to Mass or to receive the sacraments, as she had been promised by Erard, nor was she removed to a women's prison, as she had been led to believe would occur.

On Sunday, May 27, Joan was back in male clothes. According to some contemporary accounts, she had been sleeping in her gown, but wishing to answer a call of nature, she asked to be unchained from her bed. At this point one of her jailers stripped the dress from her and threw her the male garments which she had discarded, stuffing the gown into the sack. She argued with him until noon, but finally was compelled to yield; and when she returned to the bed, he refused to hand the gown back to her. It was also said that an effort had been made by an Englishman to rape her. In any case, it was in this condition that Cauchon found her when he visited the cell on May 28 to verify rumors that the Maid had once more fallen from grace.

The official report of this visit is somewhat at odds with this pathetic story. It reflects a clear determination on Joan's part to die, rather than remain in irons and be denied the benefits of her Faith. Her voices, she said, had told her "that she had done great wrong to God in confessing that what she had done was not well done." On the other hand, she did express willingness to resume women's dress if her fetters were removed and if she would be permitted to attend Mass and receive the sacrament.

The inevitable verdict which Cauchon and forty-one of the assessors rendered the next day: relapsed heretic. The sentence: "We denounce thee as a rotten member, and that thou may not vitiate others, as cast out from the unity of the Church, separate from her Body, abandoned to the secular power, as indeed by these presents, we do cast thee off, separate, and abandon thee; praying this same secular power, so far as concerns death and the mutilation of the limbs, to moderate its judgment towards thee. . . ."

The last phrase was an empty formality. "Secular justice" was already standing by in the person of the Bailiff of Rouen and the Master Executioner. The scene was the market place at Rouen, where a throng of thousands, including 800 English troops, awaited the last act. Above the stake on the high scaffold had been posted a sign: "Joan, who calls herself the Maid, liar, pernicious, deceiver of the people, sorceress . . ." On her own head had been placed a paper cap shaped like a bishop's miter, with this inscription: "Heretic, relapse, apostate, idolatress."

The gesture of turning Joan over to "secular authority" accorded with that precept of Church law which prohibited it from shedding blood (but excommunicated any secular authority which refused to do so in cases of heresy). The Bailiff waived all formalities. The executioner's assistants immediately seized Joan (once more clad in a gown), hurried her to the scaffold, and helped her mount the ladder. She was chained to the stake at the waist, and the flames leaped up and obscured her in a matter of seconds. From the pyre her voice rang out across the square as she cried out to Jesus again and again. Her head slumped forward, and then all was silent.

Hearing of the execution, John Tressart, secretary to the King of England, said, "We are lost; we have burned a saint."

Sainthood was a long time coming to Joan. Indeed, outside of Orléans, the people of France quickly forgot her. But the British fortunes in France fared poorly from then on. By 1435 Burgundy had made a separate peace with the French; and a year later, Paris freed itself of its captors and welcomed Charles VII. The latter, with a new set of advisers selected by a clever mistress, proved a surprisingly effective ruler and his armies did well in the field. By 1449, the British had fled from Rouen, and Charles set in motion the steps necessary to legitimatize the legendary maid with whom his fate was so closely linked. The shadow of the Treaty of Troyes still hung over him. It was Joan who had called him "the true heir to the throne," Joan who had engineered the anointing at Rheims. As long as the sentence of the Church stood, Charles' status was compromised by his connection with a condemned sorceress.

But only the Holy Inquisition, acting on its own initiative, could reverse its earlier decision; and the representations which Charles made to Rome were acted upon with maddening deliberation. It was not until July 7, 1456, that the Archbishop of Rheims, sitting in the great hall of the palace of the Archbishop of Rouen, before an imposing crowd of laymen and clergy, pronounced sentence: "We . . . declare the said trial and sentence to be contaminated with fraud, calumny, wickedness, contradictions, and manifest errors of fact and law, and together with the abjuration, the execution, and their consequences to have been and to be null, without value or effect, and to be quashed. . . ." So saying, the Inquisition wrote its own death warrant as a power in France, while the terror of its writ was mounting steadily elsewhere.

The record of Joan's trial is luminous with the pathos and faith of the girl who has no equal among the heroines of antiquity. Its outcome is a maze of paradoxes; the saints whom the Church Militant condemned failed her in her extremity; and the same Church Militant elevated her to sainthood in an analytical and materialistic day and age.

In these excerpts from the transcript, the Maid stands revealed as the matchless defender of her Faith against the onslaught of clericalism:

PREPARATORY INTERROGATION
MARCH 12

Q. Did not the Angel who bore the sign to your King speak to him?

A. Yes, he spoke to him; and he told my King it was necessary that I should be set to work, so that the country might be soon relieved.

Q. Was the Angel who bore the sign to your King the same Angel who had appeared before to you?

A. It is all one; and he has never failed me.

Q. Has not the Angel, then, failed you with regard to the good things of this life, in that you have been taken prisoner?

A. I think, as it has pleased Our Lord, that it is for my well-being that I was taken prisoner.

Q. Has your Angel never failed you in the good things of grace?

A. How can he fail me, when he comforts me every day? My comfort comes from Saint Catherine and Saint Margaret.

Q. Do you call them, or do they come without being called?

A. They often come without being called; and other times, if they do not come soon, I pray Our Lord to send them.

Q. Have you sometimes called them without their coming?

A. I have never had need of them without having them.

MARCH 15

Q. Have you never done anything against their command and will?

A. All that I could and knew how to do, I have done and accomplished to the best of my power. As to the matter of the fall from the keep of Beaurevoir, I did it against their command; but I could not control myself. When my Voices saw my need, and that I neither knew how, nor was able, to control myself, they saved my life and kept me from killing myself. Whatever things I did in my greatest undertakings, they always helped me; and that is a sign they are good spirits.

Q. Have you no other sign that they are good spirits?

A. Saint Michael assured me of it before the Voices came to me.

Q. How did you know it was Saint Michael?

A. By the speech and language of the Angels. I believe firmly that they were Angels.

Q. But how did you know that it was the language of the Angels?

A. I believed it at once, and I had the will to believe it. When Saint Michael came to me, he said to me: "Saint Catherine and Saint Margaret will come to thee. Follow their counsel; they have been chosen to guide thee and counsel thee in all that thou hast to do. Believe what they shall tell thee; it is the order of Our Lord."

57

Q. If the devil were to put himself in the form or likeness of an angel, how would you know if it were a good or an evil angel?

A. I should know quite well if it were Saint Michael or a counterfeit. The first time I was in great doubt if it were Saint Michael, and I was much afraid. I had seen him many times before I knew it was Saint Michael.

Q. Why did you recognize him sooner that time, when you say you believed it was he, than the first time he appeared to you?

A. The first time I was a young child, and I was much afraid. Afterwards, he had taught me so well, and it was so clear to me, that I believed firmly it was he.

Q. What doctrine did he teach you?

A. Above all things he told me to be a good child, and that God would help me—to come to the help of the King of France, among other things.

MARCH 17

Q. Will you, in respect of all your words and deeds, whether good or bad, submit yourself to the decision of our Holy Mother, the Church?

A. The Church! I love it, and would wish to maintain it with all my power, for our Christian Faith; it is not I who should be prevented from going to Church and hearing Mass! As to the good deeds I have done and my coming to the King, I must wait on the King of Heaven, who sent me to Charles, King of France, son of Charles, who was King of France. You will see that the French will soon gain a great victory, that God will send such great doings that nearly all the Kingdom of France will be shaken by them. I say it so that when it shall come to pass, it may be remembered that I said it.

Q. When will this happen?

A. I wait on Our Lord.

Q. Will you refer yourself to the decision of the Church?

A. I refer myself to God Who sent me, to Our Lady, and to all the Saints in Paradise. And in my opinion it is all one, God and the Church; and one should make no difficulty about it. Why do you make a difficulty?

Q. What do you say on the subject of the female attire which is offered to you, to go and hear Mass?

A. I will not take it yet, until it shall please Our Lord. And if it should happen that I should be brought to judgment, I beseech the lords of the Church to do me the grace to allow me a woman's smock and a hood for my head. I would rather die than revoke what God has made me do; and I believe firmly that God will not allow it to come to pass that I should be brought so low that I may not soon have succor from Him, and by miracle.

Q. As you say that you wear a man's dress by the command of God, why do you ask for a woman's smock at the point of death?

A. It will be enough for me if it be long.

Q. Do you know if Saint Catherine and Saint Margaret hate the English?

A. They love what God loves: they hate what God hates.

Q. Does God hate the English?

A. Of the love or hate God may have for the English, or of what He will do for their souls, I know nothing; but I know quite well that they will be put out of France, except those who shall die there, and that God will send victory to the French against the English.

Q. Was God for the English when they were prospering in France?

A. I do not know if God hated the French; but I believe that He wished them to be defeated for their sins, if they were in sin.

Q. Did you ever kiss or embrace Saint Catherine or Saint Margaret?

A. I have embraced them both.

Q. Did they smell good?

A. It is well to know, they smelled good.

Q. In embracing them, did you feel any heat or anything else?

A. I could not have embraced them without feeling and touching them.

Q. What part did you kiss—face or feet?

A. It is more proper and respectful to kiss their feet.

TRIAL IN ORDINARY
MARCH 31

Q. If the Church Militant tells you that your revelations are illusions or diabolical things, will you defer to the Church?

A. I will defer to God, Whose Commandment I always serve. I know well that that which is contained in my Case has come to me by the Commandment of God; . . . it is impossible for me to say otherwise. In case the Church shall prescribe to the contrary, I should not refer to any one in the world, but to God alone, Whose Commandment I always follow.

Q. Do you not then believe you are subject to the Church of God which is on earth, that is to say our Lord the Pope, to the Cardinals, the Archbishops, Bishops, and other prelates of the Church?

A. Yes, I believe myself to be subject to them; but God must be served first.

Q. Have you then command from your Voices not to submit yourself to the Church Militant, which is on earth, nor to its decision?

A. I answer nothing from my own head. What I answer is by command of my Voices; they do not order me to disobey the Church, but God must be served first.

TRIAL FOR RELAPSE
MAY 28

Q. You promised and swore not to resume a man's dress.

A. I never meant to swear that I would not resume it.

Q. Why have you resumed it?

A. Because it is more lawful and suitable for me to resume it and to wear man's dress, being with men, than to have a woman's dress. I have resumed it because the promise made to me has not been kept; that is to say, that I should go to Mass and should receive my Savior and that I should be taken out of irons.

Q. Did you not abjure and promise not to resume this dress?

A. I would rather die than be in irons!

Q. Since last Thursday,[1] have you heard your Voices at all?

A. Yes, I have heard them.

Q. What did they say to you?

A. They said to me—God has sent me word by Saint Catherine and Saint Margaret of the great pity it is, this treason to which I have consented, to abjure and recant in order to save my life! Before last Thursday, my Voices did indeed tell me what I should do and what I did on that day. When I was on the scaffold on Thursday, my Voices said to me, while the preacher was speaking: "Answer him boldly, this preacher!" And in truth he is a false preacher; he reproached me with many things I never did. If I said that God had not sent me, I should damn myself, for it is true that God has sent me. My Voices have said to me since Thursday: "Thou hast done a great evil in declaring that what thou hast done was wrong." All I said and revoked, I said for fear of the fire.

Q. On the scaffold, at the moment of your abjuration, you did admit before us, your Judges, and before many others, in the presence of all the people, that you had untruthfully boasted your Voices to be Saint Catherine and Saint Margaret.

A. I did not intend so to do or say. I did not intend to deny my apparitions—that is to say, that they were Saint Catherine and Saint Margaret. What I said was from fear of the fire: I revoked nothing that was not against the truth. I would rather do penance once for all—that is die—than endure any longer the suffering of a prison. I have done nothing against God or the Faith, in spite of all they have made me revoke. What was in the schedule of abjuration I did not understand. I did not intend to revoke anything except according to God's good pleasure. If the Judges wish, I will resume a woman's dress; for the rest, I can do no more.

[1] The day of her abjuration.

GALILEO GALILEI

(1633)

The onslaught of organized religion against scientific progress reached its climax in the city of Rome on June 22, 1633. Sick, aged, and afraid, Galileo Galilei, the greatest physicist and astronomer of his time, bowed to the Inquisition and renounced his life's work in science as a sin against God.

The same forces would clash three centuries later when the weary warrior of Fundamentalism, William Jennings Bryan, faced the crafty Clarence Darrow in a Tennessee courtroom. The stakes, too, were the same: the freedom of mankind to observe, to inquire, and to think.

From his early student days Galileo was fascinated by the laws of motion. He was only an undergraduate at the University of Pisa when he hit upon a fundamental principle concerning the movement of the pendulum. While still in his twenties, he made exhaustive inquiries into the laws of gravity. Whether the ofttold story of the experiment at the Tower of Pisa is authentic or not, he did, in the course of this research, drop two unequal weights from a height and disproved Aristotle's claim that weight governs the velocity of falling bodies.

These relatively modest challenges to accepted notions brought Galileo fame and position. At the age of twenty-five he was appointed professor of mathematics at Pisa, and three years later he moved to a similar post at Padua. But the abstract and slightly cabalistic discipline of mathematics was less to Galileo's liking than the observation of physical phenomena. He could not close his mind to the world about him and the skies above him. And when the evidence of his own eyes brought him into conflict with the teachings of Aristotle, he could not hold his tongue —even though his life depended on it.

Aristotle's notion that the earth formed the fixed center of the universe and did not rotate on its axis was at the core of Christian belief of that day. Only the very center of the world could be the stage for the all-important drama of man's salvation. And his theory had support from the Bible itself, as in the story of Joshua, who "made the sun stand still."

The Church dealt swiftly and harshly with the few who questioned Aristotle's scheme of the universe, as confirmed and embroidered by Ptolemy. In 1600, Giordano Bruno died at the stake for defending the great theoretical work of the Polish astronomer, Nicholas Copernicus, published in 1543, in which he suggested that the tracks of planets across the sky could be explained by supposing that the earth and the planets all revolved around a central sun.

Galileo had been drawn, early in his thirties, to the Copernican theory. Writing to the pioneer German astronomer Johannes Kepler in 1597, he confided that he had held these views "for many years," but had not expressed them for fear of becoming "an object of ridicule and scorn."

By 1609 he had won an appointment as first mathematician and astronomer to the court of the Duke of Tuscany. Secure in the favor of a powerful patron, he was ripe for the events which were to lead to his downfall.

In January of the following year Galileo devised a telescope. Although not its inventor, he was probably the first to use that instrument to test astronomical theories. Through its crude lenses, he observed Jupiter and, circling around it, its four satellites. Here was the solar system Copernicus had envisioned, in miniature! And he was soon writing to a fellow scholar that these small bodies move around their host "just as Venus and Mercury, and perhaps other planets, move around the sun."

Within nine months he observed the phases of Venus, seeing its shining surface pass through the same cycles as the moon. Galileo was exultant: at last, the beliefs of the Copernican philosophers were "proved by the evidence of our senses!"

The behavior of sunspots, as viewed through his telescope, led him to believe that he could deliver "a fatal blow to the Ptolemaic system." He went to Rome in 1611, bringing along several improved telescopes. Four scientific authorities of the Roman College confirmed his observations. The Pope received him graciously, and Galileo made many friends, including Cardinal Robert Bellarmine, who would later figure prominently in the story of his trial. The ever-watchful Inquisition, guardian of the Faith, did not ignore the stir he created, but held its fire.

About five years later, Galileo's book on his sunspot observations came to the attention of the Holy Office of the Inquisition. Sensing trouble, he went to Rome to mend fences. He met with an enthusiastic reception by the nobility and the intelligentsia, but the Inquisition was not numbered among his conquests. A group of experts, appointed by the Pope, branded as "formally heretical" Galileo's proposition that the sun is the center of the world and immovable; his claim that the earth is not the center of the world and moves on its axis was held to be "erroneous in the Faith." This "censure" was forwarded to the General Congregation of the Inquisition on February 25, 1616, and approved by the Pope, who, according to the Vatican file,

directed the Lord Cardinal Bellarmine to summon before him the said Galileo and admonish him to abandon the said opinion; and *in case of his refusal to obey*, that the Commissary is to intimate to him, before a notary and witnesses, a command to abstain altogether from teaching or defending this opinion and doctrine, and even from discussing it; and if he does not acquiesce therein, that he is to be imprisoned.

The meeting between Cardinal Bellarmine and Galileo was to become the cornerstone of Galileo's trial by the Inquisition seventeen years later, and a source of dispute for students of the Galileo case ever since.

The Vatican documents give the following account of the meeting:

3rd March, 1616.

The Lord Cardinal Bellarmine, having reported that Galileo Galilei, mathematician, had in terms of the order of the Holy Congregation been admonished to abandon the opinion he has hitherto held, that the sun is the center of the spheres and immovable, and that the earth moves, and had acquiesced therein . . .

Galileo's submission was important: for once he agreed to abandon the opinion which had incensed the Inquisition, he was exempt from its command "to abstain altogether from teaching or defending this opinion and doctrine and even discussing it." He could deal with it hypothetically, debate its merits as he pleased, as long as he did not adopt it as his own.

Galileo spent several months in Rome following the meeting with Cardinal Bellarmine, and took the opportunity to obtain concrete proof that he had not been formally obliged to recant, as had been widely rumored. It took the form of a letter from the Cardinal, reading:

We, Robert Cardinal Bellarmine, having heard that it is calumniously reported that Signor Galileo Galilei has in our hand abjured, and has also been punished with salutary penance, and being requested to state the truth as to this, declare, that the said Signor Galileo has not abjured, either in our hand, or the hand of any other person here in Rome, or anywhere else, so far as we know, any opinion or doctrine held by him, neither has any salutary penance been imposed upon him; but only the declaration made by the Holy Father and published by the sacred Congregation of the Index has been intimated to him, wherein it is set forth that the doctrine attributed to Copernicus, that the earth moves round the sun, and does not move from east to west, is contrary to the Holy Scriptures, and therefore cannot be defended or held. In witness whereof we have written and subscribed these presents with our hand this 26th day of May, 1616.

In other words, Bellarmine was saying, Galileo had been warned, but the affair had not required any more drastic action; and the scientist had not suffered the stigma attending the formal abjuration of a heresy.

In 1624 Galileo returned to Rome and had six audiences in as many weeks with the new Pope, Urban VIII. They evidently discussed the Copernican controversy without heat on either side, and the future looked bright for the cause of scientific inquiry.

In due course, Galileo would learn how sorely he had misjudged Urban. This was a Supreme Pontiff who declared that "the sentence of a living Pope is worth more than the decree of a hundred dead ones." Militaristic, energetic, vain, his objective was absolute power. But Galileo saw in him only the patron of arts and learning, the poet who had sent him so many cordial letters and who had enjoyed Galileo's book *The Assayer*, which in 1622 had successfully weathered an attempt to condemn it as pro-Copernican.

Galileo left Rome convinced that he was secure in papal favor and that he had won approval for the great work he had long planned—the *Dialogue on the Great World Systems*. He completed it in December 1629.

This book, which has been called "one of the most powerful levers in obtaining general recognition for the true order of the universe," was written not for the technically adept, but for educated people of all levels. It takes the form of a Socratic discourse among three people— Salviati, obviously speaking for Galileo himself; Sagredo, the intelligent, open-minded nobleman without decided views; and Simplicio, the supporter of the Ptolemaic system. The debate concerning rival theories ebbs and flows with ingenuity and wit, but the superiority of the Copernican doctrine to the teachings of Aristotle emerges all too clearly on close reading.

On its face, though, the three-way discussion purports to end inconclusively, with Simplicio voicing the pious reflection that God works in many ways, and hence that it would be rash to consider any natural phenomenon as necessary proof of a particular theory, to the exclusion of all others—a sentiment in which his companions soberly join.

Unfortunately, this little homily was a literal echo of the Pope's own words, spoken during one of his audiences with Galileo in 1624; and worse still, they were put into the mouth of a character named Simplicio. Nothing could convince Urban VIII that he was not being caricatured in Simplicio nor that the choice of the name was attributable solely to the fact that it had belonged to a contemporary of Aristotle. His wrath was unbounded.

Galileo seemed blithely unaware of—or unconcerned about—this affront to the Pontiff. He had laid careful defensive plans. And in case of trouble, he had good friends at Rome close to Urban, including the chief censor himself, Father Niccolo Riccardi, who had passed his previous book and had promised co-operation on this one.

The manuscript had been submitted to Riccardi, who, responding to pressure from some of Galileo's well-placed friends (including the Tuscan Ambassador, who was Riccardi's cousin-in-law), granted a grudging approval for a printing in Rome on condition that he make changes in the preface and conclusion and submit the completed work to Riccardi before publication.

In August, Galileo received a guarded letter from a friend in Rome urging him, for undisclosed reasons, to attempt to have the book printed in his home city of Florence "as soon as possible." Florence's Inquisitor General issued a license promptly.

Galileo then requested Riccardi to permit publication of the book at Florence, pleading that the plague ravaging Tuscany and neighboring states made it impossible to send the bulky manuscript back to Rome. Riccardi, after much delay, sent a changed preface to Galileo, instructing him to alter the style only and to conform the conclusion to it, and left the final decision to the Inquisitor at Florence, to which Riccardi's jurisdiction did not extend. A second approval from Florence was readily obtained, and the book appeared under the double imprimatur of Rome and Florence in February 1632.

The fat was in the fire. Urban VIII, who was seeing Simplicio in his looking glass every morning, raged incessantly against Galileo. In August, Galileo's publisher was instructed by the Vatican to stop selling the book. A special commission of theologians and mathematicians was convened at Rome to investigate the affair.

But the commission was confronted with the double imprimatur: Galileo's defenses seemed impregnable. How to condemn Galileo and his book without indicting the Master of the Palace and the Florentine Inquisitor who had sanctioned its publication? The problem was solved by the "discovery" in the books of the Holy Office of a document dated February 26, 1616, reading:

Friday, the 26th—At the Palace, the usual residence of the Lord Cardinal Bellarmine, the said Galileo having been summoned and brought before the said Lord Cardinal, was, in presence of the Most Revd. Michael Angelo Segnezzio, of the order of preachers, Commissary General of the Holy

65

Office, by the said Cardinal warned of the error of the aforesaid opinion, and admonished to abandon it; and immediately thereafter before me and before witnesses, the Lord Cardinal Bellarmine being still present, the said Galileo was by the said Commissary commanded and enjoined, in the name of his Holiness the Pope, and the whole Congregation of the Holy Office, to relinquish altogether the said opinion that the sun is the center of the world and immovable and that the earth moves; *nor henceforth to hold, teach, or defend it in any way whatsoever, verbally or in writing;* otherwise proceedings would be taken against him in the Holy Office; which injunction the said Galileo acquiesced in and promised to obey. Done at Rome, in the place aforesaid, in presence of Badino Nores, of Nicosia, in the Kingdom of Cyprus, and Augustino Mongardo, from a place in the Abbacy of Rottz, in the diocese of Politianeti, inmates of the said Cardinal's house, witnesses.

This second account of Galileo's meeting with Bellarmine has fascinated students of the Galileo trial ever since it was made public. It contradicts the other formal records of the 1616 proceedings and Galileo's correspondence and conduct of that period. It is not in accord with the papal order which Bellarmine had been directed to execute, permitting Galileo to teach or defend his thesis, if only as a supposition. It is completely at odds with the March 3, 1616, report of Bellarmine's session with Galileo and with the letter Bellarmine sent to Galileo. It does not square with action taken in 1616 by the Congregation of the Index with respect to other books expressing the Copernican doctrine as a hypothesis. Although a notary and witnesses are mentioned, the document is unsigned, contrary to custom. It is not an original document, like those on either side of it in the bound Vatican file, but a copy, and is inscribed on the back pages of two contemporary documents. Nor is it paginated, as are the adjacent instruments. The original (if there ever was one) has never been found.

It was supposed for a while that it was conveniently fabricated in 1632 or 1633, to furnish grounds for proceeding against Galileo; but the weight of opinion today is that it was surreptitiously inserted in the file by lesser Holy Office officials in 1616 to trap the philosopher when, as, and if he discussed the Copernican theory "in any way whatsoever."

However the deed was done, it was a godsend to the conscientious commissioners. They submitted a memorandum to the Pope charging Galileo with deviating from the permitted treatment of the Copernican theory as a hypothesis, and disposed of the imprimaturs by accusing Galileo of fraudulently concealing from the censors the newly discovered "command" of the Holy Office. Galileo was thus laid open to trial for disobedience of the Holy Office's injunction of 1616 and for heresy.

The Pope quickly referred the matter to the Inquisition, and the General Congregation of the Holy Office promptly decided to summon Galileo to Rome.

Galileo was old and sick. He had just recovered from a bout of severe illness affecting his eyesight. A certificate of three doctors, which he vainly sent to the Inquisition in hopes of delaying his trial, described him as suffering from a serious hernia with a ruptured peritoneum, and intermittent heartbeat, stomach trouble, insomnia, "flying pains about the body" and (sic!) "hypochondriacal melancholy."

He was not advised formally of the charges. Until a short time before the first hearing he was apparently sustained by his confidence that the late Cardinal Bellarmine's letter proved the limited scope of the only 1616 decree he knew anything about. But his friends close to the Vatican were fearful, and urged him to submit, although both he and they were totally unaware of the surprise which would be sprung at the hearings.

No witnesses were called. And when he produced Bellarmine's letter in his defense, no effort was made to clear up the riddle of the two accounts of his session with the Cardinal in 1616. The juggernaut rolled on; and three days after his first hearing the three counselors of the Inquisition delivered their opinions that he had violated the order of the Holy Office.

Galileo, with gout added to his other ailments, and his hernia worsening, fought on as best he could. But the following month, at a private meeting of the Holy Congregation presided over by Urban himself, it was decided to threaten torture in order to extract a complete submission from Galileo. The *Dialogue*, of course, was to be suppressed.

On June 21, he appeared once more before his judges and renounced the Copernican theory. The following day, in the large hall of the Dominican Convent of St. Maria in the center of Rome, the sentence was read to him, signed by seven of the ten cardinals who had heard his case. He was found guilty of infringing the special prohibition of 1616 and of leaving the Copernican view "undecided" and "probable" in the *Dialogue*, which was "gross error."

Assuming the genuineness of the newly discovered report of the 1616 proceedings, the sentence is technically well-founded on the first point. But the second, by reason of which he was declared "vehemently suspected of heresy," has no basis in Roman Catholic principles. The error of the Copernican doctrine had not been reduced to dogma by "infallible authority" through either of the two channels available—by the Pope speaking *ex cathedra*, or by an Ecumenical Council. It is only by one of these methods that the faithful can be required to abjure an opinion as heretical. Although a decree of the Congregation of the Index could be enforced and its disobedience punished, it is not an article of faith.

The full record of Galileo's testimony is a pathetic graph of pride going downhill, backwards. At the first hearing he is standing firm on the Bellarmine letter and saying that he did not think it necessary to inform the censor of the "order" which had just been revealed to him for the first time. At the next session, he pleads guilty to "empty ambition" and "pure heedlessness and inadvertence," and asks for the chance to revise the book to suit the Church. Then, offered an opportunity to defend himself, he submits a written *apologia*, ending with the plea that his ill-health and sufferings as a result of the trial be considered "adequate punishment." At the final hearing, he recants fully, saying, "I am in your hands, let you do with me as you will."

His sentence required him to recant his "errors and heresies" and confined him to the Inquisition's prison at his judges' pleasure. The book was, of course, banned. Galileo, kneeling before his judges, pronounced the formula of his famous abjuration. The Pope then finally relented, and after two days of confinement, permitted his release to the custody of the Tuscan Ambassador in Rome.

For the rest of his life, the aged savant was kept under strict surveillance by the Inquisition—first near Rome and then at Arcetri, where he was in effect under house arrest. In December 1637 he became completely blind, and was allowed to return to his house in Florence the following year. His researches and scientific writing continued—but never again did he venture publicly into the physics or theology of the spheres. He died in 1642, the year Isaac Newton was born.

The story persists that after his pitiable recantation, Galileo muttered under his breath the stubborn phrase, *"E pur si muove"*—"But still it moves." Mankind has need of such legends of defiance on the part of its humbled heroes, but Galileo's memory rests on firmer ground.

His trial lit a bonfire in the minds of men of learning throughout non-Catholic Europe. The *Dialogue* and other books by Galileo promptly received wide circulation in English and Latin editions published outside of Italy, and "the Copernican revolution" was well launched. By 1696, when Newton's classic *Principia Mathematica* appeared, Galileo's thesis had influenced the thinking of lay scientists everywhere. Although the Church waited until 1835 to remove the *Dialogue* from the Index, the book had long since, in the words of John H. Randall, "swept man out of his proud position as the central figure of the universe, and made him a tiny spark on a third-rate planet revolving about a tenth-rate sun drifting in an endless cosmic ocean."

The partial text of the testimony of the aged savant presented here is a dramatic account of one great man's intellectual Armageddon:

TUESDAY, APRIL 12, 1633

Galileo of Florence, son of the late Vincenzo Galileo, aged 70, having been requested to swear to speak the truth, took the oath by touching the holy objects.

Q. Does he know, or can he imagine, for what reason he was summoned?

A. I imagine that I was ordered to present myself before the Holy Office in Rome in order to give an account of my recently published book; and my reason for supposing this is that an order was issued to me and my bookseller a few days before I was summoned to Rome, prohibiting us from circulating any further copies of the book; and the bookseller was ordered by the Father Inquisitor to send the original manuscript of my book to the Holy Office in Rome.

Q. Let him state what the book is which he takes to be the cause of his summoning to Rome.

A. It is a book written in dialogue form, and treating of the constitution of the universe—that is, of the two major systems: the disposition of the heavens and of the elements.

Q. Where and when did he write the book, and during how long a time?

A. I wrote the book in Florence about ten or twelve years ago, and I spent seven or eight years at work on it, although not continuously.

Q. Has he been in Rome at any other time since the year 1616, and if so, upon what occasion?

A. I was in Rome in the year 1616, and again later in the second year of the Pontificate of His Holiness, Urban VIII, and finally, I came here three years ago for the purpose of presenting my book to be printed. The occasion of my visit in 1616 was the following: I had heard doubts raised concerning the views of Nicholas Copernicus with respect to the motion of the earth and the immobility of the sun and the order of the celestial spheres; wherefore, in order to make sure that I should hold none but holy and Catholic opinions, I came to inquire what views it was fitting to hold with regard to these matters.

Q. And he was asked to tell what decisions were reached and communicated to him at that time, in the month of February 1616.

A. In the month of February 1616, Cardinal Bellarmine told me that the views of Copernicus, since, when categorically affirmed, they stand in opposition to Holy Scripture, must neither be so held nor so defended; but that it was permissible to adopt and employ them in a hypothetical fashion. I have in my possession a document written by this same Cardinal Bellarmine on the 26th of May, 1616, in which he declares, in conformity with what I have just related, that the Copernicus view, being contrary to

69

Holy Scripture, may not be adopted nor defended; and I now present to you a copy of this document.

Q. When the aforesaid communication was made to him, were any other persons present, and who were they?

A. When Cardinal Bellarmine told me these things and informed me as I have reported concerning the view of Copernicus, there were present certain Dominican fathers; but I was unacquainted with them, and had not ever before seen them.

Q. Was any injunction concerning this matter given him by any of the fathers whom he says were there present, or by anybody else at that time? And if so, of what nature?

A. I remember that the meeting took place in this manner: Cardinal Bellarmine sent for me one morning, and told me a certain particular which I should prefer to repeat privately to His Holiness before I tell it otherwise; but in conclusion he informed me that the opinion of Copernicus must not be held or defended, since it stood counter to Holy Scripture. I cannot recall whether those Dominican fathers were present at the beginning of our talk or whether they arrived later, nor do I remember whether they were present when the Cardinal told me that the aforesaid opinion was not tenable; and it may be that some injunction was given me against holding or defending it, but if so I have no memory of it, for this was an event of some years since.

Q. If the things that were said and proposed to him at that time by way of directives were now to be read out to him, would he recall them?

A. I do not recall that anything further was said to me, nor can I answer whether, if such things as may have been said at that time were now read out to me, I should recall them; I am telling freely all that I do remember, for I do not claim that I have never in any way disobeyed those instructions—that is, that I have never in any fashion held or defended the said opinion concerning the motion of the earth and the immobility of the sun.

Q. And he was asked to say whether he remembered the gist of the aforesaid injunction given him in the presence of witnesses—namely, that he must in no way hold or defend or teach that opinion. He was asked to say whether he recalled how and by whom this injunction was given him.

A. I do not recall that any such order was communicated to me otherwise than in *viva voce* conversation by Cardinal Bellarmine, and I remember that his instructions were that I should neither hold nor defend, and it may be that he added that I should not teach, the aforesaid view. I do not remember that he did so, nor do I remember the qualification *in any way*, and yet it may be that this was included, and that I did not reflect on it nor impress the words on my memory, for the reason that only a few months later I received from Cardinal Bellarmine the document which I have presented here, and in which is set down the order not to hold or defend the said opinion. And I have no recollection of the other phrase which you now bring to my attention—namely, "and not to teach in any way"—no doubt for the reason that it is not stated in the written document which has served me as a memorandum.

Q. Following the receipt of these orders did he obtain permission to write the book he has here acknowledged as his, and which he later published?

A. After receiving the aforesaid orders, I did not seek permission to write the book which I have here recognized as mine, because I do not consider that I have in any way overstepped in it the directive given me neither to hold nor defend nor teach the aforesaid opinion, but rather to refute it.

Q. When he asked the Master of the Holy Palace for permission to print the book, did he also inform the same Most Reverend Father concerning the order which had been communicated to him on behalf of the Holy Congregation of the Index?

A. I said nothing about such an order to the Master of the Holy Palace when I sought his permission to print the book, because I did not think it necessary to do so; I felt no scruple, for in this book I had not held nor defended the doctrine proposing a moving earth and a stationary sun; indeed, in this book I expound a view contrary to that of Copernicus, and I demonstrate that his explanations are invalid and inconclusive.

After these proceedings the hearings were suspended—and a room which was to serve as prison was assigned him in the apartments of the officials in the Palace of the Inquisition; he was ordered not to depart from this room without special permission, being subject to punishment by the Holy Congregation for any breach of this order; and he was bidden to subscribe to these measures; and silence was imposed upon him under oath.

SABBATH DAY, APRIL 30, 1633

Q. Let him say what seems fitting to him.

A. When I had reflected for several days attentively and continuously on the interrogation put to me on the 16th day of the present month,[1] and in particular on the question of whether I had been forbidden sixteen years ago by order of the Holy Office to hold, defend, or teach in any fashion the view, which at that time already stood condemned, that the sun is stationary and that the earth moves, it came to my mind to reread my published *Dialogue* (as I had not ever done during the three preceding years) in order to examine carefully whether there had issued from my pen, against my firmest intention, inadvertently, any statement whereby the reader or the authorities might argue in me either some taint of disobedience or anything whatsoever else which could be conceived as contravening the orders of the Holy Church; and since by the benign consent of the authorities I was free to send my servant forth, I secured a copy of my book; and, taking it up, I set myself to a careful reading and detailed study of it. Struck by

[1] Galileo is in error about the date: the first hearing took place on the 12th, not 16th.

it, as I was, after so long an interval, as though by a new thing and the work of another writer, I freely confess that it seemed to me at several points written in such a way that a reader unfamiliar with my inmost thought would have had some cause for thinking the arguments brought forth for the false theory, the one I intended to refute, so drawn as to be more potent in confirming that theory than easy to rebut; and two of these in particular, the one concerning sunspots and the other the flux and reflux of the sea, come to the reader's ear with qualifications that seem more like robust and vigorous confirmations than is fitting from a writer who held them as inconclusive, as in truth I inwardly and truly held them and hold them to be, and who desired, as I did, to refute them. And in order to excuse myself in my own eyes for having fallen into an error so alien to my intention, unable to satisfy myself fully by remarking that when one gives the arguments of an adversary with the intention of rebutting them, one is obliged to set them forth with precision (especially when one writes in the dialogue form), and must not muffle them so as to put the adversary at a disadvantage —unable, as I say, to satisfy myself fully with this excuse, I laid the blame on the natural complacency any man feels towards his own subtlety and towards his ability to show himself sharper than the common run of men, even to the point of finding ingenious and convincing demonstrations of probability for false propositions. Wherefore, although with Cicero I may be "more avid of glory than is needful for me," if I were today faced with the task of setting forth the same arguments, there is no doubt that I should weaken them in such a way that they could not make an appearance of having that force which truly and essentially they lack. My error was, I confess, one of empty ambition and of pure heedlessness and inadvertence. And this is what I wished to say on the subject of the matter that occurred to me in rereading my book.

Following these proceedings, his signature having been entered, the gentlemen of the jury suspended the hearing, having enjoined him to silence by oath.

Returning a little later, he added:

And for further confirmation of the fact that I have not held and do not hold the condemned view that the earth moves and the sun stands still, if I am permitted, as I desire, opportunity and time to make clearer demonstration of it, I am ready to do so; and there is most appropriate occasion for it, since in the published dialogue the speakers had agreed to meet together again after a certain period of time in order to discuss various natural problems other than those treated in their earlier gatherings. Given this occasion to add one or two meetings, I promise to take up again the arguments already brought forward in favor of the aforesaid false and condemned opinion, and to refute them in the most effective way that the blessed God may grant me power to do.

Thus I beg this Holy Tribunal to concur with me in this good resolution by granting me the opportunity to carry it out.

The aforesaid Galileo, having been brought before his Paternal Eminence, the Father Commissary assigned him a period of eight days in which to frame his defense if it was his intention to do so.

Having heard this, he said:

I have heard what Your Grace has said to me, and I answer that for my defense—by which I mean, for the purpose of showing the sincerity and purity of my intention, rather than to excuse those actions in which by my own admission I have offended—I offer this written testimony, in addition to the document written by Cardinal Bellarmine in his own hand, and of which I have earlier submitted a copy written in my hand. For the rest, I yield myself in all things and fully to the well-known piety and clemency of this Tribunal.

Q. Is there anything he desires to say?

A. I have nothing to say.

Q. Does he hold, or has he ever held, the opinion that the center of the universe lies in the sun, and the earth is not the center of the universe, and that the earth moves with a diurnal motion; and if so, since when has he so held?

A. Already for a long time before the decision of the Holy Congregation of the Index, and before any directive was given me, I considered both the opinion of Ptolemy and that of Copernicus, indifferently, to be disputable; for either the one or the other might be true in nature. But, following the aforesaid decision, confirmed by the wisdom of the authorities, all ambiguity ceased for me and I held, as I still do hold, as true and indubitable Ptolemy's view, namely, that the earth is motionless and the sun in motion.

Q. And it was said to him that this [Copernican] view was discussed and defended in the book published at the time stated above, as appears from the language and tenor of the book itself; and that, indeed, it might be assumed from what he wrote and published in that book that he had continued to embrace that view after the time in question. Therefore, let him freely say whether he holds or ever held it to be the truth.

A. With regard to the writing of my published *Dialogue*, I did not undertake it because I hold Copernicus' view to be true, but rather solely for the general good, in order to set forth the natural and astronomic arguments that might be advanced on either side, and in an effort to make manifest that none of these had power to conclude affirmatively either for the one or for the other view; and that, therefore, in order to proceed securely, one must have recourse to the determinations of sublimer teachings, as can be seen clearly stated in a great many portions of that *Dialogue*. My inmost conclusion is, then, that I do not hold, nor have held since the matter was decided by the authorities, the condemned opinion.

Q. And it was said to him that it truly appears from the reasons and positive statements brought forward in his book that he assumes the earth to be in motion and the sun stationary; so that it was thought that he had, at least for a time, embraced the views of Copernicus. Therefore, unless he decides to speak the truth, the instruments of the law as befitting the situation will be employed against him.

A. I do not hold the view of Copernicus, nor have I held it since I was prompted and instructed to abandon it; for the rest, I am here in your hands, let you do with me as you will.

Q. And he was told to speak the truth, for otherwise torture would be used upon him.

A. I am here in order to obey, and I have not held that opinion since the decision of the authorities was reached, as I have said.

And as there remained nothing further to do in execution of the regulations, his signature having been taken, he was allowed to go to his dwelling.

CHARLES I
(1649)

Two weeks after Charles I lost his head, John Milton rushed into print with a tract on *The Tenure of Kings and Magistrates*. In it he quoted from the Latin poet Seneca:

> There can be slain
> No sacrifice to God more acceptable
> Than an unjust and wicked king.

Allowing for some poetic license, this pious morsel of special pleading speaks volumes about the trial of Charles and the momentous events that preceded it.

Milton's audience was a generation of Englishmen raised on the doctrine that the King reigned by the will of God. "The greatest Anglican divines of that age," according to Macaulay, "had maintained that no breach of law or contract, no excess of cruelty, rapacity, or licentiousness on the part of a rightful King, could justify the people in withstanding him by force."

Now England was being ruled by men who, but for the victory of the rebel armies against their sovereign, would have been dangling from the gibbets that lined England's highways. The trial of Charles had been designed to lay to rest the legal inhibitions and religious misgivings of all but the most ardent anti-Royalists. But his execution had nevertheless shocked many conscientious Englishmen, leaving them with a vague residue of guilt over the bloody deed.

It was not by chance, therefore, that Milton resorted to the concept of a "sacrifice to God." But for accuracy's sake, he should have made it clear that he was not referring to the God of the Anglicans, nor to the God of the Catholics. Charles Stuart was sacrificed to the God of the dissenters.

By the time Charles ascended the throne in 1625, Protestantism in his kingdom had blossomed into a wild and colorful profusion of sects.

Officially, only the Anglican creed was recognized, but its popular acceptance was anything but universal. Scotland's austere Presbyterian Kirk had been established almost half a century, and despite a superstructure of Anglican bishops appointed by the Crown, had remained relatively autonomous and politically powerful. In England itself, Charles as spiritual head of the Anglican Church had to reckon not only with the stubborn core of unreconstructed Catholics, comprising perhaps one fourth of the population, but also with Presbyterians, Puritans, Baptists, Anabaptists, Antinomians, Brownists, Seekers, Ranters, Independents, Millenarians, Fifth Monarchy Men, and a host of other splinter denominations with their own heterodox ideas about spiritual reform. And in the last analysis, it was Charles' endeavor to impose uniform religious practices and organization upon this theological hodgepodge that figured most heavily in his downfall.

From the outset he was handicapped by the legacy his sniveling buffoon of a father, James I, had left him—a war with Catholic Spain and a navy that was only a rueful reminder of its Elizabethan greatness. Crown revenues had been depleted by royal gifts and the cupidity of three generations of courtiers. Inflation had taken an equal toll: the pound had lost three quarters of its value in the past seventy-five years.

Had the English war effort enjoyed some small measure of success, Charles would have experienced less heavy weather in his early encounters with Parliament. In the eyes of his people, James had been both tardy and fainthearted in taking a hand in the mortal religious struggle that had been convulsing the European continent since 1618. The Reformation itself was in peril: Spain and Austria now seemed on the verge of crushing Protestant Holland and Denmark, which had come to the aid of their beleagured coreligionists in Germany and Bohemia.

Charles had unhappily entrusted England's fortunes in the European conflict to his late father's scandal-tainted favorite, George Villiers, Duke of Buckingham, whose courage was equaled only by his incompetence. Bidding for France's help against Spain, Buckingham had placed seven ships at the disposal of Louis XIII, only to have their guns turned against the rebellious French Protestants. Buckingham had been duped; but that explanation would hardly have satisfied the irate English, even if Charles had not taken the position that explanations were beneath the dignity of a royal minister.

Devout Protestants began to take a second look at their young King, recalling that he was, after all, the grandson of that arch-Papist, Mary of Scotland. All England had gasped when his fifteen-year-old Catholic bride, Louis XIII's sister, Henrietta Maria, arrived in England with a retinue of one bishop, forty-nine priests, and over four hundred attendants of the despised Roman Faith. And it was generally (and correctly) rumored that the marriage treaty with France was responsible for the curiously lax enforcement of the penal laws against English Catholics.

Charles' first two Parliaments gave him nothing but abuse. His administration of the anti-Papist laws and Buckingham's conduct of the war were resoundingly condemned, and the King received only a fraction of the appropriations he needed. By the time he sent his second Parliament packing in June 1626, Charles had been put on notice that there would be no further revenues until Buckingham was removed from office.

It was nothing new, by this time, for Parliament to use its taxing power as a lever to force royal concessions in other areas. Elizabeth had sidestepped these occasional democratic sorties with a curtsy and a smile. James had stormed and pouted, but had avoided a decisive conflict by somewhat ungracious but timely concessions to the popular will.

Thrown back on his own resources, Charles proceeded to raise money illegally—by forced loans, collection of customs duties, and other means equally repugnant to the wealthier classes. But not enough to keep afloat, with Spain and the royal household on his back; and his needs multiplied when Buckingham's clumsy diplomacy tripped off a war with France.

Gambling recklessly on a military victory to restore himself to popular favor, Buckingham launched an expedition to the French Coast. It wound up disastrously, bringing shame and sorrow to the English and draining what little was left in the royal Exchequer. For lack of funds, the unpaid and mutinous troops were billeted in private homes on their return from France, arousing widespread resentment.

When Parliament met again at the King's bidding in March 1628, it had blood in its eye. Some of its leaders had already sampled the conveniences of the Tower and the Fleet Prison, and they all knew that any aspersion on the Crown or its ministers could trigger a charge of treason. But with remarkable courage they drove their more timorous colleagues to enact the celebrated Petition of Right, an assertion of the dignity of man no less monumental than the Magna Carta.

By this act, the King was prohibited from levying taxes or forced loans without the consent of Parliament, from billeting soldiers upon the people, and from imprisoning anyone without a specific charge and without bail. To win the King's consent to this measure, a carrot was extended in front of the donkey in the form of a promised appropriation of about £350,000.

77

Charles' formal assent to the Petition was required to give it the force of law. Typically, he used every subterfuge at his command to trick Parliament into accepting that consent in a form which, thanks to legal technicalities, would not be binding on him. But Parliament's naked antagonism was too formidable; and before it got completely out of hand, the King grudgingly yielded. Parliament kept its word; before it adjourned, the King got his subsidy.

During the recess, Buckingham's removal from the scene at the hands of an assassin furnished Charles a priceless opportunity. He could have laid the blame for all past difficulties at the dead man's door; but Charles was too proud and too deeply committed to what Pope later called "the right of kings divine to govern wrong." Had Charles been only slightly less pigheaded and accepted the Petition of Right in good faith, he might have reaped the reward of a ripe old age.

But no sooner had Parliament gone home than it became apparent that Charles' hard-wrung assent to the Petition of Right had been a meaningless gesture. He continued without pause to collect unauthorized customs duties, and his troops remained unwelcome guests in the houses of his outraged subjects. To add fuel to the fire, he moved a step backward toward Catholicism—or so it appeared to the devout Calvinists, who constituted a powerful faction in Parliament. The trappings of papist ritual—altars, surplices, crucibles, and sacred images—were being restored to the churches under royal protection; communion tables and baptismal fonts were resuming their former positions of prominence. It began to look as if the Reformation had never occurred.

When Parliament reconvened in January 1629, it turned its guns on Charles' fiscal and religious lapses. Its vociferous month-long review of grievances came to a tumultuous and dramatic conclusion on March 2 as Sir John Eliot started to address the Commons on one of the bills he had proposed, which would assert Parliament's authority over "religious innovations" and the collection of customs duties. The Speaker, Sir John Finch, tried to shut off debate by leaving his chair, after telling the Commons that the King had commanded him to adjourn the House. Amid wild demonstrations, two members held Finch in his chair by force, while another locked the door to prevent the King's messenger from delivering the formal dissolution order. While the messenger beat vainly on the door, the resolutions were jammed through by acclamation. Then the door was opened, and Charles' third Parliament passed out of existence.

But Charles was determined to have the last word. He committed nine outstanding members of the opposition to the Tower. Denied a trial, Eliot died in prison rather than give security for good behavior;

and his martyrdom paid dividends for the Parliamentary cause in increased hostility toward the Crown.

For the next eleven years Charles kept Parliament out in pasture—the longest period of inactivity in its entire history. Peace was made with Spain and France on degrading terms; and in a remarkable about-face for a Protestant monarch, English ships were leased to Spain for the transport of her troops and payrolls around the flanks of her Calvinist and Lutheran opponents. Revenue remained a problem, although collections of customs duties mounted, thanks to a steady improvement in trade. The bottom of the barrel of royal prerogative was scraped to find additional sources of money. Fees and fines unheard of for generations were revived as a stopgap measure.

One of the most mischievous of these exactions was Charles' revival of the hoary institution of "ship money." Although this levy of ships or their monetary equivalent for the maintenance of the fleet had been traditionally confined to seaboard communities, he boldly extended it to inland cities and towns. John Hampden went to court to challenge one of the ship-money writs as an illegal tax, because it was imposed without Parliament's approval. The King's hand-picked judges threw the case out, but only by the narrowest possible margin. Hampden's daring won the applause of the entire country, but the champions of parliamentary government now realized that they could not look to the Bench to protect private rights against the King.

With neither Parliament nor judges to redress their wrongs, the English bore their cross with patience and fortitude. Buckingham's death in 1628 had moved the Queen, no longer a gawky adolescent, closer to the center of power, and her hand was seen in the lease of British ships to Spain and in the ruthless persecution of Protestant nonconformists at home.

Influential as Queen Henrietta later became, she was at that time probably responsible only for Charles' relative tolerance toward Catholics—an attitude that did not extend to Protestant dissenters. Superficially, this state of affairs was understandable. Charles' Catholic population did its best to escape notice, and occasionally even proved useful in royal diplomatic intrigue with powers adhering to the ancient faith. The English followers of Calvin and Knox, on the other hand, were an aggressive and irritating lot, constantly turning out abusive pamphlets on their illegal presses and heaping curses on the King and his court in their interminable sermons.

Charles regarded these Protestant dissenters as the prime obstacles to the establishment of uniformity in the ritual, liturgy, and organization of the Anglican Church, which had experienced some difficulty in finding its ecclesiastical bearings since the break with Rome. He entrusted the promotion of his particular brand of godliness to a prelate of prodigious energy and little discretion, William Laud, whom Charles appointed Archbishop of Canterbury in 1633. Laud made ruthless use of the Star Chamber and the Court of High Commission to bring to heel Puritans, Presbyterians, and nonconformists of every stripe. Each week brought forth new martyrs, their noses slit, their ears lopped off, their garments bloodsoaked by the lash, as object lessons to those who would speak out against the increasing weight of ceremonial in the churches or in favor of the selection of preachers by the elders of their parishes. Emigration to America provided a safety valve to the hardiest and most desperate, but it was not always kept open.

In dealing with the English dissenters, Charles had the advantage flowing from the fragmentation and disunity of the opposition. But when he tackled the Scotch Presbyterians, he ran head-on into a firmly entrenched national and religious tradition. That collision ultimately dislodged his crown.

In 1636 he issued a Book of Canons making himself sole arbiter of all ecclesiastical matters in Scotland, forbidding assemblies of clergy without royal consent, and investing his bishops with the right to appoint ministers. Rites and ceremonies were prescribed which to the Scots smacked suspiciously of popery, and the forthcoming initiation of a new and compulsory liturgy was announced.

The appearance in 1637 of the new Prayer Book—promptly dubbed "Laud's Liturgy"—confirmed the Scots in their initial revulsion for the King's program. Attempts to introduce it in the churches provoked countrywide violence. Petitions were drawn up requesting the King to recall the liturgy, but were rejected out of hand as treasonable.

As religious and nationalistic feeling coalesced, it found characteristic expression in the so-called National Covenant, a solemn compact with God pledging Scottish lives and fortunes to the defense of the Faith against innovation. During the month of March 1638, copies of the Covenant were subscribed in every city and hamlet, with a sense of pious exultation and solemn resolve, by half a million Scotsmen, including almost every Protestant nobleman. Charles' Scottish bishops fled to England, except for four who saved their skins by recanting.

A General Assembly met at Glasgow in November. Thumbing its nose at Charles' command to dissolve, it annulled the Book of Canons, abolished the system of bishoprics, and restored Presbyterianism to its pristine pre-Stuart state. Both sides saw that rebellion was at hand, and armies began to gather along the border.

In March 1639, Charles invaded Scotland. The rugged Covenanters were ready for him, and he had neither manpower nor resources equal to the task. A truce was worked out, ostensibly to explore the prospects of compromise. But neither side had its heart in the work; and as a renewal of hostilities loomed, Charles called Parliament into session, with an urgent request for funds.

Three weeks of fruitless bickering, and the King put Parliament back on the shelf. Once more he turned to face the Scots in the field, with the odds lengthened in their favor during the year's truce. The hardy Covenanters soon crossed the border and overran four northern counties. Charles sued for armistice terms and, when he learned that they involved money, was forced to summon Parliament once more. The Long Parliament, as it came to be called, would sit from November 3, 1640, until Oliver Cromwell dismissed it thirteen years later.

The opposition leaders, headed by Hampden and John Pym, viewed Charles' plight as an opportunity to settle a few old scores; the Scots could wait. Archbishop Laud and the Earl of Strafford, whom Charles had lately installed as his chief political deputy, were promptly sent to the Tower. Pym pushed through both Houses a bill of attainder condemning Strafford to death. As a legislative measure this required Charles' signature, and one week after he had openly declared to Parliament that he would never join in any move to punish Strafford for any cause, he approved the bill. When he heard the news, the condemned man muttered, "Put not your trust in princes."

On the same day, Charles assented to a bill forbidding the dissolution of Parliament without its consent. Reinforced by this law, the forces around Pym proceeded to flex their muscles. Parliament abolished the Star Chamber and the Court of High Commission. Ship money was declared illegal, and customs levies placed on a short-term basis.

The Scots were sent home happy with a complete victory in the religious arena, £200,000 and all the booty they could carry.

Charles disbanded his army. But soon rebellion broke out in Ireland. The King and Parliament had a common interest in suppressing the revolt. This meant raising a militia; but the prospect of placing an army at the disposal of the King was anathema to a Parliament which had learned to trust him to behave properly only when he was powerless. Work was accordingly resumed on the Grand Remonstrance which Parliament had been formulating for some time: a recital of political and religious grievances and a program for their correction. Within Parliament a sharp conflict of opinion developed, with the Royalists and Episcopalians lined up against the balance of Parliament.

The bill barely squeaked through. Encouraged by the close vote, and perhaps moved by rumors that the Queen was likely to be impeached for intriguing with Catholic powers abroad, Charles took the step from which he could never turn back. He sent his Attorney General down to the House of Lords to impeach Pym, Hampden, and three other opposition leaders in Commons on charges of treason. Even the upper House was dismayed by this illegal and unprecedented action: for the Attorney General had no right to institute impeachment proceedings, nor could the Lords try them. The Lords hesitated; and the Commons flatly refused to surrender its five members.

Impatient, Charles rashly compounded his folly. He staged a personal march on Commons, attended by several hundred armed men, to "pull them out by the ears." Entering the House, he found them gone; they had fled into the rabbit warrens of the city. The Speaker respectfully refused to answer his questions as to their whereabouts, and Charles, conscious of having committed a royal solecism, muttered a few words about respect for the laws, and retired ignominiously from the scene.

To Parliament and its sympathizers this was the last straw. The violent revulsion of feeling sparked by the King's act strengthened the hands of Pym in the House and of anti-Royalists throughout the country. A state of hostilities now existed between the King and Parliament, although it would be seven months before it exploded into civil war.

Within a week, the daylong demonstrations outside his window convinced Charles that he was no longer safe at Whitehall. He left London. When he returned it would be as a captive doomed to die.

The "cold war" that followed witnessed a stately minuet between King and Parliament, danced at long distance, with both of them busily preparing for armed conflict while ostensibly seeking an adjustment. Bill after bill curtailing royal prerogatives was dutifully shipped to His Majesty for approval. For his part, Charles made many concessions. But every time Parliament sought to curtail his control of the militia, the King stood firm, betraying his aggressive designs.

Parliament quietly moved to guard vital ports against seizure by the King, while the Queen departed for Holland to seek foreign military alliances and money for the inevitable fight. Royalist members of Parliament took to the countryside. On July 11, 1642, Parliament issued a declaration that the King had been guilty of the first belligerent act by raising troops without the authority of Parliament.

When war broke out in earnest, it went as most such wars go. At first the Royalists enjoyed the advantages (similar to those of the South in the American Civil War) which fall to the side with better horses and arms, and with officers practiced in the art of battle. But the financial strength of the merchants and burghers ultimately tipped the scales in favor of the fanatical "Roundheads"—the predominantly Puritan Army designed by Cromwell and whipped into shape in a complete reversal of castebound military tradition. The Scots played a vital role, too, entering into a military alliance with Parliament late in 1643 for money and the greater glory of the Kirk.

Even after the tide of battle turned against Charles, he might have saved his crown, or at least his head, by a few timely and sincere concessions. Instead he embarked upon a series of maladroit maneuvers designed to exploit the differences among the Puritan Army, the Presbyterian Scots, and the divided Parliament. It was a self-defeating game, for there are few secrets in a civil war; and although Charles started as a player, he ended up as a pawn. He was made prisoner by the Scots, who traded him to Parliament, only to have him snatched away by the Army. Once the Army established Puritan ascendancy over Parliament by purging it of its last Presbyterian die-hards, Charles knew that his time had come.

On New Year's Day, 1649, the half-empty Commons voted that the levying of war upon Parliament by a King amounted to treason. The Lords, now reduced to a handful of members, refused to go along with this novel idea; whereupon the Commons resolved that their enactments had the force of law, whether or not the Lords (or the King!) approved. On January 6, a court of 135 commissioners was set up as a special tribunal to try the King. A lawyer of no particular distinction, John Bradshaw, was nominated as presiding judge. Most of those named to the Commission refused to serve; only 52, with Cromwell as their acknowledged leader, attended its first meeting.

On Saturday, January 20, the King, handsome and stately in bearing as usual, faced his accusers. The Painted Chamber at Westminster Hall had been fitted up with six tiers of benches on a raised platform for the tribunal, with Bradshaw ensconced on a higher chair front and center. In an open space immediately in front of the benches sat the clerks at a table draped in scarlet, on which lay the crossed mace and sword symbolizing the authority of the gathering. Below the platform, facing his judges, sat Charles on a crimson velvet chair, attended by guards and servants. He had deliberately refused to remove his hat as a sign of respect for the Court; but this contingency had been anticipated, and it had been decided to ignore it.

Bradshaw directed the Solicitor General to read the indictment. Charles heard himself described as a monarch entrusted only with a "limited power to govern" who "out of a wicked design to erect and uphold in himself an unlimited and tyrannical power to rule according to his will, and to overthrow the rights and liberties of the people . . . traitorously and maliciously levied war against the present Parliament

83

and the people therein represented." There followed a recital of the principal engagements of the war. In summation, he stood accused of "all the treasons, murders, burnings, spoils, desolations, damages, and mischiefs, to this nation, acted and committed in the said wars or occasioned thereby."

The tack the King took was simple, consistent, and, above all, well founded in legal principle. By what lawful authority, he asked, was he brought here? "In the name of the Commons of England," Bradshaw replied. But he saw no Lords to make up a Parliament, said Charles calmly, and he would be untrue to his divine and hereditary trust if he acknowledged the authority of this body. He was commanded to answer the charges, but declined; and the first session adjourned.

Bradshaw tried at the sittings held the following Monday and Tuesday to extract a direct answer from the King. His motive was clear: to obtain a concession of the authority of the Court to try the case. Both he and the other lawyers on the Commission sensed the weakness of their position, legally and politically, and the King gave them no solace. On the contrary, he struck a note which endowed his hopeless cause with an air of nobility, and, paradoxically, set him up as a champion of civil rights:

But it is not my case alone, it is the freedom and liberty of the people of England, and do you pretend what you will, I stand more for their liberties, for if power without Law may make laws, may alter the fundamental laws of the Kingdom, I do not know what subject he is in England that can be sure of his life or anything that he calls his own.

The tables were turned. The tyrant had become the defender of due process of law; the people's representatives, in keeping with a pattern that was often to be duplicated in later revolutions, became the authoritarian force.

And so it went; until Bradshaw, abandoning hope of preventing the King from speaking over the heads of the Commission to posterity, declared Charles guilty *pro confesso* for failure to plead to the charge.

The Commission might have pronounced sentence then and there; but time was needed to bring its fainthearted members into line. (Its ambivalence could be seen from the continued references to Charles as "King of England" throughout the proceedings.) A private hearing was held, and thirty-two witnesses paraded before the Commission to prove Charles' complicity in the civil war. After the sentence had been whipped into shape, it was nevertheless agreed that if the King should answer the charge or say anything else worth considering before sentence was pronounced, the Court would withdraw for further deliberations.

Charles did take a new tack at the session of January 27th; he asked to be heard by the Lords and Commons. But he again fell into a verbal duel with Bradshaw about the jurisdiction of the Court—he was not denying it, but he was not acknowledging it either; and before it could be learned what was in his mind, the tribunal recessed.

It was more than likely that Charles hoped, if he could confront the full Parliament, to trade out then and there a working arrangement to preserve the monarchy—with either himself or young Prince Charles as ruler, and with the royal power severely curtailed. Had this been done, England would probably have been spared a second revolution.

But Cromwell and his fellows were equally clear about the dangers of allowing the juggernaut they had set in motion to lose its momentum. Their own fate had been sealed when they took up arms against the King; and they were no longer prepared to take his word for anything, least of all their lives. The Court reconvened, and Bradshaw intoned the sentence of death.

On January 30th, Charles was conducted to the scaffold, on a platform draped in black, which had been set up in front of the Banqueting Hall of the Palace. A sea of soldiers and commoners filled the surrounding streets. Spectators swarmed on the rooftops and in the windows of the nearby houses, where they had waited for four hours or more to catch a glimpse of the drama.

Only those close by him on the platform heard Charles' soft-spoken and dignified last words. Protesting his innocence, he nevertheless piously forgave his enemies and reiterated his belief that the liberties of the people were threatened whenever the law could be changed by the power of the sword.

He bade a calm farewell to the Bishop of London: "I go from a corruptible to an incorruptible Crown, where no disturbance can be, no disturbance in the world." Then he knelt down, and with one blow the executioner severed his head from his body. A great moan swept the crowd.

For the first time in recorded history, the misdeeds of a ruler were expiated by him in his own blood after a trial at the hands of his people. The model improvised to this end in the trial of Charles I served later generations again and again as the grip of law on the minds of men imposed a demand for judicial ritual and the cloak of legality for violent changes in government. The concept that there could be treason against the institutions and the laws of a country—and not merely against the ruling power—was born on that occasion; and it has never died.

The trial minutes tend to monotony, only because the King refused to let it get off dead center. Parliament sorely needed from Charles an acknowledgment of its power to try him. He just as stoutly refused, hinting repeatedly at the fate that awaited regicides. As a result, the exchanges between Charles and the President of the Court started and ended as a battle of wills centering around this solitary question of jurisdiction, in which Charles emerged condemned, but in the light of subsequent history, the winner.

After the restoration of the monarchy in 1660, thirty-two of the surviving participants in Charles' trial were condemned to death, but only thirteen were executed. Twenty-odd more, already dead, were also tried. These included Cromwell and Bradshaw, whose bodies were exhumed and hanged, then reburied in an unmarked grave at the foot of the scaffold.

JANUARY 20, 1649

LORD PRESIDENT. Sir, you have now heard your charge, containing such matter as appears in it; you find that in the close of it, it is prayed to the Court, in the behalf of the Commons of England, that you answer to your charge. The Court expects your answer.

KING. I would know by what power I am called hither . . . there are many unlawful authorities in the world, thieves and robbers by the highways; but I would know by what authority I was brought from thence and carried from place to place, and I know not what; and when I know what lawful authority, I shall answer. Remember I am your King, your lawful King, and what sins you bring upon your heads, and the judgment of God upon the land; think well upon it, I say, think well upon it, before you go further from one sin to a greater; therefore let me know by what lawful authority I am seated here, and I shall not be unwilling to answer. In the meantime I shall not betray my trust; I have a trust committed to me by God, by old and lawful descent; I will not betray it, to answer to a new unlawful authority; therefore resolve me that and you shall hear more of me.

LORD PRESIDENT. If you had been pleased to have observed what was hinted to you by the Court, at your first coming hither, you would have known by what authority; which authority requires you, in the name of the people of England, of which you are elected King, to answer them.

KING. No. Sir, I deny that.

LORD PRESIDENT. If you acknowledge not the authority of the Court, they must proceed.

KING. I do tell them so; England was never an elective kingdom, but an hereditary kingdom, for near these thousand years; therefore let me know by what authority I am called hither. I do stand more for the liberty of my people, than any here that come to be my pretended judges; and therefore let me know by what lawful authority I am seated here, and I will answer it; otherwise I will not answer it.

LORD PRESIDENT. Sir, how really you have managed your trust is known: your way of answer is to interrogate the Court, which beseems not you on this condition. You have been told of it twice or thrice.

KING. Here is a gentleman, Lieutenant Colonel Cobbet; ask him if he did not bring me from the Isle of Wight by force. I do not come here as submitting to the Court: I will stand as much for the privilege of the House of Commons, rightly understood, as any man here, whatsoever. I see no House of Lords here that may constitute a Parliament; and the King too should have been. Is this the bringing of the King to his Parliament? Is this the bringing an end to the treaty in the public faith of the world? Let me see a legal authority warranted by the word of God, the Scriptures, or warranted by the constitutions of the kingdom, and I will answer.

LORD PRESIDENT. Sir, you have propounded a question and have been answered. Seeing you will not answer, the Court will consider how to proceed; in the meantime, those that brought you hither are to take charge of you back again. The Court desires to know whether this be all the answer you will give or no.

KING. Sir, I desire that you would give me, and all the world, satisfaction in this: let me tell you, it is not a slight thing you are about. I am sworn to keep the peace, by the duty I owe to God and my country, and I will do it to the last breath of my body; and therefore ye shall do well to satisfy first God, and then the country, by what authority you do it; if you do it by an usurped authority, you cannot answer. There is a God in heaven that will call you and all that give you power to account. Satisfy me in that and I will answer; otherwise I betray my trust and the liberties of the people: and therefore think of that, and I shall be willing. For I do avow that it is as great a sin to withstand lawful authority as it is to submit to a tyrannical, or any other ways unlawful, authority; and therefore satisfy me that and you shall receive an answer. . . .

JANUARY 22, 1649

LORD PRESIDENT. Sir, you may remember at the last court you were told the occasion of your being brought hither, and you heard a charge read against you containing a charge of high treason and other high crimes against this realm of England. . . . You were then pleased to make some scruples concerning the authority of this Court. . . . Since that the Court hath taken into consideration what you then said; they are fully satisfied with their own authority, and they hold it fit you should stand satisfied with it too; and they do require it, that you do give a positive and particular answer to this charge that is exhibited against you. . . .

KING. When I was here last, it is very true, I made that question; truly if it were only my own particular case, I would have satisfied myself with the protestation I made the last time I was here against the legality of the Court, and that a King cannot be tried by any superior jurisdiction on earth . . . therefore when that I came here, I did expect particular reasons to know by what law, what authority, you did proceed against me here. And therefore I am a little [*hard pressed?*] to seek what to say to you in this particular, because the affirmative is to be proved, the negative often is very hard to do; but since I cannot persuade you to do it, I shall tell you my reasons as short as I can—my reasons why in conscience and the duty I owe to God first, and my people next, for the preservation of their lives, liberties, and estates I perceive I cannot answer this till I be satisfied of the legality of it. All proceedings against any man whatsoever—

LORD PRESIDENT. Sir, I must interrupt you, which I would not do, but that what you do is not agreeable to the proceedings of any court of justice. You are about to enter into argument and dispute concerning the authority of this Court, before whom you appear as a prisoner and are charged as an high delinquent. If you take upon you to dispute the authority of the Court, we may not do it, nor will any court give way unto it. You are to submit unto it; you are to give a punctual and direct answer whether you will answer your charge or no, and what your answer is.

KING. Sir, by your favor, I do not know the forms of law. I do know law and reason, though I am no lawyer professed; but I know as much law as any gentleman in England; and therefore (under favor) I do plead for the liberties of the people of England more than you do; and therefore if I should impose a belief upon any man, without reasons given for it, it were unreasonable: but I must tell you that that reason that I have, as thus informed, I cannot yield unto it.

LORD PRESIDENT. Sir, I must interrupt you; you may not be permitted. You speak of law and reason; it is fit there should be law and reason, and there is both against you. Sir, the vote of the Commons of England assembled in Parliament, it is the reason of the kingdom, and they are these that have given to that law, according to which you should have ruled and reigned. Sir, you are not to dispute our authority; you are told it again by the Court. Sir, it will be taken notice of, that you stand in contempt of the Court, and your contempt will be recorded accordingly.

KING. I do not know how a king can be a delinquent; but by any law that I ever heard of, all men (delinquents, or what you will), let me tell you, they may put in demurrers against any proceeding as legal: and I do demand that, and demand to be heard with my reasons. If you deny that, you deny reason.

LORD PRESIDENT. Sir, you have offered something to the Court. I shall speak something unto you, the sense of the Court. Sir, neither you nor any man are permitted to dispute that point; you are concluded; you may not demur to the jurisdiction of the Court. If you do, I must let you know that they overrule your demurrer. They sit here by the authority of the Commons of England, and all your predecessors, and you are responsible to them.

KING. I deny that. Show me one precedent.

LORD PRESIDENT. Sir, you ought not to interrupt while the Court is speaking to you. This point is not to be debated by you, neither will the Court permit you to do it. If you offer it by way of demurrer to the jurisdiction of the Court, they have considered of their jurisdiction; they do affirm their own jurisdiction.

KING. I say, sir, by your favor, that the Commons of England was never a court of judicature: I would know how they came to be so.

LORD PRESIDENT. Sir, you are not to be permitted to go on in that speech and these discourses. . . .

KING. Show me where ever the House of Commons was a court of judicature of that kind.

LORD PRESIDENT. Sergeant, take away the prisoner. . . .

SALEM WITCHCRAFT TRIALS

(1692)

No single settler of New England brought to its shore a more formidable reputation than Satan. The imprint of his cloven foot was not to be found in the sands of Massachusetts Bay, but it was deeply impressed on the minds and hearts of those who had come to wrest the wilderness from the Indians.

The England which they had left behind had witnessed witchcraft trials by the score. In the decade immediately preceding the landing at Plymouth Rock, the Lancashire witches had been brought to justice, and ten of them sent to the gallows in a real-life melodrama seldom surpassed in English history. Three years later, London had been rocked by the sensational disclosure of the Countess of Somerset's traffic with sorcerers to unman her first husband and snare her second. And James I, whose initial skepticism on the entire subject had been dispelled by a frightening interview with one of the famous North Berwick witches, had written his own learned treatise on demonology for the enlightenment of his subjects.

The bloodbath into which Europe had plunged in its relentless persecution of witches since the fourteenth century was ebbing by the time the American adventure started. The Inquisition had sickened of the endless procession of tens of thousands to the stake; and even the Reformation countries were beginning to doubt the soundness of the evidence on which they had condemned countless victims of local gossip and malicious falsehood to death.

But the seed of superstition lived on in the barren Puritan soil of Massachusetts long after the last witch had been extirpated in the home country. It thrived on the dark and brooding qualities of the New England winter, on the myriad and inexplicable misfortunes to which the settlers were constant prey, on the mysterious and threatening ways of the heathen savages who surrounded the isolated villages and towns. The hand of Satan was to be seen in the failure of a crop, the death of a new-born child (or calf), the untoward accident which kept a farmer from his field.

To this overwhelming pall of superstition the solemn voices which rang daily from the pulpits added the crushing consciousness of universal evil. The rigorous and sterile code of behavior which Puritanism imposed on the flock was enforced by constant reiteration of the theme of fire and brimstone. All forms of amusement that were not prohibited were regarded with suspicion; as Macaulay put it, "The Puritans hated bearbaiting, not because it gave pain to the bear, but because it gave pleasure to the spectators."

Under the heel of the ruling theocracy, the average citizen led a devout and colorless existence. It was not unusual for members of the congregation to bring notebooks to church in order to jot down the fine points of the sermon for discussion during the long week nights. The young swain wishing to win his lady's favor would present her, as often as not, with a bound volume of religious discourses. And the public snapped up the published accounts of witchcraft trials at home and abroad, coupled with homilies on these horrible manifestations of Satan's power on earth.

One best-selling author on the subject of witchcraft in the late seventeenth century was the Reverend Cotton Mather, minister of the North Church in Boston. Among the 382 books he ground out during his lifetime, the most effective were those dealing with the evil spirits that were assailing the Puritans on all sides. As credulous as he was meddlesome, he found the study of witchcraft made to order for his neurotic and oversexed spirituality.

In 1688, Boston was the scene of a drama which established him as the *deus ex machina* for the Salem witchcraft trials four years later. The teen-age daughter of a respectable mason named John Goodwin suddenly began to behave strangely, falling into fits and complaining of pains in various parts of her body. These symptoms developed shortly after she had become embroiled in a petty quarrel over some laundry with a slatternly Irish washerwoman named Glover. Soon her younger brother and two sisters were voicing similar complaints. Under the horrified eyes of four ministers from Boston and Charlestown (including Mather) their affliction worsened; they became deaf, dumb, and blind in turns; their joints spontaneously became dislocated; and they cried out piteously that they were being burnt and cut with knives. Perhaps worst of all, they could not bear to look upon the accepted catechism, but could read blasphemous literature, such as popish and Quaker books, with ease. After a day of fasting and prayer conducted by the visiting ministers, the youngest child recovered, but with the others setting Boston on its collective ear with their fits and contortions, the magistrates stepped in.

Mrs. Glover was arrested and tried under the law making witchcraft a capital offense. She refused to confess or deny the accusation—in fact, she seemed unable to comprehend what was going on. But a group of physicians declared her sane; sane enough in any case to be hanged, as she was. This did not have the anticipated effect of relieving the children's symptoms; and Mather took the eldest into his home, in order to observe her more closely. By the following year Mather had burst into print with an account of the case which enjoyed a wide audience throughout Massachusetts.

A certain Samuel Parris and his family were living in Boston at the time. The case was undoubtedly discussed in his home, and Cotton Mather's book found its way into his meager library. In these commonplace beginnings the seeds of New England's crop of witchcraft trials were sown.

In November 1689, Mr. Parris accepted a call to the ministry in the tiny village of Salem. Parris at thirty-six could look back upon a life pockmarked with disappointment. He had not quite completed a Harvard course in theology, having left the University to become a trader in the West Indies. His acceptance of so humble a pulpit as the First Church of Salem Village attests his failure as a merchant, although he possessed a skill at haggling which his parishioners found quite formidable in their business dealings with him.

The members of Parris' household in the early months of 1692 were his self-effacing wife, his nine-year-old daughter, Elizabeth, his niece, Abigail Williams, aged eleven, and two half-breed slaves whom he had brought with him from Barbados. The youngsters had little but their Puritan upbringing to keep them out of mischief during the long, harsh New England winter. Such occasional chores as they performed threw them into the company of the maid, Tituba, who may have entertained them with lurid accounts of voodoo as practiced in her native land. But when Abigail and Elizabeth began, late in February, to behave like the Goodwin children, it must be assumed that Boston, rather than Barbados, furnished the pattern they adopted for relief from boredom.

The local doctor was not very helpful. Completely baffled, he shook his head gravely and muttered something about witchcraft, just as his modern counterpart might blame a mysterious virus. The word spread through the village, and so did the malady: in no time at all, despite the fasting and prayers of the Reverend Parris and clerical reinforcements summoned from the vicinity, a handful of teen-agers were caught up in the histrionics. Barking and convulsions, desperate (but unsuccessful) lunges toward the blazing fireplace, complaints of being stuck with pins and bitten by unseen demons—all this and much more struck terror in the hearts of the onlookers. Some few turned their backs on the circus in amusement or contempt, and lived to regret it.

Several middle-aged women succumbed before long—either because they were neurotic or highly suggestible or, as in the case of Sarah Bibber, had long been subject to fits anyway and had at last found an excuse for them. There were yet others who had old scores to settle or past misfortunes to account for, and they joined the Greek chorus as the tragedy of Salem unfolded.

The teen-age dervishes could not be expected to hold the attention of their audience without fresh developments. Under the pious coercion of Parris and his fellow ministers they found a way. They lodged accusations against Tituba, a natural candidate because of her color and alien background, and Sarah Good and Sarah Osborne, two old crones whose lack of caste fit the witch-stereotype of their English ancestors. Tituba, scourged by her hysterical master, turned state's evidence at once; she confessed that she was a witch and that the two old women were her confederates. The three were promptly imprisoned.

Their bodies were carefully examined for "witches' teats" and "Devil's marks." The lore of witchcraft attached great importance to chance excrescences in the form of a supernumerary breast or an inflamed mole, for it was supposed that the witch's "familiar" (the evil spirit incarnate in the shape of an animal) suckled there. Equally incriminating were the insensitive patches of skin or moles which the faithful probed doggedly with pins: if no pain was caused, it was persuasive evidence; if no blood flowed, it was all but conclusive. Tituba was indeed found to have scars on her back which were attributed to the Devil. Whether the Reverend Parris concurred in this assumption was not recorded.

Parris assisted at the inquests, which were conducted by two "magistrates" sent down from Salem Town. John Hathorne and Jonathan Corwin were both upright men, but both were utterly devoid of legal training or background. Professional lawyers were anathema in the colony, and neither prosecuting nor defense attorneys figured in any stage of the proceedings.

The three prisoners who were arraigned in the improvised courtroom in the village church set the pattern for many who were to follow. Sarah Good, at first defiant, soon turned on Sarah Osborne, and accused her of bewitching the children. Sarah Osborne stood upon her protestations of innocence, while admitting that witches were abroad in Salem.

Tituba, her primitive instinct leading her to an alliance with authority, kept the ball rolling with a tale that sent shivers along the spines of the devout:

Yes, the Devil had bid her to serve him. Goody Osborne and Sarah Good and two other women, unidentified at this hearing, hurt the children and made Tituba do so. And there was also a tall man of Boston, with white hair, who had shown her a book in which nine names were written. But, as she could neither read nor write, she could not say whose names they were.

". . . and last night there was an appearance that said kill the children and if I would not go on hurting the children they would do worse to me."

"What is this appearance you see?"

"Sometimes it is like a hog, and sometimes like a great dog."

And sometimes it looked like a man. And the man had a yellow bird, a red cat, and a black cat, familiars all. And Sarah Good had a yellow bird.

"What meat did she give it?"

"It did suck between her fingers."

"What hath Sarah Osborne?"

"Yesterday, she had a thing like a woman, with two legs and wings."

And all the witches traveled on a stick.

Curiously, Tituba's account contained no hint of the rich voodoo lore of her native island, nor did it follow the Continental European mode which favored familiars in the shape of snakes and wild animals. It was a sedate Puritan story of the Cotton Mather variety.

Sedate, but inflammatory; for now Salem could not rest until the other witches whose names appeared in the book of the tall man from Boston had been rooted out. The youngsters had lit a forest fire. In court, while the examination was proceeding, they added fuel to it by screeching and wrenching their bodies into grotesque poses whenever they looked upon the bewildered prisoners. Sarah Good and Sarah Osborne were held for trial. The latter, ill at the time of her arrest, cheated the gallows by dying in jail.

Over the first hurdle, the children dared to break new ground and turned their accusing fingers in the direction of two respectable old churchwomen, Martha Corey and Rebecca Nurse. That these pillars of the church should be agents of Satan seemed incredible to a few, but in general, the enormity of the charge had the effect of anesthetizing the critical faculties of the community to the even more startling disclosures that followed.

In a sense the two old ladies had sealed their own fates. Martha Corey

95

had been unnecessarily outspoken about the girls' antics; Rebecca Nurse's family had clashed with Mr. Parris in a petty quarrel about his perquisites of office and had sided with the neighboring village of Topsfield in a boundary dispute which Salem Village had lost. (Before long, Rebecca's two sisters joined her in prison.)

No one yet knows why the girls next turned upon a five-year-old child, unless it was on some theory of guilt by association. To prison went Dorcas Good, daughter of Sarah; as proof of her powers, the afflicted girls showed the imprint of a small set of teeth on their bodies. The seven or eight months little Dorcas spent in jail, most of the time in chains, left an indelible mark on her, although she escaped execution.

No week passed without fresh accusations, and Salem's prison soon overflowed into the jails of communities as far away as Boston. Let a wife be defended by her husband on her preliminary hearing, as Elizabeth Procter was by John, and he was cried out upon by the writhing, caterwauling children. And even those credulous enough to join the witch hunt sometimes ended up as its quarry. Eighty-year-old Giles Corey supposed at first that there might be something to the charges against his wife, Martha: he found it difficult to pray while she was rattling off her own prayers. But he soon found himself in jail; he was a quarrelsome sort, and his neighbors seized the opportunity to settle old scores with him. Skeptics received short shrift: Edward Bishop had cured John Indian of a fit by flogging him and had declared that he could handle the rest of the afflicted with similar treatment; both he and his wife, Bridget, landed in prison.

The children set their sights a social notch higher. They cried out upon Mary English, wife of Salem's leading shipper, who had demonstrated dangerous leanings toward the Church of England.

Their audacity increasing, they proceeded to identify a former minister at Salem, George Burroughs, who had long since moved to a lonely parish in Maine, as "a little black-haired man" who had tortured the youngsters and given them his book to sign. Shortly after leaving Salem, Burroughs had been involved in a lawsuit in which he bested the uncle of Ann Putnam, one of the most talented of the "afflicted." His prodigious feats of strength, performed for the amusement of his friends, were cited as proof that he was in league with the Devil.

His arrival from Maine in close arrest spread consternation among the prisoners, many of whom had revered him as a spiritual leader throughout his stay at Salem. If their old religious mentor had indeed been a wizard, they were prepared to believe that they might at least have been used as the unwitting instruments of Satan.

To still others, Deliverance Hobbs showed the way: she confessed that she was a witch. The tale she poured out was a hysterical amalgam of all the answers which had been suggested to her in the course of endless inquisitions by the ministers, who had by this time familiarized themselves with the ways of witches to an extent that put Tituba to shame. Mrs. Hobbs' confirmation of the charges against many of her fellow prisoners had a tonic effect on the magistrates: it added substantial weight (it takes a witch to judge a witch) to the girls' evidence, and it opened the floodgates of confession by others, who saw in her example a chance to escape the gallows.

The youngsters fell in with their new confederates, adding colorful inventions to heighten interest as they confronted each fresh victim. Now they would fall into fits when the accused looked at them, and only the touch of the accused would restore their senses; they would be struck dumb; they would move their heads and bodies in mimicry of the prisoners, who were forced to stand with their hands outstretched, held by wardens, lest they endanger the girls.

The insensate cruelty of the proceedings is reflected in the account left by Captain Nathaniel Carey, a shipmaster of Charlestown, whose wife appeared voluntarily for examination upon hearing that she had been denounced:

Being brought before the justices, her chief accusers were two girls; my wife declared to the justices that she never had any knowledge of them before that day; she was forced to stand with her arms stretched out. I did request that I might hold one of her hands, but it was denied me; then she desired me to wipe the tears from her eyes, and the sweat from her face, which I did; then she desired that she might lean herself on me, saying she should faint.

Justice Hathorne replied, she had strength enough to torment these persons, and she should have strength enough to stand.

The arrest of John Alden, son of the legendary Priscilla and John, gave further proof of the long reach of the accusing arms of the children. The seventy-year-old Indian fighter and mariner had the misfortune to correspond to the image of Tituba's "tall man from Boston." After fifteen weeks in prison, he recognized that it would be futile to face his accusers and escaped, contriving to remain out of the colony until the furor subsided.

Still there had been no trials, when on May 14, 1692, Sir William Phipps, the new royal governor and a parishioner of Cotton Mather, arrived in Boston. Phipps brought with him the new charter, ending a state of suspended legal animation which had begun in 1684 when the old colonial charter was annulled, depriving the Puritan oligarchy of its stranglehold on the local government. The jails of Essex and adjoin-

97

ing counties were bulging with alleged witches, and there were no legally constituted courts to try them. Under the new charter, the colony's General Court (a representative legislative body) was to meet in October and set up a judicial system, but elections had to be held before the General Court could come into existence. Phipps, presuming that in the emergency he had powers similar to the King's, issued a commission for a Court of Oyer and Terminer to be held at once, appointing the judges on May 27.

William Stoughton, the deputy governor, who had been appointed at the instance of Cotton Mather, was the first to be named, and he presided at every trial that followed. Neither Stoughton nor any of the other six judges had received legal training of any kind. One of them, Nathaniel Saltonstall, a Cambridge graduate, refused to act as soon as he had got his first taste of the proceedings, and was supplanted.

The new Court moved swiftly. On June 2, Bridget Bishop, a poor and friendless old tavernkeeper, who had been accused of witchcraft fourteen years earlier, won the distinction of being the first to be tried under the statute prohibiting the practice of witchcraft. Cotton Mather, in his account of the trial, blandly remarked, "There was little occasion to prove the witchcraft, it being evident and notorious to all beholders."

But the Court nevertheless heard testimony against the accused—at considerably more length than it did in later cases. (Its patience wore thin as time wore on, and many convictions were obtained largely on the strength of evidence brought out in the preliminary hearings and on affidavits of the "afflicted.") The evidence in the Bishop case followed a pattern that the accusers altered only in minor details in subsequent trials. A jury of matrons had found a preternatural teat on her body. The prisoner's specter—her disembodied "shape"—had tormented the girls and had over the years wreaked strange and frightening mischief upon her neighbors. Deliverance Hobbs, now the darling of the Court, told how Mrs. Bishop tempted her to sign the Book again and whipped her with iron rods to compel her to recant her confession. And, said the witness, "this Bishop was at a general meeting of the witches in a field at Salem Village, and there partook of a diabolical sacrament in bread and wine then administered."

This mention of a Black Mass (which figured in only a few of the cases) contrasts very significantly with the lurid accounts of the diabolic assemblies reported in European witchcraft trials. The mere perversion of the ritual of the Eucharist was a far cry from the orgiastic and obscene celebrations of the Scottish and Lancashire covens, for example, with which Mather, Parris, and their cohorts must have been familiar. Perhaps the learned ministers could not bring themselves, either as a result of their own inhibitions or out of delicate concern for the tender minds of the child actors in the Salem drama, to suggest to the confessing "witches" that they had indulged in the blood sacrifices and sexual excesses of their Old World sisters. In any case, they seem to have been content with a tepid and diluted Puritan version of the lusty and shocking accounts of the Devil's nocturnal revels abroad.

The verdict in the Bishop case was sent by Stoughton, as Chief Justice of the Court, to Stoughton as acting Governor in the absence of Phipps, who was off on a summer campaign against the Indians. The sentence of death was confirmed, and the first of Salem's hangings was carried out on June 10th. The next hundred days saw eighteen more men and women executed as witches, along with two dogs.

There were, of course, avenues of escape from the gallows. The path of the Judas goat had been well defined by Tituba and Deliverance Hobbs, and fifty-five of those arrested found safety, if not solace, in confession. Margaret Jacobs, who recanted her admission of guilt (in which she implicated her grandfather and two others) found herself back in jail where, as she wrote, "I have enjoyed more felicity in spirit a thousand times than I did before in my enlargement." Torture was applied to compel others to inform against their neighbors and relatives, although its use had been forbidden by law in Massachusetts for half a century. Martha Carrier's two young sons helped her to the gallows with their forced admissions that she had made witches of them.

Pregnancy furnished a reprieve, too: a number of the prisoners escaped execution because the Court would not condemn the unborn along with their mothers.

The route taken by John Alden was followed by some whose means and connections enabled them to flee the jurisdiction. One of those who took to his heels was Dudley Bradstreet, a Justice of the Peace in Andover, who had played a dominant role in one of the uncanny sideshows of the proceedings at Salem.

Nearby Andover had early been drawn into the trials in the person of Martha Carrier, whose arrival there two years earlier had been attended by an outbreak of smallpox. "This rampant hag," as Cotton Mather called her, had been chosen by the Devil as "Queen of Hell," according to some of the confessed witches, and was supposed to have commuted on a stick between the two villages.

When, therefore, the wife of Joseph Ballard of Andover fell seriously ill in the early summer of 1692, he and a few of his similarly afflicted neighbors thought it advisable to send to Salem for some experts in "spectral evidence" to point out the oppressors of the sick. They were not disappointed. The young clairvoyants conjured up fearful tableaux of local witches sitting on people's heads and on their "lower parts," making them sick. In short order Judge Bradstreet, son of the ex-Governor, issued warrants for the arrest of some forty alleged witches, including two daughters of the senior pastor of Andover, who had foolishly expressed some doubt about the wisdom of the proceedings.

As the accusations mounted in number, Bradstreet recoiled from the bloody course that seemingly had no ending. He refused to sign any more warrants. Promptly he found himself accused of the spectral murder of nine people, and he and his wife sought refuge in flight. His brother, charged with bewitching a dog in Salem, soon followed suit.

But when word got around Andover that a Boston gentleman who had been accused by the visiting young pundits had commissioned some of his friends to serve a writ of arrest in a slander action calling for damages of £1000 against anyone who called him a witch, the visions of specters vanished from that vicinity. Later that year the traveling show from Salem briefly visited Gloucester, with the result that four women went to jail; but by and large the theater of action was confined to Salem from July on.

Meanwhile, on June 15th a dozen ministers headed by Increase Mather, Cotton's father, had begun to show concern about the naive use of spectral evidence, and had urged the Governor and his Council to exercise "a very critical and exquisite caution" in weighing the proof introduced against the accused. The Devil, they concluded, could often take the shape of innocent persons, and thereby wreak havoc even among God's anointed. But Stoughton and his fellow judges seem to have glossed over this portion of the report and taken to heart only its closing recommendation for the "speedy and vigorous prosecution of such as have rendered themselves obnoxious."

In this spirit, the judges dealt handily with an unexpected turn in the trial of Sarah Good. One of her accusers testified that she had been stabbed in the breast by the prisoner, who had snapped off part of her knife in the process. When the child produced a portion of the knife blade, a brave young man exhibited the balance of the knife, saying that it belonged to him and that he had broken it in the girl's presence the day before and thrown away the upper part. This untoward detour in the course of the judicial juggernaut resulted only in a reprimand to the accusing witness, who went right on testifying, and Sarah Good was convicted.

The sanctimonious determination of the witch-hunters was fully revealed when a jury unexpectedly brought in a verdict of acquittal against the venerable and widely respected Rebecca Nurse. Thirty-nine of her neighbors had courageously signed a testimonial to her upright character and good deeds. Despite her feebleness and deafness, her demeanor in court had counted heavily in her favor. But the outcry which the acquittal drew from her accusers led the judges to send the jury back to reconsider its verdict, after pointing out that it might have passed too lightly over a remark made by the accused when Deliverance Hobbs and her daughter were brought to the witness stand: "What? Do these persons give in evidence against me now? They used to come among us"—meaning that they had been fellow prisoners. When the prisoner was asked to explain to the jury the meaning of her comment, she failed to answer, and the jury took this as an admission that the Hobbs women had attended a witch's festival with her. Her deafness and grief had prevented her from hearing the question.

Rebecca's family sought out the Governor for a reprieve, setting forth all of the facts, and Phipps granted it. Thereupon the girls set up a fresh claim of torment and injury at the hands of Rebecca Nurse, and at the behest of "some Salem gentlemen" (probably Parris and Nicholas Noyes, minister of her own church at Salem Town, who had promptly excommunicated her) Phipps reversed his decision and the sentence of death stood.

Rebecca Nurse and Sarah Good went to the gallows on July 19th, along with three others. When Sarah Good came to the scaffold on Gallows Hill, her minister, the Reverend Noyes, urged her to confess, telling her that she knew she was a witch. "You are a liar!" Sarah shouted. "I am no more a witch than you are a wizard, and if you take away my life, God will give you blood to drink!" One of Salem's legends deals with the fulfilment of her prophecy, for in Noyes' death throes his throat filled with blood, probably as the result of a cerebral hemorrhage.

When George Burroughs and four others were hanged on August 19th, the little minister from Maine, who had evidently despaired of defending himself at his trial, almost reversed the tide of sentiment against the accused with a speech from the ladder of the gallows so touching and pious that it drew tears from the audience. To Cotton Mather, listening to the fervid prayer of the condemned man, it looked as though the ceremony was getting out of hand. The young accusers, too, were alarmed, and said that they saw the "Black Man" dictating to Burroughs as he spoke. Mather then chimed in forcefully, saying that Burroughs was no ordained minister, and that the Devil often deceived the people by taking on the appearance of an angel of light. The executions were carried out without further incident; but Burroughs had made a telling impression on many of the townfolk.

Eight more bodies adorned Gallows Hill on August 22—"eight fire-

brands of Hell," as Nicholas Noyes put it. One month later Giles Corey
cheated the gallows by allowing himself to be pressed to death.

Corey's death was the first in New England to take the form of the
old English "peine forte et dure." The law did not permit one accused
of a felony to be brought to trial without his consent, and one of the
conventional ways of obtaining acquiescence was to strip the prisoner
naked and weigh him down with stones and iron bars until he yielded.

Corey refused to stand trial, and his decision must have been a calculated one. Conviction appeared inevitable in any event, and it carried
with it the forfeiture of all one's worldly goods, and of the right to
dispose of them by will. The sheriff had moved swiftly to seize the property of those who had lost their gambles with the jury, and had sometimes not even waited for conviction before marching off with every
possession in sight. As the old man lay in a field, surrounded by his
neighbors, begging the sheriff for "More weight!" to hasten the end,
he had the grisly satisfaction of knowing that the jackals would at least
be deprived of his estate, which he had already turned over to his sons-
in-law.

By this time 150 men and women still languished in the jails of Salem
and its environs. Some had bought their lives by confessing and informing, while others resignedly awaited trial. An additional 200 had been
accused, but had not been committed for sheer lack of space.

As so often happens, the hysteria ground to a halt through its own
excesses. As far back as the day when Rebecca Nurse stood helpless and
confused before the Bench, one of the youngsters had cried out upon
the Reverend Samuel Willard, the esteemed minister of the Old South
Church in Boston. This accusation was summarily brushed aside by
the judges as an innocent mistake of identity, despite Willard's outspoken skepticism about the evidence at the trials; and he remained
free to continue his battle against the witch-mania. But the children,
emboldened by the arrest of John Alden and others of high station,
soon threw caution to the winds and hinted darkly about the strange
doings of Lady Phipps herself! The Governor was still away at the time.
Lady Phipps was in no danger; but the time of the "afflicted" was running out.

Meanwhile, common sense began to assert itself among the populace.
The cumulative impact of the terror of the past nine months was taking
effect. Word had gotten around about the use of torture to extract confessions. Each arrest had enlarged the ranks of the skeptics; each hanging had left a residue of sobriety and disgust.

The employment of confessed witches as informers likewise aroused
resentment and posed a theological puzzle. Why had they not been

hung along with those who had maintained their innocence? How could their testimony be reliable?

Favoritism rankled: why had Nathaniel Saltonstall, one of the original members of the Bench, and Margaret Thatcher, mother-in-law of Judge Jonathan Corwin, both of whom had been repeatedly named as witches, not been arrested? Why were the well-to-do who had managed to escape not been brought back for trial?

In October, the Governor found himself assailed on all sides by petitions to halt the arrests and release some of the accused from their freezing cells to the custody of their families. "We know not," one petition stated simply, "who can think himself safe, if the accusations of children, and others under a diabolical influence, shall be received against persons of good fame." ("Amen!" breathed Lady Phipps.) The Governor prohibited further arrests "without unavoidable necessity," and dismissed the Court, pending action of the General Assembly.

The new Supreme Court of Judicature, which met in January 1693, was still headed by Stoughton, with only one new face on the Bench. But Phipps had made it clear that he would not sustain convictions based on spectral evidence and the testimony of self-confessed witches. The grand jury dismissed more than half the presentments, and the few who were convicted were reprieved by the Governor. By May the slate was cleared by a proclamation pardoning all accused of witchcraft, and the spell of the witchcraft trance was dissolved throughout New England.

The grip of the Puritan theocracy, already loosened by the new royal charter, was broken forever. Cotton Mather, unrepentant and unregenerate, wandered the streets of Boston—"a general without an army," as Parrington says. Parris was driven from his pulpit by his guilt-ridden congregation; while Noyes begged and was granted forgiveness. Many of those who had participated in the delusion publicly proclaimed their error and asked pardon from those who had been wronged. But only those who survived could respond to their pleas.

It has become fashionable to speak of the Salem witchcraft trials as the prototype of every movement which seeks to quarantine or punish exponents of unpopular ideas. Comparisons of this sort involve loose thinking, both about Salem and about the activities which are thought to be analogous to it.

Witches were very real to the Puritans, and, at least in the England and Scotland from which they were but two generations removed, there were persons who practiced witchcraft in every sense except the supernatural. Witchcraft was a criminal offense; and the lesson of Salem is not that persons who commit what society has defined as a criminal act should not be punished. It is rather that the machinery and philosophy which society has evolved for the administration of justice should not be discarded in favor of the kangaroo court.

Phipps' special Court of Oyer and Terminer, which presided over the judicial murders at Salem, was devoid of any legal basis for existence. But it would have made no difference in the result if it had been a properly authorized statutory court. The shame of Salem resulted from the circumstance that the restraints normally imposed by traditional rules of evidence interpreted by trained legal minds were completely absent from the conduct of the trials.

The quibbles of the law frequently serve as the ultimate defense against popular hysteria. Self-operative principles like the presumption of innocence and the prohibition of hearsay evidence stand as dikes against the floodwaters of fear and hate. Today's candidates for persecution in the war of ideas can rely on the independence and self-discipline of the judiciary, bound to observe the rights of the accused with meticulous care dictated by precedent and tradition, to protect them (save for an occasional miscarriage of justice) against a hostile climate of public opinion. Salem remains only a salient reminder of the wholesale crimes against humanity which even the well-meaning can commit if the accused are unprotected against ignorance and malice by the judicial process.

Among the extant accounts of the trials, those of Rebecca Nurse and George Burroughs stand out as telling illustrations of man's capacity to oppress his fellows. Excerpts from the original transcripts follow:

REBECCA NURSE
MARCH 24, 1692

Preliminary examination of the accused by John Hathorne:

Q. What do you say (*speaking to one afflicted*), have you seen this woman hurt you?
A. Yes. She beat me this morning.
Q. Abigail, have you been hurt by this woman?
A. Yes.

Ann Putnam in a grievous fit cried out that she hurt her.

Q. Goody Nurse, here are two: Ann Putnam, the child, and Abigail Williams complain of your hurting them. What do you say to it?
A. I can say before my Eternal Father I am innocent, and God will clear my innocency.

Q. Here is never a one in the assembly but desires it. But if you be guilty, pray God discover you.

Then Henry Kenny rose up to speak.

Q. Goodman Kenny, what do you say?

Then he entered his complaint and further said that since this Nurse came into the house he was seized twice with an amazed condition.

Q. Here are not only these, but here is the wife of Mr. Thomas Putnam who accuseth you by creditable information and that both of tempting her to iniquity and of greatly hurting her.

A. I am innocent and clear, and have not been able to get out of doors these eight or nine days.

Q. Mr. Putnam, give in what you have to say.

Then Mr. Edward Putnam gave in his relate.

Q. Is this true, Goody Nurse?
A. I never afflicted no child, no never in my life.
Q. You see these accuse you. Is it true?
A. No.
Q. Are you an innocent person relating to this witchcraft?

Here Thomas Putnam's wife cried out: Did you not bring the black man with you? Did you not bid me tempt God and die? How oft have you eat and drunk your own damnation? What do you say to them?

A. Oh Lord, help me *and spread out her hands, and the afflicted were grievously vexed.*
Q. Do you see what a solemn condition these are in? When your hands are loose, the persons are afflicted.

Then Mary Walcott (who often heretofore said she had either bit or pinched her or hurt her) and also Elizabeth Hubbard, under the circumstances both openly accused her of hurting them.

Q. Here are then two grown persons now accuse you. What say you? Do not you see these afflicted persons and hear them accuse you?
A. The Lord knows I have not hurt them. I am an innocent person.
Q. It is very awful for all to see these agonies, and you, an old professor, thus charged with contracting with the Devil by the effects of it, and yet to see you stand with dry eyes when there are so many wet.
A. You do not know my heart.
Q. You would do well, if you are guilty, to confess; give glory to God.
A. I am as clear as the child unborn.
Q. What uncertainty there may be in apparitions I know not, yet this with me strikes hard upon you, that you are at this very present charged with familiar spirits. This is your bodily person they speak to: they say now

they see these familiar spirits come to your bodily person. Now what do you say to that?

A. I have none, sir.

Q. If you have confessed and give glory to God, I pray God clear you, if you be innocent; and if you be guilty, discover you. And therefore give me an upright answer: have you any familiarity with these spirits?

A. No. I have none but with God alone.

Q. How came you sick, for there is an odd discourse of that in the mouths of many?

A. I am sick at my stomach.

Q. Have you no wounds?

A. I have not but old age.

Q. You do know whether you are guilty and have familiarity with the Devil, and now when you are here present to see such a thing as these testify a black man whispering in your ear and birds about you. What do you say to it?

A. It is all false. I am clear.

Q. Possibly you may apprehend you are no witch, but have you not been led aside by temptations that way?

A. I have not.

Q. What a sad thing it is that a church member here and now another of Salem should be thus accused and charged.

Mr. Pope fell into a grievous fit and cried out: A sad thing, sure enough. *And then many more fell into lamentable fits.*

Q. Tell us: have not you had visible appearances more than what is common in nature?

A. I have none, nor never had in my life.

Q. Do you think these suffer voluntary or involuntary?

A. I cannot tell.

Q. That is strange. Everyone can judge.

A. I must be silent.

Q. They accuse you of hurting them, and if you think it is not unwillingly, but by design, you must look upon them as murderers.

A. I cannot tell what to think of it.

Afterwards, when this was somewhat insisted on, she said: I do not think so; *she did not understand aright what was said.*

Q. Well, then, give an answer now. Do you think these suffer against their wills, or not?

A. I do not think these suffer against their wills.

Q. Why did you never visit these afflicted persons?

A. Because I was afraid I should have fits, too.

Note: Upon the motion of her body, fits followed upon the complainants, abundantly and very frequently.

Q. Is it not an unaccountable case that when you are examined these persons are afflicted?

A. I have got nobody to look to but God.

Again, upon stirring her hands, the afflicted persons were seized with violent fits of torture.

Q. Do you believe these afflicted persons are bewitched?

A. I do think they are.

Q. When this witchcraft came upon the stage, there was no suspicion of Tituba (*Mr. Parris's Indian woman*). She professed much love to that child Betty Parris, but it was her apparition did the mischief. And why should not you also be guilty, for your apparition doth hurt also?

A. Would you have me belie myself?

She held her neck on one side and, accordingly, so were the afflicted taken.

Then authority requiring it, Samuel Parris read what he had in characters taken from Mr. Thomas Putnam's wife in her fits.

Q. What do you think of this?

A. I cannot help it—the Devil may appear in my shape.

Nurse held her neck on one side and Elizabeth Hubbard (one of the sufferers) had her neck set in that posture, whereupon another patient, Abigail Williams, cried out: Set up Goody Nurse's head, the maid's neck will be broke. *And when some set up Nurse's head, Aaron Wey observed that Betty Hubbard's was immediately righted. . . .*

JUNE 28, 1692

Petition of accused to Court of Oyer and Terminer:

The humble petition of Rebecca Nurse of Salem Village humbly showeth:

That, whereas some women did search your petitioner at Salem, as I did then conceive, for some supernatural mark; and then one of the said women, which is known to be the most ancient, skillful, prudent person of them all as to any such occurrence, did express herself to be of a contrary opinion from the rest and did then declare that she saw nothing in or about Your Honor's poor petitioner but what might arise from a natural cause; and I then rendered the said persons a sufficient known reason as to myself of the moving cause thereof, which was by exceeding weaknesses, descending partly from an overture of nature and difficult exigencies that hath befallen me in the times of my travails;

And, therefore, your petitioner humbly prays I that Your Honors would be pleased to admit of some other women to enquire into this great concern, those that are most grand, wise and skillful; namely: Mistress Higginson, Senior; Mistress Durkstone; Mistress Woodberry, two of them being midwives; Mistress Porter; together with such others as may be chosen on that account, before I am brought to my trial. All which I hope Your Honors will take into your prudent consideration and find it requisite for to do.

For my life lies now in your hands, under God, and being conscious of my own innocency, I humbly beg that I may have some liberty to manifest it to the world, partly by the means abovesaid. And your poor petitioner shall evermore pray as in duty bound, etc. Rebecca Nurse: [*her mark*] X.

JUNE 30, 1692

Depositions in Court of Oyer and Terminer:

The deposition of Samuel Parris, aged about thirty-nine years, and Nathaniel Ingersoll, aged about fifty and eight years, and Thomas Putnam, aged about forty years, all of Salem, testifieth and saith that Ann Putnam, Senior, and her daughter Ann, and Mary Walcott, and Abigail Williams were several times and grievously tortured at the examination of Rebecca Nurse, wife to Francis Nurse of Salem, before the honored magistrates, the 24 March 1692, and particularly that when her hands were at liberty some of the afflicted were pinched, and upon the motion of her head and fingers some of them were tortured; and further, that some of the afflicted then and there affirmed that they saw a black man whispering in her ear and that they saw birds fluttering about her. . . .

The deposition of Sarah Holton, relic of Benjamin Holton, deceased, who testifieth and saith that about this time three years my dear and loving husband, Benjamin Holton, deceased, was as well as ever I knew him in my life till one Saturday morning that Rebecca Nurse, who now stands charged for witchcraft, came to our house and fell a-railing at him because our pigs got into her field, though our pigs were sufficiently yoked and their fence was down in several places. Yet all we could say to her could no ways pacify her, but she continued railing and scolding a great while together, calling to her son, Benjamin Nurse, to go and get a gun and kill our pigs and let none of them go out of the field, though my poor husband gave her never a misbeholding word. And within a short time after this, my poor husband going out very early in the morning, as he was a-coming in again, he was taken with a strange fit in the entry, being struck blind and stricken down two or three times, so that when he came to himself he told me he thought he should never have come into the house any more. And all summer after he continued in a languishing condition, being much pained at his stomach and often struck blind. But about a fortnight before he died he was taken with strange and violent fits, acting very much like to our poor bewitched persons, when we thought they would have died, and the doctor that was with him could not find what his distemper was, and the day before he died he was very cheery; but about midnight he was again most violent seized upon with violent fits, till the next night about midnight he departed this life by a cruel death. . . .

The deposition of Ann Putnam, the wife of Thomas Putnam, who testifieth and saith that on the first day of June, 1692, the apparition of Rebecca Nurse did again fall upon me and almost choke me, and she told me that now she was come out of prison she had power to afflict me and that now she would afflict me all this day long and would kill me if she could, for she told me she had killed Benjamin Holton and John Fuller and Rebecca Shepard, and she also told me that she and her sister Cloyce and Edward Bishop's wife of Salem Village had killed young John Putnam's child because young John Putnam had said that it was no wonder they were witches for their mother was so before them, and because they could not avenge themselves on him they killed his child. And immediately there did appear to me six children in winding sheets which called me aunt, which did most grievously affright me; and they told me that they were my sister Baker's children of Boston and that Goody Nurse and Mistress Cary of Charlestown and an old deaf woman at Boston had murdered them and charged me to go and tell these things to the magistrates or else they would tear me to pieces; for their blood did cry for vengeance. Also, there appeared to me my own sister Bayley and three of her children in winding sheets and told me that Goody Nurse had murdered them. . . .

GEORGE BURROUGHS
MAY 9, 1692

Preliminary examination of the accused:

Being asked when he partook of the Lord's Supper, he being (as he said) in full communion at Roxbury, he answered it was so long since, he could not tell. Yet he owned he was at meeting one Sabbath, at Boston part of the day, and the other at Charlestown part of a Sabbath, when that sacrament happened to be at both, yet did not partake of either. He denied that his house at Casco was haunted, yet he owned there were toads. . . . He owned that none of his children but the eldest was baptized. The above was in private, none of the bewitched being present. At his entry into the room, many (if not all of the bewitched) were grievously tortured.

Susanna Sheldon testified that Burroughs' two wives appeared in their winding sheets and said that man killed them.

He was bid to look upon Susanna Sheldon.

He looked back and knocked down all (or most) of the afflicted who stood behind him. . . .

. . . Mary Lewes'[1] deposition going to be read, and he looked upon her and she fell into a dreadful and tedious fit. . . .

Being asked what he thought of these things, he answered it was an amazing and humbling Providence, but he understood nothing of it, and he said: Some of you may observe that when they begin to name my name they cannot name it. . . .

[1] Lewis

The bewitched were so tortured that authority ordered them to be taken away, some of them.

Sarah Bibber testified that he had hurt her, though she had not seen him personally before, as she knew. . . .

Captain Wormwood testified about the gun and the molasses. He denied that about the molasses. About the gun, he said he took it before the lock and rested it upon his breast.

John Brown testified about a barrel of cider.

He denied that his family was affrighted by a white calf in his house.

Captain Putnam testified that he made his wife enter into a covenant.

MAY 11, 1692

Abigail Hobbs, in prison, affirmed that George Burroughs, in his shape, appeared to her and urged her to set her hand to the Book, which she did, and afterwards in his own person acknowledged to her that he had made her set her hand to the Book. . . .

AUGUST 5, 1692

Depositions in Court of Oyer and Terminer:

The deposition of Mercy Lewis, who testifieth and saith that on the 7th of May 1692, at evening, I saw the apparition of Mr. George Burroughs, whom I very well knew, which did grievously torture me and urged me to write in his Book; and then he brought to me a new fashion book, which he did not used to bring, and told me I might write in that book, for that was a book that was in his study when I lived with them. But I told him I did not believe him, for I had been often in his study, but I never saw that book there. But he told me that he had several books in his study which I never saw in his study, and he could raise the Devil, and now had bewitched Mr. Shepard's daughter. And I asked him how he could go to bewitch her now he was kept at Salem. And he told me that the Devil was his servant, and he sent him in his shape to do it. Then he again tortured me most dreadfully and threatened to kill me, for he said I should not witness against him. Also he told me that he had made Abigail Hobbs a witch and several more. Then again he did most dreadfully torture me as if he would have racked me all to pieces and urged me to write in his Book or else he would kill me. But I told him I hoped my life was not in the power of his hand and that I would not write though he did kill me. The next night he told me I should not see his two wives if he could help it because I should not witness against him. This 9th May Mr. Burroughs carried me up to an exceeding high mountain and showed me all the kingdoms of the earth and told me that he would give them all to me if I would write in his Book, and if I would not, he would throw me down and break my neck. But I told him they were none of his to give, and I would not write if he throwed me down on a hundred pitchforks. . . .

ANDREW JOHNSON

(1868)

The game of politics occasionally converts the American dream into a nightmare. In Andrew Johnson's case, the long, hard road from poverty to the presidency ended in near-disaster: the White House had been booby-trapped. The trap had been laid for Abraham Lincoln, but it was sprung by Johnson.

No more likely victim could be found in that day and age. Straightforward, stubborn, and slow to seek advice, he possessed none of the political acumen displayed by Lincoln in handling his opponents. Overnight the tragedy at Ford's Theater had placed Johnson, a Southerner and a Democrat, at the head of a government dominated by Northern Republicans dedicated to continuing the Civil War on the political front. By experience and conviction a champion of the debtor, the farmer, and the small tradesman, the new President had inherited an economy in which hard money and high tariffs had become articles of faith.

The men who had set their faces against Lincoln's compassionate program for the defeated South had been lent an unwitting hand by John Wilkes Booth; the new occupant of the White House, they felt, would either be their willing tool, or would be destroyed.

By any standards, their chances of success one way or the other were good. On the very day of his inauguration as Vice President in 1864, Johnson's prestige had suffered a blow from which it would never completely recover. For Andrew Johnson was drunk at his inauguration; drunk and so slurred of speech as he delivered a disjointed and maundering address, that his friends cringed and party leaders pulled on his coattails to get him to sit down. Weakened by a recent bout of fever, Johnson had borrowed Dutch courage in the form of a couple of drinks of brandy just before the ceremony. The heat of the Senate chamber had done the rest. The incident haunted him for years and furnished grist for the mill of his opponents.

Drunkard or no, as a Southerner, and a "poor white" Southerner at that, Johnson was fair game for the charge that he had too much innate sympathy with the rebel cause, and too little for the Negro race.

But they had underestimated their man. Although he had only learned to write—under his wife's tutelage—after he reached maturity, he possessed intellectual capacity equal to his fresh responsibilities. His thirty years in public office, as Governor of Tennessee, Congressman, and United States Senator, had demonstrated his gifts as a popular stump speaker and his profound, almost reverent, mastery of American principles of government. In times of crisis he had displayed abundant moral and physical courage as well. In 1861 he had remained rooted, lonely and steadfast, to his Senate desk, while his fellow Southerners in the upper house flocked to the secessionist standard. Appointed Military Governor of Tennessee by Lincoln the following year, he had braved lynch mobs and assassins' bullets as the symbol of Union authority in an island of loyal territory surrounded by Confederate troops. He had come a long way from his days as a tailor's apprentice.

He would have need of both head and heart in the ordeal that would be uniquely his in the annals of the presidency. For the problems he faced were of unprecedented complexity, and ruthless and wily adversaries were prepared to destroy him if he attempted to solve these problems conscientiously.

The framers of the Constitution had not foreseen his peculiar difficulties. Dissident states had been provided neither with a way out of the Union, nor with a way back. Lincoln's position, forthright and strategically sound, was that they had never left; once disinfected of Confederate rule, they would be welcomed back into the fraternity. Late in 1863, he proposed his plan for their restoration to full status in the Union. He offered amnesty to all except a few classes of rebels if they would swear loyalty to the United States and obedience to its laws (including the Emancipation Proclamation). Pardoned citizens in any state numbering ten per cent of its voters in the 1860 presidential election could set up a new local government entitled to recognition in Washington.

Lincoln's program was fought at every turn by the so-called "Radical" wing of his own party, led by Charles Sumner in the Senate and Thaddeus Stevens in the House, with the aid of such implacable abolitionists as Wendell Phillips on the public platform. The arrogant Sumner, a living caricature of the Boston Brahmin, was still acting out the near-martyrdom he had earned in antislavery circles as the victim of a brutal caning by a young Southerner in 1856. For him the war would end only when full parity had been achieved between Negroes and whites. His fervent devotion to this cause was wholly philosophical; he was no more equalitarian in his personal relationships with Negroes than with his own mother, who was forced to address him as "Mr. Sumner."

Pennsylvania's Thaddeus Stevens, on the other hand, practiced what he preached. Seventy-three and ailing when Johnson took office, Stevens had bought himself a burial plot in a Negro cemetery. Consistent with a lifetime of antislavery activity, he had many years before installed a striking mulatto named Lydia Smith as head of his own household and had never risen to the bait of newspaper stories imputing to him an adulterous relationship with the dusky "Mrs. Stevens." His hatchet face and grim crescent mouth reflected the bitterness and determination of a lifetime of struggle against physical handicaps and financial reverses. Born with a hideously deformed foot, dogged by illness and bowed down by mountainous debt despite a prosperous law practice, Stevens at fifty had found in the fight against slavery the ideal outlet for his almost psychopathic spleen. The latest of his misfortunes had served only to superheat his hatred for the South: Lee's 1863 raid on Chambersburg had reduced to ashes Stevens' iron works, a venture he had sacrificed years of effort to save from creditors. The seceded states, in Stevens' view, had to be treated as "conquered lands and people, with no right to names, boundaries, territory, much less statehood."

Men like Sumner and Stevens saw Johnson's accession to the presidency as a fresh opportunity to defeat Lincoln's plan to "bind up the nation's wounds." The new President's vengeful outbursts following the assassination encouraged them mightily. "By the gods," exulted Ohio's Senator Benjamin F. Wade, "there will be no trouble now running this government."

But Wade's elation was premature; and the ensuing struggle precipitated a constitutional crisis which came within a hair's breadth of destroying the American presidency as an instrument of government.

At Johnson's first Cabinet meeting, he announced that he proposed to follow the magnanimous course Lincoln had laid out. By the next evening his Secretary of War, Edwin M. Stanton, had revealed to Senator Sumner and a group of Radicals the reconstruction measures favored by his chief.

In the conflict which culminated in Johnson's impeachment, Stanton served as the "fifth column" of the Radical forces. The spectacled, spade-bearded Pennsylvania lawyer had a gift for duplicity. As a Cabinet member under Buchanan and Lincoln he had fawned on them to the point of nausea, while criticizing them mercilessly in correspondence with their enemies.

True to form, the shrewd and able Stanton feigned general agreement with Johnson in his approach to reconstruction, but used every means at his command to thwart him. And the means were formidable: control of the army of occupation in the rebel states; authority over the Freedmen's Bureau, which managed the destinies of the liberated blacks; and a monopoly of telegraph communications with Washington. He contrived to place a number of carefully selected army men on the President's staff, assuring himself of daily reports on his chief's activities. With the War Office acting as the conduit of all White House wires, he was in a position to know the contents of all messages to and from the President, and did not hesitate, if it served his purpose, to delay transmission or delivery of urgent dispatches.

But for the time being the Radicals' hands were tied. This was April, and Congress would not meet again until December. They could only lay plans and be ready when Congress convened.

By that time eleven Southern states had trudged up the path of redemption paved by Lincoln and Johnson, and the remaining two were making progress. At Johnson's instigation, all of the eleven except Mississippi had ratified the Thirteenth Amendment, abolishing slavery, although they had rejected his suggestion that qualified Negroes be given the vote.

Twenty-two Southern Senators-elect and their fifty-eight Congressional counterparts stood ready to take their places as soon as their credentials passed muster. Democrats all, their weight in both houses would be substantial. On some issues it could prove decisive, since they would be joined by most Western Republicans in voting for lower tariffs and a continuation of the inflationary money measures so favorable to debt-ridden farmers. The threat of this coalition was anathema to the industrial East and the hard-money banking interests to which most of the Radicals owed allegiance.

Stevens and his cohorts did not need to be reminded that the Republicans had received only a minority of the popular vote in 1860. They swung into action with a crusading fervor. On the basis of the constitutional power of each house to "be the judge of the elections, returns, and qualifications of its own members," the credentials of the representatives from former rebel states were referred to committee by a strict party vote until Congress should declare "such states . . . entitled to representation." The scheme was beautiful in its simplicity: the South would be kept on the Congressional doormat until it was remodeled in the Radical image.

The Radicals were quick to point out that many who were refused their seats had recently figured prominently in the rebel cause. Former Southern generals and legislators—even Alexander H. Stephens, who had been Vice President of the Confederacy—were the logical choices of people who knew no other leaders. But logic and statesmanship did not coincide; and their election was viewed in the North as a gesture of defiance.

Even more incendiary was the enactment of the so-called "Black Codes" by almost all of the defeated states. Slavery was a dead letter; but these statutes sentencing vagrant, orphaned, and homeless blacks to virtual peonage threatened to bring it back to life. While some inconsequential civil rights were bestowed on the freedmen, they were dwarfed by the drastic punishments imposed for the slightest infractions of law.

Although the spirit of these codes could be traced to equally discriminatory laws of some Northern states, the Radicals denounced them as proof of Southern intransigence. Congress reacted by passing in 1866 a Civil Rights Act outlawing the codes and giving drastic powers of enforcement to federal officials. Johnson, thumbing his Constitution, came up with an answer as legally correct as it was impolitic: the law was a "stride towards centralization and the concentration of all legislative powers in the national government." Congress reacted violently. Refusing his offer to "cheerfully co-operate" in any protective legislation in the civil rights field "compatible with the Constitution," it promptly overrode his veto—the first time in American history that a major bill was passed over the head of the President.

But not the last. Before Johnson's term ended, the presidential veto power would be reduced to a mote in Congress' eye. Fifteen out of eighteen general bills would become law over his objection. The lines of battle had been drawn. Charles Sumner put the Radical view bluntly when he proclaimed that "by the assassination of Abraham Lincoln the Rebellion was vaulted into the presidential chair." Wendell Phillips denounced Johnson as a "Jeff Davis sycophant."

With Congress turning a deaf ear to his policy, Johnson carried his message to the people during the 1866 Congressional campaign. In August he embarked on a nationwide speaking tour—a "swing around the circle of the Union," as he called it. His opening address to a Philadelphia assembly of moderate Republicans and Democrat acknowledged the state of hostilities in Washington:

We have witnessed in one department of the government every endeavor to prevent the restoration of peace, harmony, and union. We have seen hanging upon the verge of the government, as it were, a body called, or which assumes to be, the Congress of the United States, while in fact it is a Congress of only a part of the states. . . . Instead of promoting reconciliation and harmony, its legislation has partaken of the character of penalties, retaliation, and revenge.

But the North's attitude toward the "rebs" had taken a turn for the worse. Bloody interracial riots had exploded in Memphis and New Orleans, kindling fresh fires of hatred against the South. (Stanton's failure to deliver a telegram to Johnson from the New Orleans Army Commander, requesting instructions, contributed to the massacre there of thirty-four Negroes and three of their white sympathizers.)

The campaign had gotten off to a promising start in the Middle Atlantic states, but Johnson found his westerly stops seeded with hecklers. Goaded by their taunts, he was transformed from statesman into stump speaker, and repeatedly lost his temper in rough-and-tumble exchanges with the crowd. His unbridled attacks on Stevens, Sumner, and their fellow Radicals revived the rumor that he was a drunkard. The opposition press had a field day.

Smelling victory in the air in the Congressional elections, the Radicals "waved the bloody shirt," blaming Johnson for Memphis and New Orleans. Thaddeus Stevens caustically lampooned the traveling "circus" which had just returned to Washington with a "drunken tailor" as its chief "clown." Coming on the heels of the President's loss of stature on his tour, the invective told heavily. The election dealt Johnson a crushing rebuke. With forty-two Republicans to eleven Democrats in the Senate, and a majority of ninety-four for the Republicans in the House, the new Congress would be more one-sided than any since Monroe's administration. The Radicals could look forward to a virtually veto-proof command of both houses.

And now Congress took the bit in its teeth; the Stevens-Sumner plan for holding the South in subjugation bowled along, barely pausing to brush aside Johnson's vetoes. Never in the country's history had the political game been played for such high stakes. The conquered territory was divided into five military districts, to be governed by martial law. Re-entry to the Union by former rebel states was conditioned upon their adoption of constitutions which would place the reins of government in the hands of the Negro population. Opportunists of every stripe moved into the power vacuum, winning political preferment and sudden fortune by making common cause with white and Negro Republicans. The day of the carpetbagger and scalawag was dawning. Universal Negro suffrage promised permanent Republican control of both houses of Congress.

Just to be doubly sure that the President would not use the Army to enforce his precious Constitution, Congress tacked a humiliating rider onto an Army appropriation bill, requiring him to transmit all orders to the military through Ulysses S. Grant, as General of the Armies. Significantly, any violation of the law was declared to be "a misdemeanor in office"—echoing the language of the Constitution pertaining to impeachments.

Johnson's one remaining big gun—patronage—was spiked with the passage of the Tenure of Office Act. In the early stages of his battle with Congress, most federal offices were held by supporters of the Radical wing, who gave freely of information, political support, and campaign funds to fight the President. He had been tardy in the use of reprisals; but after the "swing around the circle" he jettisoned disloyal office holders by the thousands. The Act placed Johnson in check, or so Congress thought. Civil officials whose appointment had to be confirmed by the Senate were frozen into their posts until their successors were approved. Cabinet officers were henceforth to "hold their offices respectively for and during the term of the President by whom they may have been appointed, and for one month thereafter," unless the Senate consented to their removal.

The language of the Tenure of Office Act foretold the impeachment move in which it would figure so prominently before the year was out. It provided that "every removal, appointment, or employment" contrary to its terms "shall be deemed . . . a high misdemeanor."

Johnson's cabinet unanimously condemned the law as a flagrant violation of the Constitution. Stanton's eloquence on this score so impressed the President that the cunning War Secretary was asked if he would draft the veto message. He begged off, pleading illness, but promised to give what help he could with research.

In discussions of the bill by Congress' conference committee, its effect on the four Cabinet members (including Stanton) who were holdovers from Lincoln's Cabinet had been considered clear: as appointees of the late President, they were freely removable by Johnson. The Cabinet itself voiced no concern on this score, Stanton making the point that "any man who would retain his seat in the Cabinet when his advice was not wanted was unfit for the place."

This was typical of Stanton's insincerity—for, as Sumner had openly stated, the original version of the bill was unquestionably designed to keep Stanton in his post over the President's objection. Unable to prevail against the well-reasoned objections of a number of influential senators, the Radicals had permitted it to be watered down by limiting its protection of Cabinet officers to the "term of the President by whom they may have been appointed." The language left room for the contention that Johnson was merely serving out Lincoln's unexpired term,

117

and hence Stanton could not be removed without Senate approval. Not unequivocal, to be sure; but Stanton's friends felt that, when the time came, they could sustain their interpretation. Always provided, of course, they had the votes.

As far as the House was concerned, those votes had already been counted. The idea of impeaching Johnson had been in the air for about a year. Just before the Tenure of Office Act passed, the House, which has the constitutional right to initiate impeachment proceedings, voted an inquiry by its Judiciary Committee "into the official conduct of Andrew Johnson." The margin—108 to 39—was sufficiently imposing to warrant considerable optimism on the part of Stevens, Sumner & Company.

Late that fall, with 1200 pages of testimony to its credit, the Committee reported out a resolution recommending impeachment. But it soon became evident that the case against the President added up to nothing more than nastiness to Congress and kindness to the late rebels. That wouldn't do: under the Constitution, two thirds of the Senate, which has the task of trying impeachments, must be convinced that the President has been guilty of "treason, bribery, or other high crimes and misdemeanors." Although no appeal would have been available to the President if the Senate arbitrarily decided against him even on the flimsiest of charges, the lower house had adequate regard for the conscience of the Senate to vote down the resolution 108 to 57.

A sufficiently grave incident to justify drastic action in the eyes of the Senate and the electorate was needed to tip the scales, the Radicals felt. That incident was already in the making.

Soon after the Tenure of Office Bill was assured of passage over the President's veto, Stanton had emerged as an open and irreconcilable opponent of Johnson's reconstruction policies in Cabinet discussions.

On August 1, while Congress was using the summer recess to mend political fences at home, Johnson told Grant that he had finally decided to remove Stanton. He sounded Grant out about taking over the War Office. Grant urged the President to reconsider, saying that the move would violate the Tenure of Office Act, which he thought "was intended specially to protect the Secretary of War."

Johnson pondered the problem for four days. During that period he was further enraged by the fortuitous disclosure of another instance of Stanton's duplicity. A speech by defense counsel at the recent trial of John H. Surratt revealed that in 1865 the military court that had found his mother, Mrs. Mary Surratt, guilty of complicity in Lincoln's assassination had recommended clemency. The petition for mercy was supposed to have been forwarded to the President with the other papers in Mrs.

Surratt's case, but it had never reached his desk. The lady was hanged. Johnson, who had been criticized widely for confirming the death sentence in the Surratt case, was convinced (and not without reason) that this had been more of Stanton's work, although the primary responsibility for placing the recommendation before the President fell to the War Secretary's subordinate, Judge Advocate General Joseph Holt. The incident was reminiscent of Stanton's irresponsible delay in transmitting the telegram warning of the danger of disorders in New Orleans.

His mind was made up, but he proceeded gingerly. On August 5 he requested Stanton's resignation on the basis of "public considerations of a high character." Promptly the Secretary shot back a mocking note to the White House stating that "public considerations of a high character . . . constrain me not to resign . . . before the next meeting of Congress." Johnson's next step was a half measure, calculated to allay Grant's qualms; he needed the General's prestige and support to offset Congressional reaction. Accordingly he merely suspended Stanton and installed Grant as Acting Secretary under that provision of the Tenure of Office Act permitting such action for good cause while the Senate was in recess, subject to its later approval. Stanton surrendered his office under protest, saying he had "no alternative but to submit under protest to superior force."

Johnson foresaw that the Senate, under Sumner's whip, might fight the Stanton removal, despite the luster of his successor. He consulted Grant, who agreed that the question would and should probably be resolved by the courts. The President bluntly asked Grant's pledge to stand firm in case of a showdown. But the General would agree only to notify the President of his intention to bow out of the controversy far enough in advance of an adverse Senate vote to permit a substitute to be named. Johnson had to be content with small favors from the war hero, who had his eye on the 1868 presidential nomination, and was beginning to betray a caution quite uncharacteristic of the stalwart of Cold Harbor.

When Congress reconvened in December 1867, the Radicals were smarting from their setbacks in that year's fall elections. The Democrats had scored stunning gains from Maine to California. The Republican margin for overriding vetoes appeared in grave danger of being cut back beyond the safe two-thirds mark. High-tariff and hard-money policies had taken their toll at the ballot box; the swelling of the federal bureaucracy in the administration of Congress' reconstruction program was linked in the minds of voters with the continued burden of war-born income taxes; and the waywardness of Congress in its continued warfare on the South had produced an unexpectedly adverse reaction. The

119

high political cost of civil rights for Negroes was no more congenial to some parts of the North than to the South. Kansas and Minnesota rejected Negro suffrage by popular vote. The Fourteenth Amendment, conferring equal rights under the law upon Negroes and penalizing states which deprived them of the ballot, was defeated in New York. Ohio went the whole hog, revoking its earlier ratification of the Amendment, and spurning a Negro voting clause in its own Constitution. Worst of all, it elected a Democratic legislature, which was bound to unseat Ben Wade as U. S. Senator in 1868. Every mention of Johnson's impeachment had lifted Wade's eyes toward the White House; as President of the Senate, he stood first in the line of succession. Now, unless Johnson's ouster took place quickly, he would be turned out to pasture.

A few days after the new House voted down the recommendation of its Impeachment Committee, Johnson sent the Senate his report on the removal of Stanton, in compliance with the Tenure of Office Act. Senate debate on the subject began at once, and the decision to restore Stanton to office was rushed through with little opposition. On the day following the Senate resolution, Grant advised Johnson that he had turned the War Office back to Stanton. Grant had gone over to the opposition lock, stock, and barrel.

On February 21, 1868, Johnson gave Stevens the provocation he sought: he ordered Stanton's removal as Secretary of War. Unable to induce General William T. Sherman to accept the post, he ordered Lorenzo Thomas, Adjutant General of the Army, to fill the vacancy until Stanton's successor could be chosen. Notified by Thomas of the President's action, Stanton at first seemed indecisive. But by the next morning the seventy-year-old Thomas was placed under arrest, on Stanton's complaint, for violation of the Tenure of Office Act. Released on bail, he returned to the War Department and found Stanton prepared to hold his office against siege, if need be. Courteous, but firm, as if he were addressing a small boy, Stanton refused to indulge Thomas' request to move out.

That afternoon Thad Stevens, on the strength of this new development, brought out of the House Committee a recommendation to impeach Andrew Johnson.

The capital was in an uproar. Stanton spread the rumor that the President meant to use force to eject him. The White House, meanwhile, became alarmed when it heard that General William H. Emory, Army Commander for the District of Columbia, had quietly ordered all officers of the Fifth Cavalry to report to Headquarters. Johnson summoned Emory to inquire about the report and learned that there had been no change in the disposition of troops. Emory gratuitously added that any orders to him would have to be channeled through Grant under the Army Appropriation Act rider of the previous spring. Johnson said he considered that requirement unconstitutional, and the conversation ended there. But Stanton blew it up into a fresh news story that the President had tried to give direct orders to Emory to oust Stanton by military force.

Debate on the impeachment resolution raged in the House throughout the 24th, with partisanship at fever pitch. From the floor, the President was accused of everything from treason to complicity in Lincoln's assassination. When the votes were tallied, Andrew Johnson had earned the dubious distinction of being the first and only President to be impeached. It was a straight party vote, 126–47.

Stevens and John A. Bingham, of New York, were delegated to inform the Senate of the House action, a duty which they performed the next day with mock solemnity and regret. A committee of seven members of the House was charged with preparing the Articles of Impeachment.

On February 26, Johnson was outmaneuvered in his effort to test the constitutionality of the Tenure of Office Act. When Thomas' lawyers offered to surrender him to custody in order to lay the groundwork for a quick court decision, Stanton's counsel, pretending concern for the aged warrior's health, allowed the case to be dismissed.

Three days later the House Committee offered its draft of the formal charges, all revolving around the removal of Stanton, including one which represented his version of Johnson's talk with General Emory. After Stevens had reproached the Committee members on the floor— "Never was a great malefactor so gently treated as Andrew Johnson!" —he was mollified by the addition of an Article of his own which he had evidently been unable to sell to the Committee. Cleverly contrived, this accusation laid at Johnson's door a blanket refusal to carry out the reconstruction laws and the Tenure of Office Act, based on his repeated challenges to legislation by a Congress in which the South had no voice. It was on this vague and sweeping "Omnibus Article" that Stevens pinned his highest hopes; the others, he felt, were either too trivial or too closely bound up with the ambiguous question of Johnson's control over his holdover Cabinet members.

Massachusetts' Benjamin F. Butler seized on Johnson's intemperate utterances during his 1866 speaking tour to frame yet another Article, which amounted to a charge of contempt of Congress. Although the House had once before refused to vote an impeachment on these grounds, Butler's article was adopted, probably for its value as a brush to tar the President with.

Butler's acknowledged accomplishments as a trial lawyer, coupled with a spotless Congressional record as a maligner of the President, won him the leading role for the prosecution at the impeachment trial.

The swarthy, lynx-eyed Butler exhibited all the Radical fervor that might be expected of a renegade Democrat who had voted thirty-seven times for the nomination of Jefferson Davis at the Party's 1860 presidential convention. His audacity and lack of scruple made him a formidable adversary for Johnson's defenders.

Johnson was fortunate in his choice of counsel. Leading the array of defense talent were Attorney General Henry Stanbery, who resigned his Cabinet post to devote his time exclusively to the case; Benjamin R. Curtis, a distinguished former justice of the Supreme Court; and William R. Evarts, the outstanding trial lawyer of the New York Bar.

During the week following the adoption of the eleven Articles of Impeachment, the Senate busied itself with the formulation of its own rules of procedure for the hearing. On March 4th, the House charges were formally presented by the seven "managers," as the prosecutors were called, in the hushed Senate chamber. Presiding over the proceedings was Ben Wade, who was already hopefully turning over in his mind his choices for Cabinet posts.

Wade surrendered the Chair the following day to the Chief Justice of the Supreme Court, Salmon P. Chase, as required by the Constitution. One by one, the senators then rose to take oath to "do impartial justice according to the Constitution and the laws." The potential quality of that justice became clear almost immediately. A pro-Johnson Senator challenged Wade's right as heir-apparent to sit in judgment with his fellow Senators on the President. After lengthy debate, the claim of disqualification was resoundingly voted down, and Wade was sworn.

At the heart of this debate was the question which Justice Chase posed openly the next day: was the Senate sitting as a court or as a legislative body? Chase seemed disposed to regard the Senate as a "court of impeachment"; but in the face of overwhelming opposition, he did not press the point. Perhaps his own latent presidential ambitions still smoldered; perhaps he was unsure of his footing in the shadow-area of impeachment trials. In any case, he made only a halting effort to establish himself as the final authority on the vital question of the admissibility of evidence. Instead he bowed to a rule which the Senate had adopted for the occasion, subjecting all such issues to the majority vote of the entire body. This proved to be a serious blow to Johnson's cause; for throughout the trial, defense objections to testimony were consistently smothered by the Radical bloc of votes, under Sumner's skilled leadership, while the prosecution was just as consistently upheld in its maneuvers to exclude evidence favorable to Johnson.

Much to the disappointment of the packed galleries in the Senate chamber, Johnson did not appear personally in answer to the charges. Seemingly confident of acquittal, the President remained quietly at the White House, conferring with his lawyers and friends, placidly reading books and entertaining his grandchildren. Periodically he would repair to the upstairs bedroom of his sick wife and comfort her.

By March 30th the formal preliminaries were out of the way, and Butler opened for the managers. Of the fifty-four Senators, only fourteen were considered open-minded. Twenty-eight of the Republicans and all of the twelve Democrats had already made known their opposing sentiments.

Butler had shrewdly assessed the situation. His argument from the outset was designed to divert the Senate from a strict interpretation of the Constitution's specific limitation on impeachment to "high crimes and misdemeanors," in hopes of a conviction on the strength of mere "abuse of discretionary powers from improper motives, or for any improper purpose." The trial, he claimed, should not be regarded as a judicial process, but as a simple "inquest of office"; the Senate was not sitting as a court, but as a political body, to determine Andrew Johnson's fitness to remain in the presidency.

The issue, said Butler, was "whether the presidential office itself (if it has the prerogatives and power claimed for it) ought, in fact, to exist as a part of the constitutional government of a free people." Refreshing candor; it mirrored, needless to say, Butler's confidence in the outcome.

Twenty-three days were consumed in the presentation of evidence by the managers, with thin slices of testimony sandwiched between enormous chunks of rhetoric and debate. In essence, the prosecution's proof centered about the removal of Stanton, the President's speeches, and his conversation with General Emory. Stanton remained barricaded in the War Office and was not called to testify.

General Emory furnished no help to the prosecution: his testimony was soldierly and truthful and lent no support to Stanton's lurid account of the General's encounter with the President. When Emory stepped off the stand, the Article concerning his conference with Johnson was mentally chalked off the list by both sides.

On April 9, the defense took over. In his opening address, Curtis argued that Stanton was not covered by the Tenure of Office Act, and that in any case the Act was unconstitutional. But even supposing that Johnson was mistaken in thinking the Act unconstitutional, he was duty-bound by his oath of office, Curtis argued, to test the question in court;

and this could only be done by violating the law, as John Hampden had violated the Ship-Money Act in the days of Charles I.

Defense counsel found the introduction of evidence favorable to the President an uphill climb all the way. Only old Lorenzo Thomas, among the important defense witnesses, was allowed to tell his story without persistent obstruction—the vague, slightly comic desk-warrior posed no threat to the managers, who found him an easy target for ridicule. "Call him any time," quipped Butler, "we shall always be glad to see him."

General Sherman, on the other hand, was to learn that politics could be hell, too. His account of the President's offer to him of the War Secretaryship was blocked at every turn by the House managers. In the same way, Gideon Welles, Johnson's loyal Secretary of the Navy, was never allowed to tell the story of the Cabinet's unanimous agreement with Johnson that the Tenure of Office Act was invalid and should be tested in court.

Chief Justice Chase, repenting his earlier surrender on the testimony ruling, stoutly resisted the Senate's rejection of this unquestionably pertinent evidence. By this time, he was convinced of the hollowness of the impeachment charges, and privately confided to a friend his disgust with the Senate's antics.

He was not alone. The effect upon some senators of this arrogant overreaching by the Radicals probably, in the long run, proved fatal to the prosecution. John B. Henderson of Missouri, a young Radical lawyer who had consistently voted to override Johnson's vetoes, later filed an opinion in which he said: "A verdict of guilty . . . after the exclusion of this testimony, would fail to command the respect and approval of any enlightened public judgment." The highly respected James W. Grimes of Iowa, who had fought Johnson tooth and nail, made the same point: "This evidence was clearly admissible . . . but it was rejected as incompetent testimony by a vote of the Senate. I believe that decision was erroneous; and inasmuch as there is no tribunal to revise the errors of this, and it is impossible to order a new trial of this case, I deem it proper to regard these offers to prove as having been proved."

Henderson and Grimes were two of the "doubtful Republicans" whose devotion to abstract justice had raised doubts about their voting the straight Radical line. When the trial ended on May 6th, after summations from both sides, the Senate went into closed sessions to debate the issue. Grimes did not hesitate to declare himself, along with Lincoln's former Secretary of the Treasury, William P. Fessenden of Maine, and Lyman Trumbull of Illinois, as a defector from the Radical cause.

Henderson, on the other hand, held his peace, thereby joining the pathetic company of senators who would in the next ten days be subjected to inexorable political pressure to swing their votes. The Radical leaders, smelling Johnson's blood, enlisted the press, the Party organization, abolitionist groups, and even the Methodist Church to pour brimstone on the heads of the waverers. Threats, bribes, and verbal abuse were employed shamelessly.

A telegram from Henderson's home state contained a typical veiled threat:

MEETING CALLED FOR TOMORROW NIGHT. CAN YOUR FRIENDS HOPE THAT YOU WILL VOTE FOR THE ELEVENTH ("OMNIBUS") ARTICLE? IF SO ALL WILL BE WELL.

"Say to my friends," Henderson telegraphed, "that I am sworn to do impartial justice according to the law and evidence and I will try to do it like an honest man."

Edmund G. Ross of Kansas, a newcomer to the Senate with a militant antislavery record, received word from home:

KANSAS HAS HEARD THE EVIDENCE AND DEMANDS THE CONVICTION OF THE PRESIDENT.

D. R. ANTHONY AND 1000 OTHERS.

Ross shot back this response:

I DO NOT RECOGNIZE YOUR RIGHT TO DEMAND THAT I VOTE EITHER FOR OR AGAINST CONVICTION. I HAVE TAKEN AN OATH TO DO IMPARTIAL JUSTICE ACCORDING TO THE CONSTITUTION AND LAWS, AND TRUST THAT I SHALL HAVE THE COURAGE TO VOTE ACCORDING TO THE DICTATES OF MY JUDGMENT AND FOR THE HIGHEST GOOD OF THE COUNTRY.

For the uncommitted Republicans the choice lay between country and career. They knew instinctively—and, for good measure, they were told unmistakably by Stevens—that a vote for the President was tantamount to a political death warrant.

And so it proved. Ross, Henderson, Grimes, Fessenden, Trumbull, and two others—Joseph S. Fowler of Tennessee and Peter Van Winkle of West Virginia, both of whom had been pro-Stanton at the outset—were never elected to political office again.

But when on May 16 the vote came on Stevens' Eleventh Article (considered first, because it was assumed to be strongest), they stood up to be counted; even Grimes, who had suffered a paralytic stroke three days before, struggled to his feet, pallid and suffering, and cried:

"Not guilty."

The vote was thirty-five to nineteen—one short of the two thirds required for conviction. Every vote counted.

Hopeful of winning a convert on one of the other ten articles, the Radicals swung a ten-day recess. The House launched an immediate probe of allegations that some of the recalcitrants had been bribed. (It backfired when they turned up proof that the Radicals themselves had been offering their votes for sale to the Johnson forces.) Ross and others of like mind were hounded, investigated, importuned day and night. But on May 26, when the Second and Third Articles relating to Stanton's removal were brought to a vote, he and his fellows stood firm. The vote was unchanged. The Radicals were beaten; the decision on the remaining articles was a foregone conclusion, and they elected to forego a vote.

In the White House, the President wept for joy. Stanton vacated his office and was succeeded by the popular General John M. Schofield, whose nomination Johnson strategically sent to the Senate just before the closing arguments began.

Thaddeus Stevens, whose energy had been ebbing throughout the course of the battle, did not live through the following summer. So he was spared the ultimate humiliation of seeing Andrew Johnson returned to Washington in 1875 as the new Senator from Tennessee. By that time, Sumner, too, was dead, and Wade had gone to a reward of a different sort, having become counsel to the Northern Pacific Railway. But a sufficient number of the old die-hard Radical group remained on the floor to make the occasion a dramatic one. When Andrew Johnson proceeded solemnly around the chamber shaking their hands, the Senate rang with cheers and applause. His acquittal was complete.

What almost happened in 1868 raises the hackles on the spine of any true believer in the American system of government. Had Johnson been convicted, the voice of the presidency in the affairs of the nation would have been reduced to a plaintive whisper. The dynamics of checks and balances which were designed to act as a brake upon the unbridled will of both the Legislature and the Executive would have been thrown into the discard; and the leadership which the United States, through its President, has been fated to assume in world affairs might have been subject to the whim of those colorful and power-hungry demagogues who occasionally seem to hold Congress in thrall.

Johnson's impeachment trial proved once again that democracy, American style, is not a self-operative and self-perpetuating institution. It works and survives by the grace of a handful of individuals who are willing to immolate themselves on the altar of fair play; who treasure abstract justice, and who cannot bring themselves to engage in the savage game of politics without a saving measure of sportsmanship.

The following excerpts from the impeachment trial are a fair sampling of the flavor and tone of the proceedings. The incompatibility of the judicial and legislative approaches to the issues, the obstruction of defense testimony, and the demeanor of the leading protagonists are all here. Missing are the endless, and occasionally learned, debates on questions of legal precedent, the pointless and lengthy wrangles over the admission of evidence, and the astute and often elegant closing addresses of counsel on both sides, which occupy more than two thirds of the three-volume official transcript.

APRIL 10, 1868
LORENZO THOMAS, WITNESS

MR. STANBERY . . . What happened in the War Office on the morning of the 21st of February in regard to closing the office on the succeeding day, the 22d?

A. Toward twelve o'clock I went up myself and asked Mr. Stanton, then Secretary of War, if I should close the office the next day, the 22d of February, and he directed me to do it. I issued such a circular and sent it around to the different departments.

Q. Was that an order made by you as Adjutant General?

A. Yes, sir; by his order.

Q. Was that before you had seen the President that day?

A. Yes, sir.

Q. Now, what took place after you had issued that order?

A. Very soon after I had issued it I received a note from Colonel Moore, the private secretary of the President, that the President wished to see me. I immediately went over to the White House, and saw the President. He came out of his library with two communications in his hand.

Q. He came out with two papers in his hand?

A. Yes, sir. He handed them to Colonel Moore to read. They were read to me.

Q. Read aloud?

A. Read aloud. One was addressed to Mr. Stanton, dismissing him from office, and directing him to turn over the books, papers, &c., pertaining to the War Department; the other was addressed to me, appointing me Secretary of War *ad interim*, and stating that Mr. Stanton had been directed to transfer the office. . . .

Q. What, then, was said between you and the President?

A. He said he was determined to support the Constitution and the laws, and he desired me to do the same. [*Laughter*] . . .

Q. What did you do then?

A. I went over to the War Department, went into one of my rooms, and told General Williams I wished him to go with me; I did not say for what purpose. I told him I wanted him to go with me to the Secretary of War and note what occurred.

Q. Without telling him what it was you intended?

A. I did not tell him anything about it. I then went to the Secretary's room and handed him the first paper.

Q. When you say the first paper, which was that?

A. The paper addressed to him.

Q. What took place then? Did he read it?

A. He got up when I came in, and we bade good morning to each other, and I handed him that paper, and he put it down on the corner of his table and sat down. Presently he got up and opened it and read it, and he then said, "Do you wish me to vacate the office at once, or will you give me time to remove my private property?" I said, "Act your pleasure."

Q. Did he say what time he would require?

A. No, sir; I did not ask him. I then handed him the paper addressed to me, which he read, and he asked me to give him a copy.

Q. What did you say?

A. In the meantime General Grant came in, and I handed it to him. General Grant asked me if that was for him. I said no; merely for his information. I promised a copy, and I went down.

Q. Down where? To your office?

A. Into my own room. . . .

Q. You went down and made a copy of the order?

A. I had a copy made, which I certified as Secretary of War *ad interim*. I took that up and handed it to him. He then said, "I do not know whether I will obey your instructions or whether I will resist them." Nothing more passed of any moment, and I left. . . .

Q. Was that all that occurred between you and the Secretary on that day, the 21st?

A. I think it was. [*After a pause*] No, no; I was confounding the 22d with the 21st.

Q. What further?

A. I went into the other room and he was there, and I said that I should issue orders as Secretary of War. He said that I should not; he would countermand them, and he turned to General Schriver and also to General Townsend, who were in the room, and directed them not to obey any orders coming from me as Secretary of War. . . .

Q. Did you see Stanton again that afternoon?

A. I did not.

Q. Or the President?

A. Not after I left him this time.

Q. What first happened to you the next morning?

A. The first thing that happened to me next morning was the appearance at my house of the Marshal of the District, with an assistant marshal and a constable, and he arrested me.

Q. What time in the morning was that?

A. About eight o'clock, before I had my breakfast. The command was to appear forthwith. I asked if he would permit me to see the President; I simply wanted to inform him that I had been arrested. To that he kindly assented, though he said he must not lose sight of me for a moment. I told him certainly; I did not wish to be out of his sight. He went with me to the President's and went into the room where the President was. I stated that I had been arrested, at whose suit I did not know—

MR. MANAGER BUTLER. Stop one moment. Does the presiding officer understand the ruling to go to this, to allow what occurred the next day to be brought in?

THE CHIEF JUSTICE. The Chief Justice so understands it.

MR. STANBERY. Go on, General.

THE WITNESS. He said, "Very well, that is the place I want it in— the courts." . . .

Q. When did you next go to the War Department that day?

A. I went immediately from there, first stopping at the President's on my way, and stating to him that I had given bail. He made the same answer, "Very well; we want it in the courts." I then went over to the War Office, and found the east door locked. This was on the 22d the office was closed. I asked the messenger for my key. He told me that he had not got it; the keys had all been taken away, and my door was locked. I then went up to Mr. Stanton's room, the one that he occupies as an office, where he receives. I found him there with some six or eight gentlemen, some of whom I recognized, and I understood afterward that they were all members of Congress. They were all sitting in a semiellipsis, the Secretary of War at the apex. I came in the door. I stated that I came in to demand the office. He refused to give it to me, and ordered me to my room as Adjutant General. I refused to obey. I made the demand a second and a third time. He as often refused, and as often ordered me to my room. He then said, "You may stand there; stand as long as you please." I saw nothing further was to be done, and I left the room and went into General Schriver's office, sat down and had a chat with him, he being an old friend. Mr. Stanton followed me in there, and Governor Moorhead, member of Congress from Pittsburg. He told Governor Moorhead to note the conversation, and I think he took notes at a side table. He asked me pretty much the same questions as before.

Q. State what he did ask.

A. Whether I insisted upon acting as Secretary of War, and should claim the office. I gave a direct answer, "Yes"; and I think it was at that time I said I should also require the mails. I said that on one occasion, and I think then. I do not know whether it is on the memorandum or not. Then there was some little chat with the Secretary himself.

Q. Between you and the Secretary?

A. Between me and the Secretary.

Q. Had these members of Congress withdrawn then?

A. Yes, sir.

Q. Now, tell us what happened between you and the Secretary after they withdrew.

A. I do not recollect what first occurred, but I said to him, "The next time you have me arrested"—for I had found out it was at his suit I was arrested; I had seen the paper—

MR. MANAGER BUTLER. Stop a moment. I propose, Mr. President, to object to the conversation between the Secretary and General Thomas at a time which we have not put in, because we put in only the conversation while the other gentlemen were there. This is something that took place after they had withdrawn.

MR. STANBERY. What is the difference? They did not stay to hear the whole.

THE CHIEF JUSTICE. It appears to have been immediately afterward and part of the same conversation.

MR. STANBERY. The same conversation went right on.

MR. MANAGER BUTLER. Will General Thomas say it was the same conversation?

THE WITNESS. Mr. Stanton turned to me and got talking in a familiar manner.

MR. MANAGER BUTLER. Go on, then, sir.

THE WITNESS. I said, "The next time you have me arrested, please do not do it before I get something to eat." I said I had had nothing to eat or drink that day. He put his hand around my neck, as he sometimes does, and ran his hand through my hair, and turned to General Schriver and said, "Schriver, you have got a bottle here; bring it out." [*Laughter*]

BY MR. STANBERY:

Q. What then took place?

A. Schriver unlocked his case and brought out a small vial, containing I suppose about a spoonful of whiskey, and stated at the same time that he occasionally took a little for dyspepsia. [*Laughter*] Mr. Stanton took that and poured it into a tumbler and divided it equally and we drank it together.

Q. A fair division?

A. A fair division, because he held up the glasses to the light and saw that they each had about the same, and we each drank. [*Laughter*] Presently a messenger came in with a bottle of whiskey, a full bottle; the cork was drawn, and he and I took a drink together. "Now," said he, "this at least is neutral ground." [*Laughter*]

Q. Was that all the force exhibited that day?

A. That was all.

Q. Have you ever at any time attempted to exercise any force to get into that office?

A. At no time. . . .

THOMAS CROSS-EXAMINED BY MR. MANAGER BUTLER

Q. You told Mr. Wilkeson, he tells us, that you meant to call on General Grant for a military force to take possession of the office?

A. Yes.

Q. Did you mean that when you told it, or was it merely rodomontade?

A. I suppose I did not mean it, for it never entered my head to use force.

Q. You did not mean it?

A. No, sir.

Q. It was mere boast, brag?

A. Oh, yes.

Q. How was that? Speak as loud as you did when you began.

A. I suppose so. . . .

APRIL 13, 1868

MR. JOHNSON[1] (*sending a question to the desk*). Mr. Chief Justice, I desire to put a question to General Sherman. He is in the room, I believe.

THE CHIEF JUSTICE. The Secretary will read the question. To whom does the Senator from Maryland address it?

MR. JOHNSON. General Sherman. He is in the court, I understand.

WILLIAM T. SHERMAN recalled.

The Secretary read the question of Mr. Johnson, as follows:

When the President tendered to you the office of Secretary of War *ad interim*, on the 27th of January, 1868, and on the 31st of the same month and year, did he, at the very time of making such tender, state to you what his purpose in so doing was?

MR. MANAGER BINGHAM. We object to the question as being within the ruling of the Senate, and incompetent.

THE CHIEF JUSTICE. The Chief Justice will submit the question to the Senate.

MR. DRAKE. Upon that question I ask for the yeas and nays. *The yeas and nays were ordered.* . . .

THE CHIEF JUSTICE. On this question the yeas are 26 and the nays 22. So the question is admitted and will be put to the witness. The Secretary will read the question again. . . .

THE WITNESS. He stated to me that his purpose—

MR. MANAGER BUTLER. Stay a moment. The question, Mr. Chief Justice, was whether he did state, not what he stated. We want to object to what he stated.

MR. EVARTS. Answer yes or no, General.

A. Yes.

THE CHIEF JUSTICE. The witness answers that he did.

[1] Reverdy Johnson, Senator from Maryland

BY MR. STANBERY:

Q. What purpose did he state?

MR. MANAGER BINGHAM. To that we object. . . .

MR. DAVIS. I rise to a question of order.

THE CHIEF JUSTICE. The Senator from Kentucky.

MR. DAVIS. It is that one of the managers has no right to object to a question propounded by a member of the Court. . . .

THE CHIEF JUSTICE. The Secretary will call the roll.

The question being taken by yeas and nays resulted—yeas, 26; nays, 25. . . .

THE WITNESS. The conversations were long and covered a great deal of ground; but I will endeavor to be as precise to the point as possible. The President stated to me that the relations which had grown up between the Secretary of War, Mr. Stanton, and himself—

MR. MANAGER BUTLER. Stay a moment. I must again interpose, Mr. President. The question is simply what the President stated his purpose was, and not to put in his whole declaration.

MR. JOHNSON. That is all that is asked. That is preliminary to that.

MR. CURTIS. That is all he is going to answer.

MR. MANAGER BUTLER. I pray that that may be submitted to the Senate, whether they will have the whole of the long conversation, which is nothing to the purpose.

MR. MANAGER BINGHAM. His purpose in offering General Sherman a commission. . . .

MR. MANAGER BUTLER. Yes, sir.

MR. JOHNSON. That is it.

THE WITNESS. I intended to be very precise and very short; but it appeared to me necessary to state what I began to state, that the President told me that the relations between himself and Mr. Stanton, and between Mr. Stanton and the other members of the Cabinet, were such that he could not execute the office which he filled as President of the United States without making provision *ad interim* for that office; that he had the right under the law; he claimed to have the right, and his purpose was to have the office administered in the interest of the Army and of the country; and he offered me the office in that view. He did not state to me then that his purpose was to bring it to the courts directly; but for the purpose of having the office administered properly in the interest of the Army and of the whole country.

MR. STANBERY. On both occasions, General, or the other occasion?

THE WITNESS. I asked him why lawyers could not make a case; that I did not wish to be brought as an officer of the Army into any controversy.

MR. CONKLING. Will you repeat that last answer, General?

THE WITNESS. I asked him why lawyers could not make a case, and not bring me, as an officer, into the controversy. His answer was that it was found impossible, or a case could not be made up; but, said he, "If we can bring the case to the courts it would not stand half an hour." I think that is all that he stated to me then. . . .

APRIL 17, 1868
GIDEON WELLES, WITNESS

BY MR. EVARTS:

Q. You are now Secretary of the Navy?

A. I am.

Q. At what time and from whom did you receive that appointment?

A. I was appointed in March, 1861, by Abraham Lincoln.

Q. And have held office continuously until now?

A. From that date. . . .

MR. EVARTS (*to the witness*). Please state, Mr. Welles, what communication was made by the President to the Cabinet on the subject of the removal of Mr. Stanton and the appointment of General Thomas, and what passed at that time?

THE WITNESS. As I remarked, after the departmental business had been disposed of, the President remarked, as usual, when he has anything to communicate himself, that before they separated it would be proper for him to say that he had removed Mr. Stanton and appointed the Adjutant General, Lorenzo Thomas, Secretary *ad interim*. I asked whether General Thomas was in possession. The President said he was; that Mr. Stanton required some little time to remove his writings, his papers. I said perhaps, or I asked, "Mr. Stanton, then, acquiesces?" He said he did, as he understood it. . . .

Q. Did you become aware of the passage of the civil-tenure act, as it is called, at or about the time that it passed Congress?

A. I was aware of it.

Q. Were you present at any Cabinet meeting at which, after the passage of that Act, it became the subject of consideration?

A. Yes; on two occasions.

Q. Who were present, and when was the first occasion?

A. The first occasion when it was brought before the Cabinet was Friday, I think, the 26th of February 1867. It was at a Cabinet meeting on Friday.

Q. Who were present?

A. I think all the Cabinet were.

Q. Was Mr. Stanton there?

A. Mr. Stanton was there, I think, on that occasion. I might state, perhaps, that the President said he had two bills which he wanted the advice of the Cabinet about. One of them consumed most of the time that day.

MR. MANAGER BUTLER. The point, I believe, is as to what took place there.

BY MR. EVARTS:

Q. This civil-tenure act was the subject of consideration there?

A. It was submitted.

Q. How was it brought to the attention of the Cabinet?

A. By the President.

Q. As a matter of consideration in the Cabinet?

A. For consultation; for the advice and the opinion of the members. . . .

APRIL 18, 1868

Q. At the Cabinet meetings held at the period from the presentation of the bill to the President until his message sending in his objections was completed, was the question whether Mr. Stanton was within the operation of the civil-tenure act the subject of consideration and determination?

MR. MANAGER BUTLER. Stop a moment. We object.

THE CHIEF JUSTICE. The counsel will please propose their question in writing.

MR. EVARTS. I will make an offer, with the permission of the Chief Justice.

The offer was reduced to writing, and read by the Chief Clerk, as follows:

We offer to prove that at the meetings of the Cabinet at which Mr. Stanton was present, held while the Tenure-of-Office Bill was before the President for approval, the advice of the Cabinet in regard to the same was asked by the President and given by the Cabinet; and thereupon the question whether Mr. Stanton and the other Secretaries who had received their appointment from Mr. Lincoln were within the restrictions upon the President's power of removal from office created by said Act was considered, and the opinion expressed that the Secretaries appointed by Mr. Lincoln were not within such restrictions.

MR. MANAGER BUTLER. We object, Mr. President and Senators, that this is only asking the advice of the Cabinet as to the construction of a law. . . .

THE CHIEF JUSTICE. On this question the Senator from Missouri asks for the yeas and nays.

The yeas and nays were ordered, and being taken resulted—yeas 22, nays 26. . . .

So the evidence proposed to be offered was decided to be inadmissible. . . .

Q. During those considerations and discussions was the question of the importance of having some determination judicial in its character of the constitutionality of this law considered?

MR. MANAGER BUTLER. Stay a moment; we object. . . .

THE CHIEF JUSTICE. If the question be objected to, it will be reduced to writing.

The offer of the counsel for the respondent was reduced to writing and handed to the managers. . . .

THE CHIEF JUSTICE. The Secretary will read the offer made by the counsel for the President. . . .

The offer was read as follows:

We offer to prove that at the Cabinet meetings between the passage of the Tenure-of-Civil-Office Bill and the order of the 21st of February 1868 for the removal of Mr. Stanton, upon occasions when the condition of the public service, as affected by the operation of that Bill, came up for the consideration and advice of the Cabinet, it was considered by the President and Cabinet that a proper regard to the public service made it desirable that upon some proper case a judicial determination on the constitutionality of the law should be obtained.

THE CHIEF JUSTICE. Senators, you who are of opinion that the evidence offered by the counsel for the President should be received will, when your names are called, answer yea; those of the contrary opinion, nay. The Secretary will call the roll.

The question being taken by yeas and nays resulted—yeas 19, nays 30. . . .

So the Senate ruled the offer to be inadmissible. . . .

THE DREYFUS CASE

(1894)

The facts of the Dreyfus case are unbelievable.

Justice miscarries often enough to give it a bad name; and the righting of judicial wrongs can seldom be accomplished without sturdy opposition. But when the leaders of an entire generation of France's political and military elite compromised their honor and gambled their careers to prevent the vindication of an innocent man, they left behind a record which will never be read without astonishment.

The corners of the jigsaw puzzle fall readily into place.

To begin with, there was the trauma of 1871. With a few lightning strokes, an upstart Germany had trampled the proud banners of Napoleon III's army in the dust and sent that inept monarch scuttling into exile. The gallantry of the Parisian populace during the four-month Prussian siege of the city might have salvaged a few crumbs of national pride but for its tasteless and bloody sequel, in which French soldiers fought French members of the Paris Commune, and massacred (with a ferocity they seemed to have lacked against Bismarck's brigades) over 15,000 of their countrymen. A huge indemnity had been paid to the Germans; Alsace and a good part of Lorraine had been ceded to Wilhelm I.

In every French heart the seeds of *revanche* had been sown. But the nation was oppressively conscious of her own weakness; the armed forces had to be quietly rebuilt and reinspirited, and that would take time. Discretion, too, because Bismarck's trigger was cocked; "incidents," however trivial, had to be avoided at all costs.

Then, too, there was the Panama Canal. The part played by anti-Semitism in the persecution of Dreyfus may be traced in large measure to an incomplete ditch in the fever-ridden jungles of the Isthmus. Sparked by the enthusiasm of Ferdinand de Lesseps, of Suez Canal fame, an enormous syndicate had been organized to duplicate in the wilds of Panama his earlier success. By the time De Lesseps' concept of a sea-level canal had proved impractical, the Panama Company was bankrupt and half a million Frenchmen had lost three hundred million dollars. They might have shrugged their shoulders philosophically, except for the sensational disclosure in 1891 that lavish bribes had been paid out of Company coffers to leading politicians for legislative approval of public loans, and to the press to suppress news of the Company's difficulties.

The bubble of graft and blackmail had been pricked by *Libre Parole*, a hitherto obscure, rabidly anti-Semitic sheet edited by Edouard Drumont, who would figure prominently in the frenzy of the Dreyfus affair. Drumont made great capital of the fact that a number of the principal figures in the shameless machinations of the Panama Company had been Jewish, confirming his thesis that the Jews were taking over France lock, stock, and barrel. Few convictions were obtained in the trials stemming from the scandal, but the two-year sensation raised Drumont in public esteem from a reckless mouther of slanders on a proud race to a seemingly selfless defender of the public weal, and boosted the circulation and stature of his paper. Thenceforth, the accusation of a sellout to the Jews could be counted on to produce in public officials an automatic inhibitory response rivaling that of Pavlov's dogs.

This sensitivity was aggravated by the fragmentation of French political alignments. Since the overthrow of the Emperor, political rule in the all-powerful Parliament had been maintained through a series of unstable coalitions, held together less by the bonds of conviction than by the temporary magnetic attraction of expediency. In the nineteen years between the adoption of the new Constitution and the first Dreyfus trial, twenty-seven cabinets had come and gone. The Republican form of government, which had just squeaked through in 1875, had thrice since faced the specter of monarchism. On the other side of the political spectrum, the bogies of socialism and anarchism were frightening small statesmen in their beds at night. The nightmare of the Paris Commune, dispelled at a cost of 20,000 French lives, remained all too vivid; and only three months before the Dreyfus affair started, the President of the Republic fell victim to a terrorist assassin.

The Catholic Church, at one time the most cohesive element in the national character, was still too closely identified with the Royalists and Bonapartists to contribute effectively to the strengthening of the Republic. Until 1890, it had been openly hostile to the democracy—and vice versa. Tentative moves had been made to ban the Jesuit order and to close the sectarian schools, which turned out more than half of the candidates for army colleges, the diplomatic corps, and the Bench. But the conciliatory policy of Pope Leo XIII had induced a tacit relaxation of tension, and the religious orders continued to operate openly, biding their time for a reversal of sentiment which would enable them to recover lost ground.

Within this framework the Dreyfus affair was acted out: France, her uneasy officialdom, her Church, her Army, and a vocal segment of her press, all sharing a vague paranoia—ready to be touched off by any untoward occurrence, however slight its significance.

No casting director in his right mind would have selected Alfred Dreyfus for the title role in the sordid comic opera which won a worldwide audience before it closed its twelve-year run. He lacked color; his voice was flat and toneless; worse still, he seemed incapable of communicating intensity of feeling, except to members of his immediate family. To top it off, he had a substantial private income.

Thirty-five at the time of his arrest, this Alsatian-born Jew was not ill-favored: the ends of his light-brown mustache tilted at a rakish angle, and his jaw was strong and well set. But for the fact that his blue eyes were perhaps too close together behind the rimless pince-nez he affected, he might have been considered good-looking.

Native ability, and a single-mindedness that foreclosed easy camaraderie with brother officers, had advanced him to a captaincy and earned him the distinction of being the first Jew to be posted to the Army's General Staff. In mid-September 1894, he was nearing the completion of his period of training for a high-level assignment when an agent of the Statistical Section of the Intelligence Bureau of the War Ministry lifted a letter out of the incoming-mail box of Lieutenant Colonel Max von Schwartzkoppen, German Military Attaché in Paris. The note read:

Sir, though I have no news to indicate that you wish to see me, nevertheless I am sending you some interesting items of information.

1. A note on the hydraulic brake of the 120, and on the way in which this piece behaved.

2. A note on the covering troops (some modifications will be entailed by the new plan).

3. A note on a modification in artillery formations.

4. A note relative to Madagascar.

5. The project of a firing manual for field artillery, 14th March 1894.

The last document is extremely difficult to procure, and I can only have it at my disposal during a very few days. The Minister of War has sent a limited number of copies to the several corps, and these corps are responsible for the return of it, each officer in possession of one having to return it after the maneuvers. If, then, you would like to take out of it whatever interests you, and hold it afterwards at my disposal, I will take it, unless, indeed, you would like me to have it copied *in extenso,* and then send the copy to your address.

I am just setting off to the maneuvers.

The Statistical Section possessed several notable characteristics, not the least of which was that it was steadfastly unconcerned with statistics. Its function was largely confined to counterintelligence—an operation requiring imagination, brazenness, and a high degree of technical proficiency in the falsification of documents (hopefully designed to be fed to the enemy as genuine military information). Despite the relatively low caliber of its personnel, these talents were to be utilized with deadly effect against Dreyfus.

This latest evidence of German espionage came as no surprise to the Statistical Section. It had been aware of security leaks to the Germans and their Italian allies for some time—and had done nothing to check them at the source. Top-secret documents floated around the War Office and were copied for the personal files of officers with a laxity that was nothing short of elaborate. Confronted, however, with concrete proof of commerce between a French spy and the German Military Attaché, the Statistical Section swung into action with zest, prepared to rival the intricate cerebrations of France's popular fictional sleuth, Gaboriau's Monsieur Lecoq.

The letter, or *bordereau* (schedule), was received at the Statistical Section by Major Hubert Henry. This burly, mustachioed veteran of the war with Germany and of the French campaigns overseas had risen from the ranks. His apparent devotion to his job, coupled with a peasant doggedness and shrewdness, commended him to his superiors, despite his uncouth demeanor and limited capabilities.

According to Dreyfus himself and many students of the case, Henry recognized the handwriting of the *bordereau* as that of his friend, Major Count Ferdinand Walsin-Esterhazy, a one-time translator for the Statistical Bureau. Henry's worshipful association with the socially superior Esterhazy furnishes a plausible motive for his truly monumental exertions to send Dreyfus to jail, and keep him there. But it fails to explain why Esterhazy was not instantly warned that the *bordereau* had not reached its destination.

The variety of subjects covered by the document led the Intelligence Bureau to conclude that the writer must be attached to the General Staff, while the multiple references to artillery information seemed to point to a gunner. Photographs of the document were circulated among the departmental chiefs, with instructions to compare it with the handwriting of members of their sections.

Dreyfus had served as an artillery officer, and as a staff trainee had spent time with all four bureaus of the War Office. His handwriting bore some resemblance to that of the *bordereau*. In their anxiety to find the traitor in their midst, the staff officers looked no farther. The word went up the line—to General Le Mouton de Boisdeffre, Chief of the General Staff, and to General Auguste Mercier, Minister of War: It is the Jew.

Up to this point, a few moments of analysis at depths to which military minds seldom plunge might have stopped the affair in its tracks. For the *bordereau* disclosed on its face that it could not have been written by an artilleryman. The Field Artillery Manual, described in the note as "extremely difficult to procure," had been distributed to the tune of three thousand copies throughout that arm of the service, down to the lowliest officer ranks, and did not have to be returned: no gunner would have difficulty "borrowing" it; an infantryman might. The only new 120-millimeter field gun, a howitzer, was being fitted with a hydro-pneumatic brake, as any gunnery officer would have known—not a "hydraulic" one, as the writer of the *bordereau* called it. And the language used to describe the behavior of that weapon—"*s'est conduite la pièce*"—indicative of human action, would not have come from the pen of an artilleryman, whose standard term would have been, "*s'est comportée.*"

Not for any of these reasons, but because the Foreign Minister was fearful of precipitating an incident with Germany by an ill-founded accusation of espionage, Mercier was prevailed upon by other members of the Cabinet to seek additional evidence of Dreyfus' guilt before taking action. Alfred Gobert, handwriting expert of the Bank of France, was asked to examine the documents; on October 13 he reported to General Charles Gonse, Deputy Chief of the General Staff, that Dreyfus was not their man. Gonse promptly turned over the file to Alphonse Bertillon, Chief of the Identification Department of the Judicial Police, leaving that worthy gentleman with the impression that Dreyfus was already known to be the culprit.

Bertillon had acquired quite a reputation for his system of standardized criminal identification through precise physical measurements, which is still in use (in modified form) throughout Western Europe. He had only recently set himself up as a graphologist, however; and he attacked the Dreyfus file with the headlong enthusiasm of the amateur. On the very day he got the documents he told the War Office's representative that the handwriting was Dreyfus'; then he took another ten days to prove to his own satisfaction, by a weird and incomprehensible composite of cabalistic measurements and intricate mathematical calculations, that the *bordereau* was (1) partly in Dreyfus' normal hand, and

(2) partly written by Dreyfus in a disguised script resembling his own, to make it appear that someone else was forging Dreyfus' writing! Two more experts concurred in Bertillon's opinion, while another rejected it.

On the day following Bertillon's original snap conclusion, Mercier signed the order for Dreyfus' arrest, without informing his nervous colleagues in the Cabinet.

The task of taking Dreyfus into custody was allotted to an implausible character with an even more implausible name, Major Armand Auguste Charles Ferdinand Marie Mercier, Marquis Du Paty de Clam. Du Paty, as his intimates called him, had a bizarre gift for the melodramatic. Tall, balding, his finely molded head tilted back as if to keep his monocle and mustache in place, he personified the aristocratic dilettante. Give him the simplest assignment to execute and he would invest it with all the red-velvet trappings of a paperback romance.

Dreyfus' arrest, for example. On the pretext that he had injured his finger, Du Paty induced the unsuspecting Dreyfus to write a letter for him containing many of the words of the *bordereau*. Then came the formal arrest; Du Paty told Dreyfus that the charge was high treason, and nothing more. At this point, Du Paty suddenly proffered a revolver to his prisoner, and according to the script, Dreyfus should have obligingly blown his brains out; but he heatedly protested his innocence and spoiled the scene.

Dreyfus was promptly consigned to the Cherche-Midi, where he was held incommunicado, knowing nothing of the accusation against him except that it involved the turning over of documents to a foreign power.

Lucie Dreyfus was told of her husband's arrest, but nothing of the charge or his whereabouts. Du Paty warned her to inform nobody, not even Dreyfus' family—"The only way to save him is silence!"

During the next two weeks, Dreyfus' house was literally ransacked in the hope of unearthing incriminating evidence. Du Paty drew a blank, confirming, in the labyrinth of his mind, the prisoner's guilt: only a practiced criminal would leave his house in such apple-pie order!

Three days in solitary confinement, and Dreyfus was willing to speak to anybody—even Du Paty, who showed up periodically during the next two weeks to question him. The dapper Major played intricate games with the distraught prisoner, cutting up photographs of the *bordereau* and of Dreyfus' letters into tiny fragments, mixing them together and making the accused identify which was which. He forced Dreyfus to write isolated lines of the *bordereau* in various grotesque postures, in hopes that some of the dissimilarities between his handwriting and the incriminating letter would dissolve in the process. Only after two weeks of this fantastic inquisition was the prisoner allowed to see the *bor-*

dereau. His relief on being confronted with the concrete basis for his ordeal was unmistakable; and Du Paty left the prison somewhat shaken by the prisoner's obvious confidence in his ultimate vindication.

The case seemed to rest on the unsupported (and divided) opinions of the handwriting experts. By October 31, when Du Paty turned in his written report of the investigation, Mercier might have dropped the charge but for an unexpected development.

Two days earlier *Libre Parole* had queried in its columns whether an important arrest for treason had not been made. A leak—which Mercier and his fellow Cabinet members hoped to avoid until the prisoner's guilt was definitely confirmed—had occurred. It took the form of a note slipped under Drumont's door naming Dreyfus and his place of confinement. The note was signed "Henry," which may be a good reason for believing he didn't write it. On the other hand, Henry had no reason to distrust a brother in the sacred cause of anti-Semitism.

After two other Rightist papers had joined the hue and cry, Mercier issued an announcement tending to belittle the matter, which naturally had precisely the opposite effect. The following day's *Libre Parole* carried a sensational article headed: "HIGH TREASON! ARREST OF A JEWISH OFFICER, CAPTAIN DREYFUS." The story stated that Dreyfus had confessed, and leveled an accusing finger at Mercier: "But the case will be quashed because the officer is a Jew. . . ." In no time the entire anti-administration press swelled the scurrilous chorus.

As soon as the story broke, a meeting of the full Cabinet was summoned, and on Mercier's assurance that Dreyfus was guilty, ordered him prosecuted. On November 8 the file was turned over to Major Bexon d'Ormescheville to complete the investigation and prepare a formal accusation; simultaneously the press outcry against Mercier gave way to lavish praise of his patriotism and vigilance. By November 28 he was announcing publicly that there was no doubt of Dreyfus' guilt.

Meanwhile, the Intelligence Bureau had scoured its files for every scrap of evidence that conceivably supported that proposition. An undated letter addressed a year or two before by Schwartzkoppen to his Italian counterpart, Lieutenant Colonel Panizzardi, referring to some maps which had been delivered to him by "that scoundrel D——" was resurrected; the initials coincided, and it was freshened up by inserting the date "April 16, 1894." A telegram in cipher from Panizzardi to his War Office in Rome was intercepted on November 2, 1894, and decoded at the French Foreign Ministry. It read: "If Captain Dreyfus has had no dealings with you, it would be advisable to publish an official denial to avoid comments in the press." The code had not been easy to crack, and for a few days it was thought that the last few words of the telegram might be translated: "Our emissary warned." Of the two versions, the chief of the Statistical Section, Lieutenant Colonel Jean Sandherr, chose the inaccurate but more incriminating one. Du Paty's flair for the dramatic led him to add to the spurious translation: "Precautions taken."

A few fragments referring to an unnamed German spy in the French Army and a fanciful account of Dreyfus' career in espionage, dating back to 1890, completed the dossier. Labeled secret, it was set aside for future use.

Dreyfus' family, released at last from the bond of silence by Du Paty, consulted a lawyer—the mature, respected Edgar Demange, a devout and patriotic Catholic. He saw Dreyfus, read the Act of Accusation prepared by d'Ormescheville (which did not refer to the secret file), and examined a copy of the *bordereau.* Convinced of Dreyfus' innocence, he took the case, a decision requiring moral courage of the highest order.

The court-martial proceedings began on December 19, 1894, at the Hotel du Cherche-Midi, near the prison where Dreyfus had been held for two months. Two colonels, three majors, and two captains—none of them gunners—comprised the board. Under the rules, at least five affirmative votes were required to convict.

The trial opened with a clash of cymbals. Major André Brisset, military prosecutor, demanded that the public and press be excluded from the proceedings. Demange resisted stoutly. "There are other interests involved here," Brisset intoned darkly, "than those of the defense or the prosecution." (The hulking shadow of Bismarck filled the courtroom: the German Ambassador had already denied officially any connection between Dreyfus and Schwartzkoppen, and had protested the reckless charges appearing in the French press.) Brisset prevailed; and the drama became a private affair.

The charges were read, and Dreyfus replied with perhaps too much dignity and correctness. A Frenchman on trial for treason is expected to exhibit a degree of passion suitable to the occasion. It was Dreyfus' misfortune that he could not shed his years of military discipline even to save his own skin.

From the prosecution's twenty-one military witnesses came stories of Dreyfus' curiosity about military matters in general, topped off by Du Paty's and Henry's versions of their interviews with the prisoner. Demange quietly dissected their stories, scoring his points without any forensic fireworks. Du Paty fixed the time of the writing of the *bordereau* as April 1894. How, then, did he explain the fact that the modification of artillery formations and the confidential study on Madagascar, both referred to in the letter, were not known until August of that year? He fumbled his way out of these contradictions, but the prosecution's case was left somewhat shaken.

The handwriting experts, including the redoubtable Bertillon, thoroughly confused the Court, in keeping with the hallowed tradition of expert witnesses in courts throughout the world.

By the end of the second day, Major Georges Picquart, who had been sitting in on the trial as observer for General Boisdeffre, reported to his chief: the picture looked bleak for the prosecution. The *bordereau* constituted the only solid piece of evidence; its authorship was not established beyond question; proof of motivation was weak, since Dreyfus had no need of Germany's money and had produced a few impressive character witnesses.

Ruthless measures were indicated. Henry was recalled to the stand, and testified that "a most honorable personage" had told him in March of a traitor in the Intelligence Bureau (where Dreyfus was then serving as trainee). Both Dreyfus and Demange indignantly demanded the name of his informant. Striking his breast theatrically, Henry replied: "When an officer has such a secret in his head he does not confide it even to his cap." Then, pointing to the prisoner, he cried: "And there is the man!" The presiding judge did not press Henry to identify his source, and Demange was left to wrestle with an anonymous item of hearsay.

Summing up for the defense, Demange leaned heavily on the contradictions in the expert testimony and the complete absence of proof of motive. Both he and his client confidently expected an acquittal.

In his closing speech Brisset made no bones about his parade of military gossips: "Nothing remains but the *bordereau*, but that is enough. Let the judges take up their magnifying glasses."

But the judges had just about forgotten the *bordereau*. They were mulling over the contents of the secret file which Du Paty had furtively slipped to the presiding judge with a note from Mercier, requesting that it be considered before they reached a verdict. During the luncheon recess preceding the lawyers' summations, the papers had been passed around among the judges, who presumably were wholly unaware that under the military code they had no right to see them without the knowledge or consent of the accused. Mercier had played his trump card, from his sleeve. The unanimous verdict: guilty. The sentence: degradation, forfeiture of rank, and deportation for life.

The secret file was returned to Du Paty the same day. Henry and Sandherr burned the biographical summary and the spurious translation of the Panizzardi telegram. A number of documents which had seemed

145

too dubious to submit to the Court were added to the dossier before it was placed in the Intelligence Bureau's safe.

The degradation was carried out two weeks later—Dreyfus, his uniform shredded where the insignia and stripe had been ripped away, protesting his innocence, while the crowd shouted rabidly, "Death! Death to the traitor!" Among those present was Major Picquart, who would ultimately resurrect Dreyfus from the living dead.

The phrase fits the circumstances. By a special law hastily enacted by the Chamber of Deputies, Dreyfus was exiled not to New Caledonia, the regular place of detention for political prisoners, but to Devil's Island, a barren rock off the fever-stricken, swampy coast of French Guiana, formerly used as a leper colony. There he would remain for five years, alone with his guards, shut off from the outside world.

The gratuitous cruelty of this act, the uniqueness of his solitary hell on this cursed speck of earth in the vast ocean, represented the first auspicious turn in Dreyfus' fate. Had he been consigned to waste away the years with the rest of France's deportees, he might have been forgotten and ignored. But even Napoleon's St. Helena was not as dramatically isolated as Dreyfus' walled, one-man prison. The very name of the place, with its lurid backdrop of the unexplored, steaming jungles of South America, focused a spotlight on the solitary prisoner. Framed in such a setting, he could not be consigned to oblivion, as the Army hierarchy—and indeed most of the Jewish community—devoutly desired.

Syphilis has probably never contributed to the cause of justice as heavily as when it removed Colonel Jean Sandherr from the Intelligence Bureau in July of 1895. To head it in his place, Boisdeffre installed Georges Picquart, recently promoted to lieutenant colonel. Picquart, a soft-spoken and cultivated bachelor in his early forties, was by this time well on his way to the top. Mildly anti-Semitic, he had never liked Dreyfus, and had accepted the verdict against him without reserve. As Statistical Section Chief, however, he soon realized that Dreyfus' deportation had not stopped the flow of military information to Schwartzkoppen. Another spy was apparently at large.

In March 1896—eighteen months after Dreyfus' arrest—came the first break in the case. A blue special-delivery postcard, torn into thirty-six pieces, was fished from the wastebasket of the German Military Attaché and turned over to the Bureau by one of its agents. Written in the disguised, but recognizable, hand of Schwartzkoppen's mistress, it called for a "more detailed explanation than you gave me the other day." Signed only with the initial "C," it was unstamped, and presumably had not been sent. It was addressed to "M. le Commandant Esterhazy, 27 Rue de la Bienfaisance, Paris."

The receipt of the *petit bleu*, as it was called, fired the starting gun of the grim duel between Picquart and Esterhazy which would have France holding its breath sporadically during the next few years. It was St. George and the dragon all over again: the true-blue and righteous plodder outmaneuvered and outfought by the colorful and fire-breathing reptile until the very last minute. In this battle, Dreyfus himself emerged as little more than an onlooker—in chess terms, the king whose fate hung on the moves of subordinate pieces on the board.

Esterhazy, descendant of an illegitimate member of the French branch of the illustrious Hungarian family of that name, had already carved out a checkered career—first as a papal Zouave, then in the French Foreign Legion, from which he had transferred to the regulars during the Franco-Prussian War. He had narrowly escaped court-martial for misappropriation of army funds while on duty in Tunisia; and it was characteristic of the man that he neutralized this incident by inserting in his official record a forged commendation for courage in combat. He had gambled away the 200,000-franc dowry which his comely and well-born French bride had brought him, and by the time he came to Picquart's attention, she had obtained a decree of separation against him.

For a while he had made quite a good thing of serving as second to Jewish officers involved in duels, capitalizing on his condescension by borrowing large sums from them and their coreligionists. At the same time, he managed to remain on the best of terms with Drumont and his anti-Semitic faction. Debauched and hard-pressed for money, he seemed to encounter no difficulty in attracting female admirers—a remarkable feat, for he looked more like a vulture than the eagle he fancied himself. To this day, his role in the Dreyfus case arouses grudging admiration for his quickness of wit, his uninhibited gall, and the calculating thrust of his imagination.

By the end of August, painstaking investigation by Picquart and his staff had left no doubt in his mind that Esterhazy was the author of the *bordereau* which had sent Dreyfus to Devil's Island. He urged his superior, General Gonse, Deputy Chief of the General Staff, to authorize Esterhazy's arrest and the prompt reopening of the Dreyfus case. Gonse temporized—"prudence, prudence" was his line, in keeping with military tradition in peacetime.

That indomitable dullard, Major Henry, hard-pressed to protect the honor of the Army and of his good friend Esterhazy, made the move which broke the stalemate. He leaked to *L'Eclair* an account of the trial, revealing for the first time portions of the *bordereau*, and referring to certain damaging documents which had been "handed secretly" to the Court.

To Lucie Dreyfus, who had never abandoned hope of upsetting her husband's conviction, the disclosure came as manna from heaven. She set Demange to preparing a petition to the Chamber of Deputies for a discovery of the truth about the trial.

To Picquart, the question was simple: how much farther would the War Office allow itself to be dragged into an irreversible commitment against Dreyfus, in the face of the evidence he had unearthed? For he clearly perceived that prompt confession and reparation might save the Army from public disgrace, while the continued defense of the Dreyfus verdict must ultimately spell disaster.

On the day following the appearance of the *Eclair* article, he put the case to General Gonse. The General proved intractable; Mercier's reputation was at stake: "It would be the most shocking story."

Gonse continued: "If you say nothing, no one will ever know."

To which Picquart replied: "General, what you say is contemptible. I do not know what I shall do, but in any event I shall not allow this secret to be buried with me." And, casting his lot with Dreyfus, he turned his back on his commanding officer and on the Army.

Meanwhile Henry, vaguely uneasy about the Pandora's box he had opened, was devoting his spare time to keeping the lid nailed down on Dreyfus' coffin. He dropped into the Dreyfus dossier a note from Panizzardi to Schwartzkoppen, which included the clause: "P has brought me a number of interesting things," having first changed the P to a D and added the date "March 1894." With the aid of an expert forger named Lemercier-Picard, he then proceeded to perform a more delicate operation on two other letters from Panizzardi to Schwartzkoppen: he had Lemercier-Picard write in a hand resembling Panizzardi's a substitute for the body of each letter, on paper which seemed to match that of the genuine notes. Then he pasted the original salutation and the signature to each in their proper order, adding the dates "Sept. 1896" and "14 June 1894."

The forgeries were presented to Gonse as reconstructed fragments to prove that Picquart was barking up the wrong tree. Gonse took them to his superiors, Boisdeffre and his War Minister, Billot, who accepted them at face value. The contents of the "1894" note were insignificant; but it served to authenticate the handwriting of the other. The body of the "1896" note—later known as the "*faux Henry*"—read:

I have just read that a deputy is going to make an interpellation on Dreyfus. If Rome requires new explanations, I shall say I never had relations with the Jew. That is understood. If you are ever asked, say the same, for no one must ever know what happened with him.

That clinched it: the discredited gadfly, Picquart, was sent off to eastern France on a feckless inspection of fortifications, and then on to North Africa on a concocted errand.

Henry, left in charge of the Bureau, now opened a file on Picquart, and proceeded to stuff it with forgeries implicating his absent chief in a web of conspiracy. To gild the lily still further, he dug the *petit bleu* out of the Dreyfus file, erased Esterhazy's name, and rewrote it over the erasure, to create the impression that it had been substituted for another name. A lucky find in the form of a letter from Panizzardi dated in 1895, stating that he expected to obtain the new French railway mobilization plan, was redated 1894.

Picquart, not deceived by the nature of his "mission," finally managed to return to Paris on leave. He confided his beliefs to his lawyer, Louis Leblois, and left with him a written account of his findings. But he tied the lawyer's hands, forbidding him to use the information in any way that might disclose Picquart as its source until his death.

Leblois sought out the Vice President of the Senate, Auguste Scheurer-Kestner, member of a distinguished Alsatian family, who for some time had been uneasy about Dreyfus' guilt. Given the facts in confidence, Scheurer-Kestner could do no more than advertise his belief among his colleagues and try to obtain a hearing at the War Office, where he ran up against a blank wall.

But his persistence produced a frenzy of activity there. A rendezvous was arranged with Esterhazy, at which Du Paty, wearing a false beard, assured him that he would be protected if he followed instructions. Captain Charles Lebrun-Renault, who had acted as Dreyfus' escort on the day of his degradation, was forced to sign a false declaration dictated by Du Paty relating that, just before the ceremony, Dreyfus had confessed that he was a double agent. To the forged-document factory, which resumed its functions, was added a rumor mill, circulating reports of letters from Dreyfus to the Kaiser and of marginal notes on the *bordereau* in the Kaiser's hand (complaining of the high prices demanded for information).

Esterhazy, meanwhile, daringly went over to the offensive. He wrote to General Billot and to Felix Faure, President of the Republic, accusing them of ignoring the Jewish plot against his good name. These letters were apparently inspired by Du Paty, but only Esterhazy could have been responsible for the touch of bravado in which he threatened to seek redress through his family's sovereign, the Emperor of Germany!

Still later, he wrote the President, threatening to publish the photograph of a letter stolen from a foreign embassy by Picquart (!)—"most compromising to certain diplomatic personages"—if his pleas for justice were ignored. Whatever he was talking about, he threw the War Office into a turmoil.

But the deadlock was not broken until November 1897, when Dreyfus' brother Mathieu distributed facsimiles of the *bordereau*, which had been published in *Matin* in 1896. Within a few days a stockbroker who had done business with Esterhazy identified the handwriting. Mathieu took the information to Scheurer, who felt free to pass him on to Leblois.

The knot was tied; Mathieu addressed to Billot an open letter denouncing Esterhazy as the author of the *bordereau*. The Cabinet promptly launched an investigation into that worthy, while maintaining a placid exterior to the gentlemen of the now frenetic press. Picquart was ordered back to Paris, while Schwartzkoppen left for Berlin, never to return.

The press on both sides was in full cry. The lines that would divide the entire French public into pro- and anti-Dreyfus factions began to assume definite shape and direction. A strong "revisionist" sentiment, spearheaded by a new newspaper, *L'Aurore*, with Georges Clemenceau as editor, was emerging as a potent force. In opposition, Drumont had revived the image of a worldwide Jewish conspiracy; the War Minister was accused of selling out to it in order to pay his debts. Catholic and Royalist youth demonstrations rallied to the honor of the Army and of France.

Esterhazy's following received a jolt when his ex-mistress turned over to *Figaro* a series of letters betraying his true allegiance in disquieting terms: "I would not harm a puppy, but I would kill 100,000 Frenchmen with pleasure . . ." Momentarily panicking, he tried to leave the country, but Colonel Henry stopped him at the border. Henry, for once, had acted wisely; the letters were dismissed as forgeries, and patriots vied for the privilege of buying Esterhazy a drink.

But no amount of public acclaim could stave off a court-martial for Esterhazy, based on the investigation of the *petit bleu*. It was a perfunctory affair, conducted behind closed doors. No one was surprised when on January 12, 1898, the latter-day Barabbas was released to the clamoring mob—acquitted by a unanimous Court.

The following day, General Billot ordered the arrest of Picquart, charged with disclosing confidential Army files to unauthorized civilians, i.e., his lawyer.

That same day the Dreyfus case lost its character as a French family affair. Blazoned across the face of 200,000 copies of Clemenceau's

150

Aurore was the headline "J'ACCUSE!" In the form of an open letter, France's outstanding novelist, Emile Zola, whose verbal violence had made him many enemies, took up the cudgels for Dreyfus. Nobody escaped his hammer blows, with the solitary exception of Henry, whose "absurd and culpable machinations" he attributed entirely to Du Paty. The higher-ups were not spared; Mercier, Boisdeffre, Billot, and Gonse were denounced for hushing up evidence of Dreyfus' innocence. As for the court-martial boards which had tried Dreyfus and Esterhazy:

. . . I accuse the first court-martial of having violated the law by condemning an accused man on the basis of a secret document, and I accuse the second court-martial of having, in obedience to orders, screened that illegality by committing in its turn the judicial crime of knowingly acquitting a guilty man.

He closed by inviting a suit for defamation:

I have but one passion—that of light. This I crave for the sake of humanity. . . . My fiery protest is merely the cry of my soul. Let them bring me before the Court of Assize and let an inquiry be made in broad daylight. I wait!

He would not wait long. In Parliament the next day, the Prime Minister bowed to an overwhelming demand to prosecute Zola. Only a few voices were raised in protest. Standing almost alone, Jean Jaurès broke with his own Socialist comrades who disdained to intervene for a "bourgeois writer in a bourgeois cause." Anti-Jewish riots swept the provinces, topped off by a four-day pillaging of the Jewish quarter in Algiers.

But Zola had rallied to his side the cream of the world's intelligentsia. In France three thousand names were quickly gathered for a revisionist petition, including those of Anatole France, Marcel Proust, Claude Monet, and the two Halévy brothers. Telegrams and letters poured into *Aurore's* offices from the rest of the world. Mark Twain commented acidly on French military courts in the New York *Herald*, and even the usually friendly Russian press expressed despair at the backwardness of the French. Zola had made his point, with devastating impact.

By the same token, his enemies had an enormous stake in his conviction. Craftily they confined the indictment for defamation against Zola and his publisher to his assertion that Esterhazy had been acquitted by orders from above. Thereby all inquiry into Dreyfus' case was apparently foreclosed.

Before Zola's trial commenced on February 7, 1898, a board of inquiry had recommended Picquart's dismissal from the service on the basis of his dealings with his lawyer Leblois. Picquart was slated to be the key witness at the Zola trial, and War Minister Billot thought it prudent to defer action on the board's recommendation, in hopes of influencing his testimony.

From the outset the trial resolved itself into a struggle between defense counsel and the presiding judge, Delegorgue, over the admission of testimony concerning Dreyfus. Whenever Fernand Labori, Zola's massive, mettlesome attorney, sought to turn the testimony in that direction, Delegorgue would snap: "There is no such thing as a Dreyfus affair. The question is out of order."

Nevertheless, it went well at first for Zola. Three leading handwriting experts testified that the handwriting of the *bordereau* was Esterhazy's. Bertillon's tangled analysis of the matter on the prosecution's behalf left the jury more amused than enlightened. Two witnesses were able to snake into their evidence reports which had come to them of documents which the Dreyfus judges had seen in secret.

The legal shrapnel screaming overhead unseated General Gabriel de Pellieux, who had investigated the Esterhazy case for the General Staff and ridden herd on the court-martial which acquitted him. Pellieux had been shown the *faux Henry*—and had accepted it as genuine, knowing nothing of its history. He now attempted to rush into the breach, and in his eagerness, opened it a little wider. Called at his own request, he revealed the contents of the *faux Henry* as definitive proof of Dreyfus' guilt, and asked that Generals Gonse and Boisdeffre be called to confirm his surprise disclosure. Reluctantly both of them did so, but they firmly declined to produce the document or to submit to cross-examination about it. Although the Court sustained them, the engine had to be got back on the track; and Boisdeffre accomplished this neatly with a closing appeal to the jury:

If the nation has no confidence in the chiefs of the Army, in those who are responsible for the national defense, they are ready to leave to others this heavy task. You have only to speak.

Against this sort of sword rattling, Picquart's later testimony about the *faux Henry* fell on deaf ears: ". . . this document may with good reason be put down as a forgery." The shrewdness of his deduction was matched by his courage in rejecting the carrot which had been extended to him after his own conviction. He was promptly expelled from the Army "for grave shortcomings in service."

Du Paty, Henry, Esterhazy—all retreated behind the flag, with the approval of the Court. Esterhazy stood in the box for forty minutes as Albert Clemenceau, representing Zola's publisher, threw questions at him—all of which he disdained to answer. Clemenceau finally appealed to the Court: "How is it that one cannot speak in a court of justice of an action performed by a French officer?" "Because," the Judge replied, "there is something more important than that—the honor and security of the country."

Esterhazy was carried to his cab on the shoulders of his admirers. After less than an hour's deliberation, the jury brought in a verdict of guilty. Zola received the maximum sentence: one year's imprisonment and a fine. He appealed and won on a technicality; but in July 1898, just as the re-enactment of the farce was beginning, Zola bowed to the urgent pleas of his friends, and fled to England.

A sequel unnoticed by the general public was the death—apparently by suicide—of Lemercier-Picard, Henry's assistant forger. His handiwork would soon make news.

Zola's fight had not been in vain. The few shafts of light which had illuminated his trial and the harsh reprisals taken against his witnesses left a time-bomb of doubt in the minds of many thoughtful Frenchmen: something was being covered up. Except for the die-hard Socialists, only a handful of neutrals was left in Paris. Cafe talk and dinner-party conversation (much of it preserved in Proust's A la Recherche du temps perdu) centered on the Dreyfus question. The case had become l'Affaire.

In the Chamber of Deputies the Affair continued to smolder. When Godefroy Cavaignac took over the Ministry of War with the new Brisson Cabinet in June 1898, he decided to wet down the embers once and for all. While still a member of the opposition bench, he had been challenging the Administration to come to the defense of the Army with documents which were reputed to be in its possession—including Dreyfus' "confession," as reported by Lebrun-Renault. But the authorities, more knowledgeable and therefore more circumspect, had rested on the less controversial position that the reopening of the Dreyfus case was a matter for the courts. Once in office, Cavaignac took the headlong and seemingly logical step of spreading the proof of Dreyfus' guilt on the record.

On July 7, 1898, he paraded before the astonished Chamber the Henry forgeries and the alleged confession. In recognition of the mounting volume of proof concerning the bordereau, he admitted that Esterhazy had written it and would have to be punished.

A tidy package; and with a collective sigh of relief, the Chamber voted to have his speech printed and posted in every French election district. Picquart, free of military restraint, lost no time in writing an open letter to Prime Minister Brisson, challenging the authenticity of the faux Henry and the significance of the references to a mysterious "D" in the other documents. Picquart was immediately arrested to answer criminal charges on the same grounds as those for which he had been expelled from the Army—communicating documents concerning the national defense to Leblois.

But Picquart's letter, and continued agitation in the revisionist press, led Cavaignac to direct one of his aides, General Gaudérique Roget, to undertake a thorough review of the Dreyfus file. Working late into the night of August 13, 1898, one of Roget's young assistants examined by lamplight the *faux Henry*—which only a month earlier had been posted all over France as unmistakable proof of Dreyfus' guilt. He noticed at once that the portions of the letter bearing the signature and salutation were faintly cross-hatched with blue lines, while the body of the letter had an underlying claret ruling. In that moment of perception, the Dreyfus affair went into reverse gear.

The young Captain's report quickly passed up the line; and Henry, on his return from leave, was interrogated by Cavaignac about both of the Lemercier-Picard forgeries. After an hour of severe questioning, Henry was driven into a corner.

CAVAIGNAC: Impossible! You aggravate your situation by these concealments!

HENRY: I did what I did for the good of the country.

Still irresolute, Cavaignac simply consigned the confessed forger to military prison, without preferring charges against him. The following day Esterhazy, already cashiered from the service for "personal misconduct" (!) slipped off to England. General Boisdeffre resigned. And Henry sat down in his cell to write a letter to his wife:

I am absolutely innocent; they know it, and everyone will know it later, but right now, I can't talk . . .

Then he lay down on his bed, bared his razor and cut his throat.

A brief communique had been issued to the press disclosing Henry's arrest for forgery of the *faux Henry*. Amid widespread public outcry, Cavaignac resigned rather than consent to revision; and Premier Brisson advised Lucie Dreyfus to petition for a review of her husband's case.

By all rules of dramatic construction, the Dreyfus affair should have drawn to a close at this point. But its most fantastic episodes were yet to be played out. The unregenerate anti-Semitic journals promptly fitted Henry with the garb of martyrdom: "This heroic servant of the great interests of the state" had committed the forgery only to prevent the disclosure of an even more damaging document, which would have meant war with Germany. This "plebeian" agent of the "chiefs he loved" had sinned only in "deceiving for the public good."

The War Office took steps to seal Picquart off from the Dreyfus faction. It accused him of forging Esterhazy's name on the *petit bleu*, and asked the criminal court where he was awaiting trial to surrender him to the military for court-martial. Picquart fought this move, but lost. Before a packed courtroom, he furnished himself with a life insurance policy by delivering a brief but moving valedictory:

I shall probably go tonight to the Cherche-Midi; and this is probably the last time, prior to the secret trial, that I can say a word in public. I would have people know, if there be found in my cell the rope of Lemercier-Picard or the razor of Henry, that I have been murdered. For a man like myself cannot for a moment think of suicide.

With these words, he substituted the perfidy of the Army for the guilt of Dreyfus as the central issue before the French people.

Premier Brisson, now convinced of Dreyfus' innocence, had forced through his Cabinet a grudging approval of Lucie Dreyfus' petition for review of her husband's case by the Court of Cassation's Criminal Division. Brisson paid dearly for his integrity; having lost the support of the Dreyfusists as a result of Cavaignac's ill-conceived speech and the Army's latest move against Picquart, he found himself shunned by the Right for allowing Dreyfus' case to reach the Court. His Cabinet fell; and his successor, Charles Dupuy, returned to the office he had held at the time of the original Dreyfus trial.

The Criminal Division of the Court of Cassation began reviewing the evidence on November 8, 1898, and heard over eighty witnesses, including five former War Ministers. By January 1899, it was rumored that the Dreyfusist viewpoint seemed likely to prevail; and the Drumont press joined with veterans' and Royalist organizations to forestall that result by having the case transferred to the full Court, in place of its Criminal Division alone. Dupuy bowed to the pressure, and late in February, with most of the testimony in, the Chamber passed a law entrusting such appeals to a Bench comprised of all forty-six judges of the Court's three divisions.

But the ruse miscarried. By unanimous decision, the full Court sent the case back for retrial, on the basis of the improper secret disclosure to the court-martial of the document containing the phrase "that scoundrel D——," and of expert testimony concerning the authorship of the *bordereau*, "there being no necessity to pronounce on other grounds." A new court-martial, to be convened at Rennes, was ordered to determine whether Dreyfus had conspired to hand over to a foreign power the documents mentioned in the *bordereau*.

The form of the remand and the limited scope of the decision betray

155

the difficulty the Court had in arriving at a unanimous verdict: it reeks with compromise. But for Dreyfus' purpose it sufficed, and his supporters were jubilant.

The date was June 3, 1899. On that same day the flamboyant Du Paty, who had played such a colorful part in the early scenes of the drama, was arrested, charged with forgery; and *Le Matin* published an interview between its London correspondent and Esterhazy, in which the cashiered officer confessed authorship of the *bordereau*. The generals, he said, knew about it.

Two days later, Zola returned to France. On June 9, Picquart was released from jail after 364 days of confinement, and Dreyfus left Devil's Island.

Again it would seem to be time for the curtain to come down and the house lights to go up. But the shocking denouement was yet to come. It would please Germany's sardonic von Bülow, who had remarked earlier: "It would be best for the Affair to fester, to divide the Army and scandalize Europe."

More outraged than dismayed, the anti-Dreyfusists resumed work with a will. The Court had been bribed by the Jewish conspiracy, screamed Drumont; the Army's dishonor opened the way to foreign invasion. The President of the Republic, attending the races the Sunday following the handing down of the opinion, was attacked by a young Royalist as the crowd clamored for his resignation. Violent gangs of Nationalists filled the streets, clashing with Dreyfusists at every corner. Premier Dupuy's seeming indifference to these occurrences, and his irresolution in response to Socialist demands that Mercier be prosecuted for the illegal conduct exposed by the Court's decision, led to the collapse of his ministry by mid-June.

Senator Pierre Waldeck-Rousseau, a sturdy advocate of the Dreyfus cause, managed to form a Cabinet; and its survival established the pattern of French coalition government for decades to come. Broadly based on a Republican footing, it rejected extreme Right and extreme Left. For the first time in French history, a Socialist, Alexandre Millerand, was called to a Cabinet post; and to hold the Army in check, the War Ministry was filled by the aristocratic General Gaston Galliffet, veteran of Sedan, whose patriotism and indomitable opposition to Nationalists and Communards alike made him the indispensable choice for the job.

Galliffet lost no time bluntly advising Mercier that his Army career was ended; but, he added, there would be no reprisals. For Mercier, this constituted small comfort, for his ordeal awaited him at Rennes. Dreyfus' acquittal would brand Mercier as a blackguard whose perfidy had few parallels in history.

The sleepy little city of Rennes was swollen with politicians and journalists when the court-martial convened in the bright lecture-hall of the local high school on August 8, 1899. The British press sent its top correspondents, and Queen Victoria dispatched the eminent jurist, Sir Charles Russell, to act as her personal observer. From the United States came Finley Peter Dunne ("Mr. Dooley"), whose sly lampoons of the Zola trial had earned him another shot at the French judicial system. Vienna's leading newspaper was represented by Karl Liebknecht, whose bloody imprint would someday stain the pages of German history.

Two colonels, three majors, two captains—these were the men to whom Dreyfus looked for the vindication he had grimly awaited during the four and a half years on Devil's Island. These years had taken a toll which tore an audible gasp from the audience when he entered the courtroom. The central figure in the struggle that had convulsed France was, in the words of Steevens, the *Daily Mail* correspondent, "an old, old man of thirty-nine." What was left of his hair had turned white. His new uniform hung from him grotesquely, accentuating the puppetlike, mechanical gait which carried him to his place in court. His voice had become completely toneless; the objectivity with which he customarily spoke of himself was invested with the accent of death. As the trial wore on, he occasionally exploded in denial—"I never said so!"—or a protest—"I am innocent, *mon Colonel!*"—which reminded his listeners that he had once been a man among men. These rare outbursts evoked a mixture of wonderment and horror: resurrection can be a devastating spectacle.

Dreyfus' denials of the charges against him were followed by four days' study behind closed doors of the secret file—now stuffed with almost four hundred documents, not more than twenty lines of which truthfully pertained to the accused.

Then on Saturday, August 12, Mercier took the stage, tall, slim and soldierly, his face bronzed and his gray mustache curling contemptuously upward over thin lips. In a dry, measured monotone he dug into the secret dossiers, tying them to Dreyfus with vague items of gossip. No maneuver was too desperate for his rearguard action. He introduced a false scent in the form of a letter written by an Austrian military attaché, attesting Dreyfus' guilt; several days later, the writer of the letter telegraphed the Court to deny Mercier's interpretation of its contents. He drew a wholly fictitious picture of a night in January 1895, when he and Prime Minister Dupuy had met with the President of the Republic in a frenzy of anxiety, expecting war momentarily as a result of a controversy with the German Ambassador over Dreyfus. Although General

Boisdeffre endorsed this invention, it was demolished by Jean Casimir-Perier, the former President named by Mercier. But the General remained undaunted: coolly, concisely, and in tones ringing with authority, he spun out a wild melange of hints, nuances, implications, and sheer fabrications, defending them with the tactical agility of a veteran guerrilla warrior.

Only once did Mercier launch a frontal attack: on the stroke of twelve he turned in his chair to face Dreyfus and said icily: "If I had the least doubt of his guilt, I should be the first to come to Captain Dreyfus and say to him that I was honestly mistaken." Dreyfus came to life, his face suffused with blood; rising out of his chair, he cried: "That's what you should do!"

Steevens wrote later:

None of us who heard it will ever describe it—or forget it. Men heard it that night in their sleep. It was half shriek, half sob, half despair, half snatching hope, half a fire of consuming rage, and half an anguished scream for pity.

That same evening, word reached Rennes from Paris that a Royalist-Nationalist anti-Semitic coup, planned to coincide with Mercier's appearance on the stand, had been nipped in the bud by the prompt arrest of its leaders.

In Rennes itself, feeling was running fever-high. On his way to court on Monday morning, the mercurial and overly contentious Labori, one of Dreyfus' counsel, was shot in the back by an unknown assailant; his wound was not serious, and his talents were lost to the defense for only a week. Demange, who had lived with the case since its inception, carried on alone in his absence, stolidly making his points without fanfare and without offending the Bench, in full recognition of the need to tread softly when the fate of generals hangs on the decision of a board of colonels, majors, and captains.

Called to testify for the defense, Colonel Picquart, self-possessed as ever, brought to the Court a command of the details of the Dreyfus case born of his own sacrifice. With unfailing candor and rationality, he led the Court through the maze of falsifications and machinations he had found too strong for his stomach. Although his fate was inextricably linked with the defendant's, his analysis had the earmarks of a commentary from Olympus on the peccadillos of the mortals below.

Clouds of military witnesses, including generals—Boisdeffre, Gonse, Roget—paraded past in a solid phalanx against Dreyfus; the witnesses in his behalf were of lower rank. Many had testified at the 1894 court-martial; and, not unexpectedly, their attitudes had hardened, their suspicions become certainties, in the intervening years. Missing from the procession were three of the principal figures in the drama: Esterhazy, Henry, and Du Paty—one abroad, one dead, one confined to a sickbed.

And, for days, the handwriting experts on both sides, with Bertillon frenzied as ever, reasoning like the Mad Hatter, and shuttling like a foraging bee from judge to judge with an armful of photographic enlargements.

The portly Captain Lebrun-Renault, from whom Du Paty had extracted a false account of Dreyfus' confession after the degradation ceremony, came forward with the story warmed over. Under cross-examination he faltered; but the prosecution brought up reinforcements in depth: a captain to swear that a brother officer had told him that he had been present at the confession, and a major to say that the captain had told him about it, and so on, *ad infinitum.*

Inevitably, the high stakes which had been gambled on the outcome of the case brought forth an opportunist. On September 4, as the trial was drawing to a close, a surprise witness was called by the President of the Court. Eugen Lazar von Cernusky, who described himself as a political refugee, a former officer of Austrian dragoons, confirmed that friends in the Austrian Ministry of Foreign Affairs and on the German General Staff had told him, as far back as August 1894, that Dreyfus was working for the Germans. Labori, on his feet at once, demanded that the testimony of Panizzardi and Schwartzkoppen be taken in their own countries; grandstand play or no, his application was rejected. But the defense was back the next day with a hammer blow at Cernusky: a police record of insanity, desertion, and swindling which blasted him off the witness stand. Since the Court knew that he had conferred with Generals Mercier and Roget before he testified, his departure was welcomed by all.

Thirty-three sessions and 115 witnesses after the trial opened, the judges filed out of the courtroom for their deliberations. An hour and a half later, they returned, pale and subdued. Dreyfus was absent from the room, in accordance with the military code. The President announced the verdict: Guilty, by a vote of five to two, of high treason. "But there are extenuating circumstances . . . in consequence of which the Court sentences Alfred Dreyfus to ten years' detention."

The absurdity inherent in the idea of extenuating circumstances for committing treason betrayed how far the verdict had wandered from the evidence. It amounted, indeed, as Steevens observed, to an endorsement of "the divine right of generals." The foreign press poured a hail of brimstone on France; even Queen Victoria expressed royal dismay.

But Premier Waldeck-Rousseau had had enough. He sensed that the

Affair would continue to smolder as a political issue; only the Left, which had abandoned its Marxist unconcern with the fate of the bourgeois Dreyfus, could benefit from the continuance of the struggle. Besides, he was disturbed by the swelling chorus of threats from abroad to boycott the Paris World Exhibition, scheduled to open in April 1900. It would be good business, as well as sound politics, to sweep the ashes of the Dreyfus case under the red carpet.

Ten days after the verdict was delivered, Dreyfus received a full pardon. His acceptance of it, natural enough in view of his mental and physical condition, angered many of his ardent supporters. But it paved the way for what historians have called "The Dreyfusian Revolution" in France:

A requirement of attendance for three years at state secondary schools for Army candidates broke the grip of the Catholic Church on preparatory education. The Assumptionist order, which had spearheaded the Catholic outcry against Dreyfus, was dissolved, prefacing a full-scale resumption of the long-dormant government assault on the religious congregations. Separation of Church and State entered its ultimate phase; within six years it would be complete.

The Army, too, felt the whiplash of revulsion for the role it had played. The tight little circle of high-ranking officers which had controlled nominations to the rank of general was stripped of its power, with the Minister of War taking over the function. The Statistical Section was put out of the espionage business. Military justice underwent a drastic overhaul, resulting in curtailment of the jurisdiction of courts-martial, and enlargement of the right to appeal from their verdicts to civil courts.

In the larger sense, the enthusiasms and antipathies aroused by the Affair set in motion a remolding of French political opinion which held France on a firm Republican course until the military disaster of 1940. The criminal folly of the conservative forces in their defense of the Army hierarchy sparked an egalitarian revival, with the legions of liberalism greatly strengthened by a fresh infusion of intellectuals from all classes of society. Never again would France turn back to monarchy, clerical control, or—except in defeat—military dictatorship.

Dreyfus' complete vindication might have been expected, under the circumstances, to have come about speedily. Not until July 1906, however, was he cleared of the incubus of guilt which had twice been assessed against him. On the 12th of that month, the Court of Cassation, after more than two years of painstaking review, annulled the Rennes verdict on the grounds that it rested on forged documents and perjured testimony. Fortunately the case was not sent back for retrial by court-martial, there being, in the opinion of the Court, no provable criminal charge against Dreyfus.

Both he and Picquart were reinstated promptly in the Army by Parliamentary action "to liberate the conscience of France." Picquart, accorded the rank of Brigadier General, would within six months become Minister of War under Clemenceau. Dreyfus himself lived to erase at Verdun and Chemin des Dames the memory of his disgrace—fighting against the German invader. The press notices of his death in 1935 served as a momentary reminder of a troubled France which found itself through his ordeal.

No transcript of the 1894 court-martial proceedings survives, if, indeed, it ever existed. The second court-martial was widely reported, and the excerpts from the record which follow are drawn from contemporary newspaper accounts.

AUGUST 7, 1899
ALFRED DREYFUS

PRESIDENT. Accused, stand up. You are charged with the crime of treason; of having delivered to a foreign power the documents enumerated in the *bordereau* . . . The document has already been presented to you. Do you recognize it?

A. It was shown to me in 1894. As to recognizing it, I affirm I do not. I again affirm I am innocent, as I affirmed it, as I proclaimed it in 1894. I have borne everything for five years, *mon Colonel*, but only for the honor of my name and for the sake of my wife and children. I am innocent. I swear it! I swear it! . . .

Q. Had you any relations with officers who knew the short 120 cannon?

A. I never had any conversation on the subject.

Q. Did you know the disposition of troops covering the mobilization?

A. No. In 1893, in the Fourth Bureau, I had to do with this, but not in 1894.

Q. Yes, but having known them in 1893, you were aware of them. You had the documents in your possession in 1893?

A. Yes, twice. But only for a short space of time.

Q. You had knowledge of the covering troops in 1894?

A. No, *mon Colonel*, it did not interest me. I never asked anyone about it . . .

Q. Did you have knowledge of this [artillery] manual?

A. No.

Q. There is a witness from whom you asked information about it.

A. I am sure this is a mistake. In 1894 I asked to have this witness produced, but he never appeared.

Q. He will appear soon.

A. I would also say this: In the report of Major d'Ormescheville, which you have just heard read, it is said that I had conversations with this officer in the month of February or March. Now, I saw in the depositions before the Court of Cassation that this draft of the firing manual dates from March 14 and that it was only given to the staff in the month of May. In consequence, I could not have talked about it in the month of March.

Q. It was in the month of July that Major Jannel must have given you a copy of this manual.

A. But there is mention of conversations I had with him.

Q. That doesn't matter. What I ask you is not what M. d'Ormescheville says, but what you say. Let me interrogate and don't ask me questions. The *bordereau* terminates with the following words: "I am just leaving for the maneuvers." Now, were you not at the maneuvers?

A. No, *mon Colonel.*

Q. It was customary for all probationers to go there. At what date were you informed that you would not go to the 1894 maneuvers?

A. About the end of May or the beginning of June.

Q. According to information, it was a much later date, it was August 28, 1894, when the Minister decided not to send the probationers to the maneuvers for reason of service.

A. Allow me, *mon Colonel* . . .

Q. That is to say, some days after the creation of the document known as the *bordereau.*

A. Permit me, *mon Colonel.* At the trial of 1894 I asked for the production of the official circular of the month of May 1894, by which we were informed that we were not to go to the maneuvers, but that we were to go to put in our training period with the regiments of infantry—those of the First Bureau in July and September, those of the Second in October, November, and December.

Q. In any case, there is a decision of the Minister, of September 1894, which states that the probationers would not go to the maneuvers.

A. There was one in the month of May 1894.

Q. It will have to be looked up.

M. DEMANGE. There must be a mistake.

MAJOR CARRIERE. There is no mistake. There was in the month of May an instruction warning the officers in principle, but the probationers were nevertheless to go to the maneuvers. The idea was only abandoned in the month of September on account of the special services they had to perform in connection with the preparation of the plan . . .

Q. It was you who complained to Major Jannel that the probationers did not know the artillery manual, which was in the hands of all the regimental officers. Ten copies were then sent out: two to your Bureau. Do you admit that Major Jannel lent you a copy?

A. No, *mon Colonel.*

Q. You deny it?

A. Yes. Will you permit me to make an observation?

Q. Yes.

A. I beg to point out that in July 1894, I no longer belonged to the Second Bureau, where Major Jannel was, but to the Third Bureau. Now, after the depositions to the Court of Cassation that the manual was given to all the Bureaus, I do not understand . . .

Q. In the *bordereau*, the author says that the manual is very difficult to procure. This was not true as far as artillery officers were concerned, but the staff officers found it difficult to get a copy. There is in that a coincidence with the position you held.

A. Colonel, as I said at the 1894 court-martial, it was easy to obtain this manual. Certainly, if any officer had asked for it, he would have been given it. I did not have it and I did not ask for it because I knew I was not going to the artillery maneuvers and I was doing other work. If, therefore, I did not ask for it, it was because I did not need it. But it was the easiest thing in the world for an artillery officer to procure it. Therefore, the phrase in the *bordereau* could only apply to an officer of another branch. . . .

Q. . . . During your sojourn at the War Academy, you were reproached with having used expressions unworthy of a French officer. You said that France would be happy under the domination of Germany.

A. I never said such a thing.

Q. We will come back to that later. When you were graduated from the War Academy, you were ninth on the list. However, you were very discontented and expressed your feelings in violent language. What was the reason for your discontent?

A. I gave this information back in 1894. I asked then that the people involved in this incident be called. One of my comrades at the War Academy was said to have stated that they wanted no officers of my religion at the General Staff, but it was not meant personally for me; it was only a general statement.

Q. How did you know of these words?

A. One of my comrades told me.

Q. That is curious.

A. When I heard of them after the examination, I went to the Director of the Academy, but I did not protest against the position I received. The Director received me kindly, told me that he knew of the incident and that he regretted it, but that it would not change my position. Besides, I was perfectly satisfied with it . . .

Q. Now, in September 1886, did you not follow the German maneuvers in the environs of Mulhouse?

A. Oh, no! No, *mon Colonel*, never!

Q. Did you not follow the maneuvers at Haarcheim on horseback?

A. No, *Colonel*.

Q. Did you not speak with an officer of dragoons?

A. I never spoke to a German officer.

Q. You never spoke to them of the 1886 rifle?

A. Of course not.

Q. You deny it utterly? A witness claims to have seen you there. You were known in the Fourth Bureau to be always seeking information.

A. I wanted to instruct myself.

Q. A young officer, especially when he has just left the War Academy, has the right to instruct himself, but there are limits to this. He must not push it to indiscretion. Now, you were often indiscreet: you devoted your attention to the Western Railways; you knew all these problems so well that you could deliver a lecture on them on the spur of the moment. You knew them so well that you verbally instructed Captain Boullenger. Why did you want to know all these details?

A. I gave this information to Captain Boullenger because I knew all the numbers of the lines of transport.

Q. And the mobilization?

A. As I knew all the lines of transport of the Fourth Bureau, I knew the mobilization.

Q. You interested yourself in these matters because you undoubtedly had your reasons for wanting to know them—and at a time when your chief was considerably disturbed at your indifference to your duties and disliked your presence in the Bureau because of your fondness for investigation. You went so far that you had to be called to order. One day at the Ministry of War, a lecture was given by General Ranson on the concentration of armies, an extremely confidential part of our military organization. It was forbidden to take notes, and you took them all the same.

A. I know nothing about this lecture . . .

Q. You have had relations with a lady living at 1 Rue Bizet. Do you admit these relations?

A. They were not intimate relations.

Q. But in any case you have been to her house . . . What was the nationality of this woman?

A. Austrian.

Q. She naturally spoke German.

A. Yes.

Q. She had brothers in the Austrian Army?

A. I don't know.

Q. Were you never told?

A. No.

Q. In any case, she had brothers in the Austrian Army. She was suspected of espionage. How did it come that you, an officer of the French Army . . . associated with a person of foreign nationality suspected of espionage?

A. I was ignorant of the suspicions against her, and I would like to add there that when Major Guerin appeared as a witness in the court-martial of 1895, he testified that he had never seen her name on any list of suspected persons.

164

Q. Did you not frequent other women and thereby run yourself into exaggerated expenditure?

A. Never . . .

Q. . . . Did you not gamble?

A. Never . . .

Q. Now, after your condemnation and the rejection of your appeal to a Council of Revision, Colonel Du Paty de Clam came to see you at the Cherche-Midi prison. Tell us what took place at that interview.

A. . . . He began by asking me for some unimportant information, saying to me: "Did you not give the information for the sake of making an exchange?" I replied that I had not done so, that I had never had any relations, direct or indirect, with any agent of a foreign power, that I had never known one. It was then that I said that an iniquity was committed in condemning me, that it was impossible to understand it, that there was a government with powerful means of investigation and that it was inconceivable that an innocent man should be condemned for a crime he had not committed. Then I asked that the Government employ every means at its disposal to throw light on the affair. Colonel Du Paty replied: "There are considerations which prevent certain investigations." I then replied: "I hope that in two or three years my innocence will be recognized." . . .

Q. On January 5, the day of the degradation parade, you were taken from the Cherche-Midi prison to the Ecole Militaire by Captain Lebrun-Renault . . . Did you not say to Captain Lebrun-Renault: "The Minister knows quite well that if I have delivered any documents they are without importance, in order to obtain others that were more important"?

A. I recalled the conversation with Colonel Du Paty de Clam, and I said: "The Minister sent me Lieutenant Colonel Paty de Clam to ask me if I had not given up some documents without value, in order to get more important ones."

AUGUST 14, 1899
GENERAL AUGUSTE MERCIER [MINISTER OF WAR, NOVEMBER 1893–JANUARY 1895]

THE PRESIDENT. Was there a leakage in the War Office before the arrest of Dreyfus?

A. Yes.

Q. Did they cease after his departure?

A. I can give you no information. I don't know.

Q. Can you give us evidence of the role of Esterhazy?

A. I never knew that he belonged to the Intelligence Department or had missions for counterespionage from the Minister of War.

Q. Esterhazy has admitted he was the author of the *bordereau*. From your deposition on Saturday you seem not to believe this?

A. Esterhazy is not the author of the *bordereau*. This declaration on his part is a lie. It is still my profound conviction that the *bordereau* was the work of Dreyfus.

GODEFROY CAVAIGNAC [MINISTER OF WAR, OCTOBER 1895–APRIL 1896; JUNE 1898–SEPTEMBER 1898]

Q. What do you think of the Henry forgery in relation to the facts now occupying our attention?

A. The Henry forgery, as alleged, was in order to secure a revision of the case at the Court of Cassation, and was not even alluded to there. This forgery, therefore, should remain outside the scope of the questions submitted to this court-martial. . . .

AUGUST 16, 1899
MME. HUBERT HENRY

PRESIDENT. We have thought, madam, that from your daily contacts with your husband, you might perhaps be able to give interesting information about this affair.

A. At the end of September 1894, one evening after dinner, my husband said that important papers had been given to him. As he did not return from the Ministry until late in the night, on his coming in I asked him why. He replied by unrolling a roll of narrow, transparent paper and said: "This is a grave matter which has been asked of me this evening." A few minutes afterwards he returned with these papers and letters, which he had just pieced together. He put them all in his hat so as not to forget them the following morning.

Q. What was his impression on seeing the *bordereau?*

A. He told me he did not know who wrote it. When my husband returned from conducting Dreyfus to the Cherche-Midi prison I asked him why he was in uniform. He replied, "I have just fulfilled the most painful duty an officer can carry out." He said he had conducted to the Cherche-Midi prison an officer accused of the terrible crime of treason. Then, without naming Dreyfus, he added, "I beg of you not to speak of it for some time. The wretched man is the father of a family."

Q. In the last letter you received from your husband before his death he used these words: "What a misfortune to have made myself out such a scoundrel!"

A. No, he did not say that. He said, "You know well in what interest I acted."

Q. What did he mean by those words?

A. He did not refer to any particular individual. He meant the interest of the country. "For thirty-three years I have never done anything except in the interest of my country," he told me. You know his sentiments, gentlemen. If he committed a forgery because of the intrigues of Colonel Picquart, it was to save the Army, which had been compromised by the ill will of its enemies.

166

Q. Have you ever heard that Colonel Henry was indebted to Esterhazy?

A. Oh! Never!

AUGUST 17, 1899

GENERAL GAUDÉRIQUE ROGET [CHIEF OF MILITARY SECRETARIAT UNDER CAVAIGNAC], CROSS-EXAMINATION

Q. How did you know that 600,000 francs was offered to Esterhazy if he would confess to being the author of the *bordereau?*

A. I heard it from the Court of Inquiry which tried Esterhazy, and from Esterhazy himself.

Q. Ah! It was Esterhazy who said it. Just so . . . Why was his residence searched?

A. Esterhazy at one time had the document containing the words, "Cette canaille de D——," and might therefore have had others.

Q. You admit, then, that he might have had other interesting documents?

A. When one is conducting an inquiry one must expect anything and search accordingly.

Q. Assuming that Esterhazy was the agent of the Dreyfus family and that he had agreed to take the prisoner's guilt upon himself, as suggested, how do you explain the fact that Esterhazy on several occasions wrote statements calculated to compromise the case of Dreyfus?

A. With Esterhazy one cannot ever be sure of anything. He is such an extraordinary fellow. I do not know what he may be doing today, nor what he will do tomorrow.

AUGUST 18, 1899

COLONEL GEORGES PICQUART

PICQUART. . . . I knew Esterhazy was anxious to enter the War Office, and I did not regard his desire favorably. I communicated my impressions to my chiefs, who approved all my steps, and Esterhazy's application was rejected.

His insistence, however, only increased my uneasiness about him, and I resolved to obtain a specimen of his handwriting. I was immediately struck with the similarity of his handwriting and that of the *bordereau,* and I promptly had the letters of Esterhazy which were in my possession photographed and showed the photographs to Major Du Paty de Clam and M. Bertillon between August 25th and September 5th . . .

"You realize," Du Paty de Clam maintained, "that the *bordereau* is the joint work of Alfred and Mathieu Dreyfus."

M. Bertillon said: "That is the writing of the *bordereau.*"

M. Bertillon tried to discover where I had obtained the handwriting, but the only information I imparted was that it was current and recent handwriting.

M. Bertillon then suggested that it was a tracing, and ended by saying that if it was current handwriting it could only have emanated from someone whom the Jews had been training for a year to imitate the writing of the *bordereau*.

At M. Bertillon's request I left the photographs with him. When he returned them he said he adhered to his opinion and earnestly asked to see the original. When I saw beyond a doubt that the handwriting of the *bordereau* was Esterhazy's, and realizing that the documents mentioned in it might have been supplied by Esterhazy, that the words "I am going to the maneuvers" could perfectly well apply to Esterhazy, and that Esterhazy had secretaries available to copy a document as voluminous as the firing manual, I resolved to consult the secret dossier to see what part of the treachery might be ascribed to Dreyfus, and to satisfy myself whether the dossier contained anything implicating Esterhazy.

I frankly admit that I was stupefied on reading the secret dossier. I expected to find matters of gravity in it, and found instead only a document which might as easily apply to Esterhazy as to Dreyfus, an unimportant document mentioning d'Avignon, and a document which it seemed absurd to attribute to Dreyfus—the "Cette canaille de D——" document . . .

It was then evening. I had stayed late at the office in order to examine the documents thoroughly. I thought it over during the night, and the next day I explained the whole situation to General de Boisdeffre. I took to his office the secret dossier, the facsimile of the *bordereau*, the *petit bleu*, and the principal papers connected with my investigation of Esterhazy.

. . . I still see General de Boisdeffre, as he examined the secret dossier with me, stop before he reached the end and tell me to go into the country, give an account of the affair to General Gonse, and ask his advice.

When I told General Gonse everything that had happened, he remarked: "So a mistake has been made?" . . .

When I asked General Gonse for permission to continue the investigation, emphasizing the danger of allowing the Dreyfus family to proceed with their investigation alone, the General replied that it was impossible, in his opinion and in the opinions of General de Boisdeffre and the Ministry of War, to reopen the affair. . . .

AUGUST 24, 1899
GENERAL MERCIER, RECALLED—CROSS-EXAMINATION

Q. Do you acknowledge having given orders to communicate the secret dossier to the members of the court-martial?

A. Yes. I gave the oral order to make that communication . . .

Q. . . . I ask General Mercier whether at the beginning of the affair, at the time of the conversation with M. Hanotaux, there were any charges against the accused besides that of writing the *bordereau*?

A. There were others—those of the secret dossier.

Q. Why did you not tell M. Hanotaux that there were others?

A. It is a political question; I shall not answer.

Q. . . . I now ask him why, if there were other charges against Dreyfus, he proceeded to the dictation test, and whether he acknowledges having said that if that test succeeded he would immediately have Dreyfus arrested.

A. It was an additional charge.

Q. Then the charges were insufficient?

A. I repeat that it was an additional charge, that is all.

Q. Did you say that he would not be arrested if the dictation test were not successful?

A. It is possible.

Q. Then you were not yet convinced of his guilt?

A. No, there were only presumptions.

Q. Why did you, according to your own words, precipitate Dreyfus' arrest?

A. Since there was treason, it was important to arrest the offender.

Q. Why not keep him under close surveillance?

A. That was impossible under the circumstances . . .

Q. Do you know of violent articles against you in the *Libre Parole*?

A. I am used to press attacks, and paid no attention to those of the *Libre Parole* . . .

Q. The day after the Dreyfus arrest was the *Libre Parole* full of deference to you?

A. I paid no attention to it.

Q. Are you aware of the indiscretion committed by the General Staff in revealing Dreyfus' arrest to the press?

A. I know of an indiscretion committed by the press, but not by the General Staff.

Q. Who committed it?

A. It might have come from the Dreyfus family or from the experts . . .

Q. . . . I ask General Mercier why, in 1894, the date of April or May 1894 was given to the *bordereau*.

A. I do not know why.

Q. Has not General Mercier followed this affair?

A. Not at all.

Q. Then General Mercier's conviction as to Captain Dreyfus' guilt has been formed only since the condemnation?

A. I do not understand.

Q. I repeat: if General Mercier has not followed this affair, how has he been able to form his conviction?

A. I was not called upon to interfere personally. I was kept informed about the trial, and since the beginning of the campaign I have prepared myself to answer the questions that might be put to me, but in 1894 I did not go into the details.

Q. Was not the *bordereau* a question of detail?

A. I did not have to occupy myself personally with it . . .

169

Q. Will you say what you think of Esterhazy?

A. I think and I know nothing of him and his trial.

Q. What? You know nothing of the trial in 1898?

A. I am not bound to explain or give an account of my ideas to anybody.

Q. I do not ask what you think of it, but whether you are cognizant of it.

A. I am responsible to nobody for my thoughts.

Q. But you are cognizant of it?

A. The Esterhazy trial? Not at all.

Q. You did not watch its developments? . . .

A. As a witness I abide by the decision of the court-martial, which acquitted Esterhazy.

PRESIDENT. General Mercier is not required to have an opinion on it.

AUGUST 26, 1899
ALPHONSE BERTILLON, CROSS-EXAMINATION

Q. In 1894 you contended that the *bordereau* had been signed "A. Dreyfus"?

A. I said it was possible that it had been signed. Having remarked the word "*adresse*," I voiced the hypothesis that it might be "A. Dreyfus" . . .

Q. How do you reconcile your present opinion that the *bordereau* is in an assumed handwriting with your original opinion to the contrary?

A. My first opinion was given on October 13, before the condemnation.

Q. You do not seem to understand me. In 1894 you stated that once the theory that the *bordereau* was a forged document was put aside, it had to be attributed to Dreyfus; but now you say that since it is a forged document, it may be attributed to him.

A. I had then only had the *bordereau* for ten hours, and could not form a definitive opinion, whereas a complete examination has shown me that the document was forged.

Q. At that time the fact that the document might be forged appeared to you capable of exculpating the prisoner?

A. I did not consider whether my opinion was favorable or otherwise. I was then convinced of his guilt, and I was afraid that my demonstration might be misunderstood and lead to an acquittal. I did not, however, alter my thesis.

SEPTEMBER 2, 1899
GENERAL CHARLES GONSE [ASSISTANT CHIEF OF THE GENERAL STAFF], CROSS-EXAMINATION

Q. Was not the *bordereau*, in conjunction with the *petit bleu*, the basis of Picquart's belief in Esterhazy's guilt?

A. I said to Picquart: "Don't let us trouble about handwritings at present."

Q. How could the Dreyfus and Esterhazy cases be separated, when both were based on a common document?

A. Because at that time Dreyfus had been convicted, and the *bordereau* was ascribed to him.

Q. Was it not possible to reconsider an error?

A. There was nothing to prove to me that the *bordereau* was written by Esterhazy.

Q. Will General Gonse repeat what Colonel Picquart told him about M. Bertillon's conclusions?

A. I was not acquainted with M. Bertillon's conclusions, but Picquart seems to exaggerate them.

COLONEL PICQUART, RECALLED

Q. What did you tell General Gonse concerning M. Bertillon's conclusions?

A. In a brief letter which I wrote to General Gonse in regard to M. Bertillon's conclusions, I only referred to part of his observations, and the best proof that I did not wish to exaggerate them is the fact that I asked General Gonse to order a supplemental inquiry.

THE SCOPES TRIAL

(1925)

William Jennings Bryan was probably propelled farther by his tongue than any major figure in America's history. A relatively obscure ex-Congressman when he mounted the platform of the 1896 Democratic National Convention, he catapulted himself into the presidential nomination with his "Cross of Gold" speech, articulating in resounding rhetoric the economic discontent of the West. Failing of election to the presidency three times running, he swung the 1912 nomination to Woodrow Wilson with a fervid denunciation of the "interests" supporting front-runner Champ Clark, to whom his own delegation was pledged. He thereby earned a reluctant appointment from Wilson to the post of Secretary of State, which he filled with thundering ineptitude.

Notwithstanding the pall of failure which overcast his career, he long remained a fixture in the affections of millions of farmers and humble workers throughout the country, particularly those in the hinterland whom time had more or less passed by, as time had passed him by.

Fortune smiled on him as a lecturer at Chautauqua assemblies and on the Redpath circuit, where his golden voice poured forth endless homilies on his favorite subject, the Bible. He had the common touch; as H. L. Mencken acidly remarked, "He liked people who sweated freely, and were not debauched by the refinements of the toilet." As late as 1924 the magic of the Bryan name was strong enough to win his brother a nomination for the vice presidency, although the Great Commoner himself had walked out on the convention when some of the delegates had the asperity to interrupt his utterances with cries of "Louder!"

The golden voice was gone by then; the brain had never been much to start with. But Bryan's instinctive rapport with the homely folks whose distrust of higher learning and "city people" had been imbibed with their mothers' milk remained undiminished, even by the wealth which had come to him through speculation in Florida real estate. No longer great, he was still the Commoner.

Each week thousands of admirers trooped to his Sunday outdoor Bible classes in Miami. His talks on Darwin's theory of the descent of man evoked gales of merriment from his slack-jawed audiences, as he dared the scientists to "come down out of the trees and meet the issue!" The issue, as he saw it, was not much different from that which brought Galileo to his knees: should a mere hypothesis be allowed to be taught as fact, seducing the people into the arms of agnostics and atheists?

Whether such a danger of subversion existed in the years of "normalcy" is debatable; but there is no belying the peculiar attraction that the controversy over Darwinism held for the American public in the early Twenties. It was grist for the Sunday supplements: "IS MAN A HIGH-TYPE BABOON?" Hearst's Arthur Brisbane sent a thrill of self-esteem up the spinal cords of the readers of his syndicated column when he opined that an intelligent heavyweight could thrash a roomful of gorillas in hand-to-hand combat. "Evolution"—generally pronounced with a long e—entered the common parlance for good.

The conflict, however superficial its manifestations, reached deep into the roots of America's consciousness. The impact of World War I had shaken many people loose from the absolutes by which they and their parents had been reared. Prosperity brought with it reverence for the science which was making life more comfortable and more exciting through invention, and more meaningful through the systems of self-discovery offered by Freud, Jung, and their fellows. Most of the country's churchgoers were sufficiently sold on the inherent divinity of man—especially the white man—to be unconcerned with his distant relationship with a blob of primordial slime. The old-time religion had been whittled down, in most parts of the country, to a matter of good deeds, substantial contributions to worthy causes, and regular attendance at Rotary.

But a sizable minority of the membership of the Protestant churches, particularly in the South, was profoundly committed to the literal word of the Scriptures and held out indomitably against the modern viewpoint or the lack of one. Beginning in 1921, they split openly with the "liberals," and Fundamentalism took definite shape as a movement to be reckoned with.

Indeed, it was powerful enough to force the introduction of bills in every state legislature below the Mason and Dixon line—and in several above it—condemning the teaching of evolution in the public schools. As Fundamentalism's spokesman, Bryan roamed the country addressing these bodies and urging the passage of the laws; Oklahoma, Florida, and Tennessee obliged him. It is said that in Tennessee the pundits succumbed to a classic fallacy—both houses of the Legislature passed the bill in the belief that Governor Austin Peay would spare them embarrassment by vetoing it, but he lacked the nerve to do so.

Bridging the gap between popular sentiment and his own misgivings, the Governor said at the time:

Probably the law will never be applied. It may not be sufficiently definite to admit of any specific application or enforcement. Nobody believes that it is going to be an active statute.

Much of the motivation behind this anti-intellectualism can be attributed to a desperate need for a spiritual anchor on the part of people who were adrift among the troublesome abstractions of modern Protestantism. In large measure, their revival meetings and their Sunday churchgoing represented the principal purgatives and analgesics of lives tight with boredom and racked by a sense of sin. Then, too, they may have been reluctant to accept a scientific concept which would erase some of the Biblical distinctions between them and their Negro neighbors. As Henry Steele Commager has written, "Fundamentalism and lynching seemed to go together."

Tennessee's was the only statute which made it a penal offense to expound the theory of evolution in the schools. A poorly drafted law, it forbade teachers in any school supported wholly or partly by state funds "to teach any theory that denies the story of the Divine creation of man as taught in the Bible, and to teach instead that man has descended from a lower order of animals." Under its peculiar language, it would have been perfectly lawful to spread as gospel the belief widely held among primitive people that the first man had been brought forth by a union between sky and water. But the denial of the Bible through the teaching of Darwinian theory was denominated a misdemeanor, punishable by a fine of up to five hundred dollars for each offense.

As soon as it got wind of the passage of the law, the American Civil Liberties Union announced that it would undertake the defense of any teacher who violated one of the anti-evolution statutes. On the dare of a transplanted New Yorker living in Dayton, Tennessee, John T. Scopes, twenty-four-year-old science teacher at Rhea County High School, agreed to play guinea pig in a test of the law's constitutionality. On April 24, 1925, he "polluted" some of the young minds in his care with the theory of evolution (using a state-approved textbook which had not yet been withdrawn from circulation). He was indicted one month later.

Bryan rose to the occasion like an old fire-horse, offering his services to the prosecution. To assist in the defense, the Civil Liberties Union dispatched its long-time spark plug, Arthur Garfield Hays, accompanied by two volunteers, the witty and distinguished Dudley Field Malone,

one of the leading lights of the New York Bar, and the venerable Clarence Darrow, both serving without fee at the instance of their old friend, the acidulous editor and columnist H. L. Mencken, who accompanied them to Dayton.

By the time the trial opened in the Eighteenth Tennessee Circuit Court on July 10, 1925, Dayton was sweltering in the limelight. More than a hundred members of the press were feeding stories to the entire Western world over dozens of telegraph wires especially installed for the purpose. Every revivalist within a hundred miles of the town (pop. 1800) had pitched his tent on its outskirts, to flail with the consciousness of guilt the simple folk who had flocked by the thousands from the surrounding mountains into its quiet streets, as to a county fair. Lemonade, sandwiches, and hot dogs were hawked at every corner, along with religious tracts and biology texts. Signs adorned the trees on the spacious lawn around the large red-brick courthouse: "Be Sure Your Sins Will Find You Out," and "Read Your Bible Daily For One Week," and, pithiest of all, "Be a Sweet Angel."

Once more the Peerless Leader, Bryan, his hair thinned out and graying, his white shirt cut low at the neck and his sleeves rolled up, sailed through the milling crowd, graciously acknowledging the cheers of his supporters, with his son William, Jr., in tow. Darrow, nearing seventy, his face seamed with the scars of a thousand legal battles, surprised the local gentry by his homespun appearance and his rough-and-ready demeanor: he might have been one of them, and it made them uneasy. It is disturbing to find the Devil in one's own image.

With these two protagonists dominating the scene, young Scopes faded into the background. The trial itself would be strangely transformed by the propensities of its principal combatants. Darrow, agnostic to the core, a courtroom brawler without peer, was determined to launch a frontal assault upon the faith of the Fundamentalists, instead of merely challenging their right to silence scientific opinion. Bryan committed the same error in reverse. He felt impelled to attack Darwinism as blasphemous and allowed himself to be led down the blind alley of sustaining the literal truth of Genesis, when he might easily have rested on the simple proposition that the state, which pays the piper for public education, can forbid the playing of godless music.

The two men would be addressing themselves, not so much to the jury as to their separate private worlds—Darrow to the readers of the big-city newspapers, with whose deadlines his verbal bombshells were closely synchronized, and Bryan to the faceless millions who had thrice thronged the polls to register their devotion to his image. As a result, the case was conducted at two levels, curiously intermingling the bom-

bast and showmanship of platform oratory with the desperate solemnity
of a medieval heresy trial. From one moment to the next, the atmosphere would change, as on a summer night, and the cautious affability
for which opposing lawyers are notorious would melt under the heat of
their rival brands of extremism. From start to finish, the trial would become an ideological Donnybrook unparalleled in American jurisprudence, uproariously funny and intensely violent by turns.

The courtroom was jammed to suffocation with 900 people, most of
them standees. Judge John T. Raulston, a popular local attorney of no
special competence, ascended the bench late. He had been delayed by
some photographers, he explained; and as the trial wore on, it developed
that the judge had a penchant amounting almost to an obsession for
having his picture taken. At the drop of a flashlight bulb he would halt
the proceedings to oblige a press cameraman who had thought of a fresh
grouping or a new pose. The fact that he would soon be running for
re-election may have had something to do with the judge's weakness;
or it may be that he was overwhelmed by the fame which had overtaken
a poor boy from the mountain town of Gizzard's Cove, Tennessee
(also known as Fiery Gizzard, a name Mencken fastened on gleefully
in recognition of the properties of the local brew).

The judge, flanked by two policemen waving huge fans to keep the
air and the flies circulating, ordered the day's proceedings opened with
prayer—a practice he followed throughout the trial. Some of the clergymen who performed the office proved somewhat argumentative in their
choice of texts, and Darrow protested that turning the courtroom into
a church was prejudicial to Scopes' rights. But Raulston stood firm,
leaving the old warrior glowering amid clucks of disapproval from the
scandalized Tennesseans.

At the opening session on Friday, it developed that the original indictment was probably defective, and Raulston summoned the grand
jury to formulate a new indictment on the spot. This hasty move to
ward off an anticlimax was illegal, but no objection was raised; neither
side wanted the case to turn on a technicality.

Names of the trial jury panel were drawn from a hat by a little girl
perched on a corner of the bench. Those who were chosen for the much-
coveted seats included eleven churchgoers, at least one of whom was
illiterate; but the defense lawyers had challenged none of them, since
they had abandoned hope of obtaining an acquittal except on a point
of law.

Court then recessed for the weekend. That Sunday, Bryan held forth
to a crowd of thousands on the courthouse lawn. "The God I worship
is the God of the ignorant," he cried, "as well as the God of learned

men." Such extraordinary behavior on the part of counsel in a pending case can only be explained on the ground that he had not been inside a courtroom for almost thirty years, but the defense made no point of it when the case was resumed the following day.

John R. Neal, former law professor at the University of Tennessee, who had taken up Scopes' defense on the day of his arrest, led off the Monday session with a challenge to the constitutionality of the law. Technically this move to dismiss the indictment was the heart of the defendant's case. Neal claimed that the statute violated that section of the State Constitution which read:

Knowledge, learning, and virtue being essential to the preservation of republican institutions . . . it shall be the duty of the general assembly in all future periods of this government to cherish literature and science.

He also invoked the freedom of worship clause of the U. S. Constitution, asserting that the law under which Scopes was indicted gave unlawful preference to the doctrines of Fundamentalism. Hays and Malone followed up with arguments against the vagueness of the statute and its illegality under the state's police power.

Darrow then took the floor. In shirt sleeves, his thumbs looped under his purple suspenders, he roared:

Here, we find today, as brazen and as bold an attempt to destroy learning as was ever made in the Middle Ages, and the only difference is we have not provided that they shall be burned at the stake. But there is time for that, Your Honor. We have to approach these things gradually. . . .

If today you can take a thing like evolution and make it a crime to teach it in the public schools, tomorrow you can make it a crime to teach it in the private schools, and the next year you can make it a crime to teach it from the hustings or in the church. At the next session you may ban books and the newspapers. Soon you may set Catholic against Protestant and Protestant against Protestant, and try to foist your own religion on the minds of men. If you can do one, you can do the other. . . . After a while, Your Honor, it is the setting of man against man and creed against creed until, with flying banners and beating drums, we are marching backward to the glorious ages of the sixteenth century when bigots lighted fagots to burn the men who dared to bring any intelligence and enlightenment and culture to the human mind.

The Fundamentalist position he boiled down to its *reductio ad absurdum:* "It is a crime to know more than I know." And he scored repeatedly with citations of conflict between the literal reading of the Scriptures and accepted scientific fact: even the Fundamentalists no longer believed that the earth was the center of the solar system! He taunted his audience with the contradictions in the Bible itself and with the increasingly broad areas of disagreement over its meaning among those who worshiped by it.

In proscribing the teaching of evolution, he said, the Legislature might nevertheless have been within its rights if it had merely fixed the course of study in the schools; it could not, however, penalize teaching something in the public schools that could be freely taught elsewhere.

General Ben B. McKenzie, the leading prosecuting attorney, later told Darrow outside of court that his speech was the greatest he had ever heard. But Darrow's eloquence and the cogent arguments of his associates did not register with Judge Raulston; he denied the motion to quash the indictment. Scopes entered his formal plea of not guilty. Darrow, bitter and despondent, left to Malone the opening statement to the jury.

Malone, who had been Undersecretary of State under Bryan, twitted his old chief by quoting from an article Bryan had written praising Jefferson for taking the view that "to attempt to compel people to accept a religious doctrine by act of law was to make not Christians but hypocrites." Suavely and cogently he argued that the prosecution was not entitled to a verdict of guilty unless it proved, not only that Scopes had taught the theory of evolution, but that he had also denied the Biblical version of creation. Knowing that evidence on the first point was readily at hand, Malone laid all his emphasis on the conflict within the Scriptures themselves over the origin of man, and on the compatibility of scientific knowledge with Christianity.

As its opening move, the prosecution asked the Court to take judicial notice of the Book of Genesis, as it appears in the King James version. Hays objected: No particular Bible had been specified in the statute, he argued, and there was no proof that the King James version was the one and only Bible. He referred to the history of the Holy Book, outlining the diverse sources from which it had been drawn, the changes it had undergone in successive translations, and the conflict among major religious groups as to the authorized version; but Raulston overruled his objection. King James' version, no longer accepted by Protestants in the land he had once ruled, had come into its own in Tennessee.

Seven youngsters from Scopes' class were led through an account of his teachings. Man, he had told them, had evolved with other mammals from a one-celled organism; but man differed from other mammals in that he had reasoning power, and they did not.

"There's doubt about that," remarked Darrow drily, "but we'll let it pass if he said it."

The prosecution rested its case.

179

The next day the defense sought to introduce testimony and written statements of a host of American scientists, educators, and theologians, in order to establish the soundness of the Darwinian theory and its congruity with Scripture. Before ruling on the admissibility of such evidence, Raulston allowed Dr. Maynard M. Metcalf, of Johns Hopkins University, to testify. His learned exposition of the theory of evolution left some of the local folk eying each other with fresh curiosity. From Bryan, it evoked his only extended speech of the trial. Ignoring the obvious objections to this type of opinion evidence, he mounted the stump. His rambling argument was a curious mixture of piety and crudity:

There is no place for the miracle in this train of evolution, and the Old Testament and the New are filled with miracles. . . . And that means they eliminate the Virgin Birth. . . . They believe . . . that He was born of Joseph or some other co-respondent. . . .

He had great sport with a diagram illustrating the order of species in the biology text used by Scopes (and approved by the state textbook commission). Commenting on the number of species in each class, he quipped:

I see they are round numbers, and I don't think all of these animals breed in round numbers, and so I think it must be a generalization of them. (*Laughter*)

Man, he noted with alarm, had been grouped in the book "with lions and tigers and everything that is bad." And turning to Darwin, he commented mockingly that his theory had man descending "not even from American monkeys, but from Old World monkeys." (*Laughter*)

Taking demagogic advantage of Darrow's recent connection with the Loeb-Leopold murder case, he likened Darwin to Nietzsche, whose teachings had, according to Bryan, inspired the senseless killing of young Bobby Frank. Darrow was noticeably stung by this reference, claiming that it was designed to poison the mind of the Court:

JUDGE RAULSTON. It is argument before the Court; I do not see how. . . .
DARROW. If it does not prejudice you, it does not do any good.
JUDGE RAULSTON. No, sir, it does not prejudice me.
DARROW. Then it does not do any good.
JUDGE RAULSTON. Well. . . .

And amid loud laughter and applause, Bryan took another tack.

Malone took up the cudgels for the admission of the testimony. He compared the proposed exclusion of scientific proof to the burning of the library at Alexandria by the Mohammedans, who refused to spare that great storehouse of knowledge because the Koran contained all the truth. The prosecution's position, he said, was compounded of the same ignorance and superstition

which made it possible for theologians . . . who proposed to prove the theory of Copernicus . . . to bring old Galileo to trial . . . for what purpose? For the purpose of proving a literal construction of the Bible against truth which is revealed.

Turning to face the prosecution table, Malone cried:

The truth does not need Mr. Bryan. The truth is imperishable, eternal, and immortal, and needs no human agency to support it. . . . We feel we stand with fundamental freedom in America. We are not afraid. Where is the fear?

His speech won applause equal to Bryan's. Even the crusty Mencken, rendered suddenly diffident by his admiration for his old friend's brilliance, could barely conceal his emotion. "Dudley," he said in a choked voice as he pounded the New Yorker's back, "that was the *loudest* speech I ever heard!"

But it had fallen on deaf ears. Judge Raulston ruled out the evidence at the opening of court the next day.

Darrow was furious. When Judge Raulston showed reluctance to grant an adjournment to enable the defense to formulate a new offer of proof, the old Chicago warrior could no longer contain himself. He did not understand why "every suggestion of the prosecution should meet with an endless extension of time, and a bare suggestion of anything that is perfectly competent on our part should be immediately overruled."

RAULSTON. I hope you do not mean to reflect upon the Court?
DARROW. Well, Your Honor has the right to hope.

This quip almost led to Darrow's imprisonment for contempt. His tongue-in-cheek apology won him the forgiveness of the Court, along with a brief homily on the pertinent teachings of the Bible. They shook hands, and the spectators applauded.

Following this incident Judge Raulston expressed his concern that the courtroom floor was in danger of collapsing under its unaccustomed burden of crowds, and transferred the proceedings to the lawn outside. With the audience increased to five thousand or more, the undaunted Darrow resumed the assault. He objected to a sign facing the jury, exhorting them with the words, "READ YOUR BIBLE," tacked to the courthouse wall. Darrow later wrote, "Everyone paused in awe at the audacity, but it was not a rainy day so I was taking no chance with lightning." But General McKenzie and Judge Raulston agreed that it should be removed. Hays then read into the record the affidavits of eight scientists, to establish for the purposes of appeal the nature of the testimony Raulston had refused to hear.

The trial seemed all but over; even Mencken had gone home. But on the afternoon of the seventh day of the trial, when Raulston asked the defense whether it had any more evidence to offer, Hays sprang a surprise: he asked that Bryan be called to the stand as an expert on the Bible. Logically this was the only remaining avenue of defense. Barred from establishing the truth of evolutionary teaching, the attack had to be turned on the quintessence of Fundamentalism—its literal interpretation of the Good Book. If doubt could be cast on its account of man's creation, the statute might be held to be void for uncertainty.

Bryan leaped at the challenge, stipulating only that he should have the chance to interrogate Darrow, Malone, and Hays. Judge Raulston went along with the agreement of counsel on both sides, although he was doubtful about the propriety of the proceedings.

What had happened was obvious. All of the participants were by now caught up in the public significance of the occasion; every move on both sides had been front-page news for weeks. Bryan could not resign his job as defender of the faith, even if his common sense had asserted itself. The Peerless Leader, the laurels of three great campaigns gone brittle and brown, rode forth to his last battle a Don Quixote on the spavined steed of Fundamentalism.

As a man and a legend, Bryan was destroyed by his testimony that day. Seated at a table, fanning himself incessantly, he started confidently enough; but as Darrow bore in waspishly with questions, each of them sharpened to sword's point by his years of skepticism, the Great Commoner's eye dulled, his replies became halting and puerile, and he stalled for time with increasing frequency. The laughter and prolonged applause which greeted his early sallies were succeeded by a glum and confused silence on the part of the thousands who had foregathered to see him conquer the windmill. Attorneys for the prosecution, sensing the growing disaster, did their best time and again to bring the proceedings to a halt; but the punch-drunk warrior threw their towel out of the ring and staggered back into the fray, his punches landing on empty air.

As the day wore on, even veteran newsmen cringed at the pitiable sight of the old crusader, lashed to his credo by a web of his own fashioning, as Darrow ruthlessly denuded him of all dignity, of all stature, of the reputation that had survived the years of defeat and frustration. When the session ended, Bryan left the courthouse almost alone, his face bloodless and his head bowed, his mouth filled with the taste of shame.

The next day Judge Raulston mercifully refused to let the torment continue and expunged Bryan's testimony from the record as immaterial. Darrow, reading the morning papers, knew that any further effort on his part would be anticlimactic. He asked the jury for a verdict of guilty, in order to lay the groundwork for an appeal on constitutional grounds. Bryan was thereby robbed of the opportunity to make his closing speech for the prosecution, on which he had labored for weeks.

Although under Tennessee law the fine in such cases was required to be fixed by the jury, Judge Raulston mistakenly suggested that if Scopes were found guilty, he would fix the fine at the $100 minimum, and that if the jury did not feel disposed to fix a larger fine, its verdict could be silent on the subject. The jury took the hint, leaving the amount of the fine to the Court. This error furnished the ground for reversal by the appellate court, although it went out of its way to declare the statute constitutional. But since Scopes had by that time left the school system, it suggested that he not be retried: "We see nothing to be gained by prolonging the life of this bizarre case."

The case had, indeed, shortened the life of one of its protagonists. Six days after his ordeal on the stand, Bryan died in his sleep. Even so, he had lived just a little too long; the Peerless Leader of 1896 had been publicly transformed by the swift strokes of Darrow's scalpel into a raucous-voiced simpleton.

Bryan's creed had also reached its high-water mark, although the hard-core Fundamentalists carried his banner high for another few years. In 1927, the Association of Southern Methodists recorded its opposition to "legislation that would interfere with the proper teaching of science"; and the anti-evolution laws which had been enacted became dead letters. The abasement of Galileo had been avenged.

The record of Bryan's examination, read thirty-five years later, has something of the air of a none-too-elevating high-school debate. In part, this jejune quality was inevitable, since Darrow was attacking and Bryan defending the indefensible. In part, it arose from the uncompromising fiber of the contestants, neither of whom had the slightest desire to suggest that religion and science might be harmonized.

The world has moved forward since then, in some measure because of the absurdity of this performance of Bryan's, which so starkly illuminated the moral and intellectual sterility of twentieth-century Sadduceeism.

The transcript of Bryan's testimony, slightly abridged, follows:

MR. DARROW. Do you claim that everything in the Bible should be literally interpreted?

MR. BRYAN. I believe everything in the Bible should be accepted as it is given there. Some of the Bible is given illustratively. For instance: "Ye are the salt of the earth." I would not insist that man was actually salt, or that he had flesh of salt, but it is used in the sense of salt as saving God's people.

MR. DARROW. But when you read that Jonah swallowed the whale —or that the whale swallowed Jonah, excuse me, please—how do you literally interpret that?

MR. BRYAN. When I read that a big fish swallowed Jonah—it does not say whale.

MR. DARROW. Doesn't it? Are you sure?

MR. BRYAN. That is my recollection of it, a big fish; and I believe it; and I believe in a God who can make a whale and can make a man, and make both do what He pleases.

MR. DARROW. Mr. Bryan, doesn't the New Testament say whale?

MR. BRYAN. I am not sure. My impression is that it says fish; but it does not make so much difference; I merely called to your attention that where it says fish, it does not say whale.

MR. DARROW. But in the New Testament it says whale, doesn't it?

MR. BRYAN. That may be true; I remember in my own mind what I read about it.

MR. DARROW. Now, you say, the big fish swallowed Jonah, and he remained—how long?—three days, and then he spewed him up on the land. You believe that the big fish was made to swallow Jonah?

MR. BRYAN. I am not prepared to say that. The Bible merely says it was done.

MR. DARROW. You don't know whether it was the ordinary mine-run of fish or made for that purpose?

MR. BRYAN. You may guess; you evolutionists guess.

MR. DARROW. But when we do guess, we have the sense to guess right.

MR. BRYAN. But you do not do it often.

MR. DARROW. You are not prepared to say whether that fish was made specially to swallow a man or not?

MR. BRYAN. The Bible doesn't say so. I am not prepared to say.

MR. DARROW. But you believe He made them—that He made such a fish and that it was big enough to swallow Jonah?

MR. BRYAN. Yes, sir. Let me add: One miracle is just as easy to believe as another.

MR. DARROW. It is for me.

MR. BRYAN. It is for me.

MR. DARROW. Just as hard?

MR. BRYAN. It is hard to believe for you, but easy for me. A miracle is a thing performed beyond what man can perform. When you get beyond what man can do you get within the realm of miracles; and it is just as easy to believe the miracle of Jonah as any other miracle in the Bible.

MR. DARROW. Perfectly easy to believe that Jonah swallowed the whale?

MR. BRYAN. If the Bible said so. The Bible doesn't make as extreme statements as evolutionists do.

MR. DARROW. The Bible says Joshua commanded the sun to stand still for the purpose of lengthening the day, doesn't it, and you believe it?

MR. BRYAN. I do.

MR. DARROW. Do you believe at that time the entire sun went around the earth?

MR. BRYAN. No, I believe that the earth goes around the sun.

MR. DARROW. Do you believe that the men who wrote it thought that the day could be lengthened or that the sun could be stopped?

MR. BRYAN. I don't know what they thought.

MR. DARROW. You don't know?

MR. BRYAN. I think they wrote the fact without expressing their own thoughts.

MR. DARROW. Have you an opinion as to whether or not the men who wrote that thought. . . .

MR. STEWART [ATTORNEY GENERAL A. T. STEWART]. I want to object, Your Honor. It has gone beyond the pale of any issue that could possibly be injected into this lawsuit, except by imagination. I do not think the defendant has a right to conduct the examination any further, and I ask Your Honor to exclude it.

JUDGE RAULSTON. I will hear Mr. Bryan.

MR. BRYAN. It seems to me it would be too exacting to confine the defense to the facts. If they are not allowed to get away from the facts, what have they to deal with?

JUDGE RAULSTON. Mr. Bryan is willing to be examined. Go ahead.

MR. DARROW. Have you an opinion as to whether—whoever wrote the book, I believe it was Joshua—the Book of Joshua—thought the sun went around the earth or not?

MR. BRYAN. I believe that he was inspired.

MR. DARROW. Can you answer my question?

MR. BRYAN. When you let me finish the statement.

MR. DARROW. It is a simple question, but finish it.

MR. BRYAN. You cannot measure the length of my answer by the length of your question. (Laughter)

MR. DARROW. No, except that the answer will be longer. (Laughter)

MR. BRYAN. I believe that the Bible is inspired, and an inspired author, whether one who wrote as he was directed to write understood the things he was writing about, I don't know.

MR. DARROW. Do you think whoever inspired it believed that the sun went around the earth?

MR. BRYAN. I believe it was inspired by the Almighty, and He may have used language that could be understood at that time.

MR. DARROW. So . . . it might have been subject to construction, might it not?

MR. BRYAN. It might have been used in language that could be understood then.

MR. DARROW. That means it is subject to construction?

MR. BRYAN. That is your construction. I am answering your questions.

MR. DARROW. Is that correct?

MR. BRYAN. That is my answer to it.

MR. DARROW. Can you answer?

MR. BRYAN. I might say Isaiah spoke of God sitting upon the circle of the earth.

MR. DARROW. I am not talking about Isaiah.

JUDGE RAULSTON. Let him illustrate, if he wants to, Mr. Darrow. It is your opinion that passage was subject to construction?

MR. BRYAN. Well, I think anybody can put his own construction upon it, but I do not mean necessarily that it is a correct construction. I have answered the question.

MR. DARROW. Don't you believe that in order to lengthen the day it would have been construed that the earth stood still?

MR. BRYAN. I would not attempt to say what would have been necessary, but I know this, that I can take a glass of water that would fall to the ground without the strength of my hand, and to the extent of the glass of water I can overcome the law of gravitation and lift it up; whereas, without my hand, it would fall to the ground. If my puny hand can overcome the law of gravitation, the most universally understood, to that extent, I would not set power to the hand of Almighty God that made the universe.

MR. DARROW. I read that years ago. Can you answer my question directly? If the day was lengthened by stopping, either the earth or the sun, it must have been the earth?

MR. BRYAN. Well, I should say so: yes, but it was language that was understood at that time, and we now know that the sun stood still, as it was, with the earth.

MR. DARROW. We know also the sun does stand still?

MR. BRYAN. Well, it is relatively so, as Mr. Einstein would say.

MR. DARROW. I ask you, if it does stand still?

MR. BRYAN. You know as well as I know.

MR. DARROW. Better. You have no doubt about it?

MR. BRYAN. No, no.

MR. DARROW. And the earth moves around it?

MR. BRYAN. Yes. But I think there is nothing improper if you will protect the Lord against your criticism.

MR. DARROW. I suppose he needs it?

186

MR. BRYAN. He was using language at that time that the people understood.

MR. DARROW. And that you call "interpretative"?

MR. BRYAN. No, sir, I would not call it interpretation.

MR. DARROW. I say, you would call it interpretation at this time, to say it meant something else?

MR. BRYAN. You may use your own language to describe what I have to say, and I will use mine in answering.

MR. DARROW. Now, Mr. Bryan, have you ever pondered what would have happened to the earth if it had stood still?

MR. BRYAN. No.

MR. DARROW. You have not?

MR. BRYAN. No. The God I believe in could have taken care of that, Darrow.

MR. DARROW. I see. Have you ever pondered what would naturally happen to the earth if it stood still suddenly?

MR. BRYAN. No.

MR. DARROW. Don't you know it would have been converted into a molten mass of matter?

MR. BRYAN. You testify to that when you get on the stand. I will give you a chance.

MR. DARROW. Don't you believe it?

MR. BRYAN. I would want to hear expert testimony on that.

MR. DARROW. You have never investigated that subject?

MR. BRYAN. I don't think I ever had the question asked.

MR. DARROW. Or ever thought of it?

MR. BRYAN. I have been too busy on things that I thought were of more importance than that.

MR. DARROW. You believe the story of the flood to be a literal interpretation? When was that flood?

MR. BRYAN. I wouldn't attempt to fix the date. The date is fixed, as suggested this morning.

MR. DARROW. About 4004 B.C.?

MR. BRYAN. That has been the estimate. I would not say it is accurate.

MR. DARROW. That estimate is printed in the Bible.

MR. BRYAN. Everybody knows that—at least I think most of the people know—that was the estimate given.

MR. DARROW. But what do you think that the Bible itself says? Don't you know how it is arrived at?

MR. BRYAN. I never made a calculation.

MR. DARROW. A calculation from what?

MR. BRYAN. I could not say.

MR. DARROW. From the generations of man?

MR. BRYAN. I would not want to say that.

Mr. Stewart again objected to the examination of Mr. Bryan.

MR. DARROW. He is a hostile witness.

JUDGE RAULSTON. I am going to let Mr. Bryan control.

MR. BRYAN. I want him to have all the latitude that he wants, for I am going to have some latitude when he gets through.

MR. DARROW. You can have latitude and longitude. (*Laughter*)

JUDGE RAULSTON. Order.

MR. STEWART. The witness is entitled to be examined as to the legal evidence of it. We were supposed to go into the origin of this case, and we have nearly lost the day, Your Honor.

MR. MCKENZIE. I object to it.

MR. STEWART. Your Honor, he is perfectly able to take care of this, but we are attaining no evidence. This is not competent evidence.

MR. BRYAN. These gentlemen have not had much chance. They did not come here to try this case. They came here to try revealed religion. I am here to defend it, and they can ask me any questions they please.

JUDGE RAULSTON. All right. (*Applause*)

MR. DARROW. Great applause from the bleachers!

MR. BRYAN. From those whom you call "yokels."

MR. DARROW. I have never called them yokels.

MR. BRYAN. That is, the ignorance of Tennessee, the bigotry.

MR. DARROW. You mean who are applauding?

MR. BRYAN. Those are the people whom you insult.

MR. DARROW. You insult every man of science and learning in the world because he does not believe in your fool religion.

JUDGE RAULSTON. I will not stand for that.

MR. DARROW. For what he is doing?

JUDGE RAULSTON. I am talking to both of you.

MR. STEWART. This has gone beyond the pale of a lawsuit, Your Honor. I have a public duty to perform, under my oath, and I ask the Court to stop it. Mr. Darrow is making an effort to insult the gentleman on the witness stand, and I ask that this be stopped.

JUDGE RAULSTON. To stop it now would not be just to Mr. Bryan.

MR. DARROW. How long ago was the flood, Mr. Bryan?

MR. BRYAN. Let me see Usher's calculation about it.

MR. DARROW. Surely. (*Handing a Bible to the witness*)

MR. BRYAN. I think this does not give it.

MR. DARROW. It gives an account of Noah. Where is the one in evidence? I am quite certain it is there.

MR. BRYAN. Oh, I would put the estimate where it is, because I have no reason to vary it. But I would have to look at it to give you the exact date.

MR. DARROW. I would, too. Do you remember what book the account is in?

MR. BRYAN. Genesis. It is given here as 2348 years B.C.

MR. DARROW. Well, 2348 years B.C.

MR. DARROW. You believe that all the living things that were not contained in the Ark were destroyed?

MR. BRYAN. I think the fish may have lived.

MR. DARROW. Outside of the fish?

MR. BRYAN. I cannot say.

MR. DARROW. You cannot say?

MR. BRYAN. No. I accept that just as it is. I have no proof to the contrary.

MR. DARROW. I am asking you whether you believe it.

MR. BRYAN. I do. I accept that as the Bible gives it, and I have never found any reason for denying, disputing, or rejecting it.

MR. DARROW. Let me make it definite—2348 years?

MR. BRYAN. I didn't say that. That is the time given (*indicating a Bible*), but I don't pretend to say that is exact.

MR. DARROW. You never figured it out, those generations, yourself?

MR. BRYAN. No, sir; not myself.

MR. DARROW. But the Bible you have offered in evidence says 2340 something, so that 4200 years ago there was not a living thing on the earth, excepting the people on the Ark and the animals on the Ark, and the fishes?

MR. BRYAN. There had been living things before that.

MR. DARROW. I mean at that time?

MR. BRYAN. After that.

MR. DARROW. Don't you know there are any number of civilizations that are traced back to more than 5000 years?

MR. BRYAN. I know we have people who trace things back according to the number of ciphers they have. But I am not satisfied they are accurate.

MR. DARROW. You are not satisfied there is any civilization that can be traced back 5000 years?

MR. BRYAN. I would not want to say there is, because I have no evidence of it that is satisfactory.

MR. DARROW. Would you say there is not?

MR. BRYAN. Well, so far as I know, but when 306,000,000 years is their opinion, as to how long ago life came here, I want them to be nearer, to come nearer together, before they demand of me to give up my belief in the Bible.

MR. DARROW. Do you say that you do not believe that there were any civilizations on this earth that reach back beyond 5000 years?

MR. BRYAN. I am not satisfied by any evidence that I have seen—

MR. DARROW. I didn't ask what you are satisfied with. I asked if you believed it.

MR. BRYAN. Will you let me answer it?

JUDGE RAULSTON. Go right on.

MR. BRYAN. I am satisfied by no evidence that I have found that would justify me in accepting the opinions of these men against what I believe to be the inspired Word of God.

189

MR. DARROW. And you believe every nation, every organization of men, every animal in the world, outside of the fishes . . .

MR. BRYAN. The fish, I want you to understand, is merely a matter of humor.

MR. DARROW. I believe the Bible says so. Take the fishes in?

MR. BRYAN. Let us get together and look over this.

MR. DARROW. Probably we would better. We will after we get through. You believe that all the various human races on the earth have come into being in the last 4000 years or 4200 years, whatever it is?

MR. BRYAN. No. It would be more than that.

MR. DARROW. 1237?

MR. BRYAN. Some time after creation, before the flood.

MR. DARROW. 1925 added to it?

MR. BRYAN. The flood is 2300 and something, and creation, according to the estimate there, is further back than that.

MR. DARROW. Then you don't understand me. If we don't get together on it, look at the Book. This is the year of grace 1925, isn't it? Let us put down 1925. Have you got a pencil? (*One of the defense attorneys hands Mr. Darrow a pencil.*)

MR. BRYAN. Add to that 4004?

MR. DARROW. Yes. . . .

MR. BRYAN. That is the date (*referring to the Bible*) given here on the first page, according to Bishop Usher, which I say I accept only because I have no reason to doubt it.

MR. DARROW. 1925 plus 4004 is 5929 years. Now, then, what do you subtract from that?

MR. BRYAN. That is the beginning.

MR. DARROW. I was talking about the flood.

MR. BRYAN. 2348 on that, we said.

MR. DARROW. Less than that?

MR. BRYAN. No; subtract that from 4000. It would be about 1700 years.

MR. DARROW. That is the same thing?

MR. BRYAN. No; subtracted, it is twenty-three hundred and something before the beginning of the Christian Era, about 1700 years after the creation.

MR. DARROW. If I add 2300 years, that is the beginning of the Christian Era?

MR. BRYAN. Yes, sir.

MR. DARROW. If I add 1925 to that I will get it, won't I?

MR. BRYAN. Yes, sir.

MR. DARROW. That makes 4262 years?

MR. BRYAN. According to the Bible there was a civilization before that, destroyed by the flood.

MR. DARROW. Let me make this definite. You believe that every civilization on the earth and every living thing, except possibly the fishes, that came out of the Ark, were wiped out by the flood?

MR. BRYAN. At that time.

MR. DARROW. At that time; and then, whatever human beings, including all the tribes that inhabited the world, and have inhabited the world, and who run their pedigree straight back, and all the animals have come on to the earth since the flood?

MR. BRYAN. Yes.

MR. DARROW. Within 4200 years? Do you know a scientific man on the earth that believes any such thing?

MR. BRYAN. I cannot say, but I know some scientific men who dispute entirely the antiquity of man as testified to by other scientific men.

MR. DARROW. Oh, that does not answer the question. Do you know of a single scientific man on the face of the earth that believes any such thing as you stated, about the antiquity of man?

MR. BRYAN. I don't think I have even asked one the direct question.

MR. DARROW. Quite important, isn't it?

MR. BRYAN. Well, I don't know as it is.

MR. DARROW. It might not be?

MR. BRYAN. If I had nothing else to do except speculate on what our remote ancestors were and what our remote descendants have been, but I have been more interested in Christians going on right now, to make it much more important than speculations on either the past or the future.

MR. DARROW. You do know that there are thousands of people who profess to be Christians who believe the earth is much more ancient and that the human race is much more ancient?

MR. BRYAN. I think there may be.

MR. DARROW. And you never have investigated to find out how long man has been on the earth?

MR. BRYAN. I have never found it necessary. I do not expect to find out all those things. I do not expect to find out about races.

MR. DARROW. I didn't ask you that. Now, I ask you, if you know, if it was interesting enough, or important enough for you, to try to find out, how old these ancient civilizations are?

MR. BRYAN. No. I have not made a study of it.

MR. DARROW. Don't you know that the ancient civilizations of China are six or seven thousand years old, at the very least?

MR. BRYAN. No, but they would not run back beyond the creation, according to the Bible, six thousand years.

MR. DARROW. You don't know how old they are, is that right?

MR. BRYAN. I don't know how old they are, but possibly you do. (Laughter)

MR. DARROW. Have you any idea how old the Egyptian civilization is?

MR. BRYAN. No.

MR. DARROW. Do you know of any record in the world, outside of the story of the Bible, which conforms to any statement that it is 4300 years ago or thereabouts, that all life was wiped off the face of the earth?

MR. BRYAN. I think they have found records.

MR. DARROW. Do you know of any?

MR. BRYAN. Records reciting the flood, but I am not an authority on the subject.

MR. DARROW. Mr. Bryan, don't you know that there are many old religions that describe the flood?

MR. BRYAN. No, I don't know. The Christian religion has satisfied me and I have never felt it necessary to look up some competing religion . . .

MR. DARROW. Do you know how old the Confucian religion is?

MR. BRYAN. I can't give you the exact date of it.

MR. DARROW. Do you know how old the religion of Zoroaster is?

MR. BRYAN. No, sir.

MR. DARROW. Do you know they are both more ancient than the Christian religion?

MR. BRYAN. I am not willing to take the opinion of people who are trying to find excuses for rejecting the Christian religion.

MR. DARROW. Are you familiar with James Clark's book on the ten great religions?

MR. BRYAN. No.

MR. DARROW. You don't know how old they are, all these other religions?

MR. BRYAN. I wouldn't attempt to speak correctly, but I think it is much more important to know the difference between them than to know the age.

MR. DARROW. Not for the purpose of this inquiry, Mr. Bryan. Do you know about how many people there were on this earth at the beginning of the Christian Era?

MR. BRYAN. No. I don't think I ever saw a census on that subject.

MR. DARROW. Do you know about how many people there were on this earth 3000 years ago?

MR. BRYAN. No.

MR. DARROW. Did you ever try to find out?

MR. BRYAN. When you display my ignorance, could you not give me the facts so I would not be ignorant any longer?

MR. DARROW. Can you tell me how many people there were when Christ was born? You know, some of us might get the facts and still be ignorant.

MR. BRYAN. Will you please give me that? You ought not to ask me a question that you don't know the answer to.

MR. DARROW. I can make an estimate.

MR. BRYAN. What is your estimate?

MR. DARROW. Wait until you get to me. Do you know anything

about how many people there were in Egypt 3500 years ago, or how many people there were in China 5000 years ago?

MR. BRYAN. No.

MR. DARROW. Have you ever tried to find out?

MR. BRYAN. No, sir; you are the first man I ever heard of who was interested in it. (*Laughter*)

MR. DARROW. Mr. Bryan, am I the first man you ever heard of who has been interested in the age of human societies and primitive man?

MR. BRYAN. You are the first man I ever heard speak of the number of people at these different periods.

MR. DARROW. Where have you lived all your life?

MR. BRYAN. Not near you. (*Laughter and applause*)

MR. DARROW. Nor near anybody of learning?

MR. BRYAN. Oh, don't assume you know it all.

MR. DARROW. Do you know there are thousands of books in your libraries on all those subjects I have been asking you about?

MR. BRYAN. I couldn't say, but I will take your word for it.

MR. DARROW. Did you ever read a book on primitive man? Like Tyler's *Primitive Culture*, or Boas, or any of the great authorities?

MR. BRYAN. I don't think I ever read the ones you have mentioned.

MR. DARROW. Have you read any?

MR. BRYAN. Well, I have read a little from time to time. But I didn't pursue it, because I didn't know I was to be called as a witness.

MR. DARROW. You have never in all your life made any attempt to find out about the other peoples of the earth—how old their civilizations are, how long they have existed on the earth, have you?

MR. BRYAN. No, sir, I have been so well satisfied with the Christian religion that I have spent no time trying to find argument against it.

MR. DARROW. Were you afraid you might find some?

MR. BRYAN. No, sir; I am not afraid that you will show me any.

MR. DARROW. You remember that man who said—I am not quoting literally—that one could not be content though he rose from the dead. You suppose you could be content?

MR. BRYAN. Well, will you give me the rest of it, Mr. Darrow?

MR. DARROW. No.

MR. BRYAN. Why not?

MR. DARROW. I am not interested.

MR. BRYAN. Why scrap the Bible? "They have Moses and the Prophets."

MR. DARROW. Who has?

MR. BRYAN. That is the rest of the quotation you didn't finish.

MR. DARROW. And you think if they have Moses and the Prophets, they don't need to find out anything else?

MR. BRYAN. That was the answer that was made there.

MR. DARROW. You don't care how old the earth is, how old man is, and how long the animals have been here?

193

MR. BRYAN. I am not so much interested in that.

MR. DARROW. You have never made any investigation to find out?

MR. BRYAN. No, sir, I never have.

MR. DARROW. You have heard of the Tower of Babel, haven't you?

MR. BRYAN. Yes, sir.

MR. DARROW. That tower was built under the ambition that they could build a tower up to heaven, wasn't it? And God saw what they were at and, to prevent their getting into heaven, He confused their tongues?

MR. BRYAN. Something like that. I wouldn't say to prevent their getting into heaven, He confused their tongues . . . I don't think it is necessary to believe that God was afraid they would get to heaven.

MR. DARROW. I mean that way?

MR. BRYAN. I think it was a rebuke to them.

MR. DARROW. A rebuke to them trying to go that way?

MR. BRYAN. To build that tower for that purpose.

MR. DARROW. Take that short cut?

MR. BRYAN. That is your language, not mine.

MR. DARROW. Now, when was that?

MR. BRYAN. Give us the Bible.

MR. DARROW. Yes, we will have strict authority on it—scientific authority.

MR. BRYAN. That was about 100 years before the flood, Mr. Darrow, according to this chronology. It was 2247—the date on one page is 2218 and on the other 2247, and it is described in here. . . .

MR. DARROW. That is the year 2247?

MR. BRYAN. 2218 B.C. is at the top of one page, and 2247 at the other, and there is nothing in here to indicate the change.

MR. DARROW. Well, make it 2218 then?

MR. BRYAN. All right, about.

MR. DARROW. Then you add 1500 to that.

MR. BRYAN. No, 1925.

MR. DARROW. Add 1925 to that—that would be 4143 years ago. Up to 4143 years ago, every human being on earth spoke the same language?

MR. BRYAN. Yes, sir, I think that is the inference that could be drawn from that.

MR. DARROW. All the different languages of the earth, dating from the Tower of Babel—is that right? Do you know how many languages are spoken on the face of the earth?

MR. BRYAN. No. I know the Bible has been translated into 500, and no other book has been translated into anything like that many.

MR. DARROW. That is interesting, if true. Do you know all the languages there are?

MR. BRYAN. No, sir, I can't tell you. There may be many dialects besides that and some languages, but those are all the principal languages.

MR. DARROW. There are a great many that are not principal languages?

MR. BRYAN. Yes, sir.

MR. DARROW. You haven't any idea how many there are?

MR. BRYAN. No, sir.

MR. DARROW. And you say that all those languages of all the sons of men have come on the earth not over 4150 years ago?

MR. BRYAN. I have seen no evidence that would lead me to put it any farther back than that.

MR. DARROW. That is your belief anyway? That was due to the confusion of tongues at the Tower of Babel? Did you ever study philology at all?

MR. BRYAN. No, I have never made a study of it—not in the sense in which you speak of it.

MR. DARROW. You have used language all your life?

MR. BRYAN. Well, hardly all my life—ever since I was about a year old.

MR. DARROW. And good language, too; and you never took any pains to find anything about the origin of languages?

MR. BRYAN. I never studied it as a science.

MR. DARROW. Have you ever by any chance read Max Mueller?

MR. BRYAN. No.

MR. DARROW. The great German philologist?

MR. BRYAN. No.

MR. DARROW. Or any book on that subject?

MR. BRYAN. I don't remember to have read a book on that subject, especially, but I have read extracts, of course, and articles on philology.

MR. DARROW. Mr. Bryan, could you tell me how old the earth is?

MR. BRYAN. No, sir, I couldn't.

MR. DARROW. Could you come anywhere near it?

MR. BRYAN. I wouldn't attempt to. I could possibly come as near as the scientists do, but I had rather be more accurate before I give a guess.

MR. DARROW. You don't think much of scientists, do you?

MR. BRYAN. Yes, I do, sir . . .

MR. DARROW. When was the last Glacial Age?

MR. BRYAN. I wouldn't attempt to tell you that.

MR. DARROW. Have you any idea?

MR. BRYAN. I wouldn't want to fix it without looking at some of the figures.

MR. DARROW. Do you know whether it was more than 6000 years ago?

MR. BRYAN. I think it was more than 6000 years.

MR. DARROW. Have you any idea how old the earth is?

MR. BRYAN. No.

MR. DARROW. The Book you have introduced in evidence tells you, doesn't it? (*Referring to the Bible*)

MR. BRYAN. I don't think it does, Mr. Darrow.

MR. DARROW. Let's see whether it does. Is this the one?

MR. BRYAN. That is the one, I think.

MR. DARROW. It says B.C. 4004.

MR. BRYAN. That is Bishop Usher's calculation.

MR. DARROW. Do you think the earth was made in six days?

MR. BRYAN. Not six days of twenty-four hours.

MR. DARROW. Doesn't it say so?

MR. BRYAN. No, sir.

MR. STEWART. What is the purpose of this examination?

MR. BRYAN. The purpose is to cast ridicule on everybody who believes in the Bible, and I am perfectly willing that the world shall know that these gentlemen have no other purpose than ridiculing every person who believes in the Bible.

MR. DARROW. Mr. Bryan, do you believe that the first woman was Eve?

MR. BRYAN. Yes.

MR. DARROW. Do you believe she was literally made out of Adam's rib?

MR. BRYAN. I do.

MR. DARROW. Did you ever discover where Cain got his wife?

MR. BRYAN. No, sir; I leave the agnostics to hunt for her.

MR. DARROW. You have never found out?

MR. BRYAN. I have never tried to find.

MR. DARROW. You have never tried to find?

MR. BRYAN. No.

MR. DARROW. The Bible says he got one, doesn't it? Were there other people on the earth at that time?

MR. BRYAN. I cannot say.

MR. DARROW. You cannot say? Did that never enter into your consideration?

MR. BRYAN. Never bothered me.

MR. DARROW. There were no others recorded, but Cain got a wife. That is what the Bible says. Where she came from, you don't know. All right. Does the statement, "The morning and the evening were the first day" and "The morning and the evening were the second day" mean anything to you?

MR. BRYAN. I do not think it means necessarily a twenty-four-hour day.

MR. DARROW. You do not?

MR. BRYAN. No.

MR. DARROW. What do you consider it to be?

MR. BRYAN. I have not attempted to explain it. If you will take the second chapter—let me have the Book. (*Examining the Bible*) The fourth verse of the second chapter (Genesis) says: "These are the generations of the heavens and of the earth, when they were created, in the day that the Lord God made the earth and the heavens." The word "day" there in the very next chapter is used to describe a period. I do not see that there is necessity for construing the words, "the evening and the morning," as meaning necessarily a twenty-four-hour day: "in the day when the Lord made the heaven and the earth."

MR. DARROW. Then when the Bible said, for instance, "And God called the firmament heaven. And the evening and the morning were the second day"—that does not necessarily mean twenty-four hours?

MR. BRYAN. I do not think it necessarily does.

MR. DARROW. Do you think it does or does not?

MR. BRYAN. I know a great many think so.

MR. DARROW. What do you think?

MR. BRYAN. I do not think it does.

MR. DARROW. You think these were not literal days?

MR. BRYAN. I do not think they were twenty-four-hour days.

MR. DARROW. What do you think about it?

MR. BRYAN. That is my opinion—I do not know that my opinion is better on that subject than those who think it does.

MR. DARROW. Do you not think that?

MR. BRYAN. No. But I think it would be just as easy for the kind of God we believe in to make the earth in six days as in six years or in six million years or in six hundred million years. I do not think it important whether we believe one or the other.

MR. DARROW. Do you think those were literal days?

MR. BRYAN. My impression is they were periods, but I would not attempt to argue as against anybody who wanted to believe in literal days.

MR. DARROW. Have you any idea of the length of the periods?

MR. BRYAN. No, I don't.

MR. DARROW. Do you think the sun was made on the fourth day?

MR. BRYAN. Yes.

MR. DARROW. And they had evening and morning without the sun?

MR. BRYAN. I am simply saying it is a period.

MR. DARROW. They had evening and morning for four periods without the sun, do you think?

MR. BRYAN. I believe in creation, as there told, and if I am not able to explain it, I will accept it.

MR. DARROW. Then you can explain it to suit yourself. And they had the evening and the morning before that time for three days or three periods. All right, that settles it. Now, if you call those periods, they may have been a very long time?

MR. BRYAN. They might have been.

MR. DARROW. The creation might have been going on for a very long time?

MR. BRYAN. It might have continued for millions of years.

MR. DARROW. Yes, all right. Do you believe the story of the temptation of Eve by the serpent?

MR. BRYAN. I do.

197

MR. DARROW. Do you believe that after Eve ate the apple, or gave it to Adam—whichever way it was—God cursed Eve, and at that time decreed that all womankind thenceforth and forever should suffer the pains of childbirth in the reproduction of the earth?

MR. BRYAN. I believe what it says, and I believe the fact as fully.

MR. DARROW. That is what it says, doesn't it?

MR. BRYAN. Yes.

MR. DARROW. And for that reason, every woman born of woman, who has to carry on the race—the reason they have childbirth pains is because Eve tempted Adam in the Garden of Eden?

MR. BRYAN. I will believe just what the Bible says. I ask to put that in the language of the Bible, for I prefer that to your language. Read the Bible, and I will answer.

MR. DARROW. All right, I will do that: "And I will put enmity between thee and the woman." That is referring to the serpent?

MR. BRYAN. The serpent.

MR. DARROW (*reading*). "And between thy seed and her seed; it shall bruise thy head, and thou shalt bruise his heel. Unto the woman He said, I will greatly multiply thy sorrow and thy conception; in sorrow thou shalt bring forth children; and thy desire shall be to thy husband, and he shall rule over thee." That is right, is it?

MR. BRYAN. I accept it as it is.

MR. DARROW. Do you believe that was because Eve tempted Adam to eat the fruit?

MR. BRYAN. I believe it was just what the Bible said.

MR. DARROW. And you believe that is the reason that God made the serpent to go on his belly after he tempted Eve?

MR. BRYAN. I believe the Bible as it is, and I do not permit you to put your language in the place of the language of the Almighty. You read that Bible and ask me questions, and I will answer them. I will not answer your questions in your language.

MR. DARROW. I will read it to you from the Bible: "And the Lord God said unto the serpent, Because thou hast done this, thou art cursed above all cattle, and above every beast of the field; upon thy belly shalt thou go, and dust shalt thou eat all the days of thy life." Do you think that is why the serpent is compelled to crawl upon its belly?

MR. BRYAN. I believe that.

MR. DARROW. Have you any idea how the snake went before that time?

MR. BRYAN. No, sir.

MR. DARROW. Do you know whether he walked on his tail or not?

MR. BRYAN. No, sir. I have no way to know. (*Laughter*)

MR. DARROW. Now, you refer to the bow that was put in the heaven after the flood, the rainbow. Do you believe in that?

MR. BRYAN. Read it.

MR. DARROW. All right, Mr. Bryan, I will read it for you.

MR. BRYAN. Your Honor, I think I can shorten this testimony. The only purpose Mr. Darrow has is to slur at the Bible, but I will answer his questions. I will answer it all at once, and I have no objection in the world. I want the world to know that this man, who does not believe in a God, is trying to use a court in Tennessee . . .

MR. DARROW. I object to that.

MR. BRYAN. To slur at it, and, while it will require time, I am willing to take it.

MR. DARROW. I object to your statement. I am examining you on your fool ideas that no intelligent Christian on earth believes.

THE REICHSTAG
FIRE TRIAL

(1933)

The man who kicks a pebble on a mountaintop and starts a landslide is seldom remembered, even in the annals of the buried town in the valley below. Marinus van der Lubbe was such a man. By one witless act he touched off a disaster that almost engulfed the entire world. He would be completely forgotten today but for the cloud of mystery overhanging his deed and the thunderous propaganda battle which it precipitated, culminating in that extraordinary passage-at-arms known as the Reichstag Fire trial.

A few minutes after nine o'clock on Monday evening, February 27, 1933, van der Lubbe kicked in the long, narrow panes of a large window south of the main entrance to the darkened Reichstag and dropped through the opening to the carpeted floor of the huge delegates' restaurant. Armed with only four commercial household firelighters, he set about to turn the fifty-year-old rococo structure into a flaming cauldron.

The sound of breaking glass was heard by Hans Floeter, a theological student on his way home after a day at the State Library. Looking up, he saw a shadow at the window, and seconds later, a light. Floeter ran to the nearest corner and summoned the sentry on duty, Police Sergeant Karl Buwert. Buwert rushed up the block-long automobile ramp spanning the front of the building to have a look, and Floeter—the classic bystander who hates to get involved—went home to supper.

Reaching a spot on the ramp below the smashed window, Buwert saw the fitful glare of fire inside the restaurant. At that moment he was joined by a young man in a dark coat and a Bavarian typesetter who had also spotted the intruder.

Buwert drew his gun. The intruder's movements could now be followed by the flickering light shifting from window to window in the basement below the burning restaurant. When it reached the fifth window to the right of the portal, Buwert fired. The light went out.

The young man in the dark coat was sent off to fetch assistance from the nearby Brandenburg Gate police station, and Buwert instructed some passers-by to turn in a fire alarm.

Police Lieutenant Emil Lateit, a veteran on the Berlin force, arrived with two patrolmen a jump ahead of the first fire engines. The flames in the restaurant now looked about ten feet high, and Lateit dutifully jotted down in his notebook: "9:17 . . . increasingly need help." This turned out to be an understatement. Everything that could possibly go wrong went wrong. All the doors were locked. The porter didn't have the keys and had trouble locating the house inspectors. Lateit was unfamiliar with the fire-alarm system, with the result that only two companies, consisting of eight trucks, responded to the first three alarms. The fire trucks couldn't get up the ramp because it was coated with ice, and the fire had to be fought with hand extinguishers. Later, hoses were run from the inner courtyards of the building.

Fire ladders were swung up to the front windows by about 9:22, and the firemen attacked the blaze in the restaurant with their portable equipment. Lateit had just got through the front door with a couple of policemen and assorted Reichstag employees. Hurrying past the burning hangings in the entrance foyer, they headed for the huge glass-domed assembly hall. When Lateit entered the chamber it was about 9:21, and he later testified that an "organ of flames" was shooting up from the drapes behind the President's table. Some of the furnishings on the three-tiered platform also seemed to be afire. But the seats allotted to the deputies and government officials were apparently intact. There is some question whether Lateit reported this state of affairs to the firemen, hard at work in the restaurant and in the hallways, where small fires dotted the carpeting. He admitted that at 9:25 he returned to the Brandenburg Gate station to make his report and summon reinforcements.

Moments after Lateit left the assembly hall, the house inspector and a policeman looked into the room. The drapes on the platform were still burning fiercely, and by now they could see tiny tongues of flame licking the delegates' front-row benches and other furniture in the room. But they were bent on tracking down the arsonist and continued on their way.

Some time during the next eight minutes, the assembly hall exploded in a massive burst of flame, and its glass dome was shattered by the detonation of accumulated gases within the chamber. This volcanic climax was reached before 9:31, when a "tenth-stage alarm," calling for forty fire engines, was received at the central station.

This sequence of events would assume transcendant importance in the ensuing worldwide debate that culminated in the Reichstag Fire trial. The sudden enveloping burst of flame which gutted the assembly hall was cited by each of the contending forces as conclusive proof that the other had set off the conflagration for political purposes. Only van der Lubbe, to whom nobody listened, obstinately maintained that he had done the job alone.

He was certainly alone when, a few minutes short of 9:30, two of the search party cornered him in a large anteroom northeast of the session chamber, darting about in a half-crouch, his naked torso bathed in perspiration and heaving frantically from his exertions. Veiled by the overhanging smoke, his bullet head matted with tousled hair, his long arms almost touching the floor, he must have looked in the fitful light like a creature risen from the primordial slime. He offered no resistance. In his trousers his captors found a purse, a handkerchief, a pocketknife and a pass to a local relief shelter identifying him as a Dutchman. He was wrapped in a blanket and carried off to a police station.

Sensational as his act had been, van der Lubbe would not hold the center of the stage more than a day or two. For he had stumbled, like a village oaf, into a drama of momentous significance to Germany and to the world, with a cast of characters whose names were already household words in the ministries of great nations.

Just four weeks earlier, the eighty-five-year-old President of the German Republic, Field Marshal Paul von Hindenburg, had held his nose long enough to elevate a comic-looking Austrian ex-corporal named Adolf Hitler to the chancellorship of the Reich. Conceived in perfidy, the new government was destined to eke out its precarious life in a web of intrigue. What remained to be seen at the time it came to power was who would turn out to be the spider and who the fly.

A monumental game of double-cross would decide this issue, and the principal players were old hands at the game. On the face of it, the suave, treacherous Franz von Papen seemed to hold the strongest hand, although he had scant popular backing and had been disowned by his own Catholic Center Party. Thanks to a potent combination of natural charm and aristocratic background, Papen had old Hindenburg in his pocket. During his six-month tenure as Chancellor in the latter part of 1932, he had earned the gratitude and confidence of the Rhineland industrialists and Prussian Junkers, and his strength in these quarters had not diminished in the two months that had elapsed since he had been dropped from the post. But Parliamentary support to enable him to resume the Chancellorship was lacking, and he was forced to settle for a seat behind the throne.

From this point of vantage, Papen expected to pull the strings of a puppet Hitler. Hindenburg had the same idea; he gave Papen the rarely filled post of Vice Chancellor, with the right to be present at all conferences between Hitler and the President. In addition, Papen landed the key position of Premier of the Prussian State, thereby retaining his grip on two thirds of Germany's territory and wealth. The roster of eleven ministers was dominated by five of his henchmen against two for Hitler and four for Papen's uneasy ally, the Nationalist press magnate, Alfred Hugenberg.

Hugenberg had some powerful cards of his own up his sleeve. In the November 1932 election, his Right-wing Nationalists had shown remarkable strength. Their representation in the Reichstag had risen from 37 to 52 seats, while the Nazis had suffered a 2,000,000-vote setback, losing 34 seats. With his 196 National Socialist deputies, and scattered votes from splinter groups, Hitler might hope for majority support in the 584-man Parliament—but only if Hugenberg's bloc stood with him.

This strategic position, and the enormous leverage of the Hugenberg newspaper interests, encouraged the Nationalist leader to hope he could keep Hitler in check. He despised the man, but he despised democracy and communism even more; and although democracy was losing ground steadily in Germany, the Communists had registered an alarming gain in the November election, to bring their total delegates up to the 100 mark.

Hitler had been reluctant to sit down at the table with these two veteran politicians, but figured that he had no choice. He had twice been rejected by Hindenburg when he demanded the chancellorship on the basis of Nazi showings at the polls before their November setback. Unless his luck changed, the last election foretold disaster. His Party was torn by internal dissension; the word "Socialist" in the Party label had been a spur to recruitment, but many Party members were now vociferously demanding that its promise be fulfilled. Funds were short, and there had been some notable defections from the ranks. As a last resort, Hitler had accepted a seat in the game when Papen and Hugenberg made room for him. With only two of his followers in the Cabinet— Wilhelm Frick as Minister of the Interior and Hermann Goering as Minister without Portfolio—he would not be dealing from strength. Goering was also designated Prussian Minister of the Interior, but it was generally assumed that Papen, as his superior in Prussia, would keep him under control.

From Hitler's standpoint the situation called for a finesse. He made his play immediately. Hindenburg bowed to his demand to dissolve the Reichstag, with new elections fixed for March 5. Hugenberg was apprehensive about this move lest increased Nazi strength in the Reichstag should dispense with the decisive weight of his Nationalist votes. But Hitler fobbed him off with a promise to keep the coalition Cabinet intact for at least four years, regardless of the election results.

Hitler held only a few high cards, but he played them to the hilt. All press and radio resources of the state were mobilized in the Nazi cause, with the talented Joseph Goebbels pulling out all the stops—down with the Versailles Treaty, down with communism, down with the international Jewish bankers.

The hardheaded industrialists of Germany, bemused by visions of fantastic profits to be made through large-scale rearmament, rallied to the cause with a war chest of 3,000,000 marks. And although their contributions were ostensibly earmarked for the support of the entire Right-wing coalition, they could not have misinterpreted Goering's candid fund-raising appeal: "The sacrifice requested of you is easier to bear if it is realized that the elections will certainly be the last for the next ten years, probably even for the next hundred years."

The means to bury the remnants of the Weimar Republic were at hand. Hindenburg handed Hitler the pick and shovel for the job in the form of an emergency decree signed on February 4th. By its terms, the police could ban public meetings which threatened national security, and disband any meeting at which government officials were abused. In addition, newspapers could be barred from publication for inciting to civil disobedience or publishing false reports.

With these weapons at their command, the Nazis proceeded to crack down on the opposition. Goering led the assault; as Prussia's Minister of the Interior, he controlled its police force. In short order, he replaced two thirds of its officials with his own men, and commissioned 50,000 Nazi and Nationalist roughnecks "auxiliary police," with orders to use their arms ruthlessly against "the growing excesses of the Left Radicals." Communist meetings were prohibited; Socialist and even Center Party meetings were raided; bloody street fights blossomed on every corner; opposition newspapers were systematically banned, and those which survived ran daily lists of the "enemies of the state" who had died in conflict with the Brownshirts. The sluice gates of terror were opened to full flood.

Papen and Hugenberg were shocked by the forces they had unleashed; their lion cub was behaving like the king of the jungle. Paradoxically, they were becoming increasingly solicitous in their secret hearts about the fate of the Communist Party. At the first meeting of the new coalition Cabinet, Hugenberg had proposed the complete suppression of the Party, which would have strengthened the Rightist coalition without freeing Hitler from his dependence on Nationalist support. But he had not anticipated Hitler's move for a popular election. Now both Hugenberg and Papen feared the elimination of the Communists as a potential counterweight to increased Nazi representation in the new Reichstag.

Hitler, on the other hand, had opposed at the outset the idea of outlawing the Communists. He needed the Red threat as ammunition for his campaign. Moreover, he feared that arbitrary suppression of the Communist Party might outrage the liberal Social Democrats to the point of making common cause with the extreme Left.

An unlikely prospect; but in politics anything can happen, and Hitler was taking no chances. From his viewpoint the election would serve no purpose unless his Party won a true majority in the Reichstag. And if that objective could not be attained at the polls, he had other plans.

The secret hope of the Nazis was confided by Goebbels to his diary on January 31, 1933:

At a conference with the Fuehrer we laid our plans for the fight against the Red terror. For the present, we shall avoid direct countermeasures. The Bolshevik attempt at revolution must first flare up. At the proper moment we shall strike.

All that was needed was a provocation. And as the weeks of campaigning wore on, the Nazi leadership anxiously scanned the political horizon for an incident which could be sold to the public as an "attempt at revolution." A Communist call for a general strike on January 30 gave them a momentary lift, but it turned out to be a tongue-in-cheek maneuver to expose the "decadence" of the Social Democrats to the trade unionists. Communists were becoming increasingly involved in street brawls with the Brownshirts, some of them fatal; but this sort of thing had been going on too long to be regarded by the public as the harbinger of revolt. Early in February, the Reds abandoned their Berlin party headquarters, Karl Liebknecht House, and Goering's police hopefully ransacked it on February 24th; they found nothing. Goering issued lurid press releases trumpeting the seizure of "a vast quantity of treasonable material" in the raid; but proof of the charge was another matter, and it was quickly recognized as another clumsily concocted Red scare.

Finally, one week before election day, the Reichstag went up in flames.

"A sign from heaven!" Hitler's words as he stood in a corridor of the burning Reichstag were at once an affirmation of his mystic faith in his own preordained success, and a sigh of relief that the waiting was over. Goering, first of the Nazi chieftains to reach the scene, had already told him that the conflagration was the work of a Dutch Communist. Hitler ordered the immediate arrest of all Communist Party functionaries.

Lists had been compiled in readiness for this moment. In the next few days, over 4000 Communists, most of them lowly Party workers, were taken into custody. Socialists, pacifists, and even some Nationalists were scooped up in the dragnet. The prisons soon filled to overflowing, and makeshift barbed-wire enclosures were set up to accommodate the surplus. Thus the concentration camp was born.

Meanwhile the German press dutifully developed the theme that the fire had been intended to serve as a "beacon light" for a general Communist insurrection, following precise step-by-step instructions which had been found in the police raid on Karl Liebknecht House. On the morning after the fire, the official press release declared:

According to these instructions, government buildings, castles, museums, and vitally important factories were to be set afire. . . . It is clear that it was intended that today should see the outbreak throughout Germany of a terror directed against well-known individuals, property, and the lives and persons of peaceful citizens. This terror was to signalize the commencement of civil war.

By the evening after the fire, Hitler shoved an emergency decree under Hindenburg's nose for signature. This "defensive measure against Communist acts of violence endangering the state" suspended until further notice all guarantees of civil liberties under the Constitution:

Thus, restrictions on personal liberty, freedom of speech and of the press, and the rights of assembly and association, and violations of the privacy of postal, telegraphic, and telephonic communication, as well as warrants for house-searches, orders for confiscation, and restrictions on property are permissible beyond the limits otherwise prescribed by law.

High treason and arson, formerly punishable by life imprisonment, were made capital offenses. A month later, the increased penalty was made retroactive to crimes committed after January 31, 1933. If all went well, van der Lubbe would soon be headed for the guillotine.

And so would his confederates. Despite van der Lubbe's claim of sole responsibility for the fire, the police had satisfied themselves within a few hours after his arrest that others were involved. A Reichstag cloakroom attendant volunteered the information that Communist Parliamentary leader Ernst Torgler, accompanied by one of his deputies and a secretary, had been the last to leave the building, at about 8:15 P.M. Three Nazis, two of them Reichstag members, reported seeing Torgler deep in conversation with van der Lubbe and another man on the afternoon of the 27th in a committee room frequented by the Communist faction. Learning from the morning papers that he was under suspicion, Torgler promptly surrendered to the police.

About a week later, the offer of a 10,000-mark reward brought information from a waiter in a Berlin restaurant that van der Lubbe had dined there with a group of foreigners on the afternoon of the 27th. By March 9th, the suspects were in custody, having returned to the same restaurant and been arrested on a telephone tip from the waiter. Except for the fact that they were Bulgarians, they fitted the Nazi prescription perfectly: all three were Communists and had previous criminal records, and two carried counterfeit passports under assumed names. One turned out to be really big game—Georgi Dimitrov, member of the executive committee of the Communist International and head of the Balkan Communist Federation, twice sentenced to death *in absentia* by courts in his native land.

But to Hitler and his coterie, this latest catch came as a gratuitous bonus. The prize had already been all but won—at the March 5th elections.

During the crucial week following the fire, every resource of State and Party had been marshaled by the Nazis to capitalize on the fear and hostility aroused by the senseless destruction of Germany's traditional symbol of representative government. Communist mass assemblies were forbidden by law on March 1st. Cowed by the unrestrained thuggery of Brownshirt gangs, the Social Democrats held no meetings and distributed no literature. Throughout Germany anti-Marxist demonstrations were staged nightly, uplifting the hearts and inflaming the minds of the people with the pageantry and ritual at which Goebbels excelled.

Election Day witnessed a record turnout of voters, guaranteeing a larger Reichstag than ever—the number of delegates varied with the size of the ballot. The Nazis polled 17,277,000 votes against 11,737,000 the previous November. Despite the huge increase, the figure represented a disappointing 43 per cent of the total, and Hitler could count on only 288 delegates to the parliament out of 647. The other major parties held their own, except for the Communists, who lost a fifth of their 6,000,000 votes of the previous election—mostly to the Nazis.

On arithmetic alone, Hitler's ploy had failed. But arithmetic was by this time beside the point. For, while the 52 Nationalist delegates would have been needed for majority support of the coalition Cabinet in a full Reichstag, Hitler would never face a full Reichstag again. Those Communist delegates who had not already been imprisoned were in hiding or in flight. Minus their 81 votes, the size of the Reichstag was cut to 566, giving the Nazis just five votes more than a majority. And the margin was made somewhat less squeaky by the assurance that a certain number of Social Democratic delegates would be in custody at all times. The finesse against Hugenberg had been completed.

Hitler proceeded without delay to consolidate his position. He jammed through the Cabinet and the Reichstag an "Enabling Act," giving the Cabinet a free hand for four years. Laws inconsistent with the Constitution could be enacted by an absurdly simple procedure: prepared by the Chancellor and published in the official register, they became effective the following day "unless otherwise specified." Voting as a body, the Social Democrats registered 94 votes against the Act—the death rattle of the Weimar Republic.

Within four months, the Nazi revolution would be full-blown. On April 11, Papen stepped aside as Premier of Prussia, in favor of Goering. On May 2, the Socialist trade unions went under, their property confiscated and their leaders in jail. (Two days later, Stalin reaffirmed the extension of the 1926 treaty of friendship between Germany and Russia.) On May 10, with typically sadistic humor, the Nazis seized all Socialist Party property and funds to satisfy the "claims" of the hapless unions. Two weeks later the Communist Party was formally outlawed, followed in short order by the Social Democrats. Hugenberg retired on June 27, and the next day his Party was dissolved. On July 5, the Center Party released to the press its own obituary. By July 14, Hitler made it official, with a Cabinet decree:

The National Socialist German Workers' Party constitutes the only political party in Germany.

In most of the capitals of Europe, Hitler's triumph aroused mixed feelings. A hasty dip in the turbulent waters of *Mein Kampf* was calculated to raise gooseflesh on the toughest diplomatic hide. For Hitler had made no secret of his intention to scrap the Treaty of Versailles and to restore Germany to an inside track in the armaments race. But now, because Germany was weak and he had to feel his way for a little while, Hitler spoke of peace. And he spoke, incessantly and everlastingly, of Communism.

Presenting Nazism as Germany's only alternative to Communism, Hitler struck warmly responsive chords in the hearts of the conservative leadership of Western Europe. The only fly in the propaganda ointment was the adverse reaction to Hitler's *modus operandi* in influential democratic circles abroad, ranging from uneasy suspicion to flaming indignation. The dismantling of Germany's Constitution, the persecution of liberals and Jews, and the thuggery of Hitler's private army had stirred up a storm of criticism that could not be abated by vague generalizations about the Red menace. Goebbels' new Ministry of Public Enlightenment and Propaganda pinned much of its hope for combatting this wave of hostile sentiment on the outcome of the forthcoming Reichstag Fire trial. A widely publicized judicial condemnation of the worldwide Communist conspiracy for complicity in the crime would furnish concrete justification for Hitler's repressive measures.

But Goebbels overestimated the competence of the public officials who were preparing the case for the prosecution. And he underestimated the redoubtable Willy Muenzenberg.

As Western Propaganda Chief for the Comintern, this squat, bushy-browed, lantern-jawed human dynamo had chalked up a remarkable series of successes in his twenty years in the Communist movement, subtly drawing into the orbit of Sovietism millions of trade unionists, socialists, and intellectuals throughout the world. Long before the term "popular front" was invented, he had mined that rich vein of idealism and humanitarianism which later became a mother lode for the Communist cause. His first major enterprise, the Workers' International Aid, enlisted universal support in 1921 by resort to a sure-fire appeal for famine relief in Russia; later it was channeled into aiding striking workers in other lands. In time, Muenzenberg pyramided this organization into a vast international complex of mass-circulation publications and theatrical and motion picture enterprises, which the Party elite dubbed "the Muenzenberg Trust." Less a theoretician than a tactician, he steered clear of the Party's eternal squabbles over doctrine, preferring to devote his boundless energies and formidable executive abilities to the job of enlisting liberal sentiment and backing for the Party's endeavors. By 1933, he had become the St. Christopher of fellow travelers from middle Europe to Japan, most of whom never suspected his existence.

Marked for arrest on the night of the fire, Muenzenberg had escaped the Nazi dragnet; he reached Paris early in March. Applying his sure-fire formula once again, he promptly established the "World Committee for the Relief of Victims of German Fascism," ostensibly a feeder for charitable endeavors, but actually calculated to become the headwaters of a torrential stream of philippics against the Nazi regime. The Committee letterhead was studded with the names of outstanding intellectuals, only a few of whom, like J. B. S. Haldane and Henri Barbusse, were identifiable as Communists. Most of its work was performed by a small cadre of talented Party members, based in Paris, with the assistance of professional Party workers in other capitals of Europe and America.

The Paris Secretariat set to work promptly to prepare a full-length "documented" study of Nazism in action. *The Brown Book of the Hitler*

Terror and the Burning of the Reichstag, a devastating exposé of bru-
tality and suppression of personal liberty in the Third Reich, prejudged
the issues in the impending trial, with three chapters of sensational "disclosures" about the fire. The book first appeared early in August 1933,
with an introduction by Britain's Lord Marley. Translated into seventeen languages, it found its way—largely under the imprint of non-
Communist publishers—into the hands of millions; camouflaged as a
religious tract, it was smuggled into Germany, and its clandestine circulation there rivaled the best-selling *Mein Kampf.* Its shrewd concoction
of fact, fancy, and deductive reasoning about the origins of the fire soon
received such broad acceptance that the Nazis were forced to spend considerable time at the trial attempting to refute its allegations.

The *Brown Book* charged—and in modified form the charge has
stuck to this day—that the fire originated in the mind of Joseph Goebbels as a Machiavellian propaganda stunt, and that Hermann Goering
executed the plan, with van der Lubbe serving as a willing tool.

The foundation for this accusation had been laid somewhat naively by
the Nazis themselves, scarcely before the embers of the Reichstag fire
had grown cold. The March 1 issue of the *Vossische Zeitung* cited government sources as authority for the statement that:

. . . the other criminals may have been able to escape through the subterranean passages which, in connection with the heating arrangements of
the Reichstag, link the Reichstag building itself with the building occupied
by the President of the Reichstag.

The President of the Reichstag was Hermann Goering. The official
suggestion that an undisclosed number of arsonists had made their get-
away through the residence of the No. 2 man in the Nazi hierarchy was
made to order for the wily Muenzenberg, and in the *Brown Book* the
surmise ripened into an ugly certainty. Not until it was published did
Goering think to point out that the tunnel might just as easily have
been entered from the engine house behind his residence!

The strength of Muenzenberg's position lay in the fact that, except
for the 150-yard tunnel to which the article referred, the Reichstag itself corresponded at the time of the fire to the classic locked room so
dear to the hearts of British writers of murder mysteries. No one but
van der Lubbe had been seen entering the building. Both sides stoutly
maintained that he could not have done the job alone with his pathetic handful of firelighters, and the Nazis gratuitously embellished the
story with reports of torches and incendiary material left lying about by
his supposed cohorts. Before the Bulgarians entered the scene as suspects, Goebbels hoped to make capital of the underground passage by

arguing that its existence was known only to men familiar with the geography of the building, like Torgler and his Communist deputies. But Muenzenberg turned the argument around: Who knew the tunnel better than the Reichstag President, to whose home it led? And how could anyone have escaped through the tunnel without his connivance?

This reconstruction was snapped up by the increasingly anti-Nazi foreign press, which from the outset had been skeptical of the Nazi version of the fire. And as Goebbels played one propaganda ace after another in mounting desperation, Muenzenberg trumped them with ease. To Goebbels' assertion that a Communist deputy had foretold the fire at an election meeting on February 24, Muenzenberg countered neatly with a circumstantial account of a seance held two days later by Erik Jan Hanussen, a clairvoyant close to the Berlin Nazi leadership, at which a vision of the fire had come to him. Hanussen was found murdered on April 7, and Muenzenberg cited this as proof that he knew too much. Goebbels harped on the fact that Torgler had left the Reichstag quite late on the night of the fire, but Muenzenberg got more mileage out of the curious circumstance that neither Hitler, Goering, nor Goebbels had been scheduled to speak that night, although they had been stumping the country indefatigably and the election was only one week away.

But the spearhead of Muenzenberg's attack was the so-called "Oberfohren memorandum." Seizing on some references in the *Manchester Guardian* of April 26 and 27 to a document concerning the origins of the fire, said to be circulating among German Nationalist politicians, Muenzenberg came forward with its "complete text" in the *Brown Book*, attributing its authorship to Dr. Ernst Oberfohren, Nationalist parliamentary leader, who had either been killed or committed suicide early in May.

The genuineness of the memorandum has never been established; many historians today dismiss it as a fabrication. Authentic or not, it was a masterpiece of propaganda. It had everything: a deceased dignitary (foully murdered, as Muenzenberg would have it) in the role of author, internal consistency, sex, and, above all, that exactitude as to names, dates, and places which so often passes as the hallmark of truth, when as a rule it represents precisely the opposite.

As quoted in the *Brown Book*, the Oberfohren memorandum related that Goering commissioned a group of storm troopers, headed by the boss of the Silesian SA,[1] Edmund Heines, to fire the Reichstag, giving them the run of the underground passage from the President's house:

[1] Sturmabteilung: literally, storm detachment. Popularly called "storm troopers" or "Brownshirts."

A general rehearsal had been held the previous day. Van der Lubbe went with them as the fifth or sixth man. When the observation posts in the Reichstag sent word that the air was clear, the incendiaries set to work. The starting of the fire was completed within a few minutes. Then, their work accomplished, they made their way back by the same route as they had come. Van der Lubbe alone remained behind in the Reichstag building.

Embroidering on this theme, the authors of the *Brown Book* named Goebbels as the mastermind of the plot and the Berlin SA Chief, Count Wolf von Helldorf, as the man who had "probably" accompanied van der Lubbe into the presidential palace. The Dutchman had been deliberately left behind to be captured, in order that he might "confess to everything which his employers ask him to confess." Van der Lubbe was portrayed as a defector from the Dutch Communist Party, who had fallen in with the notorious homosexual Ernst Roehm, chief of staff of the SA. Van der Lubbe's "homosexual connections with National Socialist leaders and his material dependence on them," so the story went, made him the perfect cat's-paw for the job.

It all hung together rather precariously, but before enough time had passed for sober analysis, Muenzenberg fed the press a fresh sensation.

With the aid of his right-hand man, Otto Katz, he threw together a "Committee of Inquiry into the Origins of the Reichstag Fire." The Committee numbered among its members such internationally renowned lawyers as Arthur Garfield Hays, of Scopes trial fame; Moro Giafferi, leader of the French Bar; D. N. Pritt, K.C., of England; Francesco Nitti, former Italian Prime Minister; and Wilhelm Huber, president of the Swiss National Council. The climax of this maneuver came in the form of a "countertrial" in London in September 1933. These mock judicial proceedings consumed five days of hearings before a "Commission" of prominent attorneys, in which every foreseeable aspect of the forthcoming trial in Leipzig was explored, with the Oberfohren memorandum supplying the dominant motif of the testimony of some thirty political refugees and journalists. The world press reported its sessions in detail, and with great relish.

On September 20th the Commission's findings were announced by Pritt to a huge audience in Caxton Hall. The thirty-page summation exonerated all of the accused but van der Lubbe. It concluded that the Dutchman could not have worked alone and found it "highly probable that the incendiaries made use of the subterranean passage." Since the Nazis benefited enormously from the fire, the report stated, "grave grounds exist for suspecting that the Reichstag was set on fire by or on behalf of leading personalities of the National Socialist Party." The triumph of the Muenzenberg technique was all but complete.

The State Supreme Court in Leipzig did not dare to ignore these developments when the real trial commenced the next day before a five-member tribunal. Eying the eighty foreign journalists in the gallery, Dr. Wilhelm Buenger, the President of the Court, ruefully noted the worldwide interest in the trial and the "passionate discussion and speculation in the press," adding sourly, "Attempts have been made to anticipate the result of these proceedings."

Judge Buenger took great pains to impress upon the non-German correspondents in the spacious paneled courtroom the fairness and independence of German justice. But most of them were listening with only half an ear; they were busy noting down their impressions of the defendants, who had preceded the judges into the courtroom.

The long wait in jail had taken its toll of the prisoners. During the last five months they had been held in irons. Torgler looked spent and wasted; Dimitrov's mane of black hair showed gray in the region of the temples; his fellow Bulgarians, Blagoi Popov and Vassily Tanev, acted weary and subdued.

But to those who had seen him shortly after his arrest, the change in van der Lubbe was little short of stupefying. His eyes vacant and half-closed, his head hanging on his breast, his arms falling listlessly at his sides, he seemed already to have taken leave of life. Mucus dripped constantly from his nose and half-open mouth. His court-assigned German lawyer periodically mopped his client's face, for lack of other duties to perform; for the Dutchman had refused to be represented.

Torgler alone was defended by counsel of his own choosing—Dr. Alfons Sack. A National Socialist of formidable repute as a trial lawyer, Sack outraged the Communist faction because he refused to turn the proceedings into a propaganda circus. In the best traditions of the Bar, he was interested solely in getting his client acquitted; and he undoubtedly helped Torgler by dissociating himself from the Communist tactic.

A number of foreign lawyers—some of them non-Communist—had volunteered to defend the Communists. Buenger barred them and assigned the surly Dr. Paul Teichert to represent the Bulgarians.

As it happened, this development enormously enhanced the dramatic intensity of the proceedings. For under German law at that time, defendants were entitled to put questions to witnesses, with the result that Dimitrov took over the defense, relegating Teichert to a subordinate role. Little known outside of Central Europe before his arrest, the scrappy little Bulgarian became overnight a worldwide figure, the personification of anti-Nazism. Audacious to the point of impudence, witty and eloquent by turns, alert and ruthless in cross-examination, his verbal duels with his adversaries stand to this day as models of political invective.

The Nazi case, almost seven months in the making, had been entrusted to the bald, portly Dr. Karl Werner, long-time Chief Public Prosecutor. Under German law, his function was limited, the burden of questioning the accused and examining witnesses falling on the shoulders of the Presiding Judge.

The indictment charged all of the defendants with high treason and arson. The treason count—that the defendants "attempted to alter the German Constitution by the use of violence"—was obviously designed to lay the foundation for a broad-gauge revelation of the widely advertised Communist conspiracy. But its inclusion was ill-advised, since it could only expose anew the embarrassing poverty of the evidence obtained in the widely heralded raid on the Karl Liebknecht House.

Over 100 witnesses would be heard and 10,000 pages of testimony and argument would be recorded before the verdict was rendered. All told, the Court would sit for fifty-seven days between September 21 and December 23. Any hopes Dr. Goebbels may have entertained about the propaganda value of the trial were largely dissipated when van der Lubbe started to testify on the first day. Startling as his appearance had been when he shambled into the courtroom, his behavior on the stand set off a fresh train of speculation. Foreign correspondents who had interviewed him in March recalled that he had been moderately coherent in his response to their questions; and the transcripts of his interrogations by the police bear out that impression. Now, going over the same ground, the Presiding Judge was able to extract from him little more than a series of grunts—some affirmative, some negative, some contradictory. By the close of the second day, the Nazi press was headlining defensively: "Van der Lubbe Feigns Idiocy."

Now and then he laughed, and his laughter cracked the composure of the usually stolid Judge Buenger:

BUENGER. Stand up, Lubbe! Why are you suddenly laughing . ... instead of being serious? How do you account for this? Does it have to do with these proceedings or is it something entirely different?

VAN DER LUBBE. (*Silence.*)

BUENGER. Speak up! Do you think that what is going on here is amusing? Or not?

VAN DER LUBBE. No.

BUENGER. Do you understand the trial?

VAN DER LUBBE. No.

BUENGER. Then it is not these proceedings, or what we have just

215

been talking about, that made you laugh. What is it, then? . . . Tell us!

VAN DER LUBBE. About the trial.

BUENGER. Something seems amusing to you?

VAN DER LUBBE. No.

BUENGER. If something isn't amusing, one doesn't laugh.

The marked general reaction to van der Lubbe forced the prosecutor to call a psychiatrist to the stand on the second day of the trial to confirm that he was normal. That settled it for the Court, but not for the foreign journalists. Reports spread that van der Lubbe had been drugged or hypnotized by his captors. But medical authorities have been unable to identify any known narcotic which would produce the symptoms exhibited by van der Lubbe; and had the Nazis placed him under hypnosis, they could have made better use of him as a stick to beat the Communists with.

Even when, after two months of trial, van der Lubbe spontaneously erupted with an astonishing spate of speech, he only increased the puzzlement of his audience. He spoke of "voices in his body," complained that he was fed up with "all this symbolism" and demanded a quick verdict, be it death or life imprisonment. But during this one startling outburst of comparative lucidity, he clung tenaciously to the story Judge Buenger had wormed out of him by patient questioning early in the trial.

A mason by trade, half-blinded as the result of an accident some six years earlier, van der Lubbe had wandered aimlessly all over Central Europe after breaking with the Dutch Communist Party in 1931. Reaching Berlin the previous February 18th, he seems to have talked recklessly to anyone who would listen about his intention to set fire to public buildings as a "beacon" that would spark a popular uprising against the Nazis. On February 25th he had failed miserably in successive attempts to burn down the Neukölln Welfare Office, the Town Hall, and the Palace in the Lustgarten. Most of his nights during this period had been passed in relief shelters, and except for the day preceding the fire, his movements had been traced painstakingly by the police. Dimitrov made much capital of the hours which were unaccounted for—the afternoon of February 26 and the morning of February 27—and excoriated the prosecution repeatedly on this score, especially after van der Lubbe testified that, during the period in question, he had run into a Nazi parade and perhaps even attended a Nazi meeting in a suburb of Berlin.

Van der Lubbe's detailed account of his movements on the night of the fire likewise raised more questions than it answered. Although he persisted in claiming exclusive responsibility for the crime, Nazis and

Communists alike hailed this phase of his testimony as positive proof to the contrary.

Standing on the Reichstag's first-story balcony outside the point of entry, he had lit part of a packet of firelighters. Once inside, he had pursued an antic course around the restaurant and to the lobby, setting off curtains and table tops along the way. Moving to the great hall outside the session chamber, he had found nothing inflammable and had returned to the lobby. Then, with three firelighters gone, he had stripped off his overcoat, jacket, vest, and shirt. Donning his jacket once more, he had set fire to his shirt, for use as a torch. One more turn around the restaurant and he had stumbled into a waiters' pantry where he had taken a tablecloth from a drawer, unfolded it, and transferred to it the flame from the remains of his shirt. Racing down a narrow staircase to the basement, he had kicked in the panel of the locked door to the kitchen and crawled through the hole. There he had dropped part of the burning cloth on the chopping block. Then, after setting fire to his vest and smashing the panes of a service hatch to leave the kitchen by a different route, he had landed in a washroom.

At this point Sergeant Buwert had fired the shot at the light behind the frosted glass of the ground-floor window. Buwert and his companions fixed four minutes as the maximum lapse of time between van der Lubbe's entry through the restaurant window and the firing of the shot. This account presents two major difficulties:

In the pitch-black, huge interior of the Reichstag, it seems highly improbable that the half-blind Dutchman, unfamiliar as he necessarily was with its layout, could have covered so much ground and performed so many separate actions in the time span of four minutes preceding Buwert's shot. If he had not been the actual target at which the shot was fired, who was carrying the torch in the basement?

Re-enactments of the crime by the original cast (van der Lubbe excluded) were staged in Berlin for the benefit of the Court. The time sequences checked out, in the sense that it was proved physically possible for a police official impersonating the Dutchman to cover the ground in the time allotted in broad daylight. But no effort was made to duplicate all of his actions during those few minutes, nor were allowances made for van der Lubbe's ignorance of the premises and for his severely impaired vision. Actually, nobody particularly cared. Both sides were irrevocably committed to the view that he had not acted alone; and the Dutchman's protestations were treated as an effort to protect his accomplices.

This underlying conviction was reinforced by the other facet of van der Lubbe's timetable. He testified that the assembly hall was one of the very last locations he put to the torch. Yet it was a solid mass of flame by the time he was captured, less than ten minutes later.

This facet of the testimony strongly suggests that van der Lubbe had accomplices; and the prosecution swept away all doubts in a cloud of expert testimony. In the best traditions of their craft, three experts presented three contradictory explanations of the rapid spread of the fire in the assembly chamber. But they all agreed that the evidence pointed to the use of highly inflammable agents—possibly a self-igniting fluid with a phosphorus base, possibly gasoline, or both.

The complete absence of tangible clues to back up this theory daunted none of the experts. Arson characteristically tends to destroy evidence of the means employed to commit it. And most students of the trial have endorsed the view that the Dutchman must have had help of one sort or another. Granted that its brittle drapes and antique furniture left the vaulted assembly hall particularly vulnerable to fire, it could hardly have been gutted so quickly without the use of combustible chemicals.

Dimitrov seized on the expert testimony as confirmation of the *Brown Book's* thesis. Rising from his seat in the box, he snapped, "That's just what I say! He couldn't have done it alone. Now we have Faust—who is the Mephistopheles?"

Dimitrov repeatedly harked back to this theme when he took the stand. His testimony marked the turning point of the trial; with characteristic audacity, he put the Nazis on the defensive, and they never restored the balance. Drawing on his thirty years of rough-and-tumble in trade union and political struggles, he exhibited a rare combination of intellect and insolence that left the spectators gasping. Sometimes it was more than the judges would countenance, and he was expelled from the courtroom, only to return to the fray with renewed ardor. Foreign observers in the courtroom came away with undisguised admiration for the shaggy-maned Bulgarian's "moral courage" in the heart of enemy territory.[2]

Dimitrov's attack was two-pronged. The Nazis, he argued, had the most to gain from the Reichstag fire and they alone were in a position to bring off the stunt. Time and again his questions rang changes on this proposition:

[2] Recent reports from a number of sources cast some doubt on Dimitrov's apparent heroism. A deal is said to have been made before the trial between the Gestapo and th G.P.U. to exchange Dimitrov and the other Bulgarians for three German officers who had been arrested as spies by the Soviets. Dimitrov's intimate knowledge of the inner workings of the Comintern, and the fact that the Bulgarians were allowed to cross into Russia after the trial, tend to support this suggestion.

Was the Reichstag fire not in actual fact the signal for the destruction of the working-class parties and a means of solving differences within the Hitler government?

Although this line of inquiry was consistently suppressed by the Presiding Judge, its echoes reverberated around the world—to the despair of Dr. Goebbels.

Riding the crest of Dimitrov's performance, Muenzenberg, with the aid of a tiny force of volunteers in his shabby little office in Paris, was fast outstripping the little Doctor in the propaganda race. His World Committee for the Relief of the Victims of German Fascism issued daily bulletins expounding the significance of the developments at the trial. Sales of the *Brown Book* continued brisk. Huge street demonstrations plagued German consulates and embassies in the great cities of the West. Goering was burned in effigy in Copenhagen; dockworkers in France, Belgium, and Holland let cargo rot in ships flying the swastika flag; and German trade foundered in a morass of boycotts. Men of every political stripe rallied to the cause, and things began to look up for the Communist Party organizations in the Western democracies.

Muenzenberg received no greater accolade than Buenger's words to Goering and Goebbels when they appeared in court on November 4th. The two Ministers had been summoned, Buenger said,

to express yourselves under oath concerning accusations and slanders which have been directed against Your Excellencies from certain quarters, particularly in the so-called *Brown Book*, regarding the subject matter of this trial.

But Goering would have been wise had he passed up the invitation. Inappropriately dressed in a hunting jacket, knee breeches and high brown boots, the No. 2 Nazi started out confidently enough, recounting his activities in connection with the fire. But then Dimitrov pounced: Why had Goering announced on February 28th that a Communist Party card had been found on van der Lubbe, when the arresting officials had testified to the contrary? Had not Goering steered the police away from all channels of investigation, except those which would incriminate the Communists?

The Bulgarian's close questioning threw Goering off balance. Perspiration spangled his brow; his voice became a hoarse scream:

I'll tell you what the German people know. They know that you are behaving disgracefully here, that you are a Communist scoundrel who came to Germany to burn down the Reichstag. In my eyes you are a crook who belongs on the gallows!

"The witness's outburst is quite natural," Judge Buenger interposed at this point, rebuking Dimitrov for preaching Communist propaganda. "Your only business here is to ask questions of fact."

DIMITROV. I am quite content with the Minister's answer.

GOERING. Get out, you scoundrel, get out!

DIMITROV. Are you afraid of my questions, Herr Goering?

GOERING. Get out of here, you crook!

Once more Dimitrov was dragged from the courtroom. As he reached the door, he shouted back over the general uproar: "Are you afraid, Herr Goering? Are you afraid?"

And Goering howled back, "Wait till I get my hands on you!"[3]

Forewarned by Goering's disastrous experience, Goebbels held himself in check during his appearance on the stand. He told the Court that Hitler had been his dinner guest on the night of the fire. Shortly after nine, Ernst ("Putzi") Hanfstaengl telephoned to let them know that the Reichstag was afire. According to Goebbels, he dismissed the whole thing as a practical joke, but a second call convinced him that something serious was afoot. This account coincides with the entry in Goebbels' diary for that day, and taken at face value, tends to negate his complicity in the crime.

He was less successful in explaining why many of the Nazi leaders were socializing in Berlin at the time of the fire, as if waiting for something to happen, when they should normally have been out campaigning. A Cabinet meeting kept them in the capital that day, he said. But the record showed that there had been no such meeting; and Goering had previously testified that these sessions had taken place on February 28 and March 1.

After Dimitrov's pyrotechnics, Torgler's performance at the trial assumed a pale cast. A lion in parliamentary debate, his claws had been blunted during his stay in prison. He was more than content to allow the painstaking Dr. Sack to poke holes in the prosecution case, while delicately bypassing the issue of Nazi guilt.

Sack's task had not been made particularly difficult. The witnesses against Torgler, all avowed Nazis, came to the stand in a state of unpreparedness that occasionally set even Judge Buenger's teeth on edge.

[3] An interesting passage at this session seems to have escaped notice until now. After Goering had characterized Communism as a "criminal philosophy," Dimitrov made the point that the Soviet Union's "economic orders give work to hundreds of thousands of German workers." Was the Minister aware of that? Goering answered: "I am aware, for one thing, that the Russians pay in *bills of exchange*, and I would like it better if they were honored." This sounds like a *non sequitur*, but see previous footnote.

On the afternoon of the fire, their story went, Torgler was seen at various times conversing in the corridors of the Reichstag with van der Lubbe, Dimitrov, and Popov. But on that day, Dimitrov had been on a train en route to Berlin. And the witnesses could not agree on a description of Popov's clothing, nor did they have any recollection whatsoever of what van der Lubbe was wearing. To clinch the point, Sack cited the inherent improbability of such conspiratorial meetings in the public hallways of the Reichstag, not to mention the difficulty Torgler would have had in communicating with Popov, since one spoke no Bulgarian and the other spoke no German.

The other mainstream of evidence directed against Torgler likewise dwindled to a feeble trickle in the telling. The prosecution tried to fix the time of his departure from the building at 8:40 or 8:45 P.M., but Sack proved with little difficulty that his client had been dining at a restaurant some distance away by 8:30 P.M. And a postman had passed the door of the assembly chamber at 8:55 and seen nothing out of the ordinary.

The evidence against Popov and Tanev was even less impressive. Everything considered, with over six months to prepare for trial and fairly potent means of persuasion at hand, the prosecution had little to excuse its shoddy handling of the case. It may be assumed that Goering handicapped the police and the examining magistrate by keeping a heavy hand on the tiller in the course of pretrial investigations; but sheer incompetence emerges as the only possible explanation for the sordid parade of petty criminals, perverts, and obvious perjurers upon whom the Nazis relied for proof of their charges.

Summing up on December 13 after the last witness had been heard, Prosecutor Werner had the good sense to ask the Tribunal to acquit the Bulgarians for lack of proof. With the press of the world hanging on every word, this move represented the last best hope of saving the honor of the fledgling Nazi regime. The case against Torgler was also rather thin, Werner admitted, but he must have been connected with the crime "in some manner or other." Nevertheless, Torgler was exonerated. Van der Lubbe—cat's-paw, scapegoat, dupe, or possibly the most skillful arsonist of all time—was convicted. He met his death like a dumb animal on the guillotine three days before his twenty-fifth birthday, on January 10, 1934.

Despite the stunning defeat which had been administered to the Nazis, they salvaged a few crumbs of consolation from the verdict. The *Brown Book* had been proved to be palpably wrong about van der Lubbe's sex-driven complicity with the Nazis. The Oberfohren memorandum had been fairly well discredited. And the defense had failed to

establish that the underground passage from Goering's palace had figured in the fire, as Muenzenberg claimed.

The commander of Goering's personal SS[4] detachment had testified
that he had found all entrances to the tunnel locked within an hour
after the fire started; and the night porter at the Speaker's palace had
sworn that nobody had passed through the tunnel up to the time he
learned of the fire. On the other hand, the porter admitted that he had
heard mysterious footsteps in the passage "many times, between 11 P.M.
and 1 A.M., the last time about ten days before the fire." And evidently
intruders had entered it during that ten-day interval without being heard
by him, because strips of paper and threads which he had glued to the
doors had been found torn "about six times." But this testimony left
the question in mid-air, and the defense was unable to turn it to advantage.

To those who had been stampeded into supporting Hitler's program
by the specter of Communist insurrection, the verdict furnished scant
comfort. The point of no return had been reached in the November 12,
1933, elections, held while the trial was still in progress. The Reichstag
had again been dissolved, and a single slate of candidates had been offered by the Nazis. Fear, skillful propaganda, and a sense of national
rebirth brought a record 45,000,000 voters to the polls. Only 3,400,000
—less than 8 per cent—registered their protest by depositing unmarked
ballots. Even in the concentration camps, this average held good, nine
out of ten inmates dutifully licking the hand that beat them.

Armed with this mandate, Hitler shook up the Cabinet on December
1st to give the Nazis an unmistakable majority, and a law passed the
same day declared the Nazi Party "inseparably united with the State."
The Constitution henceforth was made subordinate to the will of the
Fuehrer.

Thus German democracy breathed its last before the Reichstag trial
verdict could reveal the taint of fraud in the event which had precipitated its dissolution.

Following the acquittals, Dimitrov, Popov, and Tanev were held in
protective custody for two months, during which the world press raged
and German embassies abroad were besieged by protest marchers. On
February 15, Stalin conferred Soviet citizenship on the Bulgarians, and
less than two weeks later they were flown to Moscow. Dimitrov went on
to new and more important assignments, ending his career as Prime
Minister of postwar Bulgaria.

Torgler was less fortunate. The Nazis held him in "protective cus-

---

4 Schutzstaffel: the Elite Corps, or Blackshirts.

tody" until late in November 1936. The Party for which he had risked his life saw fit (from its haven of exile in London) to expel him in 1935. He managed somehow to survive the war, as well as the postwar barrage of Communist charges that he had collaborated with the Gestapo, which were found to be groundless.

The remarkable Muenzenberg turned his energies into other channels, the influence of his organization burgeoning as the menace of Fascism increased. But his faith in the Party was apparently shaken by the Russian purge trials. By 1938, his cautious refusals to heed urgent summonses to Moscow isolated him from the cause he had served so well. Interned as a German national by the French in 1940, he escaped, only to be killed on a country road crammed with refugees from the German invasion. The Stalinists took the trouble to label his death a suicide, thereby lending support to the theory that he was the victim of an NKVD assassin. His man Friday, Otto Katz, was hanged in Prague in 1952 as one of the "subversives" involved in the Slansky case—the Czech counterpart of the Moscow purge trials.

The verdict in the Reichstag Fire trial represented a rare exercise of Nazi justice, at a time when thousands were being imprisoned without cause and with no hope of a trial. But this judicious restraint was in accord with Nazi policy. Hitler saw that it was imperative to give a hostage to world public opinion; he had bigger fish to fry. He would not again be troubled by antiquated notions of justice. By April 1934, political cases had been completely removed from the Supreme Court's jurisdiction and placed in the hands of "People's Courts" and special courts dominated by Party members.

But the Court's decision did not dispel the almost universal belief that the Nazis had been responsible for the fire. After the June 30, 1934, purge of the SA, newspapers in London, Paris, and Prague published alleged confessions of complicity in the crime by Brownshirt functionaries who had either been killed or were in hiding. One of the most colorful accounts was attributed to the homosexual leader of the Berlin SA, Karl Ernst, who was certainly favorably situated to know the inside story. The Ernst version portrays Goering, Goebbels, and other Hitler aides racking their brains, late in February 1933, for an "incident" to serve as a pretext for polishing off the opposition. After discarding a number of ideas, including a faked attempt on Hitler's life, they came around to the notion of setting the Reichstag afire. Hitler presumably knew nothing of the plot. According to Ernst, it was Goebbels' suggestion; and with Goering's approval, Roehm, Heines, Helldorf, and Manfred Killinger, a veteran Nazi assassin, worked out the plans. Using the tunnel from Goering's house, Ernst and two SA men named Fiedler and Moh-renschild made their way into the assembly chamber at about 8:45 and left the building by the same route when van der Lubbe broke in. During that quarter hour, they doused the furniture with gasoline and with a phosphorus compound which ignited spontaneously after a short time.

This account has van der Lubbe winning his dubious niche in history by accident: he had talked loosely of his plans to a couple of SA men or underworld characters and had been steered into timing his attempt to coincide with the Nazis', without once becoming conscious of their behind-the-scenes collaboration.

The fact that Roehm, Ernst, Heines, Fiedler, and Mohrenschild all perished in the June 30th massacre does not necessarily support the inference that they were liquidated because they knew too much about the fire. Many SA men died at the same time, and some of the other alleged participants were untouched by the purge. Heines testified at the trial as one of those named in the Oberfohren memorandum and proved that he had been in Silesia on the night of the fire. This disposed of the *Brown Book* charge that he was actually on the scene with van der Lubbe, but leaves uncontradicted Ernst's charge that Heines participated in planning the fire. Helldorf's description in court of his behavior when he heard of the fire bespeaks either complete innocence or super-human self-control. After convincing himself that the Reichstag was in fact ablaze, he sent a subordinate to the scene to represent him and placidly left for his apartment to await further news. Goebbels' diary entries for that night yield no evidence of guilt. And Goering testified at Nuremberg, with the almost certain knowledge that he was facing death:

I had no reason or motive for setting fire to the Reichstag. From the artistic point of view I did not at all regret that the assembly chamber was burned; I hoped to build a better one. But I did very much regret that I was forced to find a new meeting place and . . . had to give up my Kroll Opera House . . . for that purpose. The opera seemed to me more important than the Reichstag.

But other witnesses at Nuremberg spoke to the contrary. General Franz Halder testified to hearing Goering boast at a luncheon conversation in 1942:

I am the only one who really knows the Reichstag story, because I set it on fire.

Hermann Rauschning, former Nazi leader in Danzig, told a similar tale, as did Hans Gisevius, who worked for Goering at the time of the fire.

And the private secretary to Baron Kurt von Schroeder, a Cologne banker who backed the Nazis, recalled a talk as far back as January 3, 1933, in which Goering and Papen spoke of the possibility of burning down the Reichstag as a prelude to outlawing the Communist Party.

Discounting the anxiety of these witnesses to say what they thought their captors wanted to hear, the conventional criteria for assessing guilt still point to the Nazis. Motive, means, and opportunity were all theirs. Any assistance van der Lubbe got had to pass through the tunnel, and freedom to pass without Goering's knowledge and consent was well-nigh unthinkable. The Brownshirts were experienced in the use of incendiary material. For years, one of their favorite stunts had been to set fire to the thick layers of advertising posters which decked the circular columns on Berlin's streets. And they managed to avoid capture, although plainclothesmen were stationed nearby to nab the vandals—a feat requiring more than a little expertise with delayed-action chemicals.

On this premise, the Ernst version of the fire seems well-founded—up to a point. However, Ernst's suggestion that van der Lubbe was quite unaware of his little corps of Brownshirt helpers runs afoul of the Dutchman's rather fantastic reconstruction of his first four minutes in the Reichstag. If he lied in court to make his story jibe with Police Sergeant Buwert's, he must have been covering up for known accomplices; and this secret knowledge may furnish the logical explanation for the sudden bursts of laughter which nettled old Judge Buenger. Logic dictates that these accomplices were Nazis. But that only leads to further speculation: why did this stuporous little Dutchman stick to his story to the very end?

It is, of course, conceivable that van der Lubbe really did set the fire all by himself. Fritz Tobias, a retired German civil servant, has recently reviewed the evidence exhaustively in a series of articles and makes out a moderately strong case for that position. In addition to van der Lubbe's own story, Tobias leans heavily on the speed with which other huge structures, like the Vienna Stock Exchange, have been gutted by fires of seemingly insignificant origin; the testimony that the tunnel was found locked at both ends immediately after the fire; and the difficulty of reconciling Ernst's and similar stories with the assertion of the postman, who saw nothing wrong in the assembly chamber when he passed it at 8:55 P.M.

But Tobias offers no explanation for van der Lubbe's confidence that the Reichstag would be unoccupied and unguarded at the precise moment that he forced his way into the building. Coincidence? Perhaps. Yet any police official worthy of his salt would look for an accomplice "on the inside." And he passes altogether too lightly over the inherent improbabilities of van der Lubbe's timetable.

Like the murder of the young princes in the Tower, and the theft of the Queen's necklace, the Reichstag fire will probably go down in history as a classic puzzler. The solution is of little moment, except to academicians. The trial made an indelible impression, however, upon thinking people throughout the world. By the time the proceedings ended, all but the arch-reactionaries were disenchanted with Hitler's New Order; millions of men of good will had been brought closer to the smothering embrace of Moscow; and the world had taken a giant step toward Armageddon.

The following excerpts from the minutes of the trial recall vividly the impotence of Judge Buenger's efforts to break through the shell of van der Lubbe's stubborn insistence upon his total responsibility for the fire. The appearance of Count von Helldorf, SA leader of Berlin, commands special interest for his dramatic confrontation with van der Lubbe. Goering's exchanges with Dimitrov, supplementing those reproduced in the text, give further evidence of the shrewdness and impertinence of the Bulgarian leader.

MARINUS VAN DER LUBBE
SEPTEMBER 27, 1933

BUENGER. Why did you fire these buildings?

VAN DER LUBBE. My own idea.

BUENGER. What were your reasons for doing it?

VAN DER LUBBE. I didn't know myself at the time.

BUENGER. You said, did you not, that your object was to arouse the workers struggling for freedom?

VAN DER LUBBE. No.

BUENGER. Were you ever in the Reichstag before the fire?

VAN DER LUBBE. Yes.

BUENGER. When?

VAN DER LUBBE. On the same day.

BUENGER. The day of the fire?

VAN DER LUBBE. No.

BUENGER. The day before the fire?

VAN DER LUBBE. Yes. No . . .

DIMITROV. Van der Lubbe seems to have spoken energetically enough in his examination before trial, but he is silent today. If van der Lubbe really is normal, as the psychiatrists assert, there is only one possible hypothesis for me.

BUENGER. Raise no hypotheses!

DIMITROV. Ask van der Lubbe why he answers "Yes" and "No" alternately?

226

BUENGER. The question is not admitted.

DIMITROV. Ask him who helped him—if he ever even heard the name Dimitrov?

BUENGER. He has already denied that he had confederates.

DIMITROV. Did van der Lubbe read and sign the stenographic reports of his examination by the examining magistrate?

BUENGER. This question is not admitted.

DIMITROV. Has van der Lubbe spoken to anyone but the examining magistrate about this arson business?

BUENGER. What is the purpose of that question? It is inadmissible and superfluous.

DIMITROV (to van der Lubbe). Why don't you speak? Are you bowed down with guilt because of the crime you have committed against the world proletariat?

BUENGER. Do you plead guilty to causing the fire?

VAN DER LUBBE. Yes.

BUENGER. When did you decide to do it?

VAN DER LUBBE. Can't say.

BUENGER. You said you decided on the Monday before?

VAN DER LUBBE. Can't say.

OCTOBER 4, 1933

BUENGER. You must answer Yes or No; were you outside the Reichstag about two o'clock in the afternoon?

VAN DER LUBBE. Yes.

BUENGER. Did you enter the Reichstag?

VAN DER LUBBE. No.

BUENGER. You had not been in the Reichstag before you climbed through the window in the evening?

VAN DER LUBBE. No.

BUENGER. Was it possible to get in?

VAN DER LUBBE. Can't say.

BUENGER. Then you were not there with Torgler?

VAN DER LUBBE. No.

BUENGER. Do you know Torgler?

VAN DER LUBBE. No.

BUENGER. Do you know that according to expert reports you could not have done it alone?

VAN DER LUBBE. Yes.

BUENGER. Did you fire the Reichstag alone or with others?

VAN DER LUBBE. Alone . . .

BUENGER. Did others prepare the job, so that you needed only to lay the match, as it were? Answer Yes or No.

VAN DER LUBBE. No.

BUENGER. Nobody suggested it to you?

VAN DER LUBBE. No.

BUENGER. How do you explain that two or three experts have said you could not have done it alone?

VAN DER LUBBE. Can't say.

COUNT WOLF VON HELLDORF
OCTOBER 20, 1933

HELLDORF. I think it would be best for me to describe my movements on February 27th. Until 7 P.M. I worked in the office. I was at that time leader of the SA for Berlin. Sometime between 7 and 7:30 P.M. I went out to supper with the former Chief of Staff of SA for Berlin-Brandenburg District, Professor von Arnhim. While we were having dinner the SA Headquarters telephoned to say that a fire had broken out in the Reichstag. That must have been at about 8:30.

BUENGER. But the Reichstag wasn't on fire by 8:30.

HELLDORF. Oh, well! It must have been at about 9 P.M. then! We were in the Klinger Restaurant. There is a fire station opposite and we had already remarked that fire engines were passing along the street outside. I then asked Professor von Arnhim to go at once to the scene of the fire and, if my presence were needed, to telephone me at my flat in the Nürnburger Strasse. Myself, I went straight back to my flat, and about 10 P.M. received a telephone call from Professor von Arnhim that my presence was not necessary, and that the Reichstag had been cordoned off. About one hour later, at 11 P.M., I returned to my office and held a meeting in which the Reichstag fire was discussed. Group Leader Ernst and Commander Pretzel were present. Early the following morning a large number of Communist and Social Democratic officials were arrested on my orders.

TORGLER. Did you give that order officially in your capacity as leader of the Berlin SA?

PROSECUTOR WERNER. What has that to do with the fire?

TORGLER. It is of the highest importance for the defense of my party! . . .

HELLDORF. I gave the order on my own initiative, without orders from my superiors. As a leader of the SA I could arrest enemies of the government, especially the probable incendiaries.

DIMITROV. How did you know—without investigation—that Communist and Social Democratic officials were the probable culprits?

HELLDORF. We are firmly convinced that the criminal element of society is in general Marxist. In our opinion the only possible perpetrators would be found among the Marxists, who employed the fire as a signal for insurrection.

DIMITROV. Did you notice anything that looked like an insurrection the next day?

HELLDORF. No, because we acted quickly.

DIMITROV. Who needed the Reichstag fire, the Communists or certain other people? . . .

BUENGER. Accused van der Lubbe, come forward! Raise your head, Lubbe! Look this witness in the face. Come, Lubbe, raise your head, like this! Look at the witness!

INTERPRETER. You must look at the witness.

BUENGER. Now, come! Hold up your head.

INTERPRETER. You must look at the witness. Raise your head!

PRESIDENT. Come now, hold your head up! Head up, van der Lubbe!

HELLDORF. Man, put your head up! Quick! (*Van der Lubbe obeys.*) Do you know me?

VAN DER LUBBE. No.

HERMANN GOERING
NOVEMBER 5, 1933

DIMITROV. Herr Prime Minister Goering stated on February 28th that when arrested the "Dutch Communist van der Lubbe had upon him his passport and a membership card of the Dutch Communist Party." From whom was this information derived?

GOERING. The police search all common-law criminals and report the result to me.

BUENGER. The three officials who arrested and examined van der Lubbe all agreed that no membership card of the Communist Party was discovered on him. I should like to know where the report that such a card had been found came from?

GOERING. I was told by an official. Things which were reported to me on the night of the fire, particularly those which were made in the course of explanations by officials, could not all be tested and proved. The report was made to me by a responsible official and was accepted as a fact; as it could not be immediately tested, it was announced as a fact. When I issued the first report to the press on the morning after the fire, the interrogation of van der Lubbe was not concluded. In any case I do not see that anyone has anything to complain about, because it seems to have been proved in the trial that van der Lubbe had no such card on him.

DIMITROV. I would like to ask the Minister of the Interior what steps he took to make sure that van der Lubbe's route to Henningsdorf, his stay and his meetings with other people there were investigated by the police in order to assist them in tracking down van der Lubbe's accomplices?

GOERING. As I am not an official myself but a responsible minister, it was not important that I should trouble myself with these petty, minor matters. It was my business to point out the Party and the mentality which were responsible for the crime.

DIMITROV. Afterwards, as head of the police and judiciary and as

President of the Interior, you announced to Germany and the entire world
that the Communists had burned down the Reichstag—

GOERING. Yes, indeed!

DIMITROV. —that the Communist Party—

GOERING. Yes, indeed!

DIMITROV. —had done it, that the German Communist Party along
with van der Lubbe, a foreign Communist, and other such suspects had
been identified. Is it not true that your conviction may have influenced the
entire police and judicial investigation, guiding it into this one course, and
closing off all other lines of inquiry to discover the real Reichstag arsonists?

GOERING. . . . I myself am not an official of the criminal police. As
a responsible Minister, I was not called upon to identify every petty vaga-
bond . . . The criminal police would track down the clues—don't worry!
But I ascertained that this was a political crime, and it is just as clear to me
today that the criminals were in your Party . . . If the police and judicial
investigation were influenced in any particular direction, it was the right
direction.

DIMITROV. That is your interpretation. Mine is different.

GOERING. But mine is the final one!

DIMITROV. I am only the accused, to be sure.

BUENGER. You have only to put questions.

DIMITROV. I will proceed, Mr. President. Does the Minister know
that the Party which possesses this supposed criminal philosophy rules one
sixth of the earth?—

GOERING. Unfortunately!

DIMITROV. —that the Soviet Union has diplomatic, political, and
economic relations with Germany, and that its economic orders give work
to hundreds of thousands of German workers?

GOERING. I know—

DIMITROV. Good!

GOERING. I am aware, for one thing, that the Russians pay in bills
of exchange, and I would like it better if they were honored . . . What
Russia does is of no interest to me. I am concerned only with the German
Communist Party and the foreign Communist leaders who came here to
set the Reichstag on fire.

(Cries of "Bravo" from the audience.)

DIMITROV. Of course, they shout "Bravo!" Leading an attack on the
German Communist Party is your privilege. The Communist Party has the
right to exist illegally in Germany and to fight your rule . . .

BUENGER. Dimitrov, I forbid you to propagandize for the Communists here.

DIMITROV. He's making Nazi propaganda here!

BUENGER. I forbid you most emphatically . . .

VAN DER LUBBE
NOVEMBER 23, 1933

VAN DER LUBBE (*interrupting*). I would like to ask a question . . . We have had three stages in this trial already—one in Leipzig, the second in Berlin, and now the third in Leipzig. I would like to know when the verdict will be pronounced and executed.

BUENGER. I can't tell you that yet. It is up to you, when you agree to tell us who your accomplices were.

SEUFFERT (*counsel to van der Lubbe*). Perhaps no one helped him?

VAN DER LUBBE. That was cleared up—I told you that I set fire to the Reichstag. This trial has to reach a verdict. It's eight months already and I haven't yet been understood.

BUENGER. Tell us again with whom you did this.

VAN DER LUBBE. The other defendants have confirmed that they had nothing to do with the fire and didn't set fire to the Reichstag and were never involved . . .

BUENGER. I have told you repeatedly that the Court cannot believe your testimony that you acted alone. So tell us with whom you did it . . .

VAN DER LUBBE. I can only tell you again that I set fire to the Reichstag all by myself. The testimony now in this trial has shown that Dimitrov and the others were not even there. They have indeed been involved in this trial, but they had no part in the act.

SEUFFERT. And Mr. Torgler?

VAN DER LUBBE. Not him either. (*To Torgler.*) You have to tell them yourself that you weren't involved. I am the accused and I will be sentenced to either twenty years in prison or death—but I want something done. The trouble is that all this symbolism was dragged into the Reichstag fire.

WERNER. What does the defendant mean when he speaks of "symbolism"?

SEUFFERT. He was referring to the fact that the Reichstag fire was supposed to have a symbolic significance—a signal.

VAN DER LUBBE. What did it amount to, setting the Reichstag on fire? It took ten minutes or at most a quarter of an hour. I did it all alone!

THE MOSCOW TRIALS

(1936–1938)

Historians will not hold with the view that the Second World War started on December 1, 1934. But a plausible case can be made out for that proposition by anyone who has studied the so-called "Moscow trials" and the great bloodletting which they so conspicuously and shockingly dramatized.

For it was on that day that a young Communist named Leonid Nikolayev assassinated Sergei M. Kirov in Leningrad. The shot he fired may well have lit the fuse which set off the explosion of the Nazi hordes into Poland almost five years later.

The Kirov killing had much in common with the Reichstag fire. Like the pathetic van der Lubbe, Nikolayev was fated to be painted as the insignificant but willing tool of men of greater stature. Like Hitler, Stalin used the incident to destroy the last vestiges of opposition within his country, and to establish his personal dictatorship on an unassailable footing. And in the final analysis, the finger of suspicion swung around to point directly at the Leader himself. For this charge we have support from no less a personage than Nikita Khrushchev, who in 1956 called the circumstances surrounding Kirov's murder "inexplicable and mysterious."

Mysterious, perhaps; but not inexplicable.

At 46, the ruggedly good-looking Kirov was one of the best-known members of the Communist hierarchy inside Russia, and one of the least known outside. By the scoring system which has prevailed in measuring the influence of Soviet officials, Kirov ranked no lower than third in the entire country. As a member of the Politburo and of the four-man Secretariat of the Communist Party, and as Party Secretary of the Leningrad District, he wielded enormous power. An energetic organizer and spellbinding speaker, he had labored hard and effectively in Stalin's vineyard, and was regarded by many as the heir-apparent to the all-powerful General Secretary of the Party.

He had earned his spurs the hard way. Leningrad, traditional center of revolutionary liberalism in the early days of the regime, had long been the private preserve of Gregory Zinoviev, one of Lenin's earliest and closest collaborators. A determined effort by the Zinoviev group to oust Stalin from the General Secretaryship at the 1925 Party Congress had been deftly thwarted by the simple expedient of stacking the assembly with pro-Stalin delegates. Thereupon Kirov, an old Bolshevik who had served his apprenticeship as Party Secretary of Azerbaijan, was transferred to Leningrad to eradicate Zinoviev's influence—a task which he managed so handily that Zinoviev, Lenin's "maid of all work," could be dropped from his post as head of the Comintern the following year without raising a ripple of protest.

Throughout Stalin's most trying days, in 1931–32, when it seemed that all Russia would starve as a result of the misfiring of the first Five-Year Plan, Kirov stood by his chief. He did not shrink from the Draconian measures adopted by the Party to force collectivization on the villages and wring impossible quotas of industrial production from the cities. At a time when the Kremlin was assailed by doubt that its armies of peasant conscripts could be counted on to carry out the "liquidation of the kulaks," Kirov pressed into service punitive cadres of Party zealots and secret police to exterminate the peasants who had scorched the earth of their native villages in mute resistance to the confiscation of their crops. In Leningrad proper, he ruthlessly rid the Party of laggards and dissidents who balked at the ever-mounting norms of output exacted from underfed factory workers.

But Kirov was reluctant to follow his boss blindly. Steeped in Bolshevik tradition, he remained faithful to the concept of collective rule by the leadership of the Party as represented by the Politburo, and was tolerant of dissent, provided it remained within the family and did not persist after a decision had been reached. The test of his convictions came late in 1932, when a memorandum was distributed in Party circles calling for a relaxation of the rigors of the collectivization program and demanding Stalin's removal from the General Secretaryship. Stalin interpreted this manifesto, signed by a number of Party functionaries, as proof of a plot to assassinate him. But his demand for the death penalty for this and similar "terrorist attempts" by Party members was turned down by the Politburo and the Central Committee of the Party.

Kirov figured prominently in the faction which held out for leniency to the oppositionists. Perhaps he recalled Lenin's injunction to his colleagues: "Let no blood be shed among you." Certainly he had accepted as an article of faith the tenet that expulsion from the Party and exile to the hinterland were fitting punishment for persistent opposition to

the Party line. And undoubtedly he used his powers of persuasion—
"second only to Trotsky's," it has been reported—to win over his fellow
Politburo members to a compassionate position.

In any case, the lives of the signers of the petition were spared. Along
with some other opposition leaders who had voiced criticisms of the
Five-Year Plan, such as Zinoviev and Leon Kamenev, former Chairman
of the Soviet Central Executive Committee, they were shipped off in
October 1932, to penal camps in Siberia, Kazakhstan, and other points
east. As a result of this incident, Kirov began to be looked upon as the
champion of the Party's "moderates." His elevation in 1933 to the Central Purge Commission, which had the job of keeping the Party pure,
signified the role he was expected to play as a counterweight to Stalin's
hotheads.

During 1933, Stalin was forced to make concessions to the logic of
events. The great famine and the obvious (but unpublicized) failure of
the industrialization program won the argument which Zinoviev and
Kamenev had lost, at least to the extent of allowing peasant members
of collective farms to cultivate small plots and raise some livestock for
their own benefit. That summer's bumper harvest clinched the point
for the advocates of some measure of private incentive. At about the
same time, the goals of the second Five-Year Plan were scaled down to
realistic levels, in sharp contrast with the fantastic norms Stalin had set
in 1928.

The secret of Stalin's failure had been so well masked by propaganda
that the banner under which the Party met in January 1934, for its
Seventeenth Congress bore an unconsciously ironic legend: "The Congress of Victors." The victory, if any, had been achieved at the cost of
eleven million Russian souls. Livestock was down 57 per cent from the
1928 figure. Few dogs could be found on the streets of Moscow. Hous-
ing was scarce and food still strictly rationed, although the preferential
treatment accorded Party members, managerial personnel, and "shock
workers" concealed the true state of affairs from most of the delegates at
the Congress. Still, they could point with pride to the collectivization of
60 per cent of the farms and to some small degree of industrial progress.

But beguiled though the rank-and-file delegates may have been, Joseph Stalin could not have shared their ebullience. His sharp eyes detected a pall of impending disaster on the horizon. On the very day
the Congress opened, Adolf Hitler signed a ten-year nonaggression pact
with Russia's ancient foe, Poland—an act of base ingratitude on Hitler's
part, since the Nazis were deeply indebted to the German Communists
for hoisting them, on Stalin's instructions, to the seat of power. In the
Far East, Stalin was swallowing one bitter pill after another, under un-

remitting threats of Japanese aggression. He had been forced once again to embrace Chiang Kai-shek, who had double-crossed him in 1927 and wiped out the Chinese Communist Party, after accepting misguided Russian support. A Japanese puppet state was flourishing in Manchuria, flush with the Russian border. And even as the Congress opened, Stalin was reluctantly negotiating to sell the strategic Chinese Eastern Railway to the rampaging Japanese at a shamefully huge discount, as the price for the reduction of tension.

And there was always Leon Trotsky, the brilliant wartime chief of the Red Army, founder and leader with Lenin of the Communist International, who had elected himself guardian of the revolutionary ideals which Stalin had abased and abandoned. Outmaneuvered in the struggle for succession to the mantle of the fallen Lenin, Trotsky was constitutionally incapable of accepting defeat gracefully. From his refuge in France he hurled thunderbolts of invective and searing dialectic, calculated to ignite the minds of the disaffected survivors of the famine years, expelled Party members, and old Bolsheviks who had once fought at his side. Trotsky's followers had been routed and disheartened, but his pen still penetrated the heart of his homeland. His tiny *Bulletin of the Opposition* snaked its way into Russia in the pockets of officials returning from abroad, and was read even by Stalin—who was not above adopting some of Trotsky's suggestions as his own. One issue, dated November 1932, which contained a devastatingly detailed account of the sad state of the Soviet economy, was traced to Ivan Smirnov, legendary conqueror of Kolchak's White armies during the Civil War. Smirnov was promptly thrown into prison, to emerge four years later as a defendant in the first of the Moscow trials.

Periodically Trotsky called for the removal of Stalin and his faction, unmindful of the apathy which had sapped the strength of the opposition within Russia since his expulsion in 1929. Occasionally he would boast vainly of the might of his "Fourth International" within the Soviet Union, implying that the overthrow of Stalin was near at hand. And although Trotsky's influence within Russia was limited to the realm of political philosophy, the suspicious and vengeful Stalin, mindful of the lessons of 1917, did not dare to shrug off the threat posed by his old rival. If war should come, might not the opposition rally around the exiled leader? If the domestic program should founder, would it not be remembered that Trotsky had always opposed the doctrine of "Socialism in one country," which Stalin had preached to justify the incredible harshness of the collectivization operation? Were not the newly organized collective farms themselves readily convertible into cells of counter-revolutionary activity?

236

And yet he must sit by while this "Congress of Victors," drunk with its own optimism, was expansively extending the olive branch to the late opposition. Zinoviev and Kamenev, having renounced their heresies and capitulated (for the fifth time since the Revolution), had been brought back from exile and allowed to say a few words to the delegates. Other defeated antagonists were being elected to membership on the Central Committee—Nikolai Bukharin, called by Lenin "the darling of the Party," who had fought bitterly against the excesses of the first Five-Year Plan; Yuri Pyatakov, Deputy Commissar for Heavy Industry; and Alexei Rykov, head of the Soviet Government after Lenin's death.

The "moderates" had not quite seized the throne, but they had penetrated the royal anteroom. Their crowning achievement came with the election of Kirov to the four-man Party Secretariat, marking him as their leader. Contemporary reports indicate that the Congress accorded him an ovation equal to Stalin's; and it was not considered insignificant that the announcement of the membership of the new Secretariat labeled Stalin only as "Secretary," instead of "General Secretary," the title he had borne since 1922. When the Congress disbanded on February 10, Joseph Stalin had a lot to think about.

So had the members of the Congress, if they but knew. Of its 1966 delegates, 1108 would be arrested during the next five years on charges of counterrevolutionary activity. And of the 139 members whom they elected to the Central Committee, 98 would be exterminated before the Great Purge slowed to a walk. Such were the dimensions of Stalin's wrath.

The first victim was Kirov himself. His assassination was the opening move toward the complete subjugation of the Communist Party to the will of the Leader.

The locale of the crime has been the source of much speculation. Why had Kirov remained in Leningrad for nine months after his election to the Secretariat, which ostensibly required his presence in Moscow? From the evidence available, it would seem that Kirov, embarrassed by the role of Crown Prince which had been thrust upon him, continually postponed the move, pleading unfinished business in Leningrad. But some say that Stalin deliberately kept Kirov away from the hub of Party activity, by simply failing to designate his successor in the Leningrad post. Both views bespeak a strained relationship between the two men; and taken in conjunction, they make sense. Stalin was not disposed to share the limelight with anyone; and Kirov sensibly tried to allay the suspicions of the star performer by clinging to the shelter of the wings.

But this charade could not be acted out indefinitely; and both players must have realized that the Party would read between the lines, and that Kirov's transfer to Moscow was inevitable. One former Soviet official reports that it was ordered at a Central Committee meeting in November 1934, setting the stage for the Grand Guignol which opened on the first of the following month.

Enter the misshapen instrument of destiny—Leonid Nikolayev, child of misfortune, club-footed and probably epileptic, rather anthropoid in appearance, with his enormous head, short body, and unusually long arms. Fired from a succession of minor Party jobs—he seems to have been suited for little else—turned down in his efforts to get a higher education, and refused admission to a sanitorium for treatment of his illness, he was, by 1934, penniless and hopeless. Since Leningrad had been the scene of his tribulations, he had no difficulty in fixing on Kirov as the source of all his trouble, and soon developed a full-blown persecution complex. He made no secret of his intention to revenge himself upon the man he considered his oppressor.

At least a month and a half before Kirov's death, Nikolayev fell into the hands of the Leningrad NKVD. A briefcase in his possession contained a revolver and papers disclosing his plan to assassinate Kirov. The fate of the zealous policeman who made the arrest is not recorded; but it is safe to suggest that he did not win a promotion from his NKVD boss for his diligence. For after a brief session with Vania Zaporozhets, Assistant Chief of the local NKVD, Nikolayev was released, complete with revolver. He would not be molested again; an NKVD pass gave him free access to the corridor outside Kirov's office, where he finally accomplished his mission.

A mission it was; for, although Nikolayev had his own reasons for executing it, the complicity of the NKVD in Kirov's assassination is now firmly established. Khrushchev said as much to the Twentieth Party Congress; so did Henry Yagoda, head man of the NKVD hierarchy, before he was shot in 1938. Their testimony, considered with the other facts in the case, affords no room for doubt that the Leningrad NKVD acted on the authority of Stalin himself. Zaporozhets' boldness in paving the way for the killing can only be explained on the premise that the local secret police had been under instructions to provoke, or at least to facilitate, an attempt on Kirov's life; and no one but Stalin would have dared to issue such orders.

Stalin's conduct from the moment the news of Kirov's death reached Moscow confirms this reasoning. He promptly forsook the safety of his Kremlin fortress for an unprecedented trip to Leningrad, to take personal charge of the investigation. That evening, at his instance, the Central Executive Committee issued a decree ordering immediate execution of convicted terrorists, and barring pardons or remissions of sentence.

In Leningrad, Stalin must have learned for the first time of the NKVD's incredibly clumsy handling of its assignment. Understandably, Zaporozhets would not have risked the Leader's wrath by revealing Nikolayev's earlier detention, which had almost caused the plan to miscarry; at most he would have notified Yagoda, who had equally good reasons for hushing it up. The release of Nikolayev may have conformed to the delicate precepts of sound bureaucratic practice, but it left the fingerprints of the NKVD all over the murder weapon.

It did not improve matters that the NKVD man heading Kirov's bodyguard, who managed to be absent from the assassination scene, was killed the next day in an automobile "accident" in which none of the other occupants of his car was hurt. This minor coup is also credited to Zaporozhets, who probably thought it wise to destroy a possible informant, unmindful that the incident had an informative value all its own.

Zaporozhets and eleven of his NKVD colleagues were placed under arrest, charged with failure to take "measures for the timely exposure and prevention" of the crime, "although they had every possibility of so doing." The Soviet Criminal Code prescribes no punishment for an excess of zeal.

The events of the days immediately following the murder bear the earmarks of frantic improvisation on Stalin's part, designed to cover up the NKVD's tracks. At first he tried to make it appear that White Guardists, who had allegedly slipped past the Russian border patrols to commit terrorist acts, were at fault. In the space of two weeks 104 nameless former Czarist sympathizers (dredged up from the dungeons of the NKVD) were shot without trial, and mass executions in various parts of the country decimated the already thinned-out ranks of those suspected of a lingering affection for bygone days. To the undiscriminating reader of the Soviet press, the executions appeared to put an end to speculation about the Kirov murder, although the newspaper accounts were somewhat vague on this score.

But on December 16, the wind shifted. Zinoviev, Kamenev, and five other ex-members of the Central Committee were thrown into jail, on suspicion of complicity in the plot to kill Kirov. *Izvestia* trumpeted the brilliant Karl Radek's ringing denunciation of the leaders of the late opposition, predicting that the Party would "destroy the remnants of this gang with an iron hand!" (Less than two years later, Radek would confess that he was a leader of the same "gang.")

Co-ordination was still sadly lacking, however, in the announced campaign. When Nikolayev and thirteen minor "Zinovievite" accomplices were indicted, secretly tried, and sentenced to death—all within the two-day span of December 28–29—neither the indictment nor the verdict contained a line implicating either Zinoviev or Kamenev in Kirov's assassination.

The hapless NKVD men who had been languishing in their own jails since the beginning of December were let off lightly, all things considered. After a secret trial, Zaporozhets and his immediate superior received three-year sentences, and ten of their subordinates were put away for periods ranging from two to nine years. According to some reports, they lived well in confinement, and were released before their terms expired; but Khrushchev tells us that they were all liquidated in 1937 "to cover the traces of the organizers of Kirov's killing."

By mid-January 1935, the ghastly framework of the purge was becoming discernible. Trotsky was declared to have been in contact by mail with the Nikolayev group. Zinoviev and Kamenev accepted the best of a bad bargain and acknowledged their "political and moral responsibility" for Kirov's assassination. This concession of "objective" guilt the old doctrinaire leaders found not too difficult to swallow, since, in the arcane idiom of Bolshevik thinking, all theoretical opposition to the Party line sows the seed of hostile action against its leaders.

Along with fourteen other ex-oppositionists, they received prison sentences ranging up to ten years. That they were in a position to trade at all supports the supposition that they still had the sympathy of some members of the inner circle, a few of whom apparently had the courage to speak up for lenient treatment of these pioneer Bolsheviks. Among those who urged compassion were V. V. Kuibyshev, Politburo member and Chairman of the State Planning Commission, who died suddenly within ten days after the trial; and the revered Maxim Gorki, whose growing estrangement from Stalin was punctuated at about this time by the first open attack in the Soviet press on his literary merit. Gorki succumbed to tuberculosis the following year; and the deaths of these two men were destined to furnish the most bizarre trappings for the third Moscow trial.

With the untidily managed Kirov episode out of the way, Stalin settled down in earnest to the task of consolidating his power. Andrei Zhdanov, his right-hand man, was appointed to fill Kirov's shoes in Leningrad and proceeded to ship suspected oppositionists by the tens of thousands off to the NKVD labor camps in Siberia.

Nikolai I. Yezhov, long a Stalin protégé, took over Kirov's place in the Secretariat and became head of the powerful Control Commission, charged with the purification of the Party. To assist him, a youthful Stalin henchman, Georgi Malenkov, was promoted from the ranks of Secretariat employees. Another loyal servant of the Leader, Nikita Khrushchev, was assigned to the Secretaryship of the key Moscow Party organization.

Guided by these lieutenants, the machinery for "cleansing" the Party, which had been reactivated in 1933, plowed its length and depth, cutting deep furrows in its ranks. The resultant arrests and expulsions inflicted hardship on only a minute fraction of the total population; and to the extent that it was felt, it was largely ameliorated by improvements in other spheres. The economy had caught its second wind. A retreat from orthodox Marxism had been decreed by the Kremlin: the speed-up system held full sway on the factories and farms, and special privileges were conferred upon skilled technicians and leading Party workers. The old-line theorists who remarked ruefully on these typical capitalist "abuses" were silenced, in typical Communist style, with an epithet coined by Stalin: "bourgeois egalitarianism," he called it. Meanwhile the revision of the Constitution, with its widely advertised promise of increased democratization, was going forward in the hands of a committee headed by Stalin, Bukharin, Sokolnikov, and Radek. And for the still more gullible, large helpings of patriotic pap were provided by the revival of Russia's ancient heritage. Peter the Great, Ivan the Terrible, and great military figures of the Czarist past were dusted off for use in a massive indoctrination program, making the history books obsolete.

Parallel developments in the Red Army furnish a valuable clue to the meaning of this about-face. Beginning in mid-1935, the Russian military machine was vastly enlarged and made over in the German image. Under the able leadership of Mikhail Tukhachevsky, army training theories were radically overhauled, with the emphasis on qualities of leadership instead of political orthodoxy. Later that year, pre-Revolutionary service ranks were revived and the military caste system, complete with marshals and admirals, brought back much of the pomp and glitter of Czarist days.

Unmistakably Stalin was preparing for war. Hitler's denunciation of the Versailles Treaty in March 1935, signalizing the restoration of universal military service in Germany, was the handwriting on the wall; anyone who could read realized that the little Austrian house painter included the rich resources of the Ukraine and North Caucasus in his ultimate objectives. The Japanese, too, were continuing their relentless pressure on the Outer Mongolian frontier, unappeased by the humiliating bargain Stalin had struck to cede them the Chinese Eastern Railway.

Supplementing his domestic program of readiness, Stalin embarked upon a frantic pursuit of alliances; during 1935 he concluded mutual assistance pacts with France, Czechoslovakia, and even Turkey. His able Commissar of Foreign Affairs, Maxim Litvinov, used the League of Nations skillfully as a sounding board to promote worldwide anti-Nazi sentiment and his "collective security" program. And those German Communists who were still at large must have smiled grimly when the Comintern, in July 1935, instructed Communist Parties abroad to co-operate to the hilt in a "popular front" with anti-Fascists of every shade of political coloration. As a token of the new attitude, the Bulgarian Dimitrov, popular symbol of the fight against Hitler, took over leadership of the Comintern.

But as the Fascists registered victory after victory through 1936—in the Rhineland, in Ethiopia, in Spain—without any display of resistance by the democracies, Stalin must have looked at his mutual assistance pacts with a jaundiced eye. And he may well have reasoned, with some justification, that if Russia were attacked, she might have to go it alone.

The eventuality of war brought Stalin face to face with an appraisal of his own, and his country's, strength. As time passed, the bitterness engendered by the first Five-Year Plan might be expected to subside under the weight of improved living conditions, the semblance of increased democracy, and mass propaganda. The armed forces and the technical elite would probably be faithful to the fount from which their privileges flowed. But the hard core of support would still have to come from the Party.

The Party, under the ministrations of the Control Commission and the NKVD, had been purged again and again—and the end of each purge signaled the beginning of a fresh one. There seemed to be no shortage of saboteurs, wreckers, and counterrevolutionaries; but Stalin was determined to continue the process until every last vestige of individualism had been leached out of the organization.

For Stalin realized, as an old revolutionist, that he had little to fear from those who knew only to follow; the danger lay with those who had learned to lead. He gave a free hand to Yezhov and Yagoda; and the composition of the Party changed radically as their cathartics took effect. The average age of the membership fell sharply; old-time guerrilla fighters were ruthlessly weeded out in favor of those who could give letter-perfect recitals of the latest version of the Kremlin catechism.

Ammunition for this assault had been placed in the hands of the Control Commission in the spring of 1935, when Stalin disbanded the Society of Old Bolsheviks and the Society of Former Political Prisoners and Exiles. The records of both of these venerable organizations, containing detailed biographies of their members and former members, were turned over to Yezhov and his men, simplifying the task of eliminating those who might still have a vested interest in the ideals of the Revolution.

But although the old Bolsheviks had been expelled from the Party in droves, most of them were still at large. Some held important government posts despite records of former opposition to Stalin.

It would be these men—so Stalin reasoned—the men who had turned the trick in 1917, when the Czarist defense effort was foundering, who would spearhead his overthrow when the opportunity arose. And a war, for which his country was surely not ready, would furnish them their opportunity. Convinced that his time was growing short, he directed Yagoda to mobilize the all-powerful NKVD in a drive to atomize the potential opposition leadership.

Yagoda's men had no easy task. In the spring of 1935, Stalin had hit upon the idea of a series of public trials as the chosen instrument for the chain reaction which would fuse the populace into a condition of monolithic unity. If his subjects could be taught to equate opposition with criminality, the purge could be carried forward without restraint, and without protest from the remaining Kremlin moderates. The problem he handed Yagoda was to destroy his former rivals with a succession of hammer blows, delivered with every appearance of legality—and to extract from the judicial spectacle the maximum in propaganda dividends.

The point of departure selected for this ambitious theatrical venture betrays a monumental lack of imagination in its authors. Around the nucleus of the Kirov murder, it was decided to fabricate the myth of a far-reaching Trotskyite terrorist plot, perpetrated by men whose names had become synonymous with Bolshevism. The defendants, it was charged, had conspired since 1932 to kill Stalin and seven other leaders, and had succeeded in the case of Kirov. Apparently it mattered little that every Soviet schoolboy knew that individual acts of terror were anathema in the lexicon of Bolshevism; Hitler had long since proved to the Kremlin hierarchy the effectiveness of the "big lie."

Reckless as the accusation was, the choice of the defendants for the first trial bespoke a note of caution. For most of the leaders of the "conspiracy" were already in jail or in exile for previous offenses and hence had already been partially discredited. Heading the list were Zinoviev, Kamenev, and Smirnov, followed by Gregori Evdokimov, member of the Central Committee at the time of Kirov's death; Ivan Bakayev, another former Central Committee member; Sergei Mrachkowsky, legendary Civil War hero; and Vargashak Ter-Vaganian, Armenian Bolshevik leader and noted Marxist theorist. A sprinkling of former minor Party officials and nonentities completed the roster of sixteen defendants. The choice of these lesser figures (from among a large number of candidates) was dictated by their readiness to incriminate the major defendants, and, in some instances, by their record of past residence abroad, in order to fashion a credible story of contacts with Trotsky. At least three of the so-called couriers were evidently NKVD men in good standing who posed as defendants in the expectation of handsome rewards.

The public announcement on August 15, 1936, of the arraignment of these pioneer Bolsheviks on capital charges stupefied the Russian people and startled the civilized world. Four days later the trial before the three-man Military Collegium of the Supreme Court—essentially a court-martial—commenced in a small auditorium in Moscow's Trade Union Building. Its 350 seats were deliberately filled with NKVD officials and employees, attending in shifts—an audience of insiders which could be counted on to react orthodoxly and vociferously to any departure from script by any of the defendants.

The defendants had pleaded guilty. Under Soviet law, the Court could have proceeded directly to pleas and sentence, but a full-dress hearing was conducted, ostensibly for the purpose of fixing the degree of guilt and appropriate punishment of each defendant, but actually in order to wring the last ounce of propaganda from the spectacle.

By August 24, it was all over. Andrei Vishinsky, Public Prosecutor, had demanded the supreme penalty for the "mad dogs" in the dock, and the Court sentenced all the defendants to be shot and their property confiscated. On the basis of their own testimony, this seemed to be precisely what the defendants deserved. For as each of them took the stand, he had embroidered upon his original plea with a highly circumstantial confession which excluded all consideration of mitigating circumstances. And in remarkably harmonious closing statements most of them had heaped fulsome praise on Stalin, extolling his infallible leadership and decrying their own folly in attempting to overthrow him.

The shock of the initial accusation was submerged in the reverberations of these extraordinary confessions. At first blush they appeared to corroborate each other point by point, disclosing an intricate network of diabolical cabals against the Stalin regime. Even within Russia, Party members who had become cynically acclimated to the ritual of recantation and self-criticism as a conventional observance of Party disciplinary proceedings were awed and confounded by the depths of abject self-abasement into which the leading defendants flung themselves with such extravagant abandon. And outside the country the explanations of this phenomenon were distinguished for their variety, rather than their perspicacity.

The ill-advised publication of an abridged official record of the trial, containing excerpts from the verbatim testimony, gave sophisticated analysts a chance to probe to the bottom of this judicial quagmire. At the outset it struck some as remarkable that the eight Soviet leaders marked as targets by the terrorists did not include Vyacheslav Molotov, Premier of the Soviet Union! What manner of plot was this, that it aimed at newcomers to the Politburo like Zhdanov and Postyshev, and passed over the nominal head of the government, who had ranged himself alongside the Leader since the Revolution? According to Alexander Orlov, former NKVD official, Molotov had temporarily fallen from Stalin's favor and was therefore deliberately slighted in the confessions. Whatever the cause of the omission, it strongly suggested to critical observers that the confessions had been fabricated under the guidance of a single brain—for it was otherwise inconceivable that Molotov should have been so contemptuously ignored by his political enemies.

But even more embarrassing to Stalin was the matter of the Hotel Bristol. One of the lesser defendants, Edouard Holtzmann, told about a rendezvous he had arranged in November 1932 with Trotsky's son, Leon Sedov, for the purpose of making contact with Trotsky himself:

I agreed with Sedov to be in Copenhagen within two or three days, to put up at the Hotel Bristol and meet him there. I went to the Hotel straight from the railroad station and in the lounge met Sedov. About ten A.M. we went to Trotsky.

The Iron Curtain shuts out as much information as it keeps in; else the NKVD men who prepared Holtzmann for trial would have known, as the Danish press gleefully disclosed on September 1, 1936, that the Hotel Bristol had been demolished in 1917. No hotel by that name had operated in Copenhagen since that time.

This amateurish fumble does not reflect upon Vishinsky's abilities as a prosecutor. The cases were handed over to him by the NKVD as full-blown scenarios, and he seems to have participated only slightly in their preparation. Like the accused, he was assigned a role—to lead them through their stories, prompt them, and set fire to the scenery whenever the audience showed signs of boredom. All of this he handled competently. But if the trials were to serve their purpose as propaganda, the confessions should have been screened for internal contradictions. Since he was depending upon them to support each other, he ran the foreseeable risk that disproof of a single confession might bring down the whole house of cards.

Not only were the internal contradictions numerous; worse still, objective corroboration was woefully scant. To explain how Smirnov, for example, could have played a prominent part in the plot, although he had been in prison continuously since January 1, 1933, Vishinsky spoke of a code which "was discovered by means of which, Smirnov, while in prison, got in touch with his comrades." But the code was never produced.

All told, only three pieces of documentary evidence were offered, and they only tended to demonstrate the weakness of his case. A "letter" purportedly sent to the conspirators by Trotsky and found in the false bottom of Holtzmann's suitcase, turned out to be an open letter to the Central Executive Committee published in the March 1932, *Bulletin of the Opposition*, exhorting it to fulfill Lenin's deathbed advice to the Party "to remove Stalin." This document, freely circulated outside of Russia and read at the time by the Kremlin hierarchy, was stridently condemned by Vishinsky as an "appeal to put Stalin out of the way." That Trotsky should have used Holtzmann as a courier for such widely broadcast material seemed only slightly less believable than that Holtzmann should have kept the "message" for four years in a secret compartment of his luggage.

With all the trips the conspiracy's couriers were supposed to have made abroad to receive Trotsky's instructions, it struck many observers as curious that only one passport was produced to corroborate their accounts; and that one boomeranged. It belonged to Valentin Olberg, one of the NKVD men who had been enlisted as a codefendant, whose testimony performed the vital function of linking Trotsky with the German secret police. Olberg is known to have worked for Russian counter-intelligence until 1935, ferreting out Trotskyites in Berlin and Prague, and was therefore well qualified to impersonate one.

Olberg testified that, as a Latvian, he needed help to enter Russia in order to carry out Sedov's instructions to organize a terroristic act against Stalin; and that Sedov bought him a forged Honduran passport in Czechoslovakia which enabled him to cross the Russian frontier. Vishinsky introduced this passport in evidence, together with the visiting card of the alleged Nazi agent from whom it was supposedly purchased. But in an effort to show how deeply the conspirators had penetrated Soviet life, he let Olberg testify that shortly after entering Russia in July 1935, he was employed as an instructor at the Gorki Pedagogical Institute, and held that post until he was arrested. The utter incongruity of an alien, who was not even a Communist Party member, teaching at a Soviet institute of higher education at a time when every party member's loyalty was being challenged showed the hand of the NKVD all too plainly. The visiting card, of course, proved nothing.

As points of reference, these details proved invaluable to critics of the trial. But the air of frame-up pervaded the larger picture as well. Standing in the dock were men of proven courage and conspiratorial skill who confessed that they had been dedicated for four or five years (the evidence is contradictory) to the liquidation of the Soviet leaders, with whom they had rubbed elbows repeatedly during that period. And the sum total of their accomplishments was the murder of Kirov alone! Perhaps the most humiliating aspect of the confessions to the principal defendants was their portrayal as a set of pathetically ineffectual dilettantes, talking big but accomplishing little—an account completely at odds with their known capabilities as men of action. Read in its entirety, the record of the five-day trial depicts them as characters in a Kafkaesque dream, a nightmare with the familiar theme of impotence.

Undoubtedly this served one of Stalin's underlying purposes: it caricatured the opposition and emphasized the hopelessness of its cause. But while this lesson might conceivably have been turned to account within Russia, it confirmed to outside observers that the confessions had been cut from whole cloth.

Still, there they were; and it was puzzling that so few of the defendants threw out the slightest hint of the artificiality and falsity of the prosecution's case. True, both Smirnov and Holtzmann refused to admit their personal participation in the preparation or execution of terrorist acts; but they pleaded guilty to the balance of the indictment, which sufficed from Stalin's standpoint. Only rarely did there shine through the haze of self-incriminating statements a clue to the intrinsic perfidy of the proceedings:

SMIRNOV. I listened to those instructions [*from Trotsky*] and communicated them to the center. The center accepted them but I did not take part in its work.

VISHINSKY. So when did you leave the center?

SMIRNOV. I did not intend to resign. There was nothing to resign from.

VISHINSKY. Did the center exist?

SMIRNOV. What sort of center? . . .

This sort of badinage earned Smirnov a rather rueful comment in Vishinsky's closing remarks:

The most persistent in his denials is Smirnov. He pleaded guilty only to being the leader of the Trotskyite underground center. True, he said this in a somewhat jocular way.

But if Vishinsky was occasionally nonplussed by a show of resistance, the other men in the dock could be counted on to get the runaway train back on the track. Thus Mrachkowsky, after the quoted exchange between Smirnov and Vishinsky: "Smirnov is trying to pass himself off as a simple village postman, but we regard Smirnov as Trotsky's deputy." Repeated instances of this sort give rise to the inference of a collective stake, shared by all the defendants (save possibly Smirnov), in the success of the show.

And therein may be found the key to the confessions in this first trial. The contours of that key become clearer in the light of two significant moves which Stalin made between Kirov's death and the arraignment of the defendants. On April 8, 1935, children over the age of twelve were made subject to the death penalty for offenses as slight as petty larceny and for a wide range of ill-defined political crimes. And just before the trial started, the order abolishing appeals for clemency, which had followed on the heels of the Kirov killing, was rescinded.

Except for Smirnov and the NKVD's decoy defendants, it seems highly probable that the defendants were trading their confessions for lives—their own lives or the lives of their children or grandchildren. A number of defecting Soviet officials have recorded quite circumstantial accounts of personal audiences between the major defendants and Stalin, or his deputy, Yezhov, at which these bargains were struck. Granted that there was no particular reason to accept the promises of clemency at face value, the alternative offered was far more terrifying.

But more than the mere bait of mercy was necessary to induce these tough-minded old political warriors to take the hook. Most of them had only capitulated after many months of subjection to a softening-up process, as scientific as it was fiendish—a process which, with a few refinements, came to be known in Korean War days as "brainwashing." The use of physical torture had not been officially sanctioned by this time, and it was probably not employed against these defendants. More subtle but equally effective means of subjugating them were at hand, thanks to the ground-breaking experiments of the great Ivan Pavlov in the field of conditioned reflexes.

As with Pavlov's dogs, so with Zinoviev, Kamenev, and company. Cut off from news of family and friends, deprived of sleep, adequate food, and warmth, shorn of human dignity and even of identity (except the numerals they wore), harassed week after week by endless and repetitive interrogations, they succumbed to fatigue and prolonged anxiety, losing what psychologists call the "protective brain inhibition" which helps mankind distinguish between the true and the false, the conscionable and the unconscionable. In this state, memory falters; a sense of guilt is easily inflamed by the exhumation of past errors; a promise of kindly treatment extracts extraordinary concessions; and the victim becomes so highly suggestible that he adopts as his own, ideas which may have been planted months earlier. Bombarded with an endless variety of stimuli in the form of alternating and unpredictable attitudes on the part of the inquisitors, who were often their only contacts with human beings over long stretches of solitary confinement, entrapped by provocateurs posing as fellow prisoners, flagellated verbally in round-the-clock interrogations by NKVD men working in shifts, the prisoners inevitably fell into a state of hopeless confusion and lost their former political orientation. To clinch the matter, their captors employed the old Inquisition trick of confronting them with self-styled "accomplices," to prove the futility of withholding their confessions. Small wonder that they ultimately seized the opportunity, however meager, to save themselves or their loved ones by confessing and giving Stalin more than his due.

Other solutions have been offered for the enigma of the confessions, none of which merits consideration except the politically acute hypothesis suggested by Arthur Koestler in his brilliant and searing *Darkness at Noon*. Koestler advances the theory that at least some of the defendants, facing certain death, embraced the opportunity to perform a final service to Party and country by exalting the Stalin regime and debasing the remnants of the opposition. Conceivably, after months of ceaseless harangue about the perils of Fascist invasion and the need to consolidate Soviet power around the one man who seemed destined to wield that power, a veteran Bolshevik may have felt that he could make his years of struggle and sacrifice meaningful only by stoking the fires of Communism with his own honor. But it is equally consistent with the tenor of the confessions that they may have adopted this attitude only by way of rationalization of their desperate barters with the Kremlin.

As they met their fate, some of the defendants may have reflected that Stalin had not scored a total victory after all. Trotsky would surely have his sport with the mock proceedings in the arena of world opinion; he was out of Stalin's reach and had no peer as a polemicist. And the trial itself, even to the least skeptical, had proved Stalin the victor in a power struggle, rather than an ideological conflict. He had condemned them, if their confessions were taken at face value, for conspiring, not against the Soviet Union, but against Stalin and his clique.

The Leader himself was not slow to awaken to these implications—Trotsky, now in Norway, was expounding them daily to anyone who would print them. In short order, Stalin attempted to put his nemesis out of action by asking the Norwegian Government to deport him—not extradite him as a suspected criminal, for that would have given Trotsky the chance to air the entire story before a Norwegian court. Trotsky, having been refused asylum by a number of non-Fascist countries, might have ended up in Russia; but Trygve Lie, then Norwegian Minister of Justice, interned him instead, censoring his mail and prohibiting him from action offensive to Stalin. With Trotsky silenced, Stalin took the pressure off Norway; he had other plans for the little man. Trotsky lengthened the distance between them by moving to Mexico in January 1937.

Although the trial had misfired as a propaganda weapon, a second round was unavoidable. The NKVD had planned it that way, using the confessions of Kamenev and others to implicate Bukharin, Radek, Alexis Rykov, Lenin's successor as chairman of the Council of People's Commissars, and a number of equally legendary figures. However, Yagoda seemed reluctant to risk another spectacle. In September 1936, while Stalin was vacationing with Zhdanov at a Black Sea resort, Bukharin and Radek were publicly exonerated and released from detention.

The announcement set off an explosion which blasted Yagoda out of the NKVD. In a joint telegram demanding Yezhov's appointment in his place, Stalin and Zhdanov told the Politburo:

Yagoda has definitely proved himself to be incapable of unmasking the Trotskyite-Zinovievite bloc. The OGPU [absorbed into the NKVD in 1934] is four years behind in this matter.

"Four years behind." Four years earlier, Stalin had been thwarted by Kirov and the moderates over the issue of the death penalty for the group which had petitioned for his removal as General Secretary.

Armed with this mandate, Yezhov, now holding the reins of both the secret police and the Control Commission, launched a campaign of mass repression and extermination which dwarfed everything that had preceded it. Diligent as Yagoda had been in unmasking "terrorist plots" by old Bolsheviks in every walk of life from Leningrad to Vladivostok, the volume of arrests under Yezhov increased tenfold in 1935 over the previous year. Executed or deported by the tens of thousands, without trial or after summary action of the NKVD's three-man secret tribunals, were former oppositionists, potential oppositionists, and those merely suspected of a tendency to oppose the Stalinist line. In the cellars of the NKVD the monotonous chorus, "Who recruited you? Whom did you recruit?", extorted answers even where there were no answers; for the ban on physical torture had been covertly lifted, and the price of survival was the inculpation of others.

Occasionally the results bordered on the grimly comical: some prisoners obligingly confessed to recruiting their entire villages; a ninety-year-old ex-Czarist general admitted that he had enlisted in the spy network of the Duke of Parma. In some measure, the willingness of the examiners to credit such grotesqueries was traceable to bureaucratic pressure to produce impressive statistical proof of the NKVD's effectiveness; in general, it reflected the natural tendency of false assumptions to spawn fantastic solutions.

Outside the prison walls, in the cities and villages, zealous Party workers found their integrity being measured by the number of Trotskyites, "wreckers," and "mad Fascist dogs" on whom they informed; ambitious young bureaucrats and technicians cleared away the obstacles on the road to promotion by turning in their superiors; and a host of old personal scores were settled once and for all. Such was the gory backdrop against which the succeeding show trials would be played out.

The announcement on January 17, 1937, of the indictment of another group of former Soviet leaders showed how well Stalin had assimilated the lessons of the first trial. No longer could he be charged with using the Court merely for the brazen suppression of political dissent. This time, the underlying theme of the indictment took the form of a Trotsky-inspired plot with the German and Japanese Governments to restore capitalism in Russia, and to turn over portions of the Soviet homeland in exchange for assistance from the Fascists. Coming on the heels of Hitler's famous Nuremberg speech, which staked out the Ukraine and Siberia as *Lebensraum*, and of the subsequent anti-Comintern pact between Germany and Japan, this naked exploitation of patriotism was as dexterous as it was calculating. A subordinate motif of "wrecking" activities was designed to lift the blame from Stalin's shoulders for the inadequacies of the railway system and the frequent accidents in the mineral and chemical industries—the inevitable effect of the speed-up system on a labor force recruited largely from the farms.

All this, and attempted assassinations, too—including among the chosen victims the recently rehabilitated Molotov.

Topping the list of defendants was the gaunt, goateed Yuri Pyatakov, bracketed in Lenin's testament with Bukharin as one of the "two ablest young men in the Party." As Deputy to Sergo Orjonikidze, Commissar for Heavy Industry, the indefatigable Pyatakov had made the job of his jovial, ill-educated chief a sinecure. Orjonikidze, a Politburo member and one of Stalin's closest friends, had intervened for his faithful aide, and had apparently extracted a promise of clemency from Stalin. The fee was the usual one—full confession to treasonable relations with Trotsky—and Orjonikidze induced Pyatakov to pay it. Stalin did not honor the contract; Orjonikidze lived only a few weeks after discovering that his fellow Georgian had used him as a Judas goat. On February 18 it was announced that he had suffered a fatal heart attack; but if Khrushchev can be believed, he was "forced to shoot himself." Some say NKVD chief Yezhov spared him the trouble.

The trial was held in the gaudy Hall of Columns of Trade Union House, a former Czarist noblemen's club, large enough to accommodate two thousand spectators. In the dock with Pyatakov when the trial opened on January 23, 1937, stood the colorful but erratic *Izvestia* editor and one-time member of the Central Committee, Karl Radek, caught up in the dragnet he had helped to weave. Radek had lost his taste for opposition in 1930. In succeeding years he had vaulted back into Stalin's favor by wearing his gifted pen to the nub with unstinting flattery of the Leader, coupled with violent diatribes against Trotsky. Under the circumstances, his arrest came as a surprise to the members of the Kremlin inner circle, who thought that he had found the infallible formula for survival. Faced with a hopeless situation, the resourceful Radek once again sold his literary talents—this time to his overworked NKVD masters, whose ingenuity may have been flagging. With a will born of desperation, he threw himself into the task of concocting elaborate confessions for himself and his codefendants, in line with Yezhov's specifications. Thus he won a place in history somewhere between Judas and Scheherazade.

Among the remaining fifteen defendants were names known to every student of the Revolution—Grigori Sokolnikov, Assistant Commissar for Foreign Affairs and former Central Committee member; Leonid Serebryakov, Secretary of the Party under Lenin; and the handsome sixty-year-old Civil War hero, Nikolai Muralov. According to Orlov, at least two of the lesser-known accused were NKVD men parading under false colors.

Unlike the first trial, these proceedings were attended by a full complement of the diplomatic corps and representatives of the world press. As the defendants spun out their hair-raising tales of treason, sabotage, and abortive attempts at assassination, the foreign observers listened openmouthed. American Ambassador Joseph E. Davies, an experienced attorney, and a fair number of reputable Western correspondents, reluctantly reported that the prosecution had established, beyond cavil, the existence of a gigantic Trotskyite conspiracy against the government.

They could scarcely do otherwise. The defendants showed no signs of physical mistreatment; they told their stories calmly and straightforwardly and with appropriate displays of repentance; and the deeds they recounted seemed too shocking to be utter fabrications. The Westerners, most of them handicapped by their unfamiliarity with the Russian scene, were simply not equipped to read between the lines.

As a result, when Pyatakov, for example, testified that Smirnov had recruited him to work with the conspiracy, nobody stopped to inquire why Smirnov had not incriminated Pyatakov at the first trial. And when Muralov admitted his participation in plans to assassinate Stalin, Molotov, Kirov, and others, nobody took special note of his seemingly pointless, but nevertheless vehement, denial that he had plotted the death of Sergo Orjonikidze. (Hindsight suggests that the old Bolshevik wanted to establish in advance that if anything happened to Orjonikidze, it was not the work of the opposition.)

And when Pyatakov testified that he had traveled from Germany to Norway to confer with Trotsky, the question of how he managed to escape the notice of the ubiquitous secret service went unasked. Unasked, that is, by the foreigners in Moscow; but since the neutrality-conscious Norwegian Government was involved, Pyatakov's trip promptly blossomed into another Hotel Bristol episode.

Pyatakov told of a secret flight he had taken by private plane from a Berlin field to Oslo on December 11 or 12, 1935, for a two-hour talk with Trotsky. With the lesson of the Hotel Bristol fiasco in mind, his account of this dramatic journey had been framed with deliberate vagueness, shorn of circumstantial details which could be checked. But two days after Pyatakov took the stand, the conservative Norwegian newspaper *Aftenposten* broke the story that not a single civil airplane had landed at Oslo's airport during the entire month of December 1935.

In a lame attempt to put out this brush fire, Vishinsky introduced at the January 27 session "an official communication" to the effect that the Oslo airport "receives all the year round, in accordance with international regulations, airplanes of other countries, and that the arrival and departure of airplanes is possible also in winter months." (He made no effort to conceal the source of this "official communication"—the NKVD, via the Russian Embassy in Norway.) All to no avail: on January 29, as the trial was drawing to a close, the director of the Oslo field drove the last nail home. No foreign planes, he told the press, had landed there between September 19, 1935, and May 1, 1936; the only landing in December was by a Norwegian plane, and it carried no passengers; and it was out of the question for a plane to land at the field unobserved. Vishinsky let it lie.

The following day, all but four of the defendants were condemned to death; they were executed within twenty-four hours. Sokolnikov, who had yielded promptly to the NKVD, and Radek, who had earned the highest reward ever paid for literary composition, received long prison sentences, as did two minor defendants.

If, as the Girondist politician Vergniaud said, the Revolution devours its own children, he might have added that the chefs often share the same fate. With the second trial over, the sands of time had run out for the Yagoda appointees who had cooked up the purge cases in accordance with Stalin's recipes. Yezhov, now firmly in the saddle, ousted and promptly imprisoned nearly all of the NKVD department chiefs and thousands of interrogators and other officials. Ironically, many landed in the cells of the very men they had personally interrogated; and some of these reunions must have been rather touching. During 1937 alone, over three thousand of them trod the path worn smooth by their own victims, to be executed without trial as spies, Trotskyites, and wreckers. This callous and daring move by Yezhov precipitated the defection of many important NKVD officials abroad, including Walter Krivitsky and Ignace Reiss, both of whom Stalin managed to liquidate, and Alexander Orlov, who luckily escaped the long arm of the Kremlin.

Throughout 1937, and well into 1938, the purge developed dizzying momentum—more momentum, perhaps, than the authorities intended. Millions were playing the grisly game of denunciation and counter-denunciation, multiplying enormously the number of victims whom the regime had marked for elimination. The stripping of layer after layer of top Party officials and managerial and technical personnel became such a general practice that it came to be known as "the shift system"; in some offices and factories, successive arrests carried off more than one hundred per cent of the normal complement of employees, and the turnover in the top ranks of the Party hit roughly three fourths of the hierarchy. Stalin's objectives had been broad indeed—to wipe out every iota of opposition or potential opposition in the country; but the diligent new brooms who manned the NKVD were soon infected with the universal hysteria over traitors and wreckers, and the casualties mounted to epidemic proportions.

Few ordinary prisoners could be expected to resist the interrogative methods which had succeeded in breaking so many hard-bitten old Bolshevik warriors; and few tried. At worst, unless they were Party or NKVD officials or military men, they could generally expect to receive terms of forced labor ranging up to ten years. From this abundant source, the State Administration of Camps (GULAG), operated by the NKVD, was able to supply almost all the labor required for huge segments of Soviet industry in the North and in Siberia, as well as the bulk of the manpower for the public works projects—canals, dams, railways—in which Stalin took such pride.

Trapped in the path of the juggernaut were many foreigners who had sought asylum in the Soviet Union after the collapse of the Communist Parties in their native lands. Practically every member of the Central Committee of the Polish Communist Party perished in the purge, and such storied personalities as Béla Kun, head of the abortive Soviet Republic of Hungary, and Heinz Neumann and Hermann Remmele, leading spokesmen for the German Communist Party, were shot as "Gestapo spies." A host of less distinguished and less fortunate German refugees and voluntary *emigrés* to Russia, many of them Jewish, escaped execution, only to be handed over to Hitler shortly after the Nazi-Soviet pact was signed in 1939.

By February 1937, Bukharin and Rykov, despite their exoneration six months earlier, had been returned to jail. More and more pictures of Soviet leaders disappeared daily from the walls of offices and Party meeting rooms; more and more books and pamphlets vanished from the shelves of libraries; and each empty space symbolized another arrest in the making or already effected. Higher denomination rubles had to be withdrawn from circulation when it developed that the five signatures on the bills belonged to guests of the NKVD.

In mid-1937 the Soviet earth trembled convulsively once again. On June 12, it was abruptly announced that Marshal Tukhachevsky and seven noted Soviet generals had been shot for conspiring with the Reichswehr for the overthrow of the Soviet regime. According to the official report, the generals had confessed at a closed trial, before a tribunal consisting of eight senior army officers (only two of whom survived the purge), to "habitual and base betrayal of military secrets to a certain hostile Fascist power and working as spies to encompass the downfall of the Soviet State and to restore capitalism." It is now generally agreed that they never confessed; in all likelihood, they were executed out of hand, without trial.

The implications of this decapitation of the Red Army were bound to be devastating both at home and abroad. Stalin's audacity in wielding his scythe on the flower of the military elite stood on a wholly different footing from the extirpation of his political enemies. He must have anticipated that it would set off a chain reaction of arrests and executions within the armed forces which would woefully depress public confidence in the country's readiness for war and downgrade the Soviet Army in the eyes of both the democracies and the dictatorships. He was prepared to run that risk, and even the gamble that the Army, often the crutch but sometimes the scourge of tyrants, might take action to avenge its fallen leaders and bring the fantastic carnage to a halt.

Assuming that he was neither a fool nor a madman, Stalin must have honestly believed that an Army coup was being planned at the top level. In recent years it has been revealed that in the spring of 1937 the German secret police contrived to leak "reports" of forbidden conversations between Tukhachevsky and the German General Staff back to Moscow, through the medium of the unwitting Czech Foreign Minister, Eduard Beneš, and to supply supportive and equally false documentary evidence to Stalin's personal secretariat. The fact that the grist for the Gestapo's rumor mill was supplied to it in the first instance by the NKVD itself, as German sources have since confirmed, supplies the answer to the puzzle. Stalin's fear of the Army, as the one disciplined mechanism in existence capable of seizing power, was deliberately fomented by Yezhov, who viewed the military as the only segment of the populace not subject to the NKVD's absolute control. The revival on May 17 of the system of allotting political commissars to all military units, which had been dropped twelve years earlier, lends weight to this analysis.

Had Stalin not been, as Khrushchev later put it, "morbidly suspicious," he might have considered that, had the Red Army leadership planned to move against him, it could have done so with ease in the one-month interval which elapsed between Tukhachevsky's humiliating transfer to the command of a small provincial garrison (a harbinger of worse to come) and his arrest. And he might not have swallowed the story of a plot with the Germans by a cabal which included in its number three Jewish generals.

The holocaust which hit the Army, once the regime's initial spell of nervousness had passed, reached catastrophic dimensions. The Supreme War Council lost three of its four members; 80 per cent of the country's marshals and generals, 62 out of 85 corps commanders, and more than half of the divisional and brigade commanders entered the maw of the purge, which reached all the way down to company level. Roughly 25 per cent of the 6000 top officers were executed, while the rest went to prison or labor camps. Moscow-based diplomats and their military attaches were kept busy with confidential reports to their governments on two burning questions: Will the Army remain loyal to Stalin in case of war? And, if so, is it worth anything? Even the usually sanguine Ambassador Davies had his doubts: "The opinion as to the Russian power is completely the reverse of what it was three months ago," he told the State Department in July. "This is so both as to the strength of the regime here politically and governmentally and the strength of the Red Army."

The sorry showing of the Russian Army against the Finns late in 1939 sharply reflected the debilitating effect of this wholesale bloodletting. Many years later, when Nazi records became available after World War II and yielded no hint of relationships between Tukhachevsky and the Reichswehr (but on the contrary revealed considerable contact between the Gestapo and the NKVD), Stalin may have reflected upon his folly.

With the Army and the NKVD itself caught in the toils of the purge, no segment of Soviet society was sacred. The impact on industry was particularly disastrous. Daily accounts appeared in the Soviet press of arrests and executions of factory managers and technicians for "wrecking," sabotage, and spying for foreign enemies. Production fell far below the rather modest norms set by the Second Five-Year Plan, as labor turnover in industry throughout the country continued to mount. Local Party organizations, which could normally have been relied upon to crack the whip over these laggards, were utterly demoralized by the loss of over 60 per cent of their officials by mid-1937.

One curious by-product of the purge illustrates the thoroughness of Stalin and his henchmen. Stalin's official biographers had long been engaged in repeated revisions of their accounts of his career, progressively exaggerating with each edition the part he had played in the early days of the Party struggle. Those who might bear witness to the falsity of these accounts—Stalin's old mentors and comrades-in-arms—were ruthlessly liquidated. It is perhaps more than a coincidence that one of the foremost practitioners of the art of fictionalizing Stalin's biography would soon emerge as Yezhov's successor as head of the NKVD—Lavrenti P. Beria.

Stalin's acute sensitivity to his place in history (as written in the Soviet Union) undoubtedly shaped the third show trial, Yezhov's most grotesque theatrical venture, which was staged in the Hall of Columns early in March 1938. Bukharin, Rykov, and Nikolai Krestinsky, all trusted intimates of Lenin and former members of the Politburo, headed a distinguished array of twenty-one defendants, including Christian Rakovsky, whom Lenin had placed in charge of the Ukrainian Government and who had later served as Ambassador at Paris; Arkady Rosengoltz, former Foreign Trade Commissar; Grigori Grinko, former Commissar of Finance; and a broken ex-NKVD official named Yagoda.

The presence of Yagoda in the dock invested the proceedings with a paradoxical quality which G. K. Chesterton would have recognized as unconscious plagiarism from his *The Man Who Was Thursday*. For the indictment against Yagoda labeled him a conspirator with Zinoviev, Kamenev, and the selfsame men whose trial and execution he had engineered! The serpent had begun to eat its own tail.

To add injury to insult, Yagoda was accused of having murdered his predecessor as chief of the secret police, Vyacheslav Menzhinsky, Maxim Gorki, and Gorki's son, all of whom died of natural causes, as well as Kuibyshev, whose mysterious death after the first trial, it will be recalled, had been something more than a coincidence.

The role allotted to Yagoda in this trial seems to have been that of scapegoat for crimes which, on the backstairs of the Kremlin and else-

257

where in the country and abroad, were being whispered about as having been organized by Stalin. What more effective device for stilling the ugly rumors than to admit that Yagoda had contrived the deaths of Kirov, Kuibyshev, and others, as the agent of Trotsky instead of Stalin?

And wasn't it at least a partial answer to the Trotskyite press, which had been sneering scornfully at the ridiculous picture of a vast network of terrorists with a total of one important assassination to its credit, to prove that the tally had been raised to five, through the connivance of the corrupt head of the NKVD?

As long as he was rewriting history, Stalin decided in this last major trial to go the distance. In addition to the routine accusations which had characterized the previous trials, the principal defendants (together with Trotsky) were charged with treasonable activities in league with foreign powers as far back as 1921! And Bukharin was singled out for the most extravagant invention to date: that in 1918 he had conspired to murder Lenin, Stalin, and other Bolshevik leaders.

No explanation of the recklessness of these accusations holds water, other than the megalomania which by this time had taken hold of Stalin. Their only conceivable utility was to erase from the history books the last vestige of credit to those who had led the Bolsheviks to power, except for himself and Lenin; to elevate him retroactively to the stature of Lenin's only true-blue collaborator; to enshrine permanently in Soviet theology the saintly trinity of Lenin, the Father; Stalin, the Son; and Marx, the Holy Ghost.

It speaks well for Vishinsky and for Yezhov's interrogation machine that many foreign diplomats and reporters were completely taken in by the proceedings. But some allowance must be made for the international political climate: Hitler was just about ready to formalize his annexation of Austria; the Japanese were on the rampage in China; and Westerners of good will had strong motives for blinding themselves to the vices and weaknesses of any ostensible enemy of the Fascist scourge.

In retrospect, however, their credulity appears to have exceeded all reasonable bounds. Among the coals heaped on the head of the hapless Yagoda, for example, was the masterminding of a plot to poison Stalin, Yezhov, and the members of the Politburo. One of the means he supposedly adopted against Yezhov was the spraying of poison on the walls of Yezhov's office (shades of the Medici!). How could it have escaped the attention of experienced newsmen and mature diplomats that Yagoda, who had charge of feeding the top men in the Kremlin, could easily have wiped out the lot of them with one well-spiced luncheon?

Assuming they missed this point, they might at least have cast a jaundiced eye on the lurid and gruesome accounts of the medical "murders" of the Gorkis, Kuibyshev, and Menzhinsky. According to the prosecution, these men were "cured to death" by improper treatment at the hands of four physicians acting under Yagoda's instructions. These eminent doctors included in their number Dr. Lev G. Levin, seventy-year-old senior consultant to the Kremlin's medical department, who had long attended many members of the Politburo and their families. If, as Levin confessed, Yagoda forced him to commit murder, threatening reprisals against his children and grandchildren, why could Levin not have informed on him to the intended victims or his other patients? How could Yagoda have exposed himself to this risk?

And where were Stalin's old comrade, Avel Yenukidze, former Secretary of the Central Executive Committee, and ex-Politburo member Yakovlevich Rudzutak, both heavily incriminated by the testimony as Bukharin's and Rykov's closest associates in the conspiracy? Bukharin and Rykov were tied to the assassination of Kirov and the death of Gorki only by statements attributed to Yenukidze. But this vital witness had been shot less than three months earlier, after a secret hearing, apparently unwilling to the end to participate in a public spectacle for auld lang syne. The missing Rudzutak, arrested in July 1937, had succumbed to the NKVD's powers of persuasion and then retracted his confession at his secret trial, asking that the Party's Central Committee be informed "that there is in the NKVD an as yet not liquidated center which is craftily manufacturing cases, which forces innocent people to confess. . . ." So says Khrushchev, who tells us that the plea was ignored; sentence was pronounced upon Rudzutak in twenty minutes and he was shot.

And was there nothing suspect about Rykov's confession that he was engaged in counterrevolutionary activity while he was still Premier of the Soviet Union? Or Rakovsky's admission that he had been working intermittently for the British since he took up his post as Ambassador in London in 1924? Or in the charge that Trotsky and Bukharin—in 1918 the mightiest men in Russia next to Lenin—should have sought at that time to eliminate him and the insignificant Stalin in their thirst for power?

Had Bukharin admitted the plot to kill Lenin and Stalin, as Rakovsky and Rykov supinely confessed their activities for foreign governments, it might be easier to comprehend how all of these fantastic accounts might be swallowed whole. But although he conceded complicity in a peasant revolt in the Kuban district, Bukharin stubbornly denied the plot against Lenin and Stalin in 1918, as well as the charges of espionage. The witnesses employed by Vishinsky to prove the 1918 conspiracy had been literally exhumed for the purpose—principally old Left Social Revolutionaries who had been rotting in jail since Bukharin himself had them arrested for the assassination of the German Ambassador following the Treaty of Brest-Litovsk. Did it not occur to the legally trained mind of Ambassador Davies that these prisoners would have had much to gain by unmasking Bukharin's plot during their eighteen years' imprisonment?

Bukharin fought Vishinsky with the philosophical agility and wit which had won him fame throughout the Party. Quite obviously he was prepared to die for his opposition to Stalin, but he would not permit his illustrious past to be dragged through the mire. After one of his repeated denials of the plot to kill Lenin, Vishinsky, pressing for an opening, began a question: "But the atmosphere was . . ." Cutting him short, Bukharin snapped contemptuously: "The atmosphere was the atmosphere."

But it was Krestinsky, former Deputy Foreign Minister, who furnished the most dramatic moments of the trial. Krestinsky had compliantly confessed within a week after his arrest, thus avoiding the brainwashing treatment. But on the first day of the trial, when called to plead to the indictment, he spoke up resolutely:

I plead not guilty. I am not a Trotskyite. I was never a member of the bloc of Rights and Trotskyites, of whose existence I was not aware. Nor have I committed any of the crimes with which I personally am charged; in particular, I plead not guilty to the charge of having had connections with the German intelligence service.

Consternation in the court. Vishinsky confronted the accused with the signed transcript of his confession.

"My testimony of June 5 to 9 is false from beginning to end," Krestinsky stated. But he had not recanted during his nine months in prison, Vishinsky reminded him. Why? "Because from personal experience I had arrived at the conviction that before the trial, if there was to be one, I would not succeed in refuting my testimony."

Cleaving obstinately to this position throughout the first day, Krestinsky was returned to his cell. Overnight the press section held its breath. Throughout most of the next day he was a silent figure in the courtroom; he was not called upon and he did not volunteer to speak. But after hearing Rakovsky testify that evening, dutifully involving himself and Krestinsky in Trotskyite activities, Krestinsky retracted his gesture of revolt:

Yesterday, under the influence of a momentary keen feeling of false shame, evoked by the atmosphere of the dock and the painful impression created by the public reading of the indictment, which was aggravated by my poor health, I could not bring myself to say that I am guilty . . . I admit my complete responsibility for the treason and treachery I have committed . . .

From that point on, Krestinsky was putty in Vishinsky's hands, obediently condemning himself and Trotsky as secret agents of the German General Staff since 1921.

To the general view that Krestinsky was persuaded of the error of his ways by an overnight "refresher course" with the NKVD, a footnote is in order. Orlov suggests that the repudiation was purposely staged by Stalin in order to prove to foreign critics "that in his courts not all the defendants confessed like automatons." If so, the ruse miscarried.

After an eleven-day trial, all but three of the accused received death sentences. Rakovsky and two lesser defendants, including one of the doctors, went to jail.

Stalin had made his point. The rest is anticlimax. Yezhov was ousted late in 1938, to be replaced by the sycophantic Beria, and was never heard from again. The NKVD itself underwent the last great purge of the period, and by December 1938, some of its chiefs and examiners were being tried for extracting confessions by force, as a counterrevolutionary device to foment antagonism to the government!

By the following year some of the prisoners were released, and those who remained in the jails and labor camps received somewhat better treatment. For Stalin had achieved his objectives and was now attempting to put as much distance as possible between his regime and the untoward by-products of the purge. He had diverted attention from the sacrifices he had demanded of the people and from the shortcomings of his program by conjuring up the specter of a foreign conspiracy led by Trotsky and abetted by the Fascist powers. He had made dissent the equivalent of treason; he had scourged an entire generation of potential rivals whose only crime was their nostalgia for the brave new world they had fought for in 1917. He had lifted out of obscurity a layer of young careerists who had come to maturity knowing no other leader but himself, and who had no loyalty except to him. He had laid the blame for the excesses of the purge itself on the doorstep of Yezhov and his staff. All told, he had fulfilled Trotsky's dire prophecy of 1904:

The organization of the Party takes the place of the Party itself; the Central Committee takes the place of the organization; and finally the dictator takes the place of the Central Committee . . .

In due course, Stalin took care of Trotsky, too. On August 20, 1940, in far-off Mexico, a Stalinist agent, armed with a mountaineer's ice pick, carried out the sentence which Stalin had pronounced upon him without trial.

But Stalin was by that time serving a sentence for his own crimes. The purge had left his country debilitated, its industry guided by learners, its Army led by a tiny fragment of its former elite. No family in the country had been untouched by the purge: in the two years of Yezhov's ascendance, some 7,500,000 had been arrested, and over 300,000 executed, by the most conservative estimates now available. Fear will beget conformity, but it will not promote contentment or morale, as was demonstrated by the enthusiastic reception of the German invaders as liberators in many parts of the Soviet Union in 1941, when hundreds of thousands of Russian troops surrendered without a struggle. Until they came to know the Nazis better, these subjects of Stalin were prepared to try Hitler's brand of tyranny.

The price Stalin paid for the purge was the pact with Hitler in August 1939. Hitler would not have fought a two-front war; and Stalin was woefully unprepared to fight the Nazis alone. His orchard had been pruned and disinfected unsparingly, and it bore only the grotesque fruit of appeasement. He had whipped his people with scorpions, and they saw little to choose between one dictator and another.

He signed, and Hitler moved on Poland.

The English translations of the transcripts of the trials reflect Stalin's growing confidence in their propaganda value. The record of the first trial was presented in abridged form, with much testimony paraphrased; the other two were published verbatim, omitting only testimony which would embarrass the Soviet Union in its relations with "certain foreign powers." Typical excerpts from the enormous volume of testimony adduced at the public sessions follow:

ZINOVIEV, KAMENEV AND FOURTEEN OTHERS.
("THE TROTSKYITE-ZINOVIEVITE TERRORIST CENTER")
AUGUST 19–24, 1936

AUGUST 19

I. N. SMIRNOV[1] denies Mrachkovsky's testimony to the effect that he, Smirnov, had conveyed Trotsky's instructions about terrorism to the Moscow terrorist center.

VISHINSKY. I ask leave to read Vol. XXIX, p. 115, of the record of the examination of Smirnov on August 13 by Scheinin, Examining Magistrate for cases of special importance, according to which Smirnov said that in 1931 Sedov gave terroristic directions. Here is Smirnov's testimony: "On my return to Moscow I reported this to Safonova and Mrachkovsky." Well, now, does this correspond to what you said five minutes ago?

SMIRNOV. (Remains silent.)

[1] Pioneer Bolshevik; leader of 5th Red Army in victory over Kolchak; People's Commissar for Communications, 1923–27; former member of Central Committee.

VISHINSKY. I ask that permission be given to Smirnov himself to read this passage from the evidence. As Smirnov persists in his denials, tries to evade responsibility, I ask that he read this passage from the evidence in front of everybody here.

SMIRNOV (*reading his testimony*). "In 1931, Sedov gave terroristic directions which, on my return to Moscow, I reported to Safonova and Mrachkovsky."

VISHINSKY (*to Mrachkovsky*). Mrachkovsky, did you learn about Sedov's line on terrorism from Smirnov?

MRACHKOVSKY[2]. Yes.

VISHINSKY. After Smirnov's return from Moscow, did you meet him?

MRACHKOVSKY. Yes.

VISHINSKY. Did you speak to him?

MRACHKOVSKY. Yes.

VISHINSKY. Together with Safonova?

MRACHKOVSKY. Yes.

VISHINSKY. And you knew about these directions of Sedov's?

MRACHKOVSKY. Yes, I so affirm.

VISHINSKY. Smirnov, did you hear that?

SMIRNOV. (*Remains silent.*)

VISHINSKY. Was the murder of Sergei Mironovich Kirov prepared by the center?

EVDOKIMOV. Yes.

VISHINSKY. You personally took part in these preparations.

EVDOKIMOV[3]. Yes.

VISHINSKY. Did Zinoviev and Kamenev participate with you in the preparations?

EVDOKIMOV. Yes.

VISHINSKY (*to Bakayev*). Did you meet Nikolayev in Leningrad?

BAKAYEV[4]. Yes.

VISHINSKY. Did you confer about an understanding regarding the assassination of S. M. Kirov?

BAKAYEV. There was no need for me to come to an understanding with him about it because the instructions for the assassination had been given by Zinoviev and Kamenev.

VISHINSKY. But Nikolayev told you that he had decided to assassinate S. M. Kirov, didn't he?

BAKAYEV. He did, and so did other terrorists—Levin, Mandelstamm, Kotolynov, Rumyartsev.

VISHINSKY. You discussed the assassination of Kirov?

[2] Old Bolshevik and disabled veteran of the Civil War.

[3] Former member of the Central Committee.

[4] Old Bolshevik; member of Central Committee and Central Control Commission of the Party at time of Lenin's death.

BAKAYEV. Yes.

VISHINSKY. He expressed his determination. And what was your attitude towards it?

BAKAYEV. I was for it.

VISHINSKY. How did Zinoviev and Kamenev reconcile terroristic activities with Marxism?

REINGOLD[5]. In 1932, Zinoviev, at Kamenev's apartment, in the presence of a number of members of the united Trotskyite-Zinovievite center, argued in favor of resorting to terror as follows: although terror is incompatible with Marxism, at the present moment these considerations must be abandoned. There are no other methods available of fighting the leaders of the Party and the government at the present time. Stalin combines in himself all the strength and firmness of the present Party leadership. Therefore Stalin must be put out of the way in the first place. Kamenev enlarged on this theory and said that the former methods of fighting, namely, attempts to win the masses, combinations with the leaders of the Rightists, and banking on economic difficulties, have failed. That is why the only method of struggle available is terroristic acts against Stalin and his closest comrades-in-arms, Kirov, Voroshilov, Kaganovich, Orjonikidze, Postyshev, Kossior, and the others.

Zinoviev and Kamenev were both of the opinion, and they told me about this, that on the morrow of the *coup d'état*, after the seizure of power, Bakayev should be put at the head of the G.P.U. in the capacity of chairman of the G.P.U. By the use of the G.P.U. machinery, he was to assist in covering up the traces, in doing away with, in killing, not only of employees of the People's Commissariat for Internal Affairs—the G.P.U., who might be in the possession of any threads of the conspiracy—but also all the direct perpetrators of terroristic acts against Stalin and his immediate assistants.

AUGUST 20

VISHINSKY. What appraisal should be given of the articles and statements you wrote in 1933, in which you expressed loyalty to the Party? Deception?

KAMENEV. No, worse than deception.

VISHINSKY. Worse than deception, worse than perfidy—find the word. Treason?

KAMENEV. You have found it.

VISHINSKY. Consequently, your struggle against the leaders of the Party and the government was guided by motives of a personal base character—by the thirst for personal power?

[5] Former Assistant People's Commissar of Finance. Believed to be disguised prosecution witness.

KAMENEV. Yes, by the thirst for power of our group.

VISHINSKY. Don't you think that this has nothing in common with social ideals?

KAMENEV. It has as much in common as revolution has with counterrevolution.

VISHINSKY. That is, you are on the side of counterrevolution?

KAMENEV. Yes.

VISHINSKY. Thereby you are fighting socialism as well, aren't you?

KAMENEV. You are drawing the conclusions of an historian and a prosecutor.

AUGUST 22

MRACHKOVSKY (*Closing plea*). In 1923 I became a Trotskyite. I took a despicable path, the path of deception of the Party. We must cross out past services; the past does not exist. But the present cannot be crossed out. I am a counterrevolutionary . . .

I do not ask for mitigation of my punishment. I do not want that. I want to be believed that during the investigation and in court I told the whole truth. I want to depart from life without carrying any filth with me.

Why did I take the counterrevolutionary path? My connection with Trotsky—that is what brought me to this; it is from that time on that I began to deceive the Party, to deceive its leaders . . .

Let everybody remember that not only a general, not only a prince or nobleman can become a counterrevolutionary; workers, or those who spring from the working class, like myself, can also become counterrevolutionaries.

I depart as a traitor to my Party, as a traitor who should be shot. All I ask is that I be believed when I say that during the investigation I spat out all this vomit.

EVDOKIMOV (*Closing plea*). Who will believe a single word of ours? Who will believe us, who played so detestable a comedy at the fresh grave of Kirov, whom we had killed; who will believe us who, only by accident, not through any fault of our own, did not become the assassins of Stalin and other leaders of the people? Who will believe us, who are facing the Court as a counterrevolutionary gang of bandits, as allies of Fascism, of the Gestapo? . . .

Trotsky is not here with us in the dock because he is abroad. He has two perspectives before him: either to disappear immediately and without a trace, as Azef[6] did, not only from the political arena, but from the arena of life in general, and go into oblivion, hide behind a false name as Azef did—or else, at some time, face a proletarian court.

I don't consider it possible to plead for clemency. Our crimes against

[6] Yevno Azef or Azev, leader of terrorist arm of the Social Revolutionary Party around the turn of the century, who doubled as an agent of the Czarist secret police for five years, until his exposure in 1909.

the proletarian state and against the international revolutionary movement are too great to make it possible for us to expect clemency.

PYATAKOV, RADEK AND FIFTEEN OTHERS.
("THE ANTI-SOVIET TROTSKYITE CENTER")
JANUARY 23–30, 1937

JANUARY 23

VISHINSKY. Do I rightly understand you to say that you met Sedov in Berlin in 1931 and talked about fighting the Soviet Government and the Party, that you expressed the opinion that industrialization would fail, and so on?

PYATAKOV. About the failure of industrialization I did not yet at that time say what my stand was, but at any rate I spoke about resuming the fight against the leadership, and on this question I did say what my stand was.

VISHINSKY. You considered it necessary to resume this fight?

PYATAKOV. Yes.

VISHINSKY. How is it to be explained that you so quickly consented to resume this fight against the Party and the Soviet Government?

PYATAKOV. The talk with Sedov was not the cause of this, it only served as a fresh impetus.

VISHINSKY. Consequently, you held your old Trotskyite position even before this?

PYATAKOV. Unquestionably, the old Trotskyite views still survived in me, and they subsequently grew more and more.

VISHINSKY. And by 1931 had grown sufficiently?

PYATAKOV. By 1931 there had taken shape in my mind definite differences with the leadership of the Party on the grounds of the complete removal of Trotsky from the leadership and his banishment abroad, and because Kamenev and Zinoviev were not being given any leading Party and government work.

VISHINSKY. Such was your first conversation with Sedov?

PYATAKOV. Yes.

VISHINSKY. Were you to meet Sedov again in Berlin?

PYATAKOV. During the first meeting we agreed not to meet again because it was rather difficult for me to do so. I was fairly well known in Berlin, portraits of me were published in the newspapers, and it was therefore not very convenient for me to meet. . . .

VISHINSKY. That is, for reasons of secrecy?

PYATAKOV. Yes, for those reasons. However, some time after the first meeting, I think it was three weeks later, four weeks at most, Ivan Nikitich Smirnov again came to me and said that Sedov asked, despite our agreement not to meet, to meet a second time for a very brief and very necessary talk.

VISHINSKY. So Smirnov all the time played the part of contact man, of go-between?

PYATAKOV. It was apparently easier for him to meet Sedov, so that in that sense he was a go-between for Sedov and me. At any rate, I endeavored to meet him as little as possible for reasons of secrecy, but agreed to this meeting because Sedov was very insistent about it. And we met in the same place as the first time. This time the conversation was very brief.

VISHINSKY. Was the time and place of meeting arranged by you directly with Sedov or through Smirnov?

PYATAKOV. I told Smirnov that in order not to make any further arrangements about where to meet, we would meet in the same place.

VISHINSKY. Where you had met the first time?

PYATAKOV. This second conversation was very brief; it lasted not more than ten or fifteen minutes, perhaps even less, and amounted to the following.

Without any beating about the bush, Sedov said: "You realize, Yuri Leonidovich, that inasmuch as the fight has been resumed, money is needed. You can provide the necessary funds for waging the fight." He was hinting that my business position enabled me to set aside certain government funds, or, to put it bluntly, to steal.

Sedov said that only one thing was required of me, namely, that I should place as many orders as possible with two German firms, Borsig and Demag, and that he, Sedov, would arrange to receive the necessary sums from them, bearing in mind that I would not be particularly exacting as to prices. If this were deciphered it was clear that the additions to prices that would be made on the Soviet orders would pass wholly or in part into Trotsky's hands for his counterrevolutionary purposes. There the second conversation ended.

VISHINSKY. Who named these firms?

PYATAKOV. Sedov.

VISHINSKY. Did you not inquire why he named these firms particularly?

PYATAKOV. No. He said that he had connections with these firms.

VISHINSKY. You had connections with other firms as well?

PYATAKOV. Yes, I had very many connections. But Sedov mentioned these firms, apparently because it was with them that he had connections.

VISHINSKY. Consequently, it was clear to you that these particular firms were mentioned by Sedov for specific reasons?

PYATAKOV. Of course, that is what he said.

VISHINSKY. And what was the nature of these connections?

PYATAKOV. I have just said that I do not know. He, Sedov, said that since I, Pyatakov, could not steal money, what was required of me was to place as many orders as possible with the firms I have mentioned.

VISHINSKY. And those firms were named by Sedov himself?

PYATAKOV. Yes, and he added that he would secure the necessary sum from them.

267

VISHINSKY. You did not ask how, through whom?
PYATAKOV. I considered it inconvenient to ask that.

PYATAKOV. . . . About the end of 1935 Radek received a long letter —instructions from Trotsky. In this directive Trotsky advanced two possible variants of our coming into power. The first variant was the possibility of our coming into power before a war, and the second variant, during a war. Trotsky visualized the first variant as resulting from a concentrated terrorist blow, as he said. What he had in mind was the simultaneous performance of terrorist acts against a number of leaders of the C.P.S.U. and the Soviet Government, and of course in the first place against Stalin and his immediate assistants.

The second variant, which in Trotsky's opinion was the more probable, was a military defeat. Since, as he said, war was inevitable, and moreover in the very near future—a war in the first place with Germany, and possibly with Japan—the idea therefore was to reach the necessary agreement with the governments of these countries and thus ensure that they would regard the coming to power of the bloc favorably; and that meant obtaining the necessary support to maintain ourselves in power by making a number of concessions to these countries on terms to be agreed upon beforehand. But since the question of defeatism, of military wrecking activities, of inflicting telling blows during wartime both to the rear and to the Army was here put point-blank, this very much disquieted Radek and myself. It seemed to us that the reason why Trotsky was staking on the inevitability of defeat was largely because of his isolation and ignorance of the real conditions, his ignorance of what was going on here, his ignorance of what the Red Army was like; and that was why he cherished such illusions. Both Radek and I therefore decided that it was necessary to endeavor to meet Trotsky.

VISHINSKY. Accused Radek, did you in 1935 or somewhat earlier receive two, or perhaps more, letters from Trotsky?

RADEK. One letter in April 1934 and another in December 1935.

VISHINSKY. Do their contents tally with what Pyatakov has stated here?

RADEK. In the main, yes. The first letter in substance spoke of expediting war as a desirable condition for the coming to power of the Trotskyites. The second letter elaborated on these so-called two variants—coming to power in time of peace and coming to power in the event of war.

The first letter did not deal with the social consequences of the concessions which Trotsky proposed. If a deal was to be made with Germany and Japan, then of course it would not be made purely for the sake of Trotsky's beautiful eyes. But he did not set forth any program of concessions in this letter. The second letter spoke of the social and economic policy, which Trotsky considered an essential part of such a deal for the coming to power of the Trotskyites.

VISHINSKY. In this second letter, which has been called a detailed

268

program of defeatism, was there anything about the conditions which, on coming to power, the group of the parallel center were to fulfil for the benefit of foreign states?

RADEK. The whole program was directed towards this.

VISHINSKY. Trotsky did not outline the conditions themselves?

RADEK. He did.

VISHINSKY. Did he speak concretely of territorial concessions?

RADEK. It was stated that this would probably be necessary.

VISHINSKY. What exactly?

RADEK. Territorial concessions would probably be necessary.

VISHINSKY. Of what kind?

RADEK. If peace was to be made with the Germans, we would have to satisfy them in one form or another, to consent to their expansion.

VISHINSKY. To hand over the Ukraine?

RADEK. When we read the letter we had no doubt of this. Whatever it would be called, a Hetman Ukraine or something else, it was a question of satisfying German expansion in the Ukraine.

As regards Japan, Trotsky spoke of ceding the Amur region and the Maritime Province.

JANUARY 24

VISHINSKY. Hence you were interested in hastening war and it was to your interest that the U.S.S.R. should be defeated in this war? How was this put in Trotsky's letter?

RADEK. Defeat is inevitable and it will create the conditions for our accession to power; therefore, we were interested in hastening the war. The conclusion is: we are interested in defeat.

VISHINSKY. We are reconstructing the contents of the letter.

RADEK. Undoubtedly that was the line of thought. It logically followed with indisputable clarity. But since I am giving you, the State Prosecution, evidence, I must draw a clear distinction between the phrase, as I remember it, and the precise phrase that was in the letter. But irrespective of whether it was couched in those terms or not, there is no doubt that this was the line of thought.

VISHINSKY. I ask you to reply to the question about what was your and Trotsky's attitude towards the defeat of the U.S.S.R.

RADEK. If you are asking me about Trotsky's attitude, I have answered. If you are asking me about my own, Citizen Procurator, I must say that in so far as it is a matter of establishing juridical facts I must give an answer. In so far as it is a matter of my feelings and my ethics, which did not affect my action. . . .

VISHINSKY. I am not interested in feelings, but in facts.

RADEK. The fact that I gave a visa to Trotsky's mandate. . . .

VISHINSKY. The point is not that you gave your visa to Trotsky's mandate; I am speaking of a fact: the letter which you received from

Trotsky in April 1934—this letter spoke about war, about this war being inevitable, that in this war the U.S.S.R., in Trotsky's opinion, would suffer defeat, that as a result of this war and defeat the bloc would come to power. And now I ask you: In these circumstances were you for the defeat of the U.S.S.R. or for the victory of the U.S.S.R.?

RADEK. At that time I considered defeat inevitable and thought that in the circumstances of defeat we would come to power. If you are asking me about what I wished. . . .

VISHINSKY. But were you for the defeat or for the victory of the U.S.S.R.?

RADEK. All my actions during these years testify to the fact that I aided defeat.

VISHINSKY. These actions of yours were deliberate?

RADEK. Apart from sleeping, I have never in my life committed any undeliberate actions.

VISHINSKY. And this, unfortunately, was not a dream?

RADEK. Unfortunately, this was not a dream.

VISHINSKY. It was reality?

RADEK. It was sad reality.

VISHINSKY. And what was the conclusion you drew from this?

RADEK. The conclusion to be drawn from this inevitable defeat was that now the problem of restoring capitalism was openly set before us.

VISHINSKY. That is to say, this restoration of capitalism, which Trotsky called bringing the social structure of the U.S.S.R. into line with the capitalist countries, was conceived as an inevitable result of an agreement with foreign states?

RADEK. As an inevitable result of the defeat of the U.S.S.R., of the social consequences of this defeat, and of an agreement on the basis of this defeat.

VISHINSKY. Further?

RADEK. The third condition was the most novel of all for us—that of replacing the Soviet power by what he called a Bonapartist government. And it was clear to us that this meant Fascism without its own finance capital, serving foreign finance capital.

VISHINSKY. The fourth condition?

RADEK. The fourth was the partition of the country. It was planned to surrender the Ukraine to Germany, and the Maritime Province and the Amur region to Japan.

VISHINSKY. Was there any talk at that time about any other economic concessions?

RADEK. Yes, those decisions about which I have already spoken were further amplified. The payment of indemnities in the form of supplies of food, raw materials, and fats extending over a long period of years. Then —at first he said this without giving figures, but afterwards in more definite form—a certain percentage of participation in Soviet imports to be guaranteed to the victorious countries. All this together meant the complete enslavement of the country.

VISHINSKY. Was there talk about Sakhalin oil?

RADEK. As regards Japan, we were told she must not only be given Sakhalin oil but be guaranteed oil in the event of a war with the U.S.A. It was stated that no obstacles must be raised to the conquest of China by Japanese imperialism.

VISHINSKY. And as regards the Danube countries?

RADEK. As regards the Danube and Balkan countries, Trotsky said in his letter that German Fascism was expanding and we should do nothing to prevent this. The point was, of course, to sever any of our relations with Czechoslovakia which would have contributed to the defense of that country.

VISHINSKY. And what was the conclusion?

RADEK. And therefore the conclusion: restoration of capitalism in the circumstances of 1935. For nothing at all, just for the sake of Trotsky's beautiful eyes—the country was to return to capitalism. When I read this I felt as if it were a madhouse. And, lastly, and this is no unimportant fact, formerly the position was that we were fighting for power because we were convinced that we could secure something to the country. Now we were to fight in order that foreign capital might rule, which would put us completely under its control before it allowed us to come to power. What did the directive to agree upon wrecking activities with foreign circles mean? For me this directive meant something very simple, something very comprehensible to me as a political organizer, namely that agents of foreign powers were becoming wedged in our organization, that our organization was becoming the direct representative of foreign intelligence services. We ceased to be in the slightest degree the masters of our actions. We had put up with Trotsky when he gave us directives from abroad, but in this case we were to become the agency of foreign Fascist states.

This denoted in practice that if such men as Yakov Livshitz or Serebryakov, with decades of revolutionary work behind them, could descend to wrecking, now their moral fiber would have to be utterly broken, and they would act on the instructions of the class enemy. Either they would lose their bearings, or they would become spies. If they lost their bearings, I could do nothing with them; if they became agents of foreign states, others would give them their orders. As a result, if foreign Fascism came in, this Fascism, far from letting Trotskyites get into power—they are of no use to it —would destroy the organization because it had no need to trouble itself with this crowd of anarchist intellectuals. So that even if my attitude to the country did not weigh with me, there was pure egoism. The leader of the organization told me that for the sake of power, for the phantom of power, Trotsky was ready to sacrifice the last man capable of dying for him, and I could not demand this of people who had been my associates for fifteen years. I therefore had to ask myself: what was I to do?

VISHINSKY. What did you decide?

RADEK. The first step to take would be to go to the Central Committee of the Party, to make a statement, to name all the persons. This I did not do. It was not I that went to the G.P.U., but the G.P.U. that came for me.

VISHINSKY. An eloquent reply.

RADEK. A sad reply.

VISHINSKY. That means that the following conclusion may be drawn: as long as you assumed that socialism in our country was feeble, you considered treachery permissible, that it was permissible to work for war, that it was permissible to work for the defeat of the Soviet Union, and so on. But when you saw that socialism was sufficiently powerful and strong, you decided that neither war nor defeat were possible.

RADEK. You are a profound reader of human hearts, but I must nevertheless comment on my thoughts in my own words.

VISHINSKY. I know that you have a fairly good stock of words behind which to conceal your thoughts, and it is very difficult for a man, even a good reader of human hearts, to understand you and induce you to say what you are really thinking. But I would ask you not to reason here so much as a journalist who has specialized in international affairs, but as a man accused of treason. And it is from this standpoint that I ask you the question: were you in favor of defeat in 1934?

RADEK. I have already answered that question.

VISHINSKY. Repeat it once more, if you don't mind.

RADEK. In 1934 I considered defeat inevitable.

VISHINSKY. Were you in favor of defeat in 1934?

RADEK. I considered defeat inevitable.

VISHINSKY. Were you in favor of defeat?

RADEK. If I could avert defeat, I would be against defeat.

VISHINSKY. You consider that you could not have averted it?

RADEK. I considered it an inevitable fact.

VISHINSKY. You are answering my question incorrectly. Did you accept the whole of Trotsky's line given to you in 1934?

RADEK. I accepted the whole of Trotsky's line in 1934.

VISHINSKY. Was defeat part of it?

RADEK. Yes, it was a line of defeat.

VISHINSKY. Trotsky's line included defeat?

RADEK. Yes.

VISHINSKY. Did you accept it?

RADEK. I did.

VISHINSKY. Hence, since you accepted it you were in favor of defeat?

RADEK. From the standpoint. . . .

VISHINSKY. You headed for defeat?

RADEK. Yes, of course.

VISHINSKY. That is, you were in favor of defeat?

RADEK. Of course, if I say yes, that means we headed for it.

VISHINSKY. Which of us then is putting the question rightly?

RADEK. All the same, I think that you are not putting the question rightly.

VISHINSKY. In 1934 you were not against defeat, but in favor of defeat?

RADEK. Yes, I have said so.

VISHINSKY. I want you to repeat it once more.

RADEK. As you please, you are the State Prosecutor and may demand that I repeat it ten times.

VISHINSKY. And then you were arrested?

RADEK. I was arrested, but I denied everything from beginning to end. Maybe you will ask me why?

VISHINSKY. I know that you will always find an answer. You were arrested and questioned. You gave answers?

RADEK. I denied everything from beginning to end.

VISHINSKY. You knew everything, you had the opportunity to go and tell everything?

RADEK. I had, but I decided that I would do that in the People's Commissariat of Internal Affairs. . . .

VISHINSKY. Comrade President, will you please ask the accused to answer questions and not to make speeches?

PRESIDENT. Accused Radek, you may make your two speeches: one—your speech in defense, and the other—your last plea.

VISHINSKY. Were you asked about connections with other members of the terrorist group? What did you reply?

RADEK. I denied it.

VISHINSKY. That was on September 22, 1936?

RADEK. Yes.

VISHINSKY. Were you confronted with Sokolnikov?

RADEK. Yes.

VISHINSKY. Did Sokolnikov expose you?

RADEK. Yes.

VISHINSKY. And you?

RADEK. I denied everything from beginning to end.

VISHINSKY. That was on September 22. Were you confronted with Tivel?

RADEK. I was.

VISHINSKY. What did he say?

RADEK. He said partly what was true and partly what was not true, but I denied everything.

VISHINSKY. Both what was true and what was not true?

RADEK. Yes.

VISHINSKY. Were you on November 4 questioned about various facts concerning your activity?

RADEK. Yes. I was questioned until December 4, and I denied everything.

VISHINSKY. For how many months did you deny everything?

RADEK. About three months.

VISHINSKY. The fact remains that you, who wanted to tell everything, but could not make up your mind, as you say, to surrender your people to justice, when you yourself fell into the hands of justice categorically denied everything. Is that a fact?

RADEK. Yes.

VISHINSKY. Does that not cast doubt on what you said about your vacillations and misgivings?

RADEK. Yes, if you ignore the fact that you learned about the program and about Trotsky's instructions only from me, of course, it does cast doubt on what I have said.

VISHINSKY. Accused Radek, in your testimony you say: "In 1935 . . . we resolved to call a conference, but before this, in January, when I arrived, Vitaly Putna came to me with a request from Tukhachevsky. . . ." I want to know in what connection you mention Tukhachevsky's name?

RADEK. Tukhachevsky had been commissioned by the government with some task for which he could not find the necessary material. I alone was in possession of this material. He rang me up and asked if I had this material. I had it, and he accordingly sent Putna, with whom he had to discharge this commission, to get this material from me. Of course, Tukhachevsky had no idea either of Putna's role or of my criminal role. . . .

VISHINSKY. And Putna?

RADEK. He was a member of the organization, and he did not come to talk about the organization, but I took advantage of his visit to have this talk.

VISHINSKY. So Putna came to you, having been sent by Tukhachevsky on official business having no bearing whatever on your affairs since he, Tukhachevsky, had no relations with them whatever?

RADEK. Tukhachevsky never had any relations whatever with them.

VISHINSKY. He sent Putna on official business?

RADEK. Yes.

VISHINSKY. And you took advantage of this in order to engage in your own particular affairs?

RADEK. Yes.

VISHINSKY. Do I understand you correctly, that Putna had dealings with the members of your Trotskyite underground organization, and that your reference to Tukhachevsky was made in connection with the fact that Putna came on official business on Tukhachevsky's orders?

RADEK. I confirm that, and I say that I never had and could not have had any dealings with Tukhachevsky connected with counterrevolutionary activities, because I knew Tukhachevsky's attitude to the Party and the government to be that of an absolutely devoted man.

VISHINSKY. At first you would not testify at all, and then you began to testify. Perhaps this is to be explained by some specific conditions of your arrest, perhaps pressure was brought to bear on you?

BOGUSLAVSKY[7]. No.

VISHINSKY. Perhaps it was suggested that you should testify in the way you subsequently did, in return for which your sentence would be mitigated?

BOGUSLAVSKY. No.

VISHINSKY. Consequently you began to give this testimony quite voluntarily and sincerely, because of your internal personal convictions?

BOGUSLAVSKY. Quite true; if the Court permits me, I would like to explain my motives.

VISHINSKY. What motives induced you, Boguslavsky, an old Trotskyite, who for some ten years had devoted yourself to the fight in the ranks of the Trotskyites against the Party and against the Soviet Government, and who continued your anti-Soviet Trotskyite activities until the very day of your arrest, what motives have induced you to say what you are saying, to expose people, to lay down your arms, etc. What has led you to this?

BOGUSLAVSKY. What has led me to this? In reply to the question of the Citizen Procurator, I must say that the interval of nine days between the time of my arrest—even eight days, because it was on the 6th rather than the 5th—and the 14th, was a time during which, if I may so express it, owing to my arrest, I recovered my balance and I was able to bring my still largely, if not utterly, criminal ideas, in order. This explains my stubbornness of these eight days. I must frankly say here in court that in the last few years, I mean in 1934, 1935, and 1936, the position of a criminal, in which I found myself, not only disturbed me, but weighed on me heavily.

Despite the fact that I have waged a struggle for many years, I request the Court to believe me when I say that not everything had been obliterated of that which the class I came from had given me and which had transformed me from a homeless waif into a man of politics and leader in those positions to which the Party had assigned me.

In this connection I want to mention the absolutely intolerable and incredible rottenness within the Trotskyite organization, which I could not help feeling at every step. I must confess that many things have become clear to me only at this trial, in the course of these two days, things that were absolutely unknown to me before. I cannot refrain from confessing here in court to the feelings of revulsion and disgust I experienced when Radek related here how, when the bloc with the Zinovievites had hardly

[7] Old Bolshevik. Former member of All-Ukraine and Moscow Central Executive Committee of the Party.

been formed, the fear began to be expressed that certain people in this bloc might cheat others.

The second thing is that we who conducted the work on the spot were absolutely unaware that our country was being sold to foreign capital behind our backs. I learned something about this when I was handed the indictment. But everything became clear to me only here, when I heard the testimony of Pyatakov and Radek.

VISHINSKY. Did Pyatakov and Radek conceal it from you?

BOGUSLAVSKY. They have testified here that they particularly concealed Trotsky's last directive of the end of 1935 and told nobody about it, including me.

Of course, even so I should have realized at least what every worker and collective farmer in our country realizes—where this was leading. We who held the view that it is impossible to build up socialism in one country and adopted the path of terrorism and wrecking, we should have realized that if it wasn't socialism we were intending to build, what was it? Why, there is only socialism and capitalism.

VISHINSKY. But you realized this before?

BOGUSLAVSKY. Yes, true, that is what I saw. When I was arrested I felt like a man who is on the verge of an abyss and knows that he must fall into it. For eight days, until the time I first began to give testimony, it was already quite clear to me that the time had come to put a stop to it. Of course, I realized it too late. And, indeed, everything we did was repulsive, beginning with these abominable diversive activities. "Fish begin to stink from the head down," the proverb says. And we ought to have cut off this head, but we did not. And we engaged in wrecking activities and diversive acts in order to ensure the defeat of our Union. I have committed a crime. I was guided only by what I have already spoken about. Notwithstanding the fact that my fate is now in the hands of the Court of the Soviet State, I beg the Court to believe that I was guided by this, and only this.

VISHINSKY. I am interested in knowing why you decided to give truthful testimony. Examining the record of the preliminary investigation, I see that at a number of interrogations you denied any part in underground work. Is that so?

MURALOV[8]. Yes, up to December 5. Eight months.

VISHINSKY. Why, then, in the end did you decide to give, and did give, truthful testimony? Explain the motives that led you to the decision to lay everything on the table—if you have laid everything on the table.

MURALOV. I think there were three reasons which held me back and induced me to deny everything.

One reason is political and profoundly serious; two are of an exclusively personal character. I shall begin with the least important, with my character.

[8] Civil War hero and former member of Central Control Commission of the Party.

276

I am very hot-tempered and resentful. That is the first reason. When I was arrested, I became embittered with resentment.

VISHINSKY. Were you badly treated?

MURALOV. I was deprived of my liberty.

VISHINSKY. But perhaps rough methods were used against you?

MURALOV. No, no such methods were used. I must say that in Novosibirsk and here I was treated politely and no cause for resentment was given: I was treated very decently and politely.

VISHINSKY. Was it the fact of arrest itself?

MURALOV. Instead of using other methods, they took me and put me in prison. Such is my nature.

VISHINSKY. You do not like to be put in prison?

MURALOV. No, I do not. The second reason is also of a personal nature. It is my attachment to Trotsky. It began when he was People's Commissar and I was commander of the Moscow Military Area. Then there were political affairs: a whole group of my comrades were in opposition to the Party, the majority of them being authoritative comrades well known to me, like I. N. Smirnov whom I greatly respected, V. N. Yakovlyeva, whom I regarded as a very clever woman, and quite a number of people who supported Trotsky. Of course I too was drawn into this business and began to meet them, and in the course of the work not only came close to them politically but became friends. This was the second circumstance which restrained me, so to speak. I considered it morally inadmissible to betray Trotsky, although I did not subscribe to the directive on terror and destruction. I had heart pangs all the time at the very thought of it; I considered it wrong. Friendship and political motives were involved. The third point was —well, as you know, in every affair something is carried too far.

And I reasoned that if I continued to remain a Trotskyite, especially when the others were quitting—some honestly and others dishonestly—at any rate they were not standard-bearers of counterrevolution, but I—there was a "hero" for you! . . . If I kept on this way, I might become the standard-bearer of counterrevolution. This frightened me terribly. At that time cadres, industry, the national economy were growing up before my eyes. . . . I am not blind and I am not such a fanatic.

And I said to myself, almost after eight months, that I must submit to the interests of the state for which I had fought for twenty-three years, for which I had fought actively in three revolutions, when my life hung by a thread dozens of times.

Was I to remain and continue to aggravate the affair? My name would serve as a banner to those who were still in the ranks of counterrevolution. This was what decided me, and I said: Very well, I will go and tell the whole truth. I do not know whether my answer has satisfied you or not.

JANUARY 26

VISHINSKY. What was your position at Kemerovo?

NORKIN. I was chief of the Kemerovo Combined Works Construction. In 1933 it became clear to me that the reason I was sent to Kemerovo was that I was supposed to carry on destructive work in the most important plant of the chemical industry, which is of enormous importance for defense purposes.

VISHINSKY. It was clear to you that you were sent there for that purpose?

NORKIN. It became clear.

VISHINSKY. What circumstances made this clear to you?

NORKIN. It became clear to me from the instructions I received in 1933 as a member of the Trotskyite organization from the person who was immediately directing my work, Pyatakov.

VISHINSKY. What did Pyatakov tell you?

NORKIN. In the main, his instructions were to work in the direction of retarding this construction work for the purpose of undermining the power of the state.

VISHINSKY. What have you to say about acts of diversion?

NORKIN. In 1935 I received instructions from Pyatakov to concentrate on the main units so as to achieve, without scattering our forces, the maximum results.

Accordingly, I planned to put the State District Power Station out of action by means of explosions. In February 1936 there were three explosions.

VISHINSKY. Actually occurred?

NORKIN. Yes. After that I had to abandon this operation because there was enormous pressure from the workers, and, moreover, I received instructions to stop using volatile coals, and I had to abandon this method. On the contrary, I already thought it time to take measures to ward off the blow against myself, that is to say, to bring up very sharply the question of the Kuznetsk Basin, but this did not materialize, and my request was rejected.

VISHINSKY. When were you arrested?

NORKIN. On September 30.

VISHINSKY. Did you begin to testify at once?

NORKIN. No, not at once.

VISHINSKY. You refused?

NORKIN. Yes, I refused.

VISHINSKY. Did you refuse for a long time?

NORKIN. Yes, for a fairly long time; I refused to testify for approximately two months or so.

VISHINSKY. And why did you afterwards decide to give way?

NORKIN. Because there is a limit to everything.

VISHINSKY. Perhaps pressure was brought to bear upon you?

NORKIN. I was questioned, exposed, there were confrontations.

VISHINSKY. You were confronted with evidence, facts?

NORKIN. There were confrontations.

VISHINSKY. How were you kept? What were your prison conditions like?

NORKIN. Very good. Are you asking me about outward pressure?

VISHINSKY. Yes.

NORKIN. There was no pressure whatever.

VISHINSKY. A man can be deprived of good food, deprived of sleep. We know this from the history of capitalist prisons. He can be deprived of cigarettes.

NORKIN. If that is what you are talking about, there was nothing like it.

VISHINSKY. Did they feed you well?

NORKIN. They were extremely attentive.

VISHINSKY. The evidence brought against you was weighty enough? Did that evidence play any role?

NORKIN. Of course, what played a role was that I realized the hopelessness of the struggle, and realized that it was necessary to bring the whole thing to light.

VISHINSKY. But you did not realize this on the evening of your arrest?

NORKIN. I did. This is a process that is not completed in a day. I did not arrive at the position in which I find myself now in one day. It was not that I was a member of the Party one day and became a diversionist the next. This is a prolonged process of remolding of the brain and of the perception of things.

VISHINSKY. Accused Serebryakov, do you confirm the conversation with Livshitz concerning the preparations for a terrorist act against Comrade Stalin?

SEREBRYAKOV[9]. If that conversation occurred, it could only have taken place in a most general form.

VISHINSKY (to Livshitz). When did Serebryakov tell you about this?

LIVSHITZ. In 1935 during our conversation in my railway car.

VISHINSKY. Accused Serebryakov, were you in Livshitz's railway car in 1935?

SEREBRYAKOV. I was.

VISHINSKY. Did you have a conversation with Livshitz?

SEREBRYAKOV. Yes.

VISHINSKY. What about?

SEREBRYAKOV. Mainly about wrecking work on the railways.

VISHINSKY. Were questions of terrorism mentioned there among other things?

SEREBRYAKOV. No.

[9] Secretary of Party Central Committee and Secretary of All-Russian Central Executive Committee of Soviets under Lenin.

279

VISHINSKY. You do not remember?

SEREBRYAKOV. No.

VISHINSKY. Livshitz?

LIVSHITZ. Yes, I say what I remember.

SEREBRYAKOV. I am not saying that such talk might not have taken place.

VISHINSKY. You merely plead that you do not recollect?

SEREBRYAKOV. Yes—yes, the more so since my conversation took place before I had heard from Pyatakov.

VISHINSKY. In this connection I want to ask Pyatakov, since Serebryakov pleads forgetfulness. Accused Pyatakov, do you confirm this?

PYATAKOV. I did not inform Livshitz about this specially, but he was informed about the terrorist aims and preparations; but I did not inform Livshitz about any particular preparations.

VISHINSKY. I am not referring to any special organization. Livshitz says that he learned from you that preparations were being made for a terrorist act against Stalin. Did you speak to Livshitz about this?

PYATAKOV. I do not remember.

VISHINSKY. You spoke to Livshitz about terrorist acts?

PYATAKOV. Yes.

VISHINSKY. Did you say against whom the preparations for this terrorist act were being made?

PYATAKOV. I spoke to Livshitz about terrorism, but I did not say against whom.

VISHINSKY. You confirm this?

PYATAKOV. I confirm it, but as regards preparations for a terrorist act against Stalin, I do not confirm it.

VISHINSKY. Livshitz says he learned that the center was making preparations for a terrorist act against Stalin. Do you confirm this?

PYATAKOV. No.

VISHINSKY. So you did not speak with Livshitz?

PYATAKOV. I do not think I did.

VISHINSKY. But Livshitz says that he heard about this from you. You do not confirm this then?

PYATAKOV. No, I do not confirm it.

VISHINSKY. Then permit me to ask you: were preparations being made for a terrorist act against Stalin?

PYATAKOV. Yes.

VISHINSKY. You took part in these preparations?

PYATAKOV. Yes.

VISHINSKY. So it is a fact, as Livshitz says, that preparations were being conducted for a terrorist act against Stalin? This is true?

PYATAKOV. Yes.

VISHINSKY. But you confirm the fact that preparations were being made for a terrorist act?

PYATAKOV. Yes.

VISHINSKY (*to Livshitz*). Serebryakov and Pyatakov insist that they did not have this conversation with you. Perhaps you did not have the conversation with Pyatakov and Serebryakov, but perhaps with someone else—perhaps with Sokolnikov, or perhaps with Radek?

LIVSHITZ[10]. I did not speak with Sokolnikov, and I made Radek's acquaintance for the first time here, in the dock.

VISHINSKY. Consequently, you did not know of his existence, did not know that Radek existed?

LIVSHITZ. No, I knew of him, knew of his existence, but I was not acquainted with him.

VISHINSKY. If Pyatakov and Serebryakov deny this, then, looking at the question objectively, who of the accused now seated here—or perhaps of those who will sit here in the future—who may know, who knew about this and could have told you?

LIVSHITZ. I can answer that both have forgotten about it, because I did not talk to other people on this matter, so that if I knew I could only have learned it from them.

THE PRESIDENT (*to Radek*). You raised your hand. Do you want to say something in connection with this?

RADEK. Yes.

THE PRESIDENT. You may.

RADEK. When we, the members of the center, spoke with the members —with such important members of the organization as Livshitz—we did not speak about details, we mentioned neither place, nor time, nor group. We mentioned, however, the group of persons against whom the acts were aimed. Just for this reason the difference of opinion may lie in the fact that Serebryakov or Pyatakov did not say that the act would be carried out at once, or in a month, or in six months, but among persons as important as Livshitz we used to talk, and just for this reason Livshitz cannot be telling an untruth about such things as an attempt on the life of Stalin.

VISHINSKY. Accused Livshitz, were you confronted with Pyatakov on January 17, 1937? Incidentally this will have bearing on the accused Pyatakov, so I will ask him to pay attention to this declaration. At the confrontation the question of terrorism was also referred to. (*Reads*) "QUESTION TO PYATAKOV: Did you give Livshitz directives concerning terrorism and wrecking on that occasion? ANSWER: It is difficult to recall exactly at what time I gave Livshitz these directives. QUESTION TO PYATAKOV: Is this to be understood in the sense that in general you gave such directives to Livshitz? PYATAKOV: Of course, this conversation with him took place."

At the end: "QUESTION TO PYATAKOV: Did you inform Livshitz about the preparations that were being made for terrorist acts against the leaders of the C.P.S.U.? PYATAKOV'S ANSWER: Whether I spoke specifically about this, I do not recall; in any case Livshitz knew about the terrorist activities which the center was carrying on." Is this correct?

[10] Former Assistant People's Commissar of Railways.

PYATAKOV. Yes.

VISHINSKY. Consequently, you confirm that Livshitz knew about the preparations of terrorist acts against the leaders of our Party and government, and, consequently, against Stalin.

PYATAKOV. I confirm that this was directed against certain persons, among them being Stalin.

VISHINSKY. How did Livshitz learn this?

PYATAKOV. From me, among others.

VISHINSKY. So it may be said that Livshitz could state that he knew?

PYATAKOV. No.

VISHINSKY. For me the question is clear. Livshitz spoke with you about terrorism?

PYATAKOV. Yes.

VISHINSKY. That the parallel center was making preparations for terrorism?

PYATAKOV. Yes.

VISHINSKY. That preparations for terrorism were being made against the leaders of the C.P.S.U. and consequently, against Stalin?

PYATAKOV. Yes.

VISHINSKY. So there was such a conversation with Livshitz?

PYATAKOV. Of course.

VISHINSKY. So Livshitz could conceive that when speaking about the terrorist act, you informed him that this terrorist act was being prepared against Stalin as well?

PYATAKOV. That is just what I am talking about.

JANUARY 27

MEMBER OF THE COURT RYCHKOV (to Knyazev). What spying information was handed over to the agent of the Japanese intelligence service by you in person? Was information given regarding mobilization plans?

KNYAZEV[11]. It was given.

MEMBER OF THE COURT RYCHKOV. So you revealed to the Japanese intelligence service certain data on mobilization plans?

KNYAZEV. A number of data.

MEMBER OF THE COURT RYCHKOV. Concerning one railway?

KNYAZEV. Concerning the South Urals, Perm, Transbaikal, Ussuri, and East Siberian Railways.

MEMBER OF THE COURT RYCHKOV. How many train wrecks were engineered by the Trotskyite organization under your leadership?

KNYAZEV. From thirteen to fifteen train wrecks were organized directly by us.

Yes, but the increase in train wrecks was undoubtedly connected with

[11] Former Assistant Chief of Central Traffic Division, People's Commissariat of Railways.

the wrecking activities of the Trotskyite organization in the other branches of industry as well. I remember in 1934 there were altogether about 1500 train wrecks and accidents.

MEMBER OF THE COURT RYCHKOV. Along what lines were your wrecking activities directed?

KNYAZEV. Along the lines of disrupting track maintenance. Seeing that the traffic on the South Urals Railway consisted of heavy rolling stock, I understood very well that if . . .

MEMBER OF THE COURT RYCHKOV. What did you do specifically in the way of wrecking the permanent way?

KNYAZEV. The ballast of the roadbed was weakened, which led to the subsidence of the track. This resulted in rails snapping.

MEMBER OF THE COURT RYCHKOV. And as a result were there train wrecks?

KNYAZEV. From these causes there were train wrecks on the stretch between Yakhino and Ust-Katav in December 1935, also between Yedinover and Berdyaush in February 1936.

VISHINSKY. Were there any victims as well?

KNYAZEV. There were, among the train guards.

MEMBER OF THE COURT RYCHOV. A head guard and a senior guard were killed?

KNYAZEV. Yes.

MEMBER OF THE COURT RYCHKOV. That is to say, in the first place wrecking of the permanent way?

KNYAZEV. Quite right.

MEMBER OF THE COURT RYCHKOV. And secondly?

KNYAZEV. In the traffic department.

MEMBER OF THE COURT RYCHKOV. How was wrecking work carried on to destroy the locomotives?

KNYAZEV. Powerful locomotives of the FD type were introduced in the Kurgan depot. Taking advantage of the fact that not much was known about them in this depot, the management deliberately slackened the supervision of current repairs, frequently compelled the engine drivers to leave before repairs were completed. Almost all the water gauges were reduced to a ruinous condition. As a result of this neglect, a boiler burst in January 1936 on the Rosa-Vargashi stretch. As far as I remember, the engine-driver's mate and the fireman were killed, while the engine driver was thrown about 30 meters away. The engine was put completely out of action. All these undermining, wrecking activities in the Kurgan depot were conducted by Nikolayev, Andreyev, Starostin, and Mogilny, and in the Zlatoust depot by the locomotive foreman Sumin.

MEMBER OF THE COURT RYCHKOV. The Party and the government supplied the railroad with powerful locomotives, and you Trotskyites spoiled them, put them out of action?

KNYAZEV. Yes.

VISHINSKY. What position did you hold in February 1936?

RATAICHAK. Chief of the Central Administration of the Chemical Industry.

VISHINSKY. When did you become connected with the Trotskyites, when did you become one of the Trotskyite cadres?

RATAICHAK. In 1934.

VISHINSKY. Who brought you into the Trotskyite organization?

RATAICHAK. Pyatakov. My first conversation with Pyatakov took place at the beginning of 1934, while active work began with wrecking activities connected with the construction plan for 1934.

VISHINSKY. Perhaps we had better proceed by questioning. Did you join the Trotskyite organization?

RATAICHAK. I did.

VISHINSKY. Did you receive instructions regarding wrecking work?

RATAICHAK. I did.

VISHINSKY. Did you receive instructions regarding diversive acts?

RATAICHAK. I did.

VISHINSKY. Were you connected with espionage?

RATAICHAK. I was.

VISHINSKY. Did you take part in terrorist organizations?

RATAICHAK. No.

VISHINSKY. Did you know about the terrorist organization?

RATAICHAK. I knew about Trotsky's line from Pyatakov.

VISHINSKY. Did Pyatakov tell you that he was a member of the terrorist organization, did he inform you of Trotsky's directives, including the directive about terrorism?

RATAICHAK. He did.

VISHINSKY. Terrorism against whom?

RATAICHAK. Against the leaders of the Party and the government.

VISHINSKY. That is, you knew that your organization was making preparations to commit terrorist acts against the leaders of the Party and the leaders of the government? Did you know it?

RATAICHAK. I did.

VISHINSKY. And what was your attitude towards terrorism?

RATAICHAK. I stated that at the preliminary investigation.

VISHINSKY. I am not asking you about what you said at the preliminary investigation. Answer the question. What was your attitude towards terrorism?

RATAICHAK. I did not agree with it.

VISHINSKY. Why did you not agree with it?

RATAICHAK. (*Remains silent.*)

VISHINSKY. What did not please you? Wrecking pleased you, diversive acts pleased you, espionage pleased you? Why did terrorism not please you, why did you not agree with it?

RATAICHAK. All the things you have enumerated are vile.

VISHINSKY. All are vile. But at any rate you did not dissociate yourself from the group which was engaged in terrorism, you did not leave it?

RATAICHAK. No.

VISHINSKY. Did you ever attempt to inform anybody of these abominable things?

RATAICHAK. No.

VISHINSKY. What did your diversive work consist in?

RATAICHAK. In accordance with my instructions, transmitted through Pushin, three breakdowns were arranged, one diversive act at the Gorlovka Works and two other breakdowns—one at the Nevsky Works and the other at the Voskressensk Combined Chemical Works.

VISHINSKY. Let us take the Gorlovka Works. What was this breakdown?

RATAICHAK. Owing to this breakdown certain of the installations were put out of action.

VISHINSKY. Was there a breakdown at the Gorlovka Works?

RATAICHAK. There was.

VISHINSKY. Namely?

RATAICHAK. An explosion. The department and the works as a whole were put out of action for several days. Three workers lost their lives.

VISHINSKY. When was the second case?

RATAICHAK. The second case did not involve loss of life. It was the collapse of a reserve gas line. The plant worked very unevenly for several days.

VISHINSKY. What was the third case?

RATAICHAK. The third case was in November 1934; it was an explosion in one of the departments of the air chambers, as a result of which one of the chambers was put out of action.

VISHINSKY. This was on the Linde installations?

RATAICHAK. Yes.

VISHINSKY. Did you organize it?

RATAICHAK. It was organized on my instructions.

VISHINSKY. Was anybody killed?

RATAICHAK. Two workers, I think.

VISHINSKY. Was the diversive act at the Voskressensk Combined Chemical Works performed on your instructions?

RATAICHAK. Yes.

VISHINSKY. Was there any loss of life?

RATAICHAK. No.

VISHINSKY. What about the seventeen workers killed and fifteen injured?

RATAICHAK. That was on another occasion, Citizen Procurator.

VISHINSKY. Well, let us see. When did the fire take place?

RATAICHAK. In 1936.

VISHINSKY. Was it on the night of August 1?

RATAICHAK. Yes.

VISHINSKY. Did you arrange the fire?

RATAICHAK. No.

VISHINSKY. Who arranged it?

RATAICHAK. I do not know.

VISHINSKY. You do not know?

RATAICHAK. No. I was referring to the diversive act which took place in April–May 1934, when one of the acid departments was put out of action in accordance with my instructions.

VISHINSKY. That is, there were two diversive acts: one on your instructions to put one of the departments out of order; and the other the fire on the night of August 1, 1936?

RATAICHAK. Yes.

VISHINSKY. And when was one of the departments put out of action?

RATAICHAK. In 1934, in April–May.

VISHINSKY. And did you say anything about the fire in August 1936?

RATAICHAK. I did not testify about that because I had nothing to do with it.

VISHINSKY. Did you speak about it without reference to yourself?

RATAICHAK. I had nothing to do with that fire.

VISHINSKY. And is it a fact that immediately after the fire you gave orders to proceed to the clearance work, although it involved danger to the lives of the workers?

RATAICHAK. I demanded the immediate liquidation of the consequences.

VISHINSKY. Pardon me, not liquidation. Did you demand that clearance work should be immediately proceeded with, although it involved extreme danger to human life?

RATAICHAK. Yes, I did.

VISHINSKY. Do you know that on your demand the workers undertook the clearance work?

RATAICHAK. I do.

VISHINSKY. Do you know that the wall caved in?

RATAICHAK. I was on the spot and directed the work from the start.

VISHINSKY. Don't hurry, don't run ahead. Answer the question: do you know that the wall caved in and the tower collapsed?

RATAICHAK. I do, I was on the spot myself.

VISHINSKY. And that seventeen workers were killed?

RATAICHAK. That is so.

286

VISHINSKY. Is that a fact?

RATAICHAK. Yes, it is.

VISHINSKY. And you say that you had nothing to do with it?

RATAICHAK. No, but I had to do that, Citizen Procurator, because if we had not taken this measure of precaution there was a danger that the lives of hundreds of workers might have been lost. That is why I myself directed the clearance work on the spot.

VISHINSKY. You directed it in such a way that seventeen workers were killed and fifteen were wounded. Is that so?

RATAICHAK. (*Remains silent.*)

VISHINSKY. You directed the clearance operations in such a way that seventeen workers were killed and fifteen injured.

RATAICHAK. That is true, but it was the only thing to do.

VISHINSKY. And was it the only thing to do when you blew up departments and installations and committed other diversive acts?

RATAICHAK. (*Remains silent.*)

JANUARY 29 (LAST PLEA)

RADEK. . . . This trial has revealed two important facts. The intertwining of the counterrevolutionary organizations with all the counterrevolutionary forces in the country—that is one fact. But this fact is tremendous objective proof. Wrecking work can be established by technical experts; the terrorist activities were connected with so many people that the testimony of these people, apart from material evidence, presents an absolute picture. But the trial is bicentric, and it has another important significance. It has revealed the smithy of war, and has shown that the Trotskyite organization became an agency of the forces which are fomenting a new world war.

What proofs are there in support of this fact? In support of this fact there is the evidence of two people—the testimony of myself, who received the directives and the letters from Trotsky (which, unfortunately, I burned), and the testimony of Pyatakov, who spoke to Trotsky. All the testimony of the other accused rests on our testimony. If you are dealing with mere criminals and spies, on what can you base your conviction that what we have said is the truth, the firm truth?

Naturally, the State Prosecutor and the Court, who know the whole history of Trotskyism and who know us, have no reason to suspect that we, bearing the burden of terrorism, added high treason just for our own pleasure. There is no necessity to convince you of that. We must convince, firstly, the diffused wandering Trotskyite elements in the country, who have not yet laid down their arms, who are dangerous and who must realize that we speak here shaken to the depths of our souls, and that we are speaking the truth and only the truth.

. . . All the Public Prosecutor said about the fact that not only Trotsky's directives but all the work of the Trotskyites aimed at the restoration of

287

capitalism is incontrovertibly true. The directives themselves were directives for the complete restoration of capitalism, and they did not drop from the skies: they were a summary of the fact that when people fire at the general staff of the revolution, when people undermine the economy of the country, they are undermining socialism and, that being so, they are working for capitalism.

. . . When I found myself in the People's Commissariat of Internal Affairs, the chief examining official realized at once why I would not talk. He said to me: "You are not a baby. Here you have fifteen people testifying against you. You cannot get out of it, and as a sensible man you cannot think of doing so. If you do not want to testify, it can only be because you want to gain time and look it over more closely. Very well, study it." For two and a half months I tormented the examining official. The question has been raised here whether we were tormented while under investigation. I must say that it was not I who was tormented, but I who tormented the examining officials and compelled them to perform a lot of useless work. For two and a half months I compelled the examining official, by interrogating me and by confronting me with the testimony of other accused, to open up all the cards to me, so that I could see who had confessed, who had not confessed, and what each had confessed.

This lasted for two and a half months. And one day the chief examining official came to me and said: "You are now the last. Why are you wasting time and temporizing? Why don't you say what you have to say?" And I answered: "Yes, tomorrow I shall begin my testimony." And the testimony I gave contains not a single correction from first to last. I unfolded the whole picture as I knew it, and the investigation may have corrected one or another personal mistake about the connections of some person with another, but I affirm that not a single thing I have told the examining officials has been refuted and that nothing has been added.

. . . And finally, we must say to the whole world, to all who are struggling for peace: Trotskyism is the instrument of the warmongers. We must say that with a firm voice, because we have learned it by our own bitter experience. It has been extremely hard for us to admit this, but it is an historical fact, for the truth of which we shall pay with our heads. . . . We cannot, nor can I, ask for clemency; we have no right to it. And I will say—there is no pride here; what pride can there be?—that we do not need this clemency. Life in the next few years, in the next five or ten years, when the fate of the world will be in the balance, can have meaning only under one condition, and that is if one is able to take part in the work of life, even in the roughest. But what has occurred precludes this. And in that case clemency would be only needless torture. We are a fairly closely knit crew; but when Nikolai Ivanovich Muralov, Trotsky's closest follower, of whom I was convinced that he would rather perish in prison than say a single word —when he gave testimony and explained that he did not want to die in the consciousness that his name would be a banner for every counterrevolutionary scoundrel—that is the profoundest result of this trial.

288

BUKHARIN, RYKOV, YAGODA AND EIGHTEEN OTHERS.
("THE ANTI-SOVIET BLOC OF RIGHTS AND TROTSKYITES")
MARCH 2–13, 1938

MARCH 2

BESSONOV[12]. When Krestinsky, in the late summer of 1933, came to Germany for a cure, he stayed for a long time in Berlin. He had two conversations with me which could be characterized as conversations between members of the Trotskyite organization. The first conversation was about the arrangements for the meeting between Trotsky and Krestinsky.

VISHINSKY. Who desired this meeting, Trotsky or Krestinsky?

BESSONOV. Krestinsky.

VISHINSKY. Hence, we may establish the following facts: the first is that Krestinsky traveled through Berlin.

BESSONOV. I think that was in September, or the end of August 1933.

VISHINSKY. Where was he going?

BESSONOV. To Kissingen.

VISHINSKY. What for?

BESSONOV. To take a cure. He stopped at the Trade Representation and I had a talk with him. Twice we talked on Trotskyite subjects.

VISHINSKY. And he says that he was never a Trotskyite. Perhaps he censured the Trotskyites? You heard him say here that he was not a Trotskyite. Is that right or wrong?

BESSONOV. (*Smiles.*)

VISHINSKY. Why are you smiling?

BESSONOV. I am smiling because the reason why I am standing here is that Nikolai Nikolayevich Krestinsky named me the liaison man with Trotsky. Besides him and Pyatakov nobody knew about this. And if Krestinsky had not spoken to me about this in December 1933 I would not be in the dock now.

VISHINSKY. So you think that you are obliged to him for this? Permit me to ask the accused Krestinsky.

Accused Krestinsky, did you really travel to Kissingen in 1933, in August or September?

KRESTINSKY[18]. In the beginning of September.

VISHINSKY. Do you confirm this fact?

KRESTINSKY. I do.

VISHINSKY. Did you see Bessonov?

KRESTINSKY. Yes.

VISHINSKY. Did you talk to him?

[12] Former Counselor to Soviet Trade Delegation to Germany.

[18] Former Assistant People's Commissar for Foreign Affairs; one of secretaries of Party Central Committee under Lenin.

KRESTINSKY. Yes.

VISHINSKY. What about? The weather?

KRESTINSKY. He was counselor to the Embassy in Berlin. At that time he was acting as chargé d'affaires. He informed me about the political situation in Germany, about the frame of mind of the Fascist Party, which at that time was in power, and about their program and attitude towards the U.S.S.R.

VISHINSKY. And about Trotskyite affairs?

KRESTINSKY. We did not talk about them. I was not a Trotskyite.

VISHINSKY. You never talked about them?

KRESTINSKY. Never.

VISHINSKY. That means that Bessonov is not telling the truth, and that you are telling the truth. Do you always tell the truth?

KRESTINSKY. No.

VISHINSKY. Not always. Accused Krestinsky, you and I will have to examine serious matters and there is no need to get excited. Consequently, Bessonov is not telling the truth?

KRESTINSKY. No.

VISHINSKY. But you too do not always tell the truth. Is that not so?

KRESTINSKY. I did not always tell the truth during the investigation.

VISHINSKY. But at other times you always tell the truth.

KRESTINSKY. The truth.

VISHINSKY. Why this lack of respect for the investigation, why during the investigation did you tell untruths? Explain.

KRESTINSKY. (*No reply.*)

VISHINSKY. I request Bessonov specially for Krestinsky's benefit to repeat what he said; and I would ask Krestinsky to listen carefully, to keep his ears open.

BESSONOV. I repeat, the commission which I at that time received from Krestinsky was that in my post of counselor to the Berlin Embassy of the U.S.S.R., where I, of course, enjoyed definite opportunities for the accomplishment of this commission, I was by every means open to me—naturally observing all due diplomatic decorum—to hamper, hinder, and prevent the normalization of relations between the Soviet Union and Germany along normal diplomatic lines, and in this way to compel the Germans to seek for illegal, nondiplomatic, secret, clandestine means of arriving at an agreement with the Trotskyite organization.

VISHINSKY. Did you hear that?

KRESTINSKY. Yes.

VISHINSKY. Did you have any conversations with Bessonov in May 1933?

KRESTINSKY. I had conversations with Bessonov before he left for Berlin.

VISHINSKY. You had. Do you remember what they were about?

KRESTINSKY. I do not remember the details.

VISHINSKY. You do not remember the details, but Bessonov does.

KRESTINSKY. There was not a word said about the Trotskyite stand.

VISHINSKY. Did you say what he was to do abroad, or did you not?

KRESTINSKY. Of course I did.

VISHINSKY. You did say what he was to do?

KRESTINSKY. Yes.

VISHINSKY. What was he to do?

KRESTINSKY. He was to try to create normal relations as far as possible.

VISHINSKY. As far as possible. But if it was impossible?

KRESTINSKY. If he did not succeed, it would be another matter. But he was to try.

VISHINSKY. Accused Bessonov, is what Krestinsky says true?

BESSONOV. Absolutely untrue. What is more, during this conversation Krestinsky gave me detailed organizational instructions how I was to communicate with him in the future. Apart from the official letters which the Embassy in Germany exchanges with the People's Commissariat of Foreign Affairs, I was to maintain correspondence with Krestinsky. And if in this correspondence Krestinsky were to say that his view on current questions of Soviet-German relations was such-and-such, and that he advised waiting for official instructions on this question, that would mean that I was to act in accordance with his "personal" point of view, irrespective of what the official instructions might be.

And, finally, Krestinsky referred me to Stern, his immediate subordinate along Trotskyite lines and along official lines, so that I might get addresses for the establishment of connections with Trotsky.

VISHINSKY. You hear that Bessonov speaks in fairly great detail about your conversations, which are far from bearing the character you attribute to them. What about it?

KRESTINSKY. There were no such conversations, although during the confrontation which took place in January I admitted part of the conversation.

VISHINSKY. At the confrontation with Bessonov you admitted this part?

KRESTINSKY. Yes.

VISHINSKY. So there was such a conversation?

KRESTINSKY. No.

VISHINSKY. So what Bessonov says must be understood the other way round?

KRESTINSKY. Not always.

VISHINSKY. But what about your admission?

KRESTINSKY. During the investigation I gave false testimony several times.

VISHINSKY. You said: "I did not formally belong to the Trotskyite center." Is that true or not?

KRESTINSKY. I did not belong to it at all.

VISHINSKY. You say that formally you did not belong. What is true and what is not true here? Perhaps it is all true, or it is all untrue, or only half of it is true? What percentage, how many grams of it are true?

KRESTINSKY. I did not belong to the Trotskyite center because I was not a Trotskyite.

VISHINSKY. You were not a Trotskyite?

KRESTINSKY. No.

VISHINSKY. Never?

KRESTINSKY. Yes, I was a Trotskyite until 1927.

THE PRESIDENT. At the beginning of the trial you said in reply to my question that you had never been a Trotskyite. That is what you said.

KRESTINSKY. I said that I am not a Trotskyite.

VISHINSKY. And so you were a Trotskyite until 1927?

KRESTINSKY. I was.

VISHINSKY. And when did you stop being a Trotskyite in 1927?

KRESTINSKY. Just before the Fifteenth Party Congress.

VISHINSKY. Recall the date.

KRESTINSKY. I date my rupture with Trotsky and Trotskyism from November 17, 1927, when, through Serebryakov, who had returned from America and was in Moscow, I sent Trotsky a sharp letter containing sharp criticism. . . .

VISHINSKY. That letter is not in the records. We have another letter —your letter to Trotsky.

KRESTINSKY. The letter I am referring to is in the possession of the court investigator, because it was taken from me during the search, and I request this letter to be attached to the records.

VISHINSKY. The records contain a letter dated July 11, 1927, taken from you during the search.

KRESTINSKY. But there is another letter of November 27. . . .

VISHINSKY. There is no such letter.

KRESTINSKY. That cannot be. . . .

VISHINSKY. We are just now conducting the court investigation, and you yourself said that during the preliminary investigation you did not always tell the truth. You said during the preliminary investigation that you did not formally belong to the center. That means that during the preliminary investigation you admitted that in general you were, actually speaking, a member of the Trotskyite center. Did you admit this during the preliminary investigation?

KRESTINSKY. No, I did not.

VISHINSKY. In your testimony (pp. 9 and 10) you said: "Formally I did not belong. . . ." This can be taken as meaning that you did belong, but not formally. Is that so?

KRESTINSKY. I did not belong to the Trotskyite center at all.

VISHINSKY. That means that you testified falsely?

KRESTINSKY. I have already stated that this testimony of mine does not conform to the facts.

VISHINSKY. When I interrogated you during the preliminary investigation, were you telling me the truth?

KRESTINSKY. No.

VISHINSKY. Why did you tell untruths? Did I ask you to tell untruths?

KRESTINSKY. No.

VISHINSKY. Did I ask you to tell the truth?

KRESTINSKY. You did.

VISHINSKY. Why, when I asked you to tell the truth, did you nevertheless tell untruths, compel the investigator to write them down, and then sign it? Why?

KRESTINSKY. At the preliminary investigation, before I was questioned by you, I had given false testimony.

VISHINSKY. . . . . And then you stuck to it.

VISHINSKY. Accused Rosengoltz, what grounds have you for testifying that Krestinsky is a Trotskyite, and that consequently he is not telling the truth here?

ROSENGOLTZ[14]. It is borne out by the conversations I had with him as a Trotskyite.

VISHINSKY. When did these conversations take place?

ROSENGOLTZ. They took place from 1929 onwards.

VISHINSKY. Until what year?

ROSENGOLTZ. Until quite recently.

VISHINSKY. That is?

ROSENGOLTZ. Until 1937.

VISHINSKY. Accused Grinko, what do you know about Krestinsky as a Trotskyite?

GRINKO[15]. I know.

VISHINSKY. What do you know?

GRINKO. In my conspiratorial work I had connections with Krestinsky as a conspirator, as a Trotskyite, as a member of the Right-Trotskyite, conspiratorial center, on very important questions about which I shall have to give testimony.

VISHINSKY. Can you tell us briefly what questions? Questions of supporting the Soviet power or of combating it?

GRINKO. Questions of combating the Soviet power, of establishing connections with foreign states hostile to the Soviet power.

VISHINSKY. And do you know whether Krestinsky was connected with other foreign intelligence services?

GRINKO. He helped me to establish connections with one of the foreign intelligence services.

[14] Former Commissar for Foreign Trade.
[15] Former Commissar of Finance.

VISHINSKY. So Krestinsky helped you to establish connections with a foreign intelligence service. Do you hear that, accused Krestinsky? Is it true?

KRESTINSKY. No.

VISHINSKY. Yet you testified that it was true.

VISHINSKY. When we interrogated you at the preliminary investigation, what did you say on this score?

KRESTINSKY. In giving testimony I did not refute any of my previous testimony, which I deliberately confirmed.

VISHINSKY. You deliberately confirmed it. You were misleading the Procurator. Is that so, or not?

KRESTINSKY. No.

VISHINSKY. Why did you have to mislead me?

KRESTINSKY. I simply considered that if I were to say what I am saying today—that it was not in accordance with the facts—my declaration would not reach the leaders of the Party and the government.

VISHINSKY. But you signed the protocol?

KRESTINSKY. I did.

VISHINSKY. You remember that I directly asked you whether you had any declarations or complaints to make against the investigator. Was that not so?

KRESTINSKY. It was.

VISHINSKY. Did you answer me?

KRESTINSKY. Yes.

VISHINSKY. Did I ask whether you had any complaints, or not?

KRESTINSKY. Yes, and I answered that I had no complaints.

VISHINSKY. If you were asked whether you had complaints, you should have answered that you had.

KRESTINSKY. I had in the sense that I did not speak voluntarily.

VISHINSKY (to Rosengoltz). Accused Rosengoltz, did you know that Bessonov was a Trotskyite?

ROSENGOLTZ. No, I did not.

VISHINSKY. Did not Pyatakov recommend him?

ROSENGOLTZ. I never talked to him on this subject.

VISHINSKY. But did you know Bessonov was a Trotskyite?

ROSENGOLTZ. I knew it from Krestinsky.

VISHINSKY. What did you learn from Krestinsky about Bessonov?

ROSENGOLTZ. I learnt that he was a Trotskyite and that he, Bessonov, helped Krestinsky in Trotskyite work.

VISHINSKY. Who told you that?

ROSENGOLTZ. Krestinsky told me.

VISHINSKY. Krestinsky personally?

ROSENGOLTZ. Yes, Krestinsky personally.

VISHINSKY. Do you remember in what year it was?

ROSENGOLTZ. I cannot say exactly.

VISHINSKY. Roughly, was it in 1933?

ROSENGOLTZ. Yes, roughly in that year.

VISHINSKY. Under what circumstances did he tell you this and in what connection?

ROSENGOLTZ. He was telling me about the people in the People's Commissariat of Foreign Affairs who helped him in this work, and among them mentioned Bessonov.

VISHINSKY. Accused Krestinsky, did you hear this testimony?

KRESTINSKY. I deny it.

VISHINSKY. You deny it?

KRESTINSKY. I do.

VISHINSKY. Absolutely?

KRESTINSKY. Absolutely.

VISHINSKY. Of course.

KRESTINSKY. Of course.

VISHINSKY. I have no further questions.

THE PRESIDENT. Adjournment for two hours.

VISHINSKY. Accused Rykov, do you corroborate that you knew that Krestinsky was a Trotskyite and a member of the bloc of Rights and Trotskyites?

RYKOV. That is, at that period such a complete bloc did not exist, but that he was a member of the Trotskyite organization I knew.

VISHINSKY. And he had conversations with you?

RYKOV. We discussed matters of an illegal nature.

VISHINSKY. You assert that Krestinsky knew about your affairs in the illegal organization in the Party, but Krestinsky denies it; it follows then that Rykov is now not telling the truth and that you, accused Krestinsky, are telling the truth?

KRESTINSKY. I am telling the truth.

VISHINSKY. And since when have you been telling the truth?

KRESTINSKY. On this matter?

VISHINSKY. Yes.

KRESTINSKY. Today I am telling the truth.

THE PRESIDENT. Since 12 o'clock?

KRESTINSKY. Yes, in this court.

MARCH 3

VISHINSKY (to Krestinsky). You have heard the detailed explanation Rakovsky has given of your so-called departure from Trotskyism. Do you consider Rakovsky's explanation correct?

KRESTINSKY. What he says is right.

THE PRESIDENT. You confirm what Rakovsky said?

KRESTINSKY. Yes, I do.

VISHINSKY. If what Rakovsky said is true, will you continue to deceive the Court and to deny that the testimony you gave in the preliminary investigation was true?

KRESTINSKY. I fully confirm the testimony I gave in the preliminary investigation.

VISHINSKY. Did you have an understanding with Yagoda that no repressive measures were to be adopted against the members of your underground organization?

RYKOV. Of course.

VISHINSKY. Was there an understanding with Yagoda that he was to use his official position to protect the underground organization of the Rights?

RYKOV. Yes.

VISHINSKY. And what official position did he hold at that time?

RYKOV. He was Vice Chairman, under Chairman of the OGPU, Menzhinsky.

VISHINSKY. Vice Chairman of the OGPU?

RYKOV. Yes. That is chiefly why we endeavored to keep him on a secret footing.

VISHINSKY (to the Court). Permit me to question Yagoda. Accused Yagoda, do you confirm this part of Rykov's testimony?

YAGODA. I confirm the fact, but not its formulation.

VISHINSKY. You do not like the formulation?

YAGODA. The fact is true, but not as Rykov puts it.

VISHINSKY. Was this in 1929?

YAGODA. It was.

VISHINSKY (to Rykov). Accused Rykov, you say that this was in 1929?

RYKOV. Yes, it was in 1929.

VISHINSKY. At any rate, it was when you, accused Yagoda, were Vice Chairman of the OGPU and when it was your duty to combat underground groups?

YAGODA. Yes.

VISHINSKY. Consequently, you committed direct high treason?

YAGODA. Yes.

VISHINSKY. Will it be right or wrong to say that in the period of the years 1932–33 a group was organized which we may call the Anti-Soviet Bloc of Rights and Trotskyites?

RYKOV. It was so in fact. Its organizational expression, since 1933–34, was the so-called contact center.

VISHINSKY. That's it, now; the contact center represented a further step in putting the organizational relations on a formal basis?

RYKOV. Yes. In fact and politically that is a correct way of putting it.

VISHINSKY. That is correct. And that bloc set itself the aim of—how do you formulate it?

RYKOV. It set itself the aim of overthrowing the Soviet system by forcible means, by means of treason and by means of an agreement with the Fascist forces abroad.

VISHINSKY. On what conditions?

RYKOV. On the conditions of dismembering the U.S.S.R., of severing the national republics.

VISHINSKY. You bluntly agreed to such a treasonable act as the severance of Byelorussia from the U.S.S.R. for Poland?

RYKOV. To its independence. Byelorussia was supposed to come under the protectorate of Poland.

VISHINSKY. As a vassal. (*To Bukharin*.) Accused Bukharin, do you agree with Rykov on this question?

BUKHARIN. I must say that Rykov's memory is failing him here.

VISHINSKY. Did you, like Rykov, maintain a defeatist position?

BUKHARIN. No, but I am responsible for this affair.

VISHINSKY. And was Tukhachevsky a member of this group?

BUKHARIN. I have already explained. . . .

VISHINSKY. I am asking: Were Tukhachevsky and the military group of conspirators members of your bloc?

BUKHARIN. They were.

VISHINSKY. And they discussed with the members of the bloc?

BUKHARIN. Quite right.

VISHINSKY. When members of a bloc discuss such things, it may be said that it is a plan.

BUKHARIN. It becomes a plan when all the i's are dotted.

VISHINSKY. May we say that Bukharin's standpoint was that of defeat for the U.S.S.R.?

RYKOV. Knowing Bukharin as I do, I should say that perhaps he did not consider it the only thing, but he considered it as something that could be discussed, something that could be realized under definite conditions.

VISHINSKY. I do not say the only thing possible, but one of the means—to open the gates to the enemy. Is that correct?

RYKOV. Yes, but as something possible, not indispensable.

VISHINSKY. Of course, as something possible, not indispensable; that is to say, this was not the only road along which he was pursuing his aim. Isn't that treason?

RYKOV. Yes.

VISHINSKY. Do you consider Bukharin a traitor?

RYKOV. A traitor, like myself.

VISHINSKY. Thus, when Bukharin says that he was opposed to the defeatist position, is he right or not?

RYKOV. Here I did not understand Bukharin, and do not understand him. The main thing is that a man of politics answers for his actions and for the results of his political actions. This is the one thing that must be demanded both of me and of him, and not at all the way he thinks. Then it will be of interest.

MARCH 4

VISHINSKY. And so, at the end of 1929, or rather at the beginning of 1930, you received certain instructions through Krestinsky?

ROSENGOLTZ. I have already said so.

Further, in 1933 Krestinsky received a letter from abroad. Then, when Krestinsky was abroad himself, he had a meeting. I was abroad in 1933 and had a meeting with Sedov in Felden in Austria. I had several long conversations with him near the house where I lived. I next saw Sedov in 1934 in Karlsbad.

VISHINSKY. What was the substance of your conversations?

ROSENGOLTZ. Sedov transmitted the following basic instructions from Trotsky. I shall here set forth the instructions which I received during my conversations with Sedov and which were transmitted through Krestinsky; in the main they coincided. This is with regard to connections with the Rights. It was recommended to form connections with the Rights and to carry on the work in contact with them.

VISHINSKY. With whom specifically?

ROSENGOLTZ. That I was not told. Krestinsky told me about it, but mentioned no names, except Tukhachevsky's.

VISHINSKY. But it was understood?

ROSENGOLTZ. Krestinsky said that he had instructions with regard to Rykov and Rudzutak. Sedov spoke a lot about the necessity of the maximum, the closest possible connections with Tukhachevsky, inasmuch as, in Trotsky's opinion, Tukhachevsky and the military group were to be the decisive force of the counterrevolutionary action. During the conversation it was also revealed that Trotsky entertained fears regarding Tukhachevsky's Bonapartist tendencies. In the course of one conversation Sedov said that Trotsky in this respect even expressed the fear that if Tukhachevsky successfully accomplished a military coup, it was possible that he would not allow Trotsky into Moscow, and in this connection he referred to the necessity for the greatest vigilance on our part.

VISHINSKY. How did you react to the arrest of Pyatakov in this connection?

ROSENGOLTZ. Already after the trial of Pyatakov a letter was received from Trotsky in which he put it that Tukhachevsky's military coup must be expedited to the maximum. There was a meeting in my apartment in this connection.

VISHINSKY. What sort of a letter was this? Can't you give more details?

ROSENGOLTZ. Trotsky raised several questions in it. First of all, he pointed out that if we procrastinated, the result would be that all the counterrevolutionary forces would be smashed piecemeal. Therefore, inasmuch as the cadres had already been considerably demolished, a number of possible actions should be expedited to the maximum.

VISHINSKY. For example?

ROSENGOLTZ. Two questions chiefly were raised: the first was to retaliate to the Court sentence on Pyatakov by terrorist acts.

VISHINSKY. That is, to the sentence of the Court?

ROSENGOLTZ. As a retaliation to the sentence of the Court condemning Pyatakov to be shot, it was proposed to organize terrorist acts.

VISHINSKY. Against whom?

ROSENGOLTZ. Against leaders of the Party and the government, and to expedite a military coup to the maximum.

VISHINSKY. Was there nothing else in this letter?

ROSENGOLTZ. It was demanded that Krestinsky and I should be more active.

VISHINSKY. In the preliminary investigation you testified (p. 72): "The second letter . . . In this letter Trotsky sharply criticized Pyatakov's conduct at the trial and proposed that in the event of further arrests we should not admit our guilt and refuse to give testimony." Is that correct?

KRESTINSKY. Yes.

VISHINSKY. It was so?

KRESTINSKY. Yes.

VISHINSKY. Perhaps your conduct in court two days ago was also dictated by these directions?

KRESTINSKY. No.

VISHINSKY. But you remembered these instructions of Trotsky?

KRESTINSKY. I did, but it was not this that dictated my conduct. It was connected with the facts I mentioned yesterday.

VISHINSKY. When were you arrested?

KRESTINSKY. At the end of May.

VISHINSKY. And when did you confess your guilt at the preliminary investigation?

KRESTINSKY. As to the principal crime, the one that was hardest of all for me to admit, namely, about my connections with the German intelligence service and General Seeckt, I confessed after the lapse of a week, at the first interrogation.

VISHINSKY. But for a week you denied it?

KRESTINSKY. I confessed it at the end of the first interrogation.

VISHINSKY. Was it because you wanted to carry out Trotsky's instructions that you denied your guilt?

KRESTINSKY. No. I just hoped that I would be believed and that . . .

VISHINSKY. You would succeed in the deception?

KRESTINSKY. That I would succeed in the deception and thus save myself.

VISHINSKY. But you did not succeed!

KRESTINSKY. No.

ROSENGOLTZ. Now I want to mention also that at an earlier period —in 1923, in connection with a business contact I had . . .

VISHINSKY. With whom?

ROSENGOLTZ. With German military circles. Trotsky told me to supply Seeckt with information about the Soviet air force.

VISHINSKY. And did you supply it?

ROSENGOLTZ. Yes, I supplied this information.

VISHINSKY. Accused Krestinsky, what was the connection with the Reichswehr to which Rosengoltz is referring?

KRESTINSKY. In 1921 Trotsky told me to take advantage of a meeting with Seeckt during official negotiations to propose to him, to Seeckt, that he grant Trotsky a regular subsidy for the development of illegal Trotskyite activities; at the same time he told me that, if Seeckt will put up a counterdemand that we render him services in the sphere of espionage, we should and may accept it. I shall speak later about the conversation I had with Trotsky when he gave me these instructions. I put the question before Seeckt and named the sum of 250,000 gold marks, that is $60,000 a year. General Seeckt, after consulting his assistant, the chief of staff, agreed in principle and put up the counterdemand that certain confidential and important information of a military nature should be transmitted to him, even if not regularly, by Trotsky in Moscow or through me. In addition he was to receive assistance in obtaining visas for some persons whom they needed and whom they would send to the Soviet Union as spies. This counterdemand of General Seeckt was accepted, and in 1923 this agreement had been put in effect.

VISHINSKY. Did you transmit espionage information?

KRESTINSKY. I would say, not I, but we, the Russian Trotskyites. But there were cases when I personally gave this information to General Seeckt.

VISHINSKY. You gave it personally?

KRESTINSKY. Yes. I also received money on several occasions.

VISHINSKY. From whom did you receive money?

KRESTINSKY. From General Seeckt.

VISHINSKY. Where?

KRESTINSKY. In his office. I handed over the money to Trotsky personally during my visits to Moscow.

VISHINSKY. Will you tell us how much money you received altogether?

KRESTINSKY. Beginning with 1923 until 1930 we received annually 250,000 German marks in gold.

VISHINSKY. This makes approximately 2,000,000 gold marks during these years?

KRESTINSKY. Yes, approximately 2,000,000 gold marks.

VISHINSKY. Tell us how your meeting with Trotsky in Meran was arranged.

KRESTINSKY. I stopped in Berlin for a few days on my way. In Berlin the counselor of our Embassy was Bessonov, our man, a Trotskyite who was supposed to have connections with Trotsky because when he left for Berlin in May 1933 I told him to establish such connections.

VISHINSKY. You instructed him?

KRESTINSKY. Yes, I instructed him to establish this connection. It happened that Yakubovich and Stern had left Germany and my connection was cut off. Pyatakov had a connection through his people, who were going to Germany to place orders, but this was not a regular connection and therefore it was necessary to establish a connection through the Embassy in Berlin so that we might take advantage of the diplomatic mail. And this was entrusted to Bessonov. I told him that it was necessary to inform Trotsky that I wanted to see him.

VISHINSKY. So Bessonov told us here the real truth?

KRESTINSKY. Yes.

VISHINSKY. And at first you tried to deny it?

KRESTINSKY. But this was at first, and I told you what considerations prompted me to deny it.

VISHINSKY. I am not accusing you, I only want to establish the fact.

KRESTINSKY. On the first day, when I denied my guilt, since I could not bring myself to admit it publicly, I naturally, as a logical conclusion from this, denied also what Rosengoltz and Bessonov said.

VISHINSKY. But you must agree that by this you put Bessonov in the position of a liar.

KRESTINSKY. Well, what of it? I lied myself. Since I put myself in the position of a liar, it was so much easier to put others in the same position.

VISHINSKY. That is your logic.

MARCH 5

VISHINSKY. Tell me, how would you briefly formulate your admission of guilt before the Soviet Union?

RAKOVSKY. I admit that beginning with 1924 I became a traitor to the Soviet Socialist fatherland.

301

VISHINSKY. And your activity—at first factional, then counterrevolutionary underground Trotskyite criminal activity—began in what year?

RAKOVSKY. I have been personally acquainted with Trotsky since 1903. This acquaintance grew closer and I was his intimate friend.

VISHINSKY. His political friend?

RAKOVSKY. Political when political questions were concerned.

VISHINSKY. And his personal friend?

RAKOVSKY. And personal.

VISHINSKY. And such you have remained until recently?

RAKOVSKY. And such I have remained until recently.

VISHINSKY. Consequently, for nearly thirty-five years you have been bound to Trotsky by political and personal friendship.

RAKOVSKY. Yes.

VISHINSKY. You waged a struggle against the Party and the Soviet Government?

RAKOVSKY. In 1921 the trade union discussion was, one might say, a "trial of strength." And from the end of 1924 clandestine connections were formed which came within the provisions of the Criminal Code.

VISHINSKY. From 1924 clandestine, criminal connections punishable by Soviet law, and criminal activity began?

RAKOVSKY. Which I have recounted.

VISHINSKY. Which you have admitted. For the sake of what did you Trotskyites wage this struggle against the Soviet State?

RAKOVSKY. For the sake of the seizure of power.

VISHINSKY. And further, seizure of power for what object?

RAKOVSKY. The main object was to destroy the achievements which exist at the present moment.

VISHINSKY. That is to say, in other words, to destroy the Socialist order?

RAKOVSKY. The return, I do not say openly, of the capitalist system. . . .

VISHINSKY. You won't say this openly?

RAKOVSKY. I want to say that it did not figure in my mind as an open, obvious aim, but in my subconscious mind I cannot help realizing that this is what I was after.

VISHINSKY. What premise and what historical prognosis did you act upon?

RAKOVSKY. A very indefinite prognosis. This was an adventure—if power can be seized, all right, if not . . .

VISHINSKY. But first of all you proceeded from the main Trotskyite thesis that in the U.S.S.R., taken alone, its economic and cultural level being what it is, it is impossible to build socialist society.

RAKOVSKY. This ideological premise went by the board.

VISHINSKY. It subsequently went by the board because it was replaced by some other premise?

RAKOVSKY. There was no ideological premise whatsoever.

VISHINSKY. There was no ideological premise whatsoever?

RAKOVSKY. No.

VISHINSKY. And the object was a rabid struggle against the Socialist State for the purpose of seizing power in the interests—when all's said and done, whose interests?

RAKOVSKY. Citizen Prosecutor, if I tell you that we wanted to seize power in order to hand it over to the Fascists, we would not only be the criminals we are, but we would be fools. But . . .

VISHINSKY. But?

RAKOVSKY. But when we thought it possible to seize power and to hold it without handing it over to the Fascists, it was insanity, it was a utopia.

VISHINSKY. Consequently, if you had managed to seize power it would inevitably have fallen into the hands of the Fascists?

RAKOVSKY. I share this estimate entirely.

VISHINSKY. So you wanted to seize power with the help of the Fascists?

RAKOVSKY. With the help of the Fascists.

VISHINSKY. If the Fascists secured the seizure of power for you, in whose hands would the power be?

RAKOVSKY. History knows. . . .

VISHINSKY. No, you leave history alone.

RAKOVSKY. I must say that I have pleaded guilty to this from the moment when I decided to give complete, exhaustive, and frank testimony. For eight months I denied everything and refused to testify.

VISHINSKY. Following the instructions and tactics of the Trotskyites?

RAKOVSKY. It is the application of the old revolutionary practices and the application of the counterrevolutionary practices.

VISHINSKY. What have you got to do with revolutionary practices? You have still some phraseology left, but that is another matter.

RAKOVSKY. But it cannot be denied that I once belonged to . . .

VISHINSKY. But you were arrested not once upon a time, but now, by the Soviet authorities, and you imagined that you could use against the investigation authorities of the Soviet State the old methods which you used once when you were among revolutionaries?

RAKOVSKY. It means that for eight months I continued to live with the same old Trotskyite counterrevolutionary ideology.

VISHINSKY. That is what I am saying. And not only the ideology, but the tactics as well.

RAKOVSKY. And the tactics. And then—if you will allow me, I will say.

VISHINSKY. And then, as they say, you laid down your arms.

RAKOVSKY. I will tell you what prompted me . . .

VISHINSKY. I have no objection if you will deal briefly with this, without long historical digressions. No objections, on my part.

RAKOVSKY. Very briefly. As I said, it was only in the eighth month that I began to make a clean breast of my main activities.

VISHINSKY. Criminal activities.

RAKOVSKY. My criminal activities, of course. But before this the thought frequently arose in my mind: was I doing right in denying? Nobody will deny that imprisonment, solitude in general, makes people undertake a revaluation of values. But I remember, and will never forget as long as I live, the circumstances which finally impelled me to give evidence. During one of the examinations, this was in the summer, I learnt, in the first place, that Japanese aggression had begun against China, against the Chinese people, I learnt of Germany's and Italy's undisguised aggression against the Spanish people. . . .

I learnt of the feverish preparations which all the Fascist states were making to unleash a world war. What a reader usually absorbs every day in small doses in telegrams, I received at once in a big dose. This had a stunning effect on me. All my past rose before me. Of course this past may be reduced to naught and will be obliterated by my disgraceful actions, but as an inner motive, nothing and nobody can do anything against it. All my past rose before me, my responsibilities, and it became clear to me that I myself was a party to this, that I was responsible, that I myself had helped the aggressors with my treasonable activities. I knew that I was not alone, that I was harboring illusions about them. Former heads of the government, former People's Commissars, former Assistant People's Commissars, former Ambassadors had become entangled in this web. And then I became a judge over myself, I sat in judgment over myself. This is a court which no one will reproach with being biased. I sat in judgment over myself. I had given myself to the labor movement from my youth, and where had I got to? I had reached a stage when I facilitated the vilest work with my actions, I had facilitated the Fascist aggressors' preparations to destroy culture, civilization, all the achievements of democracy, all the achievements of the working class.

That is what induced me to speak, that is what overcame my obstinacy, my false shame born of vanity, fear for my own fate, which was not worthy of a man who had once taken part in the revolutionary movement. My rancor, which all of us harbored, some to a greater and some to a lesser extent, rancor against the leadership, rancor against particular individuals, had played a great part. Rancor and ambition fell from me. I considered that from now on my duty was to help in this struggle against the aggressor, that I would go and expose myself fully and entirely, and I told the investigator that on the following day I would begin to give complete, exhaustive testimony. I must say that the testimony which I gave here is absolutely complete, sincere, and exhaustive.

VISHINSKY. And how did matters stand with regard to butter, thanks to your criminal activity?

ZELENSKY[16]. I am coming to that. I intend to speak of it.

VISHINSKY. How matters stood with butter, this is of interest to me at this stage of the investigation. You have spoken of salt, of sugar, how you held back these commodities from sale to the population by sabotage, etc. But how did matters stand with butter?

ZELENSKY. We don't sell butter in the rural districts.

VISHINSKY. I am not asking you what you sell. You were above all selling the main thing—your country. I am speaking about what measures were taken by your organization to disrupt trade and deprive the population of prime necessities. Apart from sugar and salt, do you know anything concerning butter?

ZELENSKY. I told you that the co-operatives do not sell butter in the rural districts.

VISHINSKY. You are not a co-operator, you are a member of a conspiratorial organization. Do you know anything about butter?

ZELENSKY. No.

VISHINSKY. For instance, that you did not supply cheap grades of butter?

ZELENSKY. That is another matter altogether.

VISHINSKY. What do you mean, another matter?

ZELENSKY. I can explain this to you now. I want to tell you what bore relation . . .

VISHINSKY. No, you are dividing your activities into two parts: your activity as a co-operator and your activity as a conspirator. But I want you to speak here not as a co-operator, but as a conspirator.

ZELENSKY. Quite true, but might I be allowed some continuity in my account?

VISHINSKY. You are not delivering a report here.

ZELENSKY. But in respect of the account of my criminal activity there must be some continuity?

VISHINSKY. Continuity in my opinion consists in answers being given to the questions that are put to you by the Court investigation, and I am asking you: have you any knowledge of criminal operations with regard to supplying the population with butter, particularly cheap grades of butter, or not? Operations which were effected on the orders of your "bloc of Rights and Trotskyites"; are they known to you or not?

ZELENSKY. Yes, they are.

VISHINSKY. In what did they consist?

ZELENSKY. They consisted in the following: in making butter, all the produce-purchasing organizations used the international standards fixing quality of butter.

VISHINSKY. That is not the point.

16 Old Bolshevik; Chairman of Union of Consumers' Co-operatives.

ZELENSKY. That is the point.

VISHINSKY. No.

ZELENSKY. What do you mean? This was done . . .

THE PRESIDENT. Accused Zelensky, no cross-talk and keep to the point.

VISHINSKY. You want to explain the technicalities of this business and I want to get to the bottom of this business. You said at the preliminary investigation that the destructive character of your work consisted in the following: the adopted scale of grades of butter had the result that there was only butter of the highest grade, no cheap butter reached the market.

ZELENSKY. That is what I just wanted to explain.

VISHINSKY. Is it a fact, or not?

ZELENSKY. It is.

VISHINSKY. Further. This affected the budget of the consumer. Is that so, or not?

ZELENSKY. Yes.

VISHINSKY. Did this rouse satisfaction or dissatisfaction on the part of the public?

ZELENSKY. Dissatisfaction.

VISHINSKY. Is this what you were striving for?

ZELENSKY. It was.

VISHINSKY. Did your organization strive for it?

ZELENSKY. It did.

VISHINSKY. And was the butter which was issued for sale always of good quality, or did you try to spoil its quality too?

ZELENSKY. Yes.

VISHINSKY. Were there cases when members of your organization connected with the butter business threw glass into the butter?

ZELENSKY. There were cases when glass was thrown into the butter.

VISHINSKY. Were there cases when your accomplices, fellow participators in the criminal plot against the Soviet power and the Soviet people, threw nails into the butter?

ZELENSKY. There were.

VISHINSKY. For what purpose? To make it "tastier"?

ZELENSKY. That is clear.

VISHINSKY. And who were you at that time?

ZELENSKY. The Chairman of the Centrosoyuz.

VISHINSKY. That means that it was your duty to supply the population with foodstuffs?

ZELENSKY. Yes.

VISHINSKY. And that is the way you supplied the population with foodstuffs. And did you not mix nails with the eggs?

ZELENSKY. No.

VISHINSKY. Why? It did not work? The shells interfered? Now you may continue.

ZELENSKY. I consider overcharging, short measure, and short weight to be wrecking in no less a degree.

VISHINSKY. Yes, that is a serious matter.

ZELENSKY. And I want to divulge the mechanism of this matter.

VISHINSKY. Tell us first what it consisted in and then you can go on to the mechanism.

ZELENSKY. It seems to me that the question of overcharging, short measure, and short weight should be clear to everybody; it is very obvious. It consists in the following: when a man comes into a shop to make a purchase, he is overcharged, given short measure, and short weight: that is, he is named a price higher than the one at which the goods should be sold, or is given shorter weight than he is entitled to, or is sold goods not of the proper quality.

VISHINSKY. Why is this done?

ZELENSKY. To arouse discontent among the population . . . Another important form of wrecking, also designed to arouse the discontent of the population, was the freezing of trade by dispatching goods to the wrong districts or at the wrong times. For example, there were cases when summer goods were sent in winter, and, vice versa, when winter goods arrived in the shops in summer.

VISHINSKY. That is, the public was offered felt boots in summer and summer shoes in winter?

ZELENSKY. Yes.

VISHINSKY. Was this your plan?

ZELENSKY. Yes.

VISHINSKY. Was this accidental, or was it a plan and a system?

ZELENSKY. Seeing that it was wrecking work, there can be no question of its having been accidental.

VISHINSKY. Allow me to begin the interrogation of the accused Bukharin. Formulate briefly what exactly it is you plead guilty to.

BUKHARIN. Firstly, to belonging to the counterrevolutionary "bloc of Rights and Trotskyites."

VISHINSKY. Since what year?

BUKHARIN. From the moment the bloc was formed. Even before that, I plead guilty to belonging to the counterrevolutionary organization of the Rights.

VISHINSKY. Since what year?

BUKHARIN. Roughly since 1928. I plead guilty to being one of the outstanding leaders of this bloc of Rights and Trotskyites. Consequently, I plead guilty to what directly follows from this, the sum total of crimes committed by this counterrevolutionary organization, irrespective of whether or not I knew of, whether or not I took a direct part, in any particular act.

307

Because I am responsible as one of the leaders and not as a cog of this counterrevolutionary organization.

VISHINSKY. What aims were pursued by this counterrevolutionary organization?

BUKHARIN. This counterrevolutionary organization, to formulate it briefly . . .

VISHINSKY. Yes, briefly for the present.

BUKHARIN. The principal aim it pursued, although, so to speak, it did not fully realize it, and did not dot all the i's—was essentially the aim of restoring capitalist relations in the U.S.S.R.

VISHINSKY. The overthrow of the Soviet power?

BUKHARIN. The overthrow of the Soviet power was a means to this end.

VISHINSKY. By means of?

BUKHARIN. As is known . . .

VISHINSKY. By means of a forcible overthrow?

BUKHARIN. Yes, by means of the forcible overthrow of this power.

VISHINSKY. With the help of?

BUKHARIN. With the help of all the difficulties encountered by the Soviet power; in particular, with the help of a war which prognostically was in prospect.

VISHINSKY. Which was prognostically in prospect, with whose help?

BUKHARIN. With the help of foreign states.

VISHINSKY. On condition?

BUKHARIN. On condition, to put it concretely, of a number of concessions.

VISHINSKY. To the extent of . . .

BUKHARIN. To the extent of the cession of territory.

VISHINSKY. That is?

BUKHARIN. If all the i's are dotted—on condition of the dismemberment of the U.S.S.R.

VISHINSKY. The severance of whole regions and republics from the U.S.S.R.?

BUKHARIN. Yes.

VISHINSKY. For example?

BUKHARIN. The Ukraine, the Maritime Region, Byelorussia.

VISHINSKY. In whose favor?

BUKHARIN. In favor of the corresponding states, whose geographical and political . . .

VISHINSKY. Which exactly?

BUKHARIN. In favor of Germany, in favor of Japan, and partly in favor of England.

VISHINSKY. So, that was the agreement with the circles concerned? I know of one agreement which the bloc had.

BUKHARIN. Yes, the bloc had an agreement.

VISHINSKY. And also by means of weakening the defensive power?

BUKHARIN. You see, this question was not discussed, at least not in my presence.

VISHINSKY. And what was the position with regard to wrecking?

BUKHARIN. The position with regard to wrecking was that in the end, especially under pressure of the Trotskyite part of the so-called contact center, which arose roughly in 1933, despite a number of internal differences and manipulatory political mechanics, which are of no interest to the investigation, after various vicissitudes, disputes and so on, the orientation on wrecking was adopted.

VISHINSKY. Did it tend to weaken the defensive power of our country?

BUKHARIN. Naturally.

VISHINSKY. Consequently, there was an orientation on the weakening, the undermining of defensive power?

BUKHARIN. Not formally, but essentially it was so.

VISHINSKY. But the actions and activity in this direction were clear?

BUKHARIN. Yes.

VISHINSKY. Can you say the same about diversive acts?

BUKHARIN. With regard to diversive acts—by virtue of the division of labor and my definite functions, of which you know—I mainly occupied myself with the problematics of general leadership and with the ideological side; this, of course, did not exclude either my being aware of the practical side of the matter, or the adoption of a number of practical steps on my part.

VISHINSKY. As I understand you, there was a division of labor among you.

BUKHARIN. But I, Citizen Procurator, say that I bear responsibility for the bloc.

VISHINSKY. But the bloc which you headed set itself the aim of organizing diversive acts?

BUKHARIN. As far as I can judge by various things that rise in my memory, this was made dependent on concrete circumstances and concrete conditions.

VISHINSKY. As you see from the trial, the circumstances were concrete enough. Did you and Khodjayev discuss the fact that too little wrecking was being done, and being done badly?

BUKHARIN. About accelerating wrecking there was no talk . . .

VISHINSKY. Did the bloc stand for the organization of terrorist acts, the assassination of leaders of the Party and the Soviet Government?

BUKHARIN. It did, and I think that the organization of this must be dated back roughly to 1932, the autumn.

VISHINSKY. And what was your relation to the assassination of Sergei Mironovich Kirov? Was this assassination also committed with the knowledge and on the instructions of the bloc of Rights and Trotskyites?

BUKHARIN. That I did not know.

VISHINSKY. I ask you, was this assassination committed with the

309

knowledge and on the instructions of the bloc of Rights and Trotskyites?

BUKHARIN. And I repeat that I do not know, Citizen Procurator.

VISHINSKY. You did not know about this specifically in relation to the assassination of S. M. Kirov?

BUKHARIN. Not specifically, but . . .

VISHINSKY. Permit me to question the accused Rykov.

THE PRESIDENT. You may.

VISHINSKY. Accused Rykov, what do you know about the assassination of Sergei Mironovich Kirov?

RYKOV. I know nothing about the participation of the Rights or the Right part of the bloc in the assassination of Kirov.

VISHINSKY. In general, were you aware of preparations for terrorist acts, for the assassination of members of the Party and the government?

RYKOV. As one of the leaders of the Right part of this bloc, I took part in the organization of a number of terrorist groups and in preparations for terrorist acts. As I have said in my testimony, I do not know of a single decision of the Right center, through which I was related with the bloc of Rights and Trotskyites, about the actual commission of assassinations. . . .

VISHINSKY. About the actual commission. So. Do you know that one of the aims of the bloc of Rights and Trotskyites was to organize and commit terrorist acts against leaders of the Party and the government?

RYKOV. I said more than that, I said that I personally organized terrorist groups. But you are asking me whether I knew of such aims through some third person.

VISHINSKY. I am asking whether the bloc of Rights and Trotskyites had any relation to the assassination of Comrade Kirov.

RYKOV. I have no information regarding the relation of the Right part to this assassination, and therefore I am convinced to this day that the assassination of Kirov was carried out by the Trotskyites without the knowledge of the Rights. Of course, I might not have known about it.

VISHINSKY. Were you connected with Yenukidze?

RYKOV. With Yenukidze? Very little.

VISHINSKY. Was he a member of the bloc of Rights and Trotskyites?

RYKOV. He was, since 1933.

VISHINSKY. Which part did he represent in this bloc, the Trotskyites or the Rights? To which did he gravitate?

RYKOV. He must have represented the Right part.

VISHINSKY. Very well; please be seated. Permit me to question the accused Yagoda. Accused Yagoda, do you know that Yenukidze, of whom the accused Rykov just spoke, represented the Right part of the bloc and that he had direct relation to the organization of the assassination of Sergei Mironovich Kirov?

YAGODA. Both Rykov and Bukharin are telling lies. Rykov and Yenukidze were present at the meeting of the center where the question of assassinating S. M. Kirov was discussed.

VISHINSKY. Did the Rights have any relation to this?

YAGODA. Direct relation, because it was a bloc of Rights and Trotskyites.

VISHINSKY. Did the accused Rykov and Bukharin in particular have any relation to the assassination?

YAGODA. Direct relation.

VISHINSKY. Did you, as a member of the bloc of Rights and Trotskyites, have any relation to this assassination?

YAGODA. I did.

VISHINSKY. Are Bukharin and Rykov telling the truth when they say that they knew nothing about it?

YAGODA. That cannot be so, because when Yenukidze told me that they, that is, the bloc of Rights and Trotskyites, had decided at a joint meeting to commit a terrorist act against Kirov, I categorically objected. . . .

VISHINSKY. Why?

YAGODA. I declared that I would never permit any terrorist acts. I regarded it as absolutely unnecessary.

VISHINSKY. And dangerous for the organization?

YAGODA. Of course.

VISHINSKY. Nevertheless?

YAGODA. Nevertheless Yenukidze confirmed . . .

VISHINSKY. What?

YAGODA. That at this meeting they . . .

VISHINSKY. Who were they?

YAGODA. Rykov and Yenukidze at first categorically objected . . .

VISHINSKY. To what?

YAGODA. To the commission of a terrorist act. But under the pressure of the remaining part of the bloc of Rights and Trotskyites . . .

VISHINSKY. Principally the Trotskyites?

YAGODA. Yes, under the pressure of the remaining part of the bloc of Rights and Trotskyites, they gave their consent. So Yenukidze told me.

VISHINSKY. After this, did you personally take any measures to effect the assassination of Sergei Mironovich Kirov?

YAGODA. I personally?

VISHINSKY. Yes, as a member of the bloc.

YAGODA. I gave instructions . . .

VISHINSKY. To whom?

YAGODA. To Zaporozhetz in Leningrad. That is not quite how it was.

VISHINSKY. We shall speak about that later. What I want now is to elucidate the part played by Rykov and Bukharin in this villainous act.

YAGODA. I gave instructions to Zaporozhetz. When Nikolayev was detained . . .

VISHINSKY. The first time?

YAGODA. Yes. Zaporozhetz came to Moscow and reported to me that a man had been detained . . .

VISHINSKY. In whose briefcase . . .

YAGODA. There was a revolver and a diary. And he released him.

VISHINSKY. And you approved of this?

YAGODA. I just took note of the fact.

VISHINSKY. And then you gave instructions not to place obstacles in the way of the murder of Sergei Mironovich Kirov?

YAGODA. Yes, I did. . . . It was not like that.

VISHINSKY. In a somewhat different form?

YAGODA. It was not like that, but it is not important.

VISHINSKY. Did you give instructions?

YAGODA. I have confirmed that.

VISHINSKY. And did you not count upon the arrest of Comrade Stalin in 1918?

BUKHARIN. At that time there were several talks about . . .

VISHINSKY. I am not asking about talks, but about a plan for the arrest of Comrade Stalin.

BUKHARIN. And I say that if I do not agree with your description of it as a plan, then permit me to prove to the Court how it was in actual fact. Then, it may be said, it was not a plan, but a talk.

VISHINSKY. What about?

BUKHARIN. There was the same talk about the formation of a new government of "Left Communists."

VISHINSKY. And I ask you, did you have a plan for the arrest of Comrade Stalin in 1918?

BUKHARIN. Not of Stalin, but there was a plan for the arrest of Lenin, Stalin, and Sverdlov.

VISHINSKY. All three: Lenin, Stalin, and Sverdlov?

BUKHARIN. Quite so.

VISHINSKY. And so, not Comrade Stalin, but Comrades Stalin, Lenin, and Sverdlov?

BUKHARIN. Exactly.

VISHINSKY. There was a plan of arrest?

BUKHARIN. I say that there was not a plan, but talks on the subject.

VISHINSKY. And what about the assassination of Comrades Stalin, Lenin, and Sverdlov?

BUKHARIN. Under no circumstances.

VISHINSKY. Have you lived in Austria?

BUKHARIN. I have.

VISHINSKY. For long?

BUKHARIN. 1912 to 1913.

VISHINSKY. You had no connections with the Austrian police?

BUKHARIN. None.

VISHINSKY. Have you lived in America?

BUKHARIN. Yes.

VISHINSKY. For long?

BUKHARIN. Yes.

VISHINSKY. How many months?

BUKHARIN. About seven months.

VISHINSKY. In America you were not connected with the police?

BUKHARIN. Absolutely not.

VISHINSKY. On your way from America to Russia you passed through . . .

BUKHARIN. Through Japan.

VISHINSKY. Did you stop there for long?

BUKHARIN. A week.

VISHINSKY. You were not recruited during this week?

BUKHARIN. If it pleases you to put such questions . . .

VISHINSKY. The Code of Criminal Procedure gives me the right to put such questions.

THE PRESIDENT. The Prosecutor has all the more right to put such a question because Bukharin is charged with attempting to assassinate the leaders of the Party as far back as 1918, with raising a hand against the life of Vladimir Ilyich Lenin in 1918.

VISHINSKY. I am not overstepping the Code of Criminal Procedure. If you like, you can say "no," but I may ask.

BUKHARIN. Quite right.

THE PRESIDENT. The consent of the accused is not required.

VISHINSKY. You made no connections with the police?

BUKHARIN. Absolutely.

VISHINSKY. Like Chernov in the bus. I am asking you about connections with some police authority.

BUKHARIN. I had no connections with any police authorities whatsoever.

VISHINSKY. Then why was it so easy for you to join a bloc which was engaged in espionage work?

BUKHARIN. Concerning espionage work I know absolutely nothing.

VISHINSKY. What do you mean, you don't know?

BUKHARIN. Just that.

VISHINSKY. And what was the bloc engaged in?

BUKHARIN. Two people testified here about espionage, Sharangovich and Ivanov, that is to say, two *agents provocateurs*.

VISHINSKY. Accused Bukharin, do you consider Rykov an *agent provocateur*?

BUKHARIN. No, I do not.

VISHINSKY (*to Rykov*). Accused Rykov, do you know that the bloc of Rights and Trotskyites conducted espionage work?

RYKOV. I know there were organizations that conducted espionage work.

VISHINSKY. Tell me, did the Byelorussian national-Fascist organization, which was part of your bloc of Rights and Trotskyites and which was led by the accused Sharangovich, conduct espionage work?

RYKOV. I have already spoken about that.

VISHINSKY. It conducted espionage work?

RYKOV. Yes.

VISHINSKY. You knew about this?

RYKOV. I did.

VISHINSKY. And Bukharin did not know?

RYKOV. In my opinion, Bukharin also knew.

VISHINSKY. So, accused Bukharin, it is not Sharangovich who says so, but your pal Rykov.

BUKHARIN. Nevertheless I did not know.

THE PRESIDENT. Comrade Prosecutor, have you any more questions?

VISHINSKY. I want to make myself clear to the accused Bukharin. Do you understand now why I asked you about Austria?

BUKHARIN. My connection with the Austrian police consisted in my imprisonment in an Austrian fortress.

VISHINSKY. Accused Sharangovich, you were a Polish spy, although you have been in prison?

SHARANGOVICH[17]. Yes, although I have been in prison.

BUKHARIN. I have been in a Swedish prison, twice in a Russian prison, and in a German prison.

VISHINSKY. The fact that you have been in jail is no proof that you could not have been a spy.

Accused Rykov, you confirm that after all his terms of confinement in the prisons of various countries, Bukharin, with you, knew of Sharangovich's spy connection with the Polish intelligence service? Knew about it and approved of it?

RYKOV. I knew of organizations which conducted espionage work.

VISHINSKY. The fact that Bukharin had been in various prisons did not prevent him from approving his accomplices' connections with the Polish intelligence service. You understand this?

RYKOV. No, I do not.

VISHINSKY. Bukharin understands it.

BUKHARIN. I understand, but I deny it.

MARCH 8

VISHINSKY. I request that Vol. II, p. 195, of the record be presented.

Deposition of the accused Yagoda of December 28, 1937 (p. 196 of the record):

"It is a known fact that during his last years Menzhinsky was more often ill than at work. I directed the work. It was clear that after his death I would become Chairman of the OGPU. I became accustomed to this idea

---

[17] Former Secretary of the Party Central Committee in White Russia. Believed to be prosecution witness masquerading as a defendant.

and was waiting for Menzhinsky's death, but he did not die. When I instructed Levin to get Max out of the way . . ."

VISHINSKY. Accused Levin, who is this Max?

LEVIN[18]. Maxim Alexeyevich Peshkov.[19]

VISHINSKY. "I thought, why could not the same thing be done to Menzhinsky? In one of my conversations with Levin, I spoke to him bluntly about this. He was already linked with me in preparing crimes and he could not refuse to do this."

Accused Yagoda, was Levin linked with you in preparing crimes?

YAGODA. Not in the case of Max.

VISHINSKY. In whose case?

YAGODA. Kuibyshev and Maxim Gorki.

VISHINSKY. And did you state that during the preliminary investigation?

YAGODA. I did.

VISHINSKY. "But he said that he had no access to Menzhinsky, that the physician in attendance was Kazakov, without whom nothing could be done. I instructed Levin to enlist Kazakov for this purpose."

Did you depose this, accused Yagoda?

YAGODA. I said that I did, but it is not true.

VISHINSKY. Why did you make this deposition if it is not true?

YAGODA. I don't know why.

VISHINSKY. Be seated.

"I summoned Kazakov and confirmed my orders. . . . He did his work. Menzhinsky died."

Did you depose this, accused Yagoda?

YAGODA. I did.

VISHINSKY. Hence, you met Kazakov?

YAGODA. No.

VISHINSKY. Why did you make a false deposition?

YAGODA. Permit me not to answer this question.

VISHINSKY. So you deny that you organized the murder of Menzhinsky?

YAGODA. I do.

VISHINSKY. Did you admit it in this deposition?

YAGODA. Yes.

VISHINSKY. When the Procurator of the Union interrogated you, what did you answer to this question about your part in the murder of Menzhinsky?

YAGODA. I confirmed it also then.

VISHINSKY. You confirmed it. Why did you confirm it?

YAGODA. Permit me not to answer this question.

[18] Soviet consultant to Kremlin Medical Department.
[19] Maxim Gorki's son.

VISHINSKY. Then answer my last question: Did you file any protest or complaint with regard to the preliminary investigation?

YAGODA. None.

VISHINSKY. Are you filing any now?

YAGODA. No.

VISHINSKY. Be seated.

VISHINSKY. I spoke to you about the organization of the murders you have spoken of here. As I understood you, Yagoda also explained to you the political motives which guided him?

LEVIN. He did. I have already mentioned them. He said that dissatisfaction with the Party leadership was growing within the Party.

VISHINSKY. Did Yagoda say this?

LEVIN. Yes. That this dissatisfaction was spreading throughout the country and that there was hardly a single big institution in which there were not people who were dissatisfied with this leadership and who did not consider it necessary to replace it by other people. He also spoke to me about the necessity of other people coming to power. . . .

VISHINSKY. In what way? With whose assistance?

LEVIN. Well, when he concluded this introductory historical information, he said that in order to facilitate this we must remove from the political arena certain members of the Political Bureau and Alexei Maximovich Gorki. In a second conversation he explained why Alexei Maximovich. Because Alexei Maximovich was a supporter, a staunch supporter, of the line of the Party leadership, and in particular he was a great admirer and follower of Stalin's whole policy; he was also his personal friend, would not betray him under any circumstances, and would always stand in our way and always spoil things for us. He had to be removed.

VISHINSKY. Accused Levin, Yagoda's designs to murder political leaders of our state as expressed to you bore a quite obvious and open counterrevolutionary character?

LEVIN. Yes. Everything was clear.

VISHINSKY. And your attitude towards this was not merely one of a technician, but also of a politician?

LEVIN. I do not know what you mean by that. I have never been a politician in my life.

VISHINSKY. Having learnt about this sinister plot, what should you have done?

LEVIN. I should have informed about it.

VISHINSKY. Having been invited to become a participant, and even more, an organizer, of the murder of prominent Soviet people and of the genius of Russian culture, Gorki, what should you have done if you really loved Gorki and your country?

LEVIN. Refused to do this and informed on Yagoda.

316

VISHINSKY. Why did you not do it?

LEVIN. From cowardice.

VISHINSKY. Consequently, you thought that there is no beast stronger than the cat?

LEVIN. Yes.

VISHINSKY. That the strongest and most terrible cat was Yagoda?

LEVIN. Quite right.

VISHINSKY. And what do you think now?

LEVIN. Oh, it is clear.

VISHINSKY. I further want to ask you; tell us honestly: did you think that there was no law against Yagoda?

LEVIN. I realize it perfectly clearly now. In general, when one looks back retrospectively on the past, one says to oneself: "My God, why did I not do this, why did I not do that?"

VISHINSKY. How long did your participation in this criminal activity last?

LEVIN. Three years.

VISHINSKY. Three years! You had thousands of opportunities in that time to act honestly.

LEVIN. Yes, and I did not avail myself of them.

VISHINSKY. You did not avail yourself of them because, as you say, you were a coward?

LEVIN. Yes.

VISHINSKY. Are you such a coward?

LEVIN. Yes, a coward.

VISHINSKY. And do you recall another figure in one of the earlier trials, a no less sinister one, Ivan Nikitich Smirnov? Do you know whether Yagoda was connected with him and whether he shielded him?

BULANOV[20]. Of the particular regarding Smirnov, I know precisely that when Smirnov was in prison, Yagoda sent Molchanov and through him instructed Smirnov within what limits he should keep in case of necessity, if certain testimony should be demanded of him. That is absolutely so.

VISHINSKY. And do you know what Yagoda did when Smirnov was brought from prison to Moscow?

BULANOV. I know that Yagoda departed from his usual practice. He did not usually visit prisons, but when Smirnov arrived he went to see him.

VISHINSKY. In his cell?

BULANOV. Yes.

VISHINSKY. What did he do there?

BULANOV. I heard him say to Molchanov that he, Yagoda, was easy in his mind about the way Smirnov would conduct himself in court.

VISHINSKY. That is, he coached him. What was his attitude to Kamenev after the assassination of Sergei Mironovich Kirov?

[20] Former Secretary to the NKVD and Yagoda's private secretary.

317

BULANOV. When the decision was taken to arrest Kamenev and Zinoviev, Yagoda sent me to arrest Kamenev.

VISHINSKY. Whom did he send with you?

BULANOV. I went with Pauker.

VISHINSKY. Who was this Pauker?

BULANOV. Chief of the Operations Department.

VISHINSKY. And yet, who was he?

BULANOV. A man who was completely initiated into the conspiratorial affairs and one who was exceptionally trusted. He was the connecting link with Yenukidze.

VISHINSKY. Was not Pauker a German spy?

BULANOV. I learnt later that he was a spy.

VISHINSKY. A German spy?

BULANOV. Quite so.

VISHINSKY. Accused Yagoda, did you know that Pauker was a German spy?

YAGODA. Yes, I did.

VISHINSKY. Hence, if we sum up your explanations, we may say the following:

First—that you plead guilty to the fact that your participation in the underground work of the Rights was of long standing.

YAGODA. Yes.

VISHINSKY. Second—that you plead guilty to having been one of the leaders of the underground bloc of Rights and Trotskyites.

YAGODA. Yes, I do.

VISHINSKY. Third—that, together with this bloc, you pursued the aim of overthrowing the Soviet Government and of restoring capitalism in the U.S.S.R.

YAGODA. Yes, I do. We set ourselves the task of seizing the Kremlin.

VISHINSKY. That for the purpose of overthrowing the government you chose the method of an insurrection timed primarily for the outbreak of war. Is that so?

YAGODA. No, it is not so. An armed insurrection—that was nonsense. Only these babblers here could think of that.

VISHINSKY. Well, what were you thinking of?

YAGODA. Of a "palace coup."

VISHINSKY. That is to say, of a violent coup, carried through by a small group of plotters?

YAGODA. Yes, the same as they did.

VISHINSKY. Timing it preferably for a military onslaught on the U.S.S.R. by foreign powers, or did you have various plans?

YAGODA. There was one plan, namely, to seize the Kremlin. The time was of no importance.

VISHINSKY. Was it your point of view that it was expedient in case of war to prepare and secure the defeat of the U.S.S.R.?

YAGODA. That was the point of view of the bloc, and therefore it was mine, too.

VISHINSKY. Do you also admit being guilty of espionage work?

YAGODA. No, I do not admit being guilty of this activity.

VISHINSKY. But you yourself have said that several spies were at work under your direct leadership.

YAGODA. Yes, I admit that.

VISHINSKY. Did you know they were spies?

YAGODA. Yes, I did.

VISHINSKY. Did you know they were fulfilling espionage duties?

YAGODA. Yes, I did.

VISHINSKY. So you helped them?

YAGODA. I am just as responsible for these spies as. . . .

VISHINSKY. Do you also admit being guilty of having placed state funds at Trotsky's disposal on the instructions of the bloc?

YAGODA. I do.

VISHINSKY. And do you admit being guilty of organizing and effecting terrorist acts: first—the murder of Comrade Kirov on the orders and instructions of the bloc?

YAGODA. I admit being guilty of complicity in the murder.

VISHINSKY. Do you admit being guilty of complicity in the murder or in causing the death of Menzhinsky?

YAGODA. I do.

VISHINSKY. Do you admit being guilty of organizing the murder of Kuibyshev?

YAGODA. I do.

VISHINSKY. Do you admit being guilty of the murder of Alexei Maximovich Gorki?

YAGODA. I do.

MARCH 12

RYKOV (*Last plea*). . . . I would like those who have not yet been exposed and who have not yet laid down their arms to do so immediately and openly. I would like my example to convince them of the inevitability of their being disarmed, and that they should lay down their arms at all costs and at the earliest moment, that they should realize that only by laying down their arms, even at the risk of certain privations and even arrest, can they secure any sort of relief and disencumber themselves of the monstrous burden which has been revealed by the present trial.

Salvation lies only in laying down their arms. Their only salvation, their only escape lies in helping the Party, in helping the government to expose and liquidate the remnants, the dregs of the counterrevolutionary organization, if any still happen to remain in any part of the territory of the Soviet Union.

ROSENGOLTZ (*Last plea*). . . . after all that I have lived through, after the feeling of shame which I experienced during this trial, after the monstrous crimes which I committed, I have no incentive or desire to ask for the mitigation of my sentence.

This is not a rhetorical figure. This does not mean that it is without a feeling of pain that I part with the beautiful land of the Soviets. We have beautiful new shoots now, a new generation reared by the Bolshevik Party. We have such an upsurge in the Soviet Union as no other country in the world can boast. The pain of parting is intensified by the fact that we already have absolutely real results of Socialist construction. For the first time now we have a life, a full-blooded life, scintillating with joy and color. Millions, tens of millions of people, children and citizens of the Soviet Union, including my own children sing the song:

> *Native land of mine, so beautiful . . .*
> *There is no other land the whole world over*
> *Where man walks the earth so proud and free.*

And I repeat these words, I, a prisoner, repeat these words: There is no other land the whole world over where there is such enthusiasm of labor, where such gay and joyous laughter rings, where song and dance resound so free, where there is such beautiful love; and I say: "Farewell, my native land, my own!" I want people to believe me. I want nothing from the Court, nor from people. I do not want and cannot permit myself a single word of falsehood in this, my last address to people. . . .

Long live the Bolshevik Party with the best traditions of enthusiasm, heroism, self-sacrifice, which can only be found in the world under Stalin's leadership. In the inevitable clash of two worlds, Communism will emerge victorious. Long live Communism throughout the world!

BUKHARIN (*Last plea*). . . . This trial, which is the concluding one of a series of trials, has exposed all the crimes and the treasonable activities; it has exposed the historical significance and the roots of our struggle against the Party and the Soviet Government.

I have been in prison for over a year, and I therefore do not know what is going on in the world. But, judging from those fragments of real life that sometimes reached me by chance, I see, feel, and understand that the interests which we so criminally betrayed are entering a new phase of gigantic development, are now appearing in the international arena as a great and mighty factor of the international proletarian phase. . . .

I once more repeat that I admit that I am guilty of treason to the Socialist fatherland, the most heinous of possible crimes, of the organization of kulak uprisings, of preparations for terrorist acts and of belonging to an underground, anti-Soviet organization. I further admit that I am guilty of organizing a conspiracy for a "palace coup." And this, incidentally, proves the incorrectness of all those passages in the speech for the prosecution made by Citizen the State Prosecutor, where he makes out that I adopted the pose of a pure theoretician, the pose of a philosopher, and so on. These are profoundly practical matters. I said, and I now repeat, that I was a leader and not a cog in the counterrevolutionary affairs. It follows from this, as will be clear to everybody, that there were many specific things which I could not have known, and which I actually did not know, but that this does not relieve me of responsibility. . . .

I, however, admit that I am guilty of the dastardly plan of the dismemberment of the U.S.S.R., for Trotsky was negotiating about territorial concessions, and I was in a bloc with the Trotskyites. This is a fact, and I admit it.

I categorically deny my complicity in the assassination of Kirov, Menzhinsky, Kuibyshev, Gorki, and Maxim Peshkov. According to Yagoda's testimony, Kirov was assassinated in accordance with a decision of the bloc of Rights and Trotskyites. I knew nothing about it. But what Citizen the Procurator calls logic comes here to the aid of the factual content. He asked whether Bukharin and Rykov could have stood aside from these assassinations; and he answered that they could not have stood aside because they knew about them. But not standing aside and knowing are one and the same thing. This is what in elementary logic is called tautology, that is, the acceptance of what is yet to be proved as already proven. But what is the real explanation? It might be said: Well, then, you villain, how do you explain these facts? Can you deny that some decision was adopted by some section or other with the knowledge of Yenukidze and Yagoda, or you deny even that? I cannot deny it, Citizens Judges. But if I cannot deny it, and at the same time cannot affirm it, I can make a certain conjecture. After all, you must bear in mind the secrecy of the work. The center did not hold meetings: matters were discussed as occasion arose, and given such secret methods of communication and connections with each other, such things are quite possible. . . .

Repentance is often attributed to diverse and absolutely absurd things like Tibetan powders and the like. I must say of myself that in prison, where I was confined for over a year, I worked, studied, and retained my clarity of mind. This will serve to refute by facts all fables and absurd counterrevolutionary tales.

Hypnotism is suggested. But I conducted my own defense in court from the legal standpoint too, orientated myself on the spot, argued with the State Prosecutor; and anybody, even a man who has little experience in this branch of medicine, must admit that hypnotism of this kind is altogether impossible.

This repentance is often attributed to the Dostoyevsky mind, to the specific properties of the soul ("l'âme slave," as it is called), and this can be said of types like Alyosha Karamazov, the heroes of The Idiot and other Dostoyevsky characters, who are prepared to stand up in the public square and cry: "Beat me, Orthodox Christians, I am a villain!"

But that is not the case here at all. L'âme slave and the psychology of Dostoyevsky characters are a thing of the remote past in our country, the

321

pluperfect tense. Such types do not exist in our country, or exist perhaps only on the outskirts of small provincial towns, if they do even there. On the contrary, such a psychology is to be found in Western Europe.

I shall now speak of myself, of the reasons for my repentance. Of course, it must be admitted that incriminating evidence plays a very important part. For three months I refused to say anything. Then I began to testify. Why? Because while in prison I made a revaluation of my entire past. For when you ask yourself: "If you must die, what are you dying for?"—an absolutely black vacuity suddenly rises before you with startling vividness. There was nothing to die for, if one wanted to die unrepented. And, on the contrary, everything positive that glistens in the Soviet Union acquires new dimensions in a man's mind. This in the end disarmed me completely and led me to bend my knees before the Party and the country. And when you ask yourself: "Very well, suppose you do not die; suppose by some miracle you remain alive, again what for? Isolated from everybody, an enemy of the people, in an inhuman position, completely isolated from everything that constitutes the essence of life . . ." And at once the same reply arises. And at such moments, Citizens Judges, everything personal, all the personal incrustation, all the rancor, pride, and a number of other things, fall away, disappear. And, in addition, when the reverberations of the broad international struggle reach your ear, all this in its entirety does its work, and the result is the complete internal moral victory of the U.S.S.R. over its kneeling opponents. . . . For in reality the whole country stands behind Stalin; he is the hope of the world; he is a creator. Napoleon once said that fate is politics. The fate of Trotsky is counterrevolutionary politics.

THE NUREMBERG TRIAL

(1945–1946)

It was a strange setting for Goetterdaemmerung. The high-ceilinged, paneled courtroom in Nuremberg's Palace of Justice had been freshly redecorated, and the overbright lighting lent it a slightly aseptic air. Thick carpets muffled the hubbub in the center well of the court, where prosecutors and defense counsel swarmed over tables strewn with documents. Drapes had been hung over the windows, so that the light remained of a uniform intensity throughout the day. It was as though time had been made to stand still until the drama reached its end.

Not far from the south end of the room, the prisoners' box, with its twenty-one chairs arranged in two tiers, faced the bench. Both were well elevated to afford a direct line of vision between the two. Bracketing the prisoners stood a detachment of picked troops from the 1st U.S. Infantry Division, their white helmets, belts, and gloves accentuating the formality of the occasion.

The rear third of the courtroom had been fitted out with plush seats for some three hundred press and radio reporters, with a visitors' gallery overhead.

Everywhere there were wires, terminating in individual earphones, through which everyone in the room could hear translations of the proceedings in English, French, German, or Russian by flipping a dial. Flashing red and yellow lights signaled speakers to slow down or notified them of operating breakdowns in the installation, contributing to a pervasive sense of unreality.

The choice of the rubble-strewn medieval city as the site of the trial had a suitable measure of irony. For it was here that the Nazi hierarchy had strutted and ranted at the Party rallies held each September—until 1939, when the scheduled "Peace Rally" was canceled because of urgent business elsewhere. It was from here that Julius Streicher's pornographic sheet, *Der Stürmer*, had spewed out his racist diatribes, stoking the fires of the Nazi terror. Here, too, Hermann Goering, as President of the

323

Reichstag, had proclaimed the first of the infamous anti-Jewish laws which came to bear the city's name.

Nuremberg had also witnessed Adolf Hitler's first overt hint of his determination to defy the dictates of the Versailles Treaty. On one of its green fields in the fall of 1934, he unveiled his Labor Youth Organization, a paramilitary aggregation of youngsters which left 300,000 spectators dewy-eyed when they broke into a precise and perfectly executed goose step.

The faint echo of that goose step was still audible when Hitler announced his designs on the Ukraine and parts of Siberia at the next annual Party gathering. And not too much later, the rally had served as a sounding board for the hysterical threats of Hitler and Goering against the Czechs, clearing the way for the sordid sellout at Munich.

Now, in the autumn of 1945, the klieg-lit flags and massed stormtrooper standards were gone. The hoarse cannonade of cheering voices was stilled. The sea of ramrod arms raised in salute had evaporated.

Now there was only the law.

About six months earlier, a band of Italian partisans had taken the law into its own hands and strung up the bullet-riddled body of Hitler's toady, Benito Mussolini, in Milan's Piazzale Loreto. This sort of law the Nazis could understand; it was written in the language of violence and contempt. Loath to share Mussolini's fate, Hitler and his faithful mouthpiece, Joseph Goebbels, had preferred suicide in the bunkers below the beleaguered Berlin Chancellery to the rough-and-ready justice of the advancing Russian troops. And the mild-mannered, intellectually pretentious sadist, Gestapo chief Heinrich Himmler, had taken the cyanide route out of a British prison camp, rather than risk the sure and swift retribution he expected.

Himmler was mistaken. At Nuremberg, the retribution was neither swift nor sure. Joseph Stalin would have preferred, as he proposed to Winston Churchill, that the top fifty thousand Nazis simply be taken out and hanged. But he had yielded when Churchill told him that the British people would never stand for any such action.[1]

Never before had an attempt been made to bring to book in a judicial proceeding the perpetrators of such massive iniquities against so large a segment of humanity. The crimes had no specific locale; they ranged

[1] For his own part, Churchill thought a lengthy trial would be a mistake, according to Roosevelt's personal counsel, Samuel I. Rosenman. And similar sentiments were expressed by U. S. Secretary of State Cordell Hull, Treasury Secretary Henry Morgenthau, Jr., Supreme Court Chief Justice Harlan F. Stone, and other eminent Americans. The French were already shooting collaborators without trial by the thousands.

over the entire continent of Europe and its surrounding waters. Nor did they involve merely those isolated breaches of wartime etiquette normally punishable by court-martial in keeping with widely accepted military custom. The Nazi leadership had not merely stained the tablecloth of the family of nations; they had maliciously overturned the table itself and set fire to the house.

Millions of the living and dead cried out for vengeance. And if the satisfaction of blood lust had been the sole objective, Stalin's lynch-law methods would have filled the bill. But the other major powers, prisoners of their own traditions, were loath to treat the Axis war criminals with the same savagery that they had shown toward their own victims. Poetic justice it might be, but not justice. A fair trial for the Nazi leaders could serve as an object lesson to the millions who had become strangers to the benign majesty of the law. Properly planned and executed, it could engrave in the minds of the German people the depravity and bestiality of its former leaders, demolishing the myth of a benevolent and omnipotent Hitler once and for all. And finally, the question of war guilt could be ineluctably resolved, sterilizing any stray seeds of renascent German militarism.

To achieve these ends, it was necessary to erect a social institution practically from scratch—a court to try the major offenders, and a law which would insure the conviction of the guilty without sacrificing the long-range objectives of the proceeding. Within a month after V-E Day an American team headed by Supreme Court Justice Robert H. Jackson formulated a skeletal plan. After six weeks of intensive negotiation in England, delegates of the Big Four hammered out the law—the so-called "London Charter," setting up an International Military Tribunal and defining the scope and method of its operation.

It was not smooth sailing. And if the Charter had shortcomings as a blueprint of abstract justice, its draftsmen should not be held accountable. For they were called upon to guide an untried ship of radical design on a maiden voyage at full speed through uncharted waters heavily mined with legal technicalities. It is cause for wonderment that they did not founder in the attempt, with the American and British delegates pulling for adequate protection of the defendants' rights and the Russians for a "show trial," while the French took cautious soundings in the shallows of international law.

There was immediate agreement on the composition of the Tribunal —one member and one alternate from each of the four powers. As a latent source of prejudice this was bound to stir up a cloud of criticism; but to quote Jackson:

325

The worldwide scope of the aggressions carried out by these men has left but few real neutrals. Either the victors must judge the vanquished or we must leave the defeated to judge themselves. After the First World War we learned the futility of the latter course.

Jackson was referring to the little-known World War I war crimes trials, a travesty which should have taught the Allies as early as 1920 that the Germans had signed the Treaty of Versailles in impermanent ink. Under the Treaty, the German Government agreed to hand over to Allied military tribunals some 900 persons accused of violations of the laws and customs of war—the slaughter of prisoners, unrestricted submarine warfare, the bombardment of open towns, and the like. But, as if led by a Machiavellian baton, a chorus of popular resistance and threats of widespread political disorders within Germany blackmailed the Allies into delegating the job to the Reich Supreme Court at Leipzig. As a test, forty-five of the accused were singled out for prosecution by the Germans themselves. After a year of niggling delays, only twelve offenders were actually tried; half of them went free, and the rest received sentences of two months to four years in prison.[2]

Allied demands to bring down the curtain on the farce and turn over the rest of the accused to be tried by the victors were ignored. The Germans blithely barged ahead with the proceedings, dismissing about 800 cases without trial and acquitting the remainder. War weariness and hope for improved relations with the new German Republic brought the seamy story to a futile, shoulder-shrugging conclusion; the Allies abandoned the cause entirely.

A repetition of the fiasco was out of the question. The Charter slammed the door on the trial of Germans by Germans and barred any challenge, on grounds of national bias, to the membership of the Tribunal.

But the men on the bench would merely be the architects of the final judgment. The extent to which the Allied case would win worldwide respect would depend largely on the ability of the conferees to square it with international law—an unwieldy and mercurial amalgam of customs, treaties, and generally accepted rules of universal conduct. And right from the start, the London conferees ran into trouble. For Jackson promptly launched the conference into the legal stratosphere by insisting that he would settle for nothing less than an indictment of most of the defendants on a charge of planning and waging aggressive war.

For three centuries or more, the waging of offensive war had not

[2] Soon thereafter, two of the defendants, who had been found guilty of U-boat atrocities, somehow managed to "escape," to the unconcealed delight of the entire populace.

326

been considered illegal, much less criminal. The Kellogg-Briand Pact of 1928, to be sure, renounced war as an instrument of national policy, but prescribed no punishment for violators. In most quarters, it was regarded at the time as a pious ceremonial handshake.

Jackson's fellow delegates fought shy of breaking new ground. They believed that most of the top Nazis could be convicted for recognized violations of the rules and customs of war, like the murder of prisoners and the wanton destruction of cities. But Jackson had an ax to grind: he wanted endorsement of the Roosevelt policy of aid to the Allies before Pearl Harbor. Rather than relent, he was prepared to call the whole project off:

Germany did not attack or invade the United States in violation of any treaty with us. The thing that led us to take sides in this war was that we regarded Germany's resort to war as illegal from its outset. . . . And throughout the efforts to extend aid to the peoples that were under attack, the justification was made by the Secretary of State, by the Secretary of War, Mr. Stimson, by myself as Attorney General, that . . . we were not doing an illegal thing in extending aid to peoples who were unjustly and unlawfully attacked. . . . Now it may be that we were mistaken in our attitude and philosophy and that what Germany has done is legal and right, but I am not here to confess the error. . . .

Jackson's colleagues did their tactful best to unseat him from his pet hobbyhorse. The difficulty was that it could too easily be mounted by the Germans. Once the Court started exploring the question of war guilt, what was to keep it from probing the political and economic causes of Germany's entry into war? And with the lid off this Pandora's box, the position of the prosecuting powers might well become extremely uncomfortable.

None of the other conferees went into much detail, but they all had sufficient cause for concern. For if, as Jackson hoped to prove at the trial, the Nazi regime was born to wage war, had not Stalin ordered the German Communist Party to play midwife? Had not the British ratified Germany's illegal rearmament by signing a naval limitation treaty with her in 1935? And if the seizure of Czechoslovakia had been the curtain raiser to World War II, who but Great Britain and France had spoon-fed the Czechs to the Nazi tapeworm? If the top Nazis deserved to hang for the unprovoked invasion of Poland, why should their ex-partners in the enterprise, Stalin and Molotov, go free? Was Germany guilty of a crime because she had managed to invade Norway a few steps ahead of the British?

Properly exploited by the defendants, questions like these could turn the trial into a Nazi propaganda forum. But the conferees ultimately gave

327

way to Jackson, with their fingers crossed. Leaning prayerfully on the Kellogg-Briand Pact to justify their concession, they comforted themselves with the thought that the hand-picked Bench would keep the Nazis within bounds.

At the trial, this gamble paid off poorly. Although the Court refused to permit Germany's grievances against the Versailles Treaty to be aired, fairness opened the door to more than a few illustrations of the comparative guilt of the Allies. If the record of diplomatic incest between the victors and the vanquished had not been buried under a mountain of proof of Nazi bestiality, the Jackson approach might well have proved downright disastrous.

The concession to Jackson represented only the first in a series of giant steps across the quagmire of legal theory. Once the waging of aggressive war was declared criminal, the question remained: were the victors entitled to penalize individual participants in the offense?

In modern times, international custom had fixed financial reparations from the defeated belligerent as the outside limit of reprisal. The idea of punishing heads of state or top executives for their official acts harked back to ancient days, when Tamerlane and Julius Caesar had killed and jailed captive enemy sovereigns. It had long since been discarded; Napoleon's confinement on St. Helena so troubled the British conscience that Parliament was forced to pass a law declaring that he was merely being "kept in custody . . . for the preservation of the tranquillity of Europe."

Just to make matters worse, international law furnished the accused with yet another formidable traditional defense: that they had acted under superior orders—a position which has always been close to the heart of the military. A government cannot survive, it is argued, nor can a military machine function, unless it can count on implicit and unquestioning obedience by its officers and subordinates to ostensibly lawful orders. Quite correctly, the London negotiators anticipated that all of the sins of Nazidom would be laid at the feet of Hitler, Himmler, and other leaders beyond the reach of retribution.

The conferees simply finessed both of these questions of individual culpability with a few incisive declarations in the Charter: the defendants were barred from pleading that they had acted in an official capacity, or in obedience to superior orders (except in mitigation of punishment).

With an eye to the judgment of posterity, Jackson rationalized this verbal sleight-of-hand in his opening address to the Tribunal:

Of course, the idea that a state, any more than a corporation, commits crimes is a fiction. Crimes are committed only by persons . . .

The Charter recognizes that one who has committed criminal acts may not take refuge in superior orders nor in the doctrine that his crimes were acts of states. These twin principles working together have heretofore resulted in immunity for practically everyone concerned in the really great crimes against peace and humanity. Those in lower ranks were protected against liability by the orders of their superiors. The superiors were protected because their orders were called acts of state. . . . Modern civilization puts unlimited weapons of destruction in the hands of men. It cannot tolerate so vast an area of legal irresponsibility.

Cogent as this position may be, it skewers the subjects of a totalitarian state on the prongs of a fearful dilemma. They must have the wisdom and learning to spot the illegal taint of a superior's order; the clairvoyance to foresee that it will be condemned if their country loses the war; and the courage to defy it, in an environment swarming with political police devoted to the extirpation of faintheartedness. A superhuman assignment, which only a few in Nazi Germany undertook; and of those few, almost none survived. Passive resistance was possible from a distance—as in the case of General Erwin Rommel, who consigned to a North African wastebasket Hitler's orders for the summary execution of commandos. And desperation and nausea might even move a handful of generals to cook up a plot against the Fuehrer's life. But for the average German official, it was a Hobson's choice, and a terrifying one.

Of course, for most of the leading Nazis, the question never came up. They had been Hitler's collaborators, not his pawns; they had followed his lead with enthusiasm and contrived their own diabolical embellishments on his orders. As Jackson argued, "Each of them was entrusted with broad discretion and great power"—and they abused both.

Nor could they claim that they had not been warned. As early as 1942 the Allies had publicly pledged "the punishment, through the channels of organized justice, of those guilty of or responsible for these crimes, whether they have ordered them, perpetrated them, or participated in them."

Confident of victory as they were for a long time, the Nazi chieftains nevertheless took pains to conceal their more flagrant violations of the rules of civilized warfare, in order to avoid retaliatory treatment of their own troops. As the day of reckoning approached, their fear of retribution triggered a panicky attempt to erase the traces of atrocities in their camps and prisons; but the task proved too herculean, the Allied advance too swift.

In spite of these considerations, many fair-minded individuals considered the Charter highhanded and arbitrary. The late Senator Robert

A. Taft, who would rather be righteous than President, denounced the "trial of the vanquished by the victors," in his usual uncompromising fashion:

> In these trials we have accepted the Russian idea of the purpose of trials —government policy and not justice—with little relation to the Anglo-Saxon heritage. By clothing policy in the forms of legal procedure, we may discredit the whole idea of justice in Europe for years to come.

Taft took particular exception to prosecution of the Nazis for waging aggressive war, calling the Charter *ex post facto* legislation. He had plenty of company, including such leading jurists as Jackson's colleague on the Supreme Court, William O. Douglas. But all of them overlooked the absence of such niceties in the Nazi legal system. In 1935 Hitler had the Reich criminal code amended to provide: "Whoever commits an act which the law declares punishable or which deserves punishment according to . . . *the sound feelings of the people,* will be punished." The people whose "sound feelings" were consulted were the political police; referendums had gone out of style. So it might easily be said that the rights of the Nuremberg defendants were not abrogated, in terms of Nazi concepts of law, however much they may have been ignored under the ground rules by which Americans expect to be judged.

This observation does not apply with as much force to the recognition in the Charter of the crime of *conspiring* to wage aggressive war. Although not a novel concept under Anglo-American law, the crime of conspiracy is a stranger to the Continent. There, all accessories and participants in a specific illegal act are held responsible for its direct consequences, and the German lawyers at Nuremberg stood aghast at the notion that all conspirators could be made answerable for the crimes of others committed in the course of executing their common plan, whether or not they were committed as part of the plan itself.

The conspiracy charge was designed to accomplish a twofold purpose. On the one hand, it eliminated the need to trace every link in the chain from the accused to the uniformed sadist in the camps and prisons, or to show that the defendants intended every consequence of their general program. On the other, it netted noncombatants like Schacht, Streicher, Ribbentrop, and Ley in the same catch with their military cohorts.

Historians have reason to be thankful for the conspiracy charge. The proof which it enabled the prosecution to introduce endowed the proceedings with an organic continuity, tying together every aspect of the Nazi program into an intricate but unified road map of their march toward world supremacy.

The Tribunal received the indictment on October 18. Star billing fell to Nazidom's Jack-of-all-trades, Hermann Goering. As Hitler's heir-apparent, he had exerted power and influence second only to the Fuehrer himself, until the closing days of the war. His storm troopers had helped Hitler bully his way into the chancellorship. He had founded the bestial Gestapo and invented the concentration camp. He had stage-managed the seduction of Austria and plotted the rape of Poland. His Luftwaffe had rained terror from the skies indiscriminately on civilian and military targets alike. He had presided over the marshaling of Germany's resources for aggression and had assembled for his own enrichment Europe's third largest industrial combine, dedicated to feeding the iron hounds of war.

Treatment by Allied physicians following his capture had trimmed Goering's figure down by sixty pounds and had broken the grip of his drug habit. His oversize uniform, stripped of its gaudy decorations, hung loosely on his huge frame. But he nevertheless fascinated female specta-tors in the courtroom, perhaps by his ambiguous air of sexuality, calling to mind the lurid tales which had seeped out of Germany during his palmier days.

From the start Goering had no illusions about his plight, and few about his ultimate fate. But he entered into the courtroom fray with the insouciance and bounce which were the natural legacy of a charmed and adventurous life. Whenever the defense scored a point, his deeply lined marionette's face would break into a quick smile. He was con-stantly passing notes to the other men in the box, and he kept up a run-ning commentary on the proceedings, like an unruly critic at an amateur play.

At the other end of the intellectual spectrum stood the gaunt, beetle-browed Rudolf Hess, once deputy Fuehrer of Germany, who had sat out the war in captivity since his madcap solo flight to Great Britain in May 1941. At the outset, Hess's participation in the trial was a touch-and-go affair. On the strength of Allied psychiatrists' reports that he was incapacitated by amnesia, the Tribunal seriously considered deferring his case indefinitely. But just as the Court was about to make up its mind, Hess brought off a sensation by admitting that it had all been a sham. This excess of candor cost him dearly. For ironically, under the tensions induced by the trial, he became truly amnesic and progressively paranoid; but having once cried wolf, he could hardly expect a sympa-thetic hearing the second time around.

Alongside Hess in the front row of the box sat Joachim von Ribben-trop, who as Foreign Minister had sold poisoned diplomatic champagne to Germany's hapless neighbors. Age and adversity had caught up with

Hitler's once-dapper emissary, and he had let himself go to seed. Clad in a motley combination of military and civilian castoffs, his thinning white hair unkempt, his left cheek constantly twitching, he cut a sorry figure as he shambled in and out of the courtroom. As the shadow of the gallows lengthened, he grew more and more depressed and disoriented, littering his cell each night with disjointed arguments for his defense, which his lawyers disdainfully discarded when he handed them over the next morning.

In marked contrast to Ribbentrop, his fellow diplomat, the suave, unscrupulous Franz von Papen, regarded the trial as just another distasteful test of his uncanny gift for survival. Papen had more than once been squeezed in the tight embrace of death, and was still around to joke about it. The risks he had run as a spy and saboteur for Wilhelm II in the United States had resulted in nothing worse than deportation. Marked for extinction in the Roehm purge of 1934, he had ended up suffering only the discomfort of a few days' detention. As Minister to Austria, his murder had been planned by Hess in order to provide a provocation for German intervention—but at the last minute it had proved unnecessary. Ending his checkered career as Ambassador to intrigue-ridden Turkey, he had narrowly escaped being pulverized by a bomb; the clumsy Russian cast as his assassin blew himself up instead. Since the fateful winter's day in 1933 when he hoisted the Austrian upstart into the chancellery, his luck had sustained him, and he was cheerfully trusting it to carry him through this last ordeal.

Equally confident, but not quite so jaunty, was the former Reichsbank President, Hjalmar Schacht. By his own admission, Schacht's financial wizardry with currency and credit had enabled Germany to rearm. The sixty-eight-year-old banker was a picture of outraged innocence, behaving toward his codefendants like a clergyman accidentally swept up in a raid on a brothel. A disagreement with Goering over economic policy had forced his resignation from the Reichsbank post before the war started, but by that time he had already earned his seat in the box.

Schacht had counted on his ten months' stay in concentration camps for complicity in the July 1944 attempt on Hitler's life as an automatic *laisser-passer* to freedom, and was profoundly shocked by the Allies' unwillingness to honor the ticket. Superficially it might appear that the old man had cause for complaint, but his record speaks otherwise. His belated opposition to the Fuehrer, like his earlier adherence to the Nazi cause, was apparently just another cold-blooded business judgment; Schacht had simply read the portents correctly and "sold short" on Hitler.

Papen's *sang-froid* and Schacht's aloofness set off in sharp relief the genuine remorse shown by three of the defendants for their shares in the Nazi nightmare. These three had all been in their teens at the end of World War I; they had been drawn to Hitler by a common dream of glory; and in the crisis of defeat, they had seen him transformed from demigod into man and from man into animal.

Trained as an architect, the able and sensitive Albert Speer had found an outlet for his energies in Hitler's ambitious building program during the early days of the regime. Sheer hard work and ability paid off, and by 1942 he had assumed full charge of munitions and armament production.

The turn of the tide in mid-1944 revealed to Speer the insane fury of which the Fuehrer was capable, in the form of a series of orders to scorch Europe's earth ahead of the advancing Allied forces. Slowly Speer awakened to Hitler's suicidal grand design to frame his own defeat against the backdrop of a devastated continent. Haunted by the vision of a prostrate postwar Europe, Speer embarked upon an audacious rearguard action, changing and countermanding the Fuehrer's increasingly savage commands without thought of the consequences to himself. Through his heroism, nearly half of Europe's industrial potential was rescued from wanton destruction. At the trial he said:

The sacrifices which were made on both sides after January 1945 were senseless. The dead of this period will be the accusers of the man responsible for the continuation of that fight, Adolf Hitler. The same is true of the ruined cities, which in this last phase had to lose tremendous cultural values and where innumerable dwellings suffered destruction. Many of the difficulties under which the German nation is suffering today are due to the ruthless destruction of bridges, traffic installations, trucks, locomotives, and ships. The German people remained loyal to Adolf Hitler until the end. He betrayed them with intent. He tried to throw them definitely into the abyss.

Baldur von Schirach, youngest of all the defendants, had played Pied Piper in the Nazi movement, whistling an entire generation down the dark and bloody road to war. An early convert to Alfred Rosenberg's racism, he had turned Nazi at seventeen. First as Leader of German Youth and later as Gauleiter of Vienna, he had applied his considerable talents with semireligious zeal to the brutalization of some eight million youngsters and the "purification" of Vienna, Europe's largest Jewish community.

Only when the swastika flags were lowered could Schirach see the sickening fright of the downy-faced boys fighting the last-ditch battle of Berlin, and the wasted bodies of the inmates of Auschwitz. In a voice shaking with emotion, he told the Court:

I have educated this generation in faith and loyalty to Hitler. . . . I believed that I was serving a leader who would make our people and the youth of our country great and happy. Millions of young people believed this, together with me. . . . Many died for it. Before God, before the German nation, and before my German people I alone bear the guilt of having trained our young people for a man whom I for many long years considered unimpeachable, both as a leader and as the head of the state, of creating for him a generation who saw him as I did. The guilt is mine in that I educated the youth of Germany for a man who murdered by the millions.

Hans Frank's conversion had overtones of Krafft-Ebing. Born a Catholic, this shrewd and energetic lawyer had abandoned his faith when he joined the Nazi Party. Soon after 1933, he ruthlessly made over the German system of jurisprudence in the Nazi image. With the coming of war, he was assigned to do the same to the Polish population. His worship of Hitler was apparently rooted in a latent homosexuality, which sustained him until the Fuehrer "deserted" him, as he put it, by committing suicide. In despair, he tried to follow suit by slashing his own throat and wrists. The solitude of captivity brought on apocalyptic visions and guilt-ridden dreams; the voices of those he had persecuted crowded in on him, as with Paul on the road to Damascus; and stricken with remorse, he fled back to the Church for comfort.

But even so, Frank could not bring himself to accept the complete erasure from the pages of history of the record of his dominion over the destinies of millions as Poland's Governor General. In true schizoid fashion, he turned his diary over to the American Military Government. It was loaded with damning details of his own and his codefendants' crimes. Thereby he assured himself of both the punishment which he hoped would win him absolution and of a dark niche in the hall of infamy.

Among the representatives of the armed services there had never been too much rapport; but at Nuremberg they moved in a solid phalanx to escape the gallows. They personified the classic defense of obedience to superior orders, and their position was being watched anxiously and perhaps even covertly applauded by military men of all nations.

At the trial, Jackson tried to outflank them:

We recognize that to plan warfare is the business of professional soldiers in every country. But it is one thing to plan strategic moves in the event war comes, and it is another thing to plot and bring on that war. . . . Military men are not before you because they served their country. They are here because they mastered it, along with these others, and drove it to war. . . . Politicians may have thought of them as soldiers, but soldiers knew they were politicians.

Jackson's argument sounds equitable and well-reasoned, and it certainly applied forcefully to the ubiquitous Goering, as well as Hitler's uniformed toadies, Admiral Erich Raeder and Generals Wilhelm Keitel and Alfred Jodl. But it squares neither with the Charter nor with the indictment, both of which made separate offenses of plotting aggressive war and waging it. As a result the professional soldier who had no share in the conspiracy to aggress would nevertheless be responsible for carrying out the offensive action.

This internal contradiction in the prosecution's position proved significant in the case of Admiral Karl Doenitz. The diminutive Doenitz had filled a rather routine slot in the German war machine until 1943, by which time the Nazis had left the business of conspiracy far behind. While the Tribunal quite properly acquitted Doenitz of conspiracy, it had no alternative under the Charter but to convict him of waging aggressive war. If Jackson meant what he said, he should have admitted that in regard to military men, the two charges stood and fell together.

The roster of twenty-one individual defendants in the box was rounded out by an assortment of party functionaries: hulking Ernst Kaltenbrunner, Heydrich's successor as chief of the SD, the Party's intelligence service; Fritz Sauckel, slave-labor boss; paunchy, coarse-looking Walter Funk, Minister of Economics, who followed Schacht as head of the Reichsbank; the fanatical high priests of racism, Streicher and Rosenberg, now shunned even by members of their congregation; the Austrian Quisling, Artur Seyss-Inquart, who ended up as Commissioner for the Netherlands; Ribbentrop's predecessor in the Foreign Ministry, the seventy-three-year-old career diplomat, Baron Konstantin von Neurath, later Protector of Czechoslovakia; Wilhelm Frick, legal brains of the Nazi movement, who followed Neurath in the Czech post; and Hans Fritzsche, who as Minister for Radio Propaganda seemed to have been nominated as a stand-in for his chief, the late Joseph Goebbels. Martin Bormann, Hitler's secretary, was thought to have been killed in the Berlin fighting, but was indicted and tried *in absentia* just in case.

Two others who were named in the indictment escaped trial—the fabled industrialist Gustav Krupp von Bohlen, disabled by a paralytic stroke, and Robert Ley, Minister of Labor, who strangled himself in his cell a week after the Tribunal received the indictment. Ley's suicide precipitated a frenzied shoring-up of security precautions under the mocking eye of one Hermann Goering, who had plans of his own.

In a move as novel as it was significant, a number of key Nazi groups were named as defendants. Singled out for this treatment were the Reich Cabinet, the Leadership Corps of the Nazi Party, the Gestapo, the SS, the SA, and the General Staff and High Command of the German

335

armed forces. The Allies' aim was to lay a foundation for later prosecution of individual members of these organizations through a declaration by the Tribunal which would be binding in subsequent trials, that they were criminal in purpose and method.

Widespread publicity was given to these charges to afford an opportunity to past members of these groups to be heard on the issues of collective guilt. Although the Allies intended to prosecute only prominent and voluntary participants in the condemned activities, an epidemic of unreasoning fear swept the lodge brothers, who somehow got the impression that membership alone would automatically ticket them for the gallows. In consequence, they swamped the prosecution with over 300,000 affidavits and offers of testimony. This paper deluge almost overwhelmed the Allied staffs, burdened as they were with a mountain of evidence which had to be whittled down to manageable size for the trial.

The four powers had decided at London to share the honors and burdens of prosecution, and had parceled out among themselves the areas of proof encompassed by the indictment. To Jackson fell the comprehensive "conspiracy" charge (Count I), covering the defendants' participation in a common plan to commit crimes against peace and, under a rather loose interpretation of the Charter, the other offenses specified in the indictment.

This phase of the indictment fitted together most of the scattered fragments of the Nazi jigsaw puzzle with a neatness which on casual examination looks like a conjurer's trick, but on reflection emerges as a thoughtful job of historical synthesis. With fatal inevitability it tracks the spoor of the brown-shirted predator from the first Jewish shopwindow smashed in Munich to the rubble outside the Nuremberg courthouse. The victims of totalitarianism are shown joining hands in a fraternity of fear—Catholics and Communists, Prussian autocrats and labor leaders, Jews and Jew-baiting Poles. The verbal violence of *Mein Kampf* comes to flower grotesquely in the windrows of bodies on the fields of three continents.

The British assumed the burden of proving "crimes against peace" —the planning and waging of aggressive war (Count II). This phase of the indictment followed the paper trail of broken treaty promises from Versailles to the October 1939 Nonaggression Pact with Yugoslavia, naming as dupes a dozen nations whose leaders thought they could do business with Hitler.

Count III dealt with "war crimes," and Count IV with "crimes against humanity." These accusations, closest to the hearts of the French and Russians, were handled by them jointly. Count III rested squarely on certain of The Hague and Geneva Conventions, and on the time-honored customs of warfare, designed to protect the helpless and innocent; while the less orthodox Count IV was primarily concerned with the persecution of certain political, racial, and religious groups, German as well as non-German, which were thought to stand in the way of the Nazi program of conquest. These two counts overlapped to some degree —one mass murder is pretty much like another, and the screams of the tortured defy legal analysis. But the conferees felt that the laws of war could not be stretched to apply to the issues raised by Count IV; hence the separate charges.

The solemn specifications of the indictment under Count III added up to a numbing assault on the senses, as horror was gravely heaped upon horror. They evoked the smoke of quiet villages like Lidice and Oradour-sur-Glane; the stench of freight cars packed so tight with prisoners that the dead could not fall down; the pathetic pleas of starving slave workers and the groans of tortured prisoners of war. And as an obbligato to all this, one heard the clink of money, as the Krupps and the Goerings plundered the industries and art treasures of the occupied territories.

Jackson's conspiracy count was directed against all of the defendants, but otherwise the indictment was more selective. Those who had not participated directly in the decision to go to war, like Schirach, Fritzsche, and the absent Bormann, were not charged under Count II. Schacht and Papen were considered too far removed from the conduct of the war to answer to Counts III and IV, and neither of the naval leaders was called upon to meet Count IV.

Heading the prosecution, along with Jackson, were Sir Hartley Shaw-cross, British Attorney General, and his predecessor in that post, Sir David Maxwell-Fyfe (who actually bore the brunt of the British case); Champetier de Ribes, former French Undersecretary of State; and Lieutenant General Roman A. Rudenko, Chief Prosecutor of the Ukrainian Republic. All were backed up by corps of able assistants, many still in uniform, some themselves refugees from the Nazi regime.

Arrayed against them for the defense was a battery of German attorneys, selected by the prisoners from the cream of the Bar, the Bench and the universities—including a few unregenerate Nazis. These lawyers were paid, fed, and sheltered at Allied expense. Their collective talent was hobbled somewhat by their unfamiliarity with the adversary system of criminal trials prevailing at Nuremberg. Patterned on the Anglo-American tradition, this procedure envisions a duel between rival advocates, refereed from the bench—in contrast to Continental trials, which take the form of investigations conducted by the judges with the

337

assistance of counsel. However, with the passage of time, the defense attorneys adjusted themselves to the alien scheme of things and handled themselves skillfully.

Each of the Big Four was represented on the bench by one justice and one alternate. By common consent the British member, Lord Justice Geoffrey Lawrence of the Court of Appeals, presided. The other three active members were former U.S. Attorney General Francis A. Biddle, Professor Henri Donnedieu de Vabres of Paris University, and Major General Iola T. Nikitchenko, Vice Chairman of the Soviet Supreme Court. The concurrence of three of the four was required by the Charter for conviction or sentence, with Lawrence's vote given decisive weight in case of ties. In appearance and behavior, each judge ran true to his own national stereotype—the Britisher bald, stocky, and Pickwickian; the American tall and dark, with the beady eye and sharp beak of a bald eagle; the Frenchman birdlike and mustachioed; and the Russian blond, stolid, and steely-eyed.

The trial opened on November 20 with the reading of the 25,000-word indictment. Twenty defendants were present, Kaltenbrunner being confined to his cell by illness. All pleaded not guilty, with Goering, Rosenberg, Schirach, and Sauckel adding the ambiguous phrase, "in the sense of the indictment."

More than ten months would elapse before the Court pronounced its final judgment. During that period it would sit almost uninterruptedly, except for Sundays and holidays; a total of 216 days was consumed in actual trial. Thirty-three witnesses were called to the stand by the prosecution, and the defense introduced testimony from 204, about two thirds of it in affidavit form. Nineteen of the accused took the stand themselves.

As anticipated, most of the incriminating evidence consisted of official documents, motion pictures, and photographs from the German archives, all carefully preserved with compulsive German thoroughness by the Nazi agencies, except the Gestapo (whose records were reconstructed from duplicates in other bureaus' files). Frank's and Jodl's diaries, of course, proved invaluable to the prosecution.

This accumulation of proof reached truly staggering proportions; about 4000 documents, ranging from a one-page scribbled field order to the 41 volumes of Frick's diary, had been gleaned from over 100,000 such records in Allied hands. Over heated objections from some of his subordinates, Jackson placed his main reliance on this evidence, eking it out whenever necessary by oral testimony and affidavits. Although his decision deprived the trial of much of its promised drama and color, on the whole it paid off handsomely. For the use of contemporary records to convict the Nazis out of their own mouths stamped the proceedings with an objectivity which placed the prosecution's case beyond the reach of attack by die-hards of any breed. In the course of the trial, Jackson's economy in the use of live witnesses was amply justified: former Nazi officials who testified for the Allies were confronted on cross-examination with their own unsavory backgrounds; and survivors of the terror were discredited by their patent hostility to the accused and their all-too-obvious anxiety to please their liberators.

Still, nothing is so calculated to drive spectators out of a courtroom as the drone of a lawyer's voice reading a lengthy document into the record; and Nuremberg was no exception to the rule. But slowly and painstakingly, minutes of meetings and copies of orders and transcripts of telephone conversations and reports from the field were dovetailed in a tapestry depicting methodical madness, insatiable greed, and pointless violence in dimensions never before visited upon a single generation.

Running through these documents as a dominant motif was that strangely inverted mystique which had made the Nazi social system incomprehensible to the outside world. Like participants in a Black Mass, Hitler and his circle had conjured up the New Order by turning all human values inside out, substituting evil for good, contempt for compassion, license for self-control, sadism for benevolence. Practically overnight, the nation was transformed into a malignant growth on the body of Europe, with an irreversible internal logic all its own.

The key to this parody of a society was, of course, the "master race" concept, muting the voice of conscience, dissolving all doubts, reconciling all contradictions. Thus Germany could cry out that she was being suffocated by lack of *Lebensraum*, while offering subsidies to the *Herrenvolk* to produce more babies faster. With no strain on the imagination, the "inferior" democracies could be expected to accept each successive land-grab on Hitler's renewed assurance that he had no further territorial ambitions. Aryan soldiers could be penalized for cohabiting with "subhuman" Polish girls while Polish children were kidnaped in droves to be brought up as Germans—provided, of course, that they were blond. The looting of art treasures from the "degenerate" French lost all overtones of irony, although they were ostensibly appropriated for the cultural enlightenment of their innately superior conquerors. The collection of the skulls of Russian-Jewish commissars and the conduct of bizarre pseudomedical experiments on concentration camp inmates acquired the gloss of the glorification of German science.

Inevitably, the wheels clogged from time to time. Brutal treatment of the Ukraine and Baltic populations converted native welcoming committees into fierce cores of underground resistance. The denial of medical care to Polish Jews turned them into carriers of epidemic disease to their Nazi keepers. Methodical starvation of imported slave labor brought on a decline in German munitions production. SS troops handling the bodies of crudely asphyxiated prisoners developed severe and persistent headaches, until a more humane method of genocide was devised. Rivalries sprang up among the leaders over the division of material and human plunder from the occupied countries.

But on the whole, the system worked—as long as it was fed on a diet of unbroken successes. The Fuehrer principle enabled the German people to put their consciences on ice, while they applied themselves with fearful efficiency to the enslavement and extermination of the "enemies" of their country.

The statistics were not unimpressive: twelve million civilians, half of them Jews, wiped out; almost five million impressed into slave labor; plunder running into the billions of dollars. But statistics, as Koestler has said, don't bleed. It was one of the prosecution's major tasks to reduce the numbing grandeur of German viciousness to its least common denominator.

To this end, a surprise move was made early in the trial. The court suddenly went dark and a motion picture projector proceeded to grind out films picturing the concentration camps at the time they fell into Allied hands. As in a mirror darkly, the defendants saw the stark image of the world they had made. The cameras coursed slowly over the mounds of hollow-cheeked corpses left behind in the final rout, the bones of inmates hastily buried alive, the gaping mouths of the still-warm crematorium ovens, the bales of human hair consigned to patriotic German bedding, the lamp shades made of human skin.

The dominant reaction to this gruesome display among the non-Germans at the trial was less one of pity for the victims than of astonishment at the moral anesthesia of an entire people. This response was heightened by the tone of official reports like that of SS General Juergen Stroop on the last days of the Warsaw Ghetto:

. . . I therefore decided to destroy the entire Jewish residential area by setting every block on fire. . . . Not infrequently, the Jews stayed in the burning buildings until, because of the heat and the fear of being burned alive, they preferred to jump down from the upper stories. . . . With their bones broken, they still tried to crawl across the street into blocks of buildings which had not yet been set on fire or were only partly in flames. . . . Their stay in the sewers also ceased to be pleasant after the first week. . . . A great number of Jews, who could not be counted, were exterminated by blowing up sewers and dugouts.

The longer the resistance lasted, the tougher the men of the Waffen SS,

Police, and Wehrmacht became; they fulfilled their duty indefatigably in faithful comradeship and stood together as models and examples of soldiers. . . . Only through the continuous and untiring work of all involved did we succeed in catching a total of 56,065 Jews whose extermination can be proved. To this should be added the number of Jews who lost their lives in explosions or fires but whose numbers could not be ascertained.

The depressing aftertaste of corruption left by such accounts can be only partly washed away by the occasional confirmations of the innate dignity of man which found their way into the Nuremberg record. Perhaps the most affecting of these was the prosaic description by a German engineer of an incident in the Ukraine in 1943:

Thereupon I drove to the site, accompanied by my foreman, and saw near it great mounds of earth, about thirty meters long and two meters high. Several trucks stood in front of the mounds. Armed Ukrainian militia drove the people off the trucks under the supervision of an SS man. The militia men acted as guards on the trucks and drove them to and from the pit. All these people had the regulation yellow patches on the front and back of their clothes and thus could be recognized as Jews.

My foreman and I went directly to the pits. Nobody bothered us. Now I heard the rifle shots in quick succession from behind one of the earth mounds. The people who had got off the trucks—men, women and children of all ages—had to undress upon the orders of an SS man, who carried a riding or dog whip. They had to put down their clothes in fixed places, sorted according to shoes, top clothing, and underclothing. I saw a heap of shoes of about 800 to 1000 pairs, great piles of underlinen and clothing. Without screaming or weeping these people undressed, stood around in family groups, kissed each other, said farewell, and waited for a sign from another SS man, who stood near the pit, also with a whip in his hand. During the fifteen minutes that I stood near I heard no complaint or plea for mercy. I watched a family of about eight persons, a man and a woman both about fifty with some children of about one, eight, and ten, and two grown-up daughters of about twenty and twenty-four. An old woman with snow-white hair was holding the one-year-old child in her arms and singing to it and tickling it. The child was cooing with delight. The couple was looking on with tears in their eyes. The father was holding the hand of a boy about ten years old and speaking to him softly; the boy was fighting his tears. The father pointed to the sky, stroked his head, and seemed to explain something to him. At that moment the SS man at the pit shouted something to his comrade. The latter counted off about twenty persons and instructed them to go behind the earth mound. Among them was the family I have mentioned. I well remember a girl, slim and with black hair, who as she passed close to me, pointed to herself and said, "23." I walked around the mound and found myself confronted by a tremendous grave. People were closely wedged together and lying on top of each other so that only their heads were visible.

341

Nearly all had blood running over their shoulders from their heads. Some were lifting their arms and turning their heads to show they were still alive. The pit was already two thirds full. I estimated that it already contained about 1000 people. I looked for the man who did the shooting. He was an SS man, who sat at the edge of the narrow end of the pit, his feet dangling into the pit. He had a tommy gun on his knees and was smoking a cigarette. The people, completely naked, went down some steps which were cut in the clay wall of the pit and clambered over the heads of the people lying there, to the place to which the SS man directed them. They lay down in front of the dead or injured people; some caressed those who were still alive and spoke to them in a low voice. Then I heard a series of shots.

Thus, in microcosm, Hitler's "final solution of the Jewish problem." Hans Frank, one of the principal actors in the tragedy, confessed at Nuremberg: "A thousand years will pass and this guilt of Germany will not be erased."

The crushing weight of documentary proof might have atomized the defense without resort to live witnesses. But some of the defendants took refuge in perjury, and professed shock and surprise at the handiwork of the Nazi regime, as it unfolded daily in court. In general, they tried to create the impression that they had been lowly supernumeraries in a war effort run entirely by Hitler, Goebbels, Himmler, and Bormann.

As often as not, the lie could be nailed by producing orders bearing their signatures, minutes of meetings, or other concrete evidence of their participation in the criminal act. But oral proof could not be dispensed with completely; and here the prosecution wisely used military men, as a rule, as rebuttal witnesses, taking advantage of the innate reluctance of German counsel to question the credibility of high-ranking officers. General Erwin Lahousen, who had occupied a key position in military counterintelligence, demolished Keitel and Jodl with a highly circumstantial account of their involvement in plans to bomb Warsaw and to exterminate Poland's intellectuals, churchmen, and Jews. He deposited squarely on Kaltenbrunner's doorstep the responsibility for conditions in the prison camps and for the incredibly cruel treatment of the Russian people. He dealt Keitel a particularly low blow by implicating him in a sordid plot to assassinate the French General Henri Giraud, after his escape from captivity. This caused Keitel more loss of face with the other service defendants than his crimes against civilians—the officers' code knows no national boundaries.

The military witnesses were especially helpful in illuminating the record on war guilt. Lahousen's straightforward reconstructions of the mock assault on a German radio station by a group of SS men dressed in Polish uniforms laid to rest for all time the myth of provocation for the attack that started the war. And Field Marshal Friedrich von Paulus emerged from the depths of Russia to tie Goering, Keitel, and Jodl into the preparations for the Nazi drive against the Soviets nine months before it was launched.

But in the last analysis, it was the testimony offered by the defendants themselves that stiffened the knot in the hangman's noose for most of them. The few penitents reinforced the prosecution's case with sweeping disclosures of their own and their confederates' misdeeds; and with a single exception, the others were mercilessly driven back under the lash of cross-examination from the self-righteous positions they adopted on their direct testimony. The exception was Goering, whose adroitness on the stand bespoke a clear-headedness and effrontery born of fatalism. With no illusions about the cumulative effect of the proof already recorded against him, he fought with the instinctive cunning of a trapped fox, taking full advantage of mistakes and ambiguities in the translation of German documents and of his superior knowledge of events to give the prosecutors a hard time. By the time he stepped off the stand he had managed to write his own obituary into the record: a soldier loyal to Hitler, who suffered no scruple in carrying out the Nazi program.

This is not to say that Goering escaped unscathed: he could not preserve the historical image without confessing unspeakable crimes, and even so, his soldier's honor was somewhat tarnished after Jackson took him to task concerning the looting of art treasures, and Maxwell-Fyfe raked him over the coals for his part in the murder of fifty British flyers who escaped from the Sagan prison camp. But, of all the nineteen defendants who testified in their own behalf—Hess and Frick abstained, and Bormann was missing—Goering alone achieved the dubious gangster's distinction of shouldering the blame for his own conduct and refusing aid to the prosecution against his colleagues.

Most of the other men in the box were too desperately afraid of the gallows to follow Goering's chivalrous example. Like frightened animals scattering in the face of a powerful threat, they were prepared to sacrifice each other to ward off danger, and the Allies had counted on this reaction when they decided not to trade with any of them to turn state's evidence. As witnesses against each other, they performed magnificently for the prosecution, their evidence having all the more weight because they were not testifying under a promise of leniency.

And for the benefit of posterity, they and their witnesses demolished at the same time the myth of a well-disciplined and harmonious Nazi hierarchy. One Goering witness disclosed that the No. 2 Nazi had opened negotiations with the British behind Ribbentrop's back late in 1939, while another told of Ribbentrop's countermove to prevent the parleys by causing Goering's emissary's plane to crash. Papen pinned the blame on Goering for the Roehm bloodbath in which he had been ticketed for extinction, and told of his futile suggestions to Ribbentrop in an effort to avert war. Raeder charged Goering with concocting the scandals which had driven Generals von Blomberg and Fritsch from the Army, paving the way for the toadying Keitel and the unimaginative Jodl. Schacht revealed his long-standing contempt for Goering as an "immoral, criminal type," confirming with evident relish the lurid tales of the Reichsmarshal's occasional forays into public view in toga, lipstick, and painted fingernails. Schirach outraged Rosenberg by confessing that he had never read the Nazi philosopher's magnum opus, *Myth of the Twentieth Century.* (None of the other defendants had, either.) Raeder had some unflattering comments about Doenitz and Speer. Speer repeated Hitler's characterization of Goering, in the closing days of the war, as a corrupt dope addict.

This portrait of Hitler's entourage drawn by its own members was of incalculable value in dispelling any false notions among postwar Germans about "the good old days." But still greater importance must be attached to the defendants' collective characterization of the Fuehrer himself.

Papen, Speer, and Schacht proclaimed that as patriotic Germans they had been driven to the extremity of plotting the Fuehrer's death. Schirach called him a seducer of German youth; to Schacht he was an ill-educated fanatic. Keitel disowned him for ordering escaped POW's to be turned over to the SS for execution. According to Jodl, millions of needless casualties had resulted from Hitler's rejection of Rommel's and Rundstedt's advice to sue for peace in July 1944. Von Papen spelled out chapter and verse of the Fuehrer's duplicity toward his followers in the Roehm purge. Speer revealed Hitler's proposal to use poison gas over the objections of his army chiefs and painted in vivid colors the progressive hardening of Hitler's resolve to drag his entire country down with him in flames. Fritzsche capped the climax by denouncing his chief for throwing thirteen-year-old boys into the Berlin finale against the battle-hardened Russian troops.

By the time the defense had put in its case, Adolf Hitler had been cut down to size. Little remained of the popular German conception of the Fuehrer except the fearful intuition and fanatical determination which had come within an ace of reducing the rest of the world to slavery.

But the search for historical truth could not be pursued without some loss in stature to the Allies as well. Ribbentrop disclosed the secret clause in the Nazi-Soviet pact dismembering Poland in advance of the fateful attack. Jodl showed that the British had planned to violate Norway's neutrality before the Germans landed there. Raeder invoked the Anglo-German Naval Pact as an excuse for Germany's disregard for the treaty limitations set at Versailles. Doenitz produced an affidavit from Admiral Chester W. Nimitz admitting that the United States had engaged in unrestricted submarine warfare. And the inquiry into the ill-advised Russian charges concerning the Katyn Forest massacre of Polish officers ended in a draw.

Three of the defendants actually won acquittals, thanks to the Charter itself and to the exacting standards of proof set by the Tribunal. As interpreted by the Court, the Charter barred conviction of any defendants whose conduct was not linked up directly with the intention to wage aggressive warfare or with the prosecution of the war itself. And, although the Charter was silent on the point, the Tribunal required guilt to be proved beyond a reasonable doubt.

The acquittals naturally caused the prosecution some anguish. But they stand as an eloquent rebuttal to the charge that the Tribunal was merely a well-dressed kangaroo court. The case against von Papen failed because his collaboration with Hitler in the early days and in the Anschluss adventure could not be tied in with the plan for armed aggression. Fritzsche's acquittal rested on the prosecution's failure to prove that his frankly anti-Semitic broadcasts during the latter years of the war were unmistakably intended to incite atrocities. His written confession to the charge of waging aggressive war was brushed aside when Fritzsche testified that his Russian captors had wrung it from him "after very severe confinement which had lasted for several months."

The freeing of Schacht was the bitterest pill for the prosecution (and many thinking Germans) to swallow. The financier probably owed his life to his keen instinct for seeking out high ground ahead of the changing tides of events. His break with Hitler turned out to be a shrewd calculation after all; it raised a "reasonable doubt" in the Tribunal's mind whether his services to the German war economy could be regarded as part of the general plan to wage aggressive war. The old man contemptuously accepted the verdict as confirmation of the stupidity of those who had indicted him in the first place.

In a painstakingly detailed opinion which took two days to read, the Court pronounced its judgment, acquitting these three defendants and finding the others guilty. The SA, Reich Cabinet, and the General Staff and High Command were not condemned, but the other organizations named in the indictment were held criminal, clearing the way for the trial of thousands of their members.

Sentence was pronounced on October 1, 1946, after the reading of the judgment was completed. All the defendants behaved with commenda-

345

ble restraint, except the numbed and trembling Hess, who spurned the headphones when they were handed to him.

Goering, first in line at the grim final session, figured in an unforgettable five minutes of sheer nightmare. Just as sentence was about to be pronounced on him, the sound system failed and his headphones went dead. While the mechanics tinkered frantically with the apparatus, he and Lord Chief Justice Lawrence stared at each other in mutual dismay, like friends in a dockside farewell who are drawn out of earshot as the ship pulls away from the pier. After what seemed like an eternity, the repair was completed, and the Tribunal proceeded to snuff out the last spark of life of the Third Reich, unnecessarily prolonged by the grisly incident.

Hess, Funk, and Raeder were condemned to life imprisonment. Speer and Schirach were sent to prison for twenty years, Neurath for fifteen, and Doenitz ten. All of the others, including the absent Bormann, drew sentences of death by hanging.

The disparity in the sentences raises questions common to many mass trials. Why hang Sauckel, for example, for supplying slave labor to Speer and spare the life of the "receiver"? Why let Fritzsche go and hang Streicher, both supremely vehement merchants of hate? Why spare Schacht and give Funk a life sentence for carrying out plans which Schacht had introduced and left half-executed? These queries will remain unanswered for all time; but they should not be regarded as reflections on the men on the bench, whose earnest striving for a just verdict and condign punishment are recorded in every page of the proceedings.

Late in the evening of October 15, Goering chalked up his last triumph by cheating the hangman. By some artifice which will probably never be fully explained, he had concealed a cyanide capsule in his cell, holding it against the day of reckoning, so that he might follow the suicide route taken by Hitler, Himmler, and Goebbels.

Early the next morning, the sentences of the others were executed. The bodies were cremated in secrecy—and although reports on the subject are conflicting, there is a strong temptation to accept one newsman's account that the ceremony was performed at Dachau.

A second four-power trial, with the German industrialists on the griddle, had long been discussed as a possibility, but it was dropped in the face of strong objections from the Americans and British.[3] Instead, the

[3] In the Far East, an international trial of major Japanese war criminals patterned on the main Nuremberg trial sent seven political and military leaders to the gallows, sixteen to prison for life, and two for terms of years. There were no acquittals.

four Allied commanders of the military occupation zones into which Germany had been divided authorized trials of second-echelon major war criminals by each country within its own zone.

The United States exercised this power in a series of twelve trials at Nuremberg, lasting well into 1949, in which 185 defendants faced three-man courts drawn from the American Bench and Bar. On the whole, the results were anticlimactic; the American judges imposed on the prosecution an even more rigorous standard of proof than the Tribunal had at the first trial and displayed on the whole a rather compassionate tendency to forgive and forget. Only thirteen of the defendants, most of them connected with SS extermination squads and medical experiments on concentration camp inmates, received the death penalty; eighty-five were imprisoned, eight of them for life. The British and French made little use of the authority, and the Russians apparently none at all. Special military courts convened by all four powers and other European countries tried thousands of large and small fry for run-of-the-mill atrocities.

The enactment in 1946 of "denazification laws" was designed to remove leading Nazi elements from public life and to try offenses which had not been dealt with by the Allies. In the American Zone alone, over 900,000 Germans, including the bulk of Nazi Party and SS officials, passed through the hands of tribunals set up under this system, which were manned by the Germans themselves. More than half of them were fined; 9000 received prison terms, and 22,000 were barred from holding public office. But impressive as these figures are, the leniency of the sentences against fairly notorious Nazi activists, and the acquittal of a few of the outstanding ones, alarmed those who had looked to the main Nuremberg trial as an eye-opening revelation which would convert the German people into a host of true believers.

It was, of course, too much to hope for. But the great assize at Nuremberg cannot, for that reason alone, be dismissed simply as a colorful exercise in international public relations. Its enduring importance commands much more respect than that, although not as much as some have wishfully given it.

No prospect exists, of course, that in the thermonuclear age men will be deterred from waging war by the new links in international law that were forged at the trial. Jackson conceded this in his opening address to the Tribunal:

I am too well aware of the weaknesses of juridical action alone to contend that in itself your decision under the Charter can prevent future wars. Judicial action always comes after the event. Wars are started only on the theory and in the confidence that they can be won.

But in a larger sense, the precedent at Nuremberg can serve as a key-stone in the future structure of universal peace. For to a world drugged by the determinism of Marx, Darwin, and Freud, bereft of confidence in its ability to control its own destinies, Nuremberg brought home the lesson that wars are man-made. And as a corollary, that they may be man-prevented.

As history, too, the trial justified itself magnificently. No future generation will challenge the crystal-clear record on the bestiality of Nazism, the corruptibility of the Prussian officer class, or the primary responsibility for World War II. In pragmatic terms, too, by exposing the unmitigated evil of totalitarianism, it buttressed the foundations of democracy among the free German people, preparing them to play an increasingly constructive part in the affairs of a troubled world.

In the following pertinent excerpts from the oral testimony are laid bare the mechanics of rationalization that made possible the atrocities committed under the Nazi regime. With the single exception of Speer, the witnesses hitch their wagons to the Fuehrer principle, divesting themselves of personal responsibility for their actions, simply because they accorded with German national policy.

For those interested in the technique of cross-examination, the handling of Sauckel and Seyss-Inquart by the American member of the Tribunal, Francis Biddle, deserves special attention. Only Maxwell-Fyfe, the British prosecutor, achieved comparable results in the extraction of damaging admissions from the defendants.

MARCH 11, 1946
GENERAL ERHARD MILCH, CROSS-EXAMINATION BY G. D. ROBERTS (UNITED KINGDOM)

Q. Do you know that on 24 and 25 March 1944 about eighty air-force officers, British and Dominion, with some others, escaped from the Stalag Luft III Camp?

A. I know about this from the British interrogation camp in which I was kept, where the whole case was posted up on the wall.

Q. We will come to that in a moment. Do you know that of those eighty, fifty were shot?

A. Yes.

Q. In various parts of Germany and the occupied countries from Danzig to Saarbruecken; you have heard of that?

A. I heard that about fifty were shot, but did not know where.

Q. Have you heard that, quite unusually, the bodies were never seen again, but that urns said to contain their ashes were brought back to the camp; you heard of that?

348

A. I heard of it in the camp where I was kept, from Mr. Anthony Eden's speech in the House of Commons.

Q. You heard that although these officers were reported by your government as having been shot while offering resistance or trying to escape, yet not one was wounded, and all fifty were shot dead.

A. At first I heard only the official report in Germany, that these officers had been shot while resisting or trying to escape. We did not believe this version, and there was a lot of discussion about this without precise knowledge. We were afraid that these men might have been murdered.

Q. You were afraid that murder had been committed. It does appear likely, does it not?

A. We got that impression, as the various details we heard could not be pieced together.

Q. It is quite clear that if that was murder, the order for that murder would have to come from a high level, is it not?

A. Certainly. . . .

MARCH 18, 1946
HERMANN GOERING, CROSS-EXAMINATION BY JUSTICE ROBERT H. JACKSON
(UNITED STATES)

Q. Now, the Four-Year Plan had as its purpose to put the entire economy in a state of readiness for war, had it not?

A. I have explained that it had two tasks to fulfill— 1) to safeguard German economy against crises, that is to say, to make it immune from export fluctuations, and, as regards food, from harvest fluctuations, as far as possible; and 2) to make it capable of withstanding a blockade, that is to say, in the light of experiences in the First World War, to put it on such a basis that in a second World War a blockade would not have such disastrous consequences. . . .

Q. To get a specific answer, if possible, did you not say in a letter to Schacht, dated the 18th day of December 1936, that you saw it to be your task, using these words, "within four years to put the entire economy in a state of readiness for war"? Did you say that or did you not?

A. Of course I said that.

Q. Now, do you recall the report of Blomberg in 1937 in which . . . he starts his report by saying:

"The general political position justifies the supposition that Germany need not expect an attack from any side."

A. That may have been quite possible at that moment. I took a most reassuring view of the German situation in 1937. It was after the Olympic games and at that time the general situation was extraordinarily calm. But that had nothing to do with the fact that I felt obliged, quite apart from passing fluctuations from a calmer to a more tense atmosphere, to make German economy ready for war and proof against crises or blockades, for exactly one year later incidents of a different nature occurred.

349

Q. Well now, does not Blomberg continue:

Grounds for this are, in addition to the lack of desire for war in almost all nations, particularly the Western powers, the deficiencies in the preparedness for war of a number of states, and of Russia in particular?

That was the situation in 1937, was it not?

A. That is the way Herr von Blomberg saw the situation. Concerning the readiness for war in Russia, Herr von Blomberg, in the same way as all those representatives of our Reichswehr mentality, was always really mistaken in contrast to the opinion expressed in other quarters with regard to Russian armaments. This is merely the opinion of Herr von Blomberg—not the Fuehrer's, not mine, and not the opinion of other leading people.

Q. That, however, was the report of the Commander-in-Chief of the Armed Forces on the 24th of June 1937, was it not?

A. That is correct.

Q. You organized, one month later, the Hermann Goering Works?

A. Right.

Q. And the Hermann Goering Works were concerned with putting Germany in the condition of readiness for war, were they not?

A. No, that is not right. The Hermann Goering Works were at first concerned solely with the mining of German iron ore in the region of Salzgitter and in a district in the Oberpfalz, and after the annexation, with the iron ore works in Austria. The Hermann Goering Works first established' exclusively mining and refining plants for this ore and foundries. Only much later steel works and rolling mills were added, that is to say, an industry.

Q. The Hermann Goering Works were a part of the Four-Year Plan, were they not? . . .

MARCH 21, 1946
HERMANN GOERING, CROSS-EXAMINATION BY MAXWELL-FYFE (UNITED KINGDOM)

Q. Let me remind you of the evidence that has been given before this Court, that as far as Auschwitz alone is concerned, 4,000,000 people were exterminated. Do you remember that?

A. This I have heard as a statement here, but I consider it in no way proved—that figure, I mean.

Q. If you do not consider it proved, let me remind you of the affidavit of Hoettl, who was Deputy Group Leader of the Foreign Section, of the Security Section of Amt IV of the RSHA. He says that approximately 4,000,000 Jews have been killed in the concentration camps, while an additional 2,000,000 met death in other ways. Assume that these figures—one is a Russian figure, the other a German—assume they are even 50 per cent correct, assume it was 2,000,000 and 1,000,000, are you telling this Tribunal that a Minister with your power in the Reich could remain ignorant that that was going on?

A. This I maintain, and the reason for this is that these things were kept secret from me. I might add that in my opinion not even the Fuehrer knew the extent of what was going on.

This is also explained by the fact that Himmler kept all these matters very secret. We were never given figures or any other details.

Q. But, Witness, haven't you access to the foreign press, the press department in your ministry, to foreign broadcasts? You see, there is evidence that altogether, when you take the Jews and other people, something like 10,000,000 people have been done to death in cold blood, apart from those killed in battle. Something like 10,000,000 people. Do you say that you never saw or heard from the foreign press, in broadcasts, that this was going on?

A. First of all, the figure 10,000,000 is not established in any way. Secondly, throughout the war I did not read the foreign press, because I considered it nothing but propaganda. Thirdly, though I had the right to listen to foreign broadcasts, I never did so, simply because I did not want to listen to propaganda. Neither did I listen to home propaganda.

Only during the last four days of the war did I—and this I could prove—listen to a foreign broadcasting station for the first time.

Q. You told Mr. Justice Jackson yesterday that there were various representatives in Eastern territories, and you have seen the films of the concentration camps, haven't you, since this trial started? You knew that there were millions of garments, millions of shoes, 20,952 kilograms of gold wedding rings, 35 wagons of furs—all that stuff which these people who were exterminated at Maidanek or Auschwitz left behind them. Did nobody ever tell you, under the development of the Four-Year Plan, or anyone else, that they were getting all these amounts of human material? Do you remember we heard from the Polish Jewish gentleman, who gave evidence, that all he got back from his family, of his wife and mother and daughter, I think, were their identity cards? His work was to gather up clothes. He told us that so thorough were the henchmen of your friend Himmler that it took five minutes extra to kill the women because they had to have their hair cut off as it was to be used for making mattresses. Was nothing ever told you about this accretion to German material, which came from the effects of these people who were murdered?

A. No, and how can you imagine this? I was laying down the broad outlines for the German economy, and that certainly did not include the manufacture of mattresses from women's hair or the utilization of old shoes and clothes. I leave the figure open. But, also, I do want to object to your reference to my "friend Himmler." . . .

Q. I think you told the Tribunal that right up to the end your loyalty to the Fuehrer was unshaken, is that right?

A. That is correct.

Q. Do you still seek to justify and glorify Hitler after he had ordered the murder of these fifty young flying officers at Stalag Luft Number III?

351

A. I am here neither to justify the Fuehrer Adolf Hitler nor to glorify him. I am here only to emphasize that I remained faithful to him, for I believe in keeping one's oath not in good times only, but also in bad times when it is much more difficult.

As to your reference to the fifty airmen, I never opposed the Fuehrer so clearly and strongly as in this matter, and I gave him my views about it. After that no conversation between the Fuehrer and myself took place for months.

Q. The Fuehrer, at any rate, must have had full knowledge of what was happening with regard to concentration camps, the treatment of the Jews, and the treatment of the workers, must he not?

A. I already mentioned it as my opinion that the Fuehrer did not know about details in concentration camps, about atrocities as described here. As far as I know him, I do not believe he was informed. But insofar as he . . .

Q. I am not asking about details; I am asking about the murder of four or five million people. Are you suggesting that nobody in power in Germany, except Himmler and perhaps Kaltenbrunner, knew about that?

A. I am still of the opinion that the Fuehrer did not know about these figures. . . .

Q. You heard what I read to you about Hitler, what he said to Horthy and what Ribbentrop said, that the Jews must be exterminated or taken to concentration camps. Hitler said that the Jews must either work or be shot. That was in April 1943. Do you still say that neither Hitler nor you knew of this policy to exterminate the Jews?

A. For the correctness of the document . . .

Q. Will you please answer my question. Do you still say neither Hitler nor you knew of the policy to exterminate the Jews?

A. As far as Hitler is concerned, I have said I do not think so. As far as I am concerned, I have said that I did not know, even approximately, to what extent these things were taking place.

Q. You did not know to what degree, but you knew there was a policy that aimed at the extermination of the Jews?

A. No, a policy of emigration, not liquidation of the Jews. I knew only that there had been isolated cases of such perpetrations.

Q. Thank you. . . .

GOERING, CROSS-EXAMINATION BY GENERAL R. A. RUDENKO (U.S.S.R.)

Q. These are the minutes of the conference at which you were present on the 16th of July 1941, three weeks after Germany attacked the Soviet Union. . . .

Is it correct that such a conference took place?

A. That is quite right. . . .

Q. . . . You state that with regard to the Crimea, there was some question about making the Crimea Reich territory.

A. Yes, that was discussed during that conference.

Q. All right, with regard to the Baltic provinces, there was talk about those, too?

A. Yes.

Q. All right. With regard to the Caucasus, there was talk about annexing the Caucasus also?

A. It was never a question of its becoming German. We merely spoke about very strong German economic influence in that sphere.

Q. So the Caucasus was to become a concession of the Reich?

A. Just to what degree obviously could not be discussed until after a victorious war. . . .

Q. I understand you. In that case, you considered the annexation of these regions a step to come later. As you said yourself, after the war was won you would have seized these provinces and annexed them. In principle, you have not protested.

A. Not in principle. As an old hunter, I acted according to the principle of not dividing the bear's skin before the bear was shot.

Q. I understand. And the bear's skin should be divided only when the territories were seized completely, is that correct?

A. Just what to do with the skin could be decided definitely only after the bear was shot.

Q. Luckily, this did not happen.

A. Luckily for you. . . .

Q. . . . Do you admit that as the Delegate for the Four-Year Plan you were in full charge of the working out of the plans for the economic exploitation of all the occupied territories, as well as the realization of these plans?

A. I have already admitted that I assumed responsibility for the economic policy in the occupied territories, and the directions which I had given for the exploitation of those territories. . . .

Q. With regard to your special prerogatives and rights, I am going to cite the instructions which you gave, as well as the orders you issued to some of the members who took part in a conference held on the 16th of August, and which were binding upon them. . . .

Here it says:

It seemed to me to be a relatively simple matter in former days. It used to be called plundering. It was up to the party in question to carry off what had been conquered. But today things have become more humane. In spite of that, I intend to plunder and to do it thoroughly.

Have you found the sentence?

A. Yes, I have found it, and that was exactly what I said at that conference. I emphasize that again.

Q. I just wanted to ascertain that you really said that.

A. I did say that, and now I should like to give you the reason. In making

353

that statement I meant that in former times war fed on war. Today you call it something different, but in practice it remains the same. . . .

Q. . . . You said at this conference:

I do not want to praise Gauleiter Sauckel; he does not need it. But what he has accomplished in such a short time and with such speed for the recruitment of manpower from all over Europe and setting them to work in our industries, is a unique achievement.

. . . You do not deny that this was forced labor, slavery?

A. Slavery, that I deny. Forced labor did of course partly come into it, and the reason for that I have already stated. . . .

APRIL 1, 1946
JOACHIM VON RIBBENTROP, CROSS-EXAMINATION BY MAXWELL-FYFE

Q. Witness, you were present at the interview between President Hacha and Hitler on 15 March 1939, were you not?

A. Yes, I was present.

Q. Do you remember Hitler's saying at that interview that he had given the order for German troops to march into Czechoslovakia, and that at 6 o'clock in the morning the German Army would invade Czechoslovakia from all sides?

A. I do not recall the exact words, but I know that Hitler told Hacha that he would occupy the countries of Bohemia and Moravia.

Q. Do you remember his saying what I put to you, that he had given the order for German troops to march into Czechoslovakia?

A. Yes, that is what I just said.

Q. Do you remember the Defendant Goering, as he told the Tribunal, telling President Hacha that he would order the German air forces to bomb Prague?

A. I cannot say anything about that in detail, because at that discussion I was not . . .

Q. Do you remember Hitler saying that within two days the Czech Army would not exist any more?

A. I do not recall that in detail, no; it was a very long conference. . . .

Q. If these things were said, will you agree with me that the most intolerable pressure was put on President Hacha?

A. Undoubtedly Hitler used very clear language. . . .

Q. What further pressure could you put on the head of a country except to threaten him that your army would march in, in overwhelming strength, and your air force would bomb his capital?

A. War, for instance. . . .

Q. I put to you that that agreement was obtained by threat of war. Is that not so?

A. I believe that this threat is incomparably lighter than the threats under which Germany stood for years through the Versailles Treaty and its sanctions.

Q. Well, leaving whatever it is comparatively, will you now answer my question? Do you agree that that agreement was obtained by threat of war?

A. It was obtained under a pressure, that is under the pressure of the march into Prague; there is no doubt about that. . . .

Q. Now I want you to direct your attention to the relations with Poland. . . .

Will you agree that up to the Munich Agreement, the speeches of all German statesmen were full of the most profound affection and respect for Poland? . . .

A. Yes.

Q. What was the purpose of what is shown in the Foreign Office memorandum of 26 August 1938? . . .

This method of approach towards Czechoslovakia is to be recommended also because of our relationship with Poland. The turning away of Germany from the boundary question of the southeast and her changeover to those of the east and northeast must inevitably put the Poles on the alert. After the liquidation of the Czechoslovakian question, it will be generally assumed that Poland will be the next in turn; but the later this assumption becomes a factor in international politics, the better. . . .

Does that correctly set out the endeavors of German foreign policy at that time?

A. Undoubtedly no, for, first of all, I do not know what kind of a document it is. It has apparently been prepared by some official in the Foreign Office, where sometimes such theoretical treatises were prepared and may have come to me through the State Secretary. . . .

Q. Now, when did you learn that Hitler was determined to attack Poland?

A. That Hitler contemplated a military action against Poland, I learned for the first time, as I remember, in August 1939. That, of course, he had made certain military preparations in advance to meet any eventuality becomes clear from this order regarding Danzig. But I definitely did not learn about this order, and I do not recollect now in detail whether I received at that time any military communication. I do remember that I knew virtually nothing about it.

Q. Do you tell the Tribunal that you did not know in May that Hitler's real view was that Danzig was not the subject of the dispute at all, but that his real object was the acquisition of *Lebensraum* in the East?

A. No, I did not know it in that sense. The Fuehrer talked sometimes about living space, that is right, but I did not know that he had the intention to attack Poland.

Q. Well now, just look at . . . the minutes of the conference on the 23rd day of May 1939 at the new Reich Chancellery. . . . It begins with the following words:

Danzig is not the subject of the dispute at all; it is a question of expanding our Lebensraum in the East and of securing our food supplies and of the settlement of the Baltic problem. Food supplies can be expected only from thinly populated areas. Added to the natural fertility, the German, through cultivation, will enormously increase the surplus. There is no other possibility for Europe. . . .

Are you telling the Tribunal that Hitler never explained that view to you?

A. It may be strange to say so, but I should like to say first that it looks as though I was not present during this conference. . . .

Q. Well now, just look at the very short paragraph a little further on where he says:

There is no question of sparing Poland, and we are left with no alternative but to attack Poland at the first suitable opportunity. We cannot expect a repetition of the Czech affair. There will be fighting. The task is to isolate Poland.

Do you tell the Tribunal that he never said that to his Foreign Minister? . . .

A. No, he did not do that at that time; but according to my recollection, only much later, in the summer of 1939. At that time he did say that he was resolved—and he said literally—to solve the problem one way or another. . . .

APRIL 5, 1946
FIELD MARSHAL WILHELM KEITEL, CROSS-EXAMINATION BY RUDENKO

Q. . . . I shall first of all refer to a document entitled "Directive on the Introduction of Military Jurisdiction in Region Barbarossa and on the Adoption of Special Military Measures." . . . It was drawn up on 13 May 1941, more than a month before the outbreak of war against the Soviet Union. Do you remember that in that document, drawn up before the war, instructions were given that suspect elements should immediately be brought before an officer and that he would decide whether they were to be shot? . . . Did you sign the document?

A. Yes, I have never denied that. . . .

Q. . . . Did you consider that an officer had a right to shoot people without trial or investigation?

A. In the German Army there have always been courts-martial for our own soldiers as well as for our enemies, which could always be set up, consisting of one officer and one or two soldiers, all three of whom would act as judges. That is what we call a court-martial (*Standgericht*); the only requisite is always that an officer must preside at this court. But as a matter of principle I have to repeat the statement which I have made yesterday . . .

Q. One moment! Please reply to this question. Did not this document do away with judicial proceedings in the case of so-called suspects, at the same time leaving to an officer of the German Army the right to shoot them? Is that correct?

A. In the case of German soldiers it was correct and was permitted. There is a military tribunal with judicial officers and there is a court-martial which consists of soldiers. These have the right to pass and to execute an appropriate sentence against any soldier of the German Army in court-martial proceedings.

THE PRESIDENT. You are not answering the question. The question is, what right does this document give, not what the orders in the German Army are.

Q. Can you reply to the following question? Did this document do away with judicial proceedings and did it give the German officer the right to shoot suspects, as stated herein?

A. That was an order which was given to me by Hitler. He had given me that order and I put my name under it. What that means, I explained in detail yesterday.

Q. You, a Field Marshal, signed that decree. You considered that the decree was irregular; you understood what the consequences of that decree were likely to be. Then why did you sign it?

A. I cannot say any more than that I put my name to it and I thereby, personally, assumed in my position a degree of responsibility.

Q. And one more question. This decree was dated 13 May 1941, almost a month before the outbreak of war. So you had planned the murder of human beings beforehand?

A. That I do not understand. It is correct that this order was issued about four weeks before the beginning of the campaign Barbarossa, and another four weeks earlier it had been communicated to the generals in a statement by Hitler. They knew that weeks before. . . .

Q. . . . I shall now ask you the following question: On 12 May 1941 the question of the treatment of captured Russian political commissars and military prisoners was under consideration. Do you remember that document? . . .

A. I have seen only notes on it. I do not recall the document at present but I know the facts. . . .

Q. In that case you do not deny that as far back as May, more than a month before the outbreak of war, the document had already been drafted which provided for the annihilation of Russian political commissars and military personnel? You do not deny this?

A. No, that I do not deny. That was the result of the directives which had been communicated and which had been worked out here in writing by the generals. . . .

357

Q. Defendant Keitel, I am asking you about the directive concerning the so-called Communist insurrectionary movement in the occupied territories. . . . It is an order of 16 September 1941. . . . It states:

In order to nip in the bud any conspiracy, the strongest measures should be taken at the first sign of trouble in order to maintain the authority of the occupying power and to prevent the conspiracy from spreading . . .

and furthermore:

. . . one must bear in mind that in the countries affected human life has absolutely no value and that a deterrent effect can be achieved only through the application of extraordinarily harsh measures. . . .

Do you remember this sentence?

A. Yes.

Q. You signed the order containing this statement?

A. Yes.

Q. Do you consider that necessity demanded this extremely evil order?

A. I explained some of the reasons for this order yesterday and I pointed out that these instructions were addressed in the first place to the Commander in Chief of the Wehrmacht offices in the Southeast; that is, the Balkan regions, where extensive partisan warfare and a war between the leaders had assumed enormous proportions, and secondly, because the same phenomena had been observed and established on the same or similar scale in certain defined areas of the occupied Soviet territory. . . .

Q. . . . And in this same order, . . . it is stated that:

To atone for the life of one German soldier, 50 to 100 Communists must, as a rule, be sentenced to death. The method of execution should strengthen the measure of determent.

Is that correct?

A. The German text is slightly different. It says: "In such cases, in general, the death penalty for 50 to 100 Communists may be considered adequate." . . .

Q. For one German soldier?

A. Yes. I know that and I see it here.

Q. . . . I ask you whether, when signing this order you thereby expressed your personal opinion on these cruel measures? In other words, were you in agreement with Hitler?

A. I signed the order, but the figures contained in it are alterations made personally by Hitler himself.

Q. And what figures did you present to Hitler?

A. The figures in the original were 5 to 10.

Q. In other words, the divergence between you and Hitler consisted merely in the figures and not in the spirit of the document?

A. The idea was that the only way of deterring them was to demand several sacrifices for the life of one soldier, as is stated here.

Q. You . . .

THE PRESIDENT. That was not an answer to the question. . . . Was the only difference between you and Hitler a question of figures?

A. Then I must say that with reference to the underlying principle there was a difference of opinion, the final results of which I no longer feel myself in a position to justify, since I added my signature on behalf of my department. There was a fundamental difference of opinion on the entire question. . . .

KEITEL, CROSS-EXAMINATION BY MAXWELL-FYFE

Q. . . . You remember that on the Eastern Front you captured some Frenchmen who were fighting with the Russians. Do you remember making an order about that? You captured some de Gaullists, as you called them, that is Free French people who were fighting for the Russians. Do you remember your action with regard to that?

A. I recollect the transmission of a Fuehrer order in regard to the surrender of these Frenchmen to their lawful government, which was recognized by us.

Q. That is not, of course, the part of the order I want to put to you.

Detailed investigations are to be made in appropriate cases with regard to relatives of Frenchmen fighting for the Russians. If the investigation reveals that relatives have given assistance to facilitate escape from France, then severe measures are to be taken. . . .

Can you imagine anything more dreadful than taking severe measures against the mother of a young man who has helped him to go and fight with the allies of his country? Can you imagine anything more despicable?

A. I can think of many things, since I have lost sons of my own in the war. I am not the inventor of this idea; it did not originate with me; I only transmitted it. . . .

Q. . . . Will you just look at a letter from Herr Terboven, who was in charge in Norway. . . . This is a report from Terboven for the information of the Fuehrer, and I want you to look at Paragraph 2. . . .

Now I have just received a teleprint from Field Marshal Keitel, asking for a regulation to be issued, making members of the personnel, and, if necessary their relatives, collectively responsible for cases of sabotage occurring in their establishments (joint responsibility of relatives). This demand serves a purpose and promises success only if I am actually allowed to perform executions by firing squads. If this is not possible, such a decree would have exactly the opposite effect.

359

Opposite the words "if I am actually allowed to perform executions by firing squads" there is the pencil note from you, "Yes, that is best." So that is a third example where I suggest that you, yourself, are approving and encouraging the shooting of next of kin for the act of some member of their family. What do you say to that, your own pencil mark?

A. I did make that marginal note. An order given in this matter was different. A reply was given which was different. I wrote that note.

Q. That is what I wanted to know. Why did you write this remark, "Yes, that is best," approving of a firing squad for relatives of people who had committed some occupation offense in Norway? Why did you think it was best that there should be a firing squad for the relations? Why?

A. It was not done and no order to that effect was given. A different order was given.

Q. That is not what I am asking, and I shall give you one more chance of answering it. Why did you put your pencil on that document, "Yes, that is best"?

A. I am no longer in a position to explain that today, in view of the fact that I see hundreds of documents daily. I wrote it, and I admit it now. . . .

MAY 2, 1946
HJALMAR SCHACHT, CROSS-EXAMINATION BY JACKSON

Q. . . . You gave your reasons, which you said were reasons of principle, to the Tribunal for not becoming a Party member?

A. Yes.

Q. Yesterday in court, do you recall that?

A. Yes.

Q. Now isn't it a fact that you have told the United States Prosecution Staff that you asked Hitler whether to join the Party, and that to your great relief Hitler told you not to?

A. Yes. Before I co-operated with him I wanted to find out whether he demanded that I should become a member of the Party. I was most relieved when he said I need not.

Q. So you remained out of the Party with Hitler's consent and approval?

A. Yes, of course. I think that is just another reason which will prove that I have never been a member of the Party.

Q. But you did not mention that to the Tribunal when you were giving your reasons for setting [staying?] out, that Hitler had given permission?

A. No, I thought the Tribunal would believe me anyway.

Q. When you received the Party golden swastika, you stated that it was the greatest honor that could be conferred by the Third Reich, did you not?

A. I did, yes.

Q. And while you didn't wear it in your daily life, you did wear it on official occasions, you stated, did you not?

A. Yes. It was very convenient on railroad journeys, when ordering a car, *et cetera.*

Q. From 1933 to 1942 you contributed a thousand Reichsmarks a year to the Nazi Party?

A. No. Yes, I beg your pardon; from 1937 to 1942.

Q. Didn't you say, on interrogation, that it was from 1933 to 1942?

A. No, that is an error. From 1937, after I had received the swastika. Evidently that is a misunderstanding. After I had received it I said to myself, "It would be fitting—give the people a thousand marks a year, and have done with it."

Q. For upwards of ten years, not quite ten years, you accepted and held office of one kind or another under this regime, did you not?

A. From 17 March 1933 to 21 January 1943.

Q. And as I understand you, that during this time, at least a part of the time, Hitler deceived you, and all the time you deceived Hitler.

A. No, oh no.

Q. I have misunderstood you?

A. Yes.

Q. Well now . . .

A. I believe that in the first years, at least, I did not deceive Hitler.

I not only believe so, I know it. I only started to deceive him in 1938. Until then, I always told him my honest opinion. I did not cheat him at all; on the contrary . . .

Q. What becomes, then, of your explanation that you entered his government in order to put brakes on his program? Did you tell him that?

A. Oh, no. I should hardly have done that or he would never have admitted me into the government. But I did not deceive him about it.

Q. Did he know your purpose in joining his government was to defeat his program by sabotage?

A. I did not say that I wanted to defeat his program. I said that I wanted to direct it into orderly channels. . . .

Q. Which meant slow down? Didn't it?

A. Yes.

Q. And he wanted to speed it up, isn't that right?

A. Yes, perhaps.

Q. You never allowed him to know that you had entered his government for the purpose of slowing down his rearmament program, did you?

A. It was not necessary to tell him what I was thinking. . . .

Q. Now, as to the rearmament program, you participated in that from three separate offices, did you not?

A. I do not know which offices you mean, but please go ahead.

Q. I will help you to list them. In the first place, you were Plenipotentiary for War.

A. Yes.

Q. That was the secret office at first.

361

A. Yes.

Q. You were President of the Reichsbank. That was the financial office.

A. Yes.

Q. And you were Minister of Economics, in which position you had control with the minister for the general economic situation.

A. Yes. This word "control" is such a general term that I cannot confirm your statement without question, but I was Minister of Economics.

Q. Now, let us take up first this position of Plenipotentiary for War. You have testified that this position was created for two purposes: (a) preparation for war, (b) control of the economy in event of war.

Is that correct?

A. That means preliminary planning in case war should come, and the direction of economy when war had broken out. In other words, a preparatory period and a later period in the event of war. . . .

Q. Now, those being your functions as Plenipotentiary for the War Economy, let's turn to your functions as President of the Reichsbank.

You said that the carrying out of the armament program was the principal task of the German policy in 1935, did you not?

A. Undoubtedly.

Q. There is no doubt that you voluntarily assumed the responsibility for finding financial and economic means for doing that thing.

A. No doubt. . . .

Q. And your purpose in maintaining foreign trade was to obtain enough foreign exchange to permit the imports of raw materials, not manufactured, which were required for the rearmament program. Is that not correct? . . .

A. My answer today is that that was not the only aim.

Q. Not the only aim?

A. Right.

Q. But that was the primary aim, was it not?

A. No, not at all.

Q. All right, what was the other aim?

A. To keep Germany alive, to assure employment for Germany, to obtain sufficient food for Germany.

Q. Which was your dominant aim?

A. The food supply in Germany and work for the export industry. . . .

Q. Well, on your 60th birthday Minister of War Blomberg said that, "Without your help, my dear Mr. Schacht, there could have been no rearmament," did he not?

A. Yes, those are the sort of pleasantries which one exchanges on such occasions. But there is quite a bit of truth in it. I have never denied it.

Q. That is the way it looks to me. . . .

MAY 24, 1946

BALDUR VON SCHIRACH, CROSS-EXAMINATION BY THOMAS J. DODD (UNITED STATES)

Q. . . . You told the Tribunal yesterday that the statement in the *Völkischer Beobachter*, attributed to Hitler, on 21 February 1938 was something of a mystery to you; you did not know where he got his figures from. . . . Now Hitler said, according to the press, that your naval Hitler Youth comprised 45,000 boys. Would you say that figure was too large and altogether untrue?

A. No, that is correct.

Q. That is correct?

A. That is correct.

Q. He then said, the motor Hitler Youth 60,000 boys. What do you say about that figure?

A. That is correct.

Q. And then he said that, as part of the campaign to encourage aviation, 55,000 members of the Jungvolk were trained in gliding for group activities. What do you say about that figure?

A. Glider training and model plane construction in the youth organization with—may I have the figure again—50,000 youth airmen?

Q. 55,000.

A. 55,000—yes, that is correct.

Q. That's correct. Then he says, "74,000 of the Hitler Youth are organized in its flying units." Now, what do you say about that figure?

A. You say "flying units"; those are *Fliegereinheiten*, groups of Hitler youth airmen, who—as I must emphasize again—were concerned only with gliding and the construction of model planes. There may have been such a large number at the time.

Q. Is the figure correct, 74,000?

A. It may be.

Q. Well, he lastly says, "15,000 boys passed their gliding test in the year 1937 alone." What do you say about that; is it too big or too little or not true at all?

A. No, that is probably correct.

Q. Well, now, so far you haven't disagreed with Hitler on any of these, have you?

A. No.

Q. Then, he lastly says, "Today, 1.2 million boys of the Hitler Youth receive regular instruction in small-bore rifle shooting from 7000 instructors." What's wrong with that figure, if anything?

A. It may be correct—of course, I have no documentary proof that we had 7000 young men who conducted training in small-bore rifle shooting. I discussed this small-bore rifle shooting yesterday. . . .

Q. . . . I ask you if you do not agree—that you made two suggestions at

363

least: one for the bombing of a cultural English town and the other for the wholesale evacuation of the Czechs from Vienna, because of the assassination of this man Heydrich.

A. It is true that I put the idea of such an evacuation of the Czechs into words. It is equally true, and a historical fact, that I dropped the idea and that it was never carried out. It is correct that I suggested the bombing of a British cultural site as an answer to the attempt against Heydrich and to the innumerable bombardments of German cultural places in the third year of the war, at a time when vital interests of the German people were at stake. . . .

Q. . . . Is it not a fact that Himmler assigned his SS personnel to your youth organization for the training purpose of your young people? You can answer that very simply. Did he or did he not?

A. For training purposes?

Q. Yes.

A. I am not aware of anything like that. The fact that there might have been liaison officers would not be unusual, because practically all ministries and organizations had liaison officers. What you have just suggested, however, I do not recall. . . .

Q. . . . Now, Mr. Witness, if you will look at this document, you will observe that it is a message which you sent to "Dear Party Member Bormann" in August of 1941. . . . By way of preliminary question, the SA apparently had suggested that it take over some of the training of young people, had it not, some time in the summer of 1941?

A. I said in my testimony—I think on Thursday—that already in the spring of 1939, I believe, the SA had attempted to take over the premilitary training of the youth of the two older age classes, and such attempts were probably repeated in 1941.

Q. Yes, I knew you were complaining to Bormann about it when you wrote this message. . . . If you will turn to the second page of the English text . . . what I want to call your attention to; I assume it is in capital letters in the German:

I would be happy if the SA would put personnel at my disposal for support for this purpose, similar to the way in which the SS and the police have been doing for a long time already.

. . . Did you find that sentence?

A. Yes.

Q. You say there that you would be happy if the SA would put personnel at your disposal for support of this purpose, similar to the way in which the SS and the police have been doing for a long time already, and you are referring—if you will read back to the paragraph just ahead of that sentence—to the training of the young people. You talk about Hitler schools and the training of Hitler youth. Now, it is perfectly clear, is it not, that you did have assistance from the SS, according to your own words, from the SS and police, for a long time before you sent this message?

A. During the war, yes; since the beginning of the war in 1939 we had premilitary training camps and I wanted youth instructors for these camps. Neither the Army nor the SA could supply sufficient instructors; the SS and the police could place a few young officers at my disposal.

Q. So it was only from the beginning of the war that you had personnel from the SS and police for the training of young people, was it?

A. I do not think that there would have been need for SS instructors otherwise. As I have said, we selected youth leaders from among youth itself.

Q. I ask you again, do you want the Tribunal to understand that it was only from the beginning of the war that you had the assistance of SS and police personnel assigned to your youth organization for the training of young people?

A. I cannot answer that question definitely for this reason: we had for example a training camp for skiing practice, and it was quite possible that one of the instructors was an SA man or an SS man only because by chance he happened to be one of the best sportsmen in that field. But I cannot think where such collaboration existed elsewhere.

Q. Are you able to say that you did not have SS personnel assigned for training purposes; and I am not talking about some isolated skimaster, I am talking about a regular program of assistance from the SS to you in your training of young people.

A. As far as premilitary training is concerned, it was only through this teletype message that I requested help for training purposes. Apart from that, I do not recollect any collaboration.

MAY 31, 1946
FRITZ SAUCKEL, EXAMINATION BY TRIBUNAL MEMBER, FRANCIS BIDDLE (UNITED STATES)

Q. . . . When you mentioned the 1500 district offices, were those the recruitment offices? . . .

A. They were not only recruiting offices, they were the offices of the territorial labor administration on the lowest level. . . .

Q. . . . Now I would like to know a little bit about what you call this private recruitment. Who appointed the agents who were to do private recruiting? Who appointed them? Did the employers hire agents to get workmen for them? . . .

A. In those countries, the Commissioner for Labor Allocation appointed them—I myself could not appoint them—together with the French organizations. That was an understanding, not a set appointment . . .

Q. I see. And they would be paid on, I think you said, a commission basis, is that right? They would be paid, in other words, so much per workman? Every workman they brought in, they would get a fee for that, is that right?

A. Yes. I do not know the details myself any more, but for the most part that is correct.

Q. Now, I take it when you used the word "shanghai," which you referred to and explained, that simply means private recruiting with force. That is all it means, is it not?

[*There was no response.*]

That is all it means, is it not? Private recruiting with force?

A. No . . .

Q. Now, wait a minute. Can you shanghai a man without using force? You do not mean that you shanghaied them by persuasion? Did you?

A. Yes, for I wanted to recruit these French associations in just this voluntary, friendly way, over a glass of beer or wine in a cafe, and not in the official offices. I don't mean shanghai in the bad sense as I recall its being used from my sailor days. This was a rather drastic expression, but not a concrete representation of the actual procedure. Never, Your Honor, in France or anywhere else, did I order men to be shanghaied, but rather . . .

Q. Oh, I know you did not order it. That was not my question. You mean that "shanghai" just meant that you had a friendly glass of wine with a workman and then he joined up? Was that what you meant?

A. I understand it in that way. I described it to the Central Planning Board in a somewhat drastic form in order to answer the demands made of me with some plausible counterarguments as to the efforts I was making.

Q. Why did you object to this private recruitment? What was the objection to it?

A. In this case I did not object, but it was contrary to German ideas concerning the procurement of labor. According to German principles and . . .

Q. Was it contrary to German law?

A. It was against my convictions and contrary to German laws.

Q. I did not ask you that. I am not interested for the moment in your convictions. I said: Was it contrary to German law? It was, wasn't it, against law?

A. It was in general contrary to the German labor laws. As far as possible no private recruitment was to take place. But may I say as an explanation, Your Honor, that after the workman had been won over, he nevertheless entered into an obligation on the basis of a state contract. Thus it must not be understood to mean that the worker in question came into the Reich without a contract approved by the state; a contract was granted to him just as it was to all others.

Q. You mean, a laborer that was shanghaied by private agents had the same rights, once he was in the employment, as anyone else; is that what you mean?

366

A. The same rights and assurances that everyone else had. . . .

JUNE 12, 1946
ARTUR SEYSS-INQUART, EXAMINATION BY BIDDLE

Q. Defendant, you said that you had considered that the laws of land warfare were obsolete. Do you remember?

A. Yes.

Q. Did you consider that they were all obsolete?

A. No.

Q. Which ones did you consider were obsolete?

A. I was of the opinion that the contractual stipulations for the protection of the civilian population were outdated by technical developments in weapons, for obviously certain warlike measures like total blockade, demolition bombing attacks, *et cetera*, are directed primarily at the destruction of the civilian population and consequently are only justifiable if the civilian population is considered a war potential like the troops at the front. But if that is the case, then the civilian population of the occupied countries must be considered in such a way also.

Q. And when you say "considered in such a way," you mean therefore Germany had the right to use the civilian population to fight the war, make ammunition and so forth; is that not the conclusion?

A. That is my conclusion, yes.

Q. When was that conclusion reached?

A. I believe with the increase of the bombing attacks, approximately.

Q. Never mind the increase of the bombing attacks. Just give me the date. When was it reached?

A. At the end of 1941 or the beginning of 1942. . . .

Q. Well, now, let us take up this matter of declaring forfeited the property of enemies of the state. You made those declarations, I presume, did you not, as Reich Commissioner?

A. Yes.

Q. And was that made under a decree of the Fuehrer's giving you authority to do that?

A. That was a basic practice which was current in the Reich, and if I did not get the order I nevertheless had a sort of directive . . .

Q. Now wait a minute. I did not ask you about the practice. It was made under a decree, was it not? That practice was under a decree?

A. Yes.

Q. And that decree applied to all occupied countries, did it not?

A. I do not think so. I first announced this decree in the Netherlands myself. The measures in the Netherlands came about on the basis of my directive.

Q. I understand that. I do not want to get you confused. Your action was taken under a decree of the Fuehrer, was it not, giving you that authority; is that right?

367

A. Let us say on the basis of a directive. . . .

Q. . . . Now tell us what was in it. What was in that directive?

A. It was the general directive that the property of persons who committed acts inimical to the Reich was to be confiscated. I had already issued a decree similar to this in Austria. The first one was issued in the Reich itself; that was the model.

Q. Now, you were the person in the Netherlands who had complete discretion to make the determination of who was an enemy of the Reich, did you not? That was your decision under the decree?

A. No, that was actually a matter for the police and the courts.

Q. I see.

A. I only had influence.

Q. Now, the police did not have to go to the courts to get that determination, surely, did they?

A. No. Either the police directly made a decision of this kind or the people were put at the disposal of the Court, and the Court sentenced the people on the basis of certain offenses, and then on the basis of the judgment the property suffered the legal consequences.

Q. Now, the property of the Freemasons was confiscated under that decree. What other property, of what other groups, was confiscated in the Netherlands under that directive of the Fuehrer? I do not mean individuals; I mean groups.

A. At the moment I cannot think of any others, although there were a few other groups.

Q. But, in effect—see if I state the practice correctly—the police would decide that an individual or group of individuals, on account of their words or their actions, were enemies of the Reich, and then their property would be confiscated; is that right?

A. Yes. And the decisive office at the time was that of Heydrich.

Q. The decisive factor was Heydrich?

A. And the Netherlands agencies carried through his decisions.

Q. And you carried through Heydrich's decisions; right?

A. I carried through Heydrich's decisions when it came to property rights. The association of Jehovah's Witnesses belonged to those groups.

Q. Oh, Jehovah's Witnesses belonged to the group too?

A. They were also among them.

Q. And the property of Jehovah's Witnesses was confiscated also, since they were enemies of the Reich?

A. They probably did not have very much, but what they had was confiscated because of their attitude in refusing to serve in the war effort.

Q. They refused—let me get this straight. This is interesting. Jehovah's Witnesses refused to fight or to serve in the German war effort and therefore their property was confiscated. Is that right?

A. Not quite. Jehovah's Witnesses in Germany refused to serve in the German Army. So first of all they were prohibited there, and then this prohibition was expanded for all other regions.

Q. Wait a minute. I am not talking about that. I am talking about the Netherlands. Was that true in the Netherlands?

A. Yes; but Jehovah's Witnesses in the Netherlands were not prohibited because they refused to serve in the German Army, but rather because we were against this group on principle.

Q. Oh, I see, on general principles. As pacifists, you were against them, so you confiscated their property; right?

A. Yes. . . .

JUNE 18, 1946
FRANZ VON PAPEN, CROSS-EXAMINATION BY MAXWELL-FYFE

Q. . . . I think you said that you were not certain that Hitler would eliminate opposition before he came into power. How long did it take you, after Hitler became Chancellor, to find out that his desire was to eliminate all opposition?

A. I realized that finally when I made the last attempt in my Marburg speech to hold him to the joint program, and when this attempt failed . . .

Q. That was eighteen months later, on 17 June 1934. Are you telling the Tribunal that it took you seventeen months to realize that Hitler wanted to break down the opposition?

A. No, I told the Court . . .

Q. Now will you answer my questions. Did you not know that hundreds of Social Democrats and Communists had been put in concentration camps?

A. No, I did not know there were hundreds. I knew that individual leaders had been thrown into concentration camps. . . .

Q. Defendant, you have told the Tribunal a considerable amount about your Marburg speech. Was one of your associates a gentleman called Jung?

A. Yes, that is quite correct.

Q. And—believe me I do not mean it in any offensive way—Herr Jung had helped you considerably with the composition of the Marburg speech, had he not?

A. Herr Jung quite frequently drafted outlines for speeches of mine, and the same applies to the Marburg speech.

Q. Yes. He was shot after the 30th of June, was he not?

A. Yes.

Q. He was a man for whom you had not only great affection, but for whose political views—I think you would call him a progressive conservative —you had great respect and agreement, is that not so?

A. Perfectly right, yes. . . .

Q. Well, in all—it does not matter about the names—there were two members of your staff who were shot, and three were arrested, were they not?

A. One member of my staff was shot, and two were arrested. Herr Jung was not a member of my staff.

369

Q. Herr Jung was not a member of your staff, but he was a close associate of yours. Now . . .

A. He was an associate who, as I said, quite often assisted me, when I was very busy, by drafting outlines for speeches, and with whom I exchanged conservative ideas.

Q. And, of course, it is common knowledge that General von Schleicher and his wife were also shot, and—I think my recollection is right—that General von Bredow was shot too, was he not?

A. Yes.

Q. And you were placed under arrest, as you have told us, for three days, and I think your files were taken, were they not?

A. Yes.

Q. Did this performance shake your faith in the regime?

A. My faith in what? I beg your pardon.

Q. Did this performance shake your faith in the regime and in Hitler?

A. Quite. I explained to the Tribunal yesterday that by this action the Pact of 30 January had been broken.

Q. And you offered your resignation on 2 July, I think.

A. No, I offered it even earlier.

Q. You had already offered it on 18 or 19 June, and you reaffirmed your offer on 2 July.

A. Quite right. . . .

Q. But it is correct, of course, as you write here, that you had agreed with Hitler to carry on as Vice Chancellor until September and then to be employed in the Foreign Service on this condition, is that right?

A. No, that is not correct, for I have already explained . . .

Q. It is your letter, Defendant, it is your own letter.

A. Yes, but this letter was written because Hitler had promised me a clarification, an investigation which would enable me, after my honor had been restored and all these crimes cleared up, to remain in the service of the Reich. But that was never done. . . .

JUNE 20, 1946

ALBERT SPEER, DIRECT EXAMINATION BY DR. HANS FLAECHSNER (FOR THE DEFENSE)

Q. Then, as Technical Minister, do you wish to limit your responsibility to your sphere of work?

A. No; I should like to say something of fundamental importance here. This war has brought an inconceivable catastrophe upon the German people, and indeed started a world catastrophe. Therefore it is my unquestionable duty to assume my share of responsibility for this disaster before the German people. This is all the more my obligation, all the more my responsibility, since the head of the government has avoided responsibility before the German people and before the world. I, as an important member of the leadership of the Reich, therefore, share in the total responsibility, beginning with 1942. I will state my arguments in this connection in my final remarks.

Q. Do you assume responsibility for the affairs covered by the extensive sphere of your assignments?

A. Of course, as far as it is possible according to the principles generally applied and as far as actions were taken according to my directives.

Q. Do you wish to refer to Fuehrer decrees in this connection?

A. No. Insofar as Hitler gave me orders and I carried them out, I assume the responsibility for them. I did not, of course, carry out all the orders which he gave me. . . .

Q. Herr Speer, were orders given to destroy industry in Belgium, Holland, and France?

A. Yes. In case of occupation by the Allies, Hitler had ordered a far-reaching system of destruction of war industries in all these countries; according to planned preparations, coal and mineral mines, power plants, and industrial premises were to be destroyed.

Q. Did you take any steps to prevent the execution of these orders?

A. Yes.

Q. And did you prevent them?

A. The Commander, West, was responsible for carrying out these orders, since they concerned his operational zone. But I informed him that as far as I was concerned this destruction had no sense and no purpose and that I, in my capacity of Armament Minister, did not consider this destruction necessary. Thereupon no order to destroy these things was given. By this, of course, I made myself responsible to Hitler for the fact that no destruction took place.

Q. When was that?

A. About the beginning of July 1944.

Q. How could you justify your position?

A. All the military leaders whom I knew said at that time that the war was bound to end in October or November, since the invasion had been successful.

I myself was of the same opinion in view of the fuel situation. This may be clearly seen from the memorandum, which I sent to Hitler on 30 August, in which I told him that in view of this development in the fuel situation no operational actions by the troops would be possible by October or November. The fact that the war lasted longer than that can be ascribed only to the standstill of the enemy offensive in 1944. This made it possible to throttle our fuel consumption and to give the Western Front new supplies of tanks and ammunition. In these circumstances I was perfectly willing to accept responsibility for abandoning the industries in the Western countries to the enemy in an undamaged condition, for they could be of no use to them for at least nine months, the transport system having been destroyed beforehand. . . .

Q. Did Hitler sanction these measures?

A. He could not sanction these measures for he knew nothing about them. It was a period of such hectic activity at headquarters that he never thought of checking up on the measures taken for destruction. Later, in January 1945, reports appeared in the French press on the rapid reconstruction of their undestroyed industries. Then, of course, serious charges were raised against me. . . .

Q. Herr Speer, with regard to the other occupied countries apart from France, Belgium, and Holland, did you use your influence to prevent destruction?

A. From August 1944, in the industrial installations in the Government General, the ore mines in the Balkans, the nickel works in Finland; from September 1944, in the industrial installations in Upper Italy; beginning with February 1945, in the oil fields in Hungary and the industries of Czechoslovakia. I should like to emphasize in this connection that I was supported to a great extent by Generaloberst Jodl, who quietly tolerated this policy of nondestruction.

Q. What were Hitler's intentions with regard to the preservation of industry and means of existence for the German population at the beginning of September 1944, when enemy troops approached the boundaries of the Greater German Reich from all sides?

A. He had absolutely no intention of preserving industry. On the contrary, he ordered the "scorched earth" policy with special application to Germany. That meant the ruthless destruction of all animate and inanimate property on the approach of the enemy. This policy was backed by Bormann, Ley, and Goebbels, while the various branches of the Wehrmacht and the competent ministries opposed it.

Q. Since these efforts by Speer to prevent the application of destructive measures, which had been considerably intensified, also applied to areas then considered part of the German Reich, such as Polish Upper Silesia, Alsace and Lorraine, Austria, the Protectorates of Bohemia and Moravia, I should like to have this topic admitted as part of my evidence.

Herr Speer, did the commanders of the armies in the wider German area that I have just defined have executive powers to carry out orders of destruction?

A. No. As far as industries were concerned, those executive powers were vested in me. Bridges, locks, railroad installations, *et cetera*, were the affair of the Wehrmacht.

Q. In your measures for the protection of industry, did you differentiate between the territory of the so-called Altreich and those areas which were added after 1933?

A. No. The industrial region of Upper Silesia, the remaining districts of Poland, Bohemia and Moravia, Alsace-Lorraine, and Austria, of course, were protected against destruction in the same way as the German areas. I made the necessary arrangements by personal directives on the spot—particularly in the eastern territories.

Q. What steps did you take against the scorched-earth policy?

A. I returned from a trip to the Western Front on 14 September 1944 and found the decree awaiting me that everything was to be destroyed ruthlessly. I immediately issued a counterdecree officially ordering all industrial installations to be spared. At that time I was very much upset about the fact that industries were now to be destroyed in Germany in the hopeless war situation, and I was all the more upset because I thought I had succeeded in saving the industries in the occupied western territories from destruction.

Q. . . . Herr Speer, did you succeed in getting this order carried out?

A. The scorched-earth policy was officially proclaimed in the *Völkischer Beobachter* at the same time in an official article by the Reich press chief, so that I realized quite clearly that my counterdecree could not be effective for any length of time. In this connection I used a method which is perhaps typical of the means employed by Hitler's immediate circle. In order to dissuade him from the scorched-earth policy, I made use of the faith which he induced in all his coworkers that the lost territories would be recaptured. I made him decide between the two situations: Firstly, if these industrial areas were lost, my armament potential would sink if they were not recaptured; and secondly, if they were recaptured they would be of value to us only if we had not destroyed them. . . .

Q. You emphasized a few minutes ago that up to January 1945 you tried to achieve the highest possible degree of armament. What were your reasons for giving up the idea after January 1945?

A. From January 1945 onward, a very unpleasant chapter begins: The last phase of the war and the realization that Hitler had identified the fate of the German people with his own; and from March 1945 onward, the realization that Hitler intended deliberately to destroy the means of life for his own people if the war were lost. . . .

Q. Was it possible for you to reconcile your actions during the last phase of the war with your oath and your conception of loyalty to Adolf Hitler?

A. There is one loyalty which everyone must always keep; and that is loyalty toward one's own people. That duty comes before everything. If I am in a leading position and if I see that the interests of the nation are acted against in such a way, then I too must act. That Hitler had broken faith with the nation must have been clear to every intelligent member of his entourage, certainly at the latest in January or February 1945. Hitler had once been given his mission by the people; he had no right to gamble away the destiny of the people with his own. Therefore I fulfilled my natural duty as a German. . . .

JUNE 25, 1946

KONSTANTIN VON NEURATH, CROSS-EXAMINATION BY MAXWELL-FYFE

Q. . . . Now, Defendant, you know that in the indictment in this trial we are charging you and your fellow defendants, among many other things, with genocide, which we say is the extermination of racial and national groups, or, as it has been put in the well-known book of Professor Lemkin, "a co-ordinated plan of different actions aiming at the destruction of essential foundations of the life of national groups with the aim of annihilating the groups themselves." What you wanted to do was to get rid of the teachers and writers and singers of Czechoslovakia, whom you call the intelligentsia, the people who would hand down the history and traditions of the Czech people to other generations. These were the people that you wanted to destroy by what you say in that memorandum, were they not?

A. Not quite. Here there are . . .

Q. But just before you answer, what did you mean by saying, in the last passage that I read to you, ". . . expelling those who are not useful from a racial standpoint or are enemies of the Reich, that is, the intelligentsia which has developed in the last twenty years"? Did you mean what you said? Were you speaking the truth when you said it was necessary to expel the intelligentsia? . . .

A. The class of the intelligentsia was the greatest obstacle to co-operation between Germans and Czechs. For that reason, if we wanted to achieve this co-operation, and that was still the aim of our policy, then this intelligentsia had to be reduced in some way and principally their influence had to be diminished, and that was the meaning of my explanation.

Q. Yes, you said to achieve your policy, but by achieving your policy you meant to destroy the Czech people as a national entity with their own language, history, and traditions, and assimilate them into the Greater German Reich. That was your policy, wasn't it?

A. My policy was, first of all, to assimilate Czechoslovakia, as far as possible. But in the final analysis that could not have been achieved for generations. The first thing to do was to bring about co-operation so as to have peace and order. . . .

THE OPPENHEIMER
HEARING

(1954)

According to all reports, Harry S. Truman played a better-than-average game of stud poker during his stay in the White House. This talent should have been helpful to him as President; for to an alarming degree the postwar contest between East and West more often than not turned on the "hole" cards held by each player and on his ability to bluff and to detect a bluff.

Marshal Joseph Stalin had none of the conventional vices; he could not tell the difference between a pair of treys and a full house. But he came to his first meeting with Truman a seasoned hand at the game of diplomatic poker. As history would have it, it fell to the lot of Harry Truman to bluff the wily old Georgian, and he failed—with cosmic consequences.

The scene was the East German city of Potsdam; the date, July 24, 1945. Eight days earlier Truman had received a coded message from the far-off New Mexico desert announcing the birth of the atomic bomb. Its use against Japan had already been resolved. Now, as Truman and Churchill saw it, Stalin had to be told just enough to keep up appearances, without opening the door to unwelcome demands for technical information about the bomb.

Truman waited until the close of one of the conference sessions and strolled idly over to the Generalissimo. After a few inconsequential comments, he let drop, with studied casualness, word that "a new weapon of unusual destructive force" had been developed. Stalin seemed genuinely pleased, but displayed no curiosity about details; and Truman and Churchill came away from the conference room congratulating themselves on their good fortune.

It never occurred to them that Stalin might be deliberately feigning disinterest in the recent discovery. Not until several years had passed would they learn that, since 1943, Soviet intelligence had been receiving periodic progress reports on the bomb. And the Soviet Premier's straight-faced counterbluff reinforced their belief that the bomb would remain an American monopoly for many years to come—a plausible but dangerous delusion which quickly hardened into a keystone of American postwar military and diplomatic planning.

Inevitably the awakening was rude and traumatic, carrying fear and suspicion in its train. And when it was revealed that a handful of spies had helped turn America's scientific flank, the country reacted by throwing up higher ramparts around its dwindling store of military secrets. In due course, the safeguarding of the treasure became an end in itself, developing its own ritual and its own priesthood.

In most scientific circles, the excommunication of J. Robert Oppenheimer from government service is regarded as the nadir of his country's superstitious quest for absolute safety. But the case is more than a pathological specimen of the operation of the American security system. In a broader sense it brings into focus the dilemma of the man of science in the nuclear age.

The blasts that knocked Japan out of the war catapulted J. Robert Oppenheimer at forty-one into a niche in public esteem seldom accorded to an intellectual and almost never to one so young. Newspaper headline writers, with the easy familiarity they reserve for the notable and the notorious, called him "Oppy," and practically overnight every schoolboy knew him as "the father of the atomic bomb."

Oppenheimer's modest disclaimers only served to gild the halo. His lanky, tweed-clad figure, the contemplative ice-blue eyes, the soft deliberate speech, the forthright but elegantly phrased public utterances—all contributed to the image of a latter-day scientific Prometheus whose genius had shortened the bloodiest war in history and saved hundreds of thousands of American lives.

Actually Oppenheimer had been the well-nigh indispensable man in the development of the bomb, but not for the reasons widely advertised in the press. In the early stages of the work on controlled nuclear fission, he had contributed significantly to the solution of a number of tough theoretical problems. But it was not until he was called away from academic life to take charge of the Los Alamos Laboratory that his talents received full play. He was thirty-nine. To the lonely island of activity atop the mesa in New Mexico's Jemez Mountains he attracted in the spring of 1943 a distinguished aggregation of able and resourceful scientists. Under his energetic supervision, a vast complex of experimental equipment was begged, borrowed, or requisitioned from university laboratories and placed in operation with a speed that staggered his chief, General Leslie R. Groves, of the Army Corps of Engineers. With unremitting selflessness, Oppenheimer threw himself into the nagging details of administration, catering to the whims and foibles of his small polyglot army of brainy prima donnas with all the skill of an opera-house manager, at the same time sorting, testing, catalyzing, criticizing, and stimulating the flow and application of their ideas. His gift for instilling in the doubtful, the fainthearted and the frustrated a sense of excitement in the work at hand, held turnover to a minimum and brought the venture to an unexpectedly speedy consummation. Such is the verdict of all who worked over, with, and under him, friend and foe alike.

When he left Los Alamos in November 1945, his close-cropped hair showing gray and his frame trimmed down to 120 pounds, any hopes he had of resuming his teaching career as a full-time undertaking were soon dashed. His encyclopedic knowledge of atomic energy was constantly being drawn upon by Congressional committees, the armed forces, and the State Department, and he found himself spending as much time in Washington as on the California Institute of Technology campus.

"The physicists have known sin." Oppenheimer's rueful verdict on the events that ushered in the age of nuclear power had a double meaning. On the one hand, it voiced the gnawings of conscience common to men of science who had presented a new toy of fearful potentialities to a world ill-prepared to use it wisely. On the other, it mourned the end of innocence for the theoretical physicist. No longer could the search for truth be regarded as a sublime intellectual adventure to be pursued with deliberate zeal in hushed laboratories and learned journals; he had been thrust into the fumbling world of politics and temporal power where his honest guesswork would be labeled "top secret" and might bring generals and congressmen to blows.

Whether Oppenheimer meant to include himself among the guilt-ridden is open to question. He had been among those who recommended to Truman that the bomb be dropped on Japan without warning, although leading physicists had pleaded for a harmless demonstration to convince the Japanese of the futility of further resistance. And in the Congressional fight of 1945–46 over postwar control of atomic energy, he had lined up with the Pentagon, to the puzzlement of most of his colleagues, who favored civilian regulation of the awesome new source of power.

To many of his fellow physicists Oppenheimer's neat aphorism about sin had the ring of a sermon preached on Sundays and forgotten on

377

weekdays. And his conduct was all the more surprising to those who knew something about his prewar background.

Born in 1904 to well-to-do, cultivated German-American parents, he completed his undergraduate work at Harvard as he turned twenty-one. Two years later he won his doctorate at Goettingen, specializing in nuclear physics. At the age of twenty-five he accepted concurrent appointments to the faculties of CalTech in Pasadena and the University of California at Berkeley.

It was 1929; and Oppenheimer's complete divorcement from the world outside his laboratory may be gauged by his later assertion that he learned of that year's stock-market crash "only long after the event." He studied Sanskrit; outside the scientific field his reading was confined to novels, plays, and poetry. He testified at the hearing:

I never read a newspaper or a current magazine like *Time* or *Harper's*; I had no radio, no telephone . . . the first time I ever voted was in the presidential election of 1936. . . . I had no understanding of the relations of man to his society.

The shy, introverted professor got his first glimpse of politics through the eyes of a girl. In the spring of 1936 he was introduced to Jean Tatlock, the daughter of a Berkeley professor.

We were at least twice close enough to marriage to think of ourselves as engaged. . . . She told me about her Communist Party memberships; they were on again, off again affairs, and never seemed to provide for her what she was seeking. . . . She was, as it turned out, a friend of many fellow travelers and Communists, with a number of whom I was later to become acquainted.

Unlike his brother Frank, Oppenheimer never joined the Communist Party, but under Jean's tutelage he was soon deeply embroiled in half a dozen activities "in support of humanitarian objectives." As his left-wing connections ripened into friendships, he allowed himself to be tapped for funds out of a substantial inheritance left him by his father in 1937. Although he joined few "front" organizations, he gave liberally to the Spanish Loyalist cause; and soon he was making periodic cash contributions to the Communist Party, principally, as he thought, for Spanish relief.

In 1939, Oppenheimer fell deeply in love with Katharine Puening Harrison, wife of a doctor with many friends among the CalTech faculty. Wrenching themselves loose from their alliances, they were married in November 1940, but not before they had blown up a storm of gossip and ill-feeling in the Berkeley and Pasadena circles in which they moved. Among the few who rallied to the side of the troubled lovers was a lecturer at the University of California named Haakon Chevalier. The Chevaliers soon became intimates of the Oppenheimers. The two men's politics more or less coincided, and the close association that evolved was destined to work incalculable mischief with both of their careers many years later.

Katharine brought to the union an entourage of left-wing acquaintances left over from her ill-starred first marriage to a hard-core Communist named Joe Dallet. She had held a Party card for a year or two, but after Dallet died fighting in Spain she had apparently cooled to the Marxists.

Oppenheimer's emotional attachment to the movement had likewise been shaken by such eye-openers as the Moscow purge trials, the Nazi-Soviet Pact, and Russia's subsequent aggressions against Poland and Finland. But his friendly relations with Party members and fellow travelers on and off campus continued more or less unimpaired. He was a faithful fixture at endless "Spanish relief" parties; and he saw no harm in attending a couple of "social gatherings" at which a Party official, William Schneiderman, expounded the twists and turns in Communist policy.

Nobel prizewinner Arthur Holly Compton, who was largely responsible for recruiting the young physicist into government service, says that by 1940 Oppenheimer "had evidently become convinced that Communism was dangerous." But as late as the night before Pearl Harbor, he was still chipping in to Party coffers as the spirit moved him.

Upon his enlistment in the war effort, Oppenheimer recognized the need to cut off all Communist connections. But his past record—candidly disclosed by him in his first personnel questionnaire—threatened to hold up his clearance indefinitely. Although he had been permitted to assume his post at Los Alamos while his security investigation was still pending, in view of the urgency of the situation, Army Military Intelligence was far from comfortable about his record.

The months dragged on; and to make matters worse, in June 1943 Oppenheimer took off for San Francisco—disregarding the risk to his clearance—for a meeting with his old flame, Jean Tatlock. Jean had evidently never recovered from the blow of Oppenheimer's marriage and had begged him to see her once more. He found her in a state of severe emotional stress, bordering on a breakdown. This was to be his last meeting with Jean. Seven months later she was dead.

Since Oppenheimer had been under surveillance all the while, his visit to Jean almost brought his government career to an untimely end. It took an order from General Groves in July to save his job—"irrespective of the information you have concerning Mr. Oppenheimer. He is absolutely essential to the project."

Groves' gamble paid off handsomely. The A-bomb proved to be one of the best-kept secrets of the war, at least as far as the Axis powers were concerned. Nor was Oppenheimer responsible for the leak of information that was Stalin's "hole card" at Potsdam.

Considering Oppenheimer's prewar activities, it is remarkable that the Soviet spy apparatus steered clear of him. The only semblance of an attempt to test his loyalty might have escaped the attention of the authorities altogether had Oppenheimer not chosen to report it. Thereby hangs a tangled and puzzling tale, which may well have tipped the scales against him at his trial.

A month or more before they moved to Los Alamos the Oppenheimers had the Chevaliers over to their house in Berkeley for dinner or cocktails. Oppenheimer went into the pantry to fix drinks, and Chevalier followed him. Then, according to Oppenheimer's testimony at the hearing:

He said, "I saw George Eltenton recently." Maybe he asked me if I remembered him. That Eltenton had told him that he had a method, he had a means of getting technical information to Soviet scientists. He didn't describe the means. I thought I said, "But that is treason," but I am not sure. I said anyway something, "This is a terrible thing to do." Chevalier said or expressed complete agreement. That was the end of it.

Far from the end of it, as subsequent events and the testimony at the hearing proved. Oppenheimer told no one about the encounter until he had been cleared by Military Intelligence. About a month later he learned that the security officers at the Berkeley Radiation Laboratory were concerned about the organizing activities of the left-wing Federation of Architects, Engineers, Chemists, and Technicians. Oppenheimer recalled that Eltenton, a Briton employed as a chemist by an oil company, had been one of the prime movers in the formation of FAECT. On his next visit to Berkeley he talked with the Laboratory's intelligence officer, Lieutenant Lyall Johnson. Eltenton, he said, had approached three physicists working on the bomb through a professor at Berkeley, seeking information for the Russians.

Johnson summoned his chief, Colonel Boris Pash, from Washington. The counterintelligence branch was still smarting as a result of Groves' order for Oppenheimer's clearance, and Pash, a former football coach at Hollywood High School, showed a deference and cordiality to the scientist he could scarcely have felt. But he made certain that their interview was recorded over hidden microphones.

Oppenheimer stuck to the story he had told Johnson, embroidering it with vague references to microfilm and to the Soviet consulate in San Francisco, which must have made Pash's nostrils quiver. Try as he might, Pash got nowhere in his attempts to learn the names of the three scientists who had been approached, or the identity of the intermediary. He was "absolutely certain," Oppenheimer told him, that the approach had been harmless, and he felt obliged to protect his colleagues.

Pash, needless to say, seized the opportunity to revive the debate over Oppenheimer's clearance. He reported to Los Alamos' chief security officer, Colonel John Lansdale:

This office is still of the opinion that Oppenheimer is not to be fully trusted. . . . It is believed that the only undivided loyalty he can give is to science. . . .

Despite his own belief in Oppenheimer's patriotism, Lansdale naturally dogged him for the information Pash had been seeking. He made no headway, and finally appealed to General Groves to apply pressure. After some hesitation, in December 1943, Groves ordered Oppenheimer to make a full disclosure of the incident. Oppenheimer's submission to that order appears from the record to have been half-hearted at best; for although he disclosed Chevalier's identity, he held to the main lines of the story he had told Pash. He let Groves continue to think that Chevalier had made three contacts, not including himself. Groves did not press him to name names, perhaps because, as he testified later, he suspected that Oppenheimer was covering up for his brother Frank, then employed at the Radiation Laboratory.

Oppenheimer's recollection at the hearing was that he had held nothing back from Groves and that he had confessed to the General that he had told a "cock-and-bull story" to protect Chevalier. But wires sent following this interview to Berkeley, Los Alamos, and Oak Ridge by Groves' second-in-command, Colonel Kenneth D. Nichols, indicate that Groves was still thinking in terms of three "contacts" by Chevalier.

Oppenheimer may possibly have confused the Groves interview with an interrogation by the Federal Bureau of Investigation in mid-1946, when he told a story consistent with his testimony at the hearing. By that time Chevalier had been raked over the coals by the FBI, and further concealment would have been pointless.

The FBI's renewed interest in the incident developed in the course of a security investigation preliminary to Oppenheimer's appointment to the General Advisory Committee of the newly constituted Atomic Energy Commission. Despite doubts expressed by J. Edgar Hoover concerning Oppenheimer's delay in reporting the Chevalier affair, the AEC unanimously recommended him for the post in March 1947. Later that year he was called to the directorship of the Institute for Advanced Study at Princeton. Voting for Oppenheimer in both instances was Admiral Lewis L. Strauss, who, seven years later, would write the opinion that cast Oppenheimer out of government service.

Oppenheimer wore the mantle of fame gracefully. He delivered himself of sober and well-polished pronouncements on the advancement of science and the political aspects of technology, advocating a high level of diplomacy in dealing with the new weapons, and deploring Russia's obstinate resistance in the United Nations to the Baruch plan for international control of atomic energy, which he had helped to formulate. As a member of the GAC and as consultant to the State and Defense Departments, his counsel was much in demand, and he seemed well on his way to premature stature as an elder statesman.

In the fall of 1949 his luck changed. On September 23 Truman announced that the Soviets had detonated a fission device. The Russian tortoise had overtaken the American hare.

To many scientists the news came as no surprise. They had harbored no illusions about the competence of Russian physicists, who for several decades had been making impressive strides in the exploration of the mysteries of atomic energy. But in military and diplomatic circles, where Russian mastery of the bomb had been confidently thought to be at least two years off, the shattering of our atomic monopoly had a devastating impact; and despite the outward display of official calm that attended the announcement, the air was charged with apprehension and dismay.

The next move was up to Washington. With nuclear stalemate in prospect, had the time come to re-examine our basic diplomatic and strategic assumptions? Or should we simply set out to outdistance the Russians in the race for mass-destruction devices?

Hard on the heels of the presidential announcement, a small group of scientists, led by Dr. Edward O. Lawrence and Dr. Luis Alvarez of the Berkeley Radiation Laboratory, turned up in Washington and began buttonholing key congressmen, AEC officials, and military leaders in an intensive campaign to promote the speedy development of the so-called "super"—a thermonuclear weapon with a thousand times the destructive force of the A-bomb. Since 1942, when the theory of such a device had first been explored by Oppenheimer and a team of Berkeley physicists, discussions concerning its feasibility had been held periodically at Los Alamos. But the theoretical and technical obstacles had seemed much too formidable, and the idea was "kept on the back burner," to use Oppenheimer's words, for the duration, with Dr. Hans Bethe, Dr.

Edward Teller, and a handful of associates devoting part time to its basic research problems. During the last year of the war, Oppenheimer had favored more intensive work on the "super," but shortly after Hiroshima he changed his mind. He had come to look upon the vastly more destructive H-bomb as either impracticable or immoral, or both; and he encouraged Teller, who spoke of the thermonuclear as "my baby," to leave Los Alamos early in 1946. Work continued on the weapon after Teller's departure, but it was desultory and piecemeal. By the time the Russian A-bomb went off, little progress had been made.

Late in October, AEC Chairman David Lilienthal called upon the General Advisory Committee for advice on two urgent questions: What changes, if any, should be made in the Commission's program in the light of the Soviet success? And was an all-out effort to develop the "super" advisable?

By October 29, when the Committee met, Lawrence, Alvarez, and a few like-minded scientists had made considerable headway with the Joint Congressional Committee on Atomic Energy and the Joint Chiefs of Staff in favor of the H-bomb as the only answer to the Russians. But to his surprise, Oppenheimer found his colleagues on the GAC unanimously opposed to the crash program—except for Dr. Glenn Seaborg, who was abroad and had written Oppenheimer that he was undecided. The final report advocated continued research on the thermonuclear device, but took a firm stand against according it priority over increased production of a variety of improved strategic and tactical atomic weapons.

The Committee's conclusions might have carried greater weight had they not ranged far afield from strictly scientific considerations and their military implications. A partial explanation for this excursion may be found in the policy vacuum in which it was compelled to move; for the government had committed itself neither to a strategy of mass extermination nor to a balanced offensive-defensive program. But the GAC could not ignore, either, the vision of a world laid waste by absolute weapons; and yielding to a moral imperative, it appended two annexes to the report praying for a diplomatic *détente* based on American self-restraint.

The majority annex, framed by Dr. James B. Conant and endorsed by Oppenheimer, closed with these words:

In determining not to proceed to develop the super bomb, we see a unique opportunity of providing by example some limitations on the totality of war and thus of eliminating the fear and arousing the hopes of mankind.

The language of the minority, consisting of Dr. Isador I. Rabi and Dr. Enrico Fermi, was considerably more passionate:

The fact that no limit exists to the destructiveness of this weapon makes its very existence and the knowledge of its construction a danger to humanity as a whole. It is necessarily an evil thing considered in any light. For these reasons we believe it important for the President of the United States to tell the American public and the world that we think it wrong on fundamental ethical principles to initiate the development of such a weapon.

Not that the Committee allowed the tail of scruple to wag the dog of science; quite the contrary. There was much solid stuff in the report for Harry Truman to ponder. Against a "better than even chance" that a thermonuclear device could be produced, he had to weigh the cost of triggering the new weapon with A-bombs, thereby depleting the existing nuclear stockpile and diverting plutonium piles to support an uncertain enterprise.

Even if all went well, at most it would bring about a shift of emphasis in the armaments race. Soviet scientists would surely follow the American lead and would sooner or later succeed. Thanks to America's classic reluctance to start a fight, the net result would favor the potential enemy.

Military considerations pointed to the same conclusion. All informed thinking about the "super" up to that time conjured up the picture of a huge and ponderous device, requiring an ocean-going vessel to deliver it. And to make matters worse, a weapon of such enormous destructive range had no advantage over the A-bomb except against vast and densely populated areas. On both counts, the H-bomb looked like a Pyrrhic rejoinder to Russia, where the only suitable targets would be Leningrad and perhaps, if a means could be found to transport the device inland, Moscow.

But any possibility that Truman would adopt the Committee's recommendations was eradicated by word that reached him privately from England on January 30, 1950: Klaus Fuchs had been siphoning American and British secrets to Soviet agents from 1943 to 1947. Fuchs had attended an H-bomb seminar at Los Alamos in the spring of 1946. Conceivably, now that the Russians had the A-bomb, they were hard at work on the "super."

Truman was already on the defensive. Ten days earlier a New York federal jury had convicted Alger Hiss of perjuring himself when he denied that he had turned over restricted State Department documents to a Soviet spy ring. The Republican majority in Congress was not letting the President forget that he had repeatedly dubbed the accusations against Hiss a "red herring." Charges of softness toward Communism, with which the opposition had flailed the Democrats since 1945, had reached new heights of hysteria in the nation's press.

On January 31, three days before the Fuchs story became public, Truman announced that he had ordered the AEC to "continue its work on all forms of atomic weapons, including the so-called hydrogen or super-bomb."

Timely though it was, the President's move could not turn back the tide of dread and distrust that was inundating the country. The triple hammer blows of the Hiss conviction, the Fuchs confession, and the discovery of the atomic bomb among Russia's stolen goods brought inchoate and irrational fear to millions of American hearts.

The situation was ripe for a demagogue, and there was one at hand in the person of the lynx-eyed, blue-jawed Senator from Wisconsin, Joseph R. McCarthy. Less than a week after the country learned of Fuchs' arrest, McCarthy struck his first low blow with the reckless charge that 205 Communist Party members were "still working and shaping the policy in the State Department."

Before he stood unmasked four years later as a cynical peddler of spurious news sensations, he had wreaked havoc with the nation's security system. By 1951, government servants were no longer presumed by law to be good Americans; they had to prove their loyalty beyond a reasonable doubt. And in two years loyalty alone would not be enough; the new Republican President's Executive Order 10450 authorized termination of any employment not "clearly consistent with the interests of national security." With each shift in standards, thousands who had been granted clearance found themselves required to establish their fitness anew.

For Atomic Energy Commission personnel, the change was even more drastic and came more swiftly. The 1946 Act required the Commission only to make certain that access by its personnel to restricted data "will not endanger the common defense or security." But in August 1950, Congress directed the Commission to suspend or discharge any employee if it was considered "necessary or advisable in the interest of national security."

This increasing emphasis on "security," as distinguished from "loyalty," gave free play to vicious hearts and narrow minds. In theory there were sound reasons for differentiating between them. Loyalty signifies undivided allegiance to the country and its institutions. Security relates to willingness and ability to keep secrets. The two concepts do not always coincide. Bruno Pontecorvo, who defected to the Russians in 1950, had been a model of decorum during his ten years of service on British and Canadian atomic projects, although he was a devout Communist all the while; and Colorado's Senator Edwin C. Johnson was no less loyal for his shocking breach of security in disclosing to a nationwide television audience in November 1949, that American scientists were working on the H-bomb.

Just before the ax fell on Oppenheimer, it was rumored around Washington that McCarthy had set his sights on the Atomic Energy Commission. This was bigger game than the Senator had ever stalked before, not counting presidents; and some observers say that the AEC moved against Oppenheimer just in time to forestall McCarthy's exploitation of the bulky FBI file on the scientist.

But McCarthyism cannot be held directly accountable for Oppenheimer's fall from grace. At most, the goblin from Wisconsin was blameworthy for sapping the moral stamina of a nation already in the vise of a "security syndrome," as it has been called. For Oppenheimer had made powerful enemies in other quarters. The Air Force, for example.

Korea had taught the Pentagon a bitter lesson, throwing into sharp focus the shortcomings of the A-bomb as an instrument of deterrence or reprisal. In April 1951, the armed services called upon the CalTech group to make a study of the tactical use of atomic weapons in ground warfare. This so-called Project Vista consumed about nine months of discussion and research. In its closing phase Oppenheimer participated briefly as a consultant and helped draft a portion of the intermediate report. In its final form the Vista report emphasized the need for a larger and more diversified arsenal of atomic hardware for ground troops and their air support and suggested a reallocation of our atomic stockpile for that purpose. These proposals struck the Strategic Air Command where it hurt most, threatening its virtual monopoly of atomic matériel as well as its dominant position in the scramble for military appropriations.

In the eyes of the SAC, Oppenheimer was the evil genius behind these recommendations. Earlier that year General Roscoe C. Wilson, a self-styled "big bomb man," had alerted the Air Force's Director of Intelligence to "a pattern of action" on Oppenheimer's part "that was simply not helpful to national defense." What had particularly disturbed the General were his willingness to internationalize atomic energy and his reluctance to proceed with nuclear-powered aircraft as energetically as with nuclear-powered ships. With Vista, the SAC had still another score to settle with Oppenheimer.

If anything was needed to make the SAC's smoldering resentment of Oppenheimer burst into flame, the next year's Lincoln Summer Study turned the trick. Under the auspices of the Massachusetts Institute of Technology, a group of outstanding American scientists was called together at the request of the National Security Council for a comprehensive analysis of the problems of air defense. The Study's report supplied the initial impetus to the nation's distant early warning system—a far-flung barrier of interlocking radar installations backed up by anti-aircraft devices and interceptor planes. This complex of ground defenses in depth could achieve an extraordinarily high rate of attrition against enemy bomb-carriers, according to the scientists, fully justifying the staggering expense involved. The SAC saw in these findings another sluice gate for the flow of defense dollars, siphoning them off from the construction of long-range bombers. And the prospect that the Russians might set up an equally effective system raised embarrassing questions for the airmen. Failing in its attempts to bury the report, the Strategic Air Command denounced the recommendations as a visionary plan for an "electronic Maginot line."

Although Oppenheimer had spent little time with the Summer Study, he had helped initiate the project and had lent a hand in recruiting participants for it. As with Vista, so with Lincoln—he was held responsible in Air Force circles.

In October 1952, Oppenheimer withdrew from the direct line of fire, declining reappointment to the General Advisory Committee. But he continued to serve the AEC as a special consultant, and he remained on call as a sort of Delphic oracle to over thirty government agencies. Although the volume of his contributions to scientific journals had dwindled to a trickle, his prestige was at its height. He stepped up the pace of his work at the Institute, still finding time for lectures and travel. In his speeches he addressed himself with increasing boldness to the dilemma of two mighty powers poised "like two scorpions in a bottle, each capable of killing the other, but only at the risk of his own life." The solution, he declared, lay in an informed public opinion, freer exchange of scientific data with America's major allies, and greater flexibility in the country's range of defensive and offensive measures.

These preachments were not calculated to curry favor with the new Eisenhower administration. By the end of 1953, Secretary of State John Foster Dulles was preparing to concede to the "big bomb" generals the ground they had lost in the periodic reassessments of our military posture since Korea. The "new look" with which he proposed to outstare our adversaries in the cold war was little more than the parsimonious pre-Korean policy with its face lifted: at the expense of the ground forces and local defense, the nation would henceforth rely on "a maximum deterrent at a bearable cost . . . a great capacity to retaliate instantly, by means and at times of our own choosing."

Oppenheimer's indomitable opposition to this approach had been heralded in the May, 1953, issue of *Fortune* magazine. The *Fortune* article, which contains internal evidence of having been inspired by the SAC, pictured him as the leader of a small cabal of scientists who considered the striking power of SAC a goad, rather than a deterrent, to Soviet development of counterweapons, and who held that a mutual renunciation of atomic warfare—with the United States presumably leading the way—was "essential to an easement of world tension." The Lincoln Summer Study report on continental air defense was interpreted as a tactical maneuver to stall further work on the H-bomb.

Two months after the article appeared, Oppenheimer was dropped unobtrusively as a consultant to the Defense Department's Research and Development Board. Secretary Charles E. Wilson explained the mechanics of the move at a press conference shortly after the Oppenheimer hearings started:

We dropped the whole Board. That was a real smooth way of doing that one as far as the Defense Department was concerned. (*Laughter*)

In November 1953, while Oppenheimer was lecturing in England, J. Edgar Hoover received a letter from the former executive director of the Joint Congressional Committee on Atomic Energy, William L. Borden, bluntly accusing Oppenheimer of being, "more probably than not," an espionage agent for the Soviet Union. To Hoover, whose dossier on the scientist was longer than a man's arm, the letter carried coals to Newcastle—a rehash of the material reviewed in 1947, coupled with distorted fulminations about Oppenheimer's position on the H-bomb.

Late in November, Hoover sent a digest of the Oppenheimer file to President Eisenhower, Attorney General Herbert Brownell, Defense Secretary Wilson, and AEC Chairman Strauss. On December 3, Strauss, without consulting his AEC colleagues, induced the President to order a "blank wall" placed between Oppenheimer and all classified material. Upon his return home from England later that month Oppenheimer received an urgent telephone call from Strauss summoning him to Washington.

The meeting in Strauss' office on December 21 was brief and dramatic. General Manager Kenneth D. Nichols was present, but said little. After an exchange of trivialities, Strauss soon came to the point: Oppenheimer's clearance was about to be suspended; if he did not resign his consultant's post within twenty-four hours, he would face charges. Strauss passed across the table to Oppenheimer a draft of a letter from Nichols which would initiate proceedings to revoke his clearance. For the most part its contents were familiar to Oppenheimer: the associations with Communists, the memberships in "front organizations," and the Chevalier incident. Only the concluding charge posed a fresh challenge: he was accused of vigorously opposing and retarding the development of the hydrogen bomb. These allegations, the letter stated, "until disproved, raise questions as to your veracity, conduct, and even your loyalty."

Oppenheimer left Washington without giving Strauss his decision. After he had pondered the matter overnight, he wrote Strauss from Princeton:

I have thought most earnestly of the alternative suggested. Under the circumstances, this course of action would mean that I accept and concur in the view that I am not fit to serve this government, that I have now served for some twelve years. This I cannot do.

The following day Oppenheimer received Nichols' letter officially lifting his clearance and detailing the charges. His safe was emptied of the classified information he had been permitted to store there.

According to AEC rules the proceedings were secret. But, necessarily, notice of Oppenheimer's suspension was sent to all installations with which he had been involved, and official Washington was soon buzzing with the story. Roger Robb was selected to represent the AEC at the hearing. Although he was engaged on the recommendation of the Department of Justice, anti-McCarthyites pointed out that Robb had served as attorney for radio commentator Fulton Lewis, Jr., one of the Senator's favorites.

Oppenheimer rallied to his cause the distinguished former chairman of the National War Labor Board, Lloyd K. Garrison, who was ably assisted by his law partner, Samuel J. Silverman, and by Oppenheimer's long-time personal attorney, Herbert S. Marks, ex-general counsel to the AEC. All served without fee.

The special board selected for the thankless task of trying the case was comprised of three citizens of sterling character and recognized ability. Heading the Board was the brisk, forthright, forty-five-year old Gordon Gray, successful lawyer and newspaper publisher, Secretary of the Army under Truman, and, at the time of his appointment, president of the University of North Carolina. Neither of the other members had Gray's background in public life, but each had achieved equal distinction in his chosen field. Thomas A. Morgan had spent almost twenty years guiding the destinies of the Sperry Corporation, one of the foremost producers of precision mechanisms for the AEC and the armed services. The senior member of the Board, Ward V. Evans, had headed the chemistry department at Northwestern University until his retirement in 1946, and had since been teaching at Loyola University.

389

On March 4, three days after the first American H-bomb was exploded at Bikini Atoll, Oppenheimer filed his answer to the charges. One month later the Board went into action, spending a week with prosecutor Robb poring over the voluminous FBI file and other restricted documents bearing on the case. Since they were not cleared to examine classified material, Oppenheimer and his counsel were excluded from this phase of the inquiry. However, Oppenheimer was permitted access to reports and other material he had participated in preparing.

Garrison did not protest on his client's behalf against the Board's one-sided review of the files until, in the course of the hearing, the official wraps were removed from certain documents just in time to discredit Oppenheimer and some of his witnesses. The wrangle over this seemingly sharp tactical maneuver received much attention in the press's postmortem on the case. Nichols asserted that Garrison had been given a chance to obtain the necessary security clearance before the hearings and had declined; Garrison replied that the proffer of clearance had come too late. Whatever the merits of the argument, it left an indelible blight on the outcome of the proceedings. The FBI reports and other files, which the Board examined in privacy, equaled in bulk the three thousand pages of testimony taken at the hearing itself. If Garrison had been present at the review, it would have done much to banish the shade of Dreyfus from the hearing room.

The hearings began on April 12, 1954, on the second floor of one of Washington's drab temporary wooden office buildings. Following the reading of the Nichols letter and Oppenheimer's reply, the scientist spent the first of his seven days on the witness stand. The next morning the New York *Times* broke the story, reproducing both of the documents verbatim. Oppenheimer had released the text upon being told by friendly Washington reporters that McCarthy knew of the suspension and proposed to make capital of it when the time was ripe. To the Wisconsin Senator, Oppenheimer would be much juicier headline bait than Owen Lattimore or Harry Dexter White; and Oppenheimer and his counselors felt that a voluntary disclosure would probably take the edge off any assault from that quarter. McCarthy was forced to content himself with the pronouncement that Oppenheimer should have been suspended "years ago."

The Gray Board was not unsympathetic to Oppenheimer's plight, which, indeed, strongly resembled its own. With each successive investigation, the rambunctious Senator had concentrated more and more of his fire on officials who had supposedly allowed subversives to slip through the security net. As lately as the previous December, he had loosed a withering blast at the Army's Loyalty Review Board, calculated to convince the American people that it had permitted Fort Monmouth to become an outpost of Moscow.

This was possibly the most superficial of the distant rumblings of trouble which rattled the windows of the hearing room. Hundreds of employees in all ranks of government service had been discharged for early Communist associations considerably less extensive and intimate than Oppenheimer's. If he were exonerated, they could justifiably complain of discrimination, or at the very least, maladministration.

The alternative was just as unappetizing. Oppenheimer had been cleared, first by the Army and later by the AEC, in the face of practically all of the derogatory information contained in Nichols' letter. Aside from the H-bomb imbroglio, a denial of clearance would have to rest on the same grounds. To exile Oppenheimer from government service on the strength of the twice-told tales of his early flirtations with Communism would implicitly discredit Groves and the AEC members who had made the earlier decisions—including Strauss himself. And if the H-bomb issue proved decisive at the hearing, how would it affect the solons and scientists who had agreed with him in 1949?

From a policy standpoint, of course, Oppenheimer's fellow scientists were the primary concern. With the release of the text of the charges and of Oppenheimer's reply, most of the men who guided the nation's cyclotrons and computers had reacted violently, closing ranks behind their wartime leader. Government service had never been particularly attractive to these independent spirits and inquiring minds, and the Oppenheimer case made it look even less so. How much longer would they resist the lure of academic life or of private industry? Unless Oppenheimer could be proved to have been patently disloyal, would there be enough gray matter to go around?

Finally, what would be gained by separating Oppenheimer from the mainstream of the nation's scientific life? He could not be brainwashed, nor prevented from thinking; the secrets he already knew, and those he could divine, would remain inviolate only as long as he could be trusted to keep them so. If he were turned out to pasture, that in itself would be an act of trust.

Such were the problems confronting the hearing board under its mandate to determine whether Oppenheimer's continued access to restricted data would, in the words of Eisenhower's Executive Order, "be clearly consistent with the interests of national security." An even more exacting standard was imposed by the AEC's Personnel Security Criteria, calling for an "over-all common sense judgment . . . which gives due recognition to the favorable as well as the unfavorable information concerning the individual and which balances the cost to the program of not having his services against any possible risks involved."

Clearly the Gray Board was not confined to the mere performance of a judicial function; its duties lay in the realm of executive discretion, of determining in the broadest sense what would be best for the country. But by the time the hearing had reached its midway mark, the Board had seized upon an ambiguity in the AEC criteria to lighten its burden. Under Robb's guidance it adopted the position that the "over-all common sense judgment" was an administrative matter, to be decided by Nichols, and that it could conscientiously confine itself to determining whether or not Oppenheimer was a security risk.

In its quest for the answer, the Board strayed all too often into irrelevant channels of inquiry. These excursions might have been less objectionable had the odds not been tilted against Oppenheimer from the outset. He was presumed to be unemployable—until he proved the contrary. His access to restricted information was limited. He was not afforded the opportunity to refute the "unevaluated" information in the FBI files, with its usual quotient of mistakes, rumors, and poison-pen accusations. Although he had the singularly good fortune to be confronted with many of the witnesses against him, others remained beyond the reach of cross-examination.

And the Board allowed witnesses, friendly and hostile alike, much greater latitude than its search for truth could conceivably justify. Occasionally, its permissiveness exceeded all reasonable bounds. No one interrupted to challenge former Air Force Chief Scientist David T. Griggs while he rambled through a lengthy and aimless recital of derogatory suppositions, rumors, and hearsay reports about Oppenheimer's loyalty. And no one even commented when he crowned this phase of his testimony with the remarkable admission: "I feel I have no adequate basis for judging Dr. Oppenheimer's loyalty or disloyalty."

Of course, the Board was not bound by any formal rules of evidence, because, as Chairman Gray repeatedly observed, it was conducting an inquiry, not a trial. But this hardly suffices to excuse the acceptance of testimony of this caliber. To be admissible under the AEC's rules, evidence is supposed to have "probative value." Nor was there any excuse for not summoning as witnesses the sources of Griggs's "information."[1] The rules require the Board to make "every reasonable effort . . . to obtain the best evidence reasonably available."

To be sure, the witnesses called on Oppenheimer's behalf were ac-

---

[1] The only one he named, Thomas K. Finletter, later denied that he had made the remarks attributed to him by Griggs, who then admitted that he "did not intend to imply that Mr. Finletter had concluded that Dr. Oppenheimer was disloyal."

corded equal latitude, and the combined weight of their testimony was enormously impressive. It might have gained the day for Oppenheimer had Robb only shared the Board's solemn conviction that it was engaged in an impartial investigation. In his handling of the AEC's case, Robb displayed the unrelenting zeal of an ambitious prosecuting attorney. Fairly typical of his trial tactics is this passage in which he wields a tar brush on Dr. Hans Bethe:

Q. Doctor, how many divisions were there at Los Alamos?
A. It changed somewhat in the course of time. As far as I could count the other day, there were seven . . .
Q. Which division was Klaus Fuchs in?
A. He was in my division, which was the Theoretical Division.
MR. ROBB. Thank you. That is all.

In fairness to Robb, it must be said that his task was unusually formidable. Oppenheimer's roster of witnesses included five former AEC commissioners and ten members and ex-members of the GAC. Such luminaries as Vannevar Bush, James B. Conant, Gordon Dean, Enrico Fermi, George F. Kennan, David Lilienthal, John von Neumann, and Isadore I. Rabi formed an unbroken phalanx in their defense of Oppenheimer's loyalty and integrity; while Robb was able to muster up a mere handful of intelligence officers and H-bomb-oriented scientists, only one of whom possessed comparable stature.

That one was Edward Teller, a maverick in the scientific community since the early days at Los Alamos. Assigned to Bethe's Theoretical Division there, he had displayed a marked tendency to stray from the lines of research assigned to Bethe's group in order to pursue the original and often brilliant intuitions hatched by his own restless brain. Oppenheimer had finally succumbed to his idiosyncrasies and given him a free hand to work on projects of his own choosing, with little or no relation to immediate wartime needs. This move created a vacuum which was filled by importing scientists from England—including, as fate would have it, one Klaus Fuchs.

Popularly regarded as father of the H-bomb, Teller pictured Oppenheimer as committed to the stillbirth of that weapon. And his final pronouncement on the issue before the Board must have been all the more persuasive because it was couched in such modest and judicious terms:

I believe, and that is merely a matter of belief and there is no expertness, no real information behind it, that Dr. Oppenheimer's character is such that he would not knowingly and willingly do anything that is designed to endanger the safety of this country. To the extent, therefore, that your question is directed toward intent, I would say I do not see any reason to deny clearance.

If it is a question of wisdom and judgment, as demonstrated by actions since 1945, then I would say one would be wiser not to grant clearance. I must say that I am myself a little bit confused on this issue, particularly as it refers to a person of Oppenheimer's prestige and influence.

Sincere as Teller's opinion undoubtedly was, it could not have done more damage had it been composed by an accomplished industrial board-room politician.

Oppenheimer, on the other hand, came off rather poorly as a witness in his own behalf. His ill-disguised impatience with the proceedings and his obvious distaste for reviewing his past indiscretions could not have been congenial to the members of the Board. And he proved less than a match for the bulldog Robb. His remarkable articulacy and his prodigious powers of persuasion failed him repeatedly under Robb's withering cross-examination. He sat tongue-tied while Robb wrung the last ounce of invidious inference from the unpalatable records of the men he had befriended, the women he had loved, the organizations he had supported, the young scientists he had helped along the way. All too often Oppenheimer was tripped up on questions of fact—trivial in themselves, but inflicting cumulative harm on his case. Apart from the normal incidence of faulty recollection, it sometimes seemed that these slips were the upshot of sheer inattention, as though his mind had wandered far from the hearing room, far from the nagging vagaries of the security system.

In the final analysis, it was his attitude toward that very security system that brought Oppenheimer to grief. Standing alone, the Chevalier affair might have been dismissed as a quixotic attempt to do his duty with a minimum of harm to himself and his friend. But there were other incidents which tended to support a less charitable interpretation.

Back in 1943 Oppenheimer had told Colonel Lansdale that he was not sure that he knew a Communist Party functionary named Rudy Lambert. At the hearing he admitted that prior to that time he had seen Lambert on at least half a dozen occasions and had lunched with him once or twice to discuss Oppenheimer's contributions to the Spanish Loyalists.

Even more baffling was Oppenheimer's behavior in the case of Giovanni Rossi Lomanitz, a former student of his at the University of California. This brilliant physicist was working at the Berkeley Laboratory under Lawrence when word came in the summer of 1943 that he was about to be drafted into the Army. Lawrence "yelled and screamed" over the loss of one of his key men, according to Lansdale, and Oppen-

heimer took up the cudgels for Lomanitz. After Lansdale told Oppenheimer that Lomanitz was still actively engaged in Communist Party
activities and had been "guilty of indiscretions which could not be overlooked," Oppenheimer had a talk with the young man. He found
Lomanitz defiant and intractable, and told Groves in mid-September
that he regretted his part in sponsoring Lomanitz and wanted nothing
further to do with him.

Yet by October 19, Oppenheimer was forwarding to Lansdale Lomanitz' application to return to the Berkeley Laboratory with the comment that while he could not endorse the request "in an absolute way,"
he considered Lomanitz "a man of real value whose technical service
we should make every effort to secure for the project."

Time did not cure Oppenheimer of this sort of inconstancy. In 1949
he testified before the House Un-American Activities Committee concerning Dr. Bernard Peters, of the University of Rochester. Oppenheimer told the Committee that Peters had been a member of the
German Communist Party, but had denounced it after arriving in this
country as "not sufficiently dedicated to the overthrow of government
by force and violence." (!) The story leaked to the Rochester papers,
and Peters promptly denied the charges. Some of his fellow scientists
complained to Oppenheimer that he had allowed himself to be used as
an instrument of injustice. Oppenheimer promptly wrote to the newspapers attesting Peters' loyalty and recanting his testimony before the
Committee on the strength of Peters' denial.

Robb gave Oppenheimer a hard time over this incident; and later
on Board Chairman Gray reverted to it:

Q. . . . In writing that letter, which perhaps was motivated by a desire
not to hurt the individual or to make restitution—
A. . . . I think it was wholly a question of public things. Personal things
were not involved. He was a good scientist doing, according to everyone's
account, no political work of any kind, doing no harm, whatever his views.
It was overwhelming belief (*sic*) of the community in which I lived that a
man like that ought not to be fired either for his past or for his views, unless
the past is criminal or the views lead him to wicked action. I think my effort
was to compose the flap that I had produced in order that he could stay on
and that this was not a question of my anguish about what I was doing to
him.

Gallant as this about-face may have been, if Oppenheimer was unsure of his ground, he had no more right to tell the House investigators
that Dr. Peters had been a Communist than to tell the press precisely
the opposite a few days later.

What Oppenheimer would have done had his damaging testimony

against Peters not been made public, engendering pressure from his scientific colleagues, remains an open question. To judge from his behavior toward Chevalier, he might well have held his tongue. Long after his disclosures to the FBI barred Chevalier from academic posts in the United States, Oppenheimer concealed from his friend the part he had played in destroying him. Although the two men enjoyed a warm reunion in Paris late in 1953, and had corresponded with each other in the meantime, Chevalier was not to learn the secret of his banishment until the charges against Oppenheimer were published.[2]

The Chevalier episode, as it unfolded at the hearing, was tenaciously exploited by Robb to deprive Oppenheimer of his last vestige of credibility. Nichols had simply taxed Oppenheimer with tardy reporting to the proper authorities and with refusing to identify Chevalier until ordered to do so. But Robb perceived the inherent contradiction between Oppenheimer's contention that the contact had been essentially innocent and his lurid story to Pash implicating three unnamed scientists in place of himself. Robb whipsawed Oppenheimer with this inconsistency, suggesting that his first report had been accurate and that his sworn statements to the FBI and to the Board were sheer fabrications.

Oppenheimer stoutly maintained that the later version was correct; the story he had given Pash was a "tissue of lies." The explanation? "I was an idiot," confessed the paragon of American scientists.

Robb took the tack that these episodes demonstrated a tendency in Oppenheimer to place loyalty to his friends above loyalty to his country. By this adroit maneuver he suggested that the ties of friendship might be strong enough to induce Oppenheimer to betray national secrets, although he surely recognized that none of the evidence supported this inference. He had evidently despaired quite early in the game of proving that Oppenheimer was pro-Soviet; but by hammering away at the theme of loyalty he was able to indoctrinate the Board with one of the prime tenets of the McCarthy credo: those who aren't with us are against us.

Being "with us," in this context, meant wholehearted and active enlistment in the campaign against subversion. In the lexicon of the Congressional investigations of the period, mere obedience to security regulations was not enough; those who declined to serve as beaters in the spy hunt were presumed to be security risks themselves.

This elastic conception had not been adopted, up to the time of the Oppenheimer hearing, in any formal standards for security board inquiries; but Robb was not headed off either by the Board or by Oppenheimer's counsel.

2 Chevalier has since denied Oppenheimer's account, as has Eltenton.

Emboldened by his success, he carried his thesis one step further, as he led the Board through the jungle of the H-bomb controversy of 1949.

The Nichols letter charged Oppenheimer with opposition to the "super" both before and after the President gave a green light to its production. Not only had Oppenheimer withheld his own co-operation, according to Nichols, but he had persuaded others to do so and had "definitely slowed down its development."

Nichols apparently considered Oppenheimer's stand on the H-bomb relevant only to the issue of loyalty. But Robb seized the reins and introduced a completely novel test of reliability into the security field: that dissent from the prevailing view signifies a fatal defect of character warranting discharge from public employment.

Two AEC members and three other members of the GAC confirmed Oppenheimer's testimony that in 1949 he had simply declined to recommend a "crash program" on the thermonuclear bomb in the belief that it would impede the development of fission weapons. And there was ample proof that Oppenheimer had changed his mind when Teller and his associates demonstrated the feasibility of the H-bomb in 1951. In rebuttal, Robb pounded away at the political annexes to the GAC report, pathetically ineffectual when written, and even more so by 1954, with the world's two great powers locked in deadly thermonuclear embrace.

Close to a third of the 3000-page transcript of the proceedings was devoted to the H-bomb issue, and when the case finally limped to a close after three weeks of testimony, it was the decisive factor in the Board's recommendation that Oppenheimer be jettisoned.

By a two-to-one vote, Dr. Evans dissenting, the Board held that Oppenheimer's failure to lend "enthusiastic support" to the H-bomb program following the President's decision raised a doubt "as to whether his future participation, if characterized by the same attitudes in a program relating to the national defense, would be clearly consistent with the best interests of security." Although Oppenheimer was "a loyal citizen," and had a "high degree of discretion reflecting an unusual ability to keep to himself vital secrets," he was found wanting in "understanding, acceptance, and enthusiastic support" of the security system, as evidenced by the Chevalier, Peters, and similar cases.

Dr. Evans' vigorous dissent expressed deep concern about "the effect an improper decision may have on the scientific development in our country." Not without cause; the scientific community was already up in arms over the implications of the case. With the publication of the majority opinion, with its alarming insistence upon enthusiasm for executive policy, even those who were not particularly friendly to Oppenheimer joined in the chorus of protest. While Gray and Morgan had taken note of this wave of unrest, they contented themselves with scolding scientists who "misapprehend their own duties and obligations as citizens." Nevertheless, many a loyal and law-abiding scientist undertook a fresh appraisal of his future in government service.

Oppenheimer waived his right of appeal to the Personnel Security Review Board from the findings and recommendation of the Gray Board. His contract as an AEC consultant had only a month to run, and he apparently feared that if the case were not speeded into the hands of the AEC, his term would simply be allowed to expire without a final determination by the Commission.

A day before the deadline the Commission rendered its decision. Strauss wrote the majority opinion, speaking for himself and two other commissioners, although both of them filed concurring opinions of their own. Oppenheimer was held to have fallen short of the "exemplary standards of reliability, self-discipline, and trustworthiness" required of an outstanding public servant, by reason of his "persistent and willful disregard of the obligations of security." His obstruction of inquiries by security officials, his falsehoods and evasions, were spelled out in detail, with the Chevalier affair weighing most heavily against him:

It is not clear today whether the account Dr. Oppenheimer gave to Colonel Pash in 1943 . . . or the story he told the Gray Board last month is the true version.

If Dr. Oppenheimer lied in 1943, as he now says he did, he committed the crime of knowingly making false and material statements to a federal officer. If he lied to the Board, he committed perjury in 1954.[8]

Nor did the majority take kindly to Oppenheimer's suspect associations, pointing out that he had admittedly been a fellow traveler until 1942 and had continued to see Chevalier as late as December 1953.

The Gray Board's finding that Oppenheimer had been both loyal and close-mouthed was left undisturbed by the three commissioners. But in a concurring opinion, Thomas E. Murray held adherence to the security system to be synonymous with loyalty, and on this score flatly labeled Oppenheimer disloyal.

The sole dissenter, Henry DeWolf Smyth, rejected the Thomist absolutes invoked by Murray. Referring to the "common sense" standard

[8] Five years later Strauss was denied confirmation as Secretary of Commerce by a Senate Committee which indicated that he had been less than candid in his responses to its questions about his conduct as Chairman of the AEC.

imposed on the Commission, Smyth reduced the issue to its least common denominator:

I would suggest that the system itself is nothing to worship. It is a necessary means to an end. . . . If a man protects the secrets he has in his hands and his head, he has shown essential regard for the security system.

Divided as the five Commissioners were over the question of security, they found themselves in unanimous agreement on the H-bomb question. Rejecting the position of the Gray Board, they dismissed it out of hand, perhaps in response to the mounting volume of protests against the suppression of freedom of conscience and opinion implicit in the Board's decision.

But any hope that this concession would assuage the fear and resentment that were ravaging the ranks of science was doomed to disappointment. If freedom of conscience and freedom of opinion were tolerable in relation to the building of the nation's arsenal, why should not equal latitude be permitted in the area of security? What man could consider himself safe from reprisal if he had associated with a "security risk" named Oppenheimer? Or if he chose to continue to do so in the face of the Commission's ruling?

Oppenheimer, asked to comment on the decision, said he had nothing to add to Smyth's opinion. But the liberal press had much to add, and in scientific and academic circles the reaction was vocal and rancorous. Dire predictions were voiced from all sides that many of the best brains in the country would shun government employ.

It is, of course, impossible to estimate the damage attributable to the sense of outrage and oppression felt in hundreds of government and university laboratories, and echoed in scientific and lay journals for months after the story had left the front pages of the newspapers. But if the measure to be applied to the Commission's decision is what is best for the country, no precise calculation of the harm it inflicted is necessary. Within the span of a decade, a handful of men demonstrated the practicability of controlled nuclear fission, developed the atom bomb, and mastered the mysteries of thermonuclear reactions. In the face of the acknowledged capacities of Russian science, which course entailed the greater risk—the retention of Oppenheimer or the disaffection of a single scientist whose ingenuity might represent the margin of superiority in the contest between East and West?

Still, in the climate prevailing at the time of the hearings, the myopia of the Gray Board and of the Atomic Energy Commission may be understood, even excused. Oppenheimer's record was marred by more than one instance of intellectual arrogance and downright prevarication.

Charged by the security system with predicting whether his future conduct would be "clearly consistent with the interests of the national security," it is understandable that they should have been assailed by doubt.

But they had adjudged Oppenheimer loyal to his country, and in his eleven years of government service he had never broken the seal of official silence. All things considered, it may be suggested that the Board's ritualistic concept of security, as applied in his case, left the nation less secure than ever. It may well have been the superfluous brush stroke that ruined the painting.

The qualities which make for a good public servant—intelligence, imagination, and initiative—often manifest themselves in ways that would guarantee a failing mark in a security investigation. The more rigid the nation's standards become, the more likely it is that sensitive government posts will be filled by faceless and spiritless men whose principal qualification is orthodoxy. The survival of a free society may well depend on its ability to achieve security without sterility.

The pertinent excerpts from the testimony reproduced below display Oppenheimer at his best and at his worst. He is far from his articulate and self-possessed self when accounting for his own conduct, but completely in command of the situation when abstract or scientific subjects are under consideration.

The reflections of the other pro-Oppenheimer witnesses on the problems of loyalty and national security within the framework of the cold war ranged from the intensely subjective to the philosophical and are exemplified here in the testimony of Rabi, Pike, and Kennan. The caliber of the witnesses for the AEC, except for scientists like Alvarez and Teller, was typified by Griggs, whose appearance in the following pages is supplemented in the text.

APRIL 14, 1954
J. ROBERT OPPENHEIMER, CROSS-EXAMINATION

Q. Now let us go back to your interview with Colonel Pash. Did you tell Pash the truth about this thing?

A. No.

Q. You lied to him?

A. Yes.

Q. What did you tell Pash that was not true?

A. That Eltenton had attempted to approach members of the project—three members of the project—through intermediaries.

Q. What else did you tell him that wasn't true?

A. That is all I really remember.

Q. That is all? Did you tell Pash that Eltenton had attempted to approach three members of the project—

A. Through intermediaries.

Q. Intermediaries?

A. Through an intermediary.

Q. So that we may be clear, did you discuss with or disclose to Pash the identity of Chevalier?

A. No.

Q. Let us refer, then, for the time being, to Chevalier as X.

A. All right.

Q. Did you tell Pash that X had approached three persons on the project?

A. I am not clear whether I said there were three X's or that X approached three people.

Q. Didn't you say that X had approached three people?

A. Probably.

Q. Why did you do that, Doctor?

A. Because I was an idiot.

Q. Is that your only explanation, Doctor?

A. I was reluctant to mention Chevalier.

Q. Yes.

A. No doubt somewhat reluctant to mention myself.

Q. Yes. But why would you tell him that Chevalier had gone to three people?

A. I have no explanation for that except the one already offered.

Q. Didn't that make it all the worse for Chevalier?

A. I didn't mention Chevalier.

Q. No; but X.

A. It would have.

Q. Certainly. In other words, if X had gone to three people that would have shown, would it not—

A. That he was deeply involved.

Q. That he was deeply involved. That it was not just a casual conversation.

A. Right.

Q. And you knew that, didn't you?

A. Yes.

Q. Did you tell Colonel Pash that X had spoken to you about the use of microfilm?

A. It seems unlikely. You have a record, and I will abide by it.

Q. Did you?

A. I don't remember.

Q. If X had spoken to you about the use of microfilm, that would have shown definitely that he was not an innocent contact?

A. It certainly would.

401

Q. Did you tell Colonel Pash that X had told you that the information would be transmitted through someone at the Russian consulate?

(*There was no response.*)

Q. Did you?

A. I would have said not, but I clearly see that I must have.

Q. If X had said that, that would have shown conclusively that it was a criminal conspiracy, would it not?

A. That is right.

Q. Did Pash ask you for the name of X?

A. I imagine he did.

Q. Don't you know he did?

A. Sure.

Q. Did he tell you why he wanted it?

A. In order to stop the business.

Q. He told you that it was a very serious matter, didn't he?

A. I don't recollect that, but he certainly would have.

Q. You knew that he wanted to investigate it, did you not?

A. That is right.

Q. And didn't you know that your refusal to give the name of X was impeding the investigation?

A. In actual fact I think the only person that needed watching or should have been watched was Eltenton. But as I concocted the story that did not emerge.

Q. That was your judgment?

A. Yes.

Q. But you knew that Pash wanted to investigate this?

A. Yes.

Q. And didn't you know, Doctor, that by refusing to give the name of X you were impeding the investigation?

A. I must have known that.

Q. You know now, don't you?

A. Well, actually—

Q. You must have known it then?

A. Actually the only important thing to investigate was Eltenton.

Q. What did Pash want to investigate?

A. I suppose the three people on the project.

Q. You knew, didn't you, Doctor, that Colonel Pash and his organization would move heaven and earth to find out those three people, didn't you?

A. It makes sense.

Q. And you knew that they would move heaven and earth to find out the identity of X, didn't you?

A. Yes.

Q. And yet you wouldn't tell them?

A. That is true.

Q. So you knew you were impeding them, didn't you?

A. That is right. . . .

Q. Let us move along to your interview with Colonel Lansdale on September 12.

A. Right.

Q. Did you tell him substantially the same story you told Colonel Pash?

A. I don't know whether he repeated it to me or I repeated it to him.

Q. In all events, if he repeated it to you—

A. I did not modify it.

Q. You affirmed it as the truth?

A. Yes.

Q. So you lied to him, too?

A. That is right.

Q. Did he plead with you to give him the name of X?

A. He did.

Q. Did he explain why he wanted that name?

A. I suppose he did. I don't remember.

Q. You knew why he did?

A. It didn't need explanation.

Q. Did he explain to you that either X or Eltenton might have continued to make other contacts?

A. This would have been a reasonable thing to say.

Q. Did you give him the name of X?

A. No. . . .

Q. Why did you go into such great circumstantial detail about this thing if you were telling a cock-and-bull story?

A. I fear that this whole thing is a piece of idiocy. I am afraid I can't explain why there was a consul, why there was microfilm, why there were three people on the project, why two of them were at Los Alamos. All of them seem wholly false to me.

Q. You will agree, would you not, sir, that if the story you told to Colonel Pash was true, it made things look very bad for Mr. Chevalier?

A. For anyone involved in it, yes, sir.

Q. Including you?

A. Right.

Q. Isn't it a fair statement today, Dr. Oppenheimer, that according to your testimony now you told not one lie to Colonel Pash, but a whole fabrication and tissue of lies?

A. Right.

Q. In great circumstantial detail, is that correct?

A. Right. . . .

APRIL 16, 1954

OPPENHEIMER CROSS-EXAMINATION, CONTINUED

Q. . . . Would you agree that you are or were the most experienced, most powerful, and most effective member of the opposition to the hydrogen bomb?

A. What time are we talking about?

Q. At any time.

A. Well, I would say I was not the most powerful, I was not the most experienced, and I was not the most influential. But, if you take all three factors together, perhaps I combined a little more experience, a little more power, and a little more of influence than anyone else.

Q. At what time?

A. I am thinking of the period between the Russian test and the President's decision.

Q. How about after the President's decision?

A. There was not any opposition to the hydrogen bomb.

Q. Weren't you still opposed to the development of the hydrogen bomb?

A. No. . . .

Q. Beginning in 1942 and running through at least the first year or the first meeting of the GAC, you were actively and consciously pushing the development of the thermonuclear bomb, weren't you? Isn't that your testimony?

A. Pushing is not the right word. Supporting and working on it, yes.

Q. Yes. When did these moral qualms become so strong that you opposed the development of the thermonuclear bomb?

A. When it was suggested that it be the policy of the United States to make these things at all costs, without regard to the balance between these weapons and atomic weapons as a part of our arsenal.

Q. What did moral qualms have to do with that?

A. What did moral qualms have to do with it?

Q. Yes, sir.

A. We freely used the atomic bomb.

Q. In fact, Doctor, you testified, did you not, that you assisted in selecting the target for the drop of the bomb on Japan?

A. Right.

Q. You knew, did you not, that the dropping of that atomic bomb on the target you had selected would kill or injure thousands of civilians, is that correct?

A. Not as many as turned out.

Q. How many were killed or injured?

A. 70,000.

Q. Did you have moral scruples about that?

A. Terrible ones.

Q. But you testified the other day, did you not, sir, that the bombing of Hiroshima was very successful?

A. Well, it was technically successful.

Q. Oh, technically.

A. It is also alleged to have helped end the war.

Q. Would you have supported the dropping of a thermonuclear bomb on Hiroshima?

A. It would make no sense at all.

Q. Why.

A. The target is too small. . . .

Q. Doctor, is it a fair summary of your answer—and I refer you to page 37 and the following pages of your answer—that what the GAC opposed in its October 29, 1949, meeting was merely a crash program for the development of the super?

A. Yes. I think it would be a better summary to say we opposed this crash program as the answer to the Soviet atomic bomb.

Q. What did you mean by a crash program?

A. On the basis of what was then known, that a plant be built, equipment be procured and a commitment be made to build this thing irrespective of further study and with a very high priority. A program in which alternatives would not have an opportunity to be weighed because one had to get on and because we were not going to sacrifice time. . . .

MR. GRAY. Your deep concern about the use of the hydrogen bomb, if it were developed, and therefore your own views at the time as to whether we should proceed in a crash program to develop it—your concern about this—became greater, did it not, as the practicabilities became more clear? Is that an unfair statement?

THE WITNESS. I think it is the opposite of true. Let us not say about use. But my feeling about development became quite different when the practicabilities became clear. When I saw how to do it, it was clear to me that one had to at least make the thing. Then the only problem was what would one do about them when one had them. The program we had in 1949 was a tortured thing that you could well argue did not make a great deal of technical sense. It was therefore possible to argue also that you did not want it even if you could have it. The program in 1951 was technically so sweet that you could not argue about that. It was purely the military, the political, and the humane problem of what you were going to do about it once you had it. . . .

APRIL 20, 1954
GEORGE F. KENNAN, DIRECT EXAMINATION

Q. As a result of your experience with Dr. Oppenheimer in the cases that you have reference to, what convictions, if any, did you form about him?

A. I formed the conviction that he was an immensely useful person in the councils of our government, and I felt a great sense of gratitude that we had his help. I am able to say that in the course of all these contacts and deliberations within the government I never observed anything in his conduct or his words that could possibly, it seemed to me, have indicated that he was animated by any other motives than a devotion to the interests of this country. . . .

q. An incident is referred to in 1943, in which it is said that an approach was somehow connected with a possible effort by the Russians to secure information or to secure information in their behalf, and that for some months thereafter he failed to report this incident.

What effect does that failure on his part, which he freely admits was wrong, have on your present thinking about it?

A. Mr. Marks, I have testified about him here as I have known him. I can well understand that at earlier periods in his life conflicts of conscience might have arisen, as I think they could with any sensitive person, between his feelings about his friends—perhaps his pity for them—and his governmental duties. On the other hand, I would also be inclined to bear in mind the fact that in 1943 the Soviet Union was hardly regarded by our top people in our government as an enemy. That great masses of American materials were being prepared for shipment to the Soviet Union, many of them I assume involving the transmission of official secrets. I could imagine that the implications of this may not at that time have appeared to be so sinister as they do today in retrospect, and I could also imagine if after all the information was not given in this particular instance, the man in question might have felt that no damage had been done to the government interest, and that the question of the men who had initiated such a request might be better perhaps left to their own consciences and to the process of maturity in their own development.

I don't know. I can imagine those things. For that reason I would hesitate to make definite judgments on the basis simply of what I read in the letter of indictment.

q. Would it change your opinion if I were to suggest to you that when Dr. Oppenheimer did report this incident to security officers on his own initiative, as it turned out, he didn't tell them everything about it. He still withheld the name of the friend and told them a story that was not the whole truth.

A. Mr. Marks, I do not think that that would alter anything on the statement that I just made prior to your question. I might only add to it that I could well conceive that Dr. Oppenheimer might have done things which he would think in retrospect were mistakes or which others would conclude in retrospect were mistakes, but that would not preclude in his own instance any more than it would in the case of any of the others the process of growth and the ability to recognize mistakes and to learn from them and to make fewer in the future. What I have said about his activities, his personality, the cast of his mind during the years when I knew him would, I think, not be affected.

q. These convictions that you have expressed about him, the confidence that you have expressed in him, what part is played in that judgment by the experience that you had as a Soviet expert?

406

A. I think a considerable part. One of the convictions that I have carried away from such experience as I have had with these matters in the field of Soviet work concerning the Soviet Union is that these things cannot really be judged in a fully adequate way without looking at the man as an entirety. That is, I am skeptical about any security processes that attempt to sample different portions of a man's nature separate from his whole being. I must say as one who has seen Robert Oppenheimer now over the course of several years, and more latterly outside of government, that I have these feelings and entertain them on the basis of my estimate of his personality and his character as a whole.

Q. Are they feelings or are they convictions?

A. They are on my part convictions, sir. . . .

GEORGE F. KENNAN, CROSS-EXAMINATION

MR. GRAY. If you were today director of the policy planning staff and there came to you from a staff member or from some other source, perhaps even the Secretary of State, that a certain individual had been made a member of the policy planning staff who had had close Communist associations as late as the late Thirties or perhaps early Forties, would you seriously consider adding such a person to your staff today?

THE WITNESS. It would depend, Mr. Chairman, on what I would think were his possibilities for contribution to the staff and to what extent the negative points on his record had been balanced out by a record of constructive achievement and loyalty. . . .

MR. GRAY. So I gather that you feel that perhaps the application of individual judgment increases with the stature and importance of the individual concerned. That is perhaps not a clear question.

THE WITNESS. I do feel this, that the really gifted and able people in government are perhaps less apt than the others to have had a fully conventional life and a fully conventional entry, let us say, into their governmental responsibilities. For that reason I think that while their cases have to be examined with particular care, obviously for the reasons of the great responsibilities they bear and the capabilities for damage in case one makes a mistake, nevertheless it is necessary to bear in mind in many cases, especially people who have great intellectual attainments—because those attainments often it seems to me do not always come by the most regular sort of experience in life, they are often the result of a certain amount of buffeting, and a certain amount of trial and error, and a certain amount of painful experience—I think that has to be borne in mind when one uses people of that sort. . . .

MR. GRAY. You in your testimony referred to the possible conflicts of conscience a man might have and you used the expression, I think, pity for friends who perhaps have been misguided. I am not sure those were the words, but the general import. . . .

Would you feel continued association with individuals falling in this category, for whom one would have pity and with respect to whom one might have had conflicts of conscience, was important at all in the situation?

THE WITNESS. I would think, Mr. Chairman, that it is a thing which would have to be explained, but I find great difficulty in accepting the belief that a man must rule out all those associations, whether or not they engage in any way his official responsibilities. I think there are certainly times when they are to be avoided. I suppose most of us have had friends or associates whom we have come to regard as misguided with the course of time, and I don't like to think that people in senior capacity in government should not be permitted or conceded maturity of judgment to know when they can see such a person or when they can't. If they come to you sometimes, I think it is impossible for you to turn them away abruptly or in a cruel way, simply because you are afraid of association with them, so long as what they are asking of you is nothing that affects your governmental work.

I myself say it is a personal view on the part of Christian charity to try to be at least as decent as you can to them.

I realize that it is not advisable for a man in a position of high security to be seen steadily with people about whose loyalty there is a great doubt, unless they happen to be intimates in his family or something like that. . . .

MR. GRAY. I would like to move back to the question of your attitudes toward the development of the hydrogen bomb in the period before the President's decision to proceed in January of 1950. Had you been told, Mr. Kennan, in 1949, for example, by a scientist whose judgment and capability you respected, that it was probable that a thermonuclear weapon could be developed which would be more economical in terms of the use of material and cost and the rest of it than the equivalent number of atom bombs, would you have then been in favor of developing the hydrogen bomb?

THE WITNESS. I would not have favored developing it at least until a real decision had been made in this government about the role which atomic weapons were to play generally in its arsenal of weapons. I would have had great doubts then about the soundness of doing it. That comes from philosophic considerations partly, which I exposed to the Secretary of State, which did not, I might say, meet with his agreement or with that of most of my colleagues, and the future will have to tell, but it seemed to me at the end of this atomic weapons race, if you pursued it to the end—we building all we can build, they building all they can build—stands the dilemma, which is the mutually destructive quality of these weapons, and . . . the public mind will not entertain the dilemma, and people will take refuge in irrational and unsuitable ideas as to what to do.

For that reason I have always had the greatest misgivings about the attempt to insure the security of this country by an unlimited race in the cultivation of these weapons of mass destruction and have felt that the best we could do in a world where no total security is possible is to hold just enough of these things to make it a very foolish thing for the Russians or anybody else to try to use them against us.

MR. GRAY. So you would have been in favor of stopping production of the A-bomb after we had reached a certain point with respect to the stockpile?

THE WITNESS. That is correct. . . .

MR. GRAY. . . . . You had a serious question about proceeding with the hydrogen bomb. No question that we should have done what we did with respect to the development of the atom bomb.

Is the different attitude on this due to the fact that perhaps an atom bomb properly placed could take care of a target and that a larger bomb would be unnecessarily large? Is it size? Is that the distinction you make? Is it because the civilian population may be involved more deeply?

THE WITNESS. It is because of the wonder on my part as to whether we did not already have enough of this sort of terrible ability to commit destruction. At least I had not seen it proven to me that we needed more perhaps. Perhaps there again, with some of us civilians, it becomes hard for us to absorb the mathematics of destruction involved in these things. To my mind the regular old bomb made a big enough bang, as big as anybody could want. I found it difficult—you see what has worried me, Mr. Chairman, about going ahead with this is that we would come to think of our security as embraced solely in the mathematics of whatever power of destruction we could evolve, and we would forget our security lies still very largely in our ability to address ourselves to the positive and constructive problems of world affairs, to create confidence in other people.

I am convinced that the best way to keep our allies around us is not to pay outwardly too much attention to the atomic weapons and to the prospect of war, but to come forward ourselves with plans that envisage the constructive and peaceful progress of humanity. I realize that while we do that we have to preserve an extremely alert and powerful defense posture at all times. But I believe in preserving that posture to the maximum, and talking about it to the minimum, and then limiting ourselves in our foreign policy primarily to the constructive rather than negative objectives.

I have feared that if we get launched on a program that says the only thing we are concerned to do in the development of atomic weapons is to get as much as possible as rapidly as possible, that the attentions of the public and the government will become riveted to that task at the expense of our ability to conduct ourselves profitably in positive aspects of foreign policy. That has been the nature of my worry.

I have never felt a great degree of certainty about this and I have always realized it was a very difficult problem. But it did seem to me at that time, and it seems to me still in retrospect, that one could doubt the desirability of going ahead with this weapon then from motives which were very serious and respectable motives. In other words, one could doubt it out of a devotion to the interests of our country. At least I feel that I did. . . .

DAVID E. LILIENTHAL, DIRECT EXAMINATION

Q. As a result of your experience with Dr. Oppenheimer and your knowledge of him, have you formed an opinion as to his loyalty, his integrity, his character, all the other factors that go into forming a judgment as to his loyalty, security?

A. Yes, I have.

Q. What is your opinion?

A. I have no shadow of a doubt in my mind that here is a man of good character, integrity, and of loyalty to his country.

Q. How would you assess him as a security risk?

A. I did not regard him up until the time my knowledge of the program ceased, and had no occasion to regard him, as a security risk.

Q. I think you already indicated that in March 1947 you consciously assayed the situation and came to the conclusion that he was not a security risk?

A. Yes. At that time we had this file before us and that was my conclusion, that in the light of the over-all picture, taking everything into account, the minus signs were very few indeed, and the plus signs very great indeed, and I thought he was a contribution to the security of the country. I have had no occasion since that time to change that view.

Q. Has your experience with him confirmed that view?

A. My experience from that time did confirm that view. I am sure that it is clear that he has made great contributions to the security of the country. . . .

SUMNER T. PIKE, DIRECT EXAMINATION

Q. . . . You served on the Atomic Energy Commission from 1946 to the end of 1951, did you not?

A. Exactly to December 15, 1951. . . .

Q. You have read the Commission's letter of December 23, 1953, which initiated these proceedings, containing the derogatory information about Dr. Oppenheimer?

A. Yes, I read the New York Times, which I take it gave the full letter.

Q. On the basis of your knowledge of Dr. Oppenheimer and your experiences with him, what is your opinion as to his loyalty?

A. I never had any question about his loyalty. I think he is a man of essential integrity. I think he has been a fool several times, but there was nothing in there that shook my feeling. As a matter of fact, it was a pretty good summary, it seemed to me, of the material that was turned over to us early in 1947 by the FBI, all except the last thing about the hydrogen bomb. Of course, that was not in then.

Q. The letter and, I assume, the file contained data about past associations of his.

A. Yes.

Q. In your judgment is his character and the associations of the past and his loyalty such that, if he were to continue to have access to restricted data, he would not endanger the common defense or security?

A. No, I don't think he would endanger the common defense or security the least bit.

Q. You read about the Chevalier incident in the Commission's letter and Dr. Oppenheimer's answer?

A. Yes. . . .

Q. Do you want to say why it wouldn't alter your opinion?

A. I think it was a bad incident. Taken alone it would have bothered me very much. I suspect I have been party to incidents in my life that I'd rather not have, certainly, taken out of context. This, woven into the context, however, of performance under close observation of him, many years and achievements of such size as to warrant the gratitude of this country, I don't think it should be given much weight at all. . . .

Q. When the question was put to the GAC in Mr. Lilienthal's letter, asking that consideration be given to whether in view of the Soviet success the Commission's program was adequate, and if not, in what way it should be altered or increased, would it or would it not have been a natural outgrowth of that question, considering the times and the discussions that you had, to consider the question of the hydrogen crash program?

A. I think it would have been a natural thing. If you will remember, the hydrogen question had never been dropped. It had been in charge of a small group headed by Ed Teller. Dr. Teller was never one to keep his candles hidden under bushels. He was kind of a missionary. I might say that perhaps John the Baptist is a little overexaggeration. He always felt that this program had not had enough consideration. Teller in my view was a pretty single-minded and devoted person. I would guess that it would have suited him completely if we had taken all the resources we had and devoted it to fusion bombs.

He is a very useful and a very fine man, but I always thought he was kind of lopsided, as a good many specialists are. . . .

Q. Just two more questions.

After President Truman gave the go ahead on the H-bomb program, did the GAC, as you recall, co-operate with the government and accept that decision and move forward?

A. Yes. When you say move forward, one has to remember that some of the developments in the early months were quite disappointing. The thing was attacked, I think, wholeheartedly and we were not happy, not about co-operation, but not happy about the results for some time.

Q. Did Dr. Oppenheimer, so far as you yourself knew, do anything to delay or obstruct the program?

411

A. Oh, no; rather the reverse. . . .

DR. ISADORE I. RABI, DIRECT EXAMINATION

Q. Dr. Rabi, what is your present occupation?

A. I am the Higgins professor of physics at Columbia University.

Q. What official positions do you have with the government? . . .

A. At present as chairman of the General Advisory Committee, as successor to Dr. Oppenheimer. I am a member of the Scientific Advisory Committee to ODM, which is also supposed to in some way advise the President of the United States.

I am a member of the Scientific Advisory Committee to the Ballistics Research Laboratory at Aberdeen Proving Ground. I am a member of the board of trustees of Associated Universities, Inc., which is responsible for the running of Brookhaven Laboratory. I am a consultant to the Brookhaven National Laboratory. . . .

Q. Dr. Rabi, to what extent has your work as consultant in various capacities in the government overlapped or coincided with work that Dr. Oppenheimer was performing at the same time and in the same general field?

A. Chiefly of course the General Advisory Committee, and also to a degree in project Lincoln, and particularly the summer study of, I believe, 1952.

Q. Summer study where?

A. This was a summer study at Cambridge on the question of continental defense of the United States.

Q. How long have you known Dr. Oppenheimer?

A. I think we first met in the end of 1928 and we got to know one another well in the winter and spring of 1929. I have known him on and off since. We got together very frequently during the war years and since.

Q. Do you know him intimately?

A. I think so, whatever the term may mean. I think I know him quite well. . . .

Q. To the extent that you can tell it without getting into any classified material, what was the outcome of the GAC meeting of October 1949?

A. I will try to give it as best I can.

Q. Let me break it down. First, is it fair to say that the Committee was in agreement with respect or essentially in agreement with respect to the technical factors involved in the thermonuclear situation?

A. It was hard to say whether there was an agreement or not, because what we are talking about was such a vague thing, this object, that I think different people had different thoughts about it. You could just give a sort of horseback thing and say, maybe something would come out in five years. It is that sort of thing. I know in my own case I think I took the dimmest technical view of this, and there are others who were more optimistic.

Q. I think it has been indicated here that there was some statement in the report of the GAC at that time to the effect that it was the opinion that a concerted imaginative effort might produce—that there was a 50–50 chance of success in five years.

MR. ROBB. In the interest of accuracy, I think the report says a better-than-even chance. Let me check it to make sure.

MR. GARRISON. That is correct.

BY MR. MARKS:

Q. Was that supposed to be a consensus of the views?

A. More or less. When you are talking about something as vague as this particular thing, you say a 50–50 chance in five years, where you don't know the kind of physical factors and theory that goes into the problem. I just want to give my own impression that it was a field where we really did not know what we were talking about, except on the basis of general experience. We didn't even know whether this thing contradicted the laws of physics.

Q. You didn't know what?

A. Whether it contradicted the laws of physics.

Q. In other words, it could have been altogether impossible.

A. It could have been altogether impossible. The thing we were talking about. I want to be specific. . . .

Q. After the President announced the decision to go ahead with the hydrogen bomb in January of 1950, what attitude and what steps, if any, did the GAC take with respect to the subject from then on?

A. I think we started talking about the best ways and means to do it. It was a very difficult question, because here is a statement from the President to do something that nobody knew how to do. This was just a ball of wax. So we were really quite puzzled except insofar as to try to get people to go and look at the problem.

Q. In that connection, did the GAC itself try to look into the problem?

A. Insofar as we could; yes. We had people who were quite expert and actually worked on it, chiefly of course Dr. Fermi, who went back to Los Alamos, summers and so on, and took a lot of time with it. So we had a very important expert right on the Committee. Of course, Dr. Oppenheimer knew very well the theoretical questions involved.

Q. Do you think the GAC had any usefulness in helping the work on this particular subject?

A. I think it did; I think it had a great usefulness, some way indirect and some way direct, ways of trying to bring out the solid facts. It is awfully hard to get at those facts. I recall particularly one meeting, I think it was in the summer of 1950 at Los Alamos, I am sure of the dates, where we actually got together all the knowledgeable people we could find—I think Dr. Bethe was there and Fermi—to try to produce some kind of record which would tell us where we stood. . . .

Q. If you can tell, Dr. Rabi, what was the connection or relation between the meeting you have just described at Los Alamos and another meeting that has been testified here which took place, I believe, in 1951, in the late spring at Princeton?

A. That was an entirely different meeting. At that meeting we really got on the beam, because a new invention had occurred. There we had a situation where you really could talk about it. You knew what to calculate and so on, and you were in the realm where you could apply scientific ideas which were not some extrapolation very far beyond the known. This is something which could be calculated, which could be studied, and was an entirely different thing.

Q. Why did it take that long?

A. Just the human mind.

Q. There was the President's directive in January 1950.

A. Why it took this long? One had to get rid of the ideas that were and are probably no good. In other words, there has been all this newspaper stuff about delay. The subject which we discussed in the 1949 meeting, that particular thing, has never been made and probably never will be made, and we still don't know to this day whether something like that will function.

This other thing was something quite different, a much more modest and more definite idea on which one could go. . . .

Q. . . . Do you feel that you know Dr. Oppenheimer well enough to comment on the bearing of his character, loyalty, and associations on this issue?

A. I think Dr. Oppenheimer is a man of upstanding character, that he is a loyal individual, not only to the United States, which of course goes without saying in my mind, but also to his friends and his organizations to which he is attached, let us say, to the institutions, and works very hard for his loyalties; an upright character, very upright character, very thoughtful, sensitive feeling in that respect. . . .

DR. ISADORE I. RABI, CROSS-EXAMINATION

MR. GRAY. I have one other question. You testified very clearly, I think, as to your judgment of Dr. Oppenheimer as a man, referring to his character, his loyalty to the United States, and to his friends and to institutions with which he might be identified, and made an observation about associations.

As of today would you expect Dr. Oppenheimer's loyalty to the country to take precedence over loyalty to an individual or to some other institution?

THE WITNESS. I just don't think that anything is higher in his mind or heart than loyalty to his country. This sort of desire to see it grow and develop. I might amplify my other statement in this respect, and that is something we talked of through the years. When we first met in 1929, American physics was not really very much, certainly not consonant with the great size and wealth of the country. We were very much concerned with raising the level of American physics. We were sick and tired of going to Europe as learners. We wanted to be independent. I must say I think that our generation, Dr. Oppenheimer's and my other friend (*sic*) that I can mention, did that job, and that ten years later we were at the top of the heap, and it wasn't just because certain refugees came out of Germany, but because of what we did here. This was a conscious motivation. Oppenheimer set up this school of theoretical physics, which was a tremendous contribution. In fact, I don't know how we could have carried out the scientific part of the war without the contributions of the people who worked with Oppenheimer. They made their contributions very willingly and very enthusiastically and single-mindedly.

MR. GRAY. Perhaps I could get at my question this way. You are familiar, if you have read the Nichols letter and read the summary of a file which Chairman Strauss handed you, with the Chevalier episode to some extent, I take it.

THE WITNESS. I know of the episode, yes.

MR. GRAY. Would you expect Dr. Oppenheimer today to follow the course of action he followed at that time in 1943?

THE WITNESS. You mean refuse to give information? Is that what you mean?

MR. GRAY. Yes.

THE WITNESS. I certainly do. At the present time I think he would clamp him into jail if he asked such a question.

MR. GRAY. I am sorry.

THE WITNESS. At the present time if a man came to him with a proposal like that, he would see that he goes to jail. At least that is my opinion of what he would do in answer to this hypothetical question.

MR. GRAY. Do you feel that security is relative, that something that was all right in 1943 would not be all right in 1954?

THE WITNESS. If a man in 1954 came with such a proposal, my God—it would be horrifying.

MR. GRAY. Supposing a man came to you in 1943.

THE WITNESS. I would have thrown him out.

MR. GRAY. Would you have done anything more about it?

THE WITNESS. I don't think so. Unless I thought he was just a poor jackass and didn't know what he was doing. But I would try to find out what motivated him and what was behind it, and get after that at any time. If somebody asked me to violate a law and an oath. . . .

MR. GRAY. There have been those who have testified that—men of character and standing and loyalty—that this episode should simply be disregarded. I don't think that is an unfair summary of what some of the witnesses have said. Do you feel that this is just a matter that is of no consequence?

THE WITNESS. I do not think any of it is of no consequence. I think you have to take the matter in its whole context. For example, there are men of unquestioned loyalty who do not know enough of the subject—I am talking now of the atomic energy field—so that in their ordinary speech they don't know what they are saying. They might give away very important things.

MR. GRAY. That would be true of me, I am sure.

THE WITNESS. It certainly has been true of a lot of military stuff that you see published. It makes your hair stand on end to see high officers say, and people in Congress say, some of the things they say. But with a man of Dr. Oppenheimer's knowledge, who knows the thing completely, and its implications and its importance, and the different phases, believing as I do in his fundamental loyalty, I think to whomever he talked he would know how to stay completely clear of sensitive information. . . .

MR. GRAY. . . . So this is all subjective, but would you expect without any real question in your mind that today Dr. Oppenheimer would follow the kind of course that you would approve of today with respect to this matter?

THE WITNESS. I think I can say that with certainty. I think there is no question in my mind of his loyalty in that way. You know there always is a problem of that sort. I mean the world has been divided into sheep and goats. I mean the country has been divided into sheep and goats. There are the people who are cleared and those who are not cleared. The people against whom there has been some derogatory information and what not. What it may mean and so on is difficult. It is really a question in one's personal life, should you refuse to enter a room in which a person is present against whom there is derogatory information. Of course, if you are extremely prudent and want your life circumscribed that way, no question would ever arise. If you feel that you want to live a more normal life and have confidence in your own integrity and in your record for integrity, then you might act more freely, but which could be criticized, either for being foolhardy or even worse.

In one's normal course at a university, one does come across people who have been denied clearance. Should you never sit down and discuss scientific matters with them, although they have very interesting scientific things to say? . . .

MR. GRAY. You are saying that in your judgment Dr. Oppenheimer has changed?

THE WITNESS. He has learned. . . .

DR. ISADORE I. RABI, REDIRECT EXAMINATION

Q. Dr. Rabi, Mr. Robb asked you whether you had spoken to Chairman Strauss in behalf of Dr. Oppenheimer. . . .

A. . . . I never hid my opinion from Mr. Strauss that I thought that this whole proceeding was a most unfortunate one.

DR. EVANS. What was that?

THE WITNESS. That the suspension of the clearance of Dr. Oppenheimer was a very unfortunate thing and should not have been done. In other words, there he was; he is a consultant, and if you don't want to consult the guy, you don't consult him, period. Why you have to then proceed to suspend clearance and go through all this sort of thing, he is only there when called, and that is all there was to it. So it didn't seem to me the sort of thing that called for this kind of proceeding at all against a man who had accomplished what Dr. Oppenheimer has accomplished. There is a real positive record, the way I expressed it to a friend of mine. We have an A-bomb and a whole series of it—and what more do you want, mermaids? This is just a tremendous achievement. If the end of that road is this kind of hearing, which can't help but be humiliating, I thought it was a pretty bad show. I still think so. . . .

APRIL 29, 1954
DAVID T. GRIGGS, CROSS-EXAMINATION

Q. Was that the main object of the Lincoln Summer Study, to find ways to improve our air defense?

A. Yes, sir.

Q. And did the Lincoln Study ever recommend the giving up of any part of our strategic air power?

A. No, not to my knowledge.

Q. I think you have already said, so far as your knowledge goes, Dr. Oppenheimer did not recommend that.

A. That is right. I would like to amplify my answer on that for the benefit of the Board, since this is the first mention of the Summer Study in this much detail.

We were concerned by the thing I have already mentioned, that is, the fear that the Summer Study might get into these things which we regarded as inappropriate for Lincoln, and as of questionable value to the Air Force —I refer to the giving up of our strategic air arm, and the allocation of budget between the Strategic Air Command and the Air Defense Command —but we were also very much concerned in the early days of the formation of the Lincoln Summer Study, because it was being done in such a way that, had it been allowed to go in the direction in which it was initially going, every indication was that it would have wrecked the effectiveness of the Lincoln Laboratory. This was because of the way the thing was, the Summer Study was, being handled administratively.

So far as I know, it was not because of any direct action on the part of Dr. Oppenheimer. On the other hand, I felt at the time that Dr. Oppenheimer should have been well enough informed and alert enough to see that this would be disastrous to the Lincoln Summer Study.

After having reported this to the Secretary of the Air Force, Mr. Finletter, who had been actively concerned with the Summer Study, and had been very much—excuse me, I made a mistake—I said Mr. Finletter had been actively concerned with the Summer Study. I meant to say he had been concerned with project Lincoln. He had been in touch with President Killian, and Provost Stratton of M.I.T. on the prosecution of project Lincoln. So I reported this to Mr. Finletter, and he essentially charged me with trying to find out if the Summer Study was going to be conducted in such a way as to result in a net gain to the effectiveness of Lincoln or a net loss.

If it looked to me as though it were going to be a net loss, I was asked to inform him so that steps could be taken to correct this condition, or to cancel the Summer Study if that were necessary.

I got in touch with Provost Stratton at M.I.T. I found that he hardly knew about the existence of the plan for the Summer Study. He undertook to look into it. I told him the things that worried me and worried Mr. Finletter about it. He did look into it. Some corrective action was taken in terms of discussions with people most involved and in terms of changing the organizational structure by which the Summer Study was to be introduced into the Lincoln project, and at a slightly later date Mr. Killian of M.I.T. called me and told me that he was satisfied partly as a result of the recent activities that he and Dr. Stratton had been engaged in, which I have already mentioned, and that the Lincoln Summer Study would operate to the benefit both of Lincoln and the interests of the Air Force.

He further said, since I had mentioned that one of the things we were afraid of was that the Lincoln Summer Study results might get out of hand, from our standpoint, in the sense that they might be reported directly to higher authority, such as the National Security Council, President Killian reassured me that he had taken steps so that he was sure that the Summer Study would be—I think his words were "kept in bounds."

On the basis of this assurance we had no further—that is, Mr. Finletter, myself, and General Yates, and the other Air Force people—had no further immediate worries about the Summer Study and we encouraged it.

Q. Will you tell us what part did Dr. Oppenheimer play in this?

A. Oppenheimer played the part in it that I have already mentioned, in that the Summer Study, as near as my information goes, was conceived at a meeting at which he was present, that he allowed his name, and I believe encouraged the use of his name, in recruiting for the Lincoln Summer Study. That he was closely associated with the people who were recruiting for the Summer Study and who were preparing its plans. I think that covers the question. . . .

MAY 3, 1954
J. ROBERT OPPENHEIMER, CROSS-EXAMINATION

Q. Let me turn now to the so-called Vista report, about which there has been very considerable testimony and not altogether consistent. Did you in fact prepare a draft of an introduction to chapter five of the Vista report?

A. Yes; I did. It was not a solitary labor. When I got there, I found a mass of drafts, papers, and notes. People who had written these were Christie, Bacher, Lauritsen, possibly others. But those were the principal ones. Christie had spent quite a lot of time at Los Alamos quite recently.

We went over what they wanted to say and sometimes discussed it from the point of view, did they really want to say it, and were they sure that this was what they wanted to say. I think my contribution to the writing of this was that I—well, let me back off.

The principal thing they wanted to say was that atomic weapons would be useful in the defense of Europe, in the anti-air campaign, and many other ways that you will know as much about as I do, and that for this to happen, developments of hardware, of tactics, of command structure, of habits of behavior, of exercises needed to be gone into, which would give to our tactical readiness at least a small part of the training and precision which the Strategic Air Force already had. I believe my contribution, apart from incidentals to the writing of this report, was a notion that occurred very early and I believe has remained in all drafts, and that is still basic to my own views, and that is that this is not a very fully known subject—what atomic weapons will do, either tactically or strategically, that as you go into battle, you will learn a great deal, and the primary preparation must be of two kinds. First that you have capabilities which allow you a lot of options, which give you choices that you can make at the time, and second, that you be so set up that, if your guesses have been wrong, your technical preparations are such that you can change quickly in the course of the battle. If you are wrong about the effect of a bomb on an airfield, if you are not getting away with it, that you can make the proper reassignment of fissionable material and hardware and aircraft to do what is effective. These were the two guiding ideas that I believe I brought into the organization of the report.

I then, with the help of the others, drafted a chapter—either chapter five or its introduction, I don't remember which it was called. It was a matter of some twenty pages, I believe, and had some twenty-odd recommendations.

Q. Was there in this draft at any stage the suggestion that the United States, this country, should state that it would not use atomic weapons strategically against the Soviet Union until after such weapons had been used against American cities?

A. Let me say the best of what I recollect was in there. It is related to the question you asked, but it is not identical with it. We said that we were in a coalition with the Europeans and that one of the things which we must be alert to is how the Europeans would view the destruction of their own cities by the enemy. Therefore, we needed to envisage the situation that would occur if we used our strategic air as a deterrent to the destruction of Europe's cities, as well as our own, and in that circumstance there was still a great deal that could and should be done with atomic weapons, and that we should be prepared for that contingency. We did not recommend a proclamation. . . .

Q. As long as your memory serves, did you at the time think we should have a policy, whether publicly announced or not, which would lead us to suffer atomic attack upon our cities before we would make a similar attack upon Soviet cities?

419

A. I think the question of our own cities, Mr. Gray, never came into this report, or at least was not the prominent thing. The prominent problem—

Q. I didn't ask about the report, then. I asked in your best recollection was this a view you entertained.

A. That we would welcome an attack on our own cities?

Q. No; I don't think that is an accurate restatement of my question. I said that we would suffer an attack upon our cities with the use of atomic weapons before we would ever make a strategic strike against the U.S.S.R.

A. Oh, Lord, no. I mean the very first thing we would do against the U.S.S.R. is to go after the strategic air bases and, to the extent you can, the atomic bases of the U.S.S.R. You would do everything to reduce their power to impose an effective strategic attack upon us.

Q. Which might include attacks on cities and industrial concentrations.

A. It might, although clearly they are not the forward component of the Strategic Air Command.

Q. Perhaps we are tangled up with the question of strategic?

A. I have always been clear that the thing that you do without fail and with certainty is to attack every air base that has planes on it or may have planes on it the first thing. I believe our report said that.

Q. I will try again. Did you have at that time the view that we should not use the atomic weapons against any militarily promising target which might include cities in the U.S.S.R. until after such weapons had been used against such targets in this country?

A. I think I have never been entirely clear on that. This seemed to me one of the most difficult questions before us. I am sure that I have always felt that it should be a question that we were capable of answering affirmatively and capable of thinking about at the time.

Q. This is not clear in your mind as to what our position should be, you say. Have you ever thought about it in terms of a public announcement as to policy in that regard?

A. This has always struck me as very dangerous. . . .

Q. Looking back on it, do you feel that the GAC, in consistency and with technical integrity, could have recommended something short of the crash program, but something at the same time that was more active and productive than the alternate program?

A. Indeed I do. Indeed I do. We could have very well written the report to the following effect, that the present state of the program is such and such as we see it. This we did do. That in order to get on with it, this and this and this and this would need to be done. This we did do. We could have said that the present state of fog about this is such that we don't really know just what the problem is that is to be decided. Let us get to work and remove as much of this fog as fast as possible.

We could further have said the decision as to whether this is the important, the most important, an important, an undesirable, or disastrous course involves lots of considerations of which we are dimly aware in the military

420

and political sphere, and we hope that these will be taken into account when the decision is made. We could have written such a report. . . .

Q. And your position, as reflected in the report, under no circumstances should we?

A. I think that is not quite right. I think the report itself limits itself to saying that we are reluctant, we don't think we should make a crash program, we are agreed on that, and that the statement in the majority annex that it would be better if these weapons were never brought into being was a wish, but it was not a statement that there were no circumstances under which we would also have to bring them into being.

Q. Wouldn't you say that the impression that the majority annex was calculated to give was that those who signed it were opposed to anything that would lead to the development of the hydrogen bomb?

A. That is right, under the then existing circumstances.

Q. So that really the majority, in effect, would not have been sympathetic with any acceleration of the program which would lead to the development of the bomb?

A. Of course. That does not mean that we would not have been sympathetic to studies and clarification. This was a question of whether you were going to set out to make it, test it, and have it.

May I make one other comment? This was not advice to Los Alamos as to what it should or should not study. This was not advice to the Commission as to what it should or should not build. Some such advice we gave in that report. This was an earnest, if not very profound, statement of what the men on that committee thought about the desirability of making a super-bomb.

Q. And they felt that it was undesirable?

A. We did. . . .

Q. Again, without reference to its wisdom or its folly, is it unreasonable to think that the Commission, reading this report or hearing it made, whichever form it took, would believe that the majority of the General Advisory Committee recommended that the government not proceed with steps which would lead to the production of a super-bomb?

A. That is completely reasonable. We did discuss this point with the Commission on two subsequent occasions. On one occasion we made it clear that nothing in what we had said was meant to obtain, should it be clear or should it be reasonably probable that the enemy was on this trail.

In another, we made it clear that there was a sharp distinction between theoretical study and experiment and invention and production and development on the other hand. So that the Commission, I think, had a little more than this very bald statement to go on. . . .

Q. If you will look at page four of that document, the first sentence in the last paragraph that begins on that page. . . .

There is a sentence that begins, "We are somewhat divided". . . .

From that it would appear that the majority of the members of the GAC

at that time felt unqualifiedly that they opposed not only the production but the development.

A. Right.

Q. So that my question to you is, in this proceeding there has been a lot of testimony that the GAC was opposed to a particular crash program. Isn't it clear that it was not only the crash program that the majority of the GAC found themselves in opposition to, but they were just opposed to a program at all which had to do with thermonuclear weapons?

A. I think it is very clear. May I qualify this?

Q. Yes, you may.

A. I think many things could have qualified our unqualified view. I have mentioned two of them. I will repeat them. One is indications of what the enemy was up to. One of them is a program technically very different from the one that we had before us. One of them a serious and persuasive conclusion that the political effort to which we referred to in our annexes could not be successful.

Q. Now, following the government's decision in January 1950, would it be unfair to describe your attitude toward the program as one of passive resistance?

A. Yes.

Q. That would be unfair?

A. I think so.

MR. GARRISON. Unfair, Mr. Chairman?

MR. GRAY. He said unfair to so describe it.

BY MR. GRAY:

Q. Would it be unfair to describe it as active support?

A. Active could mean many things. I was not active as I was during the war. I think it would be fairer to describe it as active support as an adviser to the Commission, active support in my job on the General Advisory Committee. Not active support in the sense that I rolled up my sleeves and went to work, and not active support in the sense that I assumed or could assume the job of attracting to the work the people who would have come to a job in response to a man's saying, "I am going to do this; will you help me?"

Q. You testified that you did not seek to dissuade anyone from working on the project.

A. Right.

Q. There have been a good many others who have given similar testimony. It also, however, has been testified that there would have been those who would have worked on the project had you encouraged them to do so.

A. There has been testimony that there were people who believed this.

Q. Yes. Do you believe that?

A. I think it possible. Let me illustrate. In the summer of 1952 there was this Lincoln Summer Study, which had to do with continental defense.

On a few limited aspects of that I know something. On most I am an ignoramus. I think it was Zacharias that testified that the reason they wanted me associated with it was that that would draw people into it. The fact that I was interested in it would encourage others. In that sense I think that if I had gone out to Los Alamos, even if I had done nothing but twiddled my thumbs, if it had been known that I had gone out to promote the super, it might have had an affirmative effect on other people's actions. I don't believe that you can well inspire enthusiasm and recruit people unless you are doing something about it yourself.

Q. Furthermore, it was fairly well known in the community—that is, the community of physicists and people who would work on this—that you had not been in favor of this program prior to the government's decision. That probably was a factor?

A. I would think inevitably so. . . .

MAY 4, 1954
JERROLD R. ZACHARIAS, DIRECT EXAMINATION

Q. . . . I would like to ask you now to describe the circumstances, or such of them as you know about, under which the Lincoln Summer Study originated and the specific purposes, if you know them, of that Summer Study.

A. I was, from the beginning of the Lincoln Laboratory, until I resigned shortly after the end of the Summer Study, associate director of the Lincoln Laboratory. . . .

Q. What were the specific purposes of the Summer Study as they were conceived by you in its inception?

A. The purpose of the Summer Study was simply this. We knew that the Russian threat might grow in a variety of ways. The types of aircraft, the types of delivery means, including ballistic missiles and so on, would increase, and we wanted to see whether the kind of air-defense planning that was going on and the air-defense work going on within Lincoln was appropriate to the growing threat. There is no sense in trying to make an air defense against yesterday's airplanes. The defense that one develops has to be against the airplanes that will be in being and threatening when the air defense is in being. Remember that technical discussion and technical work has to precede use by a number of years.

Q. Dr. Zacharias, was it ever suggested to you or intimated to you by Dr. Oppenheimer that the Summer Study should have other purposes?

A. Not that I can possibly remember.

Q. Was it ever a contemplated purpose of the Summer Study to bring about a reduction in the power of the Strategic Air Command?

A. Certainly not. . . .

Q. Was there any purpose in the Summer Study to effect a reduction in the budget of the Strategic Air Command?

A. There certainly was not.

Q. Was there ever any purpose in the Summer Study, or was any such purpose ever suggested to you, of studying or considering submarine warfare?

A. Several of us had participated in the project on antisubmarine warfare two years prior to this. We saw no reason to examine the situation again. Maybe I have not answered the question quite. You said was it ever suggested. It is very difficult to remember who suggested what. I certainly remember no emphasis at all on the antisubmarine problem. . . .

MAY 5, 1954

J. ROBERT OPPENHEIMER, CROSS-EXAMINATION

Q. Doctor, you have spoken somewhat of strategic and tactical air power and strategic and tactical uses of weapons and all that; you of course don't conceive yourself to be an expert in war, do you, or military matters?

A. Of course not. I pray that there are experts in war.

Q. Have you from time to time, however, expressed rather strong views one way or the other in the field of military strategy and tactics?

A. I am sure that I have. I don't know what specific views or instances you are referring to, but I am sure the answer to your question is "Yes."

Q. I am not referring to any for the moment.

A. I am sure the answer to your question is "Yes."

Q. Doctor, I am a little curious and I wish you would tell us why you felt it was your function as a scientist to express views on military strategy and tactics.

A. I felt, perhaps quite strongly, that having played an active part in promoting a revolution in warfare, I needed to be as responsible as I could with regard to what came of this revolution. . . .

Q. Doctor, do you think now that perhaps you went beyond the scope of your proper function as a scientist in undertaking to counsel in matters of military strategy and tactics?

A. I am quite prepared to believe that I did, but when we are talking about my counseling on military strategy and tactics, I really think I need to know whom I was counseling and in what terms. I am sure that there will be instances in which I did go beyond, but I do not wish to give the impression that I was making war plans or trying to set up military planning, nor that this practice was a very general one.

MR. GRAY. I think the witness is entitled to know whether Mr. Robb has in mind committees, panels, and other bodies on which Dr. Oppenheimer served or something else.

MR. ROBB. I was merely trying to explore in general Dr. Oppenheimer's philosophy in respect of this matter. That is what I had in mind. I was not pinpointing on any particular thing, Doctor, and I wanted to get your views on it as to proper function.

THE WITNESS. I served on a great many mixed bodies. This controversial Vista project was not a civilian project. There were a great many

424

military consultants. I learned a great deal from them. The formulation of the views of Vista depend to a very large extent on discussions, day-to-day discussions with working soldiers and staff officers. The committees in the Pentagon on which I sat were usually predominantly committees of military men. I also sat on some bodies where there were no military men. I would have thought that in an undertaking like Vista the joint intelligence, in which I played an extremely small part, of a lot of bright technical and academic people—not all scientists—and of a lot of excellent staff officers and military officers was precisely what gave value to the project. . . .

J. ROBERT OPPENHEIMER, REDIRECT EXAMINATION

Q. Do you think that a scientist can properly do his job of advising the military on the potential of newly developed weapons without having some idea of the use that they are to be put to, and some idea of the tactical and strategic use?

A. It depends. I believe we developed the atomic bomb without any idea at all of military problems. The people who developed radar needed to know precisely, or to have a very good idea of what the actual military campaign and needs were. Certainly you do a much better job if you have a feeling for what the military are up against. In peacetime it is not always clear, even to the military, what they will be up against. . . .

425

BIBLIOGRAPHY

Allen, Frederick Lewis. *Only Yesterday*. New York: Harper, 1931.

Allen, Leslie H., ed. *Bryan and Darrow at Dayton*. New York: Arthur Lee, 1925.

Alsop, Joseph and Stewart. "We Accuse!" *Harper's Magazine*, Oct. 1954.

Arendt, Hannah. *The Origins of Totalitarianism*. New York: Harcourt, Brace, 1951.

Aristophanes. *The Eleven Comedies*. New York: Liveright, 1943.

Bailey, Geoffrey. *The Conspirators*. New York: Harper, 1960.

Bancroft, George. *History of the United States*. 10 vols. Boston: Little, Brown, 1834–74.

Barker, Richard H. *Marcel Proust*. New York: Criterion, 1958.

Barmine, Alexander. *One Who Survived*. New York: Putnam, 1945.

Barrows, Chester L. *William M. Evarts*. Chapel Hill: University of North Carolina, 1941.

Bassett, John S. *A Short History of the United States*. New York: Macmillan, 1929.

Beale, Howard K. *The Critical Year*. New York: Harcourt, Brace, 1930.

Beard, Charles A. *American Government and Politics*. New York: Macmillan, 1925.

Beard, Charles A. and Mary. *The Rise of American Civilization*. New York: Macmillan, 1930.

Beck, F., and Godin, W. *Russian Purge and the Extraction of Confessions*. London: Hurst and Blackett, 1951.

Belloc, Hilaire. *Charles the First, King of England*. Philadelphia: Lippincott, 1933.

Benton, Wilbourn, and Grimm, Georg. *Nuremberg: German Views of the War Trials*. Dallas, Tex.: Southern Methodist University Press, 1955.

Berkner, Lloyd V. "Secrecy and Scientific Progress." *New Republic*, July 12, 1954.

Bernstein, Victor H. *Final Judgment*. New York: Boni and Gaer, 1947.

Blackett, P.M.S. *Fear, War and the Bomb*. New York: McGraw-Hill, 1948, 1949.

Blagoyeva, Stella D. *Dimitrov*. New York: International, 1934.

Blinzer, Josef. *The Trial of Jesus*. Westminster, Md.: Newman Press, 1959.

Bowen, Catherine Drinker. *The Lion and the Throne*. Boston: Little, Brown, 1956.

Bowers, Claude G. *The Tragic Era*. Boston: Houghton Mifflin, 1929.

Bowker, A. E. *Behind the Bar*. New York: Staples Press, 1949.

Bowra, C. M. *The Greek Experience*. Cleveland: World, 1957.

Brinton, Crane. *The Anatomy of Revolution* (rev. ed.). New York: Prentice-Hall, 1952.

Brogan, D. W. *France Under the Republic*. New York: Harper, 1940.

————. *The French Nation*. New York: Harper, 1957.

Brown, Ralph S., Jr. "Personnel Security." *The Annals*, Nov. 1953.

The Brown Book of the Hitler Terror; intro. by Lord Marley. New York: Knopf, 1933.

Bryan, William Jennings. *Memoirs*. Philadelphia: Winston, 1925.

Brzezinski, Zbigniew. *The Permanent Purge*. Cambridge, Mass.: Harvard University Press, 1956.

Bullock, Alan. *Hitler: A Study in Tyranny* (rev. ed.). New York: Harper, 1959.

Busch, Fritz-Otto. *The Five Herods*. London: Robert Hale, 1958.

Bush, Vannevar. *Modern Arms and Free Men*. New York: Simon and Schuster, 1949.

Butterfield, John and Isobel-Ann. "Joan of Arc: A Medieval View." *History Today*, Sept. 1958.

Calvocoressi, Peter. *Nuremberg—the Facts, the Law and the Consequences*. New York: Macmillan, 1948.

The Cambridge Modern History. 13 vols. New York: Macmillan, 1934.

Carr, Robert K. *The Constitution and Congressional Investigating Committees*. New York: Carrie Chapman Catt Memorial Fund, 1954.

Carter, Hodding. *The Angry Scar*. New York: Doubleday, 1959.

The Case of the Anti-Soviet Bloc of Rights and Trotskyites, March 2–13, 1938. Moscow: People's Commissariat of Justice of the U.S.S.R., 1938.

The Case of the Anti-Soviet Trotskyite Centre, January 23–30, 1937. Moscow: People's Commissariat of Justice of the U.S.S.R., 1937.

The Case of the Trotskyite-Zinovievite Terrorist Centre, August 19–24, 1936. Moscow: People's Commissariat of Justice of the U.S.S.R., 1936.

Cash, W. J. *The Mind of the South*. New York: Knopf, 1941.

Chamberlin, William Henry. *The Russian Enigma*. New York: Scribner's, 1943.

Champion, Pierre. *The Trial of Jeanne d'Arc*; trans. by W. P. Barrett. New York: Gotham House, 1932.

Chandler, Peleg W. *American Criminal Trials, vol. I*. Boston: Little, Brown, 1841.

Chapman, Guy. *The Dreyfus Case*. New York: Reynal, 1955.

Chase, Salmon P. *Inside Lincoln's Cabinet*; ed. by David Donald. New York: Longmans, Green, 1954.

Chency, Sheldon. *The Theatre*. New York: Longmans, Green, 1935.

Churchill, Winston. *Blood, Sweat and Tears*. New York: Putnam, 1941.

——. *The Second World War.* 6 vols. Boston: Houghton Mifflin, 1948–53.

Commager, Henry Steele. *The American Mind.* New Haven, Conn.: Yale University Press, 1950.

Commission of Inquiry into the Charges Made Against Leon Trotsky in the Moscow Trials. *Not Guilty.* New York: Harper, 1938.

Compton, Arthur H. *Atomic Quest.* New York: Harper, 1956.

Conybeare, Fred. C. *The Dreyfus Case.* New York: Dodd, Mead, 1898.

Cooke, Alistair. *A Generation on Trial.* New York: Knopf, 1950.

Coulton, G. G. *Medieval Panorama.* Cambridge: Cambridge University Press, 1938.

Crankshaw, Edward. *Gestapo.* New York: Viking, 1956.

——. *Russia by Daylight.* London: Michael Joseph, 1951.

Crossman, Richard. *The Charm of Politics.* New York: Harper, 1958.

Crossman, Richard, ed. *The God That Failed.* New York: Harper, 1950.

Curtis, Charles P. *The Oppenheimer Case.* New York: Simon and Schuster, 1955.

Curtiss, Mina, ed. and trans. *Letters of Marcel Proust.* New York: Random House, 1949.

Daniel-Rops, Henri. *Jesus and His Times.* New York: Dutton, 1954.

Darrow, Clarence. *The Story of My Life.* New York: Scribner's, 1932.

Davies, Joseph E. *Mission to Moscow.* New York: Simon and Schuster, 1941.

Dean, Gordon. *Report on the Atom.* New York: Knopf, 1953, 1957.

DeFord, Miriam Allen. *The Overbury Affair.* Philadelphia: Chilton, 1960.

Deutscher, Isaac. *Russia in Transition.* New York: Coward-McCann, 1957.

——. *Stalin.* New York: Oxford, 1949.

Dewar, Hugh. *Assassins at Large.* London: Wingate, 1951.

DeWitt, David Miller. *The Impeachment and Trial of Andrew Johnson.* New York: Macmillan, 1903.

Dodd, William E. *Ambassador Dodd's Diary;* ed. by Martha Dodd and William E. Dodd, Jr. New York: Harcourt, Brace, 1938.

Donald, David. "Why They Impeached Andrew Johnson." *American Heritage,* Dec. 1956 (vol. VIII, no. 1).

Dreyfus, Alfred. *Five Years of My Life, 1894–1899.* New York: McClure, Phillips, 1901.

Dreyfus, Alfred and Pierre. *The Dreyfus Case;* ed. and trans. by Donald C. McKay. New Haven, Conn.: Yale University Press, 1937.

Durant, Will. *Caesar and Christ.* New York: Simon and Schuster, 1944.

——. *The Life of Greece.* New York: Simon and Schuster, 1939.

——. *The Reformation.* New York: Simon and Schuster, 1957.

Duranty, Walter. *USSR.* Philadelphia: Lippincott, 1944.

Earle, Edward Mead, ed. *Modern France.* Princeton, N.J.: Princeton University Press, 1951.

Eisenschiml, Otto. *Why Was Lincoln Murdered?* Boston: Little, Brown, 1937.

Eliot, George Fielding, ed. *The H Bomb.* New York: Didier, 1950.

Enslin, Morton S. *The Prophet from Nazareth.* New York: McGraw-Hill, 1961.

Fabre, Lucien. *Joan of Arc.* New York: McGraw-Hill, 1954.

Fainsod, Merle. *How Russia Is Ruled.* Cambridge, Mass.: Harvard University Press, 1953.

The Federalist . . . A Collection of Essays . . . by Alexander Hamilton, John Jay, and James Madison. Washington, D.C.: National Home Library Foundation, 1937.

Feis, Herbert. *Between War and Peace: The Potsdam Conference.* Princeton, N.J.: Princeton University Press, 1960.

Finletter, Thomas K. *Power and Policy.* New York: Harcourt, Brace, 1954.

Fischer, Ruth. *Stalin and German Communism.* Cambridge, Mass.: Harvard University Press, 1948.

Florinsky, Michael T., ed. *Encyclopedia of Russia and the Soviet Union.* New York: McGraw-Hill, 1961.

Foner, Philip S. *Mark Twain, Social Critic.* New York: International Publishers, 1958.

Fosdick, Harry Emerson. *The Man from Nazareth.* New York: Harper, 1949.

Fowler, Samuel P. *An Account of the Life, Character &o. of the Rev. Samuel Parris of Salem Village . . .* Salem, Mass.: William Ives and George W. Pease, 1857.

Freeman, Kathleen. *The Paths of Justice.* New York: Roy, 1958.

Friedman, Carl J., and Brzezinski, Zbigniew. *Totalitarian Dictatorship and Autocracy.* Cambridge, Mass.: Harvard University Press, 1956.

Friess, Horace L., and Schneider, Herbert W. *Religion in Various Cultures.* New York: Holt, 1932.

Frischauer, Willi. *The Rise and Fall of Hermann Goering.* New York: Houghton Mifflin, 1951.

Fritzsche, Hans. *The Sword in the Scales.* London: Wingate, 1953.

Fromm, Bella. *Blood and Banquets.* Garden City, N.Y.: Garden City Publishing, 1944.

Galilei, Galileo. *Dialogue Concerning the Two Chief World Systems;* trans. by Stillman Drake. Berkeley: University of California Press, 1953.

Gebler, Karl von. *Galileo Galilei and the Roman Curia.* London: K. Paul, 1879.

Gedye, G. E. R. *Fallen Bastions.* London: Gollancz, 1939.

Gellhorn, Walter. *Security, Loyalty and Science.* Ithaca, N.Y.: Cornell University Press, 1950.

Gerhart, Eugene C. *America's Advocate: Robert H. Jackson.* Indianapolis, Ind.: Bobbs-Merrill, 1958.

Gilbert, G. N. *Nuremberg Diary.* New York: Farrar, Straus, 1947.

Ginger, Ray. *Six Days or Forever.* Boston: Beacon, 1958.

Ginzburg, Benjamin. "Loyalty, Suspicion and the Tightening Chain." *Reporter*, July 6, 1954.

Gisevius, Hans Berndt. "Reichstag Fire in Retrospect." *Freitag*, Mar. 4, 1960–Apr. 8, 1960.

———. *To the Bitter End.* Boston: Houghton Mifflin, 1947.

Glueck, Sheldon. *War Criminals—Their Prosecution and Punishment.* New York: Knopf, 1944.

Goldman, Eric F. *The Crucial Decade—and After.* New York: Knopf, 1956.

Guérard, Albert. *France.* Ann Arbor: University of Michigan Press, 1959.

Guignebert, Charles. *Jesus*; trans. by S. H. Hooke. London: Kegan, Paul, Trench, Trubner, 1935.

Gunther, John. *Inside Europe.* New York: Harper, 1940.

Halasz, Nicholas. *Captain Dreyfus.* New York: Simon and Schuster, 1955.

Hale, Richard W., Jr. *Democratic France.* New York: Coward-McCann, 1941.

Hale, William Harlan. *Horace Greeley.* New York: Harper, 1950.

Hamilton, Edith. *The Greek Way.* New York: Norton, 1930.

Harding, William. *Dreyfus: The Prisoner of Devil's Island.* New York: Associated Publishing, 1899.

Harper's Dictionary of Classical Literature and Antiquities. New York: Harper, 1897.

Harris, Whitney R. *Tyranny on Trial.* Dallas, Tex.: Southern Methodist University Press, 1954.

Hastings, Patrick. *Famous and Infamous Cases.* New York: Roy (undated).

Hayes, Carlton J. H. *A Political and Social History of Modern Europe.* 2 vols. New York: Macmillan, 1929.

Hays, Arthur Garfield. *City Lawyer.* Simon and Schuster, 1942.

———. *Let Freedom Ring.* New York: Boni and Liveright, 1928.

———. "The Strategy of the Scopes Defense." *The Nation*, Aug. 5, 1925.

Heiden, Konrad. *Der Fuehrer*; trans. by Ralph Manheim. Boston: Houghton Mifflin, 1944.

———. *A History of National Socialism.* New York: Knopf, 1935.

Hendrick, Burton J. *Bulwark of the Republic.* Boston: Little, Brown, 1937.

"The Hidden Struggle for the H-Bomb." *Fortune*, May, 1953.

Hilger, Gustav, and Meyer, Alfred G. *The Incompatible Allies.* New York: Macmillan, 1953.

Hyman, Harold M. *To Try Men's Souls.* Berkeley and Los Angeles: University of California Press, 1959.

International Conference on Military Trials. Washington, D.C.: U.S. State Department, 1949.

431

Jackson, Robert H. *The Case Against the Nazi War Criminals.* New York: Knopf, 1946.

———. *The Nürnberg Case.* New York: Knopf, 1947.

Jaeger, Werner. *Paidea: The Ideals of Greek Culture;* trans. from 2d German ed. by Gilbert Highet. New York: Oxford, 1939.

John, Evan (pseud.). *King Charles I.* New York: Roy (undated).

Johnson, Gerald W. *Incredible Tale.* New York: Harper, 1950.

Josephson, Matthew. *The Politicos.* New York: Harcourt, Brace, 1938.

———. *Zola and His Times.* New York: Macaulay, 1928.

Jungk, Robert. *Brighter Than a Thousand Suns;* trans. by James Cleugh. New York: Harcourt, Brace, 1956.

Kaufmann, William W., ed. *Military Policy and National Security.* Princeton, N.J.: Princeton University Press, 1956.

Kayser, Jacques. *The Dreyfus Affair;* trans. by Nora Bickley. New York: Covici, Friede, 1931.

Keenan, Joseph B., and Brown, Brendan F. *Crimes Against International Law.* Washington, D.C.: Public Affairs Press, 1950.

Kelley, Douglas M. *22 Cells in Nuremberg.* New York: Greenberg, 1947.

Kennan, George F. "The Illusion of Security." *Atlantic Monthly,* Aug. 1954.

Kennedy, John F. *Profiles in Courage.* New York: Harper, 1956.

Kenyon, J. P. *The Stuarts.* New York: Macmillan, 1959.

Kissinger, Henry A. *Nuclear Weapons and Foreign Policy.* New York: Harper, 1957.

Klausner, Joseph. *Jesus of Nazareth.* New York: Macmillan, 1926.

Knieriem, August von. *The Nuremberg Trials.* Chicago: Regnery, 1959.

Koestler, Arthur. *The Invisible Writing.* New York: Macmillan, 1954.

———. *Darkness at Noon.* New York: Macmillan, 1941.

Kravchenko, Victor A. *I Chose Freedom.* New York: Scribner's, 1946.

Krivitsky, Walter. *In Stalin's Secret Service.* New York: Harper, 1939.

Khrushchev, N. S. *Concluding Speech to the 22nd Congress, CPSU.* New York: Crosscurrents Press, 1961.

Laistner, M. L. W. *A History of the Greek World.* London: Methuen, 1957.

Lapp, Ralph E. *Atoms and People.* New York: Harper, 1956.

Leech, Margaret. *Reveille in Washington.* New York: Harper, 1941.

Leites, Nathan, and Bernant, Elsa. *Ritual of Liquidation.* Glencoe, Ill.: The Free Press, 1954.

L'Epinois, F. *Les pièces du procès de Galileo.* Rome: V. Palmé, 1877.

Lermolo, Elizabeth. *Face of a Victim.* New York: Harper, 1955.

Lindley, Ernest K. "The Oppenheimer Quandary." *Newsweek,* Apr. 26, 1954.

Lord Russell of Liverpool. *The Scourge of the Swastika.* New York: Philosophical Library, 1954.

Macaulay, Thomas Babington. *Critical and Historical Essays*. 2 vols. Every-man's Library ed. London: J. M. Dent, 1907.

————. *History of England*. 5 vols. Philadelphia: Winston (undated).

MacDonagh, Michael. *The English King*. New York: Cape and Smith, 1929.

Maclaurin, C. *Post Mortem*. London: Jonathan Cape, 1923.

Manchester, William. *Disturber of the Peace*. New York: Harper, 1950.

Mandel, Samuel, ed. *The Soviet Crucible*. Princeton: Van Nostrand, 1959.

Mann, Harvey. "Totalitarian Justice." *American Bar Association Journal*, Dec. 1938.

Manvell, Roger, and Fraenkel, Heinrich. *Dr. Goebbels—His Life and Death*. New York: Simon and Schuster, 1960.

Mather, Cotton: *The Wonders of the Invisible World*. Boston, 1693.

Mather, Increase: *A Further Account of the Trials of the New England Witches*. London: John Russell Smith, 1862.

"McCarthy, A Documented Record." *The Progressive*, Apr. 1954.

McKettrick, Eric L. *Andrew Johnson and Reconstruction*. Chicago: University of Chicago Press, 1960.

McPherson, Edward D. *The Political History of the United States of America During the Period of Reconstruction*. Washington, D.C.: Philip & Solomons, 1871.

Meier, R. L., and Rabinowitch, E. "Scientists Before and After the Bomb." *The Annals*, Nov. 1953.

Mencken, Henry L. *Prejudices: Fifth Series*. New York: Knopf, 1926.

Mill, John Stuart. *On Liberty*. New York: Holt, 1874.

Miller, William. *A New History of the United States*. New York: Braziller, 1958.

Milner, Lucille. "Education of an American Liberal." New York: *Horizon*, 1954.

Montgomery, John D. *The State versus Socrates*. Boston: Beacon, 1954.

Moorehead, Alan. *The Traitors*. New York: Scribner's, 1952.

Morison, Elting E. *Turmoil and Tradition*. Boston: Houghton Mifflin, 1960.

Muller, Herbert J. *The Uses of the Past*. New York: Oxford, 1952.

Murray, T. Douglas, ed. *Jeanne d'Arc*. New York: McClure, Phillips, 1902.

Narratives of the Witchcraft Cases; ed. by George Lincoln Burr. New York: Scribner's, 1904.

Nazi Conspiracy and Aggression. 8 vols. Washington, D.C.: U.S. Government Printing Office, 1946.

————. *Supplement*. 2 vols. 1947–48.

Nevins, Winifred S. *Witchcraft in Salem Village*. Salem: North Shore Publishing; Boston: Lee and Shepard, 1892.

Nye, Russell B. *George Bancroft*. New York: Knopf, 1944.

Ogg, Frederic A. *English Government and Politics*. New York: Macmillan, 1930.

433

Ogilvie, Charles. "Cromwell and the Execution of Charles I." *History Today*, Apr. 1959.

Oppenheimer, J. Robert. "Atomic Weapons and American Policy." *Foreign Affairs*, July 1953.

———. *The Open Mind*. New York: Simon and Schuster, 1955.

Orlov, Alexander. *The Secret History of Stalin's Crimes*. London: Jarrold's, 1954.

Paléologue, Maurice. *An Intimate Journal of the Dreyfus Case*; trans. by Eric Mosbacher. New York: Criterion, 1957.

Palfrey, John Gorham. "The Problem of Secrecy." *The Annals*, Nov. 1953.

Papen, Franz von. *Memoirs*. New York: Dutton, 1953.

Parrington, Vernon L. *The Colonial Mind*. 3 vols. New York: Harcourt, Brace, 1927.

Passant, E. J. *A Short History of Germany, 1815–1945*. Cambridge: Cambridge University Press, 1959.

Peltason, Jack. *Constitutional Liberty and Seditious Activity*. New York: Carrie Chapman Catt Memorial Fund, 1954.

A Perfect Narrative of the Whole Proceedings of the High Court of Justice in the Tryal of the King . . . London: John Playford, 1648.

Pernoud, Régine. *The Retrial of Joan of Arc*; trans. by J. M. Cohen. New York: Harcourt, Brace, 1955.

Phillipson, Coleman. *The Trial of Socrates*. London: Stevens, 1928.

Plato. *Collected Works*; trans. by Benjamin Jowett. New York: Dial, 1936.

Preliminary Commission of Inquiry into the Charges Made Against Leon Trotsky. *The Case Against Leon Trotsky*. New York: Harper, 1937.

Radin, Max. *The Trial of Jesus of Nazareth*. Chicago: University of Chicago Press, 1931.

Randall, James G., and Current, R. N. "Lincoln's Plan for Reconstruction." *American Heritage*, June 1955 (vol. VI, no. 4).

Randall, John H. *The Making of the Modern Mind*. Boston: Houghton Mifflin, 1940.

Rauch, Georg von. *A History of Soviet Russia*. New York: Praeger, 1957.

Rauschning, Hermann. *Hitler Speaks*. London: Thornton Butterworth, 1939.

Redlich, Norman. "The Truth About Spies in Government." *The Nation*, Jan. 30, 1954; Feb. 6, 1954.

Reed, Douglas. *The Burning of the Reichstag*. London: Gollancz, 1934.

Reel, A. Frank. *The Case of General Yamashita*. Chicago: University of Chicago Press, 1949.

The Reichstag Fire Trial: The Second Brown Book of the Hitler Terror; intro. by Georgi Dimitrov. London: Bodley Head, 1934.

Reinhardt, Gunther. *Crime Without Punishment*. New York: Hermitage, 1952.

Renan, Ernest. *The Life of Jesus*. New York: Modern Library, 1927.

Reuben, William A. *The Atom Spy Hoax*. New York: Action Books, 1954.

Rorty, James, and Decter, Moshe. *McCarthy and the Communists*. Boston: Beacon, 1954.

Rosenman, Samuel I. *Working with Roosevelt*. New York: Harper, 1952.

Rovere, Richard H. *Senator Joe McCarthy*. New York: Harcourt, Brace, 1959.

Sackville-West, V. *Saint Joan of Arc*. New York: Doubleday, 1936.

Santillana, Giorgio de. *The Crime of Galileo*. Chicago: University of Chicago Press, 1955.

––––––. "Galileo and J. Robert Oppenheimer." *Reporter*, Dec. 26, 1957.

Sargant, William. *Battle for the Mind*. New York: Doubleday, 1937.

Sawyer, Roland. "The Power of Admiral Strauss." *New Republic*, May 31, 1954.

Schacht, Hjalmar. *Confessions of the Old Wizard*. Boston: Houghton Mifflin, 1956.

Schachtman, Max. *Behind the Moscow Trial*. New York: Pioneer, 1936.

Schapiro, Leonard. *The Communist Party of the Soviet Union*. New York: Random House, 1959.

Schellenberg, Walter. *The Labyrinth*. New York: Harper, 1956.

Schlesinger, Arthur M., Jr. "The Oppenheimer Case." *Harper's Magazine*, Oct. 1954.

Schoen, Max. *The Man Jesus Was*. New York: Knopf, 1950.

Schuman, Frederick L. *The Nazi Dictatorship*. New York: Knopf, 1935.

Sergeant, Philip W. *Witches and Warlocks*. London: Hutchinson, 1936.

Shepley, James, and Blair, Clay, Jr. *The Hydrogen Bomb*. New York: McKay, 1954.

Shipley, Maynard. *The War on Modern Science*. New York: Knopf, 1927.

Shirer, William L. *Berlin Diary*. New York: Knopf, 1941.

––––––. *The Rise and Fall of the Third Reich*. New York: Simon and Schuster, 1960.

Smith, Homer W. *Man and His Gods*. Boston: Little, Brown, 1952.

Sowers, Herman M. "Military Policy and Democracy." *Current History*, May 1954.

Starkey, Marion R. *The Devil in Massachusetts*. New York: Knopf, 1950.

Steevens, G. W. *The Tragedy of Dreyfus*. New York: Harper, 1899.

Steinberg, Julius, ed. *Verdict of Three Decades*. New York: Duell, Sloan and Pearce, 1950.

Stern, Philip Van Doren. "The President Came Forward and the Sun Burst Through the Clouds." *American Heritage*, Feb. 1958 (vol. IX, no. 2).

Stevenson, Gertrude Scott. *Charles I in Captivity*. New York: Appleton, 1927.

Stimson, Henry L. "The Nuremberg Trial: Landmark in Law." *Foreign Affairs*, Jan. 1947.

Stone, Irving. *Clarence Darrow for the Defense.* New York: Doubleday, 1941.

Stone, Julius. *Legal Controls of International Conflict.* New York: Rinehart, 1954.

Stryker, Lloyd Paul. *Andrew Johnson, A Study in Courage.* New York: Macmillan, 1929.

Summers, Montague. *The Geography of Witchcraft.* New York: Knopf, 1927.

Tapley, Charles S. *Rebecca Nurse.* Boston: Marshall Jones, 1930.

Taylor, A. E. *Socrates.* Boston: Beacon, 1952.

Taylor, A. J. P. "Who Burnt the Reichstag?" *History Today,* Aug. 1960.

Taylor, Telford. *Grand Inquest.* New York: Simon and Schuster, 1955.

———. "The Nuremberg War Crimes Trials." *International Conciliation,* April 1949. New York: Carnegie Endowment for International Peace.

Thompson, Carol L. "What About the 'New Weapons'?" *Current History,* May 1954.

Tobias, Fritz. "Stand Up, Van der Lubbe!" *Der Spiegel,* Oct. 21, 1959–Jan. 6, 1960.

Toledano, Ralph de, and Lasky, Victor. *Seeds of Treason.* New York: Funk & Wagnalls, 1950.

Toynbee, Arnold J. *A Study of History.* 10 vols. New York: Oxford, 1934–54.

Trevelyan, C. M. *History of England.* New York: Longmans, Green, 1926.

Trevor-Roper, H. R. *The Last Days of Hitler.* New York: Macmillan, 1947.

Trial of Andrew Johnson . . . 3 vols. Washington, D.C.: Government Printing Office, 1868.

The Trial of Charles I; intro. by C. V. Wedgwood. London: Folio Society, 1959.

The Trial of Joan of Arc; trans. with an intro. by W. S. Scott. London: Folio Society, 1956.

Trial of the Major War Criminals. 42 vols. Nuremberg: International Military Tribunal, 1947–49.

Trotsky, Leon. *My Life.* Scribner's, 1930.

———. *Stalin's Frame-Up System and the Moscow Trials.* New York: Pioneer, 1950.

Tugwell, Rexford G. *A Chronicle of Jeopardy.* Chicago: University of Chicago Press, 1955.

U. S. Atomic Energy Commission. *In the Matter of J. Robert Oppenheimer: Transcript of Hearing before Personnel Security Board.* Washington, D.C.: Government Printing Office, 1954.

Upham, Charles W. *Salem Witchcraft.* 2 vols. Boston: Wiggins and Lunt, 1867.

Valtin, Jan (pseud.). *Out of the Night.* New York: Alliance, 1941.

Vaughan, Robert. *The History of England Under the House of Stuart.* 2 vols. London: Baldwin and Cradock, 1840.

Waldman, Milton. *Joan of Arc.* Boston: Little, Brown, 1935.
Wedgwood, C. V. *The Great Rebellion.* 2 vols. New York: Macmillan. 1955–59.
———. *Oliver Cromwell.* New York: Macmillan, 1956.
Weinberg, Arthur, ed. *Attorney for the Damned.* New York: Simon and Schuster, 1957.
Weissberg, Alexander. *The Accused;* trans. by Edward Fitzgerald. New York: Simon and Schuster, 1951.
Welles, Gideon. *Diary of Gideon Welles.* 3 vols. Boston: Houghton Mifflin, 1911.
West, Rebecca. *A Train of Powder.* New York: Viking, 1955.
Westin, Alan. *The Constitution and Loyalty Programs.* New York: Carrie Chapman Catt Memorial Fund, 1954.
Wharton, Michael, ed. *A Nation's Security.* London: Secker & Warburg, 1955.
What Happened in Salem; ed. with an intro. by David Levin. New York: Twayne Publications, 1952.
White, Andrew D. *The Warfare of Science with Theology in Christendom* (new ed.). New York: Braziller, 1955.
White, Theodore H. "U. S. Science: The Troubled Quest." *Reporter,* Sept. 23, 1954.
Williams, Charles. *Witchcraft.* London: Faber & Faber, 1941.
Williams, Wayne. *William Jennings Bryan.* New York: Putnam, 1936.
Wolfe, Bertram D. "The Durability of Soviet Despotism." *Commentary,* Aug. 1957.
———. *Khrushchev and Stalin's Ghost.* New York: Praeger, 1957.
———. *Three Who Made a Revolution.* New York: Dial, 1948.
Woodward, C. Vann. *Reunion and Reaction.* Boston: Little, Brown, 1951.
Woodward, W. Elliott, ed. *Records of Salem Witchcraft.* Roxbury, Mass.: Privately printed, 1864.
The World's Most Famous Court Trial: Tennessee Evolution Case. Cincinnati, O.: National Book, 1925.

Xenophon. *The Whole Works of Xenophon;* trans. by Ashley Cooper and others. Philadelphia: T. Wardle, 1842.

Young, Desmond. *Rommel.* New York: Harper, 1950.

Back files of the following periodicals were consulted and used in the preparation of the manuscript:

Atlantic Monthly, Bulletin of the Atomic Scientists, Daily Worker, New

Republic, New York *Herald,* New York *Herald* (Paris Edition), New York *Herald Tribune,* New York *Sun,* New York *Times,* New York *World-Telegram, New Yorker Staats-Zeitung, Newsweek, Saturday Review of Literature, Science, Time, The Times* (London), *U.S. News and World Report.*

INDEX

AEC. *See* Atomic Energy Commission

Aftenposten, 253

Agathon, 16

Alcibiades, 16, 17, 18

Alden, John, 97, 99, 102

Alvarez, Luis, 382–83, 400

American Civil Liberties Union, 175

Amhaaretz, 34, 35

Andover (Mass.). *See* Witchcraft trials

Anglican Church. *See* Established Church

Anytus, 17–18, 19, 21, 24, 28, 30, 31

Aristophanes, 19–20, 26

Aristotle, 61–62, 64, 65

Army Appropriation Act (U.S.), 116–17, 121

Art treasures, Nazi looting of, 339

Assayer, The, 64

Assumptionists, 160

Athens, 15, 16, 18; jury system, 18–19; law of, 18–19, 21, 24; trial procedure, 18–19, 21, 22

Atomic bomb, 375–76, 380, 382–83, 385, 386, 399, 404, 425

Atomic energy, 377, 382

Atomic Energy Commission, 381 ff., 385 ff., 388, 389, 391, 393, 397, 410, 411, 421–22; General Advisory Committee, 381 ff., 387, 393, 397, 411 ff., 420 ff.; Personnel Security Criteria, 391, 392

Atomic scientists: Soviet Union, 380, 382, 384, 399; United States, 377, 391, 395, 397–98

Atomic weapons, 382, 383, 386, 404, 408–9, 419–20

L'Aurore, 150, 151

Auschwitz, 333, 350, 351

Austria, 76, 258, 331, 333, 368

Azef, Yevno, 265, 265 n

Azerbaijan (U.S.S.R.), 234

Bakayev, Ivan: charges against, 243–44; sentence, 244; trial, 243–49, 262–66

Balkan Communist Federation, 208

Ballard, Mrs. Joseph, 99

Baltic provinces (U.S.S.R.), 353

Barabbas, 39–40, 42

"Barbarossa, Operation," 356

Barbusse, Henri, 210

Baruch Plan, 382

Beaufort, Henry, Cardinal of England, 53–54

Beauvais, Bishop of. *See* Cauchon, Pierre

Bedford, John of Lancaster, Duke of, 44, 47, 49, 50

Belgium, 371

Bellarmine, Cardinal Robert, 62, 63, 64, 65–66, 67, 69–70, 73

Beneš, Eduard, 256

Beria, Lavrenti P., 257, 261

Berkeley Radiation Laboratory, 380, 381, 394, 395

Bertillon, Alphonse, 141–42, 145, 152, 159, 167–68, 170

Bessonov, Sergei A.: testimony, 289–90; trial, 289–322

Bethe, Hans, 382, 393, 413

Bibber, Sarah, 94, 110

439

Bible, the, 175, 179. *See also* Genesis; Gospels
Biddle, Francis A., 338, 348, 365–69
Billot, Jean-Baptiste, 148, 149 ff.
Bingham, John A., 121
Birds, The, 20
Bishop, Bridget, 96, 98
Bishop, Edward, 96
Bismarck, Otto von, 137, 144
"Black Codes," 115
Black Mass, 98–99
Blomberg, Werner von, 344, 349–50, 362
Boguslavsky, Mikhail S.: testimony, 275–76; trial, 266–88
Boisdeffre, Le Mouton de, 141, 145, 146, 148, 151, 152, 154, 158, 168
Borden, William L., 388
Bordereau, 139 ff., 147, 150, 152, 153, 155, 156, 161 ff., 167 ff.
Bormann, Martin, 335, 342, 343, 364, 372; charges against, 336–37; sentence, 345–46; trial *in absentia*, 331–46, 348–74
Boston. *See* Witchcraft trials
Bradshaw, John, 83 ff.
Bradstreet, Dudley, 99, 100
"Brainwashing," 248–49
Bredow, Kurt von, 370
Brest-Litovsk, Treaty of, 260
Brisbane, Arthur, 174
Brisset, André, 144, 145
Brisson, Henri, 153 ff.
Brown Book of the Hitler Terror, The, 210–11, 212–13, 218, 219, 221, 224
Brownell, Herbert, 388
Brownshirts. *See* Sturm Abteilung
Bruno, Giordano, 62
Bryan, William Jennings, 61, 173 ff.
Bryan, William Jennings, Jr., 176
Buchanan, James, 113
Buckingham, George Villiers, Duke of, 76, 77, 78, 79
Buenger, Wilhelm, 214, 215–16, 219–20, 225

Bukharin, Nikolai, 237, 241, 250, 251, 255; charges against, 257–58; sentence, 261; trial, 257–61, 289–322
Bulanov, Pavel: testimony, 317–18; trial, 289–322
Bulletin of the Opposition, 236, 246
Bülow, Bernhard von, 156–57
Burgundians, 44, 45
Burgundy, Philip the Good, Duke of, 56
Burroughs, George, 96, 101, 109–10
Bush, Vannevar, 393
Butler, Benjamin F., 122, 123, 124, 129
Buwert, Karl, 201–2, 217, 225

Caesar, Tiberius, 37, 40
Caiaphas, High Priest, 37, 38–39, 41
California Institute of Technology, 377, 378, 386
California, University of (Berkeley), 378–79, 382, 394
Carey, Nathaniel, 97
Carrier, Martha, 99
Casimir-Perier, Jean, 158
Cassation, Court of (France), 155, 160, 162, 163, 166
Catholic Center Party, Germany, 203, 205, 209
Catholic Church, France, 138–39, 160
Catholics, English, 76, 77, 79
Caucasus, 241, 353
Cauchon, Pierre, Bishop of Beauvais, 49, 50, 51, 53, 54, 55
Cavaignac, Godefroy, 153 ff., 166
Cernusky, Eugen Lazar von, 159
Chaerophon, 26
Chambersburg (Pa.), 113
Charles I of England, 75–89; charges against, 82, 83–84; civil war, 75, 82–83; Crown revenues, 76, 77, 79; execution, 75, 85; sentence, 85; trial, 75, 83–89
Charles VI of France, 44, 58

Charles VII of France, 49, 52, 54, 56; coronation, 48, 49; Dauphin, 43, 44, 45–46, 58
Chase, Salmon P., 122, 124
Chesterton, G. K., 257
Chevalier, Haakon, 379 ff., 389, 394, 396, 396 n, 397, 398, 401 ff., 411, 415
Chiang Kai-shek, 236
China, 238, 271
Chinese Eastern Railway, 236, 241
Churchill, Winston, 324, 324 n, 375
Civil Rights Act, 1866 (U.S.), 115
Clark, Champ, 173
Clemenceau, Albert, 152
Clemenceau, Georges, 150, 161
Clouds, The, 19–20
Comintern. See Communist International
Commager, Henry Steele, quoted, 175
Communism, 205, 210
Communist International, 208, 210, 218 n, 234, 236, 242; Anti-Comintern Pact, 251
Communist Party: China, 236; Germany, 204 ff., 225, 235, 242, 255, 327, 395; Holland, 213, 216; Hungary, 255; Poland, 254; United States, 378–79, 384–85, 395
Communist Party: U.S.S.R., 237, 240–41, 242, 261; Central Committee, 234, 237, 239, 243, 259, 261, 272; Central Purge Commission, 235; Congresses, 234, 235, 237, 238; Control Commission, 240–41, 242–43; Politburo, 234, 235, 257, 258, 259; Secretariat, 233, 234, 237, 240
Compton, Arthur Holly, quoted, 379
Conant, James B., 383
Concentration camps, 207, 222, 331, 340, 350–52. See also Auschwitz; Dachau; Maidanek
Constitution, U.S., 112, 114, 115, 117, 121; Fourteenth Amendment,

120; Thirteenth Amendment, 114. See also Negroes, suffrage
Copernicus, Nicholas, 62, 69–70; theory of, 62, 64, 66, 67, 70, 72, 73, 181
Corey, Giles, 96, 102
Corey, Martha, 95, 96
Corwin, Jonathan, 94, 103
Council of Thirty, 17
CPSU. See Communist Party, U.S.S.R.
Crimea, 352
Critias, 16–17
Crito, 16, 25
Cromwell, Oliver, 7, 81, 83, 85, 86
Curtis, Benjamin R., 122, 123
Czechoslovakia, 242, 271, 327, 335, 354–55, 373–74

Dachau, 346
Daily Mail. See Steevens, G. W.
Dallett, Joseph, 379
Danzig, 355–56
Darkness at Noon, 249
Darrow, Clarence, 61, 176 ff.
Darwinism, 174, 179, 180, 197, 348; laws against teaching, 174–75
Dauphin. See Charles VII
Davies, Joseph E., 252, 256, 260
Davis, Jefferson, 115, 122
Dayton (Tenn.), 175, 176
Dean, Gordon, 393
Delegorgue, Judge, 152
de Lesseps, Ferdinand, 137
Delphic oracle, 26
Demange, Edgar, 144, 145, 148, 158
Democrats (U.S.), 114, 116, 119
Der Stürmer, 323
Devil's Island, 146, 156
Dialogue on the Great World Systems, 64–65, 67, 68, 69, 71, 73
Dimitrov, Georgi, 208, 222, 242; acquittal, 221; charges against, 215; trial, 214–21
Dissenters (England), 75–76, 79–80
Divine right, theory of, 75, 78

Doenitz, Karl, 335, 344; charges against, 334–37; sentence, 345–46; trial, 331–46, 348–74; verdict, 335
Domremy, 44, 50
d'Ormescheville, Bexon, 143, 144, 162
Dostoyevsky, Feodor, cited, 321–22
Douglas, William O., 340
Dreyfus, Alfred, 8, 139, 140 ff., 161–66; charges against, 144; first court-martial, 144–45, 161–62, 163; retrial, 155 ff.; sentence, 145–46, 159; verdict annulled, 160–61
Dreyfus, Lucie, 142, 148, 154, 155
Dreyfus, Mathieu, 150, 167
Drumont, Edouard, 138, 143, 147, 150, 155, 156
Dulles, John Foster, 387
Dunne, Finley Peter, 157
Du Paty de Clam, Armand, 142 ff., 149, 151, 152, 156, 159, 165, 167
Dupuy, Charles, 155 ff.

L'Eclair, 147–48
Eisenhower, Dwight D., 385, 387, 388
Eliot, John, 78
Elizabeth I of England, 77
Eltenton, George, 380, 396 n, 400–3
Emancipation Proclamation, 112
Emory, William H., 120–21, 123
England, Church of. See Established Church
English, Mary, 96
Erard, Guillaume, Canon of Rouen, 53–54, 55
Ernst, Karl, 224 ff.
Essenes, 34
Established Church (England), 75–76, 78, 79–80, 96
Esterhazy, Ferdinand Walsin-, 140, 147, 149 ff., 160, 165, 167 ff.
Euripides, 16
Evans, Ward V., 389, 397
Evarts, William R., 122
Evdokimov, Gregori: charges against, 243–44; sentence, 244; trial, 243–49, 262–66
Evolution. See Darwinism
Executive Order No. 10450, 385, 391

Faure, Felix, 149
Faux Henry, 148–49, 152 ff.
Federal Bureau of Investigation, 381, 390, 392, 396, 410
Federation of Architects, Engineers, Chemists and Technicians (FAECT), 380
Fermi, Enrico, 384, 393, 413
Fessenden, William P., 124–25
Fierbois (France), 46, 51
Figaro, 150, 151
"Final solution." See Genocide
Finch, John, 78
Finland, 256, 379
Finletter, Thomas K., 392 n, 417–18
Flaechsner, Hans, 370–73
Floete, Hans, 201
Fortune, 388
Fourteenth Amendment. See Constitution, U.S.
Fourth International, 236
Fowler, Joseph S., 125
France, 76, 79, 242, 327; War Ministry, Intelligence Bureau, Statistical Section, 139–40, 144, 145, 146, 160
France, Anatole, 151
Franco-Prussian War, 137
Frank, Hans, 334, 338, 342; charges against, 336–37; sentence, 345–46; trial, 331–46, 348–74
Freedmen's Bureau (U.S.), 114
Freemasons, 368
Freud, Sigmund, 174, 348
Frick, Wilhelm, 335, 343; charges against, 336–37; sentence, 345–46; trial, 331–46, 348–74
Fritsch, Werner von, 344
Fritzsche, Hans, 335, 344; acquittal, 345, 346; charges against, 336–37; trial, 331–46, 348–74

Frogs, The, 20
Fuchs, Klaus, 384–85, 393
Fundamentalism (U.S.), 174 ff., 178, 182, 183
Funk, Walter, 335; charges against, 336–37; sentence, 345–46; trial, 331–46, 348–74

GAC. *See* Atomic Energy Commission, General Advisory Committee
Galilee, 33, 34
Galileo, 8, 61–74, 174, 181, 183; astronomical theories, 62; censure, 63–64, 65–66, 70–72; charges against, 66–67; recantation, 67–68; sentence, 68; trial, 67–74
Galliffet, Gaston, 156
Garrison, Lloyd K., 389–90, 396
Genesis, Book of, 175, 179, 188 ff., 198–99
Geneva Convention, 337
Genocide, 339–42, 350–52, 373–74
Gentiles, 34, 35
Germany, 76, 326 ff., 333; Anglo-German Naval Treaty, 327, 345; Anti-Comintern Pact, 251; anti-Jewish laws, 323–24; armed forces, 255, 256, 261, 262, 300, 334–35, 340–41, 356–57, 369; denazification, 347; General Staff, 255, 335, 345; High Command, 335–36, 345; judicial system, 223, 334; laws, 205, 207, 209, 222, 330, 366; New Order, 339–40; rearmament, 327, 331, 333, 349–50, 361–62; Reich cabinet, 335, 345; secret police, 218 n, 223, 246, 255–56, 265, 324, 331, 335, 338; slave labor, 340, 346, 354, 365–66; youth movement, 324, 333–34, 363–65. *See also* Catholic Center Party; Communist Party; Hitler; National Socialist Party; Nationalist Party; Nazi-Soviet Pact; Weimar Republic
Gestapo. *See* Germany, secret police

Gethsemane, 37
Giraud, Henri, 342
Gisevius, Hans, 224
Gloucester (Mass.). *See* Witchcraft trials
Glover, Mrs., 92–93
Gobert, Alfred, 141
Goebbels, Joseph, 205, 206, 208, 210, 211 ff., 219, 220, 223, 224, 324, 335, 342, 372
Goering, Hermann, 204 ff., 209, 211, 212, 219–20, 222 ff., 229–31, 323–24, 331, 332, 335, 338, 343–44, 346, 349–54; charges against, 331, 335, 336–37; sentence, 346; trial, 331–46, 348–74
Gonse, Charles, 141, 147, 148, 151, 152, 158, 168, 170–71
Good, Dorcas, 96
Good, Sarah, 94–96, 100, 101
Goodwin, John, 92, 93
Gorki, Maxim (Alexei Maximovich Peshkov), 240, 257, 259, 315, 316, 319, 321
Gorki Pedagogical Institute, 246
Gospels, the, 39, 40, 40 n, 41–42
GPU (OGPU). *See* Soviet Union, secret police
Grand Remonstrance, 81
Grant, Ulysses S., 117 ff., 128, 131
Gray, Gordon, 389, 392, 395, 398
Great Britain, 327, 328, 331, 344; Anglo-German Naval Treaty, 327, 345
Griggs, David T., 392, 392 n, 400, 417–18
Grimes, James W., 124–25
Grinko, Grigori: charges against, 257–58; sentence, 261; trial, 257–61, 289–322
Groves, Leslie R., 377, 379 ff., 391, 395

Hacha, Emil, 354
Hague Conventions, 329, 337
Haldane, J. B. S., 210

Halder, Franz, 224
Halévy, Daniel, 151
Halévy, Elie, 151
Hampden, John, 79, 81, 82, 124
Hanfstaengl, Ernst, 220
Hanotaux, Gabriel, 168
Hanussen, Erik Jan, 212
Hathorne, John, 94, 97, 104
Hays, Arthur Garfield, 175, 178, 179, 182, 213
Heines, Edmund, 212, 224
Helldorf, Wolf von, 213, 223, 224, 226, 228–29
Henderson, John B., 124–25, 126
Henrietta Maria, Queen of England, 76–77, 79, 81–82
Henry V of England, 44
Henry VI of England, 44
Henry, Hubert, 140, 144, 145, 147 ff., 159, 166–67
Henry, Mrs. Hubert, 166–67
Hermann Goering Works, 330
Herod Antipas, 33, 36, 40 n
Hess, Rudolf, 331, 332, 343; charges against, 336–37; sentence, 345–46; trial, 331–46, 348–74
Heydrich, Reinhard, 335, 364, 368
High Commission, Court of (England), 80, 81
Himmler, Heinrich, 324, 328, 342, 351–52
Hindenburg, Paul von, 203–4, 205, 207
Hiroshima, 383, 405
Hiss, Alger, 384
Hitler, Adolf, 203 ff., 222 ff., 235, 241, 242, 243, 251, 258, 262, 324, 325, 328 ff., 339, 340, 342 ff., 351–52, 354–56, 357, 358–59, 360–61, 363, 369, 370, 371–72, 373–74
Hobbs, Abigail, 110
Hobbs, Deliverance, 96 ff., 101
Holland. See Netherlands, The
Holt, Joseph, 119
Holton, Sarah, 108
Holtzmann, Edouard, 245, 246, 247

Hoover, J. Edgar, 381, 388
Hostages, World War II, 358–59
Hotel Bristol (Copenhagen), 245, 253
Hubbard, Elizabeth, 105, 107
Hugenberg, Alfred, 204–5, 206, 209
Huguenots. See Protestants, French
Hundred Years' War, 43, 44
Hydrogen bomb, 382 ff., 393, 397, 399, 404–5, 408 ff., 420–23

Impeachment, Articles of. See Johnson, Andrew, charges against
Impeachment, law governing, 122–24
Index, Congregation of the, 66, 67–68, 71, 73
Indian, John, 96
Ingersoll, Nathaniel, 108
Inquisition, Holy, 43, 49, 50, 56, 61, 62, 63, 65, 66–67, 68, 69, 71, 91, 249; trial procedure, 50–51
Institute for Advanced Study, 382, 387
International Conference on Military Trials. See London Charter
International law, 326–27, 328, 329–30, 337, 367
International Military Tribunal, 325–26, 328, 331 ff., 336 ff.
Ireland, revolt in, 81
Isabelle de Beauvière, 44, 45
Izvestia, 239, 252

J'Accuse. See Zola
Jackson, Robert H., 325 ff., 334–35, 336, 338, 343, 347, 349–50, 360–62
Jacobs, Margaret, 99
James I of England, 76, 77, 91
Jannel, C. G. S., 162–63
Japan, 236, 241, 258, 269, 270–71, 282, 346 n, 375, 376, 377
Jaurès, Jean, 151
Jehovah's Witnesses, 368–69
Jesuits, 138

Jesus of Nazareth, 15, 33, 35–42; charges against, 37–38, 39, 41; death, 40; hearing before Pilate, 39–40, 40 n, 41–42; hearing before Sanhedrin, 37–38, 41; sentence, 40, 42

Jewish law, 36, 37–38

Jews, German: persecution of, 209–10, 333, 339–42, 350–52. See also Germany

Joan of Arc, 15, 43–60; abjuration, 54; capture, 48–49; charges against, 51, 52–53; childhood, 44–45; efforts to escape, 50; execution, 55–56; imprisonment, 49–50; military exploits, 47–49; rehabilitation trial, 44, 56; relapse, 55, 59–60; sainthood, 43, 56; sentence, 53–54, 55; trial, 51–53, 57–60; visions, 44–45, 51, 53, 55, 57–60

Jodl, Alfred, 335, 338, 342 ff., 372; charges against, 334–37; sentence, 345–46; trial, 331–46, 348–74

John of Luxembourg, Count de Ligny, 49–50

Johnson, Andrew, 111–35; acquittal, 125; charges against, 121; impeachment, 117–18, 120–35; trial procedure, 122–23, 124

Johnson, Edwin C., 386

Johnson, Lyall, 380

Judas Iscariot, 37

Jung, Carl, 174

Jung, Edgar, 369–70

Kaltenbrunner, Ernst, 335, 338, 342, 352; charges against, 336–37; sentence, 345–46; trial, 331–46, 348–74

Kamenev, Leon, 235, 237, 239, 248, 249, 262, 266, 318; charges against, 243–44; sentence, 244; trial, 243–49, 262–66

Karl Liebknecht House, 206, 207, 215

Katyn massacre, 345

Katz, Otto, 213, 223

Keitel, Wilhelm, 334–35, 342, 343, 344, 356–60; charges against, 334–37; sentence, 345–46; trial, 331–46, 348–74

Kellogg-Briand pact, 327, 328

Kennan, George F., 393, 405–10

Kenny, Henry, 105

Kepler, Johannes, 62

Khrushchev, Nikita, 233, 241, 251–52, 256, 259

Killian, James R., 417–18

Kirov, Sergei M., 233–35, 237–39, 240, 243, 247, 248, 250, 253, 258, 259, 263–64, 265, 310–12, 317, 319, 321

Knyazev, Ivan: testimony, 282–83; trial, 266–88

Koestler, Arthur, quoted, 249, 340

Korean War, 386, 387

Krestinsky, Nikolai: charges against, 257–58; sentence, 261; trial, 257–61, 289–322

Krivitsky, Walter, 254

Krupp von Bohlen und Halbach, Gustav, 335

Kuibyshev, Valerian V., 240, 258, 259, 315, 319, 321

Kun, Béla, 255

Labori, Fernand, 152, 158, 159

Lahousen, Erwin, 342–43

Lambert, Rudy, 394

Lansdale, John, 381, 394, 395, 403

Lateit, Emil, 202

Laud, William, Archbishop of Canterbury, 80, 81

Lawrence, Edward O., 382, 383, 394

Lawrence, Lord Justice Geoffrey, 338, 346

League of Nations, 242

Leblois, Louis, 149 ff., 154

Lebrun-Renault, Charles, 149, 153, 159, 165

Left Social Revolutionaries, Soviet Union, 259–60

Lemercier-Picard (Moïse Leeman), 148, 153, 154
Lenin, V. I., 234, 236, 237, 249, 251, 252, 257 ff., 313
Leningrad, 233, 234, 237 ff., 384
Leo XIII, Pope, 138
Leon of Salamis, 17
Levin, Lev G.: charges against, 259; sentence, 261; trial, 257–61, 289–322
Lewes, Mary, 109
Lewis, Mercy, 110
Ley, Robert, 330, 336, 372
Libre Parole, 138, 143, 169
Lidice (Czechoslovakia), 337
Lie, Trygvie, 250
Lilienthal, David, 383, 393, 410, 411
Lincoln, Abraham, 111, 112, 113, 115, 118, 121
Lincoln Summer Study, 386–87, 388, 412, 417–18, 422–24
Livshitz, Yakov A.: testimony, 279, 281; trial, 266–88
Lomanitz, Giovanni Rossi, 394–95
London Charter, 325, 327–30, 336, 345
Long Parliament, 81 ff.
Lorraine, 45
Los Alamos Laboratory, 376–77, 379 ff., 393, 403, 413
Louis XIII of France, 76
Loyalty oath, U.S., Civil War, 112
Lubbe, Marinus van der, 201, 203, 207–8, 211, 213, 221, 224 ff., 233; charges against, 215; sentence, 221; testimony, 226–28, 231; trial, 214–21
Lycon, 19, 21, 28

McCarthy, Joseph R., 385, 386, 389, 390, 396
McKenzie, Ben B., 179, 182
Macaulay, Thomas Babington, quoted, 75, 92
Maidanek, 351

Malenkov, Georgi, 240–41
Malone, Dudley Field, 175–76, 178 ff.
Manchester Guardian, 212
Manchuria, 236
Man Who Was Thursday, The, 257
Marks, Herbert S., 389
Marx, Karl, 258, 348
Mary, Queen of Scots, 76
Massachusetts Institute of Technology, 386, 417–18
Mather, Cotton, 92, 93, 97 ff.
Mather, Increase, 100
Matin, Le, 150, 156
Maxey (France), 45
Maxwell-Fyfe, David, 337, 343, 348, 350–52, 354–56, 359–60, 369–70, 373–74
Mein Kampf, 209, 336
Meletus, 19, 21, 24, 28, 31, 32; cross-examination of, 22, 28–30
Memphis (Tenn.), 116
Mencken, H. L., 173, 176, 181, 182
Menzhinsky, Vyacheslav, 257, 259, 296, 314–15, 319, 321
Mercier, Auguste, 141 ff., 145, 146, 148, 151, 156 ff., 165–66, 168–70
Merlin, 45
Messiah, concept of, 34, 35, 37, 38, 39
Metcalf, Maynard M., 180
Methodists (U.S.), 183
Mexico, 249, 261
Millerand, Alexandre, 156
Milton, John, quoted, 75
Molotov, Vyacheslav M., 245, 253, 327
Monet, Claude, 151
Morgan, Thomas A., 389, 398
Moscow trials, 223, 243 ff., 251 ff., 257 ff., 262 ff., 379; confessions, 244–49, 250, 251 ff., 255, 261 ff., 321–22
Mrachkowsky, Sergei: charges against, 243–44, 248; sentence, 244; trial, 243–49, 262–66

Muenzenberg, Willy, 210 ff., 222, 223
Muralov, Nikolai: charges against, 251–52; sentence, 253; trial, 251–53, 266–88
Murray, Thomas E., 398
Mussolini, Benito, 324
Myth of the Twentieth Century, 344

Napoleon I of France, 328
Napoleon III of France, 137, 138
National Covenant, 80
Nationalist Party, Germany, 204–5, 208, 209, 212
National Socialist Party, Germany, 204 ff., 208, 209, 211, 213, 222, 235, 324–25, 327, 329, 333–34, 335–36, 339–40, 360–61; annual rallies, 323–24
Nazi-Soviet Pact, 255, 262, 344, 379
Nazis. *See* National Socialist Party
Neal, John R., 178
Negroes, suffrage, 114, 116, 120
Netherlands, The, 76, 82, 335, 367–69, 371
Neumann, Heinz, 255
Neumann, John von, 393
Neurath, Konstantin von, 335, 374; charges against, 336–37; sentence, 345–46; trial, 331–46, 348–74
New Orleans (La.), 116
New York *Herald*, 151
New York *Times*, The, 390, 410
Newton, Isaac, 68
Nichols, Kenneth D., 381, 388 ff., 397, 416
Nikitchenko, Iola T., 338
Nikolayev, Leonid, 233, 238, 240, 263–64, 283, 311–12
Nimitz, Chester W., 345
NKVD. *See* Soviet Union, secret police
Norkin, Boris O.: testimony, 277–78; trial, 266–88
Norway, 249–50, 253, 327, 344–45, 359–60

Noyes, Nicholas, 101, 102, 103
Nuremberg, 323–24
Nuremberg laws. *See* Germany, anti-Jewish laws
Nuremberg trial, 224–25, 323, 331–46, 348–74; procedure, 337–38; subsequent trials, 347. *See also* War crimes, World War II; and names of individual defendants
Nurse, Rebecca, 95–96, 100–1, 102, 104–9

Oak Ridge Laboratory (Tenn.), 381
Oberfohren, Ernst, "memorandum," 212–13, 221, 224
Olberg, Valentin, 246
Oppenheimer, Frank, 378, 381
Oppenheimer, J. Robert, 376–425; AEC decision, 398–400; charges against, 388–89; hearing before Security Board, 389–99, 400–25; Security Board recommendation, 397–400; security clearance, 379 ff., 391, 410
Oppenheimer, Katharine, 378–79
Oradour-sur-Glane (France), 337
Orjonikidze, Grigori K. ("Sergo"), 251–52, 253, 264
Orléans, 45, 46, 47–48
Orlov, Alexander, 245, 252, 254, 261
Osborne, Sarah, 94–95
Outer Mongolia, 241

Palestinian coinage, 36
Panama Canal Company, 137–38
Panizzardi, Lieutenant Colonel, 143, 148, 149, 159
Papen, Franz von, 203–4, 205, 209, 225, 332, 344, 369–70; acquittal, 345; charges against, 336–37; trial, 331–46, 348–74
Paris, University of, 49, 53
Paris Commune, 137, 138
Parliament, 76 ff.; revenue measures, 77, 78
Parma, Duke of, 250

Parrington, Vernon L., quoted, 103
Parris, Elizabeth, 93
Parris, Samuel, 93 ff., 98, 101, 103, 107
Partisans, World War II, 357–60
Pash, Boris, 380–81, 396, 398, 400–3
Passover, festival of, 36, 37, 39
Pauker, Alliluyev, 318
Paul, 40, 334
Paulus, Friedrich von, 343
Pavlov, Ivan, 248
Pearl Harbor, 379
Peay, Austin, 175
Pellieux, Gabriel de, 152
Peloponnesian War, 16, 17
Peshkov, Maxim Alexeivich, 257, 258–59, 315, 321
Peters, Bernard, 395–96, 397
Petit bleu, 146–47, 149, 150, 155, 168
Petition of Right, 76–78
Phaedo, 25
Pharisees, 34, 35, 37
Phillips, Wendell, 112, 115
Phipps (or Phips), Mary, 102–3
Phipps (or Phips), William, 97–98, 101, 103, 104
Picquart, Georges, 145 ff., 158, 161, 166, 167–68, 170
Pike, Sumner T., 410–11
Pilate, Pontius, 33, 36, 40, 41, 41 n, 42; Jesus before, 39–40, 40 n, 41–42
Plato, 16, 21, 22, 25
Poitiers (France), 46, 52
Poland, 233, 235, 262, 297, 327, 331, 334, 342, 344, 345, 355–56, 379
Poles, German persecution of, 339–40
Pontecorvo, Bruno, 385
Popov, Blagoi: trial, 214–22
"Popular front," 210, 242
Potsdam Conference, 375, 380
Principia Mathematica, 68
Prisoners of war, German treatment of, 348–49, 357. See also Sagan;

Stalag Luft III
Procter, Elizabeth, 96
Procter, John, 96–97
"Project Vista," 386, 418–19, 424–25
Protestant Churches of America, 174
Protestants, French, 76
Proust, Marcel, 151, 153
Prussia, 203–4, 205, 209
Ptolemy, 62, 73
Pucelle, La, 45, 47. See also Joan of Arc
Puritans, 76, 82, 83, 91–92, 97, 103
Putna, Vitaly, 274
Putnam, Ann, 96, 104–5, 109
Putnam, Edward, 105
Putnam, Thomas, 108
Pyatakov, Yuri, 237, 289, 294, 298–99, 301; charges against, 251; sentence, 253; trial, 251–53, 266–88
Pym, John, 81, 82

Rabi, Isador I., 384, 393, 412–17
Radek, Karl, 239, 241, 250; charges against, 251; sentence, 253; trial, 251–53, 266–88
Raeder, Erich, 335, 344, 345; charges against, 334–37; sentence, 345–46; trial, 331–46, 348–74
Rakovsky, Christian: charges against, 257–58; sentence, 261; trial, 257–61, 289–322
Randall, John H., quoted, 68
Rataichak, Stanislav A.: testimony, 284–87; trial, 266–88
Raulston, John T., 177, 179 ff.
Rauschning, Hermann, 224–25
Reconstruction: Johnson plan, 113–14; Lincoln plan, 112, 113, 114; Radical plan, 114, 116–17, 119–20; Stevens plan, 113
Red Army. See Soviet Union, army
Reichstag, 204–5, 206, 208–9, 211, 222; building, 211, 212
Reichstag fire, 201–3, 211 ff., 217 ff., 222, 223 ff., 233; Committee of Inquiry into the Origins of the, 213;

Reichstag fire (*cont'd*)
counter-trial, 213; trial, 214, 226–31. *See also* Dimitrov, Georgi; Lubbe, Marinus van der; Popov, Blagoi; Tanev, Vassily; Torgler, Ernst

Reichswehr. *See* Germany, armed forces

Reiss, Ignace, 254

Remmele, Hermann, 255

Rennes (France). *See* Dreyfus, Alfred, retrial

Republicans (U.S.), 114, 116, 119; "Radical," 112 ff., 117, 119, 123 ff.

Rheims (France), 45, 48; Archbishop of, 48, 49, 56

Ribbentrop, Joachim von, 330, 331–32, 343–44, 352, 354–56; charges against, 336–37; sentence, 345–46; trial, 331–46, 348–74

Ribes, Champetier de, 337

Riccardi, Niccolo, 65

Robb, Roger, 389, 392 ff.

Roehm, Ernst, 332, 344

Roget, Gaudérique, 154, 158, 159

Roman law, 38–39

Rommel, Erwin, 329, 344

Roosevelt, Franklin D., 324 n, 327

Rosenberg, Alfred, 333, 335, 338, 344; charges against, 336–37; sentence, 345–46; trial, 331–46, 348–74

Rosengoltz, Arkady: charges against, 257–58; sentence, 261; trial, 257–61, 289–322

Ross, Edmund G., 125, 126

Rouen (France), 50, 51, 55, 56

Rouen, Canon of. *See* Erard, Guillaume

Rudenko, Roman A., 337, 352–54, 356–59

Rudzutak, Yakovlevich, 259

Rundstedt, Gerd von, 344

Russell, Charles, 157

Russia. *See* Soviet Union

Russians, German persecution of, 339, 341–42, 356–58

Rykov, Alexei, 237, 250, 255, 257, 259; charges against, 257–58; sentence, 261; trial, 257–61, 289–322

SA. *See* Sturm Abteilung

SAC. *See* United States, Strategic Air Command

Sack, Alfons, 214, 220

Sadducees, 34, 37

Sagan prison camp, 343

Saint Catherine, 45, 54, 57, 58, 59, 60

Saint Margaret, 45, 54, 57, 58, 59, 60

Saint Michael, 44–45, 52, 57

Salem (Mass.). *See* Witchcraft trials

Saltonstall, Nathaniel, 98, 103

Sandherr, Jean, 144 ff.

Sanhedrin, 37–39, 40, 41

Sauckel, Fritz, 335, 338, 354, 365–67; charges against, 336–37; sentence, 345–46; trial, 331–46, 348–74

Schacht, Hjalmar, 330, 332, 335, 344, 349, 360–62; acquittal, 345, 346; charges against, 336–37; trial, 331–46, 348–74

Scheurer-Kestner, Auguste, 149, 150

Schirach, Baldur von, 333–34, 338, 344, 363–65; charges against, 336–37; sentence, 345–46; trial, 331–46, 348–74

Schleicher, Kurt von, 370

Schneiderman, William, 379

Schofield, John M., 126

Schwartzkoppen, Max von, 139, 143, 144, 146, 148, 150, 159

Scopes, John T., 175 ff.; appeal, 183; charges against, 175, 179; sentence, 183; trial, 177–99

Scotland, 80–81, 83; Assembly, 80; Church of, 76, 80

SD (Sicherheitsdienst), 335

Seaborg, Glenn, 383

Sedov, Leon, 245, 246, 262–63, 266–67, 298

Seeckt, Hans von, 300

Seneca, quoted, 75

Serebryakov, Leonid: charges against, 251–52; sentence, 253; trial, 251–53, 266–88

Seyss-Inquart, Artur, 335, 367–69; charges against, 336–37; sentence, 345–46; trial, 331–46, 348–74

Sharangovich, Vassily, 313, 314, 314 n

Shawcross, Hartley, 337

Sheldon, Susanna, 109

Sherman, William Tecumseh, 120, 124, 131–32

Ship money, 79, 81, 124

Siberia, 251, 324

Silverman, Samuel J., 389

Smirnov, Ivan, 236, 245–48, 253, 266–67, 277, 317; charges against, 243–44; sentence, 244; trial, 243–49, 262–66

Smith, Lydia, 113

Smyth, Henry DeWolf, 398–99

Social Democratic (Socialist) Party, Germany, 205 ff.

Social Revolutionary Party, U.S.S.R., 265 n

Society of Former Political Prisoners and Exiles, 242–43

Society of Old Bolsheviks, 242–43

Socrates, 8, 15–32, 33; charges against, 19–20, 21; death of, 25; defense, 21–24, 25–32; farewell to jury, 23–24; imprisonment, 24–25; sentence, 22–23; trial, 21–24; verdict, 22

Sokolnikov, Grigori, 241; charges against, 251–52; sentence, 253; trial, 251–53, 266–88

Somerset, Frances Howard, Countess of, 91

Sophists, 20

Soviet consulate, San Francisco, 381

Soviet Union, 382, 384, 385, 406–7; Army, 236, 241, 242, 255–56, 262, 268; Central Executive Committee, 238, 246, 259; collectivization, 234, 235, 236; Constitution, 241; espionage, 384–85, 402; Five-Year Plans, 234, 235, 237, 242, 257; German attack on, 356; industrialization, 234, 235; laws, 239, 244, 248; purges, 223, 237, 239 ff., 250 ff., 256 ff., 261 ff.; secret police, 218 n, 223, 238–40, 242 ff., 248 ff., 261, 272, 288, 296, 314; State Administration of Camps, 254; Supreme Court, Military Collegium, 244. See also Communist International; Communist Party; Left Social Revolutionaries; Nazi-Soviet Pact

Spain, 76, 79, 242

Spanish Loyalists, 378, 379, 394

Sparta, 16, 18

Speer, Albert, 333, 344, 370–73; charges against, 336–37; sentence, 345–46; trial, 331–46, 348–74

SS (Schutzstaffel), 222, 222 n, 335–36, 340–44, 364–65

Stalag Luft III, 348–49, 351–52

Stalin, Joseph, 7, 209, 222, 233 ff., 324, 325, 327, 375, 380

Stanbery, Henry, 122, 127

Stanton, Edwin M., 113–14, 117, 118–19, 120, 121, 123, 126, 127–31, 132–33

Star Chamber (England), 80, 81

Steevens, G. W., quoted, 157, 158

Stephens, Alexander H., 114–15

Stevens, Thaddeus, 112–13, 114, 116, 120, 121, 125, 126

Stimson, Henry L., 327

Stoughton, William, 98, 99, 100, 103

Strafford, Thomas Wentworth, Earl of, 81

Strategic Air Command. See United States

Strauss, Lewis L., 382, 388–89, 391, 398, 398 n, 415, 416

Streicher, Julius, 323, 330, 335; charges against, 336–37; sentence,

Streicher, Julius (*cont'd*)
345–46; trial, 331–46, 348–74
Stroop, Juergen, 340–41
Sturm Abteilung (SA), 205, 206,
208, 209, 213, 223 ff., 335–36,
345, 364–65
Sumner, Charles, 112–13, 115, 116,
119, 122, 126
"Super" bomb. *See* Hydrogen bomb
Surratt, John H., 118
Surratt, Mary, 118–19
Sverdlov, Yakov M., 312

Taft, Robert A., 329–30
Tanev, Vassily, trial, 214–22
Tatlock, Jean, 378, 379
Teichert, Paul, 214
Teller, Edward, 383, 393–94, 397,
400
Temple at Jerusalem, 34, 36
*Tenure of Kings and Magistrates,
The,* 75
Tenure of Office Act (U.S.), 117–
18, 119, 120, 121, 123–24, 132,
133–34
Terboven, Josef, 359–60
Ter-Vaganian, Vargashak: charges
against, 243–44; sentence, 244;
trial, 243–49, 262–66
Thatcher, Margaret, 103
Thermonuclear bomb. *See* Hydrogen
bomb
Thirteenth Amendment. *See* Consti-
tution, U.S.
Thomas, Lorenzo, 120, 121, 124,
127–31, 133
Tituba, 93 ff., 97, 99, 107
Tobias, Fritz, 225
Torgler, Ernst, 207–8, 212, 222–23;
acquittal, 221; charges against,
215; trial, 214–21
Toynbee, Arnold, 33
Tressart, John, 56
Trotsky, Leon, 235, 236, 240, 243 ff.,
249, 251 ff., 258 ff., 265 ff.
Troyes, Treaty of, 44, 56

Truman, Harry S., 375, 377, 382,
384–85, 389, 404, 411, 413, 414
Trumbull, Lyman, 124–25
Tukhachevsky, Mikhail, 241, 255–
56, 274, 297, 298
Turkey, 242
Tuscany, Duke of, 62
Twain, Mark, 151

Ukraine, 241, 251, 257, 269, 270,
324, 341–42
United States: Air Force, 386, 392;
Army, 377, 390–91; Congress, 377,
384–85; Defense Department, 382,
388; House Un-American Activities Committee, 395; Joint Chiefs
of Staff, 383; Joint Committee on
Atomic Energy, 383, 388; Justice
Department, 389; laws, 385; Military Intelligence, 379–80; National
Security Council, 387, 418; security system, 376, 385–86, 391–92,
396–97, 399–400, 406–8, 415–16;
State Department, 256, 377, 382,
385; Strategic Air Command,
386 ff., 417, 419, 420, 423. *See
also* Atomic Energy Commission;
Executive Order 10450; Federal
Bureau of Investigation (F.B.I.)
Urban VIII, Pope, 64, 65, 67, 68, 69
U.S.S.R. *See* Soviet Union

Vabres, Henri Donnedieu de, 338
Valois, House of, 44
Van Winkle, Peter, 125
Versailles Treaty, 205, 209, 241, 324,
326, 328, 336, 345, 355
Victoria, Queen of England, 157,
159
Vienna, 33, 364
Villiers, George. *See* Buckingham
Vishinsky, Andrei, 244 ff., 253, 258,
260–61, 262 ff.
Völkische Beobachter, 363, 373
Vossische Zeitung, 211

Wade, Benjamin F., 113, 120, 122, 126

Walcott, Mary, 105

Waldeck-Rousseau, Pierre, 156, 159

Walsin-Esterhazy, Ferdinand. *See* Esterhazy

War crimes, World War I, punishment, 326, 326 n

War crimes, World War II, 326 ff., 336–37, 339–40; punishment, 324 ff., 336, 346–47. *See also* International Military Tribunal; London Charter

War guilt, World War II, 325, 327–28, 342, 348

Warsaw, 342; ghetto, 340–41

Warwick, Richard de Beauchamp, Earl of, 50, 53, 54

Weimar Republic, 205, 209, 326

Welles, Gideon, 124, 133–34

Werner, Karl, 215, 221

Wilhelm I of Germany, 149

Wilhelm II of Germany, 332

Willard, Samuel, 102

Williams, Abigail, 93, 104

Wilson, Charles E., 388

Wilson, Roscoe C., 386

Wilson, Woodrow, 173

Witchcraft: evidence, 94–95, 98, 100; executions, 99, 101–2

Witchcraft trials: Andover, 99–100; Boston, 92–93; Europe, 91; Gloucester, 100; Salem, 94–110

World Committee for the Relief of German Fascism, 210, 219

World War I, 174. *See also* War crimes

World War II, 233, 262, 327. *See also* Hostages; Partisans; War crimes; War guilt

Xanthippe, 16, 24

Xenophon, 21, 22

Yagoda, Henry, 238, 242, 243, 250, 254; charges against, 257–59; sentence, 261; trial, 257–61, 289–322

Yenukidze, Avel, 259, 310–11, 321

Yezhov, Nikolai I., 240, 242, 243, 248, 250, 252, 254, 256 ff., 261, 262

Yugoslavia, 336

Zacharias, Jerrold R., 423–24

Zaporozhets, Vania, 238, 239, 240, 311–12

Zealots, 33, 34, 37

Zelensky, Isaac A.: testimony, 305–7; trial, 289–322

Zhdanov, Andrei, 240, 250

Zinoviev, Gregory, 234, 235, 237, 239–40, 248, 257, 266, 318; charges against, 243–44; sentence, 244; trial, 243–49, 262–66

Zola, Emile, 150–51, 152, 156; *J'Accuse*, text, 151; sentence, 153; trial, 152–53, 157

I10

Travelex Travel
Assistance &
Concierge

Travelex Insurance
Services

Confirmation Number
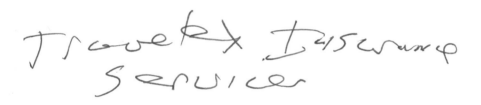

June 22-28, 06